Cite This Volume:

17 USCS § -

★ ★ ★ ★ **UNITED STATES CODE SERVICE** ★ ★ ★

Lawyers Edition

All federal laws of a general and permanent nature arranged in accordance with
the section numbering of the United
States Code and the supplements
thereto.

17 USCS
Copyrights

1978

THE LAWYERS CO-OPERATIVE PUBLISHING CO.
Rochester, New York 14603

BANCROFT-WHITNEY CO.
San Francisco, California 94107

LCP BW

ABBREVIATIONS

A	Atlantic Reporter
ALR	American Law Reports
ALR2d	American Law Reports, Second Series
ALR3d	American Law Reports, Third Series
ALR Fed	American Law Reports, Federal
Am Bankr NS	American Bankruptcy, New Series
AMC	American Maritime Cases
Am Jur	American Jurisprudence
Am Jur 2d	American Jurisprudence, Second Edition
Am Jur Legal Forms	American Jurisprudence Legal Forms
Am Jur Legal Forms 2d	American Jurisprudence Legal Forms, Second Edition
Am Jur Pl & Pr Forms	American Jurisprudence Pleading and Practice Forms
Am Jur Pl & Pr Forms (Rev ed)	American Jurisprudence Pleading and Practice Forms, Revised Edition
Am Jur Proof of Facts	American Jurisprudence Proof of Facts
Am Jur Trials	American Jurisprudence Trials
App DC	United States Court of Appeals for the District of Columbia
BTA	Board of Tax Appeals
CB	Cumulative Bulletin of the Internal Revenue Service
CFR	Code of Federal Regulations
Comr Pat	Commissioner of Patents and Trademarks
CPSC	Consumer Product Safety Commission
Ct Cl	Court of Claims
Cust & Pat App (Cust)	U.S. Court of Customs and Patent Appeals (Customs)
Cust & Pat App (Pat)	U.S. Court of Customs and Patent Appeals (Patents)
DC Dist Col	United States District Court for the District of Columbia
Dist Col App	District of Columbia Court of Appeals
Em Ct App	Emergency Court of Appeals
Ex Or	Executive Orders
Fed Proc Forms L Ed	Federal Procedural Forms Lawyers Edition

ABBREVIATIONS

F	Federal Reporter
F2d	Federal Reporter, Second Series
F Cas No	Federal Cases
Fed Reg	Federal Register
Fed Rules Serv	Federal Rules Service
FPC	Federal Power Commission
FRD	Federal Rules Decisions
FRES	Federal Regulation of Employment Service
F Supp	Federal Supplement
FTC	Federal Trade Commission
JAG	Judge Advocate General
Jud Pan Mult Lit	Rulings of the Judicial Panel on Multidistrict Litigation
LC	Labor Cases
L Ed	Lawyers Edition U.S. Supreme Court Reports
L Ed 2d	Lawyers Edition U.S. Supreme Court Reports, Second Series
L Rev	Law Review Articles
Mun Ct App Dist Col	Municipal Court of Appeals for District of Columbia
NE	Northeastern Reporter
NLRB	National Labor Relations Board
NW	Northwestern Reporter
NYS	New York Supplement
Op Atty Gen	Opinions of Attorney General
Op Comp Gen	Opinions of Comptroller General
P	Pacific Reporter
Proc	Proclamations
Rev Rul	Revenue Ruling
Rev Proc	Revenue Procedure
S Ct	Supreme Court Reporter
SE	Southeastern Reporter
SEC	Securities and Exchange Commission
So	Southern Reporter
SW	Southwestern Reporter
T Ct	United States Tax Court
TCM	Tax Court Memorandum
TD	Treasury Decisions
TMT & App Bd	Trademark Trial and Appeal Board
US	United States Reports
USPQ	United States Patents Quarterly
USTC	United States Tax Cases

FOREWORD

On October 19, 1976, President Ford signed Public Law 94-553 (90 Stat. 2541) representing the first major copyright law revision since 1909. The copyright law revision of 1976 became effective for most purposes on January 1, 1978.

The present volume has been designed to provide three vital types of information: (1) the full text of the new Copyright Act, together with appropriate legislative history notations; (2) research references to the Total Client-Service Library® and law review articles; and (3) casenotes decided under prior versions of the Act but representing viable points of law, allocated to the appropriate sections of the new Act.

The present volume represents the law as it exists today. Neither the prior statutory text nor casenotes of only historical import are reflected herein. The user of this volume is therefore advised to retain the predecessor Title 17 volume (issued in the FCA edition in combination with Title 16) until pending cases cease to call for reference to prior law. However, recognizing that the transitional need for dual coverage is only temporary, we will no longer supplement the predecessor volume and will direct our entire Title 17 supplementation effort to the present volume.

Finally, it is to be noted that the Copyright Office is currently preparing new regulations and also revising its application forms, instructions, and other printed matter to meet the needs of the new Act. Pertinent new regulations will be referenced in the USCS Advance Legislative Service and in the supplements to this volume. Readers may obtain Copyright Office materials by having their names added to the Copyright Office Mailing List. Address a written request to the Copyright Office, Library of Congress, Washington, DC 20559.

THE PUBLISHERS

TABLE OF CONTENTS

TITLE 17 — COPYRIGHTS

THE CODE OF THE LAWS

OF THE

UNITED STATES OF AMERICA

TITLE 17 — COPYRIGHTS

TABLE OF CONTENTS

CHAPTER 1. SUBJECT MATTER AND SCOPE OF COPYRIGHT

1

HISTORY; ANCILLARY LAWS AND DIRECTIVES

Other provisions:

Effective Date. Section 102 of Act Oct. 19, 1976, P. L. 94-553, 90 Stat. 2598, provided that: "This Act [which appears generally as 17 USCS §§ 101 et seq.; for full classification of this Act, consult USCS Tables volumes] becomes effective on January 1, 1978, except as otherwise expressly provided by this Act, including provisions of the first section of this Act [section 101 of Act Oct. 19, 1976, which appears as 17 USCS §§ 101 et seq.]. The provisions of sections 118, 304(b), and chapter 8 of title 17 [17 USCS §§ 118, 304(b), 801 et seq.], as amended by the first section of this Act, take effect upon enactment of this Act [enacted Oct. 19, 1976]."

Lost and expired copyrights; recording rights. Section 103 of Act Oct. 19, 1976, P. L. 94-553, 90 Stat. 2599, provided that: "This Act [which appears generally as 17 USCS §§ 101 et seq.; for full classification of this Act, consult USCS Tables volumes] does not provide copyright protection for any work that goes into the public domain before January 1, 1978. The exclusive rights, as provided by section 106 of title 17 [17 USCS § 106] as amended by the first section of this Act [section 101 of Act Oct. 19, 1976, which appears as 17 USCS §§ 101 et seq.], to reproduce a work in phonorecords and to distribute phonorecords of the work, do not extend to any nondramatic musical work copyrighted before July 1, 1909."

Authorization of appropriations. Section 114 of Act Oct. 19, 1976, P. L. 94-553, 90 Stat. 2602, provided that: "There are hereby authorized to be appropriated such funds as may be necessary to carry out the purposes of this Act [which appears generally as 17 USCS §§ 101 et seq.; for full classification of this Act, consult USCS Tables volume].

Separability of provisions. Section 115 of Act Oct. 19, 1976, P. L. 94-553, 90 Stat. 2602, provided that: "If any provision of title 17 [17 USCS §§ 101 et seq.], as amended by the first section of this Act [section 101 of Act Oct. 19, 1976, which appears as 17 USCS §§ 101 et seq.] is declared unconstitutional, the validity of the remainder of this title [17 USCS §§ 101 et seq.] is not affected."

CROSS REFERENCES

USCS Administrative Rules, Rules of Copyright Office (Library of Congress) 37 CFR Parts 201, 202; USCS Administrative Rules, Universal Copyright Convention.

§ 101. Definitions

As used in this title [17 USCS §§ 101 et seq.], the following terms and their variant forms mean the following:

An "anonymous work" is a work on the copies or phonorecords of which no natural person is identified as author.

"Audiovisual works" are works that consist of a series of related images which are intrinsically intended to be shown by the use of machines or devices such as projectors, viewers, or electronic equipment, together with accompanying sounds, if any, regardless of the nature of the material objects, such as films or tapes, in which the works are embodied.

The "best edition" of a work is the edition, published in the United States at any time before the date of deposit, that the Library of Congress determines to be most suitable for its purposes.

A person's "children" are that person's immediate offspring, whether legitimate or not, and any children legally adopted by that person.

A "collective work" is a work, such as a periodical issue, anthology, or encyclopedia, in which a number of contributions, constituting separate and independent works in themselves, are assembled into a collective whole.

A "compilation" is a work formed by the collection and assembling of preexisting materials or of data that are selected, coordinated, or arranged in such a way that the resulting work as a whole constitutes an original work of authorship. The term "compilation" includes collective works.

"Copies" are material objects, other than phonorecords, in which a work is fixed by any method now known or later developed, and from which the work can be perceived, reproduced, or otherwise communicated, either directly or with the aid of a machine or device. The term "copies" includes the material object, other than a phonorecord, in which the work is first fixed.

"Copyright owner", with respect to any one of the exclusive rights comprised in a copyright, refers to the owner of that particular right.

A work is "created" when it is fixed in a copy or phonorecord for the first time; where a work is prepared over a period of time, the portion of it that has been fixed at any particular time constitutes the work as of that time, and where the work has been prepared in different versions, each version constitutes a separate work.

A "derivative work" is a work based upon one or more preexisting works, such as a translation, musical arrangement, dramatization, fictionalization, motion picture version, sound recording, art reproduction, abridgment, condensation, or any other form in which a work may be recast, transformed, or adapted. A work consisting of editorial revisions, annotations, elaborations, or other modifications which, as a whole, represent an original work of authorship, is a "derivative work".

A "device", "machine", or "process" is one now known or later developed.

To "display" a work means to show a copy of it, either directly or by means of a film, slide, television image, or any other device or process or, in the case of a motion picture or other audiovisual work, to show individual images nonsequentially.

A work is "fixed" in a tangible medium of expression when its embodiment in a copy or phonorecord, by or under the authority of the author, is sufficiently permanent or stable to permit it to be perceived, reproduced, or otherwise communicated for a period of more than transitory duration. A work consisting of sounds, images, or both, that are being transmitted, is "fixed" for purposes of this title [17 USCS §§ 101 et seq.] if a fixation of the work is being made simultaneously with its transmission.

The terms "including" and "such as" are illustrative and not limitative.

A "joint work" is a work prepared by two or more authors with the intention that their contributions be merged into inseparable or interdependent parts of a unitary whole.

"Literary works" are works, other than audiovisual works, expressed in words, numbers, or other verbal or numerical symbols or indicia, regardless of the nature of the material objects, such as books, periodicals, manuscripts, phonorecords, film, tapes, disks, or cards, in which they are embodied.

"Motion pictures" are audiovisual works consisting of a series of related images which, when shown in succession, impart an impression of motion, together with accompanying sounds, if any.

To "perform" a work means to recite, render, play, dance, or act it, either directly or by means of any device or process or, in the case of a motion picture or other audiovisual work, to show its images in any sequence or to make the sounds accompanying it audible.

"Phonorecords" are material objects in which sounds, other than those accompanying a motion picture or other audiovisual work, are fixed by any method now known or later developed, and from which the sounds can be perceived, reproduced, or otherwise communicated, either directly or with the aid of a machine or device. The term "phonorecords" includes the material object in which the sounds are first fixed.

"Pictorial, graphic, and sculptural works" include two-dimensional and three-dimensional works of fine, graphic, and applied art, photographs, prints and art reproductions, maps, globes, charts, technical drawings, diagrams, and models. Such works shall include works of artistic craftsmanship insofar as their form but not their mechanical or utilitarian aspects are concerned; the design of a useful article, as defined in this section, shall be considered a pictorial, graphic, or sculptural work only if, and only to the extent that, such design incorporates pictorial, graphic, or sculptural features that can be identified separately from, and are capable of existing independently of, the utilitarian aspects of the article.

A "pseudonymous work" is a work on the copies or phonorecords of which the author is identified under a fictitious name.

"Publication" is the distribution of copies or phonorecords of a work to the public by sale or other transfer of ownership, or by rental, lease, or lending. The offering to distribute copies or phonorecords to a group of persons for purposes of further distribution, public performance, or public display, constitutes publication. A public performance or display of a work does not of itself constitute publication.

To perform or display a work "publicly" means—
(1) to perform or display it at a place open to the public or at any place where a substantial number of persons outside of a normal circle of a family and its social acquaintances is gathered; or
(2) to transmit or otherwise communicate a performance or display of the work to a place specified by clause (1) or to the public, by means of any device or process, whether the members of the public capable of receiving the performance or display receive it in the same place or in separate places and at the same time or at different times.

"Sound recordings" are works that result from the fixation of a series of musical, spoken, or other sounds, but not including the sounds accompanying a motion picture or other audiovisual work, regardless of the nature of the material objects, such as disks, tapes, or other phonorecords, in which they are embodied.

"State" includes the District of Columbia and the Commonwealth of Puerto Rico, and any territories to which this title [17 USCS §§ 101 et seq.] is made applicable by an Act of Congress.

A "transfer of copyright ownership" is an assignment, mortgage, exclusive license, or any other conveyance, alienation, or hypothecation of a copyright or of any of the exclusive rights comprised in a copyright, whether or not it is limited in time or place of effect, but not including a nonexclusive license.

A "transmission program" is a body of material that, as an aggregate, has been produced for the sole purpose of transmission to the public in sequence and as a unit.

To "transmit" a performance or display is to communicate it by any device or process whereby images or sounds are received beyond the place from which they are sent.

The "United States", when used in a geographical sense, comprises the several States, the District of Columbia and the Commonwealth of Puerto Rico, and the organized territories under the jurisdiction of the United States Government.

A "useful article" is an article having an intrinsic utilitarian function that is not merely to portray the appearance of the article or to convey information. An article that is normally a part of a useful article is considered a "useful article".

The author's "widow" or "widower" is the author's surviving spouse under the law of the author's domicile at the time of his or her death, whether or not the spouse has later remarried.

A "work of the United States Government" is a work prepared by an officer or employee of the United States Government as part of that person's official duties.

A "work made for hire" is—

(1) a work prepared by an employee within the scope of his or her employment; or

(2) a work specially ordered or commissioned for use as a contribution to a collective work, as a part of a motion picture or other audiovisual work, as a translation, as a supplementary work, as a compilation, as an instructional text, as a test, as answer material for a test, or as an atlas, if the parties expressly agree in a written instrument signed by them that the work shall be considered a work made for hire. For the purpose of the foregoing sentence, a "supplementary work" is a work prepared for publication as a secondary adjunct to a work by another author for the purpose of introducing, concluding, illustrating, explaining, revising, commenting upon, or assisting in the use of the other work, such as forewords, afterwords, pictorial illustrations, maps, charts, tables, editorial notes, musical arrangements, answer material for tests, bibliographies, appendixes, and indexes, and an "instructional text" is a literary, pictorial, or graphic work prepared for publication and with the purpose of use in systematic instructional activities.

(Added Oct. 19, 1976, P.L. 94-553, Title I, § 101, 90 Stat 2541.)

HISTORY; ANCILLARY LAWS AND DIRECTIVES

Effective date of section:
Section 102 of Act Oct. 19, 1976, P. L. 94-553, 90 Stat. 2598, provided that this section "becomes effective on January 1, 1978".

RESEARCH GUIDE

Am Jur:
18 Am Jur 2d, Copyright and Literary Property §§ 34, 37, 66, 77.

Annotations:
Exhibition of picture as publication. 52 L Ed 208.
Application of "works for hire" doctrine under Federal Copyright Act (17 USCS §§ 1 et seq.). 11 ALR Fed 457.
What constitutes publication of architectural plans, drawings, or designs, so as to result in loss of common-law copyright. 77 ALR2d 1048.

Law Review Articles:
Copyright Symposium, 22 New York Law School Law Review 193.

INTERPRETIVE NOTES AND DECISIONS

1. Generally
2. Best edition
3. Compilation
4. Copies
5. Derivative work
6. Display
7. Joint work
8. Motion pictures
9. Perform
10. Publication, generally
11. —Extent of publication, generally
12. — —Limited publication
13. —Public performance, generally
14. — —Drama
15. — —Lecture or speech
16. — —Music
17. —Sale, generally
18. — —Exhibition or delivery for prospective sale
19. Sound recordings
20. Works made for hire

1. Generally

Phrase "works of an author, of which copies are not reproduced for sale", as used in predecessor statute, was intended to modify "lecture," "dramatic composition" and "musical composition." Universal Film Mfg. Co. v Copperman (1914, DC NY) 212 F 301, affd (CA2 NY) 218 F 577, cert den 235 US 704, 59 L Ed 433, 35 S Ct 209.

"Component parts," as used in predecessor statute, does not mean subdivision of rights, licenses, or privileges, but refers to separate chapters, subdivisions, acts, and like of which most works are composed. New Fiction Pub. Co. v Star Co. (1915, DC NY) 220 F 994.

2. Best edition

Where only one edition of book has been published, copies thereof deposited with register of copyrights are of best edition although book might not be suitable for inclusion in "library" collection for public use. Bouve v Twentieth Century-Fox Film Corp. (1941) 74 App DC 271, 122 F2d 51, 50 USPQ 338.

Cutting out and depositing pages containing article in bound volume of encyclopedia is sufficient compliance with "best edition" provision of predecessor statute. Black v Henry G. Allen Co. (1893, CC NY) 56 F 764.

3. Compilation

"Composite works", defined in predecessor statute, are those which contain distinguishable parts which are separately copyrightable. Markham v A. E. Borden Co. (1953, CA1 Mass) 206 F2d 199, 98 USPQ 346.

Book containing comic strips printed on one side of paper only and bearing notice of copyright on title page, although each item in book bears separate copyright notice and most of items bear later release date on which date newspapers are first authorized to use material is "composite work" as defined in predecessor statute. King Features Syndicate, Inc. v Bouve (DC Dist Col) 48 USPQ 237.

"Composite work," by definition in predecessor statute, cannot also be "work made for hire," since latter presupposes that contributors are employees who are not entitled under Copyright Act to renew copyright registrations as "authors"; composite work permits both proprietor of original copyright in composite, as well as individual contributing authors, to apply for renewal. 43 OAG 2.

4. Copies

"Copy" is that which ordinary observation would cause to be recognized as having been taken from or reproduction of another. King Features Syndicate v Fleischer (1924, CA2 NY) 299 F 533.

Photograph of copyrighted piece of statuary is "copy" within predecessor statute. Bracken v Rosenthal (1907, CC Ill) 151 F 136.

5. Derivative work

Extremely brief epitomes of plots of copyrighted operas are not "a version" of copyrighted work. G. Ricordi & Co. v Mason (1913, CA2 NY) 210 F 277.

TV dramatization of copyrighted script is "derivative work." Gilliam v American Broadcasting Co. (1976, CA2) 192 USPQ 1.

6. Display

Exhibition of painting at private academy to limited number of persons subsequent to copyright thereof, but without notice of copyright, is not such publication as will constitute abandonment of owner's exclusive rights therein. Werckmeister v American Lithographic Co. (1904, CA2 NY) 134 F 321.

Exhibition of painting in art salon would not be publication unless public were permitted to make copies thereof. Werckmeister v Springer Lithographing Co. (1894, CC NY) 63 F 808.

Public exhibition of original painting, without copyright notice, is publication. Werckmeister v American Lithographic Co. (1902, CC NY) 117 F 360.

Copyright upon large figure of elk built in city street was defeated by its free public exhibition which amounted to publication and dedication thereof. Carns v Keefe Bros. (1917, DC Mont) 242 F 745.

Construction and display of model house is not such publication of architectural plans from which house was built as to terminate common-law copyright in plans; filing of architectural plans with city building department in order to procure building permit resulted in loss of common-law copyright in plans; since plans did not bear copyright notice, they were dedicated to public and statutory copyright could not be acquired thereafter. Desilva Constr. Corp. v Herrald (1962, DC Fla) 213 F Supp 184, 137 USPQ 96.

Public exhibition of painting without notice of copyright in gallery, rules of which forbid copying, is not general publication; likewise, public performance of play, public delivery of lectures, playing of song in public, and broadcast by radio of script are not general publications. King v Mister Maestro, Inc. (1963, DC NY) 224 F Supp 101, 140 USPQ 366.

Statue was open to the public to copy or photograph without restriction as to persons or purpose and without adequate notice; there was a divestive publication under an invalid copyright such as to place statue in public domain. Scherr v Universal Match Corp. (1967, DC NY) 297 F Supp 107, 160 USPQ 216, affd (CA2 NY) 417 F2d 497, 11 ALR Fed 447, 164 USPQ 225, cert den 397 US 936, 25 L Ed 2d 116, 90 S Ct 945.

Where a model of a sculpture by Pablo Picasso was put on public display without statutory notice, and where citizens were free to copy the model for their own pleasure, and camera permits were available to them, there was a general publication of this work of art wherein it became a part of the public domain, thus the monumental sculpture patented upon the original model, could not thereafter be copyrighted. Letter Edged in Black Press, Inc. v Public Bldg. Com. (1970, DC Ill) 320 F Supp 1303, 168 USPQ 559.

For work to be published, it must be reproduced, that is, there must be issuance of copies to general public; completed structure is no more copy of architectural plans than exhibition of uncopyrighted moving-picture film, performance of uncopyrighted radio script, or broadcast of uncopyrighted radio script, all of which have been held not to dedicate contents to public; as used in copyright cases, "copy" signifies tangible object that is reproduction of original work; merely viewing interior of house by limited number of people, guests of owner, is limited publication as to plans, even though exhibition of exterior to public generally loses common-law copyright to exterior design. Smith v Paul (1959) 174

Cal App 2d 744, 345 P2d 546, 77 ALR2d 1036, 123 USPQ 463.

Television station has no property interest, by copyright or otherwise, in programs broadcast by station or in any signals or programs received on defendant's community antenna system and distributed to defendant's paid subscribers by means thereof; by broadcasting programs on station, and by consenting to their rebroadcast by another station, station intentionally makes them public. Z Bar Net, Inc. v Helena Television, Inc. (Mont) 125 USPQ 595.

Annotations:

Exhibition of picture as publication. 52 L Ed 208.

7. Joint work

Canadian soldier composed the music for popular ballad, and United States citizen wrote words; there was joint authorship. G. Ricordi & Co. v Columbia Graphophone Co. (1919, DC NY) 258 F 72.

8. Motion pictures

Motion-picture photoplay is dramatic work. Tiffany Productions, Inc. v Dewing (1931, DC Md) 50 F2d 911, 9 USPQ 545.

9. Perform

Playing any substantial part of composition is performance. M. Witmark & Sons v Pastime Amusement Co. (1924, DC SC) 298 F 470, affd (CA4 SC) 2 F2d 1020.

10 Publication, generally

Serial publication of book in magazine is publication within meaning of copyright law. Holmes v Hurst (1899) 174 US 82, 43 L Ed 904, 19 S Ct 606.

Serial publication of novel in magazine in England was publication within meaning of the copyright law. Fraser v Yack (1902, CA7 Ill) 116 F 285.

"Publication" has no definite and fixed meaning and may mean one thing as related to published works and another thing as to works not reproduced for sale. As to latter, it means date of deposit. Marx v United States (1938, CA9 Cal) 96 F2d 204, 37 USPQ 380.

Republication after copies of first edition are placed on sale does not satisfy definition of "date of publication" in precedessor section. Edward B. Marks Music Corp. v Continental Record Co. (1955, CA2 NY) 222 F2d 488, 105 USPQ 171, 105 USPQ 350, cert den 350 US 861, 100 L Ed 764, 76 S Ct 101.

Courts apply different tests of publication depending on whether plaintiff is claiming protection because he did not publish, in which case distribution must be quite large to constitute publication, or whether he is claiming under copyright statute, in which case requirements of publication are quite narrow. American Visuals Corp. v Holland (1956, CA2 NY) 239 F2d 740, 111 USPQ 288.

permitting public to have access to book constitutes publication, and unless author completes title to his copyright before publication he is not entitled to protection. Ladd v Oxnard (1896, CC Mass) 75 F 703.

Advertisement in trade-paper was publication. Rigney v Dutton (1896, CC NY) 77 F 176.

Where author gave copies of his uncopyrighted pamphlet or left copies in public hotel office, this was publication. D'Ole v Kansas City Star Co. (1899, CC Mo) 94 F 840.

Article concerning terrestrial globe later copyrighted was not prior publication of globe, since no one reading article could produce globe from what it disclosed, and article did not indicate dedication to public or place globe in public domain. Geo-Physical Maps, Inc. v Toycraft Corp. (1958, DC NY) 162 F Supp 141, 117 USPQ 316.

Exhibition of moving picture is "publication." Tiffany Productions, Inc. v Dewing (1931, DC Md) 50 F2d 911, 9 USPQ 545.

Granting of motion-picture rights of unpublished play and subsequent copyright of motion picture by licensee is not publication of play. O'Neill v General Film Co. (1916) 171 App Div 854, 157 NYS 1028.

Soldier's letter to minor daughters was not dedicated to public by virtue of his military status, by virtue of necessity for having same read to them, or by virtue of being addressed to them. Property rights (literary property) in contents of letter belong to his estate. Re McCormick (Pa Or Ct) 92 USPQ 393.

Annotations:

What constitutes publication of architectural plans, drawings, or designs, so as to result in loss of common-law copyright. 77 ALR2d 1048.

11. —Extent of publication

Delivery of copies of poem to members of literary committee to enable them to decide whether it is suitable for their acceptance and presentation at public meeting is not publication of poem and does not prejudice owner's common-law rights. Press Pub. Co. v Monroe (1896, CA2 NY) 73 F 196, error dismd 164 US 105, 41 L Ed 367, 17 S Ct 40.

Publication requirement of predecessor section is complied with by placing 100 copies of publication on table in hotel for unsupervised distri-

bution at convention. American Visuals Corp. v Holland (1956, CA2 NY) 239 F2d 740, 111 USPQ 288.

One hundred sets of insurance forms not bearing copyright notice were distributed to prospective customers; distribution was not limited as to persons or purpose, only limitation being that attributable to lack of general interest in specialized subject matter; this was general publication which forfeited author's right to copyright. Continental Casualty Co. v Beardsley (1958, CA2 NY) 253 F2d 702, 117 USPQ 1, cert den 358 US 816, 3 L Ed 2d 58, 79 S Ct 25.

Over years, performer passed out great quantities of cards bearing his photograph, assumed name, slogan, and symbol; cards were "writings" and distribution amounted to publication; not having copyrighted cards, performer cannot preclude others from copying them. Columbia Broadcasting System, Inc. v Decosta (1967, CA1 RI) 377 F2d 315, 153 USPQ 649, cert den 389 US 1007, 19 L Ed 2d 603, 88 S Ct 565.

Use of author's manuscript by pupils in school for instructive purpose, did not amount to abandonment. Bartlett v Crittenden (1849, CC Ohio) F Cas No 1076; Bartlett v Crittenden (1847, CC Ohio) F Cas No 1082.

Where person makes survey of shoal at his own expense, such survey does not become public property by fact that it has been deposited in Navy Department for use of government. Blunt v Patten (1828, CC NY) F Cas No 1579.

Delivery of law reports to state for distribution prior to copyright thereof did not constitute per se publication. Myers v Callaghan (1881, CC Ill) 5 F 726.

Publication of libretto and vocal score of English comic opera in London, England, though authors retained orchestral score in manuscript, was dedication to use of public of dialogue, stage business, and words and melodies of songs as intended to be sung by one or more persons, or by chorus, comprising opera as entirety, except instrumental parts. Mikado Case (1885, CC NY) 25 F 183.

Crayon sketch of painting printed without copyright notice in catalogue of salon where painting was exhibited was not such publication as would work forfeiture of right of copyright. Werckmeister v Springer Lithographing Co. (1894, CC NY) 63 F 808.

Lending by teacher to his students mimeographed typewritten copies of parts of copyrighted text-book is both "printing" and "publication" within meaning of Copyright Act. Macmillan Co. v King (1914, DC Mass) 223 F 862.

It is not such publication as will constitute abandonment to public to give song to limited number of artists to sing prior to date of copyright. McCarthy & Fischer v White (1919, DC NY) 259 F 364.

Giving of musical composition to few musicians and leaders of orchestras to play does not constitute publication where there was no general offer or dedication to public and sending of copies to music publisher and motion-picture producer was not publication, although if either of latter had used it, or made use of it in any public way, there would have been publication. Allen v Walt Disney Productions, Ltd. (1941, DC NY) 41 F Supp 134, 50 USPQ 365.

Delivery of six copies of form to third persons is publication of form. American Institute of Architects v Fenichel (1941, DC NY) 41 F Supp 146, 51 USPQ 29.

Composer's distribution of mimeographed copies of song to members of choral groups whose performances he directed, and his permission to other choral groups to perform song, did not destroy his common-law copyright in song; there was no publication such as would put song in public domain and constitute waiver of right to obtain statutory copyright; composer's distribution of stencil copies of song was among soldier groups for whom song was written and to youth groups who sang it at their gatherings with no sale of copies was not general distribution to any one who might ask for a copy; this was not a publication. Mills Music, Inc. v Cromwell Music, Inc. (1954, DC NY) 126 F Supp 54, 103 USPQ 84.

Exhibition of literary work for particular purpose, or to limited number of persons does not thereby convert publici juris, and author retains ownership until he relinquishes it by contract or unequivocal act indicating intent to dedicate to public. Stanley v Columbia Broadcasting System, Inc. (1948, Cal App) 192 P2d 495, 77 USPQ 404, superseded (Cal) 208 P2d 9, 82 USPQ 123, subsequent op on reh 35 Cal 2d 653, 221 P2d 73, 23 ALR2d 216, 86 USPQ 520.

Mere exhibition of manuscript to others is not sufficient to deprive author of his common-law rights concerning unpublished manuscripts. French v Maguire, 55 How Prac (NY) 471.

12. — —Limited publication

Owner of common-law copyright may communicate contents of his work to others by limited publication, without forfeiting any common-law rights. Bobbs-Merrill Co. v Straus (1906, CA2 NY) 147 F 15, affd 210 US 339, 52 L Ed 1086, 28 S Ct 722.

Exhibition of motion picture in limited noncommercial way did not constitute publication. Patterson v Century Productions, Inc. (1937,

CA2 NY) 93 F2d 489, 35 USPQ 471, cert den 303 US 655, 82 L Ed 1114, 58 S Ct 759.

Publication is not limited where 200 mimeographed copies were distributed to interested persons requesting copies without any restrictions as to use or circulation except that manuscript was not to be published in book form. White v Kimmell (1952, CA9 Cal) 193 F2d 744, 92 USPQ 400, cert den 343 US 957, 96 L Ed 1357, 72 S Ct 1052.

One hundred sets of insurance forms not bearing copyright notice were distributed to prospective customers; distribution was not limited as to persons or purpose, only limitation being that attributable to lack of general interest in specialized subject matter; this was general publication which forfeited author's right to copyright. Continental Casualty Co. v Beardsley (1958, CA2 NY) 253 F2d 702, 117 USPQ 1, cert den 358 US 816, 3 L Ed 2d 58, 79 S Ct 25.

While distribution of British document to British and United States government agencies and personnel alone may not constitute publication, distribution to commercial companies without restriction on use clearly does. Garrett Corp. v United States (1970) 190 Ct Cl 858, 422 F2d 874, 164 USPQ 521, cert den 400 US 951, 27 L Ed 2d 257, 91 S Ct 242.

Restricted distribution to circumscribed class of persons of unpublished work, whether copyrighted or uncopyrighted, for purpose of arousing interest in possible sale or production, is sufficiently limited distribution to work no forfeiture of author's rights, although rights would have been forfeited had there been general publication. Burnett v Lambino (1962, DC NY) 204 F Supp 327, 133 USPQ 325.

"General" with respect to publication is of greatest significance; there can be limited publication, which is communication of work to others under circumstances showing no dedication of work to public; general publication is one which shows dedication to public so as to lose copyright; distribution only to press of advance text of speech is limited, not general, publication, since copies of speech were not offered to public. King v Mister Maestro, Inc. (1963, DC NY) 224 F Supp 101, 140 USPQ 366.

Limitation as to persons and use is test of limited publication; thus, author of book is not deprived of common-law copyright where he circulates book among his friends for their personal enjoyment. Smith v Paul (1959) 174 Cal App 2d 744, 345 P2d 546, 77 ALR2d 1036, 123 USPQ 463.

While test of whether publication is limited or general is properly one of intention, unexpressed, subjective intention of creator cannot be allowed to govern; instead, implications of his outward actions to the reasonable outsider are controlling; there may be fairly substantial but limited distribution of material susceptible of statutory copyright without putting material in public domain and without forfeiture of author's common-law copyright in it. Edgar H. Wood Associates, Inc. v Skene (1964) 347 Mass 351, 197 NE2d 886, 141 USPQ 454.

Property rights in literary production before publication are exclusively in author, and word "publication" means general publication as opposed to limited one. Berry v Hoffman (1937) 125 Pa Super 261, 189 A 516.

13. —Public performance, generally

Performance is public where there is no meaningful qualification for membership in night club to which virtually any member of general public, who has good appearance, behavior, and credit rating, would be admitted to membership. Lerner v Schectman (1964, DC Minn) 228 F Supp 354, 141 USPQ 339.

Making of recording of audition recording of radio program in presence of invited, limited audience is not publication of program to extent of abandoning it to public with right to reproduce it. Stanley v Columbia Broadcasting System, Inc. (1949, Cal) 208 P2d 9, 82 USPQ 123, subsequent op on reh 35 Cal 2d 653, 221 P2d 73, 23 ALR2d 216, 86 USPQ 520.

Public performance of work, such as delivery of speech, singing of song, or reading of script, whether given in public or over radio or television, in and of itself does not deprive unpublished work of protection accorded at common law and recognized by Copyright Act. Columbia Broadcasting System, Inc. v Documentaries Unlimited, Inc. (1964) 42 Misc 2d 723, 726, 248 NYS2d 809, 141 USPQ 310.

14. — —Drama

Author of play, who permitted performances of it to be viewed only by licensed witnesses, but did not print, sell, or circulate the play, had not published it, or in any manner abandoned or dedicated it to public. Boucicault v Hart (1875, CC NY) F Cas No 1692.

Facts must exist to indicate that author has allowed play to be represented for long period of time without license or objection, before he should be considered as having abandoned it by knowingly dedicating same to public. Boucicault v Wood (1867, CC Ill) F Cas No 1693.

Presentation of theatrical production was general publication, such as would permit others who heard it to republish from parts retained in their memory. Keene v Wheatley (1861, CC Pa) F Cas No 7644.

Public performance of drama may not be publication. Roberts v Myers (1860, CC Mass) F Cas No 11906.

Public performance of play written only in manuscript form was not publication. Palmer v De Witt, 40 How Prac 293, 32 NY Super Ct 530, affd 47 NY 532.

Performance of operas by opera company and their broadcast over radio network cannot be deemed general publication or abandonment so as to divest opera company of all rights to broadcast performances. Metropolitan Opera Ass'n v Wagner-Nichols Recorder Corp. (1950) 199 Misc 786, 101 NYS2d 483, 87 USPQ 173, affd 279 App Div 632, 107 NYS2d 795.

In determining whether common-law copyright in motion picture films vested in Alien Property Custodian was lost by distribution or exhibition of films, both in United States and abroad, without appropriate copyright notice, court holds appropriate rationalization and conclusion in cited case wherein it was held that common-law copyright in play or photoplay was not abandoned by performance thereof or by leasing of film. Brandon Films, Inc. v Arjay Enterprises, Inc. (1962) 33 Misc 2d 794, 230 NYS2d 56, 133 USPQ 165.

15. — —Lecture or speech

Delivery of lectures before audiences prior to copyrighting was limited publication not constituting abandonment of common-law rights. Nutt v National Institute, Inc. for Improv. of Memory (1929, CA2 Conn) 31 F2d 236.

Permission to take notes at delivery of lecture is not general publication. Patterson v Century Productions, Inc. (1937, CA2 NY) 93 F2d 489, 35 USPQ 471, cert den 303 US 655, 82 L Ed 1114, 58 S Ct 759.

Use of person's copyrighted work by such person, in instructing others who are permitted to take copies, does not constitute abandonment to public. Bartlette v Crittenden (1847, CC Ohio) F Cas No 1082.

Rendering of performance of radio script before microphone cannot be held to be abandonment of ownership to it by proprietors or dedication of it to public. Uproar Co. v National Broadcasting Co. (1934, DC Mass) 8 F Supp 358, 23 USPQ 254, mod on other grounds (CA1 Mass) 81 F2d 373, cert den 298 US 670, 80 L Ed 1393, 56 S Ct 835.

Statutory copyright may be obtained before publication of lectures, sermons, and addresses but as soon as publication occurs there must be compliance with requirements as to published works; ordinarily, public performance of work, such as delivery of speech or performance of play, is not publication; delivery of speech before enormous crowd, with speech being broadcast over radio and television and being recorded on movie newsreel pictures, is not general publication so as to place speech in public domain. King v Mister Maestro, Inc. (1963, DC NY) 224 F Supp 101, 140 USPQ 366.

Professor's oral delivery of lectures from prepared notes does not divest him of his common-law copyright to his lectures. Williams v Weisser (1969) 273 Cal App 2d 726, 78 Cal Rptr 542, 38 ALR3d 761, 163 USPQ 42.

16. — —Music

Music is not "performed" by playing radio receiver through four speakers in restaurant where proprietor, employees, and customers are listeners rather than performers so that copyright is not infringed and license is not required. Twentieth Century Music Corp. v Aiken (1975) 422 US 151, 45 L Ed 2d 84, 95 S Ct 2040, 186 USPQ 65.

Court assumes if conductor plays over radio it would not be abandonment just as performance of play or delivery of lecture is not abandonment of common-law copyright as it does not "publish" work and dedicate it to public. RCA Mfg. Co. v Whiteman (1940, CA2 NY) 114 F2d 86, 46 USPQ 324 cert den 311 US 712, 85 L Ed 463, 61 S Ct 393 and cert den 311 US 712, 85 L Ed 463, 61 S Ct 394.

Performance of copyrighted music on premises of nonprofit private club where drinks were sold was publicly for profit inasmuch as club was open to general public so long as such casual patrons met club's standards for appearance and behavior; performance of copyrighted material in connection with selling of drinks is performance for profit; fact that club on occasion exercised right to exclude members of general public does not mean that performance was private. Lerner v Club Wander In, Inc. (1959, DC Mass) 174 F Supp 731, 122 USPQ 595.

Fact that plaintiff's song was heard and used in school before plaintiff published it with copyright notice did not constitute publication. Freudenthal v Hebrew Pub. Co. (1942, DC NY) 44 F Supp 754, 53 USPQ 466.

Composer abandoned uncopyrighted song by permitting its wide-spread use since 1908, especially in 1917–1918, and by not objecting in 1917 to eminent composer incorporating song in march whose publication was general publication dedicating song to public use. Egner v E. C. Schirmer Music Co. (1942, DC Mass) 48 F Supp 187, 56 USPQ 214, affd (CA1 Mass) 139 F2d 398, 60 USPQ 74, cert den 322 US 730, 88 L Ed 1565, 64 S Ct 947.

Singing of composition on radio broadcast is not publication; also, making of single transcription of composition for use by radio station in broadcasting is not publication since transcription is made for limited specific purpose, not for production of other records for sale to general public. Mills Music, Inc. v Cromwell Music, Inc. (1954, DC NY) 126 F Supp 54, 103 USPQ 84.

Creator of musical composition, by performing composition over radio and also performing composition in connection with filming of motion-picture cartoons which were leased and exhibited in commercial theaters throughout world, lost common-law copyright in composition and may not maintain infringement action. Blanc v Lantz (Cal App) 83 USPQ 137.

17. —Sale, generally

Manufacture and sale of phonograph records before obtaining statutory copyright in musical compositions is not "publication" invalidating copyrights. Rosette v Rainbo Record Mfg. Corp. (1976, CA2) 192 USPQ 673.

Absolute sale of book does not amount to publication which will affect author's rights therein until book actually reaches purchaser. Black v Henry G. Allen Co. (1893, CC NY) 56 F 764.

Leasing of copies of copyrighted book is "publication." Ladd v Oxnard (1896, CC Mass) 75 F 703.

Sale of books to public upon restrictive agreement not to show them to others, was publication, and rendered author's copyright void. Larrowe-Loisette v O'Loughlin (1898, CC NY) 88 F 896.

Absolute and unrestricted sale of printed copy, especially where accompanied by filing similar copies with register of copyrights, is "publication." Atlantic Monthly Co. v Post Pub. Co. (1928, DC Mass) 27 F2d 556.

Book bearing copyright notice was actually offered for sale to public and, although number of copies offered was small, and publication was made as requisite for bringing suit to enforce registration, it cannot be said that there was no publication for had book been offered for sale without copyright notice there would have been surrender of all right to copyright. United States ex rel. Twentieth Century-Fox Film Corp. v Bouve (1940, DC Dist Col) 33 F Supp 462, 45 USPQ 411, affd 74 App DC 271, 122 F2d 51, 50 USPQ 338.

Putting work on sale to general public constitutes publication. Ross Products, Inc. v New York Merchandise Co. (1964, DC NY) 233 F Supp 260, 141 USPQ 652.

Although only small quantity of product bearing copyrightable label was sold, this constituted publication since sale was public, and since label bore no copyright notice, such publication placed label in public domain. Gray v Eskimo Pie Corp. (1965, DC Del) 244 F Supp 785, 147 USPQ 188.

Printing of book for general distribution and its distribution is a general publication. Smith v Paul (1959) 174 Cal App 2d 744, 345 P2d 546, 77 ALR2d 1036, 123 USPQ 463.

Leasing of uncopyrighted books to public generally constitutes publication. Jewelers' Mercantile Agency v Jewelers' Weekly Pub. Co. (1898) 155 NY 241, 49 NE 872.

Designer of dress loses his right of property in his creation by publishing it without obtaining statutory copyright; embodying design in dress and offering dress for general sale is publication which puts design in public demesne; if disclosure is limited as to both persons and purposes, there is no publication, but disclosure which puts product within reach of general public, so that all may have access to it without further act on part of creator, is publication even though creator attempted to limit use made of thing disclosed by persons to whom it is disclosed and even though there was no sale or even express offering for general sale. Richard J. Cole, Inc. v Manhattan Modes Co. (1956, Sup) 159 NYS2d 709, 109 USPQ 370, affd 2 App Div 2d 593, 157 NYS2d 259, 112 USPQ 193.

Author's license to motion-picture producer gave latter right to sell and rent motion picture based on author's story as well as right to publish story in magazine or newspaper; this constitutes publication of story and picture adopted therefrom, resulting in loss of author's common-law copyright, which was his until publication was authorized. Varconi v Unity Television Corp. (1958) 11 Misc 2d 191, 173 NYS2d 201, 117 USPQ 107.

18. ——Exhibition or delivery for prospective sale

Exhibition cards containing reduced size copies of photographs, but having no copyright notice thereon, used for inspection of dealers only, were not published edition. Falk v Gast Lithograph & Engraving Co. (1893, CA2 NY) 54 F 890.

Delivery of manuscript to prospective purchaser for perusal and prospective sale is not publication. Press Pub. Co. v Monroe (1896, CA2 NY) 73 F 196, error dismd 164 US 105, 41 L Ed 367, 17 S Ct 40.

Dealer's samples of calendars do not require statutory copyright notice. Gerlach-Barklow Co. v Morris & Bendien, Inc. (1927, CA2 NY) 23 F2d 159.

Printing in salon catalogue of superficial crayon sketch of painting was not "publication."

Werckmeister v Springer Lithographing Co. (1894, CC NY) 63 F 808.

Distribution of copies of pamphlet in hotel lobbies constitutes publication and renders subsequently obtained copyright invalid. D'Ole v Kansas City Star Co. (1899, CC Mo) 94 F 840.

Sheets of pictures, sent out to trade as samples, without copyright mark, are not published editions. Stecher Lithographic Co. v Dunston Lithograph Co. (1916, DC NY) 233 F 601.

Samples do not require statutory notice of copyright printed on them and cannot be considered publications, but owner of copyright has burden of showing they were samples. Basevi v Edward O'Toole Co. (1939, DC NY) 26 F Supp 41, 40 USPQ 333.

Half-tone reproduction of mezzotint engravings appeared without notice of copyright in widely circulated catalogues, but this was done only for advertising purposes and did not mislead defendants and did not result in abandonment of copyright protection of engravings. Alfred Bell & Co. v Catalda Fine Arts, Inc. (1947, DC NY) 74 F Supp 973, 75 USPQ 66.

Copyright proprietor had 100 copies of story mimeographed, but copies were not offered for sale; they were merely distributed to theatrical producers free of charge in effort to induce them to produce story; this was not publication within meaning of Copyright Act. Ilyin v Avon Publications, Inc. (1956, DC NY) 144 F Supp 368, 110 USPQ 356.

Sale of dolls by originator thereof without copyright notice was publication without copyright notice because dolls were sold to purchaser without restriction; originator cannot contend that sale to purchaser was limited publication or that purchaser is publisher. Scandia House Enterprises, Inc. v Dam Things Establishment (1965, DC Dist Col) 243 F Supp 450, 146 USPQ 342.

Neither demonstration of original drawing to prospective purchaser of fabric nor publication of design in promotional magazine article by manufacturer of dresses made from fabric, with knowledge and encouragement of copyright proprietor, was publication of design. Key West Hand Print Fabrics, Inc. v Serbin, Inc. (1965, DC Fla) 244 F Supp 287, 147 USPQ 138.

Circulation of a printed musical composition prior to obtaining copyright thereon, though author had told his agents not to sell same for limited time constituted complete dedication to public, and loss of author's exclusive right therein. Wall v Gordon (NY) 12 Abb Prac (NS) 349.

Delivery of yardage of fabric bearing design to defendant for express and limited purpose of making sample dresses is restrictive delivery only and does not constitute publication of design. Fabrics by Bus Davies, Inc. v Kay Windsor Frocks, Inc. (1960) 25 Misc 2d 48, 202 NYS2d 467, 125 USPQ 470.

Sale, or offer to sell, to any persons for purpose of "examining the title to certain specified property and for no other purpose," constitutes general publication. Vernon Abstract Co. v Waggoner Title Co. (1908) 49 Tex Civ App 144, 107 SW 919.

19. Sound recordings

Term "sound recording," as used in predecessor statute, is not unconstitutionally vague. United States v Taxe (1976, CA9 Cal) 540 F2d 961, 192 USPQ 204.

Sound recorded on video tape of television performance before February 1972 is not "sound recording" but is motion picture that suit to prevent use of video tape recording comes under copyright law and federal jurisdiction, and action is dismissed. Trophy Productions, Inc. v Telebrity, Inc. (1975, NY Sup Ct) 185 USPQ 830.

20. Works made for hire

Although advertisements in newspaper were created in whole or in part by newspaper's staff, they were works done for hire and owned by advertisers who paid for preparation. Brattleboro Publishing Co. v Winmill Publishing Corp. (1966, CA2 Vt) 369 F2d 565, 5 ALR Fed 617, 151 USPQ 666.

Work was done for hire under predecessor section where the defendant had taken initiative in engaging the plaintiff to adapt a song, and plaintiff had the power to accept, reject, or modify his work, and plaintiff in turn accepted payment for it, without protest, for 27 years, and acted in the capacity of an independent contractor, and defendant at all times had the right to direct and supervise the plaintiff's work, and the new song was revised somewhat by another employee of the defendants; the right to renew the copyright in the song thus accrued exclusively to the defendant. Picture Music, Inc. v Bourne, Inc. (1972, CA2 NY) 457 F2d 1213, cert den 409 US 997, 34 L Ed 2d 262, 93 S Ct 320.

Superman Comics is not "work for hire" giving authorship to publisher where comic was developed fully 4 years before assignment to publisher and was thereafter expanded to full length production. Siegel v National Periodical Publications, Inc. (1974, CA2 NY) 508 F2d 909, 184 USPQ 257.

Evidence of contracts between 2 companies and with third party and assignments of rights in motion picture photoplay and copyright renewal registration, without proof of control or direction over film maker or payments or agreements with

film maker, and evidence that renewer was incorporated after film was made are insufficient to allow jury to conclude that work was made for hire allowing assignee to renew as author. Epoch Producing Corp. v Killiam Shows, Inc. (1975, CA2 NY) 522 F2d 737, 187 USPQ 270, cert den 424 US 955, 47 L Ed 2d 360, 96 S Ct 1429.

Literary product of salaried employee, engaged to compile, prepare and revise, after copyright issued, belongs to employer, and employee has no more right than stranger to copy or reproduce. Colliery Engineer Co. v United Correspondence Schools Co. (1899, CC NY) 94 F 152.

"Work for hire" doctrine applies to both employees and independent contractors, and television producers have right to own copyrights to musical compositions they commissioned, and refusal to give up ownership of copyrights is not contrary to antitrust or other laws or evidence of illegal conspiracy in restraint of trade. Bernstein v Universal Pictures, Inc. (1974, DC NY) 379 F Supp 933, 183 USPQ 422, revd on other grounds (CA2 NY) 517 F2d 976.

Independent contractor supplying copyrighted design for turtle doll comes within "work for hire" doctrine even though copyright proprietor did not exercise control over design, and proprietor has title to copyright. Samet & Wells, Inc. v Shalom Toy Co. (1975, DC NY) 185 USPQ 36.

Zodiac pins are works made for hire where copyright proprietor requested and controlled creations and paid for work. Jerry De Nicola, Inc. v Genesco, Pakula & Co. (1974, DC NY) 188 USPQ 304.

Presumption that employer is author of work done for hire does not apply to independent contractor artist whose contract is repudiated for dissatisfaction with layout of historical map and who is not paid for work on map, so that copyright and title remain with artist and defendant infringes by completing and publishing work. Hughey v Palographics Co. (1976, DC Colo) 189 USPQ 527.

Work made for hire, as directed and supervised by employer and at expense of employer, establishes employer as author for copyright purposes. Goldman-Morgen, Inc. v Dan Brechner & Co. (1976, DC NY) 190 USPQ 478.

"Composite work," by definition, cannot also be "work made for hire," since latter presupposes that contributors are employees who are not entitled under Act to renew copyright registrations as "authors"; composite work permits both proprietor of original copyright in composite, as well as individual contributing authors, to apply for renewal. 43 OAG 2.

Annotations:

Application of "works for hire" doctrine under Federal Copyright Act (17 USCS §§ 1 et seq.). 11 ALR Fed 457.

§ 102. Subject matter of copyright: In general

(a) Copyright protection subsists, in accordance with this title [17 USCS §§ 101 et seq.], in original works of authorship fixed in any tangible medium of expression, now known or later developed, from which they can be perceived, reproduced, or otherwise communicated, either directly or with the aid of a machine or device. Works of authorship include the following categories:

(1) literary works;

(2) musical works, including any accompanying words;

(3) dramatic works, including any accompanying music;

(4) pantomimes and choreographic works;

(5) pictorial, graphic, and sculptural works;

(6) motion pictures and other audiovisual works; and

(7) sound recordings.

(b) In no case does copyright protection for an original work of authorship extend to any idea, procedure, process, system, method of operation, concept, principle, or discovery, regardless of the form in which it is described, explained, illustrated, or embodied in such work.
(Added Oct. 19, 1976, PL 94-553, Title I, § 101, 90 Stat 2544.)

HISTORY; ANCILLARY LAWS AND DIRECTIVES

Effective date of section:
Section 102 of Act Oct. 19, 1976, P.L. 94-553, 90 Stat. 2598 provided that this section "becomes effective on January 1, 1978".

CROSS REFERENCES

"Copies" defined, 17 USCS § 101.
"Fixation" defined, 17 USCS § 101.
"Include" defined, 17 USCS § 101.
"Literary works" defined, 17 USCS § 101.
"Motion pictures and audiovisual works" defined, 17 USCS § 101.
"Phonorecords" defined, 17 USCS § 101.
"Pictorial, graphic, and sculptural works" defined, 17 USCS § 101.
"Sound recordings" defined, 17 USCS § 101.
Scope of exclusive rights in copyrightable works, 17 USCS § 113.
Unfixed work of authorship, 17 USCS § 301.
This section referred to in 17 USCS §§ 103, 104, 301.

RESEARCH GUIDE

Am Jur:
18 Am Jur 2d, Copyright and Literary Property §§ 27, 36, 38, 40, 46, 48, 50, 51, 54, 55, 65.

Forms:
6 Federal Procedural Forms L Ed, Copyrights §§ 17:91, 17:99.

7 Am Jur Pl & Pr Forms (Rev ed), Copyright and Literary Property, Form 2.

Annotations:

Statutory copyright protection of "works of art". 98 L Ed 644.

Copyright, under federal copyright laws, of forms or form books. 8 ALR Fed 869.

Copyright, under Federal Copyright Act (17 USCS §§ 1 et seq.), in advertising materials, catalogs, and price lists. 5 ALR Fed 625.

Maps or charts as protected by copyright under federal copyright acts. 4 ALR Fed 466.

Copyright, under federal copyright laws, of architectural plans, drawings, or designs. 3 ALR Fed 793.

Law Review Articles:

Copyright Symposium, 22 New York Law School Law Review 193.

INTERPRETIVE NOTES AND DECISIONS

44. Sound recordings [17 USCS § 102(a)(7)]

V. IDEAS AND METHODOLOGY [17 USCS § 102(b)]
45. Generally
46. Facts and events
47. Particular ideas
48. Directories and lists
49. Procedures, processes and systems, generally
50. Business systems

I. IN GENERAL

1. Generally

Copyright as distinguished from literary property is wholly creature of statute. Krafft v Cohen (1941, CA3 Pa) 117 F2d 579, 48 USPQ 401.

In determining validity of copyright, starting point is Constitution; as constitutional power to enact Copyright Act derives from § 8 of Article 1, act would be void if it went beyond granting monopolies, or exclusive franchises, to authors whose works promote progress of science and useful arts; Constitution does not authorize such grant to one whose product lacks all creative originality. Chamberlin v Uris Sales Corp. (1945, CA2 NY) 150 F2d 512, 65 USPQ 544.

Literary property intended to be protected by copyrights laws is to be determined by subject matter of work only. Clayton v Stone (1829, CC NY) F Cas No 2872.

General intent of Congress, apart from proceedings in equity and from actions at law for damages for unauthorized publication of manuscript, seems to have been to enforce copyright laws by penalties, rather than by ordinary common-law remedies. Daly v Brady (1895, CC NY) 69 F 285.

Subject of statutory copyright being wholly within powers of Congress, it has full power to restrict all actions or proceedings dealing with infringement of rights secured by Copyright Act. New York Times Co. v Star Co. (1912, CC NY) 195 F 110.

In view of predecessor section, Copyright Act must be understood to cover all compositions which under Constitution can be copyrighted at all. Reiss v National Quotation Bureau (1921, DC NY) 276 F 717.

Copyrights and rights flowing therefrom are entirely creatures of statute. Loew's, Inc. v Columbia Broadcasting System, Inc. (1955, DC Cal) 131 F Supp 165, 105 USPQ 302, affd (CA9 Cal) 239 F2d 532, 112 USPQ 11, affd 356 US 43, 2 L Ed 2d 583, 78 S Ct 667, 116 USPQ 479, reh den 356 US 934, 2 L Ed 2d 764, 78 S Ct 770.

2. Construction

Copyright statutes ought to be reasonably construed, with view to effecting purposes intended by Congress; they ought not to be unduly extended by judicial construction to include privileges not intended to be conferred, or so narrowly construed as to deprive those entitled to their benefit of rights Congress intended to grant. Bobbs-Merrill Co. v Straus (1908) 210 US 339, 52 L Ed 1086, 28 S Ct 722.

Statute may be applied to new situations not anticipated by Congress, if, fairly construed, such situations come within its intent and meaning. Jerome H. Remick & Co. v American Auto. Accessories Co. (1925, CA6 Ohio) 5 F2d 411, 40 ALR 1511, cert den 269 US 556, 70 L Ed 409, 46 S Ct 19.

Copyright law, being creature of statute and conferring distinct and limited rights which do not exist at common law, must be strictly construed. White-Smith Music Pub. Co. v Apollo Co. (1906, CA2 NY) 147 F 226, affd 209 US 1, 52 L Ed 655, 28 S Ct 319.

Provisions in copyright laws should be given liberal construction in order to give effect to inherent right of author in his own work. Myers v Callaghan (1881, CC Ill) 5 F 726.

Copyright laws should be liberally construed, so as to protect rights of authors and to promote literature and art. Ford v Charles E. Blaney Amusement Co. (1906, CC NY) 148 F 642.

Copyright laws should be liberally construed and administrative act of register of copyrights should be so construed, if reasonably possible, as to carry out intention of Constitution to protect and encourage creative artists in their work. Southern Music Pub. Co. v Bibo-Lang, Inc. (1935, DC NY) 10 F Supp 972, 26 USPQ 321; Basevi v Edward O'Toole Co. (1939, DC NY) 26 F Supp 41, 40 USPQ 333.

3. Purpose

Intent and purpose of Copyright Act may not be limited by private agreement between author and his publisher. Kipling v G. P. Putnam's Sons (1903, CA2 NY) 120 F 631.

Protection must be sought either in copyright or patent field; it cannot be found in both; there is no overlapping territory, even though line of separation may be difficult of exact ascertainment. Taylor Instrument Cos. v Fawley-Brost Co. (1943, CA7 Ill) 139 F2d 98, 59 USPQ 384, cert den 321 US 785, 88 L Ed 1076, 64 S Ct 782.

Primary purpose of copyright statute is to promote progress of science and useful arts, and financial reward is secondary, and copyright claims fulfilling purpose may be granted even though they infringe other copyright claims. L.

Batlin & Son, Inc. v Snyder (1975, CA2) 187 USPQ 721.

II. WORKS OF AUTHORSHIP, GENERALLY [17 USCS § 102(a)].

4. Generally

Obtaining of patent renders subject part of public domain, except under patent, and precludes obtaining of copyright. Korzybski v Underwood & Underwood, Inc. (1929, CA2 NY) 36 F2d 727, 3 USPQ 242.

Portrait of Washington and United States shield are not susceptible of exclusive appropriations. Carr v National Capital Press, Inc. (1934) 63 App DC 210, 71 F2d 220, 21 USPQ 408.

Copyright law was extended in mid-19th century to works of art and reproductions of works of art, and extension of law did not increase scope of protection, but merely increased range of subjects covered and did not extend to protection of ideas, but merely to expressions of ideas. L. Batlin & Son, Inc. v Snyder (1975, CA2) 187 USPQ 721.

Where reproduction of picture would not be "label" while it might be "print," and picture possessed artistic merit and was also suitable for use as design, it was subject either to copyright, or might have been patented, though it could not have had such double protection, and since owner elected to copyright it, he was bound by his election. Louis De Jonge & Co. v Breuker & Kessler Co. (1910, CC Pa) 182 F 150, affd (CA3 Pa) 191 F 35, affd 235 US 33, 59 L Ed 113, 35 S Ct 6.

Trade secrets are not protected by copyright laws. Peterson System, Inc. v Morgan (1963, DC Pa) 224 F Supp 957, 140 USPQ 137.

Overlap exists between copyright law and patent law, as to some designs, and designer may secure both copyright and patent protection without election, so that design of "Spiro watch" with caricatured figure is not rejectable for such design having been copyrighted. Application of Yardley (1974, Cust & Pat App) 493 F2d 1389, 181 USPQ 331.

5. Combinations, plans, and arrangement of expressions

Any new or original plan, arrangement, or combination of materials entitled author to copyright, whether materials themselves were new or old. Nutt v National Institute, Inc. for Improv. of Memory (1929, CA2 Conn) 31 F2d 236.

New combination and novel arrangement of commonplace materials and acts is protectible by copyright. Universal Pictures Co. v Harold Lloyd Corp. (1947, CA9 Cal) 162 F2d 354, 73 USPQ 317.

Copyright is valid in fabric design copied from uncopyrighted design but broadened to cover a bolt of cloth and to repeat pattern without showing unsightly joint an embellishment requiring minimal but sufficient originality to support copyright. Soptra Fabrics Corp. v Stafford Knitting Mills, Inc. (1974, CA2 NY) 490 F2d 1092, 26 ALR Fed 402, 180 USPQ 545.

Every author of book has copyright in plan, arrangement, and combination of his materials and in his mode of illustrating his subject, if it be new and original in its substance. Emerson v Davies (1845, CC Mass) F Cas No 4436.

There may be valid copyright in plan, arrangement, combination of materials, and mode of displaying and illustrating subject, though such materials and subject be common to other writers. Greene v Bishop (1858, CC Mass) F Cas No 5763.

New and original plan, arrangement, or combination of materials will entitle author to copyright therein, whether materials themselves be old or new. Lawrence v Dana (1869, CC Mass) F Cas No 8136; Hoffman v Le Traunik (1913, DC NY) 209 F 375.

In case of literary or artistic works and works of similar character in which form, arrangement, or combination of ideas represents product of labor and skilled effort separate and apart from that entailed in development of intellectual conception involved, medium of expression is entitled to protection by copyright against its adoption by another in similar form, arrangement, and combination. Long v Jordan (1939, DC Cal) 29 F Supp 287, 43 USPQ 176.

Special arrangement of chapters for work on chemistry, that is, idea as to what proper divisions of such work should be, is not copyrightable. Colonial Book Co. v Oxford Book Co. (1942, DC NY) 45 F Supp 551, 53 USPQ 599, affd (CA2 NY) 135 F2d 463, 57 USPQ 569.

Copyright protection cannot be obtained as to ideas which are not novel, but, where idea of collecting and arranging ideas into compact course of study and instruction is novel, originator thereof is entitled to protection under copyright insofar as plan, arrangement, and form of text of publication are concerned. Powell v Stransky (1951, DC SD) 98 F Supp 434, 89 USPQ 310.

Although there is no copyrightable property right in idea, there may be property rights in particular combination of ideas where combination is reduced to concrete form. Gordon v Weir (1953, DC Mich) 111 F Supp 117, 97 USPQ 387, affd (CA6 Mich) 216 F2d 508, 104 USPQ 40.

Although ideas, abstract conceptions, and similar matters are not protectible, author's manner of treatment, expression, incidents and details, and sequence of events by which he works out and develops abstractions are copyrightable elements of his work and will be protected. Loew's, Inc. v Columbia Broadcasting System, Inc. (1955, DC Cal) 131 F Supp 165, 105 USPQ 302, affd (CA9 Cal) 239 F2d 532, 112 USPQ 11, affd 356 US 43, 2 L Ed 2d 583, 78 S Ct 667, 116 USPQ 479, reh den 356 US 934, 2 L Ed 2d 764, 78 S Ct 770.

Arrangement of contents in insurance bond, however novel arrangement may be, is not copyrightable, for novelty of arrangement is key concept in plan, and ideas and plans fall outside copyright laws. Continental Cas. Co. v Beardsley (1957, DC NY) 151 F Supp 28, 113 USPQ 181, mod on other grounds (CA2 NY) 253 F2d 702, 117 USPQ 1, cert den 358 US 816, 3 L Ed 2d 58, 79 S Ct 25.

New and original plan or combination of existing materials in public domain is sufficiently original to come within copyright protection; however, work must be original in sense that author created it by his own skill, labor, and judgment without directly copying or evasively imitating another's work; plaintiff has burden of establishing these elements when demanding preliminary injunction. Alva Studios, Inc. v Winninger (1959, DC NY) 177 F Supp 265, 123 USPQ 487.

Although mere portrayal of series of gradations of color shades, standing alone, would present doubtful case for copyright protection, court holds copyrightable a new arrangement which facilitates selection and matching of colors; this embodiment had not previously been published and was plaintiff's original creation. Pantone, Inc. v A. I. Friedman, Inc. (1968, DC NY) 294 F Supp 545, 160 USPQ 530.

The test for determining copyrightability is originality, that is, independent creation or individuality of expression, rather than novelty; and originality of even the slightest degree, even if it amounts to no more than a re-arrangement of age-old ideas, is sufficient. Trebonik v Grossman Music Corp. (1969, DC Ohio) 305 F Supp 339, 163 USPQ 352.

Copyright in executive desk calendar is valid even though work includes much that was public domain, where compilation and arrangements are original. Baldwin Cooke Co. v Keith Clark, Inc. (1974, DC Ill) 383 F Supp 650, 183 USPQ 209, affd without opinion (CA7 Ill) 505 F2d 1250 and supp op (DC Ill) 420 F Supp 404.

If format for radio program is original and novel, it may constitute protectible product of mind. Kovacs v Mutual Broadcasting System, Inc. (1950) 99 Cal App 2d 56, 221 P2d 108, 86 USPQ 547.

6. Component parts

Degree of protection afforded by copyright is determined by what is actually copyrightable in card and not by its entire contents; there is no copyright for toys, badges, or similar articles alone or fastened to book. Jackson v Quickslip Co. (1940, CA2 NY) 110 F2d 731, 45 USPQ 6.

Copyright on model airplane kit is valid as to all components of kit including plastic component parts, and copyright notice on box containing kit is proper. Monogram Models, Inc. v Industro Motive Corp. (1974, CA6 Mich) 492 F2d 1281, 181 USPQ 425, cert den 419 US 843, 42 L Ed 2d 71, 95 S Ct 76.

Monogram appearing in front of book is not subject within copyright law. Royal Sales Co. v Gaynor (1908, CC NY) 164 F 207.

Copyright of book or periodical does not include cover. Fawcett Publications, Inc. v Elliot Pub. Co. (1942, DC NY) 46 F Supp 717, 54 USPQ 367.

Characters of cartoon strips and comic books and their graphic depiction are protected as component parts of copyrighted works. Walt Disney Productions v Air Pirates (1972, DC Cal) 345 F Supp 108.

Copyright cannot be secured on ideas or public domain concepts, but can be secured on new expression of old idea, if only slightly novel. Ansehl v Puritan Pharmaceutical Co. (1932, CA8 Mo) 61 F2d 131, 15 USPQ 38, cert den 287 US 666, 77 L Ed 574, 53 S Ct 224; Eisenschiml v Fawcett Publications, Inc. (1957, CA7 Ill) 246 F2d 598, 114 USPQ 199, cert den 355 US 907, 2 L Ed 2d 262, 78 S Ct 334; Welles v Columbia Broadcasting System, Inc. (1962, CA9 Cal) 308 F2d 810, 135 USPQ 116; Roth Greeting Cards v United Card Co. (1970, CA9 Cal) 429 F2d 1106, 166 USPQ 291; Universal Athletic Sales Co. v Salkeld (1975, CA3 Pa) 511 F2d 904, 185 USPQ 76, cert den 423 US 863, 46 L Ed 2d 92, 96 S Ct 122; L. Batlin & Son, Inc. v Snyder (1975, CA2) 187 USPQ 721; L. Batlin & Son, Inc. v Snyder (1976, CA2 NY) 536 F2d 486, 189 USPQ 753, cert den 429 US 857, 50 L Ed 2d 135, 97 S Ct 156; Lewis v Kroger Co. (1952, DC W Va) 109 F Supp 484, 95 USPQ 359; Dugan v American Broadcasting Corp. (1963, DC Cal) 216 F Supp 763, 137 USPQ 238; Stratchborneo v Arc Music Corp. (1973, DC NY) 357 F Supp 1393.

So far as pictorial representations and verbal descriptions of plaintiff's fictional character are not mere delineation of benevolent Hercules, but embody arrangement of incidents and literary expressions original with author, they are proper subjects of copyright. Detective Comics, Inc. v Bruns Publications, Inc. (1940, CA2 NY) 111 F2d 432, 45 USPQ 291.

When the idea and its expression are inseparable, copying the expression will not be barred, since protecting the expression in such circumstances would confer a monopoly of the idea upon the copyright owner free of the conditions and limitations imposed by the patent law. Herbert Rosenthal Jewelry Corp. v Kalpakian (1971, CA9 Cal) 446 F2d 738, 170 USPQ 557.

When book is designed to convey information, reader may use information, whether correct or incorrect, in his own literary work, provided that his expression and treatment are distinctly his own and not merely result of copying from book; second author may adopt first author's historical ideas since copyright law only protects author's mode of expression and not his ideas. Greenbie v Noble (1957, DC NY) 151 F Supp 45, 113 USPQ 115.

Copyright does not cover idea or system of doing business, but only particular mode of expression of idea embodied in copyrighted material; public is free to use idea or method of doing business; while copyrighted description of idea may not be slavishly copied, copyright is not infringed by expression of idea which is substantially similar where similarity is necessary because idea or system being described is same. Gaye v Gillis (1958, DC Mass) 167 F Supp 416, 119 USPQ 292.

Although ideas as such are not subject to copyright, originality of slightest degree is sufficient; choice of locale for story does not, necessarily, spell originality; copyrightability lies in manner of developing idea; originality lies in pattern of work. Bradbury v Columbia Broadcasting System, Inc. (1959, DC Cal) 174 F Supp 733, 123 USPQ 10, revd on other grounds (CA9 Cal) 287 F2d 478, cert dismd 368 US 801, 7 L Ed 2d 15, 82 S Ct 19.

Distinction between "ideas" which are not protected by copyright laws and particular "expressions" which are protected is not subject to objective standard, but necessarily involves subjective determination. Goodson-Todman Enterprises, Ltd. v Kellogg Co. (1973, DC Cal) 358 F Supp 1245, 178 USPQ 573, revd on other grounds (CA9 Cal) 513 F2d 913.

Whether protectible property interest exists in literary composition reduced to concrete form depends upon originality of form and manner of expression, development of characterizations, and sequence of events; idea alone, bare, undeveloped story situation or theme, is not protectible. Weitzenkorn v Lesser (1953) 40 Cal 2d 778, 256 P2d 947, 97 USPQ 545.

Author of any product of mind has exclusive ownership therein and in expression thereof which continues so long as expressions thereof made by him remain in his possession; product

of mind is property and is intangible, incorporeal right; there cannot be property in author's idea, but there may be property in particular combination of ideas or in form in which ideas are embodied; although there can be no property in words merely generic or descriptive, person may have property right and right to exclusive use of arbitrary, fictitious, fanciful, artificial, or technical names or titles; they have special significance and are creations of mind. Johnston v Twentieth Century-Fox Film Corp. (1947) 82 Cal App 2d 796, 187 P2d 474, 76 USPQ 131.

Ideas, though in copyrighted book or play, may be copied and used, but form, sequence, or manner in which idea is developed, treated, or expressed cannot be appropriated. Stanley v Columbia Broadcasting System, Inc. (1948, Cal App) 192 P2d 495, 77 USPQ 404, superseded (Cal) 208 P2d 9, 82 USPQ 123, subsequent op on reh 35 Cal 2d 653, 221 P2d 73, 23 ALR2d 216, 86 USPQ 520.

8. Illegal or immoral matters

Handicapping systems for betting on horse races are entitled to copyright protection even if false or fraudulent. Belcher v Tarbox (1973, CA9 Cal) 486 F2d 1087, 180 USPQ 1.

Immoral production unsuited for public representation is not entitled to benefit of copyright. Martinetti v Maguire (1867, CC Cal) F Cas No 9173.

Playing cards may be subject of copyright although they are sometimes used for gambling purposes. Richardson v Miller (1877, CC Mass) F Cas No 11791.

To be entitled to copyright composition must be free from illegality or immorality. Hoffman v Le Traunik (1913, DC NY) 209 F 375.

Immoral books are not entitled to copyright protection. Simonton v Gordon (1925, DC NY) 12 F2d 116.

In determining whether work is indecent or immoral, court adopts tests in cases under postal statutes denying mailing privileges to indecent works; work must be considered as whole and have direct tendency to corrupt morals; mere vulgarity or coarseness of language does not condemn it; narrative can have no immoral tendency where derelictions end in punishment or suffering, and contrition, followed by forgiveness, although author did not have such purpose when writing. Cain v Universal Pictures Co. (1942, DC Cal) 47 F Supp 1013, 56 USPQ 8.

Book containing coupons entitling one to cash discounts on purchase of merchandise is proper subject matter for copyright protection despite fact that book is fraudulent in that it is used for sole and express purpose of falsely inducing public to believe that discounts are obtained through use of book, whereas same discounts are given to all members of public in ordinary course of business. Advisers Inc. v Wiesen-Hart, Inc. (1958, DC Ohio) 161 F Supp 831.

Obscene movie is not entitled to protection of copyright laws. Mitchell Bros. Film Group v Cinema Adult Theater (1976, DC Tex) 192 USPQ 138.

9. Literary or artistic quality

Article having none of characteristics of work of art or of literary production cannot be subject of copyright. Ehret v Pierce (1880, CC NY) 10 F 553.

To be entitled to copyright article must have some value as composition other than as advertisement. Meccano, Ltd. v Wagner (1916, DC Ohio) 234 F 912, mod on other grounds (CA6 Ohio) 246 F 603.

Right to copyright is not affected by artistic merit of work. Pellegrini v Allegrini (1924, DC Pa) 2 F2d 610.

Recent trend in copyright actions indicates tendency by courts to afford more liberal protection to copyright owner, who is not denied relief on ground that his work is not of sufficient literary quality to merit copyright protection. Gordon v Weir (1953, DC Mich) 111 F Supp 117, 97 USPQ 387, affd (CA6 Mich) 216 F2d 508, 104 USPQ 40.

Court considers differences between copyrighted ring and public domain ring and finds differences trivial and meaningless and utterly devoid of original creativity, even considering minimal standards required by copyright law, so that copyright on ring is invalid. Vogue Ring Creations, Inc. v Hardman (1976, DC RI) 410 F Supp 609, 190 USPQ 329.

10. Originality, generally

Copyright requires and protects originality of work, rather than novelty or invention. Sheldon v Metro-Goldwyn Pictures Corp. (1936, CA2 NY) 81 F2d 49, 28 USPQ 330, cert den 298 US 669, 80 L Ed 1392, 56 S Ct 835; Dorsey v Old Surety Life Ins. Co. (1938, CA10 Okla) 98 F2d 872, 119 ALR 1250, 39 USPQ 92; Ricker v General Electric Co. (1947, CA2 NY) 162 F2d 141, 73 USPQ 458; Stein v Mazer (1953, CA4 Md) 204 F2d 472, 97 USPQ 310, affd 347 US 201, 98 L Ed 630, 74 S Ct 460, 100 USPQ 325, reh den 347 US 949, 98 L Ed 1096, 74 S Ct 637; Wihtol v Wells (1956, CA7 Ill) 231 F2d 550, 109 USPQ 200; Best Medium Publishing Co. v National Insider, Inc. (1967, CA7 Ill) 385 F2d 384, 155 USPQ 550, cert den 390 US 955, 19 L Ed 2d 1150, 88 S Ct 1052, reh den 390 US 1008, 20 L Ed 2d 110, 88 S Ct 1244.

Mere priority in time in obtaining copyright does not confer monopoly, and two stories, though identical, if each is original and independent production, may both be entitled to copyright. Harold Lloyd Corp. v Witwer (1933, CA9 Cal) 65 F2d 1, cert dismd (US) 78 L Ed 1507, 54 S Ct 94.

Plaintiff's chart for analyzing handwriting contained matter in prior works but was not copied therefrom and was clearly original work within meaning of Copyright Act. Deutsch v Arnold (1938, CA2 NY) 98 F2d 686, 39 USPQ 5.

Original treatment of life of historical character, like such treatment of any material even in public domain, is protected against appropriation by others. De Acosta v Brown (1944, CA2 NY) 146 F2d 408, 63 USPQ 311, cert den 325 US 862, 89 L Ed 1983, 65 S Ct 1197 and cert den 325 US 862, 89 L Ed 1983, 65 S Ct 1198.

Fact that copyrighted doll was based on live model does not deprive it of necessary amount of originality. Rushton v Vitale (1955, CA2 NY) 218 F2d 434, 104 USPQ 158.

Plastic reproduction of public domain Uncle Sam bank is copyrightable as involving modicum of creativity in imitating original. L. Batlin & Son, Inc. v Snyder (1975, CA2) 187 USPQ 721.

Originality cannot be predicated upon similarity of locale. Echevarria v Warner Bros. Pictures, Inc. (1935, DC Cal) 12 F Supp 632, 28 USPQ 213.

Copyrighted matter must be original with copyright registrant either as author or proprietor as assignee of author; copyrighted score cards contain names of players and their numbers which originated with respective baseball clubs and not with copyright registrant which is therefore not legally entitled to register score card under Copyright Act. Penn Sportservice, Inc. v Goldstein (DC Pa) 46 USPQ 477.

Use of quotation marks by biographer to set out conversations he had with subject of biography, instead of use of narrative form, does not put matter in public domain since no stenographer was present and statement of conversations is biographer's version, result of his literary effort; if biographer was only trying to reconstruct conversations, that would be authorship; even if conversations were exact repetition, biographer's part in conversations would be original and would have contributed to creation of subject's part. Harris v Miller (DC NY) 50 USPQ 306.

Similarities and incidental details necessary to environment or setting of action are not material of which copyrightable originality consists. Cain v Universal Pictures Co. (1942, DC Cal) 47 F Supp 1013, 56 USPQ 8.

Only original work may be copyrighted; there is nothing original in use of "Sons and Daughters of Uncle Sam" or its insignia as applied to corporation of citizens of United States, "Uncle Sam" being descriptive term designating United States. Blish v National Broadcasting Co. (1942, DC Ill) 49 F Supp 346, 56 USPQ 212.

Locale is not subject of copyright protection or of common-law protection as literary property. Schwarz v Universal Pictures Co. (1945, DC Cal) 85 F Supp 270, 83 USPQ 153.

Author may not, through copyright, appropriate and withdraw from public domain idea, theme, plot, or basic characters. Tralins v Kaiser Aluminum & Chemical Corp. (1958, DC Md) 160 F Supp 511, 117 USPQ 79.

Only modicum of originality is required to justify copyright protection; thus, although Egyptian lettering may be but arrangement of letters which are part of public domain, distinguishable variation in arrangement and manner of presentation (dark background, particular size of letters, their spacing, their arrangement into three rows) combines to give product independent authorship worthy of protection against copying; this is even more evident as to drawings of products in catalog which drawings, although simple in form, present original effort at illustration of products; having gone to trouble of independently producing these illustrations and thereafter copyrighting them, plaintiff is protected against intentional copying by competitor; if it be argued that drawings contain small degree of skill and originality, answer would seem to be that so long as they contain enough skill and originality to justify another's copying them, contrary to copyright notice against such copying, such copying will be enjoined. Amplex Mfg. Co. v A. B. C. Plastic Fabricators, Inc. (1960, DC Pa) 184 F Supp 285, 125 USPQ 648.

To be copyrightable, work must be original in that author created it by his own skill, labor, and judgment, contributing something recognizably his own to prior treatments of same subject; requirements are modest; neither great novelty nor superior artistic quality is required. Doran v Sunset House Distributing Corp. (1961, DC Cal) 197 F Supp 940, 131 USPQ 94, affd (CA9 Cal) 304 F2d 251, 134 USPQ 4 and (disapproved on other grounds L. Batlin & Son, Inc. v Snyder (CA2 NY) 536 F2d 486, cert den 429 US 857, 50 L Ed 2d 135, 97 S Ct 156).

It is not novelty, but originality, which entitles author to copyright protection; originality is present in substantial and sufficient degree in conception, organization, and presentation of material whether new or old; as to what is old, only common source, not copyrighted work, except as to fair use, may be resorted to by all,

for only old lies in public domain. Addison-Wesley Publishing Co. v Brown (1963, DC NY) 223 F Supp 219, 139 USPQ 47.

Court considers differences between copyrighted ring and public domain ring and finds differences trivial and meaningless and utterly devoid of original creativity, even considering minimal standards required by copyright law, so that copyright on ring is invalid. Vogue Ring Creations, Inc. v Hardman (1976, DC RI) 410 F Supp 609, 190 USPQ 329.

11. —Proof of originality

In suit on common-law copyright by author of unpublished play charging defendant with literary larceny in production of motion picture, question of originality is one of fact, not of law, and must be established by proof. Dezendorf v Twentieth Century-Fox Film Corp. (1938, CA9 Cal) 99 F2d 850, 39 USPQ 467.

When defendant shows source of plaintiff's work is in public domain, plaintiff has burden of overcoming such proof of lack of originality. Hirsch v Paramount Pictures, Inc. (1937, DC Cal) 17 F Supp 816, 32 USPQ 233.

In determining whether there is originality, court is not governed by opinions of author or experts. Schwarz v Universal Pictures Co. (1945, DC Cal) 85 F Supp 270, 83 USPQ 153.

In determining whether plaintiff's composition is original, court must give consideration to music in public domain; perhaps, best test to determine originality is to inquire whether composition is new and different treatment of old theme or melody or is merely colorable attempt to use someone else's work as composer's own. Northern Music Corp. v King Record Distributing Co. (1952, DC NY) 105 F Supp 393, 93 USPQ 512.

Originality ordinarily is question of fact which is not to be decided on motion to dismiss, but mere allegation of originality in complaint does not create factual issue where all ideas involved have long been public property. Lewis v Kroger Co. (1952, DC W Va) 109 F Supp 484, 95 USPQ 359.

12. Plot or theme

Mere idea in plot is not copyrightable. Dymow v Bolton (1926, CA2 NY) 11 F2d 690.

Bare outline or theme of play is not copyrightable. Nichols v Universal Pictures Corp. (1930, CA2 NY) 45 F2d 119, 7 USPQ 84, cert den 282 US 902, 75 L Ed 795, 51 S Ct 216.

Theme is not subject to exclusive copyright. Shipman v R. K. O. Radio Pictures, Inc. (1938, CA2 NY) 100 F2d 533, 40 USPQ 211.

Distinctive treatment of plot or theme is copyrightable and sequence of incidents in plot in conjunction with distinctive locale and organized characterizations is protected by copyright law. Universal Pictures Co. v Harold Lloyd Corp. (1947, CA9 Cal) 162 F2d 354, 73 USPQ 317.

Where features of plot of story are old, but author rewrites and improves thereon, he is protected by copyrighting his work insofar as his embellishments and additions are original. Stodart v Mutual Film Corp. (1917, DC NY) 249 F 507.

Old plot cannot be copyrighted, but new treatment of old plot may be protected by copyright. Stephens v Howells Sales Co. (1926, DC NY) 16 F2d 805.

It is doubtful whether incidents per se can become copyrightable literary property, but it does not take many of them to make what will pass for plot and constitute action of play which can be copyrighted. Frankel v Irwin (1918, DC NY) 34 F2d 142.

Plot or mere concept of situation around which to build and develop literary or artistic adornment is not copyrightable. Wiren v Shubert Theatre Corp. (1933, DC NY) 5 F Supp 358, affd (CA2 NY) 70 F2d 1023, cert den 293 US 591, 79 L Ed 685, 55 S Ct 105, reh den 293 US 631, 79 L Ed 716, 55 S Ct 140.

Distinctive treatment of plot or theme is properly subject of copyright, as dramatic composition and sequence of incidents in plot, taken in conjunction with distinctive locale, and original characterizations, will be protected; absence of dialogue is not fatal, and theme may be in pantomime, but no broad central dramatic situation in broad outline can be protected; Copyright Act does not protect distinctive locale, mechanical devices used in production, gestures or motions or even movements of dance. Seltzer v Sunbrock (1938, DC Cal) 22 F Supp 621, 37 USPQ 491.

Test of copyrightability distinguishes between plot ideas used by author and his expression of them; only latter is copyrightable. Burnett v Lambino (1962, DC NY) 204 F Supp 327, 133 USPQ 325.

13. Titles

Title per se is not protected by copyright. Atlas Mfg. Co. v Street & Smith (1913, CA8 Mo) 204 F 398, app dismd 231 US 348, 58 L Ed 262, 34 S Ct 73; Becker v Loew's, Inc. (1943, CA7 Ill) 133 F2d 889, 56 USPQ 455, cert den 319 US 772, 87 L Ed 1720, 63 S Ct 1438, reh den 320 US 811, 88 L Ed 490, 64 S Ct 30.

Title per se is not protected by copyright. Osgood v Allen (1872, CC Me) F Cas No 10603; Donnelley v Ivers (1883, CC NY) 18 F 592;

Black v Ehrich (1891, CC NY) 44 F 793; Harper v Ranous (1895, CC NY) 67 F 904; Corbett v Purdy (1897, CC NY) 80 F 901; Glaser v St. Elmo Co. (1909, CC NY) 175 F 276; Martenet v United Artists Corp. (1944, DC NY) 56 F Supp 639, 62 USPQ 148; Shapiro Bernstein & Co. v Jerry Vogel Music Co. (1953, DC NY) 115 F Supp 754, 98 USPQ 438, 99 USPQ 381, revd on other grounds (CA2 NY) 221 F2d 569, 105 USPQ 178, adhered to (CA2 NY) 223 F2d 252, 105 USPQ 460.

Title of motion picture which has acquired distinctive meaning in motion-picture field as descriptive of film version of certain copyrighted play produced by complainant and has not been used before to designate any other full-length motion picture, may not be used by a competitor to deceive public. Warner Bros. Pictures, Inc. v Majestic Pictures Corp. (1934, CA2 NY) 70 F2d 310, 21 USPQ 405.

Copyright of "Visualized American History" did not cover use of "visualized" in title but did include book itself together with arrangement of charts, tabulations, and cartoon illustrations designed to bring information readily to reader's mind. Oxford Book Co. v College Entrance Book Co. (1938, CA2 NY) 98 F2d 688, 39 USPQ 7.

Although title to song, in itself, is not subject to copyright protection, title should be taken into account when same title is applied to work copied from song. Wihtol v Wells (1956, CA7 Ill) 231 F2d 550, 109 USPQ 200.

Title of map cannot be copyrighted. Chapman v Ferry (1883, CC Or) 18 F 539.

Copyright does not cover title to story, but name which has become descriptive, and is closely identified in public mind with work of particular author, may not, during life of copyright be used so as to mislead, either in another book or in motion picture. Patten v Superior Talking Pictures, Inc. (1934, DC NY) 8 F Supp 196, 23 USPQ 248.

Title to work probably is not protected by copyright law, but it may be protected under law of unfair competition. Loew's, Inc. v Columbia Broadcasting System, Inc. (1955, DC Cal) 131 F Supp 165, 105 USPQ 302, affd (CA9 Cal) 239 F2d 532, 112 USPQ 11, affd 356 US 43, 2 L Ed 2d 583, 78 S Ct 667, 116 USPQ 479, reh den 356 US 934, 2 L Ed 2d 764, 78 S Ct 770.

"Queen of the Flat Tops" is arbitrary, fictitious, fanciful, artificial, distinctive, and nondescriptive book title; being nondescriptive, it is product of mind; owners have right to its exclusive use for all purposes. Johnston v Twentieth Century-Fox Film Corp. (1947) 82 Cal App 2d 796, 187 P2d 474, 76 USPQ 131.

There is public or common right to use "Stowaway" as title or idea or thought conveyed as subject matter of novel, stage play, or screen portrayal. Tamas v 20th Century Fox Film Corp. (1941, Sup) 25 NYS2d 899, 48 USPQ 573.

III. FIXED IN TANGIBLE MEDIUM OF EXPRESSION [17 USCS § 102(a)]

14. Generally

As used in copyright clause (Article 1, § 8, cl 8) of Constitution, which gives Congress power to protect "writings" of authors, word "writings" need not be limited to script or printed material, but may be interpreted to include any physical rendering of the fruits of creative intellectual or aesthetic labor, including recordings of artistic performances; although area in which Congress may act is broad, nevertheless enabling provision of copyright clause does not require that Congress act in regard to all categories of materials which meet constitutional definitions. Goldstein v California (1973) 412 US 546, 37 L Ed 2d 163, 93 S Ct 2303, reh den 414 US 883, 38 L Ed 2d 131, 94 S Ct 27.

Gist of Baker v Selden (1880) 101 US 99, 25 L Ed 841, is that disclosure of copyright is reposed in public to extent necessary to achieve use of what is disclosed, whether disclosure is by descriptive words or diagrams. Crume v Pacific Mut. Life Ins. Co. (1944, CA7 Ill) 140 F2d 182, 60 USPQ 359, cert den 322 US 755, 88 L Ed 1584, 64 S Ct 1265.

In view of federal policy of encouraging intellectual creation by granting a limited monopoly at best, it is sensible to say that clause 8 of § 8 of Article I of the Constitution extends to any concrete, describable manifestation of intellectual creation; to extent that creation may be ineffable, it is ineligible for protection against copying simpliciter under either state or federal law. Columbia Broadcasting System, Inc. v Decosta (1967, CA1 RI) 377 F2d 315, 153 USPQ 649, cert den 389 US 1007, 19 L Ed 2d 603, 88 S Ct 565.

Where plaintiff incorporated in bill synopsis of unpublished uncopyrighted play containing substantially no dialogue but merely rough outline of suggested motion picture and alleged that it was disclosed to defendant who produced play based thereon, and there was no contention that any language had been copied, plaintiff would be entitled to no protection for idea of plot after he had voluntarily disclosed it to another. Clancy v Metro-Goldwyn Pictures Corp. (DC NY) 37 USPQ 406.

Artist's ideas or conceptions cannot be made subject of copyright or basis of rights; they become such only when executed and in being; when executed and sold, they are gone from his control. Grant v Kellogg Co. (1944, DC NY) 58 F Supp 48, 63 USPQ 173, affd (CA2 NY) 154 F2d 59, 75 USPQ 301.

To obtain protection author's ideas must be novel and original and must be reduced to concrete form in copyrighted writing or article; there is no copyright protection for idea, although expression of idea can be protected. Dunham v General Mills, Inc. (1953, DC Mass) 116 F Supp 152, 99 USPQ 372.

15. Particular media

Sound recordings are works that result from fixation of series of sounds, and fixation occurs when complete series of sound is first produced on final master recording that is later reproduced in published copies. United States v Taxe (1976, CA9 Cal) 540 F2d 961, 192 USPQ 204.

Book may be copyrighted, although it has not been printed. Roberts v Myers (1860, CC Mass) F Cas No 11906.

Musical composition, as idea in concrete, is not copyrightable as such, it is that which gives conception corporeal and tangible existence which is subject of copyrighting. White-Smith Music Pub. Co. v Apollo Co. (1905, CC NY) 139 F 427, affd (CA2 NY) 147 F 226, affd 209 US 1, 52 L Ed 655, 28 S Ct 319.

Typewritten pages fastened together and having printed cover and title page may be copyrighted. 28 OAG 265.

IV. PARTICULAR COPYRIGHTABLE WORKS

16. Literary works, generally [17 USCS § 102(a)(1)]

Copyright protection has been extended to literature of commerce, so that it now includes books, catalogues, mathematical tables, statistics, designs, guide books, directories, and other works of similar character. National Tel. News Co. v Western U. Tel. Co. (1902, CA7 Ill) 119 F 294.

Copyright of insurance policies did not restrict right of defendant to use plans of insurance embraced in copyrighted policies but did restrict use or copying of means of expression selected by author to extent such means of expression were original with him. Dorsey v Old Surety Life Ins. Co. (1938, CA10 Okla) 98 F2d 872, 119 ALR 1250, 39 USPQ 92.

Check is not noncopyrightable merely because it is check if in specific use it possesses requisite originality or authorship. Cash Dividend Check Corp. v Davis (1957, CA9 Cal) 247 F2d 458, 114 USPQ 32.

Greeting cards may be protected as a book. Roth Greeting Cards v United Card Co. (1970, CA9 Cal) 429 F2d 1106, 166 USPQ 291.

"Meccano Manual," instruction book accompanying mechanical toy, was proper subject of copyright. Meccano, Ltd. v Wagner (1916, DC Ohio) 234 F 912, mod on other grounds (CA6 Ohio) 246 F 603.

Plaintiff photographed edition of Books of Moses in public domain, made corrections in accents and cantillation marks on negatives, and then printed copyrighted books from printing plates made from negatives; such corrections are subject to copyright. Shulsinger v Grossman, (1954, DC NY) 119 F Supp 691, 101 USPQ 30.

Right of each organ manufacturer to advertise and sell his product includes right to compile, publish, and sell instructions for playing organ if they do not amount to copy of another's copyrighted instructions. Magnus Organ Corp. v Magnus (1967, DC NJ) 269 F Supp 981, 154 USPQ 431.

17. —Advertisements

Advertisements which are misleading and deceptive are not protected by copyright. Stone & McCarrick v Dugan Piano Co. (1915, CA5 La) 220 F 837.

Specimens of paints attached to card constitute advertisement and as such, are not copyrightable. Ehret v Pierce (1880, CC NY) 10 F 553.

Where subject of copyright is, in fact, painting, executed by artist with pencil and brush, fact that copies may be utilized for advertising purposes does not change character of original. Schumacher v Schwencke (1885, CC NY) 25 F 466.

It is matter of common knowledge that many advertisements in American publications of large circulation possess distinctive literary merit and real artistic originality; printed advertisements may be protected by copyright. Deward & Rich, Inc. v Bristol Sav. & Loan Corp. (1939, DC Va) 29 F Supp 777, 44 USPQ 26.

Mats depicting copyrighted advertisements in copyrighted book are part of copyrighted material where, without mats, copyrighted material is of little value to persons subscribing to right to use advertisements. Advertisers Exchange, Inc. v Hinkley (1951, DC Mo) 101 F Supp 801, 92 USPQ 313, affd (CA8 Mo) 199 F2d 313, 95 USPQ 124, cert den 344 US 921, 97 L Ed 710, 73 S Ct 388.

Advertisements which exhibit some original intellectual effort as to conception, composition, and arrangement are copyrightable; thus, original advertisement of dot-counting contest, which portrays merchandise given as prize in picture made up of large number of dots, is copyrightable. Gordon v Weir (1953, DC Mich) 111 F Supp 117, 97 USPQ 387, affd (CA6 Mich) 216 F2d 508, 104 USPQ 40.

When published singly in advertisement illustration from copyrighted booklet of advertisements is copyrightable printed advertisement. Metro Associated Services, Inc. v Webster City Graphic, Inc. (1953, DC Iowa) 117 F Supp 224, 100 USPQ 88.

Advertisements, whether in form of words or pictorial illustrations, may be subject of copyright despite absence of any high artistic or literary merit; however, phrases such as "This is Nature's most restful posture" or phrases emphasizing relaxing qualities of chair, which are so purely descriptive of one's product, do not comply even with slight requirement of originality in copyright law as applied to advertisements; also, while one could copyright set of original symbols or designs used as means in sale of his product, representation, either photographic or linear, of his chair with person in it does not constitute protectible novelty. Laskowitz v Marie Designer, Inc. (1954, DC Cal) 119 F Supp 541, 100 USPQ 367.

Annotations:

Copyright, under Federal Copyright Act (17 USCS §§ 1 et seq.), in advertising materials, catalogues, and price lists. 5 ALR Fed 625.

18. —Catalogues

Artistic cuts produced for use in catalogue are copyrightable matter. Campbell v Wireback (1920, CA4 Md) 269 F 372, 17 ALR 743.

Catalogue containing illustrations of garments may be copyrighted, but such copyright will not prevent another from printing catalogue in which there are illustrations of same type of garments, when such illustrations were not in fact copied from first catalogue. National Cloak & Suit Co. v Standard Mail Order Co. (1911, CC NY) 191 F 528.

Catalogue containing illustrations of goods sold is subject to copyright. Da Prato Statuary Co. v Giuliani Statuary Co. (1911, CA8 Minn) 189 F 90; J. H. White Mfg. Co. v Shapiro (1915, DC NY) 227 F 957.

Trade catalogues and tabulations of sizes and dimensions are within Copyright Act. Burndy Engineering Co. v Penn-Union Electric Corp. (1938, DC Pa) 25 F Supp 507, 39 USPQ 321.

Catalogue of plumbers' supplies is copyrightable subject matter and even if all information used in preparing catalogue is public, this does not give defendant right to reproduce photographically any portion of catalogue. R. R. Donnelley & Sons Co. v Haber (1942, DC NY) 43 F Supp 456, 52 USPQ 445.

Catalogue of marine hardware is copyrightable matter. Perkins Marine Lamp & Hardware Co. v Goodwin Stanley Co. (1949, DC NY) 86 F Supp 630, 83 USPQ 32.

Annotations:

Copyright, under Federal Copyright Act (17 USCS §§ 1 et seq.), in advertising materials, catalogues, and price lists. 5 ALR Fed 625.

19. —Forms

Inseparably included in author's bond and affidavit forms, which constitute means for practice of his insurance plan, is copyrightable language explanatory of plan; hence, forms are copyrightable. Continental Casualty Co. v Beardsley (1958, CA2 NY) 253 F2d 702, 117 USPQ 1, cert den 358 US 816, 3 L Ed 2d 58, 79 S Ct 25.

Copyright on service agreement form is invalid for lack of creativity and originality, where (1) copyright holder used legal forms in public domain in drafting his form, and (2) holder's use in service contract of language previously used in sales contract did not constitute more than trivial variation from work already in public domain. Donald v Uarco Business Forms (1973, CA8 Ark) 478 F2d 764.

Bookkeeping forms and written instructions on how to use forms are integrated work entitled to copyright protection because they convey information and are not merely blank forms. Williams & Co. v Williams & Co.-East (1976, CA9) 191 USPQ 563.

Statutory legal forms having sufficient originality are subject of copyright. Brightley v Littleton (1888, CC Pa) 37 F 103.

Blank forms of property statements for use of assessors under state law are not proper subjects of copyright. Carlisle v Colusa County (1893, CC Cal) 57 F 979.

Blank forms and blank books, usable in themselves, are not copyrightable. Amberg File & Index Co. v Shea Smith & Co. (1897, CA7 Ill) 82 F 314; Everson v Young, 26 Wash Law Rep 546.

Forms illustrating tax bookkeeping system are not copyrightable when included in copyrighted loose-leaf book describing system, since forms embody mechanics of system taught. Aldrich v Remington Rand, Inc. (1942, DC Tex) 52 F Supp 732, 59 USPQ 210.

All business, medical, legal, and other forms are not, per se, excluded from copyright protection; they are copyrightable if they convey information but not where they merely are used to

record it. Norton Printing Co. v Augustana Hospital (1967, DC Ill) 155 USPQ 133.

Copyright extends to expression of business form not to its idea. First Financial Marketing Services Group, Inc. v Field Promotions, Inc. (1968, DC NY) 286 F Supp 295.

Annotations:

Copyright, under federal copyrights laws, of forms or form books. 8 ALR Fed 869.

20. —Law reports

Written opinions delivered by United States Supreme Court may not be copyrighted. Wheaton v Peters (1834) 33 US 591, 8 L Ed 1055.

Judicial decisions are public property and not protectible by copyright. Little v Hall (1856) 59 US 165, 15 L Ed 328.

Reporter's copyright does not cover statements of cases, headnotes, and opinions prepared by judges in their official capacity; judge acting in his judicial capacity in preparing headnotes, statement of case, and opinion is not author. Banks v Manchester (1888) 128 US 244, 32 L Ed 425, 9 S Ct 36.

Reporter of volume of law reports may obtain copyright for it as author and such copyright will cover those parts of which he is author, although he has no exclusive rights in judicial opinions published. Callaghan v Myers (1888) 128 US 617, 32 L Ed 547, 9 S Ct 177.

Reporter obtaining copyright on volume of opinions of court does not obtain copyright to headnotes of opinion, when headnotes were written by judges. Chase v Sanborn (1874, CC NH) F Cas No 2628.

Copyright on law reports does not secure to owner thereof exclusive privilege to publish opinions of court. Gould v Hastings (1840, CC NY) F Cas No 5639.

Only portions of official law reports which are subject to copyright in name of individual are syllabi or statements by reporter and any statement of facts produced by original work and not filed as part of decision by court. West Publishing Co. v Edward Thompson Co. (1909, CC NY) 169 F 833, mod on other grounds (CA2 NY) 176 F 833.

Works included in reporter system and digests were duly covered by copyright. West Pub. Co. v Edward Thompson Co. (1911, CC NY) 184 F 749.

Copyright of annotator of statutes covers all that may be deemed result of his labors, such as head notes, marginal references, notes, memoranda, table of contents, indexes, and digests of judicial decisions prepared by him from original sources of information. Howell v Miller (1898, CA6 Mich) 91 F 129.

Mechanical details of reporter's arrangement of reported cases in sequence, pagination and distribution into volumes are not entitled to copyright protection. Banks Law Pub. Co. v Lawyers' Co-op Pub. Co. (1909, CA2 NY) 169 F 386, app dismd 223 US 738, 56 L Ed 636, 32 S Ct 530.

21. —Lectures

Printed lecture plan of instruction with pictorial illustrations was not copyrightable. Chautauqua School v National School (1916, CA2 NY) 238 F 151.

Interest and discount time teller is "book," and person designing and producing it is "author." Edwards & Deutsch Lithographing Co. v Boorman (1926, CA7 Ill) 15 F2d 35, cert den 273 US 738, 71 L Ed 867, 47 S Ct 247.

Series of lectures may be copyrighted although they use ideas expressed in another work. Nutt v National Institute, Inc. for Improv. of Memory (1929, CA2 Conn) 31 F2d 236.

Plaintiff's radio talks were for advertising purposes but were copyrightable as plaintiff had large following to whom lectures may have contributed something of satisfaction and benefit. Vinick v Charm Publications, Inc. (DC NY) 46 USPQ 510.

Article describing bookkeeping system, art, or manufacture created by another is subject to copyright. Aldrich v Remington Rand, Inc. (1942, DC Tex) 52 F Supp 732.

Conventional laws or rules of game are not copyrightable as such. Chamberlin v Uris Sales Corp. (1944, DC NY) 56 F Supp 987, affd (CA2 NY) 150 F2d 512.

Congress intended copyright protection for lectures, sermons, and addresses despite oral delivery thereof. King v Mister Maestro, Inc. (1963, DC NY) 224 F Supp 101, 140 USPQ 366.

22. —Letters

Private letters are protected. Bartlett v Crittenden (1849, CC Ohio) F Cas No 1076.

Right to copyright letters after writer's death is vested in personal representatives of writer and not person who received letters. Folsom v Marsh (1841, CC Mass) F Cas No 4901.

As general rule publication of letter may be restrained by its author or his executor, but in absence of some special arrangement recipient of letter is owner thereof. Baker v Libbie (1912) 210 Mass 599, 97 NE 109; Ipswich Mills v Dillon (1927) 260 Mass 453, 157 NE 604, 53 ALR 792.

Private letters are not subject to copyright by administrator of receiver. Eyre v Higbee (NY) 35 Barb 502, 22 How Prac 198.

23. —Words and phrases

Trade-marks, as such, are not subject to copyright. United States v Steffens (1879) 100 US 82, 25 L Ed 550.

List of telegraphic code words is copyrightable, so long as it is original matter. American Code Co. v Bensinger (1922, CA2 NY) 282 F 829.

List of French words with translation included in writings of author was entitled to copyright. College Entrance Book Co. v Amsco Book Co. (1941, CA2 NY) 119 F2d 874, 49 USPQ 517.

Right to use of certain words is not protected by copyright; copyright secures right to that arrangement of words which author has selected to express his ideas. Funkhouser v Loew's Inc. (1953, CA8 Mo) 208 F2d 185, 99 USPQ 448, cert den 348 US 843, 99 L Ed 664, 75 S Ct 64, reh den 348 US 890, 99 L Ed 700, 75 S Ct 209.

Brand names, trade names, slogans, and other short phrases or expressions cannot be copyrighted, even if they are distinctively arranged or printed. Kitchens of Sara Lee, Inc. v Nifty Foods Corp. (1959, CA2 NY) 266 F2d 541, 121 USPQ 359.

Book of coined words to be used for private cable code is subject to copyright. Reiss v National Quotation Bureau (1921, DC NY) 276 F 717.

Words in dictionary, usual English idioms, ideas, and character types are not subjects of copyrights. Lewys v O'Neill (1931, DC NY) 49 F2d 603, 9 USPQ 465.

Abbreviations in publication are not susceptible of copyright protection, since there is nothing unique in their composition or arrangement. Kanover v Marks (DC NY) 91 USPQ 370.

Copyright or literary rights do not extend to words or phrases isolated from their context. O'Brien v Chappel & Co. (1958, DC NY) 159 F Supp 58, 116 USPQ 340.

Common phrases are generally not susceptible to copyright protection. Stratchborneo v Arc Music Corp. (1973, DC NY) 357 F Supp 1393.

24. Musical works, generally [17 USCS § 102(a)(2)]

Musical composition, which is copy of another piece but with variations which experienced writer of music might easily make, cannot be copyrighted. Jollie v Jaques (1850, CC NY) F Cas No 7437.

Musical composition is not subject to copyright, when it is combination of parts of older compositions. Reed v Carusi (1845, CC Md) F Cas No 11642.

Orchestral accompaniment for noncopyrighted oratorio is subject to copyright. Thomas v Lennon (1883, CC Mass) 14 F 849.

Addition of alto to well-known musical composition is not such new and original work as entitles person adding such alto to copyright. Cooper v James (1914, DC Ga) 213 F 871.

Similarity of musical compositions did not preclude copyrights. Arnstein v Edward B. Marks Music Corp. (1935, DC NY) 11 F Supp 535, 27 USPQ 127, affd (CA2 NY) 82 F2d 275, 28 USPQ 426.

Slight variations in use of rhythm or harmony, of accent and tempo, may result in popular song subject of copyright. Hirsch v Paramount Pictures, Inc. (1937, DC Cal) 17 F Supp 816, 32 USPQ 233.

Distinctive style in interpretations of musical numbers gives interpreter distinct, exclusive, and separable property right in his unique rendition. Waring v Dunlea (1939, DC NC) 26 F Supp 338, 41 USPQ 201.

Specific bass is too simple to be copyrightable; it is mechanical application of simple harmonious chord; purpose of copyright law is to protect creation, not mechanical skill. Shapiro, Bernstein & Co. v Miracle Record Co. (1950, DC Ill) 91 F Supp 473, 85 USPQ 39.

Musical composition is made up of rhythm, harmony, and melody, but rhythm and harmony have been in public domain for so long that neither can be subject of copyright, hence originality must be found in melody; separate works alike in every respect can be copyrighted without denial of anyone's rights, for copyright does not give monopoly of ideas, but second song must be innocently and independently composed. Northern Music Corp. v King Record Distributing Co. (1952, DC NY) 105 F Supp 393, 93 USPQ 512.

Inconsequential melodic and harmonic embellishments such as are frequently improvised by any competent musician are de minimis contributions and do not qualify for copyright protection since they are technical improvisations in common vocabulary of music. McIntyre v Double-A Music Corp. (1958, DC Cal) 166 F Supp 681, 119 USPQ 106, motion den (DC Cal) 179 F Supp 160.

Rhythmic annotations indicating manner of performance of chants are integral part of musical composition which may be copyrightable under predecessor section; remedy against unauthorized copying of published literary property must be sought under this law; there is no special reservation of rights in typography of published work, and this may be copied except insofar as copyright makes copying of work itself unlawful. Desclee & Cie., S. A. v Nemmers (1961, DC Wis) 190 F Supp 381, 128 USPQ 186.

Prior statute applies to songs fixed after 15 February 1972 on tape recordings including earlier songs. United States v Taxe (1974, DC Cal) 380 F Supp 1010, 184 USPQ 5, affd in part and vacated in part on other grounds (CA9 Cal) 540 F2d 961.

There can be no conversion of musical idea that has been copyrighted and only claim of copyright proprietor to musical idea is claim under copyright laws, and claim for broadcast of music in commercial is barred by contract with composer. Jackson v Stone & Simon Advertising, Inc. (1974, DC Mich) 188 USPQ 564.

If performer of musical composition, in consummating work by transforming it into sound, contributes by his interpretation something of novel, intellectual, or artistic value, he has participated in creation of product in which he is entitled to right of property which in no way overlaps or duplicates that of author in the musical composition. Waring v WDAS Broadcasting Station, Inc. (1937) 327 Pa 433, 194 A 631, 35 USPQ 272.

25. —Arrangements or performances

Person having right to use copyrighted song has right to make orchestration of song for use in operetta, and to have such orchestration copyrighted. Edmonds v Stern (1918, CA2 NY) 248 F 897.

Copyright may be obtained upon music taken from opera and subsequently rewritten by arranger to include alterations and additions original with him. Atwill v Ferrett (1846, CC NY) F Cas No 640.

Pianoforte arrangement of orchestral score of opera made by system of selection and culling, creating nothing original, is not protectible by copyright. Mikado Case (1885, CC NY) 25 F 183.

Pianoforte arrangement of orchestral score of opera is original musical composition and subject to copyright. Carte v Evans (1886, CC Mass) 27 F 861.

New arrangements of words and music of old song are entitled to protection. Italian Book Co. v Rossi (1928, DC NY) 27 F2d 1014.

Composition, to be subject of copyright, must have sufficient originality to make it new work rather than copy of old, with minor changes which any skilled musician might make; it must be result of some original or creative work. Norden v Oliver Ditson Co. (1936, DC Mass) 13 F Supp 415, 28 USPQ 183.

Before one having limited right to record song may have its recorded musical arrangement thereof protected as right against competitor, arrangement must have distinctive characteristic, aside from composition itself, of such character that any person hearing it played would become aware of distinctiveness of arrangement. Supreme Records, Inc. v Decca Records, Inc. (1950, DC Cal) 90 F Supp 904, 85 USPQ 405.

Fact that defendants applied for copyright registration of same arrangement, in which application they represented that arrangement contained original, copyrightable material, does not estop defendants from denying originality of plaintiff's work, since defendants' representations did not mislead plaintiff or place him at disadvantage in instant litigation. McIntyre v Double-A-Music Corp. (1959, DC Cal) 179 F Supp 160, 124 USPQ 27.

26. —Words and music

Whenever song is copyrighted as musical composition, both words and music are protected; and, as these do not constitute indivisible whole, owner may limit use of his copyright either to music or to words, or he may allow both to be used. Standard Music Roll Co. v Mills (1917, CA3 NJ) 241 F 360.

Orchestral score of operetta may be copyrighted separately from words and music of song whicn formed part of operetta, when such score is substantially new and distinct composition. Edmonds v Stern (1918, CA2 NY) 248 F 897.

Mere fact that copyrighted poem is adapted to be set to music does not make it, in form written, musical composition; many prose compositions have been set to music. Corcoran v Montgomery Ward & Co. (1941, CA9 Cal) 121 F2d 572, 50 USPQ 274, cert den 314 US 687, 86 L Ed 550, 62 S Ct 300.

Copyright of musical composition protects words of song. M. Witmark & Sons v Standard Music Roll Co. (1914, DC NJ) 213 F 532, affd (CA3 NJ) 221 F 376.

Music of popular ballad, which was written by another than one who wrote words was not independent composition. G. Ricordi & Co. v Columbia Graphophone Co. (1919, DC NY) 258 F 72.

Copyright of adaptation of English text to Russian music, if valid, does not cover music. Norden v Oliver Ditson Co. (1936, DC Mass) 13 F Supp 415, 28 USPQ 183.

Musical composition as idea or intellectual conception is not subject to copyright, either as to words or music; jingle, as subject of copyright, should be considered as single original work from standpoint of its melody and lyrics, and not disjointedly, or from standpoint of intellectual conception thereby expressed. Smith v George E. Muehlebach Brewing Co. (1956, DC Mo) 140 F Supp 729, 110 USPQ 177.

Copyright of musical composition consisting of both words and music integrated in single work protects against unauthorized use of words alone, as well as against unauthorized use of music alone or of combination of music and words. Stratchborneo v Arc Music Corp. (1973, DC NY) 357 F Supp 1393.

27. Dramatic works, generally [17 USCS § 102(a)(3)]

Photoplay taken from book is dramatization. Kalem Co. v Harper Bros. (1911) 222 US 55, 56 L Ed 92, 32 S Ct 20.

Scene of play having literary quality is protectible by copyright. Daly v Webster (1893, CA2 NY) 56 F 483; Chappell & Co. v Fields (1914, CA2 NY) 210 F 864.

Copyright may not only protect dialogue of drama, but also all such means of expression as author used to give dramatic significance to scenes of his work. Sheldon v Metro-Goldwyn Pictures Corp. (1936, CA2 NY) 81 F2d 49, 28 USPQ 330, cert den 298 US 669, 80 L Ed 1392, 56 S Ct 835.

Mere motions, voice, and postures of actors and mere stage business are not subject of copyright protection; but sequence having literary quality in that it contains story and has dramatic composition may be protected. Universal Pictures Co. v Harold Lloyd Corp. (1947, CA9 Cal) 162 F2d 354, 73 USPQ 317.

Many of separate rights of copyright owner may be used as basis for securing new and separate copyrights; for example, copyright owner of novel has right to dramatize it, and he may secure copyright on dramatic scenario based upon copyright. Herwig v United States (1952) 122 Ct Cl 493, 105 F Supp 384, 93 USPQ 421.

Dramatic composition, composed from old material, but put in new form, may be copyrighted. Boucicault v Fox (1862, CC NY) F Cas No 1691.

Railroad scene from author's composition "Under the Gaslight" was dramatic composition, since written play, without use of spoken language by characters is "dramatic composition." Daly v Palmer (1868, CC NY) F Cas No 3552.

Series of scenes consisting of artists' models in seductive poses is not "dramatic composition." Martinetti v Maguire (1867, CC Cal) F Cas No 9173.

Drama taken from old play but with changes in dialogue, characters, scenery, and dramatic situations, and original title may be copyrighted, and any one else may be restrained from using such title on another drama based on same play. Aronson v Fleckenstein (1886, CC Ill) 28 F 75.

Exhibitions of woman changing costumes was not "dramatic composition" subject to copyright. Barnes v Miner (1903, CC NY) 122 F 480.

Voice, motions, and postures of actors and mere stage business have no literary quality and cannot be copyrighted. Bloom & Hamlin v Nixon (1903, CC Pa) 125 F 977; Savage v Hoffmann (1908, CC NY) 159 F 584.

Dramatic sketch consisting of series of recitations and songs to be recited or sung by same person dressed in different costumes was dramatico-musical composition. Green v Luby (1909, CC NY) 177 F 287.

Partial invalidity of copyright for play does not preclude valid portion of copyright from protection. Stodart v Mutual Film Corp. (1917, DC NY) 249 F 507, affd (CA2 NY) 249 F 513.

Content of dramatic or literary composition is not copyrightable, but form and sequence of its treatment is copyrightable. Rush v Oursler (1930, DC NY) 39 F2d 468, 5 USPQ 320.

Where pamphlets describing exhibition roller skate race with rules for conduct of race were copyrighted as books, in narrative form with no fixed plot or story, and no distinctive characters possessing individual personalities or names, mere fact that race as staged would be entertaining or thrilling does change essential nature of composition to drama since there is no definite story structure. Seltzer v Sunbrock (1938, DC Cal) 22 F Supp 621, 37 USPQ 491.

Neither choice of distinct locale for play or story is subject of appropriation, nor are mechanical devices used in production, gestures of actors, or movement of dance or spectacle. Supreme Records, Inc. v Decca Records, Inc. (1950, DC Cal) 90 F Supp 904, 85 USPQ 405.

Copyright owner's protectible property in play consists of development, treatment, and expression of such elements as theme, locale, settings, situations, ideas, bare basic plots, and ordinarily characters; elements in themselves are not protectible; it is expression of ideas, not ideas themselves, that is protected. Gethers v Blatty (1968, DC Cal) 283 F Supp 303, 157 USPQ 297.

Although it might be possible that author could so carefully delineate character as to secure protectible property interest in character, generally it is held that character is not included within monopoly of copyright. Burtis v Universal Pictures Co. (1953) 40 Cal 2d 823, 256 P2d 933, 97 USPQ 567.

Although dramatic core of actual life events included in author's book is not protectible, plaintiff's original dramatic arrangement and development thereof may be protectible, if compensation was promised, despite author's disclosure of story outlines. Beardsley v Columbia Broadcasting System, Inc. (Cal 2d) 137 USPQ 260.

28. —Accompanying music

Where song was published and copyrighted separate and apart from previously copyrighted dramatico-musical composition of which it was part, and no notice was printed on republished song that it was taken from copyrighted comic opera, benefit of copyright of dramatico-musical composition was lost as to that song. Herbert v Shanley Co. (1916, CA2 NY) 229 F 340, revd on other grounds 242 US 591, 61 L Ed 511, 37 S Ct 232.

Topical song which is part of dramatic composition is proper subject of copyright. Henderson v Tompkins (1894, CC Mass) 60 F 758.

Song, that has dramatic features in it, may be considered dramatic composition. M. Witmark & Sons v Pastime Amusement Co. (1924, DC SC) 298 F 470, affd (CA4 SC) 2 F2d 1020.

29. —Props or accessories

Patented mechanical contrivance used in scene in play cannot be included in copyright of play. Freligh v Carroll (CC NY) F Cas No 5092a.

Imitation river used in connection with stage play in which real water is used is not proper subject of copyright. Serrana v Jefferson (1888, CC NY) 33 F 347.

30. Pantomimes and choreographic works [17 USCS § 102(a)(4)]

Musical choreographic composition which combines music and action in such manner as to provoke emotion, portray character and have theme, or tell story is copyrightable under predecessor section; however, "dramatic or dramatico-musical composition," as used in predecessor statute, includes only those representations and exhibitions which tend to promote progress of science and useful arts; where performance contains nothing of literary, dramatic, or musical character which is calculated to elevate, cultivate, inform, or improve moral or intellectual natures of audience, it does not tend to promote progress of science or useful arts; not everything put on stage can be subject to copyright; although specific choreographic performance was amusing and entertaining to many, it is not subject to common-law copyright protection since it did not tend to promote progress of science and useful arts. Dane v M. & H. Co. (NY Sup Ct) 136 USPQ 426.

31. Pictorial, graphic, and sculptural works, generally [17 USCS § 102(a)(5)]

Congress intended scope of copyright statute to include more than traditional fine arts. Mazer v Stein (1954) 347 US 201, 98 L Ed 630, 74 S Ct 460, 100 USPQ 325, reh den 347 US 949, 98 L Ed 1096, 74 S Ct 637.

Painting, if it possess artistic merit and be suitable, also, for use as design, may, at owner's election, be protected either by copyright or by patent. De Jonge & Co. v Breuker & Kessler Co. (1911, CA3 Pa) 191 F 35, affd 235 US 33, 59 L Ed 113, 35 S Ct 6.

Works of art need not disclose originality to be copyrightable. Gerlach-Barklow Co. v Morris & Bendien, Inc. (1927, CA2 NY) 23 F2d 159.

Copyright on work of art does not protect subject, but only treatment of subject. F. W. Woolworth Co. v Contemporary Arts, Inc. (1951, CA1 Mass) 193 F2d 162, 92 USPQ 4, affd 344 US 228, 97 L Ed 276, 73 S Ct 222, 95 USPQ 396, motion den 350 US 810, 100 L Ed 727, 76 S Ct 37.

Cardboard star which stands because of folded flaps is not work of art. Bailie v Fisher (1958) 103 App DC 331, 258 F2d 425, 117 USPQ 334.

Troughs, waves, and lines in molded shoe bottom are not independent works of art apart from utilitarian function of shoe bottom and are not copyrightable. SCOA Industries, Inc. v Famolare, Inc. (1976, DC NY) 192 USPQ 216.

Engraving of billiard table used for advertisement purposes was not "work of art." Collender v Griffiths (1873, CC NY) F Cas No 3000.

Artist cannot acquire such exclusive right to conception embodied and expressed in his picture as to preclude others from exercise of their own creative genius or artistic skill, or from availing themselves of any part of genial contribution of artistic production. Johnson v Donaldson (1880, CC NY) 3 F 22.

Painting about seven inches long by four and one-half inches wide, may be copyrighted. Schumacher v Schwencke (1885, CC NY) 25 F 466.

Copyright protection existing for original art does not extend to protecting lamp which employs copy of protected art as part of its ornamentation. Stein v Rosenthal (1952, DC Cal) 103 F Supp 227, 92 USPQ 402, affd (CA9 Cal) 205 F2d 633, 98 USPQ 180.

If object is clearly work of art, its utility will not preclude registration; however, wrist watch is not work of art even if it is difficult to tell time by it. Vacheron & Constantin-Le Coultre Watches, Inc. v Benrus Watch Co. (1957, DC NY) 155 F Supp 932, affd in part and revd in part on other grounds (CA2 NY) 260 F2d 637.

Copyright on work of art does not protect subject, such as horse, but only treatment of subject. Blazon, Inc. v Deluxe Game Corp. (1965, DC NY) 268 F Supp 416, 156 USPQ 195.

Typeface design can be work of art so that long-standing interpretation of Copyright Act to prevent registration of typeface designs is erro-

neous, although mandamus is denied because of legislative history and long-standing practice. Eltra Corp. v Ringer (1976, DC Va) 194 USPQ 198.

Annotations:

Statutory copyright protection of "works of art." 98 L Ed 644.

32. —Advertising illustrations

Picture may be subject to copyright notwithstanding its use for advertising purposes; chromolithographs used as circus posters are pictorial illustrations and entitled to copyright. Bleistein v Donaldson Lithographing Co. (1903) 188 US 239, 47 L Ed 460, 23 S Ct 298.

Cuts of baths, printed in trade catalogue, were not prints connected with fine arts and were not subject to copyright. J. L. Mott Iron Works v Clow (1897, CA7 Ill) 82 F 316.

Cuts originally designed and prepared by persons of skill and artistic capacity were entitled to copyright registry, although used to embellish advertising matter. Campbell v Wireback (1920, CA4 Md) 269 F 372, 17 ALR 743.

Labels on which are printed receipts may be copyrighted although intended for advertising purposes. Fargo Mercantile Co. v Brechet & Richter Co. (1924, CA8 ND) 295 F 823.

Chromo of evident artistic merit, although used for advertising purposes, is copyrightable. Yuengling v Schile (1882, CC NY) 12 F 97.

Chromos or lithographs may be copyrighted, even though they are intended for advertising articles of commerce and possess little artistic merit, when pictures in their details and designs are in fact pictorial illustrations or works connected with fine arts. Stecher Lithographic Co. v Dunston Lithograph Co. (1916, DC NY) 233 F 601.

33. —Architectural plans

In a suit for infringement of copyright in architectural drawings for residence, the exclusive right to copy what is copyrighted belongs to the architect, even though the plans give him no unique claim on any feature of the structure they detail; court remands for determination of whether the defendant copied the floor plan set forth in an advertising promotional booklet distributed by plaintiff, and if so, such copying would constitute an infringement of plaintiff's copyright privileges. Imperial Homes Corp. v Lamont (1972, CA5 Fla) 458 F2d 895, 173 USPQ 519.

One who has worked out embodiment of design for work of art or plans for large building program possesses property right in his original production. Ketcham v New York World's Fair 1939, Inc. (1940, DC NY) 34 F Supp 657, 46 USPQ 307, affd (CA2 NY) 119 F2d 422, 49 USPQ 756.

Copyright of architectural plans does not encompass buildings themselves, but is limited only to plans; architect does not have exclusive right to build structures embodied in his technical writings; only monopoly which copyright gives author of architectural plans is exclusive right to reproduce design as artistic figure; architectural plans, including drawings and models, are copyrightable under specified class of drawings or plastic works of scientific or technical nature. Desilva Constr. Corp. v Herrald (1962, DC Fla) 213 F Supp 184, 137 USPQ 96.

Design by architect is subject to protection of common law until it is published by erection of building having such design. Gendell v Orr (Pa) 36 Leg Int 412, 13 Phila 191.

Annotations:

Copyright, under federal copyright laws, of architectural plans, drawings, or designs. 3 ALR Fed 793.

34. —Cartoons

Comic cartoon in magazine embodies conception of humor or surprise or incredulity—whatsoever cartoonist is aiming at—and what owner of copyright is entitled to is protection of that embodiment of his concept. Detective Comics, Inc. v Bruns Publications, Inc. (1939, DC NY) 28 F Supp 399, 41 USPQ 182, mod on other grounds (CA2 NY) 111 F2d 432, 45 USPQ 291.

35. —Charts and guides

Chart for analyzing handwriting is copyrightable. Deutsch v Arnold (1938, CA2 NY) 98 F2d 686, 39 USPQ 5.

Chart is copyrightable if it is object of explanation but not if object of use; chart for recording temperature is not copyrightable since it is mechanical element of instrument and is indispensable in its operation, neither teaching nor explaining use of art, but being art itself. Taylor Instrument Cos. v Fawley-Brost Co. (1943, CA7 Ill) 139 F2d 98, 59 USPQ 384, cert den 321 US 785, 88 L Ed 1076, 64 S Ct 782.

Both plaintiff's and defendants' airline guides key timetables to maps, but keying was common in railway and airline guides before plaintiff, so plaintiff may not monopolize it to exclusion of defendants. Official Aviation Guide Co. v American Aviation Associates (1945, CA7 Ill) 150 F2d 173, 65 USPQ 553, cert den 326 US 776, 90 L Ed 469, 66 S Ct 267, reh den 326 US 811, 90 L Ed 495, 66 S Ct 335.

Charts on which machine records in writing variable temperatures and pressures are not copyrightable since charts function as working mechanical elements of and essential parts of machine which is useless without charts. Brown Instrument Co. v Warner (1947) 82 App DC 232, 161 F2d 910, 73 USPQ 427, cert den 332 US 801, 92 L Ed 380, 68 S Ct 101.

Diagrammatic instruction sheet accompanying crude model of steamship, parts of which are to be assembled according to instructions, was proper subject of copyright. Ideal Aeroplane & Supply Co. v Brooks (1936, DC NY) 18 F Supp 936, 33 USPQ 193.

Had defendant made use of plaintiff's color chart with written description and directions for world's fair, plaintiff would be entitled to recover as his disclosure constitutes substantial intellectual property and it is law that individual has property right in his original unpublished intellectual productions. Ketcham v New York World's Fair 1939, Inc. (1940, DC NY) 34 F Supp 657, 46 USPQ 307, affd (CA2 NY) 119 F2d 422, 49 USPQ 756.

Drawing interpreting plumbing code shows sufficient originality to sustain copyright which is not defective because it follows interpretation of board of health or because there may be some wrong interpretation. Borthwick v Stark-Davis Co. (DC Or) 38 USPQ 327.

Illustrative drawings of electrical devices in catalogue are proper subject of copyright. Burndy Engineering Co. v Penn-Union Electric Corp. (1938, DC Pa) 25 F Supp 507, 39 USPQ 321.

Annotations:

Maps or charts as protected by copyright under federal copyright acts. 4 ALR Fed 466.

36. —Designs

Dichotomy of protection for aesthetic is not beauty and utility but art for copyright and invention of original and ornamental design for design patents; there is nothing in Copyright Act to support argument that intended use or use in industry of article eligible for copyright bars or invalidates registration. Mazer v Stein (1954) 347 US 201, 98 L Ed 630, 74 S Ct 460, 100 USPQ 325, reh den 347 US 949, 98 L Ed 1096, 74 S Ct 637.

Photostatic copies of pencilled art work are in copyrightable form; predecessor section does not warrant any limitation on copyrighting of work merely because it may subsequently achieve more perfect or final form. American Visuals Corp. v Holland (1956, CA2 NY) 239 F2d 740, 111 USPQ 288.

Publication of copyrighted design printed on textiles occurs on sale of textiles to dress manufacturers; notice of copyright at that time is constructive notice to all dress manufacturers, provided notice is sufficient; in that event, copier acts at his peril if he takes design from finished dress; such result may well be considered necessary to carry out Congressional intent to give copyright protection to reproductions on textiles of works of art; absence of notice is defense, with burden on copier to show that it could have been embodied in design without impairing its market value. Peter Pan Fabrics, Inc. v Dixon Textile Corp. (1960, CA2 NY) 280 F2d 800, 125 USPQ 39, on remand (DC NY) 188 F Supp 235 and (ovrld on other grounds Chappell & Co. v Frankel (CA2 NY) 367 F2d 197).

Work copyrighted was not merely single rose square from which textile design was created, but composite design itself, which depends for its aesthetic effect upon both rose figure and manner in which reproductions of that figure are arranged in checkerboard relation to each other upon fabric; work was sufficiently original for copyright protection, even though checkerboard configuration, considered apart from original component squares, does not possess even modest originality that copyright laws require. H. M. Kolbe Co. v Armgus Textile Co. (1963, CA2 NY) 315 F2d 70, 99 ALR2d 390, 137 USPQ 9.

Printing of trade name or trade-mark on copyrighted design did not affect copyright. Hoague-Sprague Corp. v Frank C. Meyer Co. (1929, DC NY) 31 F2d 583.

Design or pattern for dress goods, whether stamped on paper or on goods itself, is not copyrightable as design for work of art. Kemp & Beatley, Inc. v Hirsch (1929, DC NY) 34 F2d 291.

Design for cemetery monument was entitled to copyright as design for work of art. Jones Bros. Co. v Underkoffler (1936, DC Pa) 16 F Supp 729.

Design printed on fabric from which dresses are manufactured is not copyrightable. Verney Corp. v Rose Fabric Converters Corp. (1949, DC NY) 87 F Supp 802, 83 USPQ 386.

Owner of patentable design on glassware may invoke protection of Copyright Act since design is work of art. William A. Meier Glass Co. v Anchor Hocking Glass Corp. (1951, DC Pa) 95 F Supp 264, 88 USPQ 249.

Design printed on dress fabric is proper subject of copyright both as work of art and as print. Peter Pan Fabrics, Inc. v Brenda Fabrics, Inc. (1959, DC NY) 169 F Supp 142, 120 USPQ 158.

Design printed upon blouse fabric is proper subject of copyright as work of art, although fish, sailor suits, and ice cream parlor trappings are in public domain, designs depicting them are copyrightable since artist's contribution is sufficient to qualify designs as distinguishable variations, that is there is sufficient originality in designs to warrant copyright. Scarves by Vera, Inc. v United Merchants & Mfrs., Inc. (1959, DC NY) 173 F Supp 625, 121 USPQ 578.

Ornamental box which presents novel and original design and which can be used as container for rings or other small items of jewelry is copyrightable. Dan Kasoff, Inc. v Gresco Jewelry Co. (1962, DC NY) 204 F Supp 694, 133 USPQ 438, affd (CA2 NY) 308 F2d 806, 135 USPQ 209.

Copyright protection extends to plaintiff's designs as productions of originality and novelty, since plaintiff does not claim rights to all toy banks in form of dogs, but only rights in its particular novel and original renditions; by its treatment of subjects, plaintiff has contributed something recognizably its own which is by no means trivial. Royalty Designs, Inc. v Thrifticheck Service Corp. (1962, DC NY) 204 F Supp 702, 133 USPQ 148.

Fact that characters in copyrighted design are replicas of people of specific historical era in appearance and dress is not fatal to claim of originality. John Wolf Textiles Inc. v Andris Fabrics Inc. (DC NY) 139 USPQ 365.

Defendants borrowed plaintiff's ideas and made substantial deviations from plaintiff's expression of ideas by crossbreeding plaintiff's expressions with those found in design form book; as result, defendants' designs are aesthetic mutations, reflecting major changes and significant alterations that keep clear of plaintiff's expression. Condotti, Inc. v Slifka (1963, DC NY) 223 F Supp 412, 139 USPQ 373.

Copyright on molded shoe bottom covers only molded bicycle design and not troughs, waves, and lines having no separate identity as works of art. SCOA Industries, Inc. v Famolare, Inc. (1976, DC NY) 192 USPQ 216.

"Art" is not confined to traditional art forms, and encompasses industrial design of lighting fixture shaped to have aesthetically pleasing line and form so that design is copyrightable even though serving functional and utilitarian purpose and having no specifically separate decorative effect. Esquire, Inc. v Ringer (1976, DC Dist Col) 194 USPQ 30.

Design for typeface can be work of art within Copyright Act, but is not registrable because of legislative history and long-standing practice. Eltra Corp. v Ringer (1976, DC Va) 194 USPQ 198.

Register of copyrights has authority to enter claim in painting which is made merely as first step in production of lithograph as "work of art" within meaning of predecessor section, provided painting itself is work of art. 28 OAG 557.

Design printed on fabric is subject of copyright and is entitled to common-law protection if it remains unpublished. Fabrics by Bus Davies, Inc. v Kay Windsor Frocks, Inc. (1960) 25 Misc 2d 48, 202 NYS2d 467, 125 USPQ 470.

37. —Jewelry

Costume jewelry is copyrightable subject matter entitled to protection under Copyright Act. Boucher v Du Boyes, Inc. (1958, CA2 NY) 253 F2d 948, 117 USPQ 156, cert den 357 US 936, 2 L Ed 2d 1550, 78 S Ct 1384.

Although it might be thought that invocation of power of government to protect designs against infringement implied some merit other than faint trace of "originality," it is settled that practically anything novel can be copyrighted. Dan Kasoff, Inc. v Novelty Jewelry Co. (1962, CA2 NY) 309 F2d 745, 135 USPQ 234.

Relative artistic merit of work is not material in determining eligibility for copyright; costume jewelry may express artistic conception no less than painting or statue; simply because costume jewelry is commonplace fashion accessory, not an expression of "pure" or "fine" art, does not preclude finding that such jewelry is "work of art" within meaning of Copyright Act. Trifari, Krussman & Fishel, Inc. v Charel Co. (1955, DC NY) 134 F Supp 551, 107 USPQ 48.

Costume jewelry is subject to copyright. Hollywood Jewelry Mfg. Co. v Dushkin (1955, DC NY) 136 F Supp 738, 108 USPQ 354.

Copyright may be obtained for original design of costume jewelry as work of art; fact that design is used in manufacturing cheap jewelry does not deprive original design of benefits of copyright. Dan Kasoff, Inc. v Palmer Jewelry Mfg. Co. (1959, DC NY) 171 F Supp 603, 120 USPQ 445.

Rendition of T-shirt as jewelry pendant requires exercise of artistic craftsmanship and results in distinguishable variation from ordinary public domain T-shirt so that result is copyrightable even though T-shirts are in public domain. Cynthia Designs, Inc. v Robert Zentall, Inc. (1976, DC NY) 416 F Supp 510, 191 USPQ 35.

38. —Labels and prints

Clause of Constitution under which Congress is authorized to legislate for protection of authors does not have any reference to labels which simply designate or describe articles to which they are attached, and which have no value separated from articles, and no possible influence upon science or useful arts. Higgins v Keuffel (1891) 140 US 428, 35 L Ed 470, 11 S Ct 731.

While single illustration of trade-mark of manufacturer or jobber may not be copyrightable, this does not preclude valid copyright upon book containing compilation of such illustrations. Jeweler's Circular Pub. Co. v Keystone Pub. Co. (1922, CA2 NY) 281 F 83, 26 ALR 571, cert den 259 US 581, 66 L Ed 1074, 42 S Ct 464.

Picture was copyrightable even though its theme was taken from another. Gerlach-Barklow Co. v Morris & Bendien, Inc. (1927, CA2 NY) 23 F2d 159.

Card consisting of portrait of Washington, United States shield with eagle atop it, and words George Washington Bicentennial, may be copyrighted as original combination, but these features when standing alone are not subject to copyright. Carr v National Capital Press, Inc. (1934) 63 App DC 210, 71 F2d 220, 21 USPQ 408.

Upon compliance with copyright law, any person has exclusive right to print and vend copyrighted work which may include prints and pictorial illustrations including prints or labels used for articles of merchandise; prints and labels published in connection with sale or advertising of articles of merchandise are copyrightable; not every commercial label is copyrightable; it must contain appreciable amount of original text or pictorial material; familiar symbols or designs, mere variations of typographic ornamentation, lettering or coloring, and mere listings of ingredients or contents are not copyrightable. Kitchens of Sara Lee, Inc. v Nifty Foods Corp. (1959, CA2 NY) 266 F2d 541, 121 USPQ 359.

Ninth circuit follows liberal rather than strict rule of what constitutes copyrightable matter; labels which go beyond mere trade-mark are copyrightable; if label has some value as composition, it is no longer mere label. Drop Dead Co. v S. C. Johnson & Son, Inc. (1963, CA9 Cal) 326 F2d 87, 139 USPQ 465, cert den 377 US 907, 12 L Ed 2d 177, 84 S Ct 1167.

Greeting cards may be protected as a print. Roth Greeting Cards v United Card Co. (1970, CA9 Cal) 429 F2d 1106, 166 USPQ 291.

Print of object to be cut up, embroidered, and made into entirely different article, such as balloon or hanging basket, is not copyrightable. Rosenbach v Dreyfuss (1880, DC NY) 2 F 217.

Prints and pictorial illustrations in illustrated business catalogue are protectible. National Cloak & Suit Co. v Kaufman (1911, CC Pa) 189 F 215; Da Prato Statuary Co. v Giuliani Statuary Co. (1911, CA8 Minn) 189 F 90; Wireback v Campbell (1919, DC Md) 261 F 391, affd (CA4 Md) 269 F 372, 17 ALR 743.

Cigar labels containing name and cut of photograph of dealer are not "writings." M. B.

Fahey Tobacco Co. v Senior (1917, DC Pa) 247 F 809, mod on other grounds (CA3 Pa) 252 F 579.

Box manufacturer could obtain copyright on label designated as "footwear," and made for shoe manufacturer. Hoague-Sprague Corp. v Frank C. Meyer Co. (1929, DC NY) 31 F2d 583.

Prints and pictorial illustrations may be subject to registration under copyright law where they represent personal reaction of individual upon nature; very modest grade of art has in it something irreducible which may be copyrighted unless there is restriction in words of Copyright Act; agent for engraver presented to plaintiff stock labels and recommended label as type or pattern for those printed; pictorial part was precisely that employed in well-known and much used labels; texts on label were such as were then in use and well-known; there was slight variation in arrangement of text in relation to picture and difference in scroll about medallion or vignette; there was nothing original in this; copyright is invalid. Bobrecker v Denebeim (1939, DC Mo) 28 F Supp 383, 42 USPQ 194.

Copyright protection is afforded if picture is (1) original, created by author's own skill, labor, and judgment, and (2) meritorious, connected with fine arts; although not work of art in ordinary sense, picture is distinctive, humorous, not likely to be forgotten, brings enjoyment, and is copyrightable; that it amuses instead of instructs does not destroy copyrightability. Stuff v La Budde Feed & Grain Co. (1941, DC Wis) 42 F Supp 493, 52 USPQ 23.

Picture of animal's head on beer label is copyrightable; although textual part of label is eligible for copyright registration as matter of art when it aids or augments pictorial illustration, "Stag Beer" and "Extra Pale Pilsener" on the label are not such originality and contribution to fine arts as to entitle them to copyright protection. Griesedieck Western Brewery Co. v Peoples Brewing Co. (1944, DC Minn) 56 F Supp 600, 63 USPQ 74, affd (CA8 Minn) 149 F2d 1019, 66 USPQ 1.

Label placed upon woolen piece goods is not copyrightable where it consists merely of maker's name, "100% Virgin Wool," and three separate fleurs de lis. Forstmann Woolen Co. v J. W. Mays, Inc. (1950, DC NY) 89 F Supp 964, 85 USPQ 200.

"Stepping Tones" with fanciful representation of girl dancing on top of phonograph record has enough originality to be copyrightable. Silvers v Russell (1953, DC Cal) 113 F Supp 119, 98 USPQ 376.

Component illustrations are separately copyrightable and each illustration is protected by copyright of whole booklet; therefore, unauthorized publication of any illustration is infringement even though illustration bears minute proportion to whole booklet. Metro Associated Services, Inc. v Webster City Graphic, Inc. (1953, DC Iowa) 117 F Supp 224, 100 USPQ 88.

To extent that any elements of playing cards are copyrightable, they are copyrightable as prints. Freedman v Grolier Enterprises, Inc. (1973, DC NY) 179 USPQ 476.

39. —Maps

There is no exclusive right to signs and keys on maps. Perris v Hexamer (1879) 99 US 674, 25 L Ed 308.

Automobile road map was proper subject of copyright. General Drafting Co. v Andrews (1930, CA2 NY) 37 F2d 54, 4 USPQ 72.

Outline map of United States with state boundaries is in public domain and is not copyrightable. Christianson v West Pub. Co. (1945, CA9 Cal) 149 F2d 202, 65 USPQ 263.

For map to be copyrightable, its preparation must involve modicum of creative work instead of mere gathering of information from other maps. Amsterdam v Triangle Publications, Inc. (1951, CA3 Pa) 189 F2d 104, 89 USPQ 468.

Although maps as such are entitled to limited copyright protection, court of appeals cannot say as matter of law that plaintiff's map involved such high degree of creation that, even if copied by defendant, plaintiff's copyright was infringed. Axelbank v Rony (1960, CA9 Cal) 277 F2d 314, 125 USPQ 262.

Chart which corrected error common to prior like charts, and which was based upon author's own discovery, was copyrightable. Blunt v Patten (1828, CC NY) F Cas No 1580.

Copyright of statistical atlas covers maps contained therein. Black v Henry G. Allen Co. (1890, CC NY) 42 F 618.

Map may be copyrighted even though all material was secured from other uncopyrighted publications, when it constitutes new arrangement of old material. Woodman v Lydiard-Peterson Co. (1912, CC Minn) 192 F 67, affd (CA8 Minn) 204 F 921, reh den (CA8 Minn) 205 F 900.

One using government geological survey map and introducing thereon choice of principal cities was not entitled to copyright. Andrews v Guenther Pub. Co. (1932, DC NY) 60 F2d 555.

Map is copyrightable as original work; guide material on back of a map is copyrightable as compilation of arrangement of matter in public domain. Freedman v Milnag Leasing Corp. (1937, DC NY) 20 F Supp 802, 35 USPQ 184.

Fundamental map outlines of United States are in public domain, not subject to copyright; plaintiff's original idea of illustrating, by outline map of United States, defendant's national reporter system, is not entitled to protection; only embodiment of idea can be copyrighted; use of arbitrary colors, numbers, or symbols on map, explained by reference to key, is not copyrightable. Christianson v West Pub. Co. (1944, DC Cal) 53 F Supp 454, 60 USPQ 279, affd (CA9 Cal) 149 F2d 202, 65 USPQ 263.

At best, originality as to maps is narrow in scope, because of nature of art which consists merely of depicting, on map, in accepted form, topography of terrain; originality is more limited even than slight degree of originality required in copyrighted works in general. Hayden v Chalfant Press, Inc. (1959, DC Cal) 177 F Supp 303, 123 USPQ 475, affd (CA9 Cal) 281 F2d 543, 126 USPQ 483.

Although maps are copyrightable, they are entitled to only limited copyright protection; thus, outline of island and names of areas, cities, and hotels are in public domain and not copyrightable; even if copyright proprietor's naming of certain places and descriptions of activities and points of interest can be termed original, originality is so slight that it cannot be basis of valid copyright; moreover, such types of designation and description are not within contemplation of statute and are not copyrightable even if original. Carter v Hawaii Transp. Co. (1961, DC Hawaii) 201 F Supp 301, 133 USPQ 65.

Copyright Act recognizes maps as copyrightable material, but, as with all such materials, they are subject to requirement of originality; however, since physical facts to be portrayed, and in most cases some actual portrayal of them, are already in public domain, originality cannot mean novelty; copy of something in public domain will support copyright if it is a distinguishable variation; by labor expended in laying out map outlines on grid drawings, and in exercise of judgment in selection, from comparison of many sources, of place names to be shown, cartographer produced work which owed its origin to its author; such work is copyrightable. C. S. Hammond & Co. v International College Globe, Inc. (1962, DC NY) 210 F Supp 206, 135 USPQ 56.

Map showing originality and creativity in numbering, legibility, and clarity of streets is copyrightable. Newton v Voris (1973, DC Or) 364 F Supp 562, 180 USPQ 262.

Copyright by artist in layout for historical map is valid as covering particular tangible expression of illustrated concepts, and copyright is infringed by defendant who hired other artist to complete work and did not pay plaintiff for work. Hughey v Palographics Co. (1976, DC Colo) 189 USPQ 527.

Annotations:

Maps or charts as protected by copyright under federal copyright acts. 4 ALR Fed 466.

40. —Photographs

Photographs are entitled to copyright; Burrow-Giles Lithographic Co. v Sarony (1884) 111 US 53, 28 L Ed 349, 4 S Ct 279; Thornton v Schreiber (1888) 124 US 612, 31 L Ed 577, 8 S Ct 618.

Whether photograph is mere manual reproduction of subject matter, or original work of art, is question of fact. Bolles v Outing Co. (1897, CA2 NY) 77 F 966, affd 175 US 262, 44 L Ed 156, 20 S Ct 94.

After photograph has become public property it cannot again be made subject of copyright by etching slight and colorable alteration in negative, which was not done in good faith for purpose of producing new work of art. Snow v Laird (1900, CA7 Ill) 98 F 813.

When photograph has been produced and copyrighted, any other artist may use same model for his pictures even though, by chance, pose, background, light, and shade of new picture may be similar, provided he does not copy from copyrighted photograph in order to obtain similar picture. Gross v Seligman (1914, CA2 NY) 212 F 930.

Photographer is entitled to copyright photographs which were taken gratuitously and for his own benefit. Lumiere v Pathe Exchange, Inc. (1921, CA2 NY) 275 F 428.

Reproduction of photograph for use in advertising is proper subject of copyright. Ansehl v Puritan Pharmaceutical Co. (1932, CA8 Mo) 61 F2d 131, 15 USPQ 38, cert den 287 US 666, 77 L Ed 574, 53 S Ct 224.

Photograph, if it be also artistic production, result of original intellectual conception on part of author, may be copyrighted, and without protection of statute it cannot continue to be author's exclusive property, after it has been printed and offered to public for sale. Bamforth v Douglass Post Card & Mach. Co. (1908, CC Pa) 158 F 355.

Mere copy of photograph does not come within domain of legislation under constitutional power of Congress as provided for in § 8 of Article 1 of Constitution. M. B. Fahey Tobacco Co. v Senior (1917, DC Pa) 247 F 809, mod on other grounds (CA3 Pa) 252 F 579.

Courts liberally extend copyright protection and ordinary photographs of familiar scenes are protected if photographer uses skill and judgment in arrangement, grouping, and lighting. Stuff v La Budde Feed & Grain Co. (1941, DC Wis) 42 F Supp 493, 52 USPQ 23.

41. —Sculpture

Use or intended use in industry of statuette eligible for copyright does not bar or invalidate its copyright registration. Mazer v Stein (1954) 347 US 201, 98 L Ed 630, 74 S Ct 460, 100 USPQ 325, reh den 347 US 949, 98 L Ed 1096, 74 S Ct 637.

Doll head, was assumed, with difficulty, to be work of art. E. I. Horsman & Aetna Doll Co. v Kaufman (1922, CA2 NY) 286 F 372, cert den 261 US 615, 67 L Ed 828, 43 S Ct 361.

Model airplane kits having originality in expression and embodiment of design and structure of kit are copyrightable subject matter. Monogram Models, Inc. v Industro Motive Corp. (1974, CA6 Mich) 492 F2d 1281, 181 USPQ 425, cert den 419 US 843, 42 L Ed 2d 71, 95 S Ct 76.

Ladies' chart for cutting coats and dresses was legitimate subject of copyright as book. Drury v Ewing (1862, CC Ohio) F Cas No 4095.

Representation of elk of prodigious proportions built of wooden frame covered with chicken wire, canvassed, plastered and painted, intended for street decoration is not subject to copyright. Carns v Keefe Bros. (1917, DC Mont) 242 F 745.

Design of statuette of figures of two saints standing on either side of crucifix, may be copyrighted, but such copyright does not give exclusive right to subject, be it saint, crucifix, or anything or any personality which may be subject of artist's brush or sculptor's chisel. Pellegrini v Allegrini (1924, DC Pa) 2 F2d 610.

Sculpture of animal is copyrightable subject matter. Contemporary Arts, Inc. v F. W. Woolworth Co. (1950, DC Mass) 93 F Supp 739, 86 USPQ 476, affd (CA1 Mass) 193 F2d 162, 92 USPQ 4, affd 344 US 228, 97 L Ed 276, 73 S Ct 222, 95 USPQ 396, motion den 350 US 810, 100 L Ed 727, 76 S Ct 37.

Statue is properly copyrightable as work of art where photographs deposited with copyright office are photographs of mere statue alone without electrical assemblies, lamp shades, or lamp mounting stubs, even though statues are sold wired with electrical assemblies to which lamp shades are attached. Stein v Rosenthal (1952, DC Cal) 103 F Supp 227, 92 USPQ 402, affd (CA9 Cal) 205 F2d 633, 98 USPQ 180.

Although flower is creation of nature, its likeness may be copyrighted as work of art; since artificial lilac made of polyethylene reflects originality and substantial degree of skill and inde-

pendent judgment, it is proper subject for copyright. Prestige Floral, Societe Anonyme v California Artificial Flower Co. (1962, DC NY) 201 F Supp 287, 132 USPQ 350.

Copyright does not protect dahlia itself but merely creator's impression, treatment, or reproduction thereof in polyethylene. Prestige Floral, Societe Anonyme v Zunino-Altman, Inc. (1962, DC NY) 203 F Supp 649, 133 USPQ 75, affd (CA2 NY) 301 F2d 286, 133 USPQ 58.

Although reproductions of creations of nature such as dancers, dogs, and artificial flowers have been given copyright protection where they represented some originality in their treatment of the subject, instant materials are not copyrightable since they do not represent creations of nature, but merely patterns of arranging floral components for decorative purposes, and plaintiff has shown no originality in patterns of arrangements it chose. Gardenia Flowers, Inc. v Joseph Markovits, Inc. (1968, DC NY) 280 F Supp 776, 157 USPQ 685.

There is no requirement that creator of copyrighted work possess any special talent; accidental or laboriously contrived creation, if it qualifies objectively, is doubtless enough; however, court's appraisal of alleged creator of copyrighted artificial flower model is a factor in the case because it influences court's finding that he is not the creator he was alleged to be and because it affects the independently material point that object in question, a routine assembly of old elements, is probably not copyrightable. Florabelle Flowers, Inc. v Joseph Markovits, Inc. (1968, DC NY) 296 F Supp 304, 160 USPQ 611.

42. Motion pictures and other audiovisual works, generally [17 USCS § 102(a)(6)]

Motion-pictures are entitled to copyright. Edison v Lubin (1903, CA3 Pa) 122 F 240, app dismd 195 US 624, 49 L Ed 349, 25 S Ct 790; Harper & Bros. v Kalem Co. (1909, CA2 NY) 169 F 61, affd 222 US 55, 56 L Ed 92, 32 S Ct 20; Metro-Goldwyn-Mayer Distributing Corp. v Bijou Theatre Co. (1933, DC Mass) 3 F Supp 66, 17 USPQ 124; American Mutoscope & Biograph Co. v Edison Mfg. Co. (1905, CC NJ) 137 F 262.

Motion picture representing launching of vessel was subject to copyright. Edison v Lubin (1903, CA3 Pa) 122 F 240, app dismd 195 US 624, 49 L Ed 349, 25 S Ct 790.

"Comic accretion," "gags," and "stage business" may be so combined with events as to become subject to copyright protection, but original combination of 57 motion-picture scenes constituting sequence of vital importance to story, containing character, dialogue, and action, cannot be termed mere comedy accretion. Universal Pictures Co. v Harold Lloyd Corp. (1947, CA9 Cal) 162 F2d 354, 73 USPQ 317.

Motion-picture photoplay film is entitled to protection against unauthorized exhibition whether it is dramatic work or is dramatization of nondramatic work. Metro-Goldwyn-Mayer Distributing Corp. v Bijou Theatre Co. (1933, DC Mass) 3 F Supp 66, 17 USPQ 124.

Radio, motion picture, and television have great value, are subject of popular demand, and are as such subject of property rights and deserve protection of equity. Waring v Dunlea (1939, DC NC) 26 F Supp 338, 41 USPQ 201.

Motion-picture "shorts" were comedy but had story, not of great intellectual value but which showed originality, and were entitled to protection under Copyright Act. Vitaphone Corp. v Hutchinson Amusement Co. (1939, DC Mass) 28 F Supp 526, 42 USPQ 431.

Although news event (death of President Kennedy) may not be copyrighted, motion picture film of that event is copyrightable. Time Inc. v Bernard Geis Associates (1968, DC NY) 293 F Supp 130, 159 USPQ 663.

Movie found to be obscene is not entitled to protection of copyright laws so that relief sought by owners for infringement is denied. Mitchell Bros. Film Group v Cinema Adult Theater (1976, DC Tex) 192 USPQ 138.

When book or drama is dedicated to public, anyone may prepare and copyright motion-picture photoplay founded thereon; but such copyright will not give owner thereof exclusive right to motion-picture rights in book or drama. O'Neill v General Film Co. (1916) 171 App Div 854, 157 NYS 1028.

43. —Television

Interview-master of ceremonies technique and lecture by traveler are in public domain and cannot be appropriated so as to exclude others; thus, first one to show foreign scenes on television cannot pre-empt right to do so. Television Adventure Films Corp. v KCOP Television, Inc. 137 USPQ 254.

44. Sound recordings [17 USCS § 102(a)(7)]

Copyright protection does not extend to phonograph records comprising performance of public domain literary property or musical compositions. Neal v Thomas Organ Co. (1963, CA9 Cal) 325 F2d 978, 140 USPQ 103, cert den 379 US 828, 13 L Ed 2d 37, 85 S Ct 55.

V. IDEAS AND METHODOLOGY [17 USCS § 102(b)]

45. Generally

Copyright protection is given only to expression of idea—not to idea itself. Mazer v Stein (1954) 347 US 201, 98 L Ed 630, 74 S Ct 460, 100 USPQ 325, reh den 347 US 949, 98 L Ed 1096, 74 S Ct 637.

Lecturer may use ideas expressed in another work, for it is not subject that is protected, but treatment of subject. Nutt v National Institute, Inc. for Improv. of Memory (1929, CA2 Conn) 31 F2d 236.

Copyright of playwright does not prevent use of his "ideas." Nichols v Universal Pictures Corp. (1930, CA2 NY) 45 F2d 119, 7 USPQ 84, cert den 282 US 902, 75 L Ed 795, 51 S Ct 216.

Purpose of copyright to promote literary progress would be frustrated if author could prevent others from using common ideas. Becker v Loew's, Inc. (1943, CA7 Ill) 133 F2d 889, 56 USPQ 455, cert den 319 US 772, 87 L Ed 1720, 63 S Ct 1438, reh den 320 US 811, 88 L Ed 490, 64 S Ct 30.

Copyright protects only to extent of what is taught or explained; unlike patent, information disclosed is lodged in public domain, where its use is unrestricted. Crume v Pacific Mut. Life Ins. Co. (1944, CA7 Ill) 140 F2d 182, 60 USPQ 359, cert den 322 US 755, 88 L Ed 1584, 64 S Ct 1265.

Concrete incidents are protected by copyright law although law gives no monopoly of general ideas. MacDonald v Du Maurier (1944, CA2 NY) 144 F2d 696, 62 USPQ 394, later app (DC NY) 75 F Supp 653 and later app (DC NY) 75 F Supp 655.

Statutes do not protect intellectual conception apart from thing produced. Christianson v West Pub. Co. (1945, CA9 Cal) 149 F2d 202, 65 USPQ 263.

Copyright does not pre-empt field as against others who choose different means of expressing same idea; in this respect, it differs from patent which protects inventor against any unauthorized use of discovery itself. Alexander v Irving Trust Co. (1955, DC NY) 132 F Supp 364, 106 USPQ 74, affd (CA2 NY) 228 F2d 221, 108 USPQ 24, cert den 350 US 996, 100 L Ed 860, 76 S Ct 545.

Substantial similarity is not one of ideas as such, but of embodiment of these ideas in written or other form, since author cannot obtain copyright on his ideas apart from their expression; fundamental idea of original work may even be borrowed as long as specific details of author's literary efforts are not copied. Richards v Columbia Broadcasting System, Inc. (1958, DC Dist Col) 161 F Supp 516, 117 USPQ 174.

Neither common law nor statutory copyright extends protection to idea as such; however, ideas may be subject of contract to pay for their use. Desny v Wilder (1956) 46 Cal 2d 715, 299 P2d 257, 110 USPQ 433.

Ideas as such are not subject to copyright; copyright does not pre-empt field as against others who choose different means of expressing same idea; however, there may be protectible interest in idea or combination of ideas which is reduced to "concrete" form; even then it is only form in which ideas are expressed that is protected; law does not award originator monopoly in ideas themselves. Herwitz v National Broadcasting Co. (1962, DC NY) 210 F Supp 231, 135 USPQ 96.

46. Facts and events

Copyright of news protects form of expression but not facts, since facts are public property. International News Service v Associated Press (1918) 248 US 215, 63 L Ed 211, 39 S Ct 68, 2 ALR 293.

News and telegraphic market quotations on ticker tape are not subject to copyright. National Tel. News Co. v Western U. Tel. Co. (1902, CA7 Ill) 119 F 294.

There can be no copyright of news facts, for such are public property. Davies v Bowes (1913, DC NY) 209 F 53, affd (CA2 NY) 219 F 178; Chicago Record-Herald Co. v Tribune Asso. (1921, CA7 Ill) 275 F 797; Gilmore v Sammons (1925, Tex Civ App) 269 SW 861, error dismd.

Printed pamphlet, furnishing valuable information as to dimensions of piston rings is subject to copyright. No-Leak-O Piston Ring Co. v Norris (1921, CA4 Md) 277 F 951.

Neither historical facts nor errors in fact are copyrightable per se. Oxford Book Co. v College Entrance Book Co. (1938, CA2 NY) 98 F2d 688, 39 USPQ 7.

Where series of events portrayed in book purport to represent real occurrences, form of expression is only thing protected by copyright. Collins v Metro-Goldwyn Pictures Corp. (1939, CA2 NY) 106 F2d 83, 42 USPQ 553.

Well-known incidents and experiences which are common to all may be the ingredients of story or play, and although book is copyrighted containing these incidents, they still may be used in story written by another. Stevenson v Harris (1917, DC NY) 238 F 432.

Facts of history which necessarily must be dealt with in similar manner by all historians are not copyrightable. Caruthers v R. K. O. Radio Pictures, Inc. (1937, DC NY) 20 F Supp 906, 35 USPQ 115, 35 USPQ 542.

One who narrates matters of fact may be protected by copyright as to his arrangement, manner, and style, but not as to material or ideas. Oliver v St. Germain Foundation (1941, DC Cal) 41 F Supp 296, 51 USPQ 20.

Plaintiff's copyrighted book "Famous First Facts" containing bare statements of historical facts is not infringed by defendant's advertisements entitled "First Facts" each containing one fact obtained from book, since wording of items is not same and plaintiff does not own facts; name "First Facts" is not subject to copyright protection; publications have nothing in common, there is no competition, and plaintiff cannot be injured. Kane v Pennsylvania Broadcasting Co. (1947, DC Pa) 73 F Supp 307, 73 USPQ 258.

No one has legal right to exclusive use of historical facts in public domain. Funkhouser v Loew's, Inc. (1952, DC Mo) 108 F Supp 476, 96 USPQ 115, affd (CA8 Mo) 208 F2d 185, 99 USPQ 448, cert den 348 US 843, 99 L Ed 664, 75 S Ct 64, reh den 348 US 890, 99 L Ed 700, 75 S Ct 209.

No one has right of property in historical or biographical event; any one may publish biographies or photographs of public figures or narratives of historical events; no one can have monopoly of idea of publishing history of particular wars or of other events, but one can acquire property right in specific embodiment of idea. Curtis v Time, Inc. (1957, DC Dist Col) 147 F Supp 505, 112 USPQ 248, affd 102 App DC 148, 251 F2d 389, 116 USPQ 119.

Author of biographical novel has right to use another's copyrighted biography as guide where author checks fundamental records himself by going to sources; facts concerning actual life of historic character are in public domain and are not entitled to copyright protection; however, fictionalizing of events in life is author's original treatment of life and is subject to protection. Greenbie v Noble (1957, DC NY) 151 F Supp 45, 113 USPQ 115.

Copyright proprietor has neither monopoly of scientific information with which book deals nor monopoly of idea of expounding information in simple language comprehensible by lay readers. Ricker v General Electric Co. (1947, CA2 NY) 162 F2d 141, 73 USPQ 458.

Magazine's statements concerning attributes of consumer goods are not copyrightable since they are bald statements of fact which could hardly be stated in any different fashion; they are pedestrian expressions with no independent creative stature; they describe facts and nothing more. Consumers Union of United States, Inc. v Hobart Mfg. Co. (1961, DC NY) 199 F Supp 860, 131 USPQ 438.

Though facts concerning actual life of historic character are in public domain and are not entitled to copyright protection, copyright holder has exclusive right to exploit form of his expression; association, arrangement, and combination of ideas and thoughts and their form of expression may entitle particular composition to protection. Holdredge v Knight Publishing Corp. (1963, DC Cal) 214 F Supp 921, 136 USPQ 615.

Protectible literary property may be created out of unprotectible material such as historical events; creation in technical sense is not essential to vest one with ownership of rights in intellectual property. Desny v Wilder (1956) 46 Cal 2d 715, 299 P2d 257, 110 USPQ 433.

47. Particular ideas

Mere idea of depicting more common kinds of automobile accidents in form of story in cartoon form is not copyrightable. American Visuals Corp. v Holland (1958, CA2 NY) 261 F2d 652, 119 USPQ 482.

Ideas or known concepts cannot be protected by copyright, but new expression of public domain idea in form of Uncle Sam bank is copyrightable insofar as differing from original. L. Batlin & Son, Inc. v Snyder (1975, CA2) 187 USPQ 721.

Ideas as such and means for expressing ideas, such as warrants to be issued for state insurance, are not proper subjects of copyright. Long v Jordan (1939, DC Cal) 29 F Supp 287, 43 USPQ 176.

Author of scientific article published in professional journal is not entitled to monopoly of ideas presented therein. Alexander v Irving Trust Co. (1955, DC NY) 132 F Supp 364, 106 USPQ 74, affd (CA2 NY) 228 F2d 221, 108 USPQ 24, cert den 350 US 996, 100 L Ed 860, 76 S Ct 545.

One cannot get copyright or literary rights to idea of having actors appear in black and white costumes. O'Brien v Chappel & Co. (1958, DC NY) 159 F Supp 58, 116 USPQ 340.

Mere idea of basing quiz program on motion pictures, even if it were original, is not subject to protection under copyright laws. Richards v Columbia Broadcasting System, Inc. (1958, DC Dist Col) 161 F Supp 516, 117 USPQ 174.

Idea of Santa Claus as part of Christmas motif belongs to public domain and cannot be withdrawn by copyright, but reproduction of idea in different combinations, adaptations, arrangements, or mediums of expression which are sufficiently original is protected by copyright laws. Barton Candy Corp. v Tell Chocolate Novelties Corp. (1959, DC NY) 178 F Supp 577, 123 USPQ 425.

Idea of doll on pole in display box may be appropriated by any manufacturer; what he may not appropriate is copyright proprietor's tangible expression of that idea. Uneeda Doll Co. v P &

M Doll Co. (1965, DC NY) 241 F Supp 675, 145 USPQ 326, affd (CA2 NY) 353 F2d 788, 148 USPQ 7.

Idea of printing point count value on honor cards of bridge deck is so restrictive that it necessarily requires particular form of expression and is not copyrightable. Freedman v Grolier Enterprises, Inc. (1973, DC NY) 179 USPQ 476.

48. Directories and lists

Jewelry trade directory showing cuts of trademarks used, respectively, by listed jewelers, was subject to copyright. Jeweler's Circular Pub. Co. v Keystone Pub. Co. (1922, CA2 NY) 281 F 83, 26 ALR 571, cert den 259 US 581, 66 L Ed 1074, 42 S Ct 464.

List of code words is copyrightable. American Code Co. v Bensinger (1922, CA2 NY) 282 F 829.

Consolidated index of tariffs of various carriers on corresponding subject is proper subject of copyright. Guthrie v Curlett (1929, CA2 NY) 36 F2d 694, 4 USPQ 1.

Lists of names, addresses, and other information contained in applications for registration of motor vehicles in office of state Commissioner of Motor Vehicles is copyrightable. New Jersey Motor List Co. v Barton Business Service (1931, DC NJ) 57 F2d 353, 13 USPQ 43.

Book containing list of hotels was "directory" and subject to copyright. American Travel & Hotel Directory Co. v Gehring Publishing Co. (1925, DC NY) 4 F2d 415.

49. Procedures, processes and systems, generally

System of spelling words with less than usual number of letters, such as "Steno-Short-Type System" is not copyrightable, though description of such system might be subject of copyright. Brief English Systems, Inc. v Owen (1931, CA2 NY) 48 F2d 555, 9 USPQ 20, cert den 283 US 858, 75 L Ed 1464, 51 S Ct 650.

Although basic materials and arithmetical problems may have been old and in public domain, arrangements and combinations contained in sets of copyrighted flash cards used to teach arithmetic were more than mere compilations; combinations of problems selected, together with test sheets and instructions, were more analogous to educational book; arrangement, plan, and manner in which materials were put together constitute novelty; copyright is valid. Gelles-Widmer Co. v Milton Bradley Co. (1963, CA7 Ill) 313 F2d 143, 136 USPQ 240, cert den 373 US 913, 10 L Ed 2d 414, 83 S Ct 1303.

Although substance of contest is not copyrightable, it does not follow that contest rule contains no original creative authorship; copyright attaches to form of expression; however, since uncopyrightable subject matter, substance of contest, is narrow, contest rule requires, if not only one form of expression, at best only limited number. Morrissey v Procter & Gamble Co. (1967, CA1 Mass) 379 F2d 675, 154 USPQ 193.

Copyright of book describing "short hand" system did not give exclusive right to system, so as to prevent others from describing same system in their own language. Griggs v Perrin (1892, CC NY) 49 F 15.

Description of plan or method of coupon system is subject to copyright, as contrasted with coupons themselves. Mutual Advertising Co. v Refo (1896, CC-SC) 76 F 961.

Letter indexes provided with leaves arranged loosely, so that they may be separated, and letters indexed or temporarily filed in their proper places do not constitute "book," and are not proper subject of copyright. Amberg File & Index Co. v Shea Smith & Co. (1896, CC Ill) 78 F 479, affd (CA7 Ill) 82 F 314.

Person can acquire no exclusive rights in particular distribution of playing cards, in problem of play or principles of contract bridge applicable to its solution. Russell v Northeastern Pub. Co. (1934, DC Mass) 7 F Supp 571, 23 USPQ 123.

Books describing game or sporting event and rules thereof as ideas are not copyrightable, and system of staging game or spectacle is not covered; idea of staging purportedly transcontinental roller skating race having distinctive treatment of theme ought to be protected by copyright law only if theme be essential part of true dramatic composition. Seltzer v Sunbrock (1938, DC Cal) 22 F Supp 621.

Forms, arrangement, and format involved in use of system or method are not protected by copyright. Kanover v Marks (DC NY) 91 USPQ 370.

Copyright gives no protection with respect to techniques and methods; it gives no exclusive right to practice or use arts and methods described in copyrighted work. Dunham v General Mills, Inc. (1953, DC Mass) 116 F Supp 152, 99 USPQ 372.

Cases holding that games, sports, and similar systems and plans are not copyrightable seem to spring from Baker v Selden, 101 US 99; that case made clear distinction between writings describing plans, methods, or systems, and plans or systems themselves; former were held subject to copyright, latter, if at all, to patent protection; therefore, court dismisses action for infringement of copyrighted brochure describing betting system and for unfair competition since statutes and

court decisions give no protection by copyright to sports, games, or similar systems as distinguished from publications describing them and since sport involved is so elementary and ordinary that it is in public domain and to afford protection would be to give author monopoly out of proportion to originality involved. Briggs v New Hampshire Trotting & Breeding Asso., Inc. (1960, DC NH) 191 F Supp 234, 128 USPQ 465.

System for playing bridge is idea which cannot be copyrighted, although book containing system may be copyrighted. Downes v Culbertson (1934) 153 Misc 14, 275 NYS 233.

50. Business systems

Neither system of bookkeeping nor blank account books is subject of copyright. Baker v Selden (1880) 101 US 99, 25 L Ed 841.

Copyright of pamphlet describing plan for organizing and operating burial association does not confer right to plan disclosed. Burk v Johnson (1906, CA8 Kan) 146 F 209.

One cannot copyright system or method of selling product, but may copyright original symbols or designs used as means of effecting sale of product. Kaeser & Blair, Inc. v Merchants' Asso. (1933, CA6 Ohio) 64 F2d 575, 17 USPQ 357.

Bank night theater scheme, being in no sense writing, could not be copyrighted. Affiliated Enterprises, Inc. v Gruber (1936, CA1 Mass) 86 F2d 958, 32 USPQ 94.

Copyright of insurance policies did not restrict right of defendant to use plans of insurance embraced in copyrighted policies but did restrict use or copying of means of expression selected by author to extent such means of expression were original with him. Dorsey v Old Surety Life Ins. Co. (1938, CA10 Okla) 98 F2d 872, 119 ALR 1250, 39 USPQ 92.

Method of advertising cannot be copyrighted, and owner of copyright on paint card cannot sue to prevent anyone else from advertising paint by attaching pieces of colored paper to card. Ehret v Pierce (1880, CC NY) 10 F 553.

System, plan, method, and arrangement of originator of compilation of credit ratings derives no protection from statutory copyright of book in which they are set forth. Burnell v Chown (1895, CC Ohio) 69 F 993.

System or means of doing business or of accomplishing certain result is not generally copyrightable; Copyright protection covers form of expression, not underlying act or system. Norton Printing Co. v Augustana Hospital (1967, DC Ill) 155 USPQ 133.

§ 103. Subject matter of copyright: Compilations and derivative works

(a) The subject matter of copyright as specified by section 102 [17 USCS § 102] includes compilations and derivative works, but protection for a work employing preexisting material in which copyright subsists does not extend to any part of the work in which such material has been used unlawfully.

(b) The copyright in a compilation or derivative work extends only to the material contributed by the author of such work, as distinguished from the preexisting material employed in the work, and does not imply any exclusive right in the preexisting material. The copyright in such work is independent of, and does not affect or enlarge the scope, duration, owner-ship, or subsistence of, any copyright protection in the preexisting material. (Added Oct. 19, 1976, P. L. 94-553, Title I, § 101, 90 Stat 2545.)

HISTORY; ANCILLARY LAWS AND DIRECTIVES

Effective date of section:

Section 102 of Act Oct. 19, 1976, P. L. 94-553, 90 Stat. 2598 provided that this section "becomes effective on January 1, 1978".

CROSS REFERENCES

"Compilations" defined, 17 USCS § 101.
"Derivative works" defined, 17 USCS § 101.
Copyrightable subject matter, 17 USCS § 102.
This section referred to in 17 USCS §§ 104, 301.

RESEARCH GUIDE

Am Jur:

18 Am Jur 2d, Copyright and Literary Property §§ 26, 39, 42, 49, 115.

Annotations:

Copyright, under Federal Copyright Act (17 USCS §§ 1 et seq.), in advertising materials, catalogs, and price lists. 5 ALR Fed 625.

INTERPRETIVE NOTES AND DECISIONS

I. COMPILATIONS [17 USCS § 103(a)]

1. Generally
2. Literary works, generally
3. —Catalogues
4. —Directories and lists
5. —Law reports
6. —Periodicals
7. Musical works, generally
8. —Arrangements
9. Pictorial, graphic, and sculptural works, generally
10. —Reproductions

II. DERIVATIVE WORKS [17 USCS § 103(b)]

11. Generally
12. Literary works, generally
13. —New editions
14. —Translations
15. Musical works, generally
16. —Arrangements
17. Dramatic works
18. Pictorial, graphic, and sculptural works, generally
19. —Maps
20. Motion pictures and other audiovisual works

I. COMPILATIONS [17 USCS § 103(a)]

1. Generally

Compilation is sum total of words and phrases as arranged by author and copyright is valid because of originality of combination; when statute allows compilation to be copyrighted, no one can copy phrases or sequences which are original with author or appropriate any other part of copyrighted work, whether that part is in public domain or not. Hartfield v Peterson (1937, CA2 NY) 91 F2d 998, 34 USPQ 305.

Aggregation of standard provisions, including some required by statute forming copyrighted insurance policy is not susceptible of infringement as to such provisions. Dorsey v Old Surety Life Ins. Co. (1938, CA10 Okla) 98 F2d 872, 119 ALR 1250, 39 USPQ 92.

All writings of author are entitled to copyright and this includes composite and cyclopedic works, directories, gazetteers, and other compilations. College Entrance Book Co. v Amsco Book Co. (1941, CA2 NY) 119 F2d 874, 49 USPQ 517.

Information as to air travel on file with Civil Aeronautics Authority and distributed by airlines in publicly accessible timetables is not copyrightable per se. Official Aviation Guide Co. v American Aviation Associates (1945, CA7 Ill) 150 F2d 173, 65 USPQ 553, cert den 326 US 776, 90 L Ed 469, 66 S Ct 267, reh den 326 US 811, 90 L Ed 495, 66 S Ct 335.

Composite works relating to handicapping systems for betting on horse races and containing extracts from past performance records are not denied copyright protection for containing in part matter copyrighted by another. Belcher v Tarbox (1973, CA9 Cal) 486 F2d 1087, 180 USPQ 1.

Compilation of material forming shipper's guide is copyrightable. Bullinger v Mackey (1879, CC NY) F Cas No 2127.

Arithmetic book which is compilation of materials from other sources combined with author's own genius to illustrate subject results in new and original plan and arrangement, capable of copyright. Emerson v Davies (1845, CC Mass) F Cas No 4436.

Old materials, when subsequently collected, arranged, and combined in new and original form may be copyrighted. Lawrence v Dana (1869, CC Mass) F Cas No 8136.

"Compilation" consists of selected abstracts from different authors. Story v Holcombe (1847, CC Ohio) F Cas No 13497.

Compilation showing financial standing of local businessmen was not proper subject of copyright. Burnell v Chown (1895, CC Ohio) 69 F 993.

Mere compilation of facts is protected by copyright law, as well as original matter showing invention. American Trotting Register Ass'n v Gocher (1895, CC Ohio) 70 F 237.

Compilation of credit ratings and financial standings is subject to copyright. Ladd v Oxnard (1896, CC Mass) 75 F 703.

Predecessor section makes it possible to copyright compilation of trade-marks, although trademarks themselves cannot be copyrighted. Jewelers' Circular Pub. Co. v Keystone Pub. Co. (1921, DC NY) 274 F 932, affd (CA2 NY) 281 F 83, 26 ALR 571, cert den 259 US 581, 66 L Ed 1074, 42 S Ct 464.

Copyright of collection of works, some of which have been previously copyrighted, protects only what is original in new collection. Andrews v Guenther Pub. Co. (1932, DC NY) 60 F2d 555.

Account of single event is copyrightable as compilation only when it has individuality of expression or reflects peculiar skill and judgment. Triangle Publications, Inc. v New England Newspaper Pub. Co. (1942, DC Mass) 46 F Supp 198, 54 USPQ 171.

While compilation need not be sole product of maker, something more than compilation of information procured by others is required to make map copyrightable; there must be originality resulting from independent effort of maker in acquiring reasonably substantial portion of information; reduction in size by use of mechanical instrument is not original idea; omission of towns, highways, or other markings superfluous for maker's purpose is no indication of originality; free-hand location of highways is not new information; mere contraction of edge of map to bring in additional area is not sufficient original work. Marken & Bielfeld, Inc. v Baughman Co. (1957, DC Va) 162 F Supp 561, 117 USPQ 332.

Although it has been said that copyright on compilation protects all matter embodied therein in which copyright is already subsisting, this means only that, because of copyright on compilation, no one can copy old material from that compilation; it does not mean that one cannot go back to source; that is protected only by copyright on original. C. S. Hammond & Co. v International College Globe, Inc. (1962, DC NY) 210 F Supp 206, 135 USPQ 56.

Compilation and arrangement of public domain material in executive desk calendar is copyrightable where compilation and arrangement is original. Baldwin Cooke Co. v Keith Clark, Inc. (1974, DC Ill) 383 F Supp 650, 183 USPQ 209, affd without op (CA7 Ill) 505 F2d 1250 and supp op (DC Ill) 420 F Supp 404.

Composite works involve contributions by several authors and are mutually exclusive of works done for hire where employer is sole "author" so that Register of Copyrights properly refuses renewal registration claiming contradictory rights under both composite work and work done for hire in comic books. Opinion of Atty. Gen. (1974) 183 USPQ 624.

2. Literary works, generally

Even though some of material was in public domain, arrangement, expression, and manner of presentation thereof are copyrightable since they were not in public domain. Flick-Reedy Corp. v Hydro-Line Mfg. Co. (1965, CA7 Ill) 351 F2d 546, 146 USPQ 694, cert den 383 US 958, 16 L Ed 2d 301, 86 S Ct 1222.

Combining of several old materials and methods to form book does not constitute new and original work. Bullinger v Mackey (1879, CC NY) F Cas No 2127.

There may be no copyright in subject matter of book which is open to public, but book itself may be subject to copyright. Centennial Catalogue Co. v Porter (1876, CC Pa) F Cas No 2546.

Notes to edition of Latin grammar selected from various authors and arranged was original work which would entitle author thereof to copyright in their actual form and combination. Gray v Russell (1839, CC Mass) F Cas No 5728.

Compilation, made from voluminous public documents, and so arranged as to show readily date and order of certain historic events, may be copyrighted, because such publications require labor, care, and some skill in their preparation. Hanson v Jaccard Jewelry Co. (1887, CC Mo) 32 F 202.

Treatise printed with author's consent and forming part of "Encyclopedia Britannica" may not be reprinted, without author's consent, as part of unauthorized reprint of such encyclopedia. Black v Henry G. Allen Co. (1890, CC NY) 42 F 618.

Copyrights in books, secured by publication with prescribed notice of copyright duly affixed thereto, secure to copyright proprietor copyright in every copyrightable component part of books just as if parts had been separately published with notice of copyright. King Features Syndicate, Inc. v Bouve (DC Dist Col) 48 USPQ 237.

3. —Catalogues

Protection extends to original achievement in publication of trade catalogue. Markham v A. E. Borden Co. (1953, CA1 Mass) 206 F2d 199, 98 USPQ 346.

Copyright of catalogue protects each cut contained therein. Da Prato Statuary Co. v Giuliani Statuary Co. (1911, CA8 Minn) 189 F 90.

Copyright of catalogue containing trademarks, copyrights trade-marks as they appear in catalogue. Jewelers' Circular Pub. Co. v Keystone Pub. Co. (1921, DC NY) 274 F 932, affd (CA2 NY) 281 F 83, 26 ALR 571, cert den 259 US 581, 66 L Ed 1074, 42 S Ct 464.

Where Italian registration of copyright in picture was subsequent to registration in United States of catalogue containing picture and of course subsequent to date of publication claimed in United States registration, copyright of picture as component part of catalogue was valid. Basevi v Edward O'Toole Co. (1939, DC NY) 26 F Supp 41, 40 USPQ 333.

Each original description and illustration in copyrighted catalogue is component part protected by predecessor section. Harry Alter Co. v A. E. Borden Co. (1954, DC Mass) 121 F Supp 941, 102 USPQ 2.

Trade catalogue is composite work. Unistrut Corp. v Power (1958, DC Mass) 175 F Supp 294, affd in part and vacated in part on other grounds (CA1 Mass) 280 F2d 18.

Copyright of entire catalog protects each illustration therein as if each had been individually copyrighted; therefore, there is only one copyright which can be infringed regardless of how many illustrations are copied by infringer. Hedeman Products Corp. v Tap-Rite Products Corp. (1964, DC NJ) 228 F Supp 630, 141 USPQ 381.

Prints and pictorial illustrations, including illustrations of articles of manufacture or merchandise, are copyrightable material. Such illustrations may be individually protected in a catalogue by obtaining a copyright on catalogue as "copyrightable parts." Blumcraft of Pittsburgh v Newman Bros., Inc. (1968, DC Ohio) 159 USPQ 166.

Copyright Act protects each of component portions of copyrighted catalogue. Walco Products, Inc. v Kittay & Blitz, Inc. (1972, DC NY) 354 F Supp 121.

Annotations:

Copyright, under Federal Copyright Act (17 USCS §§ 1 et seq.), in advertising materials, catalogues, and price lists. 5 ALR Fed 625.

4. —Directories and lists

Originality in compilation of directory does not mean entirely new conception of directory; any one may produce directory of restaurants, but he must "start from scratch," do own collecting, own appraisal, and own description and editing. Adventures in Good Eating, Inc. v Best Places to Eat, Inc. (1942, CA7 Ill) 131 F2d 809, 56 USPQ 242.

Compilation of war records made from voluminous public documents is entitled to copyright. Hanson v Jaccard Jewelry Co. (1887, CC Mo) 32 F 202.

"Official form chart of races," printed in daily periodical and containing information and statistics relative to horse racing was proper subject of copyright. Egbert v Greenberg (1900, CC Cal) 100 F 447.

Author of street directory for portion of city cannot, by incorporating material in new street directory for entire city, prolong protection for earlier compilation; single daily race chart is not copyrightable as compilation because majority of items can be collected without labor, skill or judgment by any spectator and does not result from labor of assembling, connecting, and categorizing facts which in nature occurred in isolation. Triangle Publications, Inc. v New England Newspaper Pub. Co. (1942, DC Mass) 46 F Supp 198, 54 USPQ 171.

Copyrighter of directory has right to protection. Chain Store Business Guide, Inc. v Wexler (1948, DC NY) 79 F Supp 726, 77 USPQ 656.

It is one function of copyright system to clothe with copyright protection compilation of facts; thus, compiler of directory can, by copyrighting it, obtain protection against competitor who merely copies his work; however, he cannot obtain protection against one who publishes article upon distribution of residents in relation to national origin and who used compilation from directory for locating concentrations of persons bearing names characteristic of various national origins; directory cases are exceptions to rule that facts are not proper subject of copyright; exception does not go so far as to prohibit noncompetitive use of facts set forth in copyrighted collection. Consumers Union of United States, Inc. v Hobart Mfg. Co. (1960, DC NY) 189 F Supp 275, 125 USPQ 296.

Plaintiff expended substantial efforts in gathering, assembling, and synthesizing of data relating to automotive items which it selected for marketing; plaintiff then condensed such data and created for its catalog original descriptions, in text and pictures, of features of items which it stocked and sold; catalog possesses such degree of originality as is required to entitle plaintiff to copyright protection. B & B Auto Supply, Inc. v Plesser (1962, DC NY) 205 F Supp 36, 133 USPQ 247.

Telephone directories and portions of telephone directories are copyrightable, including separate directory for town or suburb extracted from larger directory. Southwestern Bell Tel. Co. v Nationwide Independent Directory Service, Inc. (1974, DC Ark) 371 F Supp 900, 182 USPQ 193.

Property right in unpublished manuscript which is entitled to protection is limited to particular statement or compilation and does not extend to plan adopted for imparting information; it does not prevent another person from making independent collection of same facts or information and using it as his own; right secured to author embraces form, sequence, and manner of composition in which he expresses ideas but not ideas themselves. Turner v Century House Publishing Co. (1968, NY Sup Ct) 159 USPQ 699.

Annotations:

Copyright, under Federal Copyright Act (17 USCS §§ 1 et seq.), in advertising materials, catalogues, and price lists. 5 ALR Fed 625.

5. —Law reports

Copyright of annotated statutes covers everything that may fairly be deemed result of compiler's own labors; compiler of volume of annotated statutes may obtain valid copyright upon such book to extent of matters contained therein which are product of his work. Howell v Miller (1898, CA6 Mich) 91 F 129.

Arrangement of reported cases in sequence, their paging and distribution into volumes, are not features of such importance as to entitle reporter to copyright protection of details. Banks Law Pub. Co. v Lawyers' Co-op Pub. Co. (1909, CA2 NY) 169 F 386, app dismd 223 US 738, 56 L Ed 636, 32 S Ct 530.

Mere aggregation of weekly reporters into volumes does not constitute new work, but compilation of new and larger digests does constitute new work entitled to copyright. West Pub. Co. v Edward Thompson Co. (1910, CA2 NY) 176 F 833.

Use of prior copyrighted statutory compilations prior to independent research constitutes infringement of copyright. W. H. Anderson Co. v Baldwin Law Pub. Co. (1928, CA6 Ohio) 27 F2d 82.

Book of court rules of practice, annotated with reference to court's decisions, is new compilation which may be copyrighted, although previously rules were published in book with annotations and rules themselves were only slightly revised. Banks v McDivitt (1875, CC NY) F Cas No 961.

Compilation of statutes may be so original as to entitle author to copyright on account of skill and judgment displayed in combination and analysis thereof, but such compiler cannot obtain copyright for publication of laws only, and legislature cannot confer such exclusive privilege upon him. Davidson v Wheelock (1886, CC Minn) 27 F 61.

6. —Periodicals

Where several parts of story had been dedicated to public, through their publication in magazine, story could be copyrighted when several parts were bound together in one book. Holmes v Hurst (1899) 174 US 82, 43 L Ed 904, 19 S Ct 606.

When work is once copyrighted, there is no authority for second grant to author for same work and such second copyright will be inoperative. Caliga v Inter Ocena Newspaper Co. (1907, CA7 Ill) 157 F 186, affd 215 US 182, 54 L Ed 150, 30 S Ct 38.

Copyright of periodical protects pictures therein as "component parts." Mail & Express Co. v Life Pub. Co. (1911, CA2 NY) 192 F 899.

Cut not separately copyrighted is not protected by copyright on newspaper alone. Bennett v Boston Traveler Co. (1900, CA1 Mass) 101 F 445.

Publisher's copyright does not attach to commercial advertising and listings in magazine. Official Aviation Guide Co. v American Aviation Associates (1945, CA7 Ill) 150 F2d 173, 65 USPQ 553, cert den 326 US 776, 90 L Ed 469, 66 S Ct 267, reh den 326 US 811, 90 L Ed 495, 66 S Ct 335.

Where a magazine has purchased the right of first publication under circumstances which show that the author has no intentions to donate his work to the public, copyright notice in the magazine's name is sufficient to obtain a valid copyright on behalf of the beneficial owner, the author or proprietor; fact that the arrangement between the author or proprietor and the magazine publisher is in the nature of a "partial assignment" does not require a different result. Goodis v United Artists Television, Inc. (1970, CA2 NY) 425 F2d 397, 165 USPQ 3.

Newspapers composed in large part of noncopyrightable matter were not entitled to general copyright. Tribune Co. v Associated Press (1900, CC Ill) 116 F 126.

Copyright of magazine covers articles therein written or owned by proprietor of magazine. Ford v Charles E. Blaney Amusement Co. (1906, CC NY) 148 F 642.

When periodical contains articles or pictures made by persons who have not transferred their rights to publisher, publisher's copyright in periodical does not cover them, link from artist to publisher being missing from publisher's supposed title. Kaplan v Fox Film Corp. (1937, DC NY) 19 F Supp 780, 33 USPQ 469.

Issues of periodicals are original works and therefore copyrightable. Detective Comics, Inc. v Bruns Publications, Inc. (1939, DC NY) 28 F Supp 399, 41 USPQ 182, mod on other grounds (CA2 NY) 111 F2d 432, 45 USPQ 291.

Each fashion magazine cover is proper subject of copyright, if each cover is artistic composition, demonstrating originality and good taste, being distinctive of magazine and product of publisher's labor; furthermore, cover of each magazine indicates particular feature emphasized in that issue; such relation between cover and text makes cover integral part of magazine falling within protection of copyright of latter as copyrightable component part. Conde Nast Publications, Inc. v Vogue School of Fashion Modeling, Inc. (1952, DC NY) 105 F Supp 325, 94 USPQ 101.

General copyright in issue of periodical does not protect rights in contributed article therein unless such rights had been previously assigned to publisher; article is protected where author assigned all rights to publisher in first instance under express condition that, after registration of copyright in publisher's name, publisher would reassign all rights to author. Morse v Fields (1954, DC NY) 127 F Supp 63, 104 USPQ 54.

7. Musical works, generally

One may be entitled to copyright on his work where, by his own intellectual labors, he has arranged and compiled old materials to produce composition new and original in itself. Atwill v Ferrett (1846, CC NY) F Cas No 640.

If musical composition is made up of different parts of older musical compositions with only slight and unimportant alterations and additions, producer thereof is not author. Reed v Carusi (1845, CC Md) F Cas No 11642.

8. —Arrangements

Pianoforte arrangement of orchestral score of opera made by system of selection and culling, creating nothing original, is not protectible by copyright. Mikado Case (1885, CC NY) 25 F 183.

New arrangements of words and music of old song are entitled to protection. Italian Book Co. v Rossi (1928, DC NY) 27 F2d 1014.

9. Pictorial, graphic, and sculptural works, generally

Book and descriptive map sold with book were one production; copyright of book covering also map. Lydiard-Peterson Co. v Woodman (1913, CA8 Minn) 204 F 921, reh den (CA8 Minn) 205 F 900.

"Manuscript" did not include picture. Parton v Prang (1872, CC Mass) F Cas No 10784.

Maps in statistical atlas are covered by copyright of book as whole. Black v Henry G. Allen Co. (1890, CC NY) 42 F 618.

Cut and description of monogram appearing in copyrighted booklet was not so protected by copyright on booklet that others could not lawfully reproduce cut as saleable article. Royal Sales Co. v Gaynor (1908, CC NY) 164 F 207.

Pictorial history of United States, work of compilers employed by copyright holder is properly subject of copyright. Yale University Press v Row, Peterson & Co. (1930, DC NY) 40 F2d 290, 5 USPQ 530.

Gift novelty in form of book made of cardboard resembling traveling bag with words "They're Off," with picture of jockey on race horse and "Greetings from Chicago" or some other city and "It's in the Bag," and when its flap was opened there appeared pair of doll's rubber panties marked "So What," was not afforded copyright protection as book by addition of lettered pants to previous publication. Jackson v Quickslip Co. (1939, DC NY) 27 F Supp 338, 41 USPQ 464, affd (CA2 NY) 110 F2d 731, 45 USPQ 6.

Book containing comic strips printed on one side of paper only and bearing notice of copyright on title page, although each item in book bears separate copyright notice and most of items bear later release date on which date newspapers are first authorized to use material, is book within meaning of that term and is composite work. King Features Syndicate, Inc. v Bouve (DC Dist Col) 48 USPQ 237.

Where application specified class as book, plaintiff did not protect copyright for works of art or for prints or pictorial illustrations, which may have been contained in book, as it made no application and was issued no certificate therefor. Advertisers Exchange, Inc. v Anderson (1943, DC Iowa) 52 F Supp 809, 59 USPQ 391, affd (CA8 Iowa) 144 F2d 907, 63 USPQ 39.

10. —Reproductions

Although embroidered design, which plaintiff copied on fabric, was in public domain, plaintiff's contribution to reproduction of design sufficed to meet modest requirement made of copyright proprietor that his work contain some substantial, not merely trivial, originality, inasmuch as plaintiff's creation of three-dimensional effect, giving something of impression of embroidery on flat fabric, required effort and skill. Millworth Converting Corp. v Slifka (1960, CA2 NY) 276 F2d 443, 125 USPQ 506.

Reproduction of painting may be independently copyrightable, and such copyright will support suit for infringement of reproduction. Home Art, Inc. v Glensder Textile Corp. (1948, DC NY) 81 F Supp 551, 79 USPQ 12.

Reproductions of work of art constitute distinct class of copyrightable material. Leigh v Gerber (1949, DC NY) 86 F Supp 320, 82 USPQ 271.

Reproduction on reduced scale of three-dimensional work of art is copyrightable where it embodies and resulted from reproducer's skill and originality in producing accurate scale reproduction of original; in work of sculpture, this reduction requires far more than abridgement of written classic. Alva Studios, Inc. v Winninger (1959, DC NY) 177 F Supp 265, 123 USPQ 487.

Ornamental design, which is reproduction of work of art, printed on dress fabrics is proper subject of copyright; there is sufficient originality in design to warrant copyright; although floral patterns are in public domain, plaintiff has contributed enough originality in design to qualify it as distinguishable variation. Peter Pan Fabrics, Inc. v Candy Frocks, Inc. (1960, DC NY) 187 F Supp 334, 126 USPQ 171.

Plaintiff performed independent research to locate engravings of famous deceased composers suitable for reproduction on sweatshirts; it found suitable engravings in library, copied them, and produced necessary art work for production of prints on sweatshirts; although engravings were in public domain, plaintiff's art work is sufficiently original and changed from engravings to be copyrightable. Eagle-Freedman-Roedelheim Co. v Allison Mfg. Co. (1962, DC Pa) 204 F Supp 679, 133 USPQ 357.

Necessary degree of creativity is not supplied through innovations which are solely utilitarian or mechanical; thus, fact that plaintiff added practical features to component parts of conventional flower arrangements does not overcome absence of creativity inherent in arrangements. Gardenia Flowers, Inc. v Joseph Markovits, Inc. (1968, DC NY) 280 F Supp 776, 157 USPQ 685.

Plastic reproduction on reduced scale of public domain work of art in form of Uncle Sam bank is not validly copyrighted, because reproduction does not contain "substantial", rather than "merely trivial" variation from original and is not sufficiently original to support copyright, which cannot be based on physical skill or special training without differing by more than merely trivial variation. L. Batlin & Son, Inc. v Snyder (1976, CA2 NY) 536 F2d 486, 189 USPQ 753, cert den 429 US 857, 50 L Ed 2d 135, 97 S Ct 156.

Lithographic reproduction of original paintings, in the form of post cards, made in Germany, are subject to registration. 28 OAG 150.

II. DERIVATIVE WORKS [17 USCS § 103(b)]

11. Generally

Copyright of publication consisting of new, original matter incorporated in and with uncopyrighted publication of foreign author is not void, but will be afforded protection only as to original work therein. American Code Co. v Bensinger (1922, CA2 NY) 282 F 829.

While copy of something in public domain will not, if it be merely copy, support copyright, distinguishable variation will; though it present same theme. Gerlach-Barklow Co. v Morris & Bendien, Inc. (1927, CA2 NY) 23 F2d 159.

Where new work is based on work already in public domain, valid copyright may not exist in new work unless it shows more than trivial variation from old work; however, if new work is independently created, it is entitled to copyright even though it is identical to work in public domain. Donald v Uarco Business Forms (1973, CA8 Ark) 478 F2d 764.

Work cannot qualify as derivative work to support federal jurisdiction where original work was not copyrighted and copyright claims are common law. Simon & Flynn, Inc. v Time, Inc. (1975, CA2 NY) 513 F2d 832, 185 USPQ 325.

Infringement may result from copying work based on material in public domain when material so taken has been transformed by first borrower so as to entitle him to claim originality. Hirsch v Paramount Pictures, Inc. (1937, DC Cal) 17 F Supp 816, 32 USPQ 233.

Copyright laws protect not only original works, but also reproductions of works in public domain in different adaptations, arrangements, or mediums of expression. Allegrini v De Angelis (1944, DC Pa) 59 F Supp 248, 64 USPQ 165, affd (CA3 Pa) 149 F2d 815, 65 USPQ 589.

When author adds new and original material to matter in public domain, copyright on entire work is valid, but author is entitled to protection only as to such added material. Lake v Columbia Broadcasting System, Inc. (1956, DC Cal) 140 F Supp 707, 110 USPQ 173.

Edition of public domain work that contains new matter is entitled to derivative copyright on new matter only when such new matter is not trivial. Grove Press, Inc. v Collectors Publication, Inc. (1967, DC Cal) 264 F Supp 603, 152 USPQ 787.

12. Literary works, generally

Article substantially based on uncopyrighted but published work of another was not entitled to copyright. Du Puy v Post Tel. Co. (1914, CA3 NJ) 210 F 883.

Editor may procure successive copyrights on same book, where he has materially revised it; copyright covers whole book and later copyrights cover supplemental material only; there cannot be two copyrights on same material. Adventures in Good Eating, Inc. v Best Places to Eat, Inc. (1942, CA7 Ill) 131 F2d 809, 56 USPQ 242.

Book is not "derivative work" because story is taken from folklore, and derivative work requires substantial copying from copyrighted work. Reyher v Children's Television Workshop (1976, CA2 NY) 533 F2d 87, 190 USPQ 387.

Author who reworks previously published plot is not entitled to copyright protection of plot but is entitled to copyright protection of his manner of stating plot. Stodart v Mutual Film Corp. (1917, DC NY) 249 F 507.

Where copyrighted book contains new treatment of old plot, one copying book has burden of proving that his plot was taken from some source in public domain. Stephens v Howells Sales Co. (1926, DC NY) 16 F2d 805.

Copyright protects exclusive use of theme presented in original way with novelty of treatment or embellishment. Nutt v National Institute, Inc. for Improv. of Memory (1929, CA2 Conn) 31 F2d 236.

Book is copyrightable as distinguishable variation from author's prior edition and other books in public domain where, in numerous instances, letters, words, or lines of text were added, deleted, or rearranged; also, it contains substantial number of unique changes which did not appear in prior books; even if author secured all material for his prayer book from publications in public domain, book was product of his own labor, judgment, money, and skill, and as such was copyrightable as new version of work in public domain. Ziegelheim v Flohr (1954, DC NY) 119 F Supp 324, 100 USPQ 189.

Where book based on story heard from another is derivative work, copyright protects only material contributed by author of book, as distinguished from preexisting story plot. Reyher v Children's Television Workshop (1975, DC NY) 387 F Supp 869, affd (CA2 NY) 533 F2d 87.

13. —New editions

Copyright of new edition of author's works does not operate to extend or enlarge prior copyrights or remove from public domain works which he has dedicated to public, but protects only what is original in new edition. Kipling v G. P. Putnam's Sons (1903, CA2 NY) 120 F 631.

New edition, with minor changes, of copyrighted catalogue is "new work" subject to copyright. Sieff v Continental Auto Supply, Inc. (1941, DC Minn) 39 F Supp 683, 50 USPQ 19.

14. —Translations

There is no requirement in Copyright Act that there be some special notice where copyrighted work consists in part of translation of words spoken or written by any person. Toksvig v Bruce Pub. Co. (1950, CA7 Wis) 181 F2d 664, 85 USPQ 339.

English translation from Hebrew of Books of Moses was proper subject of copyright. Lesser v Sklarz (1859, CC NY) F Cas No 8276a.

Person has right to make independent translation of his own from French play, although another translation had been made from same play and copyrighted, provided new translation does not include parts of copyrighted one. Stevenson v Fox (1915, DC NY) 226 F 990.

15. Musical works, generally

Plaintiff heard tune similar to melody score of his copyrighted work; however, it was original work on plaintiff's part when, 30 years later, he devised calculated melody score, thus putting it in shape for all to read; copyright is valid; predecessor section specifically provides for protection of work of composer growing out of creations of those who came before. Wihtol v Wells (1956, CA7 Ill) 231 F2d 550, 109 USPQ 200.

To be entitled to copyright musical composition must be new and original work, and not copy of piece already produced, with additions and variations, which writer of music with experience and skill might readily make. Jollie v Jaques (1850, CC NY) F Cas No 7437.

Where author of song permits its use in book of songs, it is reasonable that he intends that song may be included in future editions of same book even though some of songs in original work were omitted or new songs were added. Gabriel v McCabe (1896, CC Ill) 74 F 743.

Addition of alto parts to music in sacred hymnal does not result in such original composition as can be copyrighted. Cooper v James (1914, DC Ga) 213 F 871.

Differences from earlier composition were insufficient to make latter adaptation or arrangement. Fred Fisher, Inc. v Dillingham (1924, DC NY) 298 F 145.

Adaptation of foreign composer's music to English words chosen by arranger was insufficient to constitute originality and another was free to use music as it appeared in such copy in making adaptation of another English text to music. Norden v Oliver Ditson Co. (1936, DC Mass) 13 F Supp 415, 28 USPQ 183.

By changing title to song, making slight variation in bass of accompaniment, and adding additional chorus in march time, original chorus being in common time, song is not subject to copyright as "new work" under predecessor section, since there is no change in tune or lyrics. Shapiro, Bernstein & Co. v Jerry Vogel Music Co. (1947, DC NY) 73 F Supp 165, 74 USPQ 264.

Following copyright of music, proprietor had words written to accompany music and copyrighted song as new work under predecessor section; copyright served to protect words. Shapiro, Bernstein & Co. v Jerry Vogel Music Co. (1953, DC NY) 115 F Supp 754, 98 USPQ 438, 99 USPQ 381, revd on other grounds (CA2 NY) 221 F2d 569, 105 USPQ 178, adhered to (CA2 NY) 223 F2d 252, 105 USPQ 460.

In applying rule that copyright is valid where author adds original material to material in public domain, originality means that material added must have aspects of novelty and be something more than trivial addition or variation; if what is added does not give some value to public domain composition, or serve some purpose other than to merely emphasize what is present in public domain, it is not entitled to copyright; if all that author of musical composition does is to add mechanical application of sound to word that is itself not copyrightable, and adds same to descriptive phrase in public domain, without use of even most simple harmonious chords, he has no musical composition subject to copyright. Smith v George E. Muehlehach Brewing Co. (1956, DC Mo) 140 F Supp 729, 110 USPQ 177.

16. —Arrangements

Person having right to use copyrighted song has right to make orchestration of song for use in operetta, and to have such orchestration copyrighted. Edmonds v Stern (1918, CA2 NY) 248 F 897.

Copyright may be obtained upon music taken from opera and subsequently rewritten by arranger to include alterations and additions original with him. Atwill v Ferrett (1846, CC NY) F Cas No 640.

Pianoforte arrangement of orchestral score of opera is original musical composition and subject to copyright. Carte v Evans (1886, CC Mass) 27 F 861.

Composition, to be subject of copyright, must have sufficient originality to make it new work rather than copy of old, with minor changes which any skilled musician might make; it must be result of some original or creative work. Norden v Oliver Ditson Co. (1936, DC Mass) 13 F Supp 415, 28 USPQ 183.

Before one having limited right to record song may have its recorded musical arrangement thereof protected as right against competitor, arrangement must have distinctive characteristic, aside from composition itself, of such character that any person hearing it played would become aware of distinctiveness of arrangement. Supreme

Records, Inc. v Decca Records, Inc. (1950, DC Cal) 90 F Supp 904, 85 USPQ 405.

Fact that defendants applied for copyright registration of same arrangement, in which application they represented that arrangement contained original, copyrightable material, does not estop defendants from denying originality of plaintiff's work, since defendants' representations did not mislead plaintiff or place him at disadvantage in instant litigation. McIntyre v Double-A-Music Corp. (1959, DC Cal) 179 F Supp 160, 124 USPQ 27.

17. Dramatic works

Person making dramatization of work in public domain acquires exclusive right only to that part which is original work. McCaleb v Fox Film Corp. (1924, CA5 La) 299 F 48.

Copyright is not voided just because source of material is in public domain, but protection is limited to new and original contribution of author. Axelbank v Rony (1960, CA9 Cal) 277 F2d 314, 125 USPQ 262.

Play based on novel was original work. Boucicault v Fox (1862, CC NY) F Cas No 1691.

New and original plan, arrangement, or combination of materials will entitle author to copyright therein, whether materials themselves be old or new. Hoffman v Le Traunik (1913, DC NY) 209 F 375.

Opera based on novel and drama is substantially new and distinct composition, being piece of property wholly separate and independent from novel and drama, and is subject of copyright; copyright on opera does not expire with expiration of copyright on novel. G. Ricordi & Co. v Paramount Pictures, Inc. (1950, DC NY) 92 F Supp 537, 86 USPQ 452, mod (CA2 NY) 189 F2d 469, 89 USPQ 289, cert den 342 US 849, 96 L Ed 641, 72 S Ct 77.

Play, which dramatizes novel, is copyrightable as new work; copyright on play exists and protects all new matter therein, independently of ownership of original or renewal copyrights on novel. Davis v E. I. Du Pont De Nemours & Co. (1965, DC NY) 240 F Supp 612, 145 USPQ 258.

18. Pictorial, graphic, and sculptural works, generally

Where original photograph is given to public, same picture, with cane etched in hand of one of figures, cannot be copyrighted. Snow v Laird (1900, CA7 Ill) 98 F 813.

Copyright of comic strip of later exploit of "Superman" is valid, insofar as picture differs from those going before, even though later exploit is so similar to prior exploit that publication of later by stranger would be infringement.

National Comics Publications, Inc. v Fawcett Publications, Inc. (1951, CA2 NY) 191 F2d 594, 90 USPQ 274.

Reproduction of public domain Uncle Sam bank is copyrightable insofar as differing from original bank. L. Batlin & Son, Inc. v Snyder (1975, CA2) 187 USPQ 721.

Copyright of design of miniature religious shrine, which was adaptation of work in public domain, was valid to extent of new features originated by plaintiffs and combination or arrangement of new features with original shrine. Allegrini v De Angelis (1944, DC Pa) 59 F Supp 248, 64 USPQ 165, affd (CA3 Pa) 149 F2d 815, 65 USPQ 589.

Although it is impossible to draw two identical proofs from same mezzotint plate, all proofs carry same interpretation of original work and may be considered same work rather than individual works which must each be copyrighted. Alfred Bell & Co. v Catalda Fine Arts, Inc. (1947, DC NY) 74 F Supp 973, 75 USPQ 66.

Even though original model for Last Supper diorama is in public domain, plaintiffs' photograph of plaintiffs' diorama of Last Supper can be copyrighted in same way that engraving of painting in public domain may be copyrighted. Hesse v Brunner (1959, DC NY) 172 F Supp 284, 121 USPQ 141.

Owner of copyright on two-dimensional cartoons has right to make three-dimensional figures or dolls therefrom or to license another to do so; copyright upon work in one medium may be asserted affirmatively by copyright owner to obtain protection against infringement accomplished in a different medium; copyright upon work in one medium empowers owner to copy work in a different medium. Geisel v Poynter Products, Inc. (1968, DC NY) 295 F Supp 331, 160 USPQ 590.

Defendant's process of purchasing at retail plaintiff's greeting cards and stationery containing copyrighted pictorial art work, making decals of such art work from each item purchased, and using each decal to transfer art work to ceramic plaques which were sold by defendant—an individual piece of plaintiff's art work being purchased for each decal and plaque produced by defendant—does not result in "compilation," "adaptation," or "arrangement" of copyrighted material. C. M. Paula Co. v Logan (1973, DC Tex) 355 F Supp 189.

Art design from previously copyrighted book but having additional slogan is new derivative work supporting new copyright date so that notice for date of derivative work is not defective. American Greetings Corp. v Kleinfab Corp. (1975, DC NY) 400 F Supp 228, 188 USPQ 297.

19. —Maps

Automobile road map based on geological survey maps was proper subject of copyright. General Drafting Co. v Andrews (1930, CA2 NY) 37 F2d 54, 4 USPQ 72.

New editions of maps may be copyrighted. Farmer v Calvert Lithographing Co. (1872, CC Mich) F Cas No 4651.

Map drawn from other uncopyrighted publications, but containing original features constituted new arrangement of old material and was copyrightable. Woodman v Lydiard-Peterson Co. (1912, CC Minn) 192 F 67, affd (CA8 Minn) 204 F 921, reh den (CA8 Minn) 205 F 900.

Guide material on back of map is copyrightable as compilation of arrangement of matter in public domain. Freedman v Milnag Leasing Corp. (1937, DC NY) 20 F Supp 802, 35 USPQ 184.

Annual revisions of road map are proper subjects of copyright; copyright attaches only to new matter; design and setting of map are part of presentation or portrayal and are protected by copyright. Crocker v General Drafting Co. (1943, DC NY) 50 F Supp 634, 58 USPQ 60.

Copyright of map is void as duplicate since only change from copyright of proprietor's prior copyrighted map is obvious change of highway route number. Market & Bielfeld, Inc. v Baughman Co. (1957, DC Va) 162 F Supp 561, 117 USPQ 332.

In order not to give cartographer permanent monopoly which would enable him, without renewing copyright, to begin new copyright period every year, courts limit copyrightability of periodic revisions of maps to new matter appearing on them. Hayden v Chalfant Press, Inc. (1959, DC Cal) 177 F Supp 303, affd (CA9 Cal) 281 F2d 543.

20. Motion pictures and other audiovisual works

Matters in public domain are not copyrightable, and copyright of story containing such matters is limited to novel features of story. Harold Lloyd Corp. v Witwer (1933, CA9 Cal) 65 F2d 1, cert dismd (US) 78 L Ed 1507, 54 S Ct 94.

Motion picture as derivative work separately copyrighted relative to original novel under agreement specifying that rights in motion picture extend under renewal copyright in novel does not infringe renewal copyright secured by child of author and assigned to plaintiff, and existence of separate rights in motion picture after renewal of copyright in novel does not "affect the force or validity of any subsisting copyright" in novel, but new derivative works cannot be created without license under renewal copyright. Rohauer v Killiam Shows, Inc. (1977, CA2) 192 USPQ 545.

Where, in motion picture, same use is made of same series of events to excite, by representation, same emotion, in same sequence, as in copyrighted picture, such motion picture infringes upon other. International Film Service Co. v Affiliated Distributors, Inc. (1922, DC NY) 283 F 229.

§ 104. Subject matter of copyright: National origin

(a) Unpublished works.

The works specified by sections 102 and 103 [17 USCS §§ 102 and 103], while unpublished, are subject to protection under this title [17 USCS §§ 101 et seq.] without regard to the nationality or domicile of the author.

(b) Published works.

The works specified by sections 102 and 103 [17 USCS §§ 102 and 103], when published, are subject to protection under this title [17 USCS §§ 101 et seq.] if—

(1) on the date of first publication, one or more of the authors is a national or domiciliary of the United States, or is a national, domiciliary, or sovereign authority of a foreign nation that is a party to a copyright treaty to which the United States is also a party, or is a stateless person, wherever that person may be domiciled; or

(2) the work is first published in the United States or in a foreign nation that, on the date of first publication, is a party to the Universal Copyright Convention; or

(3) the work is first published by the United Nations or any of its specialized agencies, or by the Organization of American States; or

(4) the work comes within the scope of a Presidential proclamation. Whenever the President finds that a particular foreign nation extends, to works by authors who are nationals or domiciliaries of the United States or to works that are first published in the United States, copyright protection on substantially the same basis as that on which the foreign nation extends protection to works of its own nationals and domiciliaries and works first published in that nation, the President may by proclamation extend protection under this title [17 USCS §§ 101 et seq.] to works of which one or more of the authors is, on the date of first publication, a national, domiciliary, or sovereign authority of that nation, or which was first published in that nation. The President may revise, suspend, or revoke any such proclamation or impose any conditions or limitations on protection under a proclamation.

(Added Oct. 19, 1976, P. L. 94-553, Title I, § 101, 90 Stat. 2545.)

HISTORY; ANCILLARY LAWS AND DIRECTIVES

References in text:

For the "Universal Copyright Convention", referred to in para. (2) of subsec. (b), see USCS Administrative Rules, Copyright Convention.

Effective date of section:

Section 102 of Act Oct. 19, 1976, P. L. 94-553, 90 Stat. 2598 provided that this section "becomes effective on January 1, 1978".

Other provisions:

Universal Copyright Convention. The UNESCO International Copyright Convention, adopted by the Intergovernmental Copyright Conference at Geneva, Switzerland on Sept. 6, 1952, entered into force for the United States on Sept. 16, 1955. For the text of the Universal Copyright Convention, see USCS Administrative Rules, Copyright Conv.

Particular Proclamations, Treaties and Conventions establishing copyright relations between the United States of America and other countries.

(Revised to January 1, 1976)

By virtue of presidential proclamations, treaties, and conventions, the United States has established copyright relations with various other countries. This note is an attempt to present a complete and annotated list of those countries. Treaties and conventions on the subject of copyright relations in force January 1, 1961, are also included in the following table under appropriate country or subject headings.

Proclamations by the President of the United States extending copyright protection, upon compliance with the provisions of the United States copyright law, to the works of foreign authors prior to July 1, 1909, were issued pursuant to section 13 of Act March 3, 1891 (26

Stat. 1106) and those issued subsequent to July 1, 1909, were issued under the provisions of sections 1(e) and 8(b) of Act March 4, 1909 (35 Stat. 1075) and as later amended. Section 8(b) was amended by Act December 18, 1919 (41 Stat. 368) and the Act of September 25, 1941 (55 Stat. 732). Those sections of Act March 4, 1909, as amended, became sections 1(e) and 9(b), respectively, of Title 17 of the United States Code when it was codified and enacted into positive law by Act July 30, 1947 (61 Stat. 652). A number of the proclamations were preceded or accompanied by exchanges of diplomatic notes which served as the basis for their issuance. Such exchanges of notes, if in force January 1, 1958, and if printed in the official pamphlet series, are included in the footnotes to the table.

The period for compliance with the conditions and formalities prescribed by the copyright law was extended by proclamation with respect to certain works in the case of a number of countries because of the disruption or suspension of facilities essential for such compliance during World War I and World War II. In the case of World War I this period was extended by proclamations issued under Act December 18, 1919 (41 Stat. 368) to fifteen months after the proclamation of peace, as to works published after August 1, 1914, and before the proclamation of peace. In the case of World War II, this period was extended by proclamations issued under Act September 25, 1941 (55 Stat. 732) until such time as terminated or suspended, either by the terms of the proclamation itself or by the issuance of a subsequent proclamation. A number of the proclamations issued under the 1919 Act and all of the proclamations issued under the 1941 Act or section 9(b) of title 17 of the United States Code refer to rights previously granted.

KEY TO SYMBOLS

PROCLAMATIONS

P   Proclamation issued pursuant to section 13 of the Act of March 3, 1891, Section 8(b) of the Act of March 4, 1909, and as amended, or Section 9(b) of Title 17 of the United States Code.

Pm   Proclamation including mechanical reproduction rights for music under Section 1(e) of the United States copyright law.

Px   Proclamation providing an extension of time under the Act of December 18, 1919, for compliance with the conditions and formalities prescribed by the United States copyright law.

Pmx   Proclamation specifically including provisions similar to those contained in both "Pm" and "Px" proclamations.

Pxx   Proclamation providing an extension of time under the Act of September 25, 1941, for compliance with the conditions and formalities prescribed by the United States copyright law.

Po   Proclamation specifically issued for the purpose of terminating a proclamation issued under the Act of September 25, 1941.

TREATIES AND CONVENTIONS

BAC   Buenos Aires Convention. Convention on literary and artistic copyright signed at the Fourth International Conference of American States at Buenos Aires August 11, 1910.

MCC   Mexico City Convention. Convention on literary and artistic copyrights signed at the Second International Conference of American States at Mexico January 27, 1902.

UCC   Universal Copyright Convention. Done at Geneva September 6, 1952.

UCC   Universal Copyright Convention, revised. Done at Paris July 24, 1971.

C   Bilateral convention.

Cm   Bilateral convention including provisions covering mechanical reproduction rights for music.

T   Treaty relating in part to copyright.

PROCLAMATIONS, TREATIES, AND CONVENTIONS ESTABLISHING COPYRIGHT RELATIONS BETWEEN THE UNITED STATES AND OTHER COUNTRIES

Country	Document	Date of document	Date effective	Reference
Algeria	UCC	Sept. 6, 1952	Aug. 28, 1973	6 UST 2731.
	UCC rev.	July 24, 1971	July 10, 1974	25 UST 1341.
Andorra	UCC	Sept. 6, 1952	Sept. 16, 1955	6 UST 2731.
Argentina	Pm	Aug. 23, 1934	Aug. 23, 1934	49 Stat. 3413.
	BAC	Aug. 11, 1910	Apr. 19, 1950	38 Stat. 1785.
	UCC	Sept. 6, 1952	Feb. 13, 1953	6 UST 2731.
Australia[1]	Pm	Apr. 3, 1918	Mar. 15, 1918	40 Stat. 1764,
	Pxx[2]	Dec. 29, 1949	Dec. 29, 1949	64 Stat. A385.
	UCC	Sept. 6, 1952	Feb. 13, 1953	6 UST 2731.
Austria[3]	P	Sept. 20, 1907	Sept. 20, 1907	35 Stat. 2155.
	P	Apr. 9, 1910	July 1, 1909	36 Stat. 2685.
	Px	May 25, 1922	May 25, 1922	42 Stat. 2273.

Country	Document	Date of document	Date effective	Reference
	Pm	Mar. 11, 1925	Aug. 1, 1920	44 Stat. 2571.
	UCC	Sept. 6, 1952	July 2, 1957	6 UST 2731.
Bangladesh	UCC	Sept. 6, 1952	Aug. 5, 1975	6 UST 2731.
Belgium	P	July 1, 1891	July 1, 1891	27 Stat. 981.
	P	Apr. 9, 1910	July 1, 1909	36 Stat. 2685.
	Pm	June 14, 1911	July 1, 1909	37 Stat. 1688.
	UCC	Sept. 6, 1952	Aug. 31, 1960	6 UST 2731.
Bolivia	BAC	Aug. 11, 1910	May 15, 1914	38 Stat. 1785.
Brazil	BAC	Aug. 11, 1910	Aug. 31, 1915	38 Stat. 1785.
	Pm	Apr. 2, 1957	Apr. 2, 1957	8 UST 424.
	UCC	Sept. 6, 1952	Jan. 13, 1960	6 UST 2731.
	UCC rev.	July 24, 1971	Dec. 11, 1975	25 UST 1341.
Bulgaria	UCC	Sept. 6, 1952	June 7, 1975	6 UST 2731.
	UCC rev.	July 24, 1971	June 7, 1975	25 UST 1341.
Cameroon	UCC	Sept. 6, 1952	May 1, 1973	6 UST 2731.
	UCC rev.	July 24, 1971	July 10, 1974	25 UST 1341.

Country	Document	Date of document	Date effective	Reference
Canada[1]	Pm	Dec. 27, 1923	Jan. 1, 1924	43 Stat. 1932.
	UCC	Sept. 6, 1952	Aug. 10, 1962	6 UST 2731.
Chile	P	May 25, 1896	May 25, 1896	29 Stat. 880.
	P	Apr. 9, 1910	July 1, 1909	36 Stat. 2685.
	Pm	Nov. 18, 1925	July 1, 1925	44 Stat. 2590.
	BAC	Aug. 11, 1910	June 14, 1955	38 Stat. 1785.
	UCC	Sept. 6, 1952	Sept. 16, 1955	6 UST 2731.
China	T[4]	Oct. 8, 1903	Jan. 13, 1904	33 Stat. 2208.
	T[4]	Nov. 4, 1946	Nov. 30, 1948	63 Stat. 1299.
Colombia	BAC	Aug. 11, 1910	Dec. 23, 1936	38 Stat. 1785.
Costa Rica	P	Oct. 19, 1899	Oct. 19, 1899	31 Stat. 1955.
	P	Apr. 9, 1910	July 1, 1909	36 Stat. 2685.
	MCC	Jan. 27, 1902	June 30, 1908	35 Stat. 1934.
	BAC	Aug. 11, 1910	Nov. 30, 1916	38 Stat. 1785.
	UCC	Sept. 6, 1952	Sept. 16, 1955	6 UST 2731.
Cuba	P	Nov. 17, 1903	Nov. 17, 1903	33 Stat. 2324.
	P	Apr. 9, 1910	July 1, 1909	36 Stat. 2685.

Country	Document	Date of document	Date effective	Reference
	Pm	Nov. 27, 1911	May 29, 1911	37 Stat. 1721.
	UCC	Sept. 6, 1952	June 18, 1957	6 UST 2731.
Czechoslovakia....	Pm	Apr. 27, 1927	Mar. 1, 1927	45 Stat. 2906.
	UCC	Sept. 6, 1952	Jan. 6, 1960	6 UST 2731.
Danzig	Pm	Apr. 7, 1934	Apr. 7, 1934	48 Stat. 1737.
Denmark[5]	IP	May 8, 1893	May 8, 1893	28 Stat. 1219.
	P	Apr. 9, 1910	July 1, 1909	36 Stat. 2685.
	Pmx	Dec. 9, 1920	Dec. 9, 1920	41 Stat. 1810.
	Pxx	Feb. 4, 1952	Feb. 4, 1952	66 Stat. C20.
	UCC	Sept. 6, 1952	Feb. 9, 1962	6 UST 2731.
Dominican Republic	MCC	Jan. 27, 1902	June 30, 1908	35 Stat. 1934.
	BAC	Aug. 11, 1910	Oct. 31, 1912	38 Stat. 1785.
Ecuador	BAC	Aug. 11, 1910	Aug. 31, 1914	38 Stat. 1785.
	UCC	Sept. 6, 1952	June 5, 1957	6 UST 2731.
El Salvador.......	MCC	Jan. 27, 1902	June 30, 1908	35 Stat. 1934.
Fiji.............	UCC	Sept. 6, 1952	May 4, 1963	6 UST 2731.

Country	Document	Date of document	Date effective	Reference
Finland	Pm	Dec. 15, 1928	Jan. 1, 1929	45 Stat. 2980.
	Pxx	Nov. 16, 1951	Nov. 16, 1951	66 Stat. C5.
	UCC	Sept. 6, 1952	Apr. 16, 1963	6 UST 2731.
France[6]	P	July 1, 1891	July 1, 1891	27 Stat. 981.
	P	Apr. 9, 1910	July 1, 1909	36 Stat. 2685.
	Pm	May 24, 1918	May 24, 1918	40 Stat. 1784.
	Pxx	Mar. 27, 1947	Mar. 27, 1947	61 Stat. 1057.
	Po	May 26, 1950	Dec. 29, 1950	64 Stat. A413.
	UCC	Sept. 6, 1952	Jan. 14, 1956	6 UST 2731.
	UCC rev.	July 24, 1971	July 10, 1974	25 UST 1341.
German Dem. Rep.	UCC	Sept. 6, 1952	Oct. 5, 1973	6 UST 2731.
Germany[5]	P	Apr. 15, 1892	Apr. 15, 1892	27 Stat. 1021.
	P	Apr. 9, 1910	July 1, 1909	36 Stat. 2685.
	Pm	Dec. 8, 1910	Dec. 8, 1910	36 Stat. 2761.
	Px	May 25, 1922	May 25, 1922	42 Stat. 2271.
Germany, Fed. Rep..............	Pxx	July 12, 1967	July 12, 1967	18 UST 2369.
	UCC	Sept. 6, 1952	Sept. 16, 1955	6 UST 2731.

Country	Document	Date of document	Date effective	Reference
	UCC rev.	July 24, 1971	July 24, 1974	25 UST 1341.
Ghana	UCC	July 24, 1971	Aug. 22, 1962	25 UST 1341.
Greece	Pm	Feb. 23, 1932	Mar. 1, 1932	47 Stat. 2502.
	UCC	Sept. 6, 1952	Aug. 24, 1963	6 UST 2731.
Guatemala	MCC	Jan. 27, 1902	June 30, 1908	35 Stat. 1934.
	BAC	Aug. 11, 1910	Mar. 28, 1913	38 Stat. 1785.
	UCC	Sept. 6, 1952	Oct. 28, 1964	6 UST 2731.
Haiti	BAC	Aug. 11, 1910	Nov. 27, 1919	38 Stat. 1785.
	UCC	Sept. 6, 1952	Sept. 16, 1955	6 UST 2731.
Holy See	UCC	do	Oct. 5, 1955	Do.
Honduras	MCC	Jan. 27, 1902	June 30, 1908	35 Stat. 1934.
	BAC	Aug. 11, 1910	Apr. 27, 1914	38 Stat. 1785.
Hungary[6]	Cm[7]	Jan. 30, 1912	Oct. 16, 1912	37 Stat. 1631.
	Px	June 3, 1922	June 3, 1922	42 Stat. 2277.
	T[8,9]	Feb. 10, 1947	Sept. 15, 1947	61 Stat. 2065.
	UCC	Sept. 6, 1952	Jan. 23, 1971	6 UST 2731.
	UCC rev.	July 24, 1971	July 10, 1974	25 UST 1341.

Country	Document	Date of document	Date effective	Reference
Iceland	UCC	Sept. 6, 1952	Dec. 18, 1956	6 UST 2731.
India[1,10]	Pm	Oct. 21, 1954	Aug. 15, 1947	5 UST 2529.
	UCC	Sept. 6, 1952	Jan. 21, 1958	6 UST 2731.
Ireland[1]	Pm[11]	Sept. 28, 1929	Oct. 1, 1929	46 Stat. 3005.
	UCC	Sept. 6, 1952	Jan. 20, 1959	6 UST. 2731.
Israel[12]	Pm	May 4, 1950	May 15, 1948	64 Stat. A402.
	UCC	Dec. 16, 1952	Sept. 16, 1955	6 UST 2731.
Italy............	P[13]	Oct. 31, 1892	Oct. 31, 1892	27 Stat. 1043.
	P	Apr. 9, 1910	July 1, 1909	36 Stat. 2685.
	Pm[13]	May 1, 1915	May 1, 1915	39 Stat. 1725.
	Px	June 3, 1922	June 3, 1922	42 Stat. 2276.
	T[14]	Feb. 10, 1947	Sept. 15, 1947	61 Stat. 1245.
	Pxx	Dec. 12, 1951	Dec. 12, 1951	66 Stat. C13.
	UCC	Sept. 6, 1952	Jan. 24, 1957	6 UST 2731.
Japan............	C[15]	Nov. 10, 1905	May 10, 1906	34 Stat. 2890.
	C[16]	May 19, 1908	Aug. 16, 1908	35 Stat. 2044.
	T[17]	Sept. 8, 1951	Apr. 28, 1952	3 UST 3169.

Country	Document	Date of document	Date effective	Reference
	Pm[18]	Nov. 10, 1953	Apr. 28, 1952	5 UST 118.
	UCC	Sept. 6, 1952	Apr. 28, 1956	6 UST 2731.
Kenya	UCC	Sept. 6, 1952	Sept. 7, 1966	6 UST 2731.
	UCC rev.	July 24, 1971	July 10, 1974	25 UST 1341.
Khmer Rep.	UCC	Sept. 6, 1952	Sept. 16, 1955	6 UST 2731.
Korea	C[19]	May 19, 1908	Aug. 16, 1908	35 Stat. 2041.
Laos	UCC	Sept. 6, 1952	Sept. 16, 1955	6 UST 2731.
Lebanon	UCC	Sept. 6, 1952	Oct. 17, 1959	6 UST 2731.
Liberia.	UCC	Sept. 6, 1952	July 27, 1956	6 UST 2731.
Leichtenstein	UCC	Sept. 6, 1952	Jan. 22, 1959	6 UST 2731.
Luxembourg	P	June 29, 1910	June 29, 1910	36 Stat. 2716.
	Pm	June 14, 1911	do	37 Stat. 1689.
	UCC	Sept. 6, 1952	Oct. 15, 1955	6 UST 2731.
Malawi	UCC	Sept. 6, 1952	Oct. 26, 1965	6 UST 2731.
Malta.	UCC	Sept. 6, 1952	Nov. 19, 1968	6 UST 2731.
Mauritius	UCC	Sept. 6, 1952	Mar. 12, 1968	6 UST 2731.

Country	Document	Date of document	Date effective	Reference
Mexico	P	Feb. 27, 1896	Feb. 27, 1896	29 Stat. 877.
	P	Apr. 9, 1910	July 1, 1909	36 Stat. 2685.
	UCC	Sept. 6, 1952	May 12, 1957	6 UST 2731.
	UCC rev.	July 24, 1971	Oct. 31, 1975	25 UST 1341.
Monaco	Pm	Oct. 15, 1952	Oct. 15, 1952	67 Stat. C16.
	UCC	Sept. 6, 1952	Sept. 16, 1955	6 UST 2731.
	UCC rev.	July 24, 1971	Dec. 13, 1974	25 UST 1341.
Morocco	UCC	Sept. 6, 1952	May 8, 1972	6 UST 2731.
	UCC rev.	July 24, 1971	Jan. 28, 1976	25 UST 1341.
Netherlands and Possessions[20]	P	Nov. 20, 1899	Nov. 20, 1899	31 Stat. 1961.
	P	Apr. 9, 1910	July 1, 1909	36 Stat. 2685.
	Pm	Feb. 26, 1923	Oct. 2, 1922	42 Stat. 2297.
New Zealand[1]	Pm	Feb. 9, 1917	Dec. 1, 1916	39 Stat. 1815.
	Px	May 25, 1922	May 25, 1922	42 Stat. 2274.
	Pxx	Apr. 24, 1947	Apr. 24, 1947	61 Stat. 1055.
	Po	May 26, 1950	Dec. 29, 1950	64 Stat. A414.
	UCC	Sept. 6, 1952	Sept. 11, 1964	6 UST 2731.

Country	Document	Date of document	Date effective	Reference
Nicaragua . . . . MCC		Jan. 27, 1902	June 30, 1908	35 Stat. 1934.
	BAC	Aug. 11, 1910	Dec. 15, 1913	38 Stat. 1785.
	UCC	Sept. 6, 1952	Aug. 16, 1961	6 UST 2731.
Nigeria . . . . UCC		Sept. 6, 1952	Feb. 14, 1962	6 UST 2731.
Norway . . . . P		July 1, 1905	July 1, 1905	34 Stat. 3111.
	P	Apr. 9, 1910	July 1, 1909	36 Stat. 2685.
	Pm	June 14, 1911	Sept. 9, 1910	37 Stat. 1687.
	UCC	Sept. 6, 1952	Jan. 23, 1963	6 UST 2731.
	UCC rev.	July 24, 1971	Aug. 7, 1974	25 UST 1341.
Pakistan . . . . UCC		July 24, 1971	Sept. 16, 1955	25 UST 1341.
Palestine (excluding Trans-Jordan)	Pm 1933	Sept. 29, 1933	Oct. 1, 1713.	48 Stat.
	Pxx[12]	Mar. 10, 1944	Mar. 10, 1944	58 Stat. 1129.
	Po[12]	May 26, 1950	Dec. 29, 1950	64 Stat. A412.
Panama . . . . BAC		Aug. 11, 1910	Nov. 25, 1913	38 Stat. 1785.
	UCC	Sept. 6, 1952	Oct. 17, 1962	6 UST 2731.
Paraguay . . . . BAC		Aug. 11, 1910	Sept. 20, 1917	38 Stat. 1785.
	UCC	Sept. 6, 1952	Mar. 11, 1962	6 UST 2731.

Country	Document	Date of document	Date effective	Reference
Peru............	BAC	Aug. 11, 1910	Apr. 30, 1920	38 Stat. 1785.
	UCC	Sept. 6, 1952	Oct. 16, 1963	6 UST 2731.
Philippines	Pm	Oct. 21, 1948	Oct. 21, 1948	62 Stat. 1568.
	UCC[21]	Sept. 6, 1952		6 UST 2731.
Poland......:....	Pm	Feb. 14, 1927	Feb. 16, 1927	44 Stat. 2634.
Portugal	P	July 20, 1893	July 20, 1893	28 Stat. 1222.
	P	Apr. 9, 1910	July 1, 1909	36 Stat. 2685.
	UCC	Sept. 6, 1952	Dec. 25, 1956	6 UST 2731.
Rumania	Pm[22]	May 14, 1928	May 14, 1928	45 Stat. 2949.
	T[9, 23]	Feb. 10, 1947	Sept. 15, 1947	61 Stat. 1757.
Senegal	UCC	Sept. 6, 1952	July 10, 1974	6 UST 2731.
	UCC rev.	July 24, 1971	July 10, 1974	25 UST 1341.
South Africa[1]	Pm	June 26, 1924	July 1, 1924	43 Stat. 1957.
Spain[5]	P[14]	July 10, 1895	July 10, 1895	29 Stat. 871.
	P	Apr. 9, 1910	July 1, 1909	36 Stat. 2685.
	Pm	Oct. 10, 1934	Oct. 10, 1934	49 Stat. 3420.
	UCC	Sept. 6, 1952	Sept. 16, 1955	6 UST 2731.

Country	Document	Date of document	Date effective	Reference
	UCC rev.	July 24, 1971	July 10, 1974	25 UST 1341.
Sweden	P	May 26, 1911	June 1, 1911	37 Stat. 1682.
	Pm	Feb. 27, 1920	Feb. 1, 1920	41 Stat. 1787.
	UCC	Sept. 6, 1952	July 1, 1961	6 UST 2731.
	UCC rev.	July 24, 1971	July 10, 1974	25 UST 1341.
Switzerland.......	P	July 1, 1891	July 1, 1891	27 Stat. 981.
	P	Apr. 9, 1910	July 1, 1909	36 Stat. 2685.
	Pm	Nov. 22, 1924	July 1, 1923	43 Stat. 1976.
	UCC	Sept. 6, 1952	Mar. 30, 1956	6 UST 2731.
Thailand	T[25]	Dec. 16, 1920	Sept. 1, 1921	42 Stat. 1928.
	T[25]	Nov. 13, 1937	Oct. 1, 1938	53 Stat. 1731.
	T[25]	May 29, 1966	June 8, 1968	19 UST 5843.
Tunisia	P	Oct. 4, 1912	Oct. 4, 1912	37 Stat. 1765.
	UCC	Sept. 6, 1952	June 19, 1969	6 UST 2731.
	UCC rev.	July 24, 1971	June 10, 1975	25 UST 1341.
Union of Soviet Socialist Reps.	UCC	Sept. 6, 1952	May 27, 1973	6 UST 2731.
United Kingdom ..	UCC	Sept. 6, 1952	Sept. 27, 1957	6 UST 2731.
	UCC rev.	July 24, 1971	July 10, 1974	25 UST 1341.

Country	Document	Date of document	Date effective	Reference
United Kingdom and Possessions[1]	P	July 1, 1801	July 1, 1891	27 Stat. 981.
	P	Apr. 9, 1910	July 1, 1909	36 Stat. 2685.
United Kingdom and the British Dominions, Colonies and Possessions with the exception of Canada, Australia, New Zealand, South Africa and Newfoundland[1]	Pm	Jan. 1, 1915	Jan. 1, 1915	38 Stat. 2044.
	Pmx	Apr. 10, 1920	Feb. 2, 1920	41 Stat. 1790.
United Kingdom, certain British[1]	Pxx	Mar. 10, 1944	Mar. 10, 1944	58 Stat. 1129.
Territories[1] and Palestine[12]	Po	May 26, 1950	Dec. 29, 1950	64 Stat. A412.
Uruguay	BAC	Aug. 11, 1910	Dec. 17, 1919	38 Stat. 1785.
Venezuela	UCC	Sept. 6, 1952	Sept. 30, 1966	6 UST 2731.
Yugoslavia	UCC	Sept. 6, 1952	May 11, 1966	6 UST 2731.
UCC rev.	1971	July 24, 1974	July 10, 1341.	25 UST
Zambia	UCC	Sept. 6, 1952	June 1, 1965	6 UST 2731.

FOOTNOTES

[1]The proclamations of July 1, 1891 and April 9, 1910 apply to "Great Britain and the British possessions", but the proclamations of January 1, 1915 and April 10, 1920 specifically except Australia, Canada, Newfoundland, New Zealand and South Africa. The proclamations of March 10, 1944 and May 26, 1950 enumerate the various British territories to which they apply, excluding the areas specifically excepted in the proclamations of 1915 and 1920. Proclamations establishing

individual copyright relations with Australia, Canada, Ireland, New Zealand, Palestine, and South Africa are listed separately. (See also footnotes 2, 11, 12.)

The proclamation of December 27, 1923 regarding Canada is considered as applying to Newfoundland at the present time.

The copyright proclamations of July 1, 1891, April 9, 1910, January 1, 1915, April 10, 1920, and March 10, 1944 regarding Great Britain and possessions each applied when issued to the areas now within the boundaries of Burma, Ceylon, India, and Pakistan. See footnote 10 with respect to India. No announcement has been made as to the application of the proclamations to Burma, Ceylon, and Pakistan since they acquired their new status.

[2]The proclamation of December 29, 1949 extends for one year from its date the period of time for compliance by citizens of Australia with the conditions and formalities prescribed by the copyright law of the United States.

[3]The United States entered into treaties restoring friendly relations with Austria, Germany, and Hungary at Vienna on August 24, 1921 (42 Stat. 1946; TS 659); at Berlin on August 25, 1921 (42 Stat. 1939; TS 658) and at Budapest on August 29, 1921 (42 Stat. 1951; TS 610), respectively. By virtue of these treaties the United States became entitled to the benefits of the provisions relative to copyright protection in the treaties of peace signed by Austria, Germany and Hungary at Saint-Germain-en-Laye on September 10, 1919, at Versailles on June 28, 1919, and at Trianon on June 4, 1920, respectively. (See also footnote 7.)

[4]The Treaty of Friendship, Commerce and Navigation (Art. IX) together with the Protocol (par. 5) signed at Nanking November 4, 1946, and the reservation and understandings in the ratification by the United States (TIAS 1871) govern present copyright relations between the United States and China. Although Article XXIX of this Treaty lists the earlier Treaty as to Commercial Relations signed at Shanghai October 8, 1903 (33 Stat. 2208, TS 430) as superseded by the 1946 Treaty, the ratification by the United States provides in part that the 1946 Treaty is subject to the following reservation and understandings: "The Government of the United States of America does not accept Section 5(c) of the Protocol relating to protection against translations of literary and artistic works, and with the understanding that United States interests in this respect will be interpreted in accordance with the provisions of the Treaty as to Commercial Relations signed at Shanghai, October 8, 1903, until further negotiations and agreement concerning translations are forthcoming."

[5]Treaties and Conventions containing provisions relative to copyright protection in territories ceded to the United States are not included in this table: for example, the Treaty of Peace with Spain signed at Paris December 10, 1898 (30 Stat. 1754; TS 343), Art. XIII (see also footnote 25); and the Convention with Denmark for the Cession to the United States of the Danish West Indies, signed at New York, August 4, 1916 (39 Stat. 1706; TS 629), Art. 9.

[6]The Department of State has made no announcement as to the application of the proclamations of July 1, 1891, April 9, 1910, May 24, 1918, and March 27, 1947 to Cambodia, Laos, and Viet-Nam.

[7]Copyright Convention signed at Budapest January 30, 1912 (TS 571). This Convention was continued in force following World War I by notice given by the United States on May 27, 1922 to Hungary in pursuance of Article 224 of the Treaty of Trianon concluded on June 4, 1920 (III Redmond 3539), to the benefits of which the United States became entitled by the Treaty of August 29, 1921 establishing friendly relations between the United States and Hungary (42 Stat. 1951; TS 660). The Convention of 1912 was kept in force or revived following World War II by notice given on March 9, 1948 by the United States to Hungary pursuant to Article 10 of the Treaty of Peace with Hungary (61 Stat. 2065; Department of State Bulletin March 21, 1948; p. 382).

[8]Treaty of Peace with Hungary (Annex IV A) dated at Paris February 10, 1947 (TIAS 1651).

[9]Except with respect to rights of third parties, the provisions relating to protection of copyright in the annexes to the Treaties of Peace with Hungary, Italy, and Rumania dated at Paris February 10, 1947, are bilateral in character. For example, the provisions of Annex IV A of the Treaty of Peace with Hungary, relate in general, to copyright relations between Hungary on the one part, and each of the other ratifying or adhering States, on the other part. Those provisions do not pertain to copyright relations between those other States, except for third party rights (see also footnotes 13 and 19). Annex IV of the Treaty of Peace with Bulgaria dated at Paris February 10, 1947 (61 Stat. 1915; TIAS 1650) contains similar provisions; however, there are no general copyright relations between the United States and Bulgaria.

[10]The proclamation of October 21, 1954 affirms the existence of copyright relations with India after August 15, 1947 (the effective date of the Indian Independence Act), as before that date (see footnote 1).

[11]The Department of State has determined that the entry into force on April 18, 1949 of the Republic of Ireland Act had no effect upon the proclamation of September 28, 1929 regarding the Irish Free State (Eire). Copyright relations with Ireland are therefore governed by that proclamation (see also footnote 1).

[12]The proclamations of March 10, 1944 and May 26, 1950 regarding Great Britain and possessions, also specifically refer to Palestine, excluding Trans-Jordan.

[13]The exchanges of notes between the United States and Italy, on the basis of which the proclamations of October 31, 1892 and May 1, 1915 were issued, were the subject of a note delivered on March 12, 1948 to the Italian Foreign Office by the American Embassy at Rome with respect to prewar bilateral treaties and other international agreements which the United States desired to keep in force or revive pursuant to Article 44 of the Treaty of Peace with Italy. The note stated in part "that the Government of the United States of America wishes to include the reciprocal copyright arrangement between the United States

and Italy effected pursuant to the exchange of notes signed at Washington October 28, 1892 and the exchange of notes signed at Washington September 2, 1914, February 12, March 4 and March 11, 1915, among the prewar bilateral treaties and other international agreements with Italy which the United States desires to keep in force or revive. Accordingly, it is understood that the aforementioned arrangement will continue in force and that the Government of each country will extend to the nationals of the other country treatment as favorable with respect to copyright as was contemplated at the time the arrangement was entered into by the two countries". (Department of State Bulletin, April 4, 1918, p. 455.)

[14]Treaty of Peace with Italy (Annex XV A) dated at Paris January 10, 1947 (TIAS 1648).

[15]Copyright Convention, signed at Tokyo November 10, 1905 (TS 450). This convention is considered as having been abrogated on April 22, 1953, pursuant to the provisions of Article 7 of the Treaty of Peace with Japan signed at San Francisco September 8, 1951 (TIAS 2490), since it was not included in the notification which was given on behalf of the United States Government to the Japanese Government on April 22, 1953, indicating the prewar bilateral treaties or conventions which the United States wished to continue in force or revive.

[16]Convention between the United States and Japan for reciprocal protection of inventions, designs, trademarks and copyrights in China and other countries where either contracting party may exercise extraterritorial jurisdiction, signed at Washington May 19, 1908 (TS 507).

This convention is considered as having been abrogated on April 22, 1953, pursuant to the provisions of Article 7 of the Treaty of Peace with Japan signed at San Francisco September 8, 1951 (TIAS 2490), since it was not included in the notification which was given on behalf of the United States Government to the Japanese Government on April 22, 1953, indicating the prewar bilateral treaties or conventions which the United States wished to continue in force or revive.

[17]Treaty of Peace with Japan (Articles 12, 14 and 15) signed at San Francisco September 8, 1951 (TIAS 2490). (See also footnotes 15, 16 and 19.)

[18]The proclamation of November 10, 1953 extends benefits under the copyright law for a period of four years from the coming into force of the Treaty of Peace with Japan (TIAS 2490). That period expired April 28, 1956.

[19]Copyright Convention with Japan for reciprocal protection in Korea of inventions, designs, trademarks and copyrights signed at Washington May 19, 1908 (TS 506).

This convention is considered as having been abrogated on April 22, 1953, pursuant to the provisions of Article 7 of the Treaty of Peace with Japan signed at San Francisco September 8, 1951 (TIAS 2490), since it was not included in the notification which was given on behalf of the United States Government to the Japanese Government on April 22, 1953, indicating the prewar bilateral treaties or conventions which the United States wished to continue in force or revive.

[20]The Department of State has made no announcement as to the application of the proclamations of November 20, 1899, April 9, 1910 and February 26, 1923 to Indonesia since it acquired its new status.

[21]An instrument of accession was deposited by the Philippine Government August 19, 1955. In a communication received by the State Department January 17, 1956, UNESCO stated that by a note dated November 14, 1955, the Philippine Government informed the Director General that "the President of the . . . Philippines has directed the withdrawal of the . . . accession . . . to the Universal Copyright Convention prior to the date of November 19, 1955, at which time the Convention would become effective" for the Philippines. The Director General notified the Philippine Government that he "proposed to submit their communication to the States concerned, upon whom it is incumbent to declare what legal inference they intend to draw from it."

[22]In a note delivered February 26, 1948 to the Rumanian Minister for Foreign Affairs by the American Minister at Bucharest with respect to prewar bilateral treaties and other international agreements which the United States desired to keep in force or revive pursuant to Article 10 of the Treaty of Peace with Rumania (see footnotes 9 and 24), the following statement was made regarding the proclamation of May 14, 1928 and the exchange of notes on which it is based: "It shall be understood that the reciprocal copyright arrangement between the United States and Rumania effected pursuant to the exchange of notes signed at Bucharest May 13 and October 13, 1928 and at Washington May 12 and 19, 1928 and the proclamation issued May 14, 1928 by the President of the United States of America will continue in force." (Department of State Bulletin, March 14, 1948, p. 356).

[23]Treaty of Peace with Rumania, dated at Paris, February 10, 1947 (TIAS 1649).

[24]The proclamation of July 10, 1895, regarding Spain was based upon an arrangement between the United States and Spain effected by an exchange of notes signed at Washington July 6 and 15, 1895. An agreement restoring the arrangement of July 6 and 15, 1895 was effected by an exchange of notes signed at Madrid January 29 and November 18 and 26, 1902 (II Malloy 1710), following the Treaty of Peace between the United States and Spain signed at Paris December 10, 1898 (30 Stat. 1754; TS 343). The latter treaty also contains in Article XIII the following provisions: "The rights of property secured by copyrights and patents acquired by Spaniards in the Island of Cuba, and in Puerto Rico, the Philippines and other ceded territories, at the time of the exchange of ratifications of this treaty, shall continue to be respected. Spanish scientific, literary and artistic works, not subversive of public order in the territories in question, shall continue to be admitted free of duty into such territories, for the period of ten years, to be reckoned from the date of the exchange of ratifications of this treaty."

[25]Treaty of friendship, commerce and navigation, protocol and exchanges of notes, signed at Bangkok November 13, 1937 (Art. 9 of the Treaty) (TS 940). This treaty replaces the treaty of friendship, commerce and navigation between the United States and Thailand signed at

Washington December 16, 1920 (TS 655), Article XII of which contains provisions relating to copyright protection. The treaty of amity and economic relations with three exchanges of notes between the United States and Thailand signed at Bangkok May 29, 1966 (TIAS 6540) replaces the treaty of Nov 13, 1937. Article V. 2 contains provisions relating to copyright.

Copyright extension to Federal Republic of Germany. Proclamation No. 3792 of July 12, 1967, 32 Fed. Reg. 10341, provided:

"WHEREAS the President is authorized, in accordance with the conditions prescribed in Section 9 of Title 17 of the United States Code [former 17 USCS § 9; see 17 USCS § 104] which includes the provisions of the act of Congress approved March 4, 1909, 35 Stat. 1075, as amended by the act of September 25, 1941, 55 Stat. 732, to grant an extension of time for fulfillment of the conditions and formalities prescribed by the copyright laws of the United States of America, with respect to works first produced or published outside the United States of America and subject to copyright or to renewal of copyright under the laws of the United States of America, by nationals of countries which accord substantially equal treatment to citizens of the United States of America; and

"WHEREAS satisfactory official assurances have been received that, since April 15, 1892, citizens of the United States have been entitled to obtain copyright in Germany for their works on substantially the same basis as German citizens without the need of complying with any formalities, provided such works secured protection in the United States; and

"WHEREAS, pursuant to Article 2 of the Law No. 8, Industrial, Literary and Artistic Property Rights of Foreign Nations and Nationals, promulgated by the Allied High Commission for Germany on October 20, 1949, literary or artistic property rights in Germany owned by United States nationals at the commencement of or during the state of war between Germany and the United States of America which were transferred, seized, requisitioned, revoked or otherwise impaired by war measures, whether legislative, judicial or administrative, were, upon request made prior to October 3, 1950, restored to such United States nationals or their legal successors; and

"WHEREAS, pursuant to Article 5 of the aforesaid law, any literary or artistic property right in Germany owned by a United States national at the commencement of or during the state of war between Germany and the United States of America was, upon request made prior to October 3, 1950, extended in term for a period corresponding to the inclusive time from the date of the commencement of the state of war, or such later date on which such right came in existence, to September 30, 1949; and

"WHEREAS, by virtue of a proclamation by the President of the United States of America dated May 25, 1922, 42 Stat. 2271, German citizens are and have been entitled to the benefits of the act of Congress approved March 4, 1909, 35 Stat. 1075, as amended, including the benefits of Section 1(e) of the aforementioned Title 17 of the United

States Code [former 17 USCS §§ 1 et seq.; see 17 USCS §§ 101 et seq.]; and

"WHEREAS, a letter of February 6, 1950, from the Chancellor of the Federal Republic of Germany to the Chairman of the Allied High Commission for Germany established the mutual understanding that reciprocal copyright relations continued in effect between the Federal Republic of Germany and the United States of America:

"Now, THEREFORE, I, LYNDON B. JOHNSON, President of the United States of America, by virtue of the authority vested in me by Section 9 of Title 17 of the United States Code [former 17 USCS § 9; see 17 USCS § 104], do declare and proclaim:

"(1) That, with respect to works first produced or published outside the United States of America: (a) where the work was subject to copyright under the laws of the United States of America on or after September 3, 1930, and on or before May 5, 1956, by an author or other owner who was then a German citizen; or (b) where the work was subject to renewal of copyright under the laws of the United States of America on or after September 3, 1939, and on or before May 5, 1956, by an author or other person specified in Sections 24 and 25 of the aforesaid Title 17 [former 17 USCS §§ 24, 25; see 17 USCS §§ 301 et seq.] who was then a German citizen, there has existed during several years of the aforementioned period such disruption and suspension of facilities essential to compliance with conditions and formalities prescribed with respect to such works by the copyright law of the United States of America as to bring such works within the terms of Section 9(b) of the aforesaid Title 17 [former 17 USCS § 9(b); see 17 USCS § 104]; and

"(2) That, in view of the reciprocal treatment accorded to citizens of the United States by the Federal Republic of Germany, the time within which persons who are presently German citizens may comply with such conditions and formalities with respect to such works is hereby extended for one year after the date of this proclamation [proclaimed July 12, 1967].

"It shall be understood that the term of copyright in any case is not and cannot be altered or affected by this proclamation [this note]. It shall also be understood that, as provided by Section 9(b) of Title 17, United States Code [former 17 USCS § 9(b); see 17 USCS § 104], no liability shall attach under that title [former 17 USCS §§ 1 et seq.; see 17 USCS §§ 101 et seq.] for lawful uses made or acts done prior to the effective date of this proclamation [proclaimed July 12, 1967] in connection with the above-described works, or with respect to the continuance for one year subsequent to such date of any business undertaking or enterprise lawfully undertaken prior to such date involving expenditure or contractual obligation in connection with the exploitation, production, reproduction, circulation or performance of any such works."

Proclamations issued by President under predecessor provisions.
Act Oct. 19, 1976, P. L. 94-553, Title I, § 104, 90 Stat 2599, provided: "All proclamations issued by the President under section 1(e) or 9(b) of title 17 [former 17 USCS §§ 1(e) or 9(b)] as it existed on December 31, 1977, or under previous copyright statutes of the United States, shall

continue in force until terminated, suspended, or revised by the President."

CROSS REFERENCES

Copyrightable subject matter, 17 USCS § 102.
Compilations and derivative works, 17 USCS § 103.

RESEARCH GUIDE

Am Jur:

18 Am Jur 2d, Copyright and Literary Property §§ 28, 31, 32, 58, 64, 73–76.

INTERPRETIVE NOTES AND DECISIONS

1. Generally
2. Unpublished works [17 USCS § 104(a)]
3. Published works, generally [17 USCS § 104(b)]
4. —Musical works
5. —Translations
6. —Reciprocity

1. Generally

Nonresident alien artist himself not possessing right to copyright cannot assign right to copyright. Bong v Alfred S. Campbell Art Co. (1909) 214 US 236, 53 L Ed 979, 29 S Ct 628.

Literary works of stateless person are subject to copyright, and therefore "Mein Kampf" by Hitler was entitled to copyright. Houghton Mifflin Co. v Stackpole Sons, Inc. (1939, CA2 NY) 104 F2d 306, 42 USPQ 96, cert den 308 US 597, 84 L Ed 499, 60 S Ct 131.

It is general rule that author, even alien author, must take certain formal steps to obtain American copyright. Machaty v Astra Pictures, Inc. (1952, CA2 NY) 197 F2d 138, 93 USPQ 51, cert den 334 US 827, 97 L Ed 644, 73 S Ct 29.

Only slight evidence is necessary to make prima facie proof of citizenship and residence; certificate of librarian and other evidence was sufficient to warrant conclusion that complainant was "citizen or resident" of United States when he applied for copyright. Patterson v J. S. Ogilvie Pub. Co. (1902, CC NY) 119 F 451.

Canadian soldier, who came to New York City with all his property, and with intent to remain there was domiciled in United States and entitled to copyright. G. Ricordi & Co. v Columbia Graphophone Co. (1919, DC NY) 258 F 72.

Buenos Aires Copyright Convention of 1910 provided that foreigners must look to our copyright laws for enforcement of rights in this country. Portuondo v Columbia Phonograph Co. (1937, DC NY) 81 F Supp 355, 36 USPQ 104.

Hostilities between nations suspend intercourse and deprive citizens of the hostile nations of any right to privilege of copyright. 22 OAG 268.

German citizen who had strictly complied with provisions of Copyright Act at any time after law became effective, but before date of proclamation of President as provided for in that provision of predecessor section, not only was vested with copyright, but could maintain action for any infringement which occurred prior to date of proclamation. 29 OAG 64.

2. Unpublished works [17 USCS § 104(a)]

Mere license to perform play given by foreign author does not grant authority to licensee to copyright. Saake v Lederer (1909, CA3 Pa) 174 F 135.

Copyright in 1940, as unpublished work, of play in German is not voided by fact that English translations later published bear copyright date later than 1940; translations were "new works" within predecessor section and were thus entitled to separate copyright; Copyright Office regulations (37 C.F.R. 202.2) have reference only to subsequent publication of work upon which unpublished copyright was secured; year date required in "new work" is year of publication of "new work," not year of registration of prior unpublished work. Brecht v Bentley (1960, DC NY) 185 F Supp 890, 126 USPQ 356.

3. Published works, generally [17 USCS § 104(b)]

Book in English language by American authors is in public domain where it is published only in foreign country; plaintiffs never applied for registration of copyright on French edition of book and may not sue for infringement. G. P. Putnam's Sons v Lancer Books, Inc. (1965, DC NY) 239 F Supp 782, 144 USPQ 530.

4. —Musical works

Publication in foreign country of song produced and copyrighted there did not prevent later copyright of same song in United States, there having been no intervening rights. Italian Book Co. v Cardilli (1918, DC NY) 273 F 619.

5. —Translations

Book written in French language was published in France in 1949; thereafter, plaintiff translated book into English and, in 1952, published portion of translation in United States with proper copyright notice; such copyright was not dissipated by fact that revision of complete translation was published by plaintiff in France in 1954 with only French copyright notice. Grove Press, Inc. v Greenleaf Publishing Co. (1965, DC NY) 247 F Supp 127, 147 USPQ 31.

Book written in French was translated into English by United States citizen and then published in France, and translation cannot be copyrighted in United States where ad interim copyright was not obtained, if translator was author of translation; however, if translator was employee for hire of French publisher, rather than independent writer, publisher was author and may obtain copyright. Olympia Press v Lancer Books, Inc. (1967, DC NY) 267 F Supp 920, 153 USPQ 349.

6. —Reciprocity

Provision as to proclamation by President is condition and not directory; no right is conferred independently of presidential proclamation. Bong v Alfred S. Campbell Art Co. (1909) 214 US 236, 53 L Ed 979, 29 S Ct 628.

Presidential proclamation is conclusive evidence as to existence of reciprocal relations. Chappell & Co. v Fields (1914, CA2 NY) 210 F 864.

Court must take judicial notice of existence of reciprocal relations. Ohman v New York City (1909, CC NY) 168 F 953.

Reciprocity proviso as to foreign authors does not affect foreigner domiciled in United States. G. Ricordi & Co. v Columbia Graphophone Co. (1919, DC NY) 258 F 72.

Domiciled alien cannot protect work of which copies are not reproduced for sale unless his sovereign extends reciprocal rights to Americans. Leibowitz v Columbia Graphone Co. (1923, DC NY) 298 F 342.

In absence of separate proclamation of existence of reciprocal conditions as to mechanical production alien cannot avail himself of copyright laws of United States, and complaint for enforcement of copyright is fatally defective in not alleging affirmatively that proclamation to that effect was made. Portuondo v Columbia Phonograph Co. (1937, DC NY) 81 F Supp 355.

Presidential proclamation does not create right but is only evidence of existence of conditions under which rights and privileges may be exercised and is conclusive evidence on that point. 28 OAG 222.

Under predecessor section, President is required to determine by proclamation existence of reciprocal conditions upon which alien authors and composers may acquire general privileges, and date when reciprocal condition was actually met by laws of any foreign nation is one which should be inserted in proclamation. 29 OAG 209.

§ 105. Subject matter of copyright: United States Government works

Copyright protection under this title [17 USCS §§ 101 et seq.] is not available for any work of the United States Government, but the United States Government is not precluded from receiving and holding copyrights transferred to it by assignment, bequest, or otherwise.
(Added Oct. 19, 1976, P. L. 94-553, Title I, § 101, 90 Stat 2546.)

HISTORY; ANCILLARY LAWS AND DIRECTIVES

Effective date of section:

Section 102 of Act Oct. 19, 1976, P. L. 94-553, 90 Stat. 2598 provided that this section "becomes effective on January 1, 1978".

CROSS REFERENCES

"Any work of the United States Government" defined, 17 USCS § 101.

RESEARCH GUIDE

Am Jur:

18 Am Jur 2d, Copyright and Literary Property §§ 29, 41, 99.

INTERPRETIVE NOTES AND DECISIONS

Copy of public official document, although few sentences and words had been changed, is not subject to copyright; article taken from government official bulletin is not protectible by copyright. Du Puy v Post Tel. Co. (1914, CA3 NJ) 210 F 883.

General Pershing's official report to government in 1919 was not matter subject to copyright protection. Eggers v Sun Sales Corp. (1920, CA2 NY) 263 F 373.

Government officer's written records, executed in discharge of official duties, are public documents owned by government; however, rough notes kept by explorer's associate and later used as basis for associate's private journal belong to associate since they are his private and personal writings, unofficial in character; this is especially true since explorer was carrying out his duty of making official record of expedition. United States v First Trust Co. (1958, CA8 Minn) 251 F2d 686, 116 USPQ 172.

In light of the voluntary nature of servicemen's work, the compensation received, though assuredly minimal, and the absence of any concrete evidence of legislative intent to exclude from the coverage of this section any works created by military personnel while fulfilling their obligation to serve their country, the government did not violate any right of the servicemen when it agreed that third party could copy statue they created while in service. Scherr v Universal Match Corp. (1969, CA2 NY) 417 F2d 497, 11 ALR Fed 447, 164 USPQ 225, cert den 397 US 936, 25 L Ed 2d 116, 90 S Ct 945.

Work distributed personally by Army psychiatrist with permission of author does not become government publication, even if Army copying facilities were used, so that copyright in work is abandoned by lack of copyright notice on distributed copies. Bell v Combined Registry Co. (1976, CA7 Ill) 536 F2d 164, 191 USPQ 493, cert den (US) 50 L Ed 2d 612, 97 S Ct 530.

Artist attached to government expedition, who has agreed that United States shall have exclusive right to any sketches or drawings made while on expedition, may not later obtain valid copyright upon his works composed while attached to expedition. Heine v Appleton (1857, CC NY) F Cas No 6324.

Copyright to map prepared by executive assistant to Secretary of Interior and another government employee from government data is held in trust for government; because of his position, assistant's direction that map bear copyright notice in his name was carried out but this does not show title in him; credit given to him by government on reprinting map, does not show title since giving credit to public official is not unusual; government's seeking permission to reprint was natural since copyright was in assistant's name. Sawyer v Crowell Pub. Co. (1942, DC NY) 46 F Supp 471, 54 USPQ 225, affd (CA2 NY) 142 F2d 497, 61 USPQ 389, cert den 323 US 735, 89 L Ed 589, 65 S Ct 74.

Government employee who prepares and delivers speech on his own time on subject relating to or bearing directly on his employment may claim proprietary interest in speech and copyright it as protection against its unauthorized use where speech does not fall within purview of his official duties. Public Affairs Associates, Inc. v Rickover (1967, DC Dist Col) 268 F Supp 444, 153 USPQ 598.

§ 106. Exclusive rights in copyrighted works

Subject to sections 107 through 118 [17 USCS §§ 107–118], the owner of copyright under this title [17 USCS §§ 101 et seq.] has the exclusive rights to do and to authorize any of the following:

(1) to reproduce the copyrighted work in copies or phonorecords;

(2) to prepare derivative works based upon the copyrighted work;

(3) to distribute copies or phonorecords of the copyrighted work to the public by sale or other transfer of ownership, or by rental, lease, or lending;

(4) in the case of literary, musical, dramatic, and choreographic works, pantomimes, and motion pictures and other audiovisual works, to perform the copyrighted work publicly; and

(5) in the case of literary, musical, dramatic, and choreographic works, pantomimes, and pictorial, graphic, or sculptural works, including the individual images of a motion picture or other audiovisual work, to display the copyrighted work publicly.

(Added Oct. 19, 1976, P. L. 94-553, Title I, § 101, 90 Stat. 2546.)

HISTORY; ANCILLARY LAWS AND DIRECTIVES

Effective date of section:

Section 102 of Act Oct. 19, 1976, P. L. 94-553, 90 Stat. 2598 provided that this section "becomes effective on January 1, 1978".

CROSS REFERENCES

"Copies" defined, 17 USCS § 101.
"Derivative work" defined, 17 USCS § 101.
"Display" defined, 17 USCS § 101.
"Perform" defined, 17 USCS § 101.
"Phonorecords" defined, 17 USCS § 101.
"Publicly" defined, 17 USCS § 101.
"Transmit" defined, 17 USCS § 101.
Limitations, qualifications, or exemptions on copyright owner's exclusive rights, 17 USCS §§ 107–118.
Ceasing of copyright owner's rights with respect to particular copy or phonorecord once he has parted with ownership of it, 17 USCS § 109.
Performing rights in sound recordings, 17 USCS § 114.
Use of copyrighted work in computer systems, 17 USCS § 117.
Ownership of copyright, 17 USCS § 201.
This section referred to in 17 USCS §§ 101 note, 107–109, 112–118, 201, 301, 501, 506, 602.

RESEARCH GUIDE

Am Jur:

18 Am Jur 2d, Copyright and Literary Property §§ 21, 22, 24–26, 47, 49, 97, 104, 111–113, 115, 119–122, 128, 137, 152.

58 Am Jur 2d, Newspapers, Periodicals, and Press Associations § 35.

74 Am Jur 2d, Telecommunications § 181.

Annotations:

What is a prohibited performance of a copyrighted musical composition. 61 L Ed 511.

Right to republish advertising material originally appearing in plaintiff's publication. 55 ALR3d 180.

Unfair competition by direct reproduction of literary, artistic, or musical property. 40 ALR3d 566.

Copyright: Abandonment of statutory copyright. 84 ALR2d 462.

Law Review Articles:

Copyright Symposium, 22 New York Law School Law Review 193.

INTERPRETIVE NOTES AND DECISIONS

I. IN GENERAL

1. Generally
2. Construction
3. Federal jurisdiction
4. Rights in ideas, procedures or systems

II. SPECIFIC RIGHTS

5. Generally
6. Right to reproduce copies, generally [17 USCS § 106(1)]
7. —Phonorecords
8. —Transfer as affecting right to copy
9. Right to prepare derivative works, generally [17 USCS § 106(2)]
10. —Transfer as affecting right to derive
11. Right to distribute copies [17 USCS § 106(3)]
12. Right to perform, generally [17 USCS § 106(4)]
13. —Dramatic works
14. —Motion pictures and audiovisual works
15. —Musical works
16. Right to display, generally [17 USCS § 106(5)]
17. —Motion pictures and audiovisual works

III. LOSS OF RIGHTS

18. Generally
19. Abandonment or public dedication, generally
20. —Intent to abandon
21. —Publication, performance or display as abandonment
22. —Transfer or grant as abandonment
23. Expiration of rights

I. IN GENERAL

1. Generally

Although objective of copyright clause of Constitution is to facilitate granting of rights na-

tional in scope, nevertheless copyright clause does not indicate that all writings are necessarily of national interest or that state legislation is, in all cases, unnecessary or precluded; when Congress grants exclusive right or monopoly under federal copyright law, no citizen or state may escape its reach. Goldstein v California (1973) 412 US 546, 37 L Ed 2d 163, 93 S Ct 2303, reh den 414 US 883, 38 L Ed 2d 131, 94 S Ct 27.

Copyright is property in notion and has no corporeal tangible substance. Stephens v Cady (1853) 55 US 528, 14 L Ed 528.

Unlicensed use of copyrighted work is no infringement of holder's rights, and limited scope of copyright monopoly, like limited copyright duration, reflects balance of competing claims upon public interest to encourage creative work and promote broad public availability. Twentieth Century Music Corp. v Aiken (1975) 422 US 151, 45 L Ed 2d 84, 95 S Ct 2040, 186 USPQ 65.

It has become settled law that protection under copyright law is granted only to those who perform conditions essential to perfect copyright title. De Jonge & Co. v Breuker & Kessler Co. (1911, CA3 Pa) 191 F 35, affd 235 US 33, 59 L Ed 113, 35 S Ct 6.

Holder of copyright has no monopoly by virtue of issued copyright itself, but his rights are measured by statute. Lydiard-Peterson Co. v Woodman (1913, CA8 Minn) 204 F 921, reh den (CA8 Minn) 205 F 900.

Right of author to monopoly of his publications is determined by copyright statute. American Code Co. v Bensinger (1922, CA2 NY) 282 F 829.

Copyright statute extends author's sole and exclusive right by reserving writing from public domain for effective period of the copyright. Warner Bros. Pictures, Inc. v Columbia Broadcasting System, Inc. (1954, CA9 Cal) 216 F2d

945, 104 USPQ 103, cert den 348 US 971, 99 L Ed 756, 75 S Ct 532.

It is contrary to public interest to permit anyone to buy up copyright to anything written about himself, using ownership to restrain others from publishing biographical material concerning him. Rosemont Enterprises, Inc. v Random House, Inc. (1966, CA2 NY) 366 F2d 303, 23 ALR3d 122, 150 USPQ 715, cert den 385 US 1009, 17 L Ed 2d 546, 87 S Ct 714.

Property intended to be protected by copyright acts is exclusive right of author in his writings. Clayton v Stone (1829, CC NY) F Cas No 2872.

Author must comply with copyright laws in order to secure exclusive right to his works. The Mark Twain Case (1883, CC Ill) 14 F 728; Holmes v Donohue (1896, CC Ill) 77 F 179.

Holders of domestic copyrights may refrain from licensing at all, and content themselves with right of excluding others from use of their property. Paine v Electrical Research Products, Inc. (1939, DC NY) 27 F Supp 780, 41 USPQ 575.

Copyright is intangible, incorporeal right in nature of privilege or franchise and is enjoyable as legal estate, as other movable personal property; it will not be considered joint estate unless specifically stated. Stuff v La Budde Feed & Grain Co. (1941, DC Wis) 42 F Supp 493, 52 USPQ 23.

Rights possessed by copyright owner are purely statutory. Miller v Goody (1954, DC NY) 125 F Supp 348, 103 USPQ 292.

Although copyright protection is afforded author of legal forms as against copying disseminators of this information, right to exact royalties from users of forms generally is denied. Continental Cas. Co. v Beardsley (1957, DC NY) 151 F Supp 28, 113 USPQ 181, mod on other grounds (CA2 NY) 253 F2d 702, 117 USPQ 1, cert den 358 US 816, 3 L Ed 2d 58, 79 S Ct 25.

Rights granted upon compliance with Copyright Act are separate and independent; they may be retained by owner or disposed of by him to others either singly or in their entirety. Schwartz v Broadcast Music, Inc. (1959, DC NY) 180 F Supp 322, 124 USPQ 34.

Except for copyright, published musical composition would be public property usable by any one in any way. Gay v Robbins Music Corp. (1942, Sup) 38 NYS2d 337, 55 USPQ 461.

Copyright is right available only to author or proprietor of literary property; its purpose is to secure to him exclusive right to that property; it is distinct from property copyrighted and its assignment will no more effect transfer of property than sale of property will effect assignment

of copyright; it has been described as intangible, incorporeal right in nature of privilege or franchise independent of author's manuscript or printer's plate; in case of copyrighted play, copyright is distinct from play and is exercised by playright or owner for own exclusive benefit. McClintic v Sheldon (1943) 182 Misc 32, 43 NYS2d 695, 59 USPQ 41, revd on other grounds 269 App Div 356, 55 NYS2d 879, affd without opinion 295 NY 682, 65 NE2d 328.

Antitrust Laws [15 USCS §§ 1 et seq.] do not apply to copyrights. Metro-Goldwyn-Mayer Distributing Corp. v Cocke (1933, Tex Civ App) 56 SW2d 489.

2. Construction

Author's exclusive rights are absolute when perfected. Gilmore v Anderson (1889, CC NY) 38 F 846.

Distribution of intellectual property or work is capable of limitation, and restrictions on use of interpretations are not unreasonable or against public policy. Waring v Dunlea (1939, DC NC) 26 F Supp 338, 41 USPQ 201.

Courts have taken broad view of copyright protection in order to give to copyright proprietor exclusive right to any lawful use of his property whereby he may get a profit out of it. Loew's, Inc. v Columbia Broadcasting System, Inc. (1955, DC Cal) 131 F Supp 165, 105 USPQ 302, affd (CA9 Cal) 239 F2d 532, 112 USPQ 11, affd 356 US 43, 2 L Ed 2d 583, 78 S Ct 667, 116 USPQ 479, reh den 356 US 934, 2 L Ed 2d 764, 78 S Ct 770.

3. Federal jurisdiction

After owner has transferred his title to copyrighted books under agreement restricting use, he cannot invoke jurisdiction of federal courts under copyright laws to prevent violation of agreement; and where court does not have jurisdiction otherwise suit will be dismissed. Harrison v Maynard, M. & Co. (1894, CA2 NY) 61 F 689.

Where author secured copyright of unpublished dramatic composition under predecessor section, he is restricted to remedies provided by statute for any infringement of that right, and federal district court is only court in which he may seek such redress originally. Loew's Inc. v Superior Court of Los Angeles County (1941) 18 Cal 2d 419, 115 P2d 983, 50 USPQ 641.

4. Rights in ideas, procedures or systems

Copyright of pamphlet relating to plans for formation of burial associations did not confer exclusive right to organize and operate under plan disclosed in such pamphlet. Burk v Johnson (1906, CA8 Kan) 146 F 209.

Copyright on form of insurance policy does not prevent others from offering insurance coverage similar to that of copyrighted policy. Miner v Employers Mut. Liability Ins. Co. (1956) 97 App DC 152, 229 F2d 35, 108 USPQ 100.

Production of jeweled bee pins is a larger private reserve than Congress intended to be set aside in the public market without a patent, and therefore such pins represent an idea that defendants were free to copy. Herbert Rosenthal Jewelry Corp. v Kalpakian (1971, CA9 Cal) 446 F2d 738, 170 USPQ 557.

Exclusive right to employ certain advertising method cannot be acquired under copyright laws. Ehret v Pierce (1880, CC NY) 10 F 553.

Person who bestows his skill and time in surveys, research, and observation necessary to making of correct map, does not thereby prevent any other person from using same means to accomplish same end; natural objects, public records, and surveys from which map is made are open to examination of any one, but no person has right to sit down and copy the map of another. Chapman v Ferry (1883, CC Or) 18 F 539.

Copyright owner has exclusive right to form of his work, but not to subject thereof. Pellegrini v Allegrini (1924, DC Pa) 2 F2d 610.

Author cannot build story around historical incident and claim exclusive right to use of incident. Echevarria v Warner Bros. Pictures, Inc. (1935, DC Cal) 12 F Supp 632, 28 USPQ 213.

Copyright of song protects theme, story, and unique arrangement of words and phrases. Gingg v Twentieth Century-Fox Film Corp. (1944, DC Cal) 56 F Supp 701, 62 USPQ 121.

Defendant did not copy plaintiff's copyrighted game; fact that basis for each of defendant's rules may be found in plaintiff's and that two playing boards are similar is not strange since each applied to well-known game played by many for many years on same board and under same rules which were common public knowledge and property prior to copyright. Chamberlin v Uris Sales Corp. (1944, DC NY) 56 F Supp 987, 62 USPQ 375, affd (CA2 NY) 150 F2d 512, 65 USPQ 544.

Use, absent copying, of another's directory solely for mail solicitation purposes is not within protection of copyright laws; one who copyrights compilation or directory of names cannot gain monopoly, under copyright statute, over business dealings with those listed. Caldwell-Clements, Inc. v Cowan Publishing Corp. (1955, DC NY) 130 F Supp 326, 105 USPQ 116.

Copyright does not give its owner exclusive right to use basic material, but only exclusive

right to reproduce his individual presentation of material; so long as there is no copying, actual or implied, owner has no cause for complaint if later artist produces identical presentation of material by his independent efforts. Rochelle Asparagus Co. v Princeville Canning Co. (1959, DC Ill) 170 F Supp 809.

Plaintiffs who designed method for measuring auto tops and placed same in their copyrighted catalogue did not acquire exclusive right to methods set forth in catalogue. Buob v Brown Carriage Co. (1919) 11 Ohio App 266.

II. SPECIFIC RIGHTS

5. Generally

"Copying" proscription of Copyright Act applies generally to books and periodicals in spite of earlier copyright laws proscribing only acts of "printing," "reprinting," and "publishing" relative to books and periodicals, although the extent of the "copying" proscription of Copyright Act is conditioned by "fair use" doctrine. Williams & Wilkins Co. v United States (1973) 203 Ct Cl 74, 487 F2d 1345, 21 ALR Fed 151, affd 420 US 376, 43 L Ed 2d 264, 95 S Ct 1344.

6. Right to reproduce copies, generally [17 USCS § 106(1)]

Copyright is exclusive right of author or publisher of reproducing copies. Perris v Hexamer (1879) 99 US 674, 25 L Ed 308.

"Vend" does not enlarge scope of copyright over right granted by word "copy" in predecessor section. Corcoran v Montgomery Ward & Co. (1941, CA9 Cal) 121 F2d 572, 50 USPQ 274, cert den 314 US 687, 86 L Ed 550, 62 S Ct 300.

Copyrighting of illustration merely precludes another from copying it, not from making his own. Christianson v West Pub. Co. (1945, CA9 Cal) 149 F2d 202, 65 USPQ 263.

Lectures, oral or written, cannot be published without consent of lecturer, though taken down when delivered. Bartlett v Crittenden (1849, CC Ohio) F Cas No 1076; Bartlette v Crittenden (1847, CC Ohio) F Cas No 1082.

Recipient of letter, may, in vindication, publish so much thereof, but no more, without consent of author, as is required to vindicate his character or reputation or free him from unjust obloquy and reproach occasioned by author; any other or further publication breaches rights of author. Folsom v Marsh (1841, CC Mass) F Cas No 4901.

Unlike patent law, which gives patent owner absolute ownership of patented domain, copyright law gives copyright owner no right other than to prevent copying. Gordon v Weir (1953,

DC Mich) 111 F Supp 117, 97 USPQ 387, affd (CA6 Mich) 216 F2d 508, 104 USPQ 40.

When letters are valuable as literary productions, they cannot be published without consent of author. Hoyt v Mackenzie (NY) 3 Barb Ch 320.

Property right of sender in letter is well recognized, and publication may be prevented by injunction. Re Ryan's Estate (1921) 115 Misc 472, 188 NYS 387.

Annotations:

Unfair competition by direct reproduction of literary, artistic, or musical property. 40 ALR3d 566.

7. —Phonorecords

Composers are given exclusive right of recording their copyright musical compositions and like right was granted to authors of copyrighted dramatic works. Corcoran v Montgomery Ward & Co. (1941, CA9 Cal) 121 F2d 572, 50 USPQ 274, cert den 314 US 687, 86 L Ed 550, 62 S Ct 300.

One who copyrights musical composition by publishing written copies thereof with copyright notice has exclusive right to make records thereof. Capitol Records, Inc. v Mercury Records Corp. (1955, CA2 NY) 221 F2d 657, 105 USPQ 163.

Owners of copyrighted tape recordings are entitled to preliminary injunction against defendants' use in their stores of coin-operated electronic systems whereby customers purchase blank tapes and obtain recordings of plaintiffs' tapes furnished by defendants, since prima facie case of irreparable harm to warrant preliminary injunctive relief is established by showing that defendants' customers obtained copies of plaintiffs' $6.00 tapes at a cost of less than $2.00; defendants' activities are not outside scope of predecessor statute because individual rather than mass-duplication was involved, or because reproductions were made by self-service of customers rather than defendants' active reproduction—electronic tape reproducing system not being comparable to photocopy machine in public library. Elektra Records Co. v Gem Electronic Distributors, Inc. (1973, DC NY) 360 F Supp 821.

Amendments to Copyright Act to protect musical reproductions from tape piracy are not unconstitutional as denying of freedom of speech or due process. United States v Bodin (1974, DC Okla) 375 F Supp 1265, 183 USPQ 345.

United States has right to sue for destruction of equipment used in tape piracy of copyrighted musical works as parens patriae, as enforcer of its copyright laws, and as protector of copyrights under international treaties. United States v Brown (1975, DC Miss) 400 F Supp 656, 189 USPQ 612.

8. —Transfer as affecting right to copy

Right to print does not pass with execution sale of plate. Stephens v Cady (1853) 55 US 528, 14 L Ed 528; Stevens v Gladding (1855) 58 US 447, 15 L Ed 155.

There is no distinction, independent of statute, between literary property and property of any other description, and author of literary property possesses right of sale, and such sale may be absolute or conditional, and with or without qualifications or restrictions. Maurel v Smith (1921, CA2 NY) 271 F 211.

Contract whereby orchestra agreed to perform at night club contained clause prohibiting reproduction of such performances; although clause had no self-contained provision for its termination, it does not follow that parties intended, or that contract should be interpreted to mean, that clause should remain in effect in perpetuity; it is more reasonable to infer intent that prohibition at most should be limited to specific term provided for main affirmative performance bargained for; even if clause could be construed to have any legal effect subsequent to complete performance of affirmative provisions of contract, it does not follow that contract should be interpreted as intended or effective to transfer orchestra's exclusive right to make recordings of its live performances. Walsh v Radio Corp. of America (1960, CA2 NY) 275 F2d 220, 124 USPQ 390.

Absolute and unconditional sale and delivery of a painting carries with it right of reproduction and sale. Parton v Prang (1872, CC Mass) F Cas No 10784.

Absent specific reservation thereof, right to reproduce original painting goes with artist's sale of painting; likewise, if painting is copy of earlier painting by same artist, its sale, without specific reservation of right to reproduce copy, carries with it right to reproduce both copy and original. Grandma Moses Properties, Inc. v This Week Magazine (1953, DC NY) 117 F Supp 348, 99 USPQ 455.

Copyright grants to author exclusive right of multiplying copies of what he has written or printed. Richards v Columbia Broadcasting System, Inc. (1958, DC Dist Col) 161 F Supp 516, 117 USPQ 174.

Copyright embraces right of one to make copies of literary work and to publish and vend same to exclusion of others. Brunner v Stix, Baer & Fuller Co. (1944) 352 Mo 1225, 181 SW2d 643.

Mere fact that artist gave right to make copies of his oil painting to another does not dedicate such painting to public. Oertel v Wood (NY) 40 How Prac 10.

Absolute sale by artist of painting without reservation of right to reproduce painting, passes such right to vendee. Pushman v New York Graphic Soc. (1942) 287 NY 302, 39 NE2d 249, 52 USPQ 273.

9. Right to prepare derivative works, generally [17 USCS § 106(2)]

Reproduction of words of poem in combination with music is not dramatization of poem. Corcoran v Montgomery Ward & Co. (1941, CA9 Cal) 121 F2d 572, 50 USPQ 274, cert den 314 US 687, 86 L Ed 550, 62 S Ct 300.

Publication of brief synopsis of copyrighted opera by another than owner of copyright thereof not violation. G. Ricordi & Co. v Mason (1912, DC NY) 201 F 184, affd on basis of opinion below (CA2 NY) 210 F 277.

Memoranda taken from text books and used in tutoring students constituted "versions" of substantial portions of book. Macmillan Co. v King (1914, DC Mass) 223 F 862.

Former copyright law did not give copyright owner exclusive right to novelize play. Fitch v Young (1911, DC NY) 230 F 743, affd (CA2 NY) 239 F 1021.

Author of copyrighted poem is entitled to protection of name of production under which it has become known to public as against one who uses name alone, and not body of work, in production of moving picture. Paramore v Mack Sennett, Inc. (1925, DC Cal) 9 F2d 66.

Copyright statute affords protection against infringement of copyrighted idea by its manufacture in other media. Jones Bros. Co. v Underkoffler (1936, DC Pa) 16 F Supp 729, 31 USPQ 197.

Copyright owner has right to refuse consent to any compilation, adaptation or arrangement by others of copyrighted work. National Geographic Soc. v Classified Geographic, Inc. (1939, DC Mass) 27 F Supp 655, 41 USPQ 719.

As incident to proprietorship over copyrights covering music, proprietor has right to have words written for music. Shapiro Bernstein & Co. v Jerry Vogel Music Co. (1953, DC NY) 115 F Supp 754, 98 USPQ 438, revd on other grounds (CA2 NY) 221 F2d 569, 105 USPQ 178, adhered to (CA2 NY) 223 F2d 252, 105 USPQ 460.

Trust upon translator's copyright will not be implied in favor of author. Rolland v Henry Holt & Co. (1957, DC NY) 152 F Supp 167, 113 USPQ 253.

Copying substance of copyrighted design produced through different medium is prohibited.

Walco Products, Inc. v Kittay & Blitz, Inc. (1972, DC NY) 354 F Supp 121.

Copyright in telephone directory extends to extracting information from larger directory for town included in larger directory. Southwestern Bell Tel. Co. v Nationwide Independent Directory Service, Inc. (1974, DC Ark) 371 F Supp 900, 182 USPQ 193.

Copyright of motion picture based on published book or drama gives owner of such copyright exclusive right to his motion-picture dramatization, but does not give exclusive right to all motion-picture rights in book or drama. O'Neill v General Film Co. (1916) 171 App Div 854, 157 NYS 1028.

Stage performing rights of drama carry with it right to produce play in motion pictures. Hart v Fox (1917, Sup) 166 NYS 793.

Annotations:

Right to republish advertising material originally appearing in plaintiff's publication. 55 ALR3d 180.

10. —Transfer as affecting right to derive

Contract granting "sole and exclusive right to dramatize said book for presentation on stage" does not include motion-picture rights. Klein v Beach (1917, CA2 NY) 239 F 108.

Owners of copyright on book or play may make motion pictures of story, or lawfully assign such right to others. National Picture Theatres, Inc. v Foundation Film Corp. (1920, CA2 NY) 266 F 208.

Purchaser of painting had right to republish it by chromo. Parton v Prang (1872, CC Mass) F Cas No 10784.

Contract for "exclusive right of producing dramatic version on the stage" does not convey motion-picture rights. Harper Bros. v Klaw (1916, DC NY) 232 F 609.

Published sheet music or orchestral arrangement which alone is "sold" in vending of composition is not "song" but graphic portrayal of spiritual creation; song remains property of proprietor and to it is attached right of public performance for profit; sale of sheet music or orchestrations does not necessarily suppose or involve their use as instruments in public performance for profit without license, there being other uses. Remick Music Corp. v Interstate Hotel Co. (1944, DC Neb) 58 F Supp 523, 63 USPQ 327, affd (CA8 Neb) 157 F2d 744, 71 USPQ 138, cert den 329 US 809, 91 L Ed 691, 67 S Ct 622, reh den 330 US 854, 91 L Ed 1296, 67 S Ct 769.

There is no illegal monopoly under section 2 of Sherman Antitrust Act [15 USCS § 2] even if dramatist guild makes it mandatory, in transactions for purchasing rights to make motion picture from copyrighted plays owned by its members, that there be restriction on time before which picture may be released, since guild members control only small portion of plays. Inge v Twentieth Century-Fox Film Corp. (1956, DC NY) 143 F Supp 294, 111 USPQ 153.

Author's grant of right to translate and adapt drama into English, and to perform in that language, does not convey motion-picture rights. Underhill v Schenck (1921) 114 Misc 520, 187 NYS 589, mod on other grounds 201 App Div 46, 193 NYS 745, mod on other grounds 238 NY 7, 143 NE 773, 33 ALR 303.

Copyright owner of play (1) may grant licenses to use play on stage, in motion pictures, or otherwise; he is paid for award of rights to another, proceeds constituting moneys derived from stage production or photoplay exhibition pursuant to contract; (2) he may prevent unauthorized persons from appropriating or using it, or obtain redress from them for such unauthorized use, or both; he is paid for infliction of wrongs on himself, proceeds constituting reparations for injury to his property pursuant to Copyright Act. McClintic v Sheldon (1943) 182 Misc 32, 43 NYS2d 695, 59 USPQ 41, revd on other grounds 269 App Div 356, 55 NYS2d 879, affd without opinion 295 NY 682, 65 NE2d 328.

11. Right to distribute copies [17 USCS § 106(3)]

Exclusive right to multiply and vend copies of intellectual work is given by statutory copyright laws only. Bentley v Tibbals (1915, CA2 NY) 223 F 247.

"Vend" does not enlarge scope of copyright over right granted by word "copy" in predecessor section. Corcoran v Montgomery Ward & Co. (1941, CA9 Cal) 121 F2d 572, 50 USPQ 274, cert den 314 US 687, 86 L Ed 550, 62 S Ct 300.

Restriction of sales to subscribers only is protected; Copyright Act protects copyright-owner's plan of sales from interference by other dealers offering surreptitiously obtained copies of copyrighted work without his consent. Henry Bill Pub. Co. v Smythe (1886, CC Ohio) 27 F 914.

Owner of copyright is czar in his own domain, may sell or not as he chooses, may fix such prices as he pleases, and is not required to deal equally or fairly with purchasers. Buck v Hillsgrove Country Club, Inc. (1937, DC RI) 17 F Supp 643, 33 USPQ 134; Buck v Del Papa (1937, DC RI) 17 F Supp 645.

Predecessor section gives copyright owner not only exclusive right to copy but also to vend copyrighted work. Shapiro, Bernstein & Co. v

Bleeker (1963, DC Cal) 224 F Supp 595, 140 USPQ 111.

Copyright owner can grant to another exclusive right to sell copyrighted right in specified territory. Davis v Vories (1897) 141 Mo 234, 42 SW 707.

12. Right to perform, generally [17 USCS § 106(4)]

Monopoly of right to reproduce compositions of any author is not limited to words; pictures are included and court assumes that it covers performances of orchestra conductor and skill and art by which phonographic record maker makes possible proper recording. RCA Mfg. Co. v Whiteman (1940, CA2 NY) 114 F2d 86, 46 USPQ 324, cert den 311 US 712, 85 L Ed 463, 61 S Ct 393 and cert den 311 US 712, 85 L Ed 463, 61 S Ct 394.

As matter of pleading, when composer composes his composition with unlimited copyright notice, it may fairly be inferred that he had written work for purpose of securing all rights attainable under Copyright Act, including exclusive right publicly to perform it for profit. Hubbell v Royal Pastime Amusement Co. (1917, DC NY) 242 F 1002.

ASCAP and BMI do not misuse or unlawfully extend copyright by granting blanket licenses to CBS where evidence fails to show that direct licensing for each composition is impractical or that ASCAP and BMI would refuse direct licensing. Columbia Broadcasting System, Inc. v American Soc. of Composers (1975, DC NY) 400 F Supp 737, 187 USPQ 431.

Annotations:

What is a prohibited performance of a copyrighted musical composition. 61 L Ed 511.

13. —Dramatic works

Sale of story without reservation to publisher, and copyright by him, carries with it right of dramatization. Dam v Kirk La Shelle Co. (1910, CA2 NY) 175 F 902 (ovrld on other grounds Sheldon v Metro-Goldwyn Pictures (CA2 NY) 106 F2d 45, affd 309 US 390, 84 L Ed 825, 60 S Ct 681).

Actors in play, who later sought to represent such play from memory were not within rule which permits presentation of play obtained by process of memory alone. Shook v Rankin (1875, CC Minn) F Cas No 12805.

Court cannot decide, upon demurrer, that there is no dramatic right in series of cartoons. Empire City Amusement Co. v Wilton (1903, CC Mass) 134 F 132.

Right of dramatizing novel can be reserved by its author, when sole right to print it has been sold to publisher, who, as proprietor, has taken out copyright on novel. Ford v Charles E. Blaney Amusement Co. (1906, CC NY) 148 F 642.

Although song may not be dramatic composition, copyright owner has right to dramatize it. M. Witmark & Sons v Pastime Amusement Co. (1924, DC SC) 298 F 470, affd (CA4 SC) 2 F2d 1020.

Copyright owner's exclusive right to dramatize nondramatic work includes monopoly in presentation of such work in dramatic form on radio broadcast. Warner Bros. Pictures, Inc. v Columbia Broadcasting System, Inc. (1951, DC Cal) 102 F Supp 141, 92 USPQ 54, affd in part and revd in part on other grounds (CA9 Cal) 216 F2d 945, 104 USPQ 103, cert den 348 US 971, 99 L Ed 756, 75 S Ct 532.

Copyright on musical play protects proprietors' original arrangement and expression of ideas in play, including proprietors' development of plot, characters, sequences of scenes and incidents, and interplay of characters, which possessed originality. Breffort v I Had A Ball Co. (1967, DC NY) 271 F Supp 623, 155 USPQ 391.

Where author acquires under statute right to exclusive representation for profit of dramatic composition deposited with register, he likewise must be restricted to remedies provided for in infringement of that right. Loew's Inc. v Superior Court of Los Angeles County (1941) 18 Cal 2d 419, 115 P2d 983, 50 USPQ 641.

Under copyright laws of United States, author has exclusive right to dramatize his works. Gillette v Stoll Film Co. (1922) 120 Misc 850, 200 NYS 787.

Copyright owner of play has two spheres of influence; on the one hand he may grant licenses to use play on stage or in motion pictures or otherwise; on other he may prevent unauthorized persons from appropriating or using it, or obtain redress from them for such unauthorized use, or both. McClintic v Sheldon (1943) 182 Misc 32, 43 NYS2d 695, 59 USPQ 41, revd on other grounds 269 App Div 356, 55 NYS2d 879, affd without opinion 295 NY 682, 65 NE2d 328.

14. —Motion pictures and audiovisual works

Photoplay taken from book constitutes dramatization. Kalem Co. v Harper Bros. (1911) 222 US 55, 56 L Ed 92, 32 S Ct 20.

Owner of copyright of motion-picture film has right to exhibit picture and to grant exclusive or restrictive license to others to exhibit, but he cannot dictate that other pictures may not be shown with licensed film or admission price which shall be paid for entertainment which includes features other than particular picture licensed. Interstate Circuit, Inc. v United States

(1939) 306 US 208, 83 L Ed 610, 59 S Ct 467, 40 USPQ 299.

Exclusive rights of author in his "writings" include motion-picture rights. Harper & Bros. v Kalem Co. (1909, CA2 NY) 169 F 61, affd 222 US 55, 56 L Ed 92, 32 S Ct 20.

Valid copyright of novel gives owner thereof exclusive right to make dramatizations of it upon stage or in form of motion pictures. Photo-Drama Motion Picture Co. v Social Uplift Film Corp. (1915, CA2 NY) 220 F 448.

It has become settled by decisions, under earlier copyright laws, that copyright of dramatization covers photo-play presentation of same subject. United States v Motion Picture Patents Co. (1915, DC Pa) 225 F 800, app dismd 247 US 524, 62 L Ed 1248, 38 S Ct 578.

Motion-picture photoplay film is entitled to protection against unauthorized exhibition whether it is dramatic work or is dramatization of nondramatic work. Metro-Goldwyn-Mayer Distributing Corp. v Bijou Theatre Co. (1933, DC Mass) 3 F Supp 66, 17 USPQ 124.

Contract grants sole and exclusive right to make and exhibit motion-picture versions of copyrighted play in any manner and method now or at any time hereafter known; since television is known method of exhibiting motion pictures, right to televise motion pictures is granted unless limitation or reservation is expressly and clearly imposed; "live television" is less competitive than televising motion pictures. Wexley v KTTV, Inc. (1952, DC Cal) 108 F Supp 558, 95 USPQ 308, affd (CA9 Cal) 220 F2d 438, 105 USPQ 86.

Author's action to enforce rights in motion picture based on his story is barred by laches where he delayed for 18 years, after knowledge of exhibition of picture, in asserting rights. Varconi v Unity Television Corp. (1958) 11 Misc 2d 191, 173 NYS2d 201, 117 USPQ 107.

15. —Musical works

Playing of copyrighted music in restaurant for entertainment of guests during meal times was public performance for profit and infringement. Herbert v Shanley Co. (1917) 242 US 591, 61 L Ed 511, 37 S Ct 232.

Copyright Act gives exclusive right to perform copyrighted musical composition in public for profit. Gibbs v Buck (1939) 307 US 66, 83 L Ed 1111, 59 S Ct 725, 41 USPQ 162.

Person giving public performance of copyrighted musical composition on rolls not showing copyright notice was liable, though manufacturers of rolls had paid fees allowed by law. Lutz v Buck (1930, CA5 Tex) 40 F2d 501, 5 USPQ 452, cert den 282 US 880, 75 L Ed 776, 51 S Ct 83.

Monopoly given copyright owner is to perform work for profit. Associated Music Publishers, Inc. v Debs Memorial Radio Fund (1944, CA2 NY) 141 F2d 852, 61 USPQ 161, cert den 323 US 766, 89 L Ed 613, 65 S Ct 120.

Mimicry of song should be done in good faith and not as attempt to evade owner's copyright. Bloom & Hamlin v Nixon (1903, CC Pa) 125 F 977.

Person entitled to copyright for song which is part of dramatico-musical composition has exclusive right to publicly present it. Green v Luby (1909, CC NY) 177 F 287.

Right under copyright to perform musical compositions is not trade or commerce within the Sherman AntiTrust Act [15 USCS §§ 1–7, 15 note]; playing of excerpts from copyrighted musical composition, as accompaniment to pictures, in motion-picture theater charging for admission, was performance for profit, although no separate charge was made for music. Harms v Cohen (1922, DC Pa) 279 F 276.

Use by operator of player piano on one occasion of copyrighted music rolls, in theater to which admission was charged, rendered theater owner liable, though use was without his knowledge and against his orders. M. Witmark & Sons v Calloway (1927, DC Tenn) 22 F2d 412.

Right of public performance for profit assured to proprietor of copyrighted musical composition includes (1) right to perform composition by himself and with no license to others, (2) right to license performance by one and deny privilege to others, (3) right to fix prices and terms on which license is granted, (4) right to limit public performance for profit to certain places, and (5) right utterly to forbid public performance for profit; proprietor may exercise one right and forbear to exercise others. Remick Music Corp. v Interstate Hotel Co. (1944, DC Neb) 58 F Supp 523, 63 USPQ 327, affd (CA8 Neb) 157 F2d 744, 71 USPQ 138, cert den 329 US 809, 91 L Ed 691, 67 S Ct 622, reh den 330 US 854, 91 L Ed 1296, 67 S Ct 769.

Possession of matrices for making phonograph records does not carry with it right to performance; right to reproduce performances engraved on matrices is intangible and its situs is at domicile of its owner. Capitol Records, Inc. v Mercury Record Corp. (1952, DC NY) 109 F Supp 330, 95 USPQ 177, (CA2 NY) 221 F2d 657, 105 USPQ 163.

Nominal value of public performance rights to three copyrighted songs as to which plaintiffs seek declaratory judgment makes court reluctant to grant such relief; songs were selected at random from many others for purpose of action; maxim de minimis non curat lex applies. Broad-

cast Music, Inc. v Taylor (1945) 10 Misc 2d 9, 55 NYS2d 94, 65 USPQ 503.

Orchestra leader has no property interest in his rendition of musical compositions; in absence of palming off or confusion, others may meticulously duplicate or imitate his renditions. Miller v Universal Pictures Co. (1960) 11 App Div 2d 47, 201 NYS2d 632, 126 USPQ 303, amd on other grounds 13 App Div 2d 473, 214 NYS2d 645, affd without opinion 10 NY2d 972, 224 NYS2d 662, 180 NE2d 248.

Purchase of sheet music or recordings does not carry with it right to publicly perform copyrighted compositions for profit. Taylor v State (1948) 29 Wash 2d 638, 188 P2d 671, 76 USPQ 275.

16. Right to display, generally [17 USCS § 106(5)]

Protection given copyright proprietor extends to other modes or forms of using or exhibiting his work. Loew's, Inc. v Columbia Broadcasting System, Inc. (1955, DC Cal) 131 F Supp 165, 105 USPQ 302, affd (CA9 Cal) 239 F2d 532, 112 USPQ 11, affd 356 US 43, 2 L Ed 2d 583, 78 S Ct 667, 116 USPQ 479, reh den 356 US 934, 2 L Ed 2d 764, 78 S Ct 770.

17. —Motion pictures and audiovisual works

Photographs of scenes of play used for purpose of advertising do not constitute representation amounting to publication of such play. O'Neill v General Film Co. (1916) 171 App Div 854, 157 NYS 1028.

III. LOSS OF RIGHTS

18. Generally

If author has valid copyright, fact that his book is bound up in volume with 50 other books will not invalidate his copyright. Black v Henry G. Allen Co. (1890, CC NY) 42 F 618.

Where author copyrights play under one title and produces it under another, he, or his assignee do not forfeit copyright title thereto as to persons with full knowledge of all facts. Collier v Imp Films Co. (1913, DC NY) 214 F 272.

Article concerning terrestrial globe later copyrighted was not prior publication of globe, since no one reading article could produce globe from what it disclosed, and article did not indicate dedication to public or place globe in public domain. Geo-Physical Maps, Inc. v Toycraft Corp. (1958, DC NY) 162 F Supp 141, 117 USPQ 316.

When copyright owner improperly obtains second copyright on same article, second copyright is invalid, but works no forfeiture of earlier copyright. Uneeda Doll Co. v Regent Baby Products Corp. (1972, DC NY) 355 F Supp 438.

Owner of manuscript may part with possession of it without parting with his author's rights. O'Neill v General Film Co. (1916) 171 App Div 854, 157 NYS 1028.

19. Abandonment or public dedication, generally

Plaintiffs cannot be said to have abandoned claim for copyright infringement by bringing action for unfair competition in state court. Leo Feist, Inc. v Song Parodies, Inc. (1944, CA2 NY) 146 F2d 400, 64 USPQ 92.

Copies of survey chart given to Navy Department and placed in public archives did not effect public dedication of chart, so that anyone could copy it. Blunt v Patten (1828, CC NY) F Cas No 1579.

Copyrighted drama cannot be dedicated to public by publication of novel based on such drama. Shook v Rankin (1875, CC Ill) F Cas No 12804.

Publication of novel adapted from play is not abandonment of right to exclusively re-present drama. Shook v Rankin (1875, CC Minn) F Cas No 12805.

Where there is question of abandonment of legal right once existing, testimony must be reasonably conclusive of fact before party will be deprived of his rights under law. Myers v Callaghan (1881, CC Ill) 5 F 726.

Publication of lithographic copies of copyrighted painting does not effect abandonment of exclusive rights to print and vend such copies. Schumacher v Schwencke (1887, CC NY) 30 F 690.

Manual for using certain toy, copyrighted in 1912, does not cause abandonment of copyright on manual issued in 1911, when subsequently issued manual was new book. Meccano, Ltd. v Wagner (1916, DC Ohio) 234 F 912, mod on other grounds (CA6 Ohio) 246 F 603.

Newspaper accounts of presentation of play do not constitute dedication by owner thereof to public. O'Neill v General Film Co. (1916) 171 App Div 854, 157 NYS 1028.

Soldier's letter to minor daughters was not dedicated to public by virtue of his military status, by virtue of necessity for having same read to them, or by virtue of being addressed to them; property rights (literary property) in contents of letter belong to his estate. Re McCormick (Pa Or Ct) 92 USPQ 393.

Annotations:

Copyright: Abandonment of statutory copyright. 84 ALR2d 462.

20. —Intent to abandon

Rights gained under copyright law may be abandoned; however, abandonment must be manifested by some overt act indicative of purpose to surrender rights and allow public to copy; mere lack of action is insufficient. Hampton v Paramount Pictures Corp. (1960, CA9 Cal) 279 F2d 100, 84 ALR2d 454, 125 USPQ 623, cert den 364 US 882, 5 L Ed 2d 103, 81 S Ct 170.

Reproduction of a floor plan from a copyrighted set of architectural drawings in an advertising brochure does not constitute a waiver or abandonment of the copyright by plaintiff, and copying such reproduction constitutes an infringement of the copyright; the exclusive right to copy what is copyrighted belongs to the architect, even though the plans give him no unique claim on any feature of the structure detailed. Imperial Homes Corp. v Lamont (1972, CA5 Fla) 458 F2d 895, 173 USPQ 519.

To constitute abandonment there must be clear, unequivocal, and decisive act of person entitled to exclusive rights in production, showing determination not to have rights which he relinquished. Harper & Bros. v M. A. Donohue & Co. (1905, CC Ill) 144 F 491, affd (CA7 Ill) 146 F 1023.

Where defendant, which contracted for use for specific time of duly-copyrighted book of advertisements bearing notice of copyright, continued to use material beyond contract time, fact that copyright owner furnished for defendant's convenience mats for printing, which did not contain copyright notice, did not constitute abandonment. Deward & Rich, Inc. v Bristol Sav. & Loan Corp. (1939, DC Va) 29 F Supp 777, 44 USPQ 26.

Court does not agree that there can be no general publication unless author so intends, but holds that intentional surrender is not necessary to forfeiture of copyright. Gardenia Flowers, Inc. v Joseph Markovits, Inc. (1968, DC NY) 280 F Supp 776, 157 USPQ 685.

Forced filing of architectural plans in building department of municipality constitutes only limited publication of copyright and gives no person right to use copy thereof; plans do not become public record in sense that public has right to use them; plans are open to public inspection for purpose of determining whether building will comply with law, but not for purpose of giving anyone right to use them. Smith v Paul (1959) 174 Cal App 2d 744, 345 P2d 546, 77 ALR2d 1036, 123 USPQ 463.

Intent to abandon rights in literary work in such degree as to afford protection against charge of plagiarism is question of fact. Hirsch v Twentieth Century-Fox Film Corp. (1955) 207 Misc 750, 144 NYS2d 38, 105 USPQ 253, app dismd 1 App Div 2d 808, 152 NYS2d 401.

Architect does not abandon copyright in plans for building, although plans are seen by builder and contractors; moreover, requirement of deposit for contractor to obtain plans to examine does not evince intention to sell them but intention that they be returned; also, right is not lost where architect files plans with city so that building permit can issue. Ashworth v Glover (1967) 20 Utah 2d 85, 433 P2d 315, 156 USPQ 219.

21. —Publication, performance or display as abandonment

Public representation of dramatic composition, not printed and published, does not deprive owner of his right, save by operation of statute. Ferris v Frohman (1912) 223 US 424, 56 L Ed 492, 32 S Ct 263.

Owner of written scenario of play may perform play and motion picture based thereon, and also license others to do same without prejudicing its ownership. Universal Film Mfg. Co. v Copperman (1914, CA2 NY) 218 F 577, cert den 235 US 704, 59 L Ed 433, 35 S Ct 209.

Delivery of a lecture before audiences prior to copyright does not deprive author of protection of copyright laws by later application. Nutt v National Institute, Inc. for Improv. of Memory (1929, CA2 Conn) 31 F2d 236.

Proof that complainant's play was performed some six nights with author's consent, and for his profit, but while in manuscript form was not evidence of abandonment. Boucicault v Fox (1862, CC NY) F Cas No 1691.

Author of play, who permitted performances of it to be viewed only by licensed witnesses, but did not print, sell, or circulate play, had not published it, or in any manner abandoned or dedicated it to public. Boucicault v Hart (1875, CC NY) F Cas No 1692.

Facts must exist to indicate that author has allowed play to be represented for long period of time without license or objection, before he should be considered as having abandoned it by knowingly dedicating same to public. Boucicault v Wood (1867, CC Ill) F Cas No 1693.

Mere representation of unpublished play does not of itself dedicate it to public; it cannot be true that lecturer has no rights of property in his unpublished and unprinted lecture, or that clergyman has no rights of property in his unpublished sermon merely because he has repeated it to audience. Crowe v Aiken (1870, CC Ill) F Cas No 3441.

Exhibition of painting in art salon would not be publication unless public were permitted to make copies thereof. Werckmeister v Springer Lithographing Co. (1894, CC NY) 63 F 808.

Limited publication of song in Italy does not preclude subsequent American copyright of same song. Italian Book Co. v Cardilli (1918, DC NY) 273 F 619.

Delivery of lecture before audiences prior to copyright is limited publication and does not deprive author of protection of copyright statute by later application. National Institute, Inc. v Nutt (1928, DC Conn) 28 F2d 132, affd (CA2 Conn) 31 F2d 236.

Rendering of performance of radio script before microphone cannot be held to be abandonment of ownership to it by proprietors or dedication of it to public. Uproar Co. v National Broadcasting Co. (1934, DC Mass) 8 F Supp 358, 23 USPQ 254, mod on other grounds (CA1 Mass) 81 F2d 373, 28 USPQ 250, cert den 298 US 670, 80 L Ed 1393, 56 S Ct 835.

Inclusion of author's work in compilation gives compiler no copyright thereof; it does not forfeit author's registered copyright or put his unpublished work in public domain, if he did not authorize its publication. Mills Music, Inc. v Cromwell Music, Inc. (1954, DC NY) 126 F Supp 54, 103 USPQ 84.

Performance of operas by opera company and their broadcast over radio network cannot be deemed general publication or abandonment so as to divest opera company of all rights to broadcast performances. Metropolitan Opera Ass'n v Wagner-Nichols Recorder Corp. (1950) 199 Misc 786, 101 NYS2d 483, 87 USPQ 173, affd 279 App Div 632, 107 NYS2d 795.

Public performance of play, exhibition of picture, or sale of copy of film for public presentation did not constitute abandonment or deprive owner of his rights. Dior v Milton (1956) 9 Misc 2d 425, 155 NYS2d 443, 110 USPQ 563, affd 2 App Div 2d 878, 156 NYS2d 996, 113 USPQ 210.

Production of play, delivery of lecture, playing of musical composition, exhibition of painting, or performance over radio do not constitute publication which operates as abandonment to public use. Waring v WDAS Broadcasting Station, Inc. (1937) 327 Pa 433, 194 A 631, 35 USPQ 272.

22. —Transfer or grant as abandonment

Distribution of copies of work with consent of author and without copyright notice is abandonment of copyright and defense to infringement suit. Bell v Combined Registry Co. (1976, CA7 Ill) 536 F2d 164, 191 USPQ 493, cert den (US) 50 L Ed 2d 612, 97 S Ct 530.

After author grants exclusive right to use operetta in United States, author cannot make public dedication by publication preventing protection of rights of grantee. Goldmark v Kreling (1888, CC Cal) 35 F 661.

Author of copyrighted book did not abandon his copyright by failing to buy in at execution sale type plates and impression sheets to be used in publishing his work. Patterson v J. S. Ogilvie Pub. Co. (1902, CC NY) 119 F 451.

When owner of copyright licenses publication of copyrighted material by licensee under new copyright there is abandonment of former. West Publishing Co. v Edward Thompson Co. (1909, CC NY) 169 F 833, mod on other grounds (CA2 NY) 176 F 833.

Where one acquires right to elaborate on original story, he is not given right to discard whole story and apply title and name of author to wholly dissimilar tale. Curwood v Affiliated Distributors, Inc. (1922, DC NY) 283 F 219.

Copyright of compilation of songs does not copyright song in compilation which was printed by publisher merely as licensee of composer, and such publication and sale with composer's consent dedicated song to public. Egner v E. C. Schirmer Music Co. (1943, CA1 Mass) 139 F2d 398, 60 USPQ 74, cert den 322 US 730, 88 L Ed 1565, 64 S Ct 947.

When unpublished manuscript is levied on by sheriff, right of author is only suspended, and not destroyed. Banker v Caldwell (1859) 3 Minn 94.

Granting of motion-picture rights of unpublished play and subsequent copyright of motion picture by licensee is not publication of play. O'Neill v General Film Co. (1916) 171 App Div 854, 157 NYS 1028.

23. Expiration of rights

Upon expiration of copyright on book any person has right to publish copyright book and fairly use its generic name. G. & C. Merriam Co. v Ogilvie (1908, CA1 Mass) 159 F 638, cert den 209 US 551, 52 L Ed 922, 28 S Ct 761.

On expiration of copyright of novel any person may use plot for play, copy or publish it, or make any other use of it he sees fit, subject to limitation that right must be so exercised as not to deceive public into believing that they are buying particular thing that was produced under copyright. Atlas Mfg. Co. v Street & Smith (1913, CA8 Mo) 204 F 398, app dismd 231 US 348, 58 L Ed 262, 34 S Ct 73.

Where play based on copyrighted novel is copyrighted, no one can, so long as copyright on play is effective, produce another by copying from such play although copyright of the novel has expired; but anyone is free to produce another play based on novel which is no longer protected. Glaser v St. Elmo Co. (1909, CC NY) 175 F 276.

§ 107.   Limitations on exclusive rights: Fair use

Notwithstanding the provisions of section 106 [17 USCS § 106], the fair use of a copyrighted work, including such use by reproduction in copies or phonorecords or by any other means specified by that section, for purposes such as criticism, comment, news reporting, teaching (including multiple copies for classroom use), scholarship, or research, is not an infringement of copyright. In determining whether the use made of a work in any particular case is a fair use the factors to be considered shall include—

(1) the purpose and character of the use, including whether such use is of a commercial nature or is for nonprofit educational purposes;

(2) the nature of the copyrighted work;

(3) the amount and substantiality of the portion used in relation to the copyrighted work as a whole; and

(4) the effect of the use upon the potential market for or value of the copyrighted work.

(Added Oct. 19, 1976, P. L. 94-553, Title I, § 101, 90 Stat. 2546.)

HISTORY; ANCILLARY LAWS AND DIRECTIVES

Effective date of section:

Section 102 of Act Oct. 19, 1976, P. L. 94-553, 90 Stat. 2598 provided that this section "becomes effective on January 1, 1978".

CROSS REFERENCES

Reproduction by libraries or archives, 17 USCS § 108.

Broad insulation against unwarranted liability for infringement by innocent teachers and other non-profit users, 17 USCS § 504(c).

This section referred to in 17 USCS §§ 106, 108, 117, 118, 501, 504.

RESEARCH GUIDE

Forms:

6 Federal Procedural Forms L Ed, Copyrights § 17:97.

Annotations:

Extent of doctrine of "fair use" under Federal Copyright Act. 23 ALR3d 139.

Law Review Articles:

Free, Fair Use and The New Act. 22 New York Law School Law Review 497.

Rosenfield, The Constitutional Dimension of "Fair Use" In Copyright Law. 50 Notre Dame Lawyer 790.

INTERPRETIVE NOTES AND DECISIONS

I. IN GENERAL

1. Generally
2. Burlesque or parody as fair use
3. Criticism, comment or review as fair use
4. Intent of user

II. FACTORS TO BE CONSIDERED

5. Purpose or character of use [17 USCS § 107(1)]
6. Nature of copyrighted work [17 USCS § 107(2)]
7. Amount and substantiality of work used [17 USCS § 107(3)]
8. Effect of use on market [17 USCS § 107(4)]

I. IN GENERAL

1. Generally

"Fair use" means that others may copy theme or ideas of work, but not its expression. Sheldon v Metro-Goldwyn Pictures Corp. (1936, CA2 NY) 81 F2d 49, 28 USPQ 330, cert den 298 US 669, 80 L Ed 1392, 56 S Ct 835.

Court-created doctrine of "fair use" demonstrates that Copyright Act does not cover all copying, and some forms of copying are universally deemed immune from liability. Williams & Wilkins Co. v United States (1973) 203 Ct Cl 74, 487 F2d 1345, 21 ALR Fed 151, affd 420 US 376, 43 L Ed 2d 264, 95 S Ct 1344.

Overall factors to be considered in applying "fair use" doctrine are: (a) purpose and character of use, (b) nature of copyrighted work, (c) amount and substantiality of material used in relation to copyrighted work as whole, and (d) effect of use on copyright owner's potential market for and value of work. Williams & Wilkins Co. v United States (1973) 203 Ct Cl 74, 487 F2d 1345, 21 ALR Fed 151, affd 420 US 376, 43 L Ed 2d 264, 95 S Ct 1344.

Some tests to be applied on question of fair use are: (1) extent and relative value of extracts, (2) purpose and whether quoted portions might be used as substitute for original work, (3) effect on distribution and objects of original work. Broadway Music Corp. v F-R Pub. Corp. (1940, DC NY) 31 F Supp 817, 45 USPQ 309.

Motion to dismiss complaint on ground that defendant's use is "fair use" is denied since determination of "fair use" should not be resolved on affidavits but is best left to trial judge. New York Tribune, Inc. v Otis & Co. (1941, DC NY) 39 F Supp 67, 49 USPQ 361.

Subsequent authors, publishers and general public may use copyrighted works in reasonable manner without consent of copyright owner on theory that such use is "fair use" of copyrighted material. Greenbie v Noble (1957, DC NY) 151 F Supp 45, 113 USPQ 115.

Almost total copying of copyrighted work cannot be considered "fair use," and addition of variations to make "better" production cannot justify infringement. Robert Stigwood Group, Ltd. v O'Reilly (1972, DC Conn) 346 F Supp 376, 175 USPQ 403, 23 ALR Fed 961, revd on other grounds (CA2 Conn) 530 F2d 1096, cert den 429 US 848, 50 L Ed 2d 121, 97 S Ct 135.

Annotations:

Extent of doctrine of "fair use" under Federal Copyright Act. 23 ALR3d 139.

2. Burlesque or parody as fair use

Doctrine of fair use does not apply to copying substance of copyrighted dramatic work and presenting it, with few variations, as burlesque. Benny v Loew's, Inc. (1956, CA9 Cal) 239 F2d 532, 112 USPQ 11, affd 356 US 43, 2 L Ed 2d 583, 78 S Ct 667, 116 USPQ 479, reh den 356 US 934, 2 L Ed 2d 764, 78 S Ct 770.

In historical burlesque, part of content is used to conjure up general image of original; such limited taking is permitted under doctrine of fair use; doctrine permits burlesque to go somewhat farther so long as taking is not substantial; burlesque is not per se defense. Columbia Pictures Corp. v National Broadcasting Co. (1955, DC Cal) 137 F Supp 348, 107 USPQ 344.

Using entire "Mickey Mouse March" in sound track of movie during sex scene is not fair use or excusable as parody where entire work is used, and use is preliminarily enjoined. Walt Disney Productions v Mature Pictures Corp. (1975, DC NY) 389 F Supp 1397, 186 USPQ 48.

3. Criticism, comment or review as fair use

While police were searching premises of bookbinder for evidence of alleged crime, plaintiff's copyrighted book of poems, which bookbinder had bound, was found; editor accompanying police copied one poem and published it in full in newspaper as part of article describing search and alleged crime; publication of entire poem was neither reasonable quotation or extract from book nor in nature of article by reviewer or commentator. Phillips v Constitution Publishing Co. (DC Ga) 72 USPQ 69.

While critics may quote extensively from copyrighted works in order to comment effectively, almost total copying of copyrighted work cannot be considered "fair use" where use far exceeds any reasonable reproduction for purposes of criticism, comment, or review. Robert Stigwood Group, Ltd. v O'Reilly (1972, DC Conn) 346 F Supp 376, 175 USPQ 403, 23 ALR Fed 961, revd on other grounds (CA2 Conn) 530 F2d 1096, cert den 429 US 848, 50 L Ed 2d 121, 97 S Ct 135.

4. Intent of user

Evidence showing close similarity between complainant's and defendant's work was sufficient to make out prima facie case of unfair use by defendant. West Pub. Co. v Lawyers' Co-op. Pub. Co. (1897, CA2 NY) 79 F 756.

Copying of all, or substantially all, of copyrighted song cannot be held to be fair use merely because infringer had no intent to infringe. Wihtol v Crow (1962, CA8 Iowa) 309 F2d 777, 135 USPQ 385.

If "fair use" is to constitute defense it must be determined by consideration of all evidence in case; extent and relative value of copyrighted material, purpose for claimed "fair use," and effect on distribution and objects of original work are some elements entering into determination of issue and, while intent to infringe is not essential to plaintiff's cause of action, nevertheless defendant's intention bears on question of "fair use." New York Tribune, Inc. v Otis & Co. (1941, DC NY) 39 F Supp 67, 49 USPQ 361.

Fair use does not apply to copying of manuals for computers and components to appropriate creative efforts for copier's own profit. Telex Corp. v International Business Machines Corp. (1973, DC Okla) 367 F Supp 258, 179 USPQ 777, affd in part and revd in part on other grounds (CA10 Okla) 510 F2d 894, cert dismd 423 US 802, 46 L Ed 2d 244, 96 S Ct 8.

II. FACTORS TO BE CONSIDERED

5. Purpose or character of use [17 USCS § 107(1)]

Use of plaintiff's publication to verify proper abbreviations and spelling is not unfair. Official Aviation Guide Co. v American Aviation Associates (1945, CA7 Ill) 150 F2d 173, 65 USPQ 553, cert den 326 US 776, 90 L Ed 469, 66 S Ct 267, reh den 326 US 811, 90 L Ed 495, 66 S Ct 335.

Doctrine of fair use of copyrighted material appears in cases having to do with compilations, listings, digests, and like, and is concerned with use made of prior compilations, listings, and digests; some cases held that writer may be guided by earlier copyrighted works, may consult original authorities, and may use those which he considers applicable in support of his own original text, but even in such cases it is generally held that, if he appropriates fruits of another's labors, without alteration and without independent research, he violates rights of copyright owner. Benny v Loew's, Inc. (1956, CA9 Cal) 239 F2d 532, 112 USPQ 11, affd 356 US 43, 2 L Ed 2d 583, 78 S Ct 667, 116 USPQ 479, reh den 356 US 934, 2 L Ed 2d 764, 78 S Ct 770.

Compiler of directory or like may make fair use of existing compilation serving same purpose if he first makes honest, independent canvass, merely compares and checks his own compilation with that of copyrighted publication, and publishes result after verifying additional items derived from copyrighted publication. G. R. Leonard & Co. v Stack (1967, CA7 Ill) 386 F2d 38, 156 USPQ 161.

Photographic representations, in defendants' catalog of copyrighted article were not "fair use" since defendants' sole purpose was to appropriate plaintiff's design either outright or by frivolous variation. Tennessee Fabricating Co. v Moultrie Mfg. Co. (1970, CA5 Ga) 421 F2d 279, 164 USPQ 481, cert den 398 US 928, 26 L Ed 2d 91, 90 S Ct 1819.

Extensive photocopying by government libraries of medical journal articles at request of individuals and other libraries is fair use where proprietor of copyright in journal articles copied has not shown it is harmed by copying practices, where medicine and medical research will be injured by holding copying practices to be infringements, and where accommodating interests of science with interests of publishers calls for legislative solution. Williams & Wilkins Co. v United States (1973) 203 Ct Cl 74, 487 F2d 1345, 21 ALR Fed 151, affd 420 US 376, 43 L Ed 2d 264, 95 S Ct 1344.

There may be publication of infringing articles although defendant issued such articles only to his own pupils, and to them only upon agreement that they should be returned to him within limited time. Macmillan Co. v King (1914, DC Mass) 223 F 862.

Law permits those working in field of science or art to make use of ideas, opinions, or theories and in certain cases even exact words in copyrighted books in that field, and implies consent of copyright owner to fair use of publication for advancement of science or art, but this does not warrant defendant's use, to advertise its tobacco, of statements from book of plaintiff who is physician. Henry Holt & Co. v Liggett & Myers Tobacco Co. (1938, DC Pa) 23 F Supp 302, 37 USPQ 449.

"Fair use" may be made of copyrighted article, and what is fair use depends on circumstances of each particular case. Karll v Curtis Pub. Co. (1941, DC Wis) 39 F Supp 836, 51 USPQ 50.

Copyrighted hand puppets were sold without any contractual limitations as to use; defendant purchased puppets from retailer and manipulated them on its television program; there is no infringement since use was fair use, was of type for which puppets were intended, and was reasonable. Mura v Columbia Broadcasting System, Inc. (1965, DC NY) 245 F Supp 587, 147 USPQ 38.

Arranging, printing copies, making recordings, and making thousands of performances of copyrighted musical compositions without authorization for promoting state fair is not defendable as

"fair use". Mills Music, Inc. v Arizona (1975, DC Ariz) 187 USPQ 22.

6. Nature of copyrighted work [17 USCS § 107(2)]

Question of fair use, which is question of fact, usually arises in connection with scientific or other works dealing with common subject matter; thus, writings dealing with same historical event are expected to have similarity of treatment. Eisenschiml v Fawcett Publications, Inc. (1957, CA7 Ill) 246 F2d 598, 114 USPQ 199, cert den 355 US 907, 2 L Ed 2d 262, 78 S Ct 334.

It is reasonable and customary for biographers to confer to and utilize earlier works dealing with same subject and occasionally to quote directly from such works. Rosemont Enterprises, Inc. v Random House, Inc. (1966, CA2 NY) 366 F2d 303, 150 USPQ 715, 23 ALR3d 122, cert den 385 US 1009, 17 L Ed 2d 546, 87 S Ct 714.

Willingness of copyright proprietor of medical journal articles to license government libraries copying articles does not alter conclusion that unlicensed copying is fair use, because Copyright Act does not provide for compulsory licensing and copyright proprietors would otherwise have full rights of injunction against libraries other than government libraries. Williams & Wilkins Co. v United States (1973) 203 Ct Cl 74, 487 F2d 1345, 21 ALR Fed 151, affd 420 US 376, 43 L Ed 2d 264, 95 S Ct 1344.

Copying of form from copyrighted form book and delivery of six copies to persons with whom defendant is dealing is not infringement but fair use; when plaintiff put on general market a book of forms, he implied right to their private use, especially in view of notice on cover. American Institute of Architects v Fenichel (1941, DC NY) 41 F Supp 146, 51 USPQ 29.

Statement in copyrighted tax manual that it is hoped that it will assist counties, cities, and taxing districts, is invitation to use and adoption, and use of forms in book is not unlawful. Aldrich v Remington Rand, Inc. (1942, DC Tex) 52 F Supp 732, 59 USPQ 210.

Doctrine of fair use arises from essential nature of copyright; all persons may make fair use of copyrighted work; occasionally, courts refer to right to use noncopyrightable material in copyrighted work as "fair use"; in this meaning, question is only conventional one of whether material was copyrightable; primarily, however, fair use relates to extent to which copyrightable material may be used without express license; in field of science and fine arts, broad scope is given to fair use; criticism is important and proper exercise of fair use; as one draws away from fields of science or fine arts, and enters fields where business competition exists, scope of fair use is narrowed but still exists; purpose for which use is made is of major importance, in consideration with other factors, in arriving at sound determination of extent of fair use; broader scope is permitted doctrine where field of learning is concerned and much narrower scope where taking is solely for commercial gain. Loew's, Inc. v Columbia Broadcasting System, Inc. (1955, DC Cal) 131 F Supp 165, 105 USPQ 302, affd (CA9 Cal) 239 F2d 532, 112 USPQ 11, affd 356 US 43, 2 L Ed 2d 583, 78 S Ct 667, 116 USPQ 479, reh den 356 US 934, 2 L Ed 2d 764, 78 S Ct 770.

Concept of fair use has been established and applied in cases involving scientific, medical, and historical materials; though technically infringement, it is allowed on ground that appropriation is reasonable and customary; whether use is fair use is matter of fact; thus, use of copyrighted book as source for article on historical personage could be termed fair, but use is not fair where article is not only based in large part on book but also mirrors manner and style in which copyright owner set down factual and historical material and expressed her thoughts and conclusions. Holdredge v Knight Publishing Corp. (1963, DC Cal) 214 F Supp 921, 136 USPQ 615.

Fair use by insubstantial copying is recognized for biographical works; fair use doctrine is applicable to biographic work to encourage public benefit in historical and biographical works and covers insubstantial copying from biography of Rosenbergs in work differing in every other respect. Gardner v Nizer (1975, DC NY) 391 F Supp 940, 185 USPQ 485, mod on other grounds (DC NY) 396 F Supp 63.

7. Amount and substantiality of work used [17 USCS § 107(3)]

If all common material in books was result of copying by defendant, only answer to charge of tortious plagiarism is that common matter was in public domain or was so trifling as not to count; since common matter is not so trifling that it can be ignored, question is whether borrowing, although substantial, was fair use; borrowing series of concrete incidents and details was not fair use. MacDonald v Du Maurier (1944, CA2 NY) 144 F2d 696, 62 USPQ 394, later app (DC NY) 75 F Supp 653 and later app (DC NY) 75 F Supp 655.

Large numbers of copies of medical journal articles made by government libraries at requests of individuals and other libraries are fair use in spite of volume of copying, considering large number of medical journals involved and reasonable limitations imposed by libraries on copying practices. Williams & Wilkins Co. v United States (1973) 203 Ct Cl 74, 487 F2d 1345, 21 ALR Fed 151, affd 420 US 376, 43 L Ed 2d 264, 95 S Ct 1344.

Although what was appropriated for defendants' play was comparatively small part of plaintiff's two volume biography, it formed substantial part of play and most of taking was verbatim; substantial taking is not matter of lines or inches but exists when part taken had merely value and formed greater part of one act of play. Harris v Miller (DC NY) 50 USPQ 306.

Broadcasting one entire part of four-part musical composition, time consumed being third of time required for performance of whole work, is not fair use. Associated Music Publishers, Inc. v Debs Memorial Radio Fund, Inc. (1942, DC NY) 46 F Supp 829, 54 USPQ 461, affd (CA2 NY) 141 F2d 852, 61 USPQ 161, cert den 323 US 766, 89 L Ed 613, 65 S Ct 120.

It is not fair use to copy four bars from copyrighted musical composition where such four bars are portion of composition upon which popular appeal and commercial success of composition depend. Robertson v Batten, Barton, Durstine & Osborn, Inc. (1956, DC Cal) 146 F Supp 795, 111 USPQ 251.

Use in novel of one seventh of page copied from 142 page copyrighted history is fair use, since copied portion represents neither substantial nor material part of history, was insignificant in value and extent of copyrighted material, and did not prejudice sale, diminish profits, or supersede objects of original work; copied material had no effect on sale of novel and did not relate to theme of history; copyright proprietor could not be damaged by publication of novel; action is de minimis. Toulmin v Rike-Kumler Co. (DC Ohio) 137 USPQ 533, affd (CA6 Ohio) 316 F2d 232, 137 USPQ 499, cert den 375 US 825, 11 L Ed 2d 58, 84 S Ct 66.

Using entire "Mickey Mouse March" in sound track of movie during sex scene is not fair use or excusable as parody where entire work is used, and use is preliminarily enjoined. Walt Disney Productions v Mature Pictures Corp. (1975, DC NY) 389 F Supp 1397, 186 USPQ 48.

Fair-use defense applies to copying of less than 3 percent of copyrighted letters in manner forming insignificant part of work, especially where matter copied is of historical interest and evidence does not show reduction of market for copyrighted letters. Meeropol v Nizer (1976, DC NY) 417 F Supp 1201, 191 USPQ 346, application den (US) 50 L Ed 2d 729, 97 S Ct 687.

8. Effect of use on market [17 USCS § 107(4)]

Both plaintiff's and defendant's books meet exactly same demand on same market and defendant unquestionably copied to avoid trouble or expense of independent work; this is unfair use. College Entrance Book Co. v Amsco Book Co. (1941, CA2 NY) 119 F2d 874, 49 USPQ 517.

Publication, without music, as part of epitaph of actress of chorus of song, written 24 years before concerning her, is fair use where there was no intent to infringe and defendant's use did not impair value of song or harm plaintiff in its distribution and part published could not be used for song. Broadway Music Corp. v F-R Pub. Corp. (1940, DC NY) 31 F Supp 817, 45 USPQ 309.

Magazine article concerning football team made fair use of copyrighted official team song by printing chorus as part of article since authorship of song was attributed to its author where article was not competitive with song and no music was set forth in article, reference to chorus being purely incidental and relatively unimportant to article as whole. Karll v Curtis Pub. Co. (1941, DC Wis) 39 F Supp 836, 51 USPQ 50.

Textbooks and scientific works present special problems and require special treatment in applying doctrine of fair use; those who for their own requirements avail themselves of instruction given in texts or who apply the art described therein do no more than act upon license author grants and do not thereby infringe; however, another's use of same methods of statement, whether in words or illustrations, in book published by other for teaching art infringes copyright; thus, it is not fair use, and defendant infringes, where defendant publishes book of solutions to problems in plaintiff's copyrighted textbook, especially since defendant's book profits defendant alone and since availability to students of book of solutions adversely affects prospects of collegiate adoption of textbook. Addison-Wesley Publishing Co. v Brown (1963, DC NY) 223 F Supp 219, 139 USPQ 47.

Despite exclusive rights granted by Copyright Act, courts recognize that copying or other appropriation of copyrighted work will not entail liability if it is reasonable or "fair"; doctrine is equitable and is so flexible as virtually to defy definition. Fair use presupposes good faith and fair dealing. Hope for commercial gain is not a significant factor; in view of public interest in having the fullest information available on murder of President Kennedy, it is fair use for defendant to make artistic copies of plaintiff's copyrighted photographs of death, and to include such copies in serious book on the subject, especially since book is not bought because of pictures, but because of defendant's theory and there is little, if any, injury to plaintiff, which is not in competition with defendant. Time Inc. v Bernard Geis Associates (1968, DC NY) 293 F Supp 130, 159 USPQ 663.

Copying is not excused under fair use doctrine because of amount copied, extensive paraphrasing, and commercial effect of plagiarization. Meredith Corp. v Harper & Row, Publishers, Inc. (1974, DC NY) 378 F Supp 686, 182 USPQ 609, affd (CA2 NY) 500 F2d 1221.

Fair use defense does not apply to copying of compilation of executive desk calendar by company active in desk calendar business for many years. Baldwin Cooke Co. v Keith Clark, Inc. (1974, DC Ill) 383 F Supp 650, 183 USPQ 209, affd without opinion (CA7 Ill) 505 F2d 1250 and supp op (DC Ill) 420 F Supp 404.

§ 108. Limitations on exclusive rights: Reproduction by libraries and archives

(a) Notwithstanding the provisions of section 106 [17 USCS § 106], it is not an infringement of copyright for a library or archives, or any of its employees acting within the scope of their employment, to reproduce no more than one copy or phonorecord of a work, or to distribute such copy or phonorecord, under the conditions specified by this section, if—

(1) the reproduction or distribution is made without any purpose of direct or indirect commercial advantage;

(2) the collections of the library or archives are (i) open to the public, or (ii) available not only to researchers affiliated with the library or archives or with the institution of which it is a part, but also to other persons doing research in a specialized field; and

(3) the reproduction or distribution of the work includes a notice of copyright.

(b) The rights of reproduction and distribution under this section apply to a copy or phonorecord of an unpublished work duplicated in facsimile form solely for purposes of preservation and security or for deposit for research use in another library or archives of the type described by clause (2) of subsection (a), if the copy or phonorecord reproduced is currently in the collections of the library or archives.

(c) The right of reproduction under this section applies to a copy or phonorecord of a published work duplicated in facsimile form solely for the purpose of replacement of a copy or phonorecord that is damaged, deteriorating, lost, or stolen, if the library or archives has, after a reasonable effort, determined that an unused replacement cannot be obtained at a fair price.

(d) The rights of reproduction and distribution under this section apply to a copy, made from the collection of a library or archives where the user makes his or her request or from that of another library or archives, of no more than one article or other contribution to a copyrighted collection or periodical issue, or to a copy or phonorecord of a small part of any other copyrighted work, if—

(1) the copy or phonorecord becomes the property of the user, and the library or archives has had no notice that the copy or phonorecord would be used for any purpose other than private study, scholarship, or research; and

(2) the library or archives displays prominently, at the place where orders are accepted, and includes on its order form, a warning of copyright in accordance with requirements that the Register of Copyrights in accordance with requirements that the Register of Copyrights shall prescribe by regulation.

(e) The rights of reproduction and distribution under this section apply to the entire work, or to a substantial part of it, made from the collection of a library or archives where the user makes his or her request or from that of another library or archives, if the library or archives has first determined, on the basis of a reasonable investigation, that a copy or phonorecord of the copyrighted work cannot be obtained at a fair price, if—

(1) the copy or phonorecord becomes the property of the user, and the library or archives has had no notice that the copy or phonorecord would be used for any purpose other than private study, scholarship, or research; and

(2) the library or archives displays prominently, at the place where orders are accepted, and includes on its order form, a warning of copyright in accordance with requirements that the Register of Copyrights shall prescribe by regulation.

(f) Nothing in this section—

(1) shall be construed to impose liability for copyright infringement upon a library or archives or its employees for the unsupervised use of

reproducing equipment located on its premises: *Provided,* That such equipment displays a notice that the making of a copy may be subject to the copyright law;

(2) excuses a person who uses such reproducing equipment or who requests a copy or phonorecord under subsection (d) from liability for copyright infringement for any such act, or for any later use of such copy or phonorecord, if it exceeds fair use as provided by section 107 [17 USCS § 107];

(3) shall be construed to limit the reproduction and distribution by lending of a limited number of copies and excerpts by a library or archives of an audiovisual news program, subject to clauses (1), (2), and (3) of subsection (a); or

(4) in any way affects the right of fair use as provided by section 107 [17 USCS § 107], or any contractual obligations assumed at any time by the library or archives when it obtained a copy or phonorecord of a work in its collections.

(g) The rights of reproduction and distribution under this section extend to the isolated and unrelated reproduction or distribution of a single copy or phonorecord of the same material on separate occasions, but do not extend to cases where the library or archives, or its employee—

(1) is aware or has substantial reason to believe that it is engaging in the related or concerted reproduction or distribution of multiple copies or phonorecords of the same material, whether made on one occasion or over a period of time, and whether intended for aggregate use by one or more individuals or for separate use by the individual members of a group; or

(2) engages in the systematic reproduction or distribution of single or multiple copies or phonorecords of material described in subsection (d): *Provided,* That nothing in this clause prevents a library or archives from participating in interlibrary arrangements that do not have, as their purpose or effect, that the library or archives receiving such copies or phonorecords for distribution does so in such aggregate quantities as to substitute for a subscription to or purchase of such work.

(h) The rights of reproduction and distribution under this section do not apply to a musical work, a pictorial, graphic or sculptural work, or a motion picture or other audiovisual work other than an audiovisual work dealing with news, except that no such limitation shall apply with respect to rights granted by subsections (b) and (c), or with respect to pictorial or graphic works published as illustrations, diagrams, or similar adjuncts to works of which copies are reproduced or distributed in accordance with subsections (d) and (e).

(i) Five years from the effective date of this Act, and at five-year intervals thereafter, the Register of Copyrights, after consulting with representatives of authors, book and periodical publishers, and other owners of copyrighted materials, and with representatives of library users and librarians, shall submit to the Congress a report setting forth the extent to which this section has achieved the intended statutory balancing of the rights of creators, and the needs of users. The report should also describe any problems that may have arisen, and present legislative or other recommendations, if warranted.

(Added Oct. 19, 1976, PL 94-553, Title I, § 101, 90 Stat 2546.)

HISTORY; ANCILLARY LAWS AND DIRECTIVES

References in text:
"Effective date of this Act", referred to in subsec. (i), is Jan. 1, 1978; see section 102 of Act Oct. 19, 1976, set out as a note preceding 17 USCS § 101.

Effective date of section:
Section 102 of Act Oct. 19, 1976, P.L. 94-553, 90 Stat. 2598 provided that this section "becomes effective on January 1, 1978".

CROSS REFERENCES

Fair use, 17 USCS § 107.
Librarian insulation from unwarranted liability for copyright infringement, 17 USCS § 504(c).
This section referred to in 17 USCS §§ 106, 117, 501, 602.

RESEARCH GUIDE

Annotations:
Unauthorized photocopying by library as infringement of copyright. 21 ALR Fed 212.

INTERPRETIVE NOTES AND DECISIONS

Extensive photocopying by government libraries of medical journal articles at request of individuals and other libraries is fair use where proprietor of copyright in journal articles copied has not shown it is harmed by copying practices, where medicine and medical research will be injured by holding copying practices to be infringements, and where accommodating interests of science with interests of publishers calls for legislative solution. Williams & Wilkins Co. v United States (1973) 203 Ct Cl 74, 487 F2d 1345, 21 ALR Fed 151, affd 420 US 376, 43 L Ed 2d 264, 95 S Ct 1344.

Annotations:
Unauthorized photocopying by library as infringement of copyright. 21 ALR Fed 212.

§ 109. Limitations on exclusive rights: Effect of transfer of particular copy or phonorecord

(a) Notwithstanding the provisions of section 106(3) [17 USCS § 106(3)], the owner of a particular copy or phonorecord lawfully made under this title [17 USCS §§ 101 et seq.], or any person authorized by such owner, is entitled, without the authority of the copyright owner, to sell or otherwise dispose of the possession of that copy or phonorecord.

(b) Notwithstanding the provisions of section 106(5) [17 USCS § 106(5)], the owner of a particular copy lawfully made under this title [17 USCS §§ 101 et seq.], or any person authorized by such owner, is entitled, without the authority of the copyright owner, to display that copy publicly, either directly or by the projection of no more than one image at a time, to viewers present at the place where the copy is located.

(c) The privileges prescribed by subsections (a) and (b) do not, unless authorized by the copyright owner, extend to any person who has acquired possession of the copy or phonorecord from the copyright owner, by rental, lease, loan, or otherwise, without acquiring ownership of it.
(Added Oct. 19, 1976, PL 94-553, Title I, § 101, 90 Stat 2548.)

HISTORY; ANCILLARY LAWS AND DIRECTIVES

Effective date of section:

Section 102 of Act Oct. 19, 1976, P.L. 94-553, 90 Stat. 2598 provided that this section "becomes effective on January 1, 1978".

CROSS REFERENCES

Exclusive right of display, 17 USCS § 106(5).
Fair use, 17 USCS § 107.
Exemption of certain performances and displays as limitations on exclusive rights, 17 USCS § 110.
Secondary transmissions as limitations on exclusive rights, 17 USCS § 111.
Disposition of phonorecord legally made under compulsory licensing, 17 USCS § 115.
Ownership of copyright as distinct from ownership of material object, 17 USCS § 202.
This section referred to in 17 USCS §§ 106, 117, 501.

INTERPRETIVE NOTES AND DECISIONS

Exclusive right to print, publish and vend does not create right to impose, by notice in book, limitation on price at which book shall be sold at retail by future purchasers. Bobbs-Merrill Co. v Straus (1908) 210 US 339, 52 L Ed 1086, 28 S Ct 722.

Copyright laws do not confer upon holder of copyright any further right after he has exercised his right to "vend." Straus & Straus v American Publishers' Asso. (1913) 231 US 222, 58 L Ed 192, 34 S Ct 84.

One who purchases unbound copyrighted volumes from copyright owner has right to bind and resell them. Kipling v G. P. Putnam's Sons (1903, CA2 NY) 120 F 631.

Lawful monopolist, owner of patent or copyright, cannot prevent purchasers from reselling at whatever prices they please. United States v Aluminum Co. of America (1945, CA2 NY) 148 F2d 416, 65 USPQ 6.

Person has right to buy and sell copyrighted books at any price he sees fit, when he has no knowledge of agreement between owner of copyright and sales agent that books were not to be sold under specified price. Clemens v Estes (1885, CC Mass) 22 F 899.

Right to control retail sale prices of books is not protected by copyright laws. Bobbs-Merrill Co. v Snellenburg (1904, CC Pa) 131 F 530.

Copyright law does not give publisher and owner of copyrighted book right to combine with other copyright owners for purpose of not permitting sale of any books to cut-price dealer. Mines v Scribner (1906, CC NY) 147 F 927.

Owner of copyright on certain set of books which have been sold by him cannot claim exclusive right to subsequent sale of such books when second-hand. Bureau of Nat. Literature v Sells (1914, DC Wash) 211 F 379.

Averment in answer that defendant obtained motion pictures from third persons who obtained license from plaintiff stated issuable defense. Pathe Exchange, Inc. v International Alliance, T.S.E., etc. (1932, DC NY) 3 F Supp 63.

Statute secures to copyright proprietor exclusive right to multiply copies but right to vend is confined to first sale of any one copy and cannot restrict future sale. Fawcett Publications, Inc. v Elliot Pub. Co. (1942, DC NY) 46 F Supp 717, 54 USPQ 367.

Copyright proprietor has no right of control over use or disposition of individual copies of copyrighted work once he has sold or otherwise disposed of them. C. M. Paula Co. v Logan (1973, DC Tex) 355 F Supp 189.

Where owner of copyright and plates for book sold set of plates and agreed that purchaser could sell books and that books should not be sold below certain price, this contract was binding on one who subsequently bought copyright and remainder of plates. Murphy v Christian Press Ass'n Pub. Co. (1899) 38 App Div 426, 56 NYS 597.

§ 110. Limitations on exclusive rights: Exemption of certain performances and displays

Notwithstanding the provisions of section 106 [17 USCS § 106], the following are not infringements of copyright:

(1) performance or display of a work by instructors or pupils in the course of face-to-face teaching activities of a nonprofit educational institution, in a classroom or similar place devoted to instruction, unless, in the case of a motion picture or other audiovisual work, the performance, or the display of individual images, is given by means of a copy that was not lawfully made under this title [17 USCS §§ 101 et seq.], and that the person responsible for the performance knew or had reason to believe was not lawfully made;

(2) performance of a nondramatic literary or musical work or display of a work, by or in the course of a transmission, if—

(A) the performance or display is a regular part of the systematic instructional activities of a governmental body or a nonprofit educational institution; and

(B) the performance or display is directly related and of material assistance to the teaching content of the transmission; and

(C) the transmission is made primarily for—

(i) reception in classrooms or similar places normally devoted to instruction, or

(ii) reception by persons to whom the transmission is directed because their disabilities or other special circumstances prevent their attendance in classrooms or similar places normally devoted to instruction, or

(iii) reception by officers or employees of governmental bodies as a part of their official duties or employment;

(3) performance of a nondramatic literary or musical work or of a dramatico-musical work of a religious nature, or display of a work, in the course of services at a place of worship or other religious assembly;

(4) performance of a nondramatic literary or musical work otherwise than in a transmission to the public, without any purpose of direct or indirect commercial advantage and without payment of any fee or other

compensation for the performance to any of its performers, promoters, or organizers, if—

(A) there is no direct or indirect admission charge; or

(B) the proceeds, after deducting the reasonable costs of producing the performance, are used exclusively for educational, religious, or charitable purposes and not for private financial gain, except where the copyright owner has served notice of objection to the performance under the following conditions;

(i) the notice shall be in writing and signed by the copyright owner or such owner's duly authorized agent; and

(ii) the notice shall be served on the person responsible for the performance at least seven days before the date of the performance, and shall state the reasons for the objection; and

(iii) the notice shall comply, in form, content, and manner of service, with requirements that the Register of Copyrights shall prescribe by regulation;

(5) communication of a transmission embodying a performance or display of a work by the public reception of the transmission on a single receiving apparatus of a kind commonly used in private homes, unless—

(A) a direct charge is made to see or hear the transmission; or

(B) the transmission thus received is further transmitted to the public;

(6) performance of a nondramatic musical work by a governmental body or a nonprofit agricultural or horticultural organization, in the course of an annual agricultural or horticultural fair or exhibition conducted by such body or organization; the exemption provided by this clause shall extend to any liability for copyright infringement that would otherwise be imposed on such body or organization, under doctrines of vicarious liability or related infringement, for a performance by a concessionnaire, business establishment, or other person at such fair or exhibition, but shall not excuse any such person from liability for the performance;

(7) performance of a nondramatic musical work by a vending establishment open to the public at large without any direct or indirect admission charge, where the sole purpose of the performance is to promote the retail sale of copies or phonorecords of the work, and the performance is not transmitted beyond the place where the establishment is located and is within the immediate area where the sale is occurring;

(8) performance of a nondramatic literary work, by or in the course of a transmission specifically designed for and primarily directed to blind or other handicapped persons who are unable to read normal printed material as a result of their handicap, or deaf or other handicapped persons who are unable to hear the aural signals accompanying a transmission of visual signals, if the performance is made without any purpose of direct or indirect commercial advantage and its transmission is made through the facilities of: (i) a governmental body; or (ii) a noncommercial educational broadcast station (as defined in section 397

of title 47) [47 USCS § 397]; or (iii) a radio subcarrier authorization (as defined in 47 CFR 73.293–73.295 and 73.593–73.595); or (iv) a cable system (as defined in section 111(f)) [17 USCS § 111(f)].

(9) performance on a single occasion of a dramatic literary work published at least ten years before the date of the performance, by or in the course of a transmission specifically designed for and primarily directed to blind or other handicapped persons who are unable to read normal printed material as a result of their handicap, if the performance is made without any purpose of direct or indirect commercial advantage and its transmission is made through the facilities of a radio subcarrier authorization referred to in clause (8)(iii), *Provided,* That the provisions of this clause shall not be applicable to more than one performance of the same work by the same performers or under the auspices of the same organization.

(Added Oct. 19, 1976, PL 94-553, Title I, § 101, 90 Stat 2549.)

HISTORY; ANCILLARY LAWS AND DIRECTIVES

Effective date of section:
Section 102 of Act Oct. 19, 1976, P.L. 94-553, 90 Stat. 2598 provided that this section "becomes effective on January 1, 1978".

CROSS REFERENCES

Copyright owner's exclusive right to make dramatizations, adaptations, or other derivative works, 17 USCS § 106(2).
Copyright owner's cause of action against unauthorized distributor, 17 USCS § 106(3).
Public display to viewers present at place where copy is located, 17 USCS § 109(b).
This section referred to in 17 USCS §§ 106, 111, 112, 117, 118, 501.

RESEARCH GUIDE

Annotations:
Construction and application of so-called "charitable and educational exemption" of Copyright Act (17 USCS § 104). 23 ALR Fed 974.

Law Review Articles:
Korman, Performance rights in music under §§ 110 and 118 of the 1976 Copyright Act. 22 New York Law School Law Rev 521.

INTERPRETIVE NOTES AND DECISIONS

1. Generally
2. Educational or instructional use [17 USCS § 110(1,2)]
3. Religious performance [17 USCS § 110(3)]
4. Single receiver performance [17 USCS § 110(5)]
5. Vending establishment performance [17 USCS § 110(7)]

1. Generally

Where copyright owner has licensed broadcaster to perform copyrighted musical composition publicly for profit, reception of radio broadcast of composition by owner of restaurant, which broadcast is heard by owner, his employees and his customers through several ceiling speakers, even though it may be assumed that reception occurred publicly for profit, does not constitute "performance" of copyrighted work, and thus does not constitute copyright infringement. Twentieth Century Music Corp. v Aiken (1975) 422 US 151, 45 L Ed 2d 84, 95 S Ct 2040.

2. Educational or instructional use [17 USCS § 110(1,2)]

Nonprofit corporation which operates radio broadcasting station for philanthropic and educational purposes infringed by broadcasting on sustaining program quarter of copyrighted musical composition; third of radio time is sold to advertisers; sustaining programs build up listener appeal and provide inducement to advertisers; it is not important whether profit from advertising programs go to corporation, its employees, or advertisers since performance of composition was for profit and copyright owner had right to preclude each of them; corporation's station manager was also liable since he was paid for services and exercised own judgment in choosing music broadcast. Associated Music Publishers, Inc. v Debs Memorial Radio Fund (1944, CA2 NY) 141 F2d 852, 61 USPQ 161, cert den 323 US 766, 89 L Ed 613, 65 S Ct 120.

Use of person's copyrighted work by such person, in instructing others who are permitted to take copies, does not constitute abandonment to public. Bartlette v Crittenden (1847, CC Ohio) F Cas No 1082.

Predecessor section amounts to protection in favor of those persons who do not perform publicly for profit musical composition—as in case of street parades, school, educational, or similar public occasions and exhibitions. Hubbell v Royal Pastime Amusement Co. (1917, DC NY) 242 F 1002.

Student organization showed bootleg film of Charlie Chaplin's "Modern Times" on campus and using university facilities; university cannot be held vicariously liable for violation of copyright, for it derived no financial benefit from the exhibition. Roy Export Co. Establishment v Trustees of Columbia University (1972, DC NY) 344 F Supp 1350.

Annotations:

Construction and application of so-called "charitable and educational exemption" of Copyright Act (17 USCS § 104). 23 ALR Fed 974.

3. Religious performance [17 USCS § 110(3)]

Predecessor provision granting "charitable and educational exemption" to performances by church choirs or vocal societies, includes performances of opera or rock opera; rock opera company did not qualify as exempt church choir where performances were not given in churches or as part of church services but rather were highly professional productions presented in school auditoriums and theaters across country; mere fact that performers were under direction of several priests did not turn professional touring company into church choir; nor did rock opera company qualify as exempt vocal society where there was no evidence that members of company had clearly marked identity as unit distinguished by similar beliefs, particular concerns and same interests. Robert Stigwood Group, Ltd. v O'Reilly (1972, DC Conn) 346 F Supp 376, 23 ALR Fed 961, 175 USPQ 403, revd on other grounds (CA2 Conn) 530 F2d 1096, cert den 429 US 848, 50 L Ed 2d 121, 97 S Ct 135.

4. Single receiver performance [17 USCS § 110(5)]

Copyright holder granting to radio broadcasting station license to perform musical composition cannot bring suit against cafe owner for infringement when cafe owner permits song to be heard in his cafe through his radio receiver. Buck v Debaum (1929, DC Cal) 40 F2d 734.

Playing radio receiver through four speakers in restaurant for employees and customers is not "performance" although public and for profit, and does not infringe copyright or require license from copyright holder. Twentieth Century Music Corp. v Aiken (1975) 422 US 151, 45 L Ed 2d 84, 95 S Ct 2040, 186 USPQ 65.

Hotel proprietor, in entertaining his guests, through instrumentality of radio receiving set and loud speakers installed in hotel and under his control, is liable for unauthorized use of copyrighted musical composition, though he does not select pieces played from broadcasting station or have any contractual relation with such station, since his act amounts to performance within meaning of the statute. Buck v Jewell-La Salle Realty Co. (1931) 283 US 191, 75 L Ed 971, 51 S Ct 410, 76 ALR 1266.

Cafe owner tuning in on radio for entertainment of his patrons and giving them rendition of copyrighted musical composition as to which broadcasting station had license was not liable to copyright owner. Buck v Debaum (1929, DC Cal) 40 F2d 734.

Playing at motion-picture theater without separate charge for music is performance for profit. M. Witmark & Sons v Pastime Amusement Co. (1924, DC SC) 298 F 470, affd (CA4 SC) 2 F2d 1020.

Hotel proprietor installing two-channel radio system, making available programs of two radio stations, with amplifying apparatus, output of which is led through cable and fed into distribution wires having termini in some 1900 individual guest rooms, concealed in night tables, on face of each of which is switch with designation plate above, containing figures 1 and 2, enabling guest by turning knob to either figure to tune in on whichever of two available programs is desired was liable for unauthorized public performance of copyrighted musical composition broadcast on one of such programs, though turning of knob and selection of program is done by guest. Society of European Stage Authors & Composers, Inc. v New York Hotel Statler Co. (1937, DC NY) 19 F Supp 1, 34 USPQ 6.

5. Vending establishment performance [17 USCS § 110(7)]

Prior statute does not authorize playing of record over store's loud speaker system of copyrighted musical composition even in connection with sale of authorized records of such composition; musical compositions are publicly performed for profit since playing of records is commercially beneficial to store in that it aids in creating attractive shopping atmosphere. Chappell & Co. v Middletown Farmers Market & Auction Co. (1964, CA3 Pa) 334 F2d 303, 142 USPQ 54.

Department store maintaining radio department in which it sells at retail radio equipment is liable as for performing "publicly for profit" copyrighted song, where it maintains broadcasting station, for which it charges no admission fees to dining hall connected therewith, and expense of broadcasting is charged as general expenses of business; and it is no defense that song is thereby advertised. M. Witmark & Sons v L. Bamberger & Co. (1923, DC NJ) 291 F 776.

§ 111. Limitations on exclusive rights: Secondary transmissions

(a) Certain secondary transmissions exempted. The secondary transmission of a primary transmission embodying a performance or display of a work is not an infringement of copyright if—

(1) the secondary transmission is not made by a cable system, and consists entirely of the relaying, by the management of a hotel, apartment house, or similar establishment, of signals transmitted by a broadcast station licensed by the Federal Communications Commission, within the local service area of such station, to the private lodgings of guests or residents of such establishment, and no direct charge is made to see or hear the secondary transmission; or

(2) the secondary transmission is made solely for the purpose and under the conditions specified by clause (2) of section 110 [17 USCS § 110]; or

(3) the secondary transmission is made by any carrier who has no direct or indirect control over the content or selection of the primary transmission or over the particular recipients of the secondary transmission, and whose activities with respect to the secondary transmission consist solely of providing wires, cables, or other communications channels for the use of others: *Provided,* That the provisions of this clause extend only to the activities of said carrier with respect to secondary transmissions and do not exempt from liability the activities of others with respect to their own primary or secondary transmissions; or

(4) the secondary transmission is not made by a cable system but is made by a governmental body, or other nonprofit organization, without any purpose of direct or indirect commercial advantage, and without charge to the recipients of the secondary transmission other than assessments necessary to defray the actual and reasonable costs of maintaining and operating the secondary transmission service.

(b) Secondary transmission of primary transmission to controlled group. Notwithstanding the provisions of subsections (a) and (c), the secondary transmission to the public of a primary transmission embodying a performance or display of a work is actionable as an act of infringement under section 501 [17 USCS § 501], and is fully subject to the remedies provided by sections 502 through 506 and 509 [17 USCS §§ 502–506, 509], if the primary transmission is not made for reception by the public at large but is controlled and limited to reception by particular members of the public: *Provided,* however, That such secondary transmission is not actionable as an act of infringement if—

(1) the primary transmission is made by a broadcast station licensed by the Federal Communications Commission; and

(2) the carriage of the signals comprising the secondary transmission is required under the rules, regulations, or authorizations of the Federal Communications Commission; and

(3) the signal of the primary transmitter is not altered or changed in any way by the secondary transmitter.

(c) Secondary transmissions by cable systems. (1) Subject to the provisions of clauses (2), (3), and (4) of this subsection, secondary transmissions to the public by a cable system of a primary transmission made by a broadcast station licensed by the Federal Communications Commission or by an appropriate governmental authority of Canada or Mexico and embodying a performance or display of a work shall be subject to compulsory licensing upon compliance with the requirements of subsection (d) where the carriage of the signals comprising the secondary transmission is permissible under the rules, regulations, or authorizations of the Federal Communications Commission.

(2) Notwithstanding the provisions of clause (1) of this subsection, the willful or repeated secondary transmission to the public by a cable system of a primary transmission made by a broadcast station licensed by the Federal Communications Commission or by an appropriate governmental authority of Canada or Mexico and embodying a performance or display of a work is actionable as an act of infringement under section 501 [17 USCS § 501], and is fully subject to the remedies provided by sections 502 through 506 and 509 [17 USCS §§ 502–506, 509], in the following cases:

(A) where the carriage of the signals comprising the secondary transmission is not permissible under the rules, regulations, or authorizations of the Federal Communications Commission; or

(B) where the cable system has not recorded the notice specified by subsection (d) and deposited the statement of account and royalty fee required by subsection (d).

(3) Notwithstanding the provisions of clause (1) of this subsection and subject to the provisions of subsection (e) of this section, the secondary transmission to the public by a cable system of a primary transmission

made by a broadcast station licensed by the Federal Communications Commission or by an appropriate governmental authority of Canada or Mexico and embodying a performance or display of a work is actionable as an act of infringement under section 501 [17 USCS § 501], and is fully subject to the remedies provided by sections 502 through 506 and sections 509 and 510 [17 USCS §§ 502–506, 509, 510], if the content of the particular program in which the performance or display is embodied, or any commercial advertising or station announcements transmitted by the primary transmitter during, or immediately before or after, the transmission of such program, is in any way willfully altered by the cable system through changes, deletions, or additions, except for the alteration, deletion, or substitution of commercial advertisements performed by those engaged in television commercial advertising market research: *Provided,* That the research company has obtained the prior consent of the advertiser who has purchased the original commercial advertisement, the television station broadcasting that commercial advertisement, and the cable system performing the secondary transmission: *And provided further,* That such commercial alteration, deletion, or substitution is not performed for the purpose of deriving income from the sale of that commercial time.

(4) Notwithstanding the provisions of clause (1) of this subsection, the secondary transmission to the public by a cable system of a primary transmission made by a broadcast station licensed by an appropriate governmental authority of Canada or Mexico and embodying a performance or display of a work is actionable as an act of infringement under section 501 [17 USCS § 501], and is fully subject to the remedies provided by sections 502 through 506 and section 509 [17 USCS §§ 502–506, 509], if (A) with respect to Canadian signals, the community of the cable system is located more than 150 miles from the United States-Canadian border and is also located south of the forty-second parallel of latitude, or (B) with respect to Mexican signals, the secondary transmission is made by a cable system which received the primary transmission by means other than direct interception of a free space radio wave emitted by such broadcast television station, unless prior to April 15, 1976, such cable system was actually carrying, or was specifically authorized to carry, the signal of such foreign station on the system pursuant to the rules, regulations, or authorizations of the Federal Communications Commission.

(d) Compulsory license for secondary transmissions by cable systems. (1) For any secondary transmission to be subject to compulsory licensing under subsection (c), the cable system shall, at least one month before the date of the commencement of operations of the cable system or within one hundred and eighty days after the enactment of this Act [enacted Oct. 19, 1976], whichever is later, and thereafter within thirty days after each occasion on which the ownership or control or the signal carriage complement of the cable system changes, record in the Copyright Office a notice including a statement of the identity and address of the person who owns or operates the secondary transmission service or has power to exercise primary control over it, together with the name and location of the primary transmitter or primary transmitters whose signals are regularly carried by the cable system, and thereafter, from time to time, such further information as the Register of Copyrights, after consultation with the Copyright Royalty Tribunal (if and when the Tribunal has been constituted), shall prescribe by regulation to carry out the purpose of this clause.

(2) A cable system whose secondary transmissions have been subject to compulsory licensing under subsection (c) shall, on a semiannual basis, deposit with the Register of Copyrights, in accordance with requirements that the Register shall, after consultation with the Copyright Royalty Tribunal (if and when the Tribunal has been constituted), prescribe by regulation—

(A) a statement of account, covering the six months next preceding, specifying the number of channels on which the cable system made secondary transmissions to its subscribers, the names and locations of all primary transmitters whose transmissions were further transmitted by the cable system, the total number of subscribers, the gross amounts paid to the cable system for the basic service of providing secondary transmissions of primary broadcast transmitters, and such other data as the Register of Copyrights may, after consultation with the Copyright Royalty Tribunal (if and when the Tribunal has been constituted), from time to time prescribe by regulation. Such statement shall also include a special statement of account covering any nonnetwork television programming that was carried by the cable system in whole or in part beyond the local service area of the primary transmitter, under rules, regulations, or authorizations of the Federal Communications Commission permitting the substitution or addition of signals under certain circumstances, together with logs showing the times, dates, stations, and programs involved in such substituted or added carriage; and

(B) except in the case of a cable system whose royalty is specified in subclause (C) or (D), a total royalty fee for the period covered by the statement, computed on the basis of specified percentages of the gross receipts from subscribers to the cable service during said period for the basic service of providing secondary transmissions of primary broadcast transmitters, as follows:

(i) 0.675 of 1 per centum of such gross receipts for the privilege of further transmitting any nonnetwork programming of a primary transmitter in whole or in part beyond the local service area of such primary transmitter, such amount to be applied against the fee, if any, payable pursuant to paragraphs (ii) through (iv);

(ii) 0.675 of 1 per centum of such gross receipts for the first distant signal equivalent;

(iii) 0.425 of 1 per centum of such gross receipts for each of the second, third, and fourth distant signal equivalents;

(iv) 0.2 of 1 per centum of such gross receipts for the fifth distant signal equivalent and each additional distant signal equivalent thereafter; and

in computing the amounts payable under paragraph (ii) through (iv), above, any fraction of a distant signal equivalent shall be computed at its fractional value and, in the case of any cable system located partly within and partly without the local service area of a primary transmitter, gross receipts shall be limited to those gross receipts derived from subscribers located without the local service area of such primary transmitter; and

(C) if the actual gross receipts paid by subscribers to a cable system for the period covered by the statement for the basic service of providing secondary transmissions of primary broadcast transmitters total $80,000 or less, gross receipts of the cable system for the purpose of this subclause shall be computed by subtracting from such actual gross receipts the amount by which $80,000 exceeds such actual gross receipts, except that in no case shall a cable system's gross receipts be reduced to less than $3,000. The royalty fee payable under this subclause shall be 0.5 of 1 per centum, regardless of the number of distant signal equivalents, if any; and

(D) if the actual gross receipts paid by subscribers to a cable system for the period covered by the statement, for the basic service of providing secondary transmissions of primary broadcast transmitters, are more than $80,000 but less than $160,000, the royalty fee payable under this subclause shall be (i) 0.5 of 1 per centum of any gross receipts up to $80,000; and (ii) 1 per centum of any gross receipts in excess of $80,000 but less than $160,000, regardless of the number of distant signal equivalents, if any.

(3) The Register of Copyrights shall receive all fees deposited under this section and, after deducting the reasonable costs incurred by the Copyright Office under this section, shall deposit the balance in the Treasury of the United States, in such manner as the Secretary of the Treasury directs. All funds held by the Secretary of the Treasury shall be invested in interest-bearing United States securities for later distribution with interest by the Copyright Royalty Tribunal as provided by this title [17 USCS §§ 101 et seq.]. The Register shall submit to the Copyright Royalty Tribunal, on a semiannual basis, a compilation of all statements of account covering the relevant six-month period provided by clause (2) of this subsection.

(4) The royalty fees thus deposited shall, in accordance with the procedures provided by clause (5), be distributed to those among the following copyright owners who claim that their works were the subject of secondary transmissions by cable systems during the relevant semiannual period:

(A) any such owner whose work was included in a secondary transmission made by a cable system of a nonnetwork television program in whole or in part beyond the local service area of the primary transmitter; and

(B) any such owner whose work was included in a secondary transmission identified in a special statement of account deposited under clause (2)(A); and

(C) any such owner whose work was included in nonnetwork programing consisting exclusively of aural signals carried by a cable system in whole or in part beyond the local service area of the primary transmitter of such programs.

(5) The royalty fees thus deposited shall be distributed in accordance with the following procedures:

(A) During the month of July in each year, every person claiming to be entitled to compulsory license fees for secondary transmissions shall file a claim with the Copyright Royalty Tribunal, in accordance with requirements that the Tribunal shall prescribe by regulation. Notwithstanding any provisions of the antitrust laws, for purposes of this clause any claimants may agree among themselves as to the proportionate division of compulsory licensing fees among them, may lump their claims together and file them jointly or as a single claim, or may designate a common agent to receive payment on their behalf.

(B) After the first day of August of each year, the Copyright Royalty Tribunal shall determine whether there exists a controversy concerning the distribution of royalty fees. If the Tribunal determines that no such controversy exists, it shall, after deducting its reasonable administrative costs under this section, distribute such fees to the copyright owners entitled, or to their designated agents. If the Tribunal finds the existence of a controversy, it shall, pursuant to chapter 8 of this title [17 USCS §§ 801 et seq.], conduct a proceeding to determine the distribution of royalty fees.

(C) During the pendency of any proceeding under this subsection, the Copyright Royalty Tribunal shall withhold from distribution an amount sufficient to satisfy all claims with respect to which a controversy exists, but shall have discretion to proceed to distribute any amounts that are not in controversy.

(e) **Nonsimultaneous secondary transmissions by cable systems.** (1) Notwithstanding those provisions of the second paragraph of subsection (f) relating to nonsimultaneous secondary transmissions by a cable system, any such transmissions are actionable as an act of infringement under section 501 [17 USCS § 501], and are fully subject to the remedies provided by sections 502 through 506 and sections 509 and 510 [17 USCS §§ 502–506, 509, 510], unless—

(A) the program on the videotape is transmitted no more than one time to the cable system's subscribers; and

(B) the copyrighted program, episode, or motion picture videotape, including the commercials contained within such program, episode, or picture, is transmitted without deletion or editing; and

(C) an owner or officer of the cable system (i) prevents the duplication of the videotape while in the possession of the system, (ii) prevents unauthorized duplication while in the possession of the facility making the videotape for the system if the system owns or controls the facility, or takes reasonable precautions to prevent such duplication if it does not own or control the facility, (iii) takes adequate precautions to prevent duplication while the tape is being transported, and (iv) subject to clause (2), erases or destroys, or causes the erasure or destruction of, the videotape; and

(D) within forty-five days after the end of each calendar quarter, an owner or officer of the cable system executes an affidavit attesting (i) to the steps and precautions taken to prevent duplication of the videotape, and (ii) subject to clause (2), to the erasure or destruction of all videotapes made or used during such quarter; and

(E) such owner or officer places or causes each such affidavit, and affidavits received pursuant to clause (2)(C), to be placed in a file, open to public inspection, at such system's main office in the community where the transmission is made or in the nearest community where such system maintains an office; and

(F) the nonsimultaneous transmission is one that the cable system would be authorized to transmit under the rules, regulations, and authorizations of the Federal Communications Commission in effect at the time of the nonsimultaneous transmission if the transmission had been made simultaneously, except that this subclause shall not apply to inadvertent or accidental transmissions.

(2) If a cable system transfers to any person a videotape of a program nonsimultaneously transmitted by it, such transfer is actionable as an act of infringement under section 501 [17 USCS § 501], and is fully subject to the remedies provided by sections 502 through 506 and 509 [17 USCS §§ 502–506, 509], except that, pursuant to a written, nonprofit contract providing for the equitable sharing of the costs of such videotape and its transfer, a videotape nonsimultaneously transmitted by it, in accordance with clause (1), may be transferred by one cable system in Alaska to another system in Alaska, by one cable system in Hawaii permitted to make such nonsimultaneous transmissions to another such cable system in Hawaii, or by one cable system in Guam, the Northern Mariana Islands, or the Trust Territory of the Pacific Islands, to another cable system in any of those three territories, if—

(A) each such contract is available for public inspection in the offices of the cable systems involved, and a copy of such contract is filed, within thirty days after such contract is entered into, with the Copyright Office (which Office shall make each such contract available for public inspection); and

(B) the cable system to which the videotape is transferred complies with clause (1)(A), (B), (C)(i), (iii), and (iv), and (D) through (F); and (C) such system provides a copy of the affidavit required to be made in accordance with clause (1)(D) to each cable system making a previous nonsimultaneous transmission of the same videotape.

(3) This subsection shall not be construed to supersede the exclusivity protection provisions of any existing agreement, or any such agreement hereafter entered into, between a cable system and a television broadcast station in the area in which the cable system is located, or a network with which such station is affiliated.

(4) As used in this subsection, the term "videotape", and each of its variant forms, means the reproduction of the images and sounds of a program or programs broadcast by a television broadcast station licensed by the Federal Communications Commission, regardless of the nature of the material objects, such as tapes or films, in which the reproduction is embodied.

(f) Definitions. As used in this section, the following terms and their variant forms mean the following:

A "primary transmission" is a transmission made to the public by the transmitting facility whose signals are being received and further transmitted by the secondary transmission service, regardless of where or when the performance or display was first transmitted.

A "secondary transmission" is the further transmitting of a primary transmission simultaneously with the primary transmission, or nonsimultaneously with the primary transmission if by a "cable system" not located in whole or in part within the boundary of the forty-eight contiguous States, Hawaii, or Puerto Rico: *Provided, however,* That a nonsimultaneous further transmission by a cable system located in Hawaii of a primary transmission shall be deemed to be a secondary transmission if the carriage of the television broadcast signal comprising such further transmission is permissible under the rules, regulations, or authorizations of the Federal Communications Commission.

A "cable system" is a facility, located in any State, Territory, Trust Territory, or Possession, that in whole or in part receives signals transmitted or programs broadcast by one or more television broadcast stations licensed by the Federal Communications Commission, and makes secondary transmissions of such signals or programs by wires, cables, or other communications channels to subscribing members of the public who pay for such service. For purposes of determining the royalty fee under subsection (d)(2), two or more cable systems in contiguous communities under common ownership or control or operating from one headend shall be considered as one system.

The "local service area of a primary transmitter", in the case of a television broadcast station, comprises the area in which such station is entitled to insist upon its signal being retransmitted by a cable system pursuant to the rules, regulations, and authorizations of the Federal Communications Commission in effect on April 15, 1976, or in the case of a television broadcast station licensed by an appropriate governmental authority of Canada or Mexico, the area in which it would be entitled to insist upon its signal being retransmitted if it were a television broadcast station subject to such rules, regulations, and authorizations. The "local service area of a primary transmitter", in the case of a radio broadcast station, comprises the primary service area of such station, pursuant to the rules and regulations of the Federal Communications Commission.

A "distant signal equivalent" is the value assigned to the secondary transmission of any nonnetwork television programing carried by a cable system in whole or in part beyond the local service area of the primary transmitter of such programing. It is computed by assigning a value of one to each independent station and a value of one-quarter to each network station and noncommercial educational station for the nonnetwork programing so carried pursuant to the rules, regulations, and authorizations of the Federal Communications Commission. The foregoing values for independent, network, and noncommercial educational stations are subject, however, to the following exceptions and limitations. Where the rules and regulations of the Federal Communications Commission require a cable system to omit the further transmission of a particular program and such rules and regulations also permit the substitution of another program embodying a performance or display of a work in place of the omitted transmission, or where such rules and regulations in effect on the date of enactment of this Act [enacted Oct. 19, 1976) permit a cable system, at its election, to effect such deletion and substitution of a nonlive program or to carry additional programs not transmitted by primary transmitters within whose local service area the cable system is located, no value shall be assigned for the substituted or additional program; where the rules, regulations, or authorizations of the Federal Communications Commission in effect on the date of enactment of this Act [enacted Oct. 19, 1976] permit a cable system, at its election, to omit the further transmission of a particular program and such rules, regulations, or authorizations also permit the substitution of another program embodying a performance or display of a work in place of the omitted transmission, the value assigned for the substituted or additional program shall be, in the case of a live program, the value of one full distant signal equivalent multiplied by a fraction that has as its numerator the number of days in the year in which such substitution occurs and as its denominator the number of days in the year. In the case of a station carried pursuant to the late-night or specialty programming rules of the Federal Communications Commission, or a station carried on a part-time basis where full-time carriage is not possible because the cable system lacks the activated channel capacity to retransmit on a full-time basis all signals which it is authorized to carry, the values for independent, network, and noncommercial educational stations set forth above, as the case may be, shall be multiplied by a fraction which is equal to the ratio of the broadcast hours of such station carried by the cable system to the total broadcast hours of the station.

A "network station" is a television broadcast station that is owned or operated by, or affiliated with, one or more of the television networks in the United States providing nationwide transmissions, and that transmits a substantial part of the programming supplied by such networks for a substantial part of that station's typical broadcast day.

An "independent station" is a commercial television broadcast station other than a network station.

A "noncommercial educational station" is a television station that is a noncommercial educational broadcast station as defined in section 397 of title 47 [47 USCS § 397].
(Added Oct. 19, 1976, P. L. 94-553, Title I, § 101, 90 Stat. 2550.)

HISTORY; ANCILLARY LAWS AND DIRECTIVES

References in text:
"Antitrust laws", referred to in subsec. (d)(5)(A), appear generally as 15 USCS §§ 1 et seq.

Effective date of section:
Section 102 of Act Oct. 19, 1976, P. L. 94-553, 90 Stat. 2598 provided that this section "becomes effective on January 1, 1978".

CROSS REFERENCES

"Transmission program" defined, 17 USCS § 101.
"Transmit" defined, 17 USCS § 101.
Instructional transmission, 17 USCS § 110(2).
Copyright Royalty Tribunal, 17 USCS § 801.
Noncommercial educational broadcast station, 47 USCS § 397.
This section referred to in 17 USCS §§ 106, 110, 117, 501, 510, 801, 804, 809.

RESEARCH GUIDE

Law Review Articles:
Meyer, The Feat of Houdini or How the New Act distangles the CATV-Copyright Knot. 22 New York Law School Law Rev 545.

INTERPRETIVE NOTES AND DECISIONS

1. Generally
2. Source of primary transmissions
3. Function of secondary transmitter

1. Generally

Community antenna systems are not performers of television programs which they carry within meaning of predecessor section, since they merely receive program for their subscribers who cannot have large antennas needed for reception; therefore, community antenna system which received and passed on to its subscribers certain copyrighted motion pictures without license was not infringer. Fortnightly Corp. v United Artists Television, Inc. (1968) 392 US 390, 20 L Ed 2d

1176, 88 S Ct 2084, reh den 393 US 902, 21 L Ed 2d 190, 89 S Ct 65.

Preparation of video tapes of copyrighted materials infringed upon the rights of copyright owner, and dissemination of programs through cable system constitutes an infringement. Walt Disney Productions v Alaska Television Network, Inc. (1969, DC Wash) 310 F Supp 1073, 164 USPQ 211.

2. Source of primary transmissions

Importation by CATV systems of "distant" signals from one community into another do not constitute a "performance" under Copyright Act; CATV system does not lose its status as nonbroadcaster, and thus "nonperformer", for copyright purposes when signals it carries are from distant rather than local sources. Teleprompter Corp. v Columbia Broadcasting System, Inc. (1974) 415 US 394, 39 L Ed 2d 415, 94 S Ct 1129.

3. Function of secondary transmitter

Mere quantitative contribution cannot be the proper test to determine copyright liability in the context of television broadcasting; resolution of issue depends upon a determination of function

that alleged infringer (CATV) plays in total process of television broadcasting and reception; CATV operators, like viewers and unlike broadcasters, do not perform copyrighted programs that they receive and carry. Fortnightly Corp. v United Artists Television, Inc. (1968) 392 US 390, 20 L Ed 2d 1176, 88 S Ct 2084, reh den 393 US 902, 21 L Ed 2d 190, 89 S Ct 65.

Development and implementation by CATV systems of program orientation, sale of commercials, and interconnection with other CATV systems, even though they may allow CATV systems to compete more effectively with broadcasters for television market, are simply extraneous to determination of copyright infringement liability relative to reception and retransmission of broadcasters' programs; even though origination service and reception service are sold to subscriber as package by a CATV system, they remain separate and different operations and system does become "performer" of broadcast programming when it offers both origination and reception service but remains nonperformer when it offers only reception service. Teleprompter Corp. v Columbia Broadcasting System, Inc. (1974) 415 US 394, 39 L Ed 2d 415, 94 S Ct 1129.

§ 112.   Limitations on exclusive rights: Ephemeral recordings

(a) Notwithstanding the provisions of section 106 [17 USCS § 106], and except in the case of a motion picture or other audiovisual work, it is not an infringement of copyright for a transmitting organization entitled to transmit to the public a performance or display of a work, under a license or transfer of the copyright or under the limitations on exclusive rights in sound recordings specified by section 114(a) [17 USCS § 114(a)], to make no more than one copy or phonorecord of a particular transmission program embodying the performance or display, if—

(1) the copy or phonorecord is retained and used solely by the transmitting organization that made it, and no further copies or phonorecords are reproduced from it; and

(2) the copy or phonorecord is used solely for the transmitting organization's own transmissions within its local service area, or for purposes of archival preservation or security; and

(3) unless preserved exclusively for archival purposes, the copy or phonorecord is destroyed within six months from the date the transmission program was first transmitted to the public.

(b) Notwithstanding the provisions of section 106 [17 USCS § 106], it is not an infringement of copyright for a governmental body or other nonprofit organization entitled to transmit a performance or display of a work, under section 110(2) [17 USCS § 110(2)] or under the limitations on exclusive rights in sound recordings specified by section 114(a) [17 USCS § 114(a)], to make no more than thirty copies or phonorecords of a particular transmission program embodying the performance or display, if—

(1) no further copies or phonorecords are reproduced from the copies or phonorecords made under this clause; and

(2) except for one copy or phonorecord that may be preserved exclusively for archival purposes, the copies or phonorecords are destroyed within seven years from the date the transmission program was first transmitted to the public.

(c) Notwithstanding the provisions of section 106 [17 USCS § 106], it is not an infringement of copyright for a governmental body or other nonprofit organization to make for distribution no more than one copy or phonorecord, for each transmitting organization specified in clause (2) of this subsection, of a particular transmission program embodying a performance of a nondramatic musical work of a religious nature, or of a sound recording of such a musical work, if—

(1) there is no direct or indirect charge for making or distributing any such copies or phonorecords; and

(2) none of such copies or phonorecords is used for any performance other than a single transmission to the public by a transmitting organization entitled to transmit to the public a performance of the work under a license or transfer of the copyright; and

(3) except for one copy or phonorecord that may be preserved exclusively for archival purposes, the copies or phonorecords are all destroyed within one year from the date the transmission program was first transmitted to the public.

(d) Notwithstanding the provisions of section 106 [17 USCS § 106], it is not an infringement of copyright for a governmental body or other nonprofit organization entitled to transmit a performance of a work under section 110(8) [17 USCS § 110(8)] to make no more than ten copies or phonorecords embodying the performance, or to permit the use of any such copy or phonorecord by any governmental body or nonprofit organization entitled to transmit a performance of a work under section 110(8) [17 USCS § 110(8)], if—

(1) any such copy or phonorecord is retained and used solely by the organization that made it, or by a governmental body or nonprofit organization entitled to transmit a performance of a work under section 110(8) [17 USCS § 110(8)], and no further copies or phonorecords are reproduced from it; and

(2) any such copy or phonorecord is used solely for transmissions authorized under section 110(8) [17 USCS § 110(8)], or for purposes of archival preservation or security; and

(3) the governmental body or nonprofit organization permitting any use of any such copy or phonorecord by any governmental body or non-

profit organization under this subsection does not make any charge for such use.

(e) The transmission program embodied in a copy or phonorecord made under this section is not subject to protection as a derivative work under this title [17 USCS §§ 101 et seq.] except with the express consent of the owners of copyright in the preexisting works employed in the program. (Added Oct. 19, 1976, P. L. 94-553, Title I, § 101, 90 Stat. 2558.)

HISTORY; ANCILLARY LAWS AND DIRECTIVES

Effective date of section:
Section 102 of Act Oct. 19, 1976, P. L. 94-553, 90 Stat. 2598 provided that this section "becomes effective on January 1, 1978".

CROSS REFERENCES

Copyrightability of derivative work, 17 USCS § 103.
Nonprofit organization free to transmit performance or display of work, 17 USCS § 110(2).
Exemption in case of transmissions to blind and deaf, 17 USCS § 110(8).
Compulsory license, 17 USCS § 111.
"Local service area" defined, 17 USCS § 111(f).
Transmission of sound recording, 17 USCS § 114.
This section referred to in 17 USCS §§ 106, 117, 501.

§ 113. Scope of exclusive rights in pictorial, graphic, and sculptural works

(a) Subject to the provisions of subsections (b) and (c) of this section, the exclusive right to reproduce a copyrighted pictorial, graphic, or sculptural work in copies under section 106 [17 USCS § 106] includes the right to reproduce the work in or on any kind of article, whether useful or otherwise.

(b) This title [17 USCS §§ 101 et seq.] does not afford, to the owner of copyright in a work that portrays a useful article as such, any greater or lesser rights with respect to the making, distribution, or display of the useful article so portrayed than those afforded to such works under the law, whether title 17 [17 USCS §§ 101 et seq.] or the common law or statutes of a State, in effect on December 31, 1977, as held applicable and construed by a court in an action brought under this title [17 USCS §§ 101 et seq.].

(c) In the case of a work lawfully reproduced in useful articles that have been offered for sale or other distribution to the public, copyright does not include any right to prevent the making, distribution, or display of pictures or photographs of such articles in connection with advertisements or commentaries related to the distribution or display of such articles, or in connection with news reports. (Added Oct. 19, 1976, P. L. 94-553, Title I, § 101, 90 Stat. 2560.)

HISTORY; ANCILLARY LAWS AND DIRECTIVES

Effective date of section:

Section 102 of Act Oct. 19, 1976, P. L. 94-553, 90 Stat. 2598 provided that this section "becomes effective on January 1, 1978".

CROSS REFERENCES

"Pictorial, graphic, and sculptural works" defined, 17 USCS § 101.
"Useful article" defined, 17 USCS § 101.
This section referred to in 17 USCS §§ 106, 117, 501.

RESEARCH GUIDE

Am Jur:

18 Am Jur 2d, Copyright and Literary Property § 48.

Forms:

6 Federal Procedural Forms L Ed, Copyrights § 17:54.

Annotations:

Statutory copyright protection of "works of art". 98 L Ed 644.

INTERPRETIVE NOTES AND DECISIONS

Statuettes of male and female dancing figures made of semivitreous china are copyrightable as works of art notwithstanding that they are intended for use and are used as bases for table lamps, with electric wiring, sockets, and lamp shades attached. Mazer v Stein (1953) 347 US 201, 98 L Ed 630, 74 S Ct 460.

Copyrightability of reproduction of coin bank requires judgment of fact as to modicum of novelty and creativity, and where skill and judgment is required to make reproduction, it is copyrightable insofar as differing from original.

L. Batlin & Son, Inc. v Snyder (1975, CA2) 187 USPQ 721.

Defendant is free to copy plaintiff's merchandise or its own merchandise, but it cannot copy plaintiff's copyrighted copy of it. Blumcraft of Pittsburgh v Newman Bros., Inc. (1968, DC Ohio) 159 USPQ 166.

Where plaintiff develops artistic idea used on ashtrays in pursuance of defendant's commission and order, and sells ashtrays to defendant, right to reproduce idea thus created is vested in defendant. Otten v Curtis Publishing Co. (NY Sup Ct) 91 USPQ 222.

§ 114. Scope of exclusive rights in sound recordings

(a) The exclusive rights of the owner of copyright in a sound recording are limited to the rights specified by clauses (1), (2), and (3) of section 106 [17 USCS § 106(1)–(3)], and do not include any right of performance under section 106(4) [17 USCS § 106(4)].

(b) The exclusive right of the owner of copyright in a sound recording under clause (1) of section 106 [17 USCS § 106(1)] is limited to the right to duplicate the sound recording in the form of phonorecords, or of copies of motion pictures and other audiovisual works, that directly or indirectly recapture the actual sounds fixed in the recording. The exclusive right of the owner of copyright in a sound recording under clause (2) of section 106 [17 USCS § 106(2)] is limited to the right to prepare a derivative work in which the actual sounds fixed in the sound recording are rearranged, remixed, or otherwise altered in sequence or quality. The exclusive rights of the owner of copyright in a sound recording under clauses (1) and (2) of section 106 [17 USCS § 106(1) and (2)] do not extend to the making or duplication of another sound recording that consists entirely of an independent fixation of other sounds, even though such sounds imitate or simulate those in the copyrighted sound recording. The exclusive rights of the owner of copyright in a sound recording under clauses (1), (2), and (3) of section 106 [17 USCS § 106(1)–(3)] do not apply to sound recordings included in educational television and radio programs (as defined in section 397 of title 47) [47 USCS § 397] distributed or transmitted by or through public broadcasting entities (as defined by section 118(g) [17 USCS § 118(g)]): *Provided,* That copies or phonorecords of said programs are not commercially distributed by or through public broadcasting entities to the general public.

(c) This section does not limit or impair the exclusive right to perform publicly, by means of a phonorecord, any of the works specified by section 106(4) [17 USCS § 106(4)].

(d) On January 3, 1978, the Register of Copyrights, after consulting with representatives of owners of copyrighted materials, representatives of the broadcasting, recording, motion picture, entertainment industries, and arts organizations, representatives of organized labor and performers of copyrighted materials, shall submit to the Congress a report setting forth recommendations as to whether this section should be amended to provide for performers and copyright owners of copyrighted material any performance rights in such material. The report should describe the status of such rights in foreign countries, the views of major interested parties, and specific legislative or other recommendations, if any.

(Added Oct. 19, 1976, P. L. 94-553, Title I, § 101, 90 Stat. 2560.)

HISTORY; ANCILLARY LAWS AND DIRECTIVES

Effective date of section:
Section 102 of Act Oct. 19, 1976, P. L. 94-553, 90 Stat. 2598 provided that this section "becomes effective on January 1, 1978".

CROSS REFERENCES

Exclusive right of owner of copyright in sound recording, 17 USCS § 106(2).
Right of performance, 17 USCS § 106(4).
"Public broadcasting entity" defined, 17 USCS § 118(g).
This section referred to in 17 USCS §§ 106, 112, 117, 501.

RESEARCH GUIDE

Forms:
6 Federal Procedural Forms L Ed, Copyrights § 17:53.

Annotations:
Making, selling, or distributing counterfeit or "bootleg" tape recordings or phonograph records as violation of federal law. 25 ALR Fed 207.

Law Review Articles:
Meyers, Sound Recordings and the new Copyright Act. 22 New York Law School Law Rev 573.

INTERPRETIVE NOTES AND DECISIONS

One who acquires right of mechanical reproduction of musical work, either by contract, or by complying with prescribed requirements, does not acquire right of publicly performing for profit copyrighted work. Irving Berlin, Inc. v Daigle (1929, CA5 La) 31 F2d 832.

Possession of matrices for making phonograph records does not carry with it right to performance; right to reproduce performances engraved on matrices is intangible and its situs is at domicile of its owner. Capitol Records, Inc. v Mercury Record Corp. (1952, DC NY) 109 F Supp 330, 95 USPQ 177, affd (CA2 NY) 221 F2d 657, 105 USPQ 163.

Annotations:

Making, selling, or distributing counterfeit or "bootleg" tape recordings or phonograph records as violation of federal law. 25 ALR Fed 207.

§ 115. Scope of exclusive rights in nondramatic musical works: Compulsory license for making and distributing phonorecords

In the case of nondramatic musical works, the exclusive rights provided by clauses (1) and (3) of section 106 [17 USCS § 106(1)–(3)], to make and to distribute phonorecords of such works, are subject to compulsory licensing under the conditions specified by this section.

(a) **Availability and scope of compulsory license.** (1) When phonorecords of a nondramatic musical work have been distributed to the public in the United States under the authority of the copyright owner, any other person may, by complying with the provisions of this section, obtain a compulsory license to make and distribute phonorecords of the work. A person may obtain a compulsory license only if his or her primary purpose in making phonorecords is to distribute them to the public for private use. A person may not obtain a compulsory license for use of the work in the making of phonorecords duplicating a sound recording fixed by another, unless: (i) such sound recording was fixed lawfully; and (ii) the making of the phonorecords was authorized by the owner of copyright in the sound recording or, if the sound recording was fixed before February 15, 1972, by any person who fixed the sound recording pursuant to an express license from the owner of the copyright in the musical work or pursuant to a valid compulsory license for use of such work in a sound recording.

(2) A compulsory license includes the privilege of making a musical arrangement of the work to the extent necessary to conform it to the style or manner of interpretation of the performance involved, but the arrangement shall not change the basic melody or fundamental character of the work, and shall not be subject to protection as a derivative work under this title [17 USCS §§ 101 et seq.], except with the express consent of the copyright owner.

(b) **Notice of intention to obtain compulsory license.** (1) Any person who wishes to obtain a compulsory license under this section shall, before or within thirty days after making, and before distributing any phonorecords of the work, serve notice of intention to do so on the copyright owner. If the registration or other public records of the Copyright Office do not identify the copyright owner and include an address at which notice can be served, it shall be sufficient to file the notice of intention in the Copyright Office. The notice shall comply, in form, content, and manner of service, with requirements that the Register of Copyrights shall prescribe by regulation.

(2) Failure to serve or file the notice required by clause (1) forecloses the possibility of a compulsory license and, in the absence of a negotiated license, renders the making and distribution of phonorecords actionable as acts of infringement under section 501 [17 USCS § 501] and fully subject to the remedies provided by sections 502 through 506 and 509 [17 USCS §§ 502–506, 509].

(c) Royalty payable under compulsory license. (1) To be entitled to receive royalties under a compulsory license, the copyright owner must be identified in the registration or other public records of the Copyright Office. The owner is entitled to royalties for phonorecords made and distributed after being so identified, but is not entitled to recover for any phonorecords previously made and distributed.

(2) Except as provided by clause (1), the royalty under a compulsory license shall be payable for every phonorecord made and distributed in accordance with the license. For this purpose, a phonorecord is considered "distributed" if the person exercising the compulsory license has voluntarily and permanently parted with its possession. With respect to each work embodied in the phonorecord, the royalty shall be either two and three-fourths cents, or one-half of one cent per minute of playing time or fraction thereof, whichever amount is larger.

(3) Royalty payments shall be made on or before the twentieth day of each month and shall include all royalties for the month next preceding. Each monthly payment shall be made under oath and shall comply with requirements that the Register of Copyrights shall prescribe by regulation. The Register shall also prescribe regulations under which detailed cumulative annual statements of account, certified by a certified public accountant, shall be filed for every compulsory license under this section. The regulations covering both the monthly and the annual statements of account shall prescribe the form, content, and manner of certification with respect to the number of records made and the number of records distributed.

(4) If the copyright owner does not receive the monthly payment and the monthly and annual statements of account when due, the owner may give written notice to the licensee that, unless the default is remedied within thirty days from the date of the notice, the compulsory license will be automatically terminated. Such termination renders either the making or the distribution, or both, of all phonorecords for which the royalty has not been paid, actionable as acts of infringement under section 501 [17 USCS § 501] and fully subject to the remedies provided by sections 502 through 506 and 509 [17 USCS §§ 502–506, 509].

(Added Oct. 19, 1976, P. L. 94-553, Title I, § 101, 90 Stat. 2561.)

HISTORY; ANCILLARY LAWS AND DIRECTIVES

Effective date of section:
Section 102 of Act Oct. 19, 1976, P. L. 94-553, 90 Stat. 2598 provided that this section "becomes effective on January 1, 1978".

Other provisions:
Operation under compulsory license before January 1, 1978. Act Oct. 19, 1976, P. L. 94-553, Title I, § 106, 90 Stat. 2599, provided: "In any case where, before January 1, 1978, a person has lawfully made parts of instruments serving to reproduce mechanically a copyrighted work under the compulsory license provisions of section 1(e) of title 17 [former 17 USCS § 1(e)] as it existed on December 31, 1977, such person may continue to make and distribute such parts embodying the same mechanical reproduction without obtaining a new compulsory license under the terms of section 115 of title 17 [17 USCS § 115] as amended by the first section of this Act [section 101 of Act Oct. 19, 1976, which appears as 17 USCS §§ 101 et seq.]. However, such parts made on or after January 1, 1978, constitute phonorecords and are otherwise subject to the provisions of said section 115 [17 USCS § 115]."

CROSS REFERENCES

Acts of infringement, 17 USCS § 501.
Remedies for infringement, 17 USCS §§ 502–506.
Copyright Royalty Tribunal, 17 USCS § 801.
This section referred to in 17 USCS §§ 106, 115 note, 117, 501, 708, 801, 804.

RESEARCH GUIDE

Am Jur:
18 Am Jur 2d, Copyright and Literary Property §§ 93, 97.

Annotations:
Making, selling, or distributing counterfeit or "bootleg" tape recordings or phonograph records as violation of federal law. 25 ALR Fed 207.

Law Review Articles:
The Sound Recording Act of 1971. 40 George Washington LR 964, July 1972.

INTERPRETIVE NOTES AND DECISIONS

1. Generally
2. Duplication of previous recordings [17 USCS § 115(a)]
3. Notice and report requirements [17 USCS § 115(b)]
4. Royalties required, generally [17 USCS § 115(c)]
5. —Damages for noncompliance

1. Generally
Object of compulsory license provision is pre-vention of monopoly or favoritism in granting of right to reproduce musical work mechanically; license to use song as may be needed "in the manufacture of sound records in any form whatsoever" does not give licensee right to include in sale of its music rolls printed copies of words of song. Standard Music Roll Co. v Mills (1917, CA3 NJ) 241 F 360.

One who has become "compulsory licensee" of right to make phonograph records of song, and paid royalties under such license is estopped from denying its licensor's title. G. Ricordi & Co. v Columbia Graphophone Co. (1920, CA2 NY) 263 F 354.

Once copyright owner makes musical work available to any record manufacturer, it becomes subject to compulsory licensing provisions of Copyright Act and may be copied by others simply upon giving notice of intention and thereafter paying statutory royalty. Shapiro, Bernstein & Co. v Remington Records, Inc. (1959, CA2 NY) 265 F2d 263, 121 USPQ 109.

Where copyrights cover mechanical reproductions of musical compositions under predecessor section, copyright holder has no right to exclusive use thereof once it knowingly acquiesces in their use; any person who complies with compulsory licensing provisions may manufacture records containing copyrighted songs without becoming liable as infringer. American Metropolitan Enterprises, Inc. v Warner Bros. Records, Inc. (1968, CA2 NY) 389 F2d 903, 157 USPQ 69.

Where master records, matrices, and stampers were manufactured in United States and then shipped to Canada where final records were made, records were manufactured in United States and plaintiff was entitled to recover for manufacture of such records. G. Ricordi & Co. v Columbia Graphophone Co. (1920, DC NY) 270 F 822.

Practical effect of predecessor section is to limit bargaining rights of copyright proprietor (1) as to persons with whom he may refuse to contract, (2) as to times when he may contract, (3) as to duration of contract, and (4), most importantly, as to maximum royalty he may receive, irrespective of commercial value of particular musical composition. ABC Music Corp. v Janov (1960, DC Cal) 186 F Supp 443, 126 USPQ 429.

Defendant's preparation of tapes (which are sent by defendant to persons abroad to be used by said persons to manufacture phonograph records), which contain renditions of plaintiff's copyrighted musical compositions, violates predecessor statute; defendant's act in producing tapes in United States involves defendant as joint tort feasor in "manufacture." Famous Music Corp. v Seeco Records, Inc. (1961, DC NY) 201 F Supp 560, 132 USPQ 342.

Compulsory license provision of predecessor section does not authorize defendants to make mechanical reproductions of plaintiffs' copyrighted musical compositions in United States although records embodying such compositions

have been made and sold abroad. Beechwood Music Corp. v Vee Jay Records, Inc. (1964, DC NY) 226 F Supp 8, 140 USPQ 409, affd (CA2 NY) 328 F2d 728, 140 USPQ 499.

Widow of orchestra leader granted to motion picture producer right to portray leader in photoplay and to simulate leader's style of playing; agreement made no reference to making recordings from photoplay's sound track; negative covenant, that producer should not so use sound track as to compete with widow's royalty-yielding license to third party to sell original recordings of orchestra, is not implied; producer made sound track under copyright licenses which widow neither controlled nor granted; widow had no protectible interest as such in leader's renditions, and recording of sound tracks for commercial purposes did not involve new medium of entertainment; license to third party was in existence and known to all parties at time of contract with producer and, if widow wished to restrict producer's use of sound track, she should have expressly so provided in contract. Miller v Universal Pictures Co. (1960) 11 App Div 2d 47, 201 NYS2d 632, 126 USPQ 303, amd on other grounds 13 App Div 2d 473, 214 NYS2d 645, affd 10 NY2d 972, 224 NYS2d 662, 180 NE2d 248.

A manufacturing defendant is entitled to avail himself of the compulsory license provisions of the copyright laws. Duchess Music Corp. v Stern (1971, DC Ariz) 331 F Supp 127, 170 USPQ 391, revd on other grounds (CA9 Ariz) 458 F2d 1305, 22 ALR Fed 475, cert den 409 US 847, 34 L Ed 2d 88, 93 S Ct 52.

The copyright constitutional provisions must be construed broadly to cover technical advances unknown and not anticipated at the time of adoption of the constitution; 1971 amendments to the copyright act to cover sound recordings is such an advance and is valid; fact that the 1909 revision contained a compulsory licensing provision in respect to copyrighted musical compositions while the 1971 revision does not make similar provisions in respect to sound recordings does not invalidate the 1971 amendments. Shaab v Kleindienst (1972, DC Dist Col) 345 F Supp 589.

Annotations:

Making, selling, or distributing counterfeit or "bootleg" tape recordings or phonograph records as violation of federal law. 25 ALR Fed 207.

2. Duplication of previous recordings [17 USCS § 115(a)]

Ricordi v Columbia, 270 F 822, did not hold that all first eight steps stated therein must be taken to constitute defendant manufacturer of phonograph record; likewise, defendants' reliance on Marks v Foullon, 77 USPQ 502, as establishing that defendant, who performs only ninth step, is not manufacturer, is unfounded since that case was dealing with meaning of "manufacturer" for purposes of statutory royalty imposed upon authorized manufacturers rather than with word "manufacture" as act of infringement, which is tort; all persons concerned with infringement are jointly and severally liable; whether separate act performed by each defendant constitutes "manufacture" in latter sense, two defendants, acting in concert, manufactured infringing discs inasmuch as one defendant produced master stamper which other defendant used to press infringing records. Reeve Music Co. v Crest Records, Inc. (1960, CA2 NY) 285 F2d 546, 128 USPQ 24.

Defendant's manufacture of cassette and tape recordings of phonograph records legitimately issued by plaintiffs from plaintiffs' copyrighted musical compositions does not fall within the compulsory license provision; making of exact and identical copies of copyrighted compositions does not constitute "similar use" under this section. Duchess Music Corp. v Stern (1972, CA9 Ariz) 458 F2d 1305, 22 ALR Fed 475, cert den 409 US 847, 34 L Ed 2d 88, 93 S Ct 52.

Bootleg tapes which are reproductions of another's recordings, and which are marketed under different label, are not protected by the Copyright Act. United States v Shultz (1973, CA6 Tenn) 482 F2d 1179, 25 ALR Fed 201.

Compulsory licensing provisions do not give tape pirate right to copy and sell licensed recorded works of musical compositions, and possible antitrust violations or unclean hands of plaintiff are insufficient to alter this conclusion. Edward B. Marks Music Corp. v Colorado Magnetics, Inc. (1974, CA10 Okla) 497 F2d 285, 181 USPQ 129, cert den 419 US 1120, 42 L Ed 2d 819, 95 S Ct 801.

Compulsory license provisions protect rights of composer and publisher and do not allow making identical copy of recorded version of copyrighted musical composition, because such use is not "similar" to use made by original licensee in making original recording. Jondora Music Publishing Co. v Melody Recordings, Inc. (1974, CA3 NJ) 506 F2d 392, 184 USPQ 326, cert den 421 US 1012, 44 L Ed 2d 680, 95 S Ct 2417.

Dubbing tape recorded copies from successful records and selling copies in competition with music publishers is not protected by compulsory license provision and infringes copyright, and this meets congressional intent, encourages creativity and competition, and is consistent with judicial authority. Fame Publishing Co. v Alabama Custom Tape, Inc. (1975, CA5 Ala) 507 F2d 667, 184 USPQ 577, cert den 423 US 841, 46 L Ed 2d 61, 96 S Ct 73.

Maker of mechanical records under compulsory license clause may use copyrighted original composition in their manufacture but he cannot copy and duplicate records made by another licensee. Aeolian Co. v Royal Music Roll Co. (1912, DC NY) 196 F 926.

Tape piracy provisions of Copyright Act are not unconstitutional as denying freedom of speech or not granting tape pirates compulsory license; Act never granted compulsory license to parties dubbing recordings. United States v Bodin (1974, DC Okla) 375 F Supp 1265, 183 USPQ 345.

Compulsory license provisions do not permit infringer to reproduce sound recordings, so that counterclaim by alleged recording infringer for damages from plaintiff's false marking of symbol "P" is dismissed. Columbia Broadcasting System, Inc. v Newman (1974, DC NM) 184 USPQ 18.

Tape pirates are not entitled to avail themselves of compulsory licensing provision and infringe copyright because tape piracy is not "similar use" contemplated by compulsory licensing provision. Heilman v Levi (1975, DC Wis) 391 F Supp 1106, 185 USPQ 682.

Compulsory licensing provisions allow "similar use" of recorded music, but do not allow tape piracy by dubbing duplicates directly from previous recordings. GAI Audio of New York, Inc. v Columbia Broadcasting System, Inc. (1975) 27 Md App 172, 340 A2d 736, 188 USPQ 75.

3. Notice and report requirements [17 USCS § 115(b)]

Failure to file notice of license to use music only of song is no defense to suit for infringement of copyright of words. Standard Music Roll Co. v Mills (1917, CA3 NJ) 241 F 360.

Correspondence between owner and reproducer did not create personal license, but was sufficient as notice. Leo Feist, Inc. v American Music Roll Co. (1918, CA3 Pa) 251 F 245.

Notice given during pendency of infringement suit, is effective. G. Ricordi & Co. v Columbia Graphophone Co. (1920, CA2 NY) 263 F 354.

Copyright owners' failure to comply with required notice bars collection of statutory royalties for mechanical reproduction of musical composition; Trading with the Enemy Act [50 USCS Appx. §§ 1 et seq.] does not clothe attorney general with power to avoid these conditions, which are set up by copyright statute and which have not been repealed; rule that terms of copyright statute must be substantially complied with or no advantage can be taken of its provision is applicable. Biltmore Music Corp. v Kittinger (1956, CA9 Cal) 238 F2d 373, 111 USPQ 228, cert den 352 US 954, 1 L Ed 2d 243, 77 S Ct 327.

"Notice of use" provision of predecessor section is designed to notify all other persons that musical composition has become available for mechanical reproduction; however, statute is silent as to when notice shall be filed beyond necessary implication that it must be done before suit is instituted if successful defense is to be avoided; court holds that failure to file timely notice of use bars suit for acts of infringement occurring prior to time notice was filed, but not for acts occurring afterwards. Norbay Music, Inc. v King Records, Inc. (1961, CA2 NY) 290 F2d 617, 129 USPQ 336.

Since plaintiff licensed others to reproduce mechanically words and music of copyrighted song, plaintiff's failure to file notice of use bars action wherein complaint charges that defendant mechanically reproduced copyrighted composition. Stasny Music Corp. v Santly-Joy, Inc. (1957, DC NY) 156 F Supp 795, 116 USPQ 137, affd (CA2 NY) 249 F2d 957, 116 USPQ 130.

Parties may substitute private licensing agreements for protection afforded by predecessor section; fact that they departed from exact terms of statute by varying accounting period, lowering royalties for songs, and dispensing with notice requirements does not support contention that agreement was private licensing agreement enforceable in state courts only; absent clear showing that parties did not intend relationship to be governed by statute's compulsory license provisions, it will not be presumed that departure from exact terms of statute was intended as waiver of its protection. Joy Music, Inc. v Seeco Records, Inc. (1958, DC NY) 166 F Supp 549, 119 USPQ 460.

Relatively minor variations from provisions of predecessor section are not sufficient to make private licensing agreement since parties intended that their relationship be governed by compulsory license provisions and not by private licensing agreement. Shapiro, Bernstein & Co. v Gabor (1966, DC NY) 266 F Supp 613, 152 USPQ 170.

Notice of intention to use should be filed before musical works are reproduced; it is too late for one, who acquired illegal records, to file notice four days before being sued for infringement; payment of royalty is based on number of albums manufactured, not upon number manufactured and sold. Payments tendered on basis of number manufactured and sold may be rejected.

Pickwick Music Corp. v Record Productions, Inc. (1968, DC NY) 292 F Supp 39, 159 USPQ 228.

It is no excuse that the defendants relied upon a custom or trade practice of awaiting completion of manufacture and distribution of a recording before filing a notice of intention to use copyrighted material. Leo Feist, Inc. v Apollo Records N. Y. Corp. (1969, DC NY) 300 F Supp 32, 163 USPQ 24, affd (CA2 NY) 418 F2d 1249.

Where a district court cannot, as it interprets the copyright laws, prohibit future manufacture of tape recordings which serve to reproduce a plaintiff's copyrighted compositions, it can nonetheless require a close compliance with the compulsory license reporting provision of the laws. Duchess Music Corp. v Stern (1971, DC Ariz) 331 F Supp 127, 170 USPQ 391, revd on other grounds (CA9 Ariz) 458 F2d 1305, 22 ALR Fed 475, cert den 409 US 847, 34 L Ed 2d 88, 93 S Ct 52.

In view of provisions requiring statutory copyright holder of musical composition to file notice of use of composition on records, thereby authorizing others to manufacture records upon payment of royalties, common law copyright holder who sells records of unpublished compositions may not recover against infringing record manufacturer until statutory copyright is obtained and notice of use is filed, whereupon suit may be maintained for subsequent infringements. Rosette v Rainbo Record Mfg. Corp. (1973, DC NY) 354 F Supp 1183, affd (CA2 NY) 546 F2d 461.

4. Royalties required, generally [17 USCS § 115(c)]

Defendant offered no testimony before master in support of item of royalty and therefore court must consider schedule of defendant's costs of manufacture amended by plaintiff's exception to royalties, thus reducing costs by amount allowed for royalties. Davilla v Brunswick-Balke Collender Co. (1938, CA2 NY) 94 F2d 567, 36 USPQ 398, cert den 304 US 572, 82 L Ed 1536, 58 S Ct 1040.

Relief against seller of unauthorized records of copyrighted music is not restricted to injunction, but seller is liable for royalty; however, general damage provisions are not applicable to infringement of musical copyright by mechanical reproduction; basic royalty is both maximum and minimum; there is no discretion as to this basic amount. Shapiro, Bernstein & Co. v Goody (1957, CA2 NY) 248 F2d 260, 115 USPQ 36, cert den 355 US 952, 2 L Ed 2d 529, 78 S Ct 536.

Although "complete defense" provision of predecessor section applies by its terms only to actions for "infringement," bar is not avoided by suing for "royalties" under that such section rather than for infringement; since once-recorded composition is available to all third parties upon payment of two-cent royalty, manufacture at this point can be "unauthorized" only in that third party fails to make required payments; thus, nonpayment of statutory royalty is infringement; therefore, "complete defense" provision applies to all actions for unpaid statutory royalties, however they may be named. Norbay Music, Inc. v King Records, Inc. (1961, CA2 NY) 290 F2d 617, 129 USPQ 336.

Exclusive right to perform copyrighted musical composition for profit is limited by compulsory license provision, which provides that, once composition is recorded, anyone else may record it on paying two cents for each record manufactured. Miller v Goody (1954, DC NY) 125 F Supp 348, 103 USPQ 292.

There is clear unmistakable intent in predecessor section that number manufactured, not number sold, is royalty criterion; although copyright holder may agree to accept less than statute entitles him to, custom and usage whereby holder is paid only for phonograph records made and sold, rather than for records manufactured, cannot change meaning of language of statute or add gloss thereto so as to dilute rights conferred. Southern Music Publishing Co. v Seeco Records, Inc. (1960, DC NY) 200 F Supp 704, 132 USPQ 682.

Custom and usage may not be invoked to relieve defendant of clear-cut obligations imposed by predecessor section; thus, fact that plaintiffs may have accepted payments for certain period on basis of sales, rather than on basis of records manufactured as required by statute, does not require continuance of waiver of payments of royalties on records manufactured but not sold. Famous Music Corp. v Seeco Records, Inc. (1961, DC NY) 201 F Supp 560, 132 USPQ 342.

5. —Damages for noncompliance

Defendants having deliberately frustrated proof of amount of their statutory liability for manufacturing records of copyrighted musical compositions, either by failing to disclose facts reasonably known to them or by failing to keep accurate production records, number of records manufactured may be proven by expert opinion testimony; court has wide discretion in receiving evidence, whether by way of expert opinion or otherwise, where defendants availed themselves of benefits of Copyright Act, but failed to comply with its burdens; all doubts as to volume of unknown production should be resolved strictly against defendants; court will not permit commercial piracy to produce illegal gains immune from recovery. Shapiro, Bernstein & Co. v Remington Records, Inc. (1959, CA2 NY) 265 F2d 263, 121 USPQ 109.

Tendency is not to look for piracy or willfulness as requisite to increased award under predecessor section, but rather to hold that mere violation of statutory obligations imposed upon record manufacturers who appropriate to themselves compulsory license is sufficient to justify treble-damage award. ABC Music Corp. v Janov (1960, DC Cal) 186 F Supp 443, 126 USPQ 429.

§ 116. Scope of exclusive rights in nondramatic musical works: Public performances by means of coin-operated phonorecord players

(a) Limitation on exclusive right. In the case of a nondramatic musical work embodied in a phonorecord, the exclusive right under clause (4) of section 106 [17 USCS § 106(4)] to perform the work publicly by means of a coin-operated phonorecord player is limited as follows:

(1) The proprietor of the establishment in which the public performance takes place is not liable for infringement with respect to such public performance unless—

(A) such proprietor is the operator of the phonorecord player; or

(B) such proprietor refuses or fails, within one month after receipt by registered or certified mail of a request, at a time during which the certificate required by clause (1)(C) of subsection (b) is not affixed to the phonorecord player, by the copyright owner, to make full disclosure, by registered or certified mail, of the identity of the operator of the phonorecord player.

(2) The operator of the coin-operated phonorecord player may obtain a compulsory license to perform the work publicly on that phonorecord player by filing the application, affixing the certificate, and paying the royalties provided by subsection (b).

(b) Recordation of coin-operated phonorecord player, affixation of certificate, and royalty payable under compulsory license. (1) Any operator who wishes to obtain a compulsory license for the public performance of works on a coin-operated phonorecord player shall fulfill the following requirements:

(A) Before or within one month after such performances are made available on a particular phonorecord player, and during the month of January in each succeeding year that such performances are made available on that particular phonorecord player, the operator shall file in the Copyright Office, in accordance with requirements that the Register of Copyrights, after consultation with the Copyright Royalty Tribunal (if and when the Tribunal has been constituted), shall prescribe by regulation, an application containing the name and address of the operator of the phonorecord player and the manufacturer and serial number or other explicit identification of the phonorecord player, and deposit with the Register of Copyrights a royalty fee for the current calendar year of $8 for that particular phonorecord player. If such performances are made available on a particular phonorecord player for the first time after July 1 of any year, the royalty fee to be deposited for the remainder of that year shall be $4.

(B) Within twenty days of receipt of an application and a royalty fee pursuant to subclause (A), the Register of Copyrights shall issue to the applicant a certificate for the phonorecord player.

(C) On or before March 1 of the year in which the certificate prescribed by subclause (B) of this clause is issued, or within ten days after the date of issue of the certificate, the operator shall affix to the particular phonorecord player, in a position where it can be readily examined by the public, the certificate, issued by the Register of Copyrights under subclause (B), of the latest application made by such operator under subclause (A) of this clause with respect to that phonorecord player.

(2) Failure to file the application, to affix the certificate, or to pay the royalty required by clause (1) of this subsection renders the public performance actionable as an act of infringement under section 501 [17 USCS § 501] and fully subject to the remedies provided by sections 502 through 506 and 509 [17 USCS §§ 502–506, 509].

(c) Distribution of royalties. (1) The Register of Copyrights shall receive all fees deposited under this section and, after deducting the reasonable costs incurred by the Copyright Office under this section, shall deposit the balance in the Treasury of the United States, in such manner as the Secretary of the Treasury directs. All funds held by the Secretary of the

Treasury shall be invested in interest-bearing United States securities for later distribution with interest by the Copyright Royalty Tribunal as provided by this title [17 USCS §§ 101 et seq.]. The Register shall submit to the Copyright Royalty Tribunal, on an annual basis, a detailed statement of account covering all fees received for the relevant period provided by subsection (b).

(2) During the month of January in each year, every person claiming to be entitled to compulsory license fees under this section for performances during the preceding twelve-month period shall file a claim with the Copyright Royalty Tribunal, in accordance with requirements that the Tribunal shall prescribe by regulation. Such claim shall include an agreement to accept as final, except as provided in section 810 of this title [17 USCS § 810], the determination of the Copyright Royalty Tribunal in any controversy concerning the distribution of royalty fees deposited under subclause (A) of subsection (b)(1) of this section to which the claimant is a party. Notwithstanding any provisions of the antitrust laws, for purposes of this subsection any claimants may agree among themselves as to the proportionate division of compulsory licensing fees among them, may lump their claims together and file them jointly or as a single claim, or may designate a common agent to receive payment on their behalf.

(3) After the first day of October of each year, the Copyright Royalty Tribunal shall determine whether there exists a controversy concerning the distribution of royalty fees deposited under subclause (A) of subsection (b)(1). If the Tribunal determines that no such controversy exists, it shall, after deducting its reasonable administrative costs under this section, distribute such fees to the copyright owners entitled, or to their designated agents. If it finds that such a controversy exists, it shall, pursuant to chapter 8 of this title [17 USCS §§ 801 et seq.], conduct a proceeding to determine the distribution of royalty fees.

(4) The fees to be distributed shall be divided as follows:

(A) to every copyright owner not affiliated with a performing rights society, the pro rata share of the fees to be distributed to which such copyright owner proves entitlement.

(B) to the performing rights societies, the remainder of the fees to be distributed in such pro rata shares as they shall by agreement stipulate among themselves, or, if they fail to agree, the pro rata share to which such performing rights societies prove entitlement.

(C) during the pendency of any proceeding under this section, the Copyright Royalty Tribunal shall withhold from distribution an amount sufficient to satisfy all claims with respect to which a controversy exists, but shall have discretion to proceed to distribute any amounts that are not in controversy.

(5) The Copyright Royalty Tribunal shall promulgate regulations under which persons who can reasonably be expected to have claims may, during the year in which performances take place, without expense to or

harassment of operators or proprietors of establishments in which phonorecord players are located, have such access to such establishments and to the phonorecord players located therein and such opportunity to obtain information with respect thereto as may be reasonably necessary to determine, by sampling procedures or otherwise, the proportion of contribution of the musical works of each such person to the earnings of the phonorecord players for which fees shall have been deposited. Any person who alleges that he or she has been denied the access permitted under the regulations prescribed by the Copyright Royalty Tribunal may bring an action in the United States District Court for the District of Columbia for the cancellation of the compulsory license of the phonorecord player to which such access has been denied, and the court shall have the power to declare the compulsory license thereof invalid from the date of issue thereof.

(d) Criminal penalties. Any person who knowingly makes a false representation of a material fact in an application filed under clause (1)(A) of subsection (b), or who knowingly alters a certificate issued under clause (1)(B) of subsection (b) or knowingly affixes such a certificate to a phonorecord player other than the one it covers, shall be fined not more than $2,500.

(e) Definitions. As used in this section, the following terms and their variant forms mean the following:

(1) A "coin-operated phonorecord player" is a machine or device that—

(A) is employed solely for the performance of nondramatic musical works by means of phonorecords upon being activated by insertion of coins, currency, tokens, or other monetary units or their equivalent;

(B) is located in an establishment making no direct or indirect charge for admission;

(C) is accompanied by a list of the titles of all the musical works available for performance on it, which list is affixed to the phonorecord player or posted in the establishment in a prominent position where it can be readily examined by the public; and

(D) affords a choice of works available for performance and permits the choice to be made by the patrons of the establishment in which it is located.

(2) An "operator" is any person who, alone or jointly with others:

(A) owns a coin-operated phonorecord player; or

(B) has the power to make a coin-operated phonorecord player available for placement in an establishment for purposes of public performance; or

(C) has the power to exercise primary control over the selection of the musical works made available for public performance on a coin-operated phonorecord player.

(3) A "performing rights society" is an association or corporation that licenses the public performance of nondramatic musical works on behalf

of the copyright owners, such as the American Society of Composers, Authors and Publishers, Broadcast Music, Inc., and SESAC, Inc.
(Added Oct. 19, 1976, P. L. 94-553, Title I, § 101, 90 Stat. 2562.)

HISTORY; ANCILLARY LAWS AND DIRECTIVES

References in text:

"Antitrust laws", referred to in subsec. (c)(2), appear generally as 15 USCS §§ 1 et seq.

Effective date of section:

Section 102 of Act Oct. 19, 1976, P. L. 94-553, 90 Stat. 2598 provided that this section "becomes effective on January 1, 1978".

CROSS REFERENCES

Compulsory license for making and distributing phonorecords, 17 USCS § 115.
Register of Copyrights, 17 USCS § 701.
Copyright Royalty Tribunal, 17 USCS § 801.
Judicial review procedures after action by Copyright Royalty Tribunal, 17 USCS § 810.
This section referred to in 17 USCS §§ 106, 117, 501, 801, 804, 809.

INTERPRETIVE NOTES AND DECISIONS

Performance of music by juke box and by live band is performance for profit where admission fee is charged. Quackenbush Music, Ltd. v Wood (1974, DC Tenn) 381 F Supp 904, 184 USPQ 210.

ASCAP and BMI do not misuse or unlawfully extend copyright by granting blanket licenses to CBS where evidence fails to show that direct licensing for each composition is impractical or that ASCAP and BMI would refuse direct licensing. Columbia Broadcasting System, Inc. v American Soc. of Composers, (1975, DC NY) 400 F Supp 737, 187 USPQ 431.

§ 117. Scope of exclusive rights: Use in conjunction with computers and similar information systems

Notwithstanding the provisions of sections 106 through 116 and 118 [17 USCS §§ 106–116, 118], this title [17 USCS §§ 101 et seq.] does not afford to the owner of copyright in a work any greater or lesser rights with respect to the use of the work in conjunction with automatic systems capable of storing, processing, retrieving, or transferring information, or in conjunction with any similar device, machine, or process, than those afforded to works under the law, whether title 17 [17 USCS §§ 101 et seq.] or the common law or statutes of a State, in effect on December 31, 1977, as held applicable and construed by a court in an action brought under this title [17 USCS §§ 101 et seq.].
(Added Oct. 19, 1976, P. L. 94-553, Title I, § 101, 90 Stat. 2565.)

HISTORY; ANCILLARY LAWS AND DIRECTIVES

Effective date of section:
Section 102 of Act Oct. 19, 1976, P. L. 94-553, 90 Stat. 2598 provided that this section "becomes effective on January 1, 1978".

CROSS REFERENCES

Exclusive rights in copyrighted works, 17 USCS § 106.
Limitations on exclusive rights, 17 USCS §§ 107–116, 118.
This section referred to in 17 USCS §§ 106, 501.

§ 118. Scope of exclusive rights: Use of certain works in connection with noncommercial broadcasting

(a) The exclusive rights provided by section 106 [17 USCS § 106] shall, with respect to the works specified by subsection (b) and the activities specified by subsection (d), be subject to the conditions and limitations prescribed by this section.

(b) Not later than thirty days after the Copyright Royalty Tribunal has been constituted in accordance with section 802 [17 USCS § 802], the Chairman of the Tribunal shall cause notice to be published in the Federal Register of the initiation of proceedings for the purpose of determining reasonable terms and rates of royalty payments for the activities specified by subsection (d) with respect to published nondramatic musical works and published pictorial, graphic, and sculptural works during a period beginning as provided in clause (3) of this subsection and ending on December 31, 1982. Copyright owners and public broadcasting entities shall negotiate in good faith and cooperate fully with the Tribunal in an effort to reach reasonable and expeditious results. Notwithstanding any provision of the antitrust laws, any owners of copyright in works specified by this subsection and any public broadcasting entitites, respectively, may negotiate and agree upon the terms and rates of royalty payments and the proportionate division of fees paid among various copyright owners, and may designate common agents to negotiate, agree to, pay, or receive payments.

(1) Any owner of copyright in a work specified in this subsection or any public broadcasting entity may, within one hundred and twenty days after publication of the notice specified in this subsection, submit to the Copyright Royalty Tribunal proposed licenses covering such activities with respect to such works. The Copyright Royalty Tribunal shall proceed on the basis of the proposals submitted to it as well as any other relevant information. The Copyright Royalty Tribunal shall permit any interested party to submit information relevant to such proceedings.

(2) License agreements voluntarily negotiated at any time between one or more copyright owners and one or more public broadcasting entities shall be given effect in lieu of any determination by the Tribunal: *Provided,* That copies of such agreements are filed in the Copyright

Office within thirty days of execution in accordance with regulations that the Register of Copyrights shall prescribe.

(3) Within six months, but not earlier than one hundred and twenty days, from the date of publication of the notice specified in this subsection the Copyright Royalty Tribunal shall make a determination and publish in the Federal Register a schedule of rates and terms which, subject to clause (2) of this subsection, shall be binding on all owners of copyright in works specified by this subsection and public broadcasting entities, regardless of whether or not such copyright owners and public broadcasting entities have submitted proposals to the Tribunal. In establishing such rates and terms the Copyright Royalty Tribunal may consider the rates for comparable circumstances under voluntary license agreements negotiated as provided in clause (2) of this subsection. The Copyright Royalty Tribunal shall also establish requirements by which copyright owners may receive reasonable notice of the use of their works under this section, and under which records of such use shall be kept by public broadcasting entities.

(4) With respect to the period beginning on the effective date of this title [17 USCS §§ 101 et seq.] and ending on the date of publication of such rates and terms, this title [17 USCS §§ 101 et seq.] shall not afford to owners of copyright or public broadcasting entities any greater or lesser rights with respect to the activities specified in subsection (d) as applied to works specified in this subsection than those afforded under the law in effect on December 31, 1977, as held applicable and construed by a court in an action brought under this title [17 USCS §§ 101 et seq.].

(c) The initial procedure specified in subsection (b) shall be repeated and concluded between June 30 and December 31, 1982, and at five-year intervals thereafter, in accordance with regulations that the Copyright Royalty Tribunal shall prescribe.

(d) Subject to the transitional provisions of subsection (b)(4), and to the terms of any voluntary license agreements that have been negotiated as provided by subsection (b)(2), a public broadcasting entity may, upon compliance with the provisions of this section, including the rates and terms established by the Copyright Royalty Tribunal under subsection (b)(3), engage in the following activities with respect to published nondramatic musical works and published pictorial, graphic, and sculptural works:

(1) performance or display of work by or in the course of a transmission made by a noncommercial educational broadcast station referred to in subsection (g); and

(2) production of a transmission program, reproduction of copies or phonorecords of such a transmission program, and distribution of such copies or phonorecords, where such production, reproduction, or distribution is made by a nonprofit institution or organization solely for the purpose of transmissions specified in clause (1); and

(3) the making of reproductions by a governmental body or a nonprofit institution of a transmission program simultaneously with its transmission as specified in clause (1), and the performance or display of the contents of such program under the conditions specified by clause (1) of section 110 [17 USCS § 110], but only if the reproductions are used for performances or displays for a period of no more than seven days from the date of the transmission specified in clause (1), and are destroyed before or at the end of such period. No person supplying, in accordance with clause (2), a reproduction of a transmission program to governmental bodies or nonprofit institutions under this clause shall have any liability as a result of failure of such body or institution to destroy such reproduction: *Provided,* That it shall have notified such body or institution of the requirement for such destruction pursuant to this clause: *And provided further,* That if such body or institution itself fails to destroy such reproduction it shall be deemed to have infringed.

(e) Except as expressly provided in this subsection, this section shall have no applicability to works other than those specified in subsection (b).
(1) Owners of copyright in nondramatic literary works and public broadcasting entities may, during the course of voluntary negotiations, agree among themselves, respectively, as to the terms and rates of royalty payments without liability under the antitrust laws. Any such terms and rates of royalty payments shall be effective upon filing in the Copyright Office, in accordance with regulations that the Register of Copyrights shall prescribe.
(2) On January 3, 1980, the Register of Copyrights, after consulting with authors and other owners of copyright in nondramatic literary works and their representatives, and with public broadcasting entities and their representatives, shall submit to the Congress a report setting forth the extent to which voluntary licensing arrangements have been reached with respect to the use of nondramatic literary works by such broadcast stations. The report should also describe any problems that may have arisen, and present legislative or other recommendations, if warranted.

(f) Nothing in this section shall be construed to permit, beyond the limits of fair use as provided by section 107 [17 USCS § 107], the unauthorized dramatization of a nondramatic musical work, the production of a transmission program drawn to any substantial extent from a published compilation of pictorial, graphic, or sculptural works, or the unauthorized use of any portion of an audiovisual work.

(g) As used in this section, the term "public broadcasting entity" means a noncommercial educational broadcast station as defined in section 397 of title 47 [47 USCS § 397] and any nonprofit institution or organization engaged in the activities described in clause (2) of subsection (d).
(Added Oct. 19, 1976, P. L. 94-553, Title I, § 101, 90 Stat. 2565.)

HISTORY; ANCILLARY LAWS AND DIRECTIVES

References in text:

"Antitrust laws", referred to in subsecs. (b) and (e)(1), appear generally as 15 USCS §§ 1 et seq.

"Effective date of this title", referred to in subsec. (b)(4), is Jan. 1, 1978; see section 102 of Act Oct. 19, 1976, which appears as a note preceding 17 USCS § 101.

Effective date of section:

Act Oct. 19, 1976, P. L. 94-553, Title I, § 102, 90 Stat. 2598, provided in part that this section takes "effect upon enactment of this Act [enacted Oct. 19, 1976]."

CROSS REFERENCES

Performance or display in course of teaching activities in nonprofit educational institution, 17 USCS § 110(1).
Remedies for infringement, 17 USCS §§ 502–505.
Register of Copyrights, 17 USCS § 701.
Copyright Royalty Tribunal, 17 USCS § 801.
This section referred to in 17 USCS §§ 101 note, 106, 114, 117, 501, 504, 801, 804.

RESEARCH GUIDE

Law Review Articles:

Korman, Performance rights in music under §§ 110 and 118 of the 1976 Copyright Act. 22 New York Law School Law Rev 521.

CHAPTER 2.   COPYRIGHT OWNERSHIP AND TRANSFER

---

§ 201.   Ownership of copyright

(a) Initial ownership. Copyright in a work protected under this title [17 USCS §§ 101 et seq.] vests initially in the author or authors of the work. The authors of a joint work are co-owners of copyright in the work.

(b) Works made for hire. In the case of a work made for hire, the employer or other person for whom the work was prepared is considered the author for purposes of this title [17 USCS §§ 101 et seq.], and, unless the parties have expressly agreed otherwise in a written instrument signed by them, owns all of the rights comprised in the copyright.

(c) Contributions to collective works. Copyright in each separate contribution to a collective work is distinct from copyright in the collective work as a whole, and vests initially in the author of the contribution. In the absence of an express transfer of the copyright or of any rights under it, the owner of copyright in the collective work is presumed to have acquired only the privilege of reproducing and distributing the contribution as part of that particular collective work, any revision of that collective work, and any later collective work in the same series.

(d) Transfer of ownership. (1) The ownership of a copyright may be transferred in whole or in part by any means of conveyance or by operation of law, and may be bequeathed by will or pass as personal property by the applicable laws of intestate succession.

(2) Any of the exclusive rights comprised in a copyright, including any subdivision of any of the rights specified by section 106 [17 USCS § 106], may be transferred as provided by clause (1) and owned separately. The owner of any particular exclusive right is entitled, to the extent of that right, to all of the protection and remedies accorded to the copyright owner by this title [17 USCS §§ 101 et seq.].

(e) Involuntary transfer. When an individual author's ownership of a copyright, or of any of the exclusive rights under a copyright, has not previously been transferred voluntarily by that individual author, no action by any governmental body or other official or organization purporting to seize, expropriate, transfer, or exercise rights of ownership with respect to

the copyright, or any of the exclusive rights under a copyright, shall be given effect under this title [17 USCS §§ 101 et seq.].
(Added Oct. 19, 1976, P. L. 94-553, Title I, § 101, 90 Stat. 2568.)

HISTORY; ANCILLARY LAWS AND DIRECTIVES

Effective date of section:

Section 102 of Act Oct. 19, 1976, P. L. 94-553, 90 Stat. 2598 provided that this section "becomes effective on January 1, 1978".

CROSS REFERENCES

"Collective work" defined, 17 USCS § 101.
"Joint work" defined, 17 USCS § 101.
"Transfer of copyright ownership" defined, 17 USCS § 101.
"Works made for hire" defined, 17 USCS § 101.
Copyright notice, 17 USCS § 404.

RESEARCH GUIDE

Am Jur:

6 Am Jur 2d, Assignments §§ 75, 89, 90.
18 Am Jur 2d, Copyright and Literary Property § 23.

Forms:

6 Federal Procedural Forms L Ed, Copyrights § 17:96.

Annotations:

Application of "works for hire" doctrine under Federal Copyright Act (17 USCS §§ 1 et seq.). 11 ALR Fed 457.

Law Review Articles:

Copyright Symposium, 22 New York Law School Law Review 193.

INTERPRETIVE NOTES AND DECISIONS

I.   INITIAL OWNERSHIP [17 USCS § 201(a)]
A. In General (notes 1–3)
B. Particular Initial Owners (notes 4–9)

II.   WORKS MADE FOR HIRE [17 USCS § 201(b)]
A. In General (notes 10 & 11)
B. Particular Works (notes 12–19)

III.   CONTRIBUTIONS TO COLLECTIVE WORKS [17 USCS § 201(c)]

IV.   TRANSFER OF OWNERSHIP, GENERALLY [17 USCS § 201(d)(1)]
A. In General (notes 23–27)
B. Particular Transfers (notes 28–38)

V.   TRANSFER OF OWNERSHIP OF PARTICULAR RIGHTS [17 USCS § 201(d)(2)] (notes 39–48)

VI.   INVOLUNTARY TRANSFER [17 USCS § 201(e)] (notes 49–51)

I. INITIAL OWNERSHIP [17 USCS § 201(a)]

A. In General

1. Generally
2. Title determination, generally
3. —Equitable title

B. Particular Initial Owners

4. Authors, generally
5. —Of compilations
6. Of derivative works
7. Co-authors
8. Photographers
9. Publishers and printers

I. INITIAL OWNERSHIP [17 USCS § 201(a)]

A. In General

1. Generally

"Proprietor," not author, stands in no better status in acquiring copyright than does author. Houghton Mifflin Co. v Stackpole Sons, Inc. (1939, CA2 NY) 104 F2d 306, 42 USPQ 96, cert den 308 US 597, 84 L Ed 499, 60 S Ct 131.

Proprietors of books, though not authors, were entitled to benefits of copyright acts. Lawrence v Dana (1869, CC Mass) F Cas No 8136.

"Proprietor" as used in copyright laws is one who has lawfully acquired, by purchase or otherwise, exclusive rights of author. Yuengling v Schile (1882, CC NY) 12 F 97.

Although not corporeal, but existing in contemplation of law, copyright is enjoyable as legal estate, as other movable property. Simmons v Sikes (1932, Tex Civ App) 56 SW2d 193, error dismd w o j.

2. Title determination, generally

Uncopyrighted news is quasi property as between two parties engaged in vending it. International News Service v Associated Press (1918) 248 US 215, 63 L Ed 211, 39 S Ct 68, 2 ALR 293.

Partnership may obtain copyright by firm name, even though such name indicates corporation. Campbell v Wireback (1920, CA4 Md) 269 F 372, 17 ALR 743.

Ownership of unpublished composition presumptively includes privilege of publication and of securing statutory copyright. Gerlach-Barklow Co. v Morris & Bendien, Inc. (1927, CA2 NY) 23 F2d 159.

Federal court is without jurisdiction to foreclose mortgage on copyright. Republic Pictures Corp. v Security-First Nat. Bank (1952, CA9 Cal) 197 F2d 767, 94 USPQ 291.

Corporation can secure copyright. Mutual Advertising Co. v Refo (1896, CC SC) 76 F 961.

Failure to produce receipt or document of title to map is not conclusive of ownership but is of some consequence. Sawyer v Crowell Pub. Co.

(1942, DC NY) 46 F Supp 471, 54 USPQ 225, affd (CA2 NY) 142 F2d 497, 61 USPQ 389, cert den 323 US 735, 89 L Ed 589, 65 S Ct 74.

Since facts are equivocal and participants are dead, it is necessary to rely on interpretation and inference to reach conclusion as to ownership of dialogue of operetta. Brown v Select Theatres Corp. (1944, DC Mass) 56 F Supp 438, 62 USPQ 240.

Federal court does not have jurisdiction under 28 USCS § 1338(a) of action seeking declaration that plaintiff has interest as coauthor in defendants' copyrighted musical composition inasmuch as no issue is presented as to validity or infringement of copyright and diversity of citizenship is lacking; plaintiff merely claims that he is entitled to assignment of interest in copyright and accounting for share of proceeds earned by composition. Harrington v Mure (1960, DC NY) 186 F Supp 655, 126 USPQ 506.

Long and continued possession and assertion of exclusive right to drama raises every presumption of title. Hart v Fox (1917, Sup) 166 NYS 793.

Action by music publisher owning copyrights against American Society of Composers, Authors, and Publishers seeking declaratory judgment of rights in musical compositions after 1950 under contract with composers before assignment to publisher is dismissed on motion for lack of justiciable controversy although complaint alleges that American Society of Composers, Authors, and Publishers claims right beyond 1950. Denton & Haskins Corp. v Taylor (1943, Sup) 42 NYS2d 18, 58 USPQ 95.

Action against American Society of Composers and Publishers and five composer members to determine title to public performance rights in three songs composed by members, but copyrighted by plaintiff, is not res judicata as against other American Society of Composers and Publishers composers, who composed other songs copyrighted by plaintiff, but who are not parties to suit. Broadcast Music, Inc. v Taylor (1945) 10 Misc 2d 9, 55 NYS2d 94.

3. —Equitable title

Owner of the equitable title of copyright is not mere licensee, and he may sue in equity, particularly where owner of legal title is infringer, or one of infringers, thus occupying position hostile to plaintiff. Ted Browne Music Co. v Fowler (1923, CA2 NY) 290 F 751.

Although cases recognized standing of equitable owner of copyright to sue for infringement, federal court has no original jurisdiction to hear and decide claim of title to copyright; such incidental power as it has to do so must depend upon its power to adjudicate infringement claim

where, as preliminary matter, court may permit plaintiff to establish facts as to his ownership interest on which his right to sue for infringement depends; where claim of infringement is absent, federal courts are without jurisdiction to determine questions of title dependent on general common-law or equitable principles, and plaintiffs, in absence of diversity, must look to state courts to decide such issues. Cresci v Music Publishers Holding Corp. (1962, DC NY) 210 F Supp 253, 135 USPQ 189.

Action brought in equity for damages and for assignment of copyright in book is improperly dismissed as seeking remedies available at law and is remanded to chancery because both common law and statutory copyright are distinct from matter copyrighted and require equity jurisdiction for copyright transfer. Hughes Tool Co. v Fawcett Publications, Inc. (1974, Del Sup Ct) 181 USPQ 525.

B. Particular Initial Owners

4. Authors, generally

Judge may not secure copyright in his judicial opinions; state may not obtain copyright on its courts opinions, for it may not properly be called citizen or resident; court reporter not being author of judicial decisions may not obtain copyright thereon. Banks v Manchester (1888) 128 US 244, 32 L Ed 425, 9 S Ct 36.

Married woman was entitled to copyright protection, as against defendant's contention that her husband was owner of copyrighted book by virtue of his marital rights. Belford v Scribner (1892) 144 US 488, 36 L Ed 514, 12 S Ct 734.

Legal title to copyright vests in person in whose name copyright is taken out; it may, however, be held by him in trust for true owner, and question of true ownership is one of fact, dependent upon circumstances of case. Bisel v Ladner (1924, CA3 Pa) 1 F2d 436.

Author, or his assignee, of unpublished play has right of property in manuscript and its incorporeal contents. Crowe v Aiken (1870, CC Ill) F Cas No 3441.

Where events of person's life were given to writer, to enable him to write biography of such person, person giving facts is not author of biography and is therefore not entitled to copyright. De Witt v Brooks (CC NY) F Cas No 3851.

Person to whom letter was addressed was not entitled to copyright. Folsom v Marsh (1841, CC Mass) F Cas No 4901.

Where author of book continues to be owner thereof, he is entitled to copyright. Lawrence v Dana (1869, CC Mass) F Cas No 8136.

Authors, proprietors, and lawful assigns only are entitled to copyright. Yuengling v Schile (1882, CC NY) 12 F 97.

Person may be author of musical composition although there are short parts of it that are similar to composition previously published, when these parts are not continuous and are not extended. Blume v Spear (1887, CC NY) 30 F 629.

Copyright may be taken out in name of trustee for benefit of another who is "author or proprietor." Hanson v Jaccard Jewelry Co. (1887, CC Mo) 32 F 202.

Validity of copyright on biography does not depend on whether or not author of work was designated by subject as his special biographer. Gilmore v Anderson (1889, CC NY) 38 F 846.

Although bill fails to allege authorship, except by implication arising from words "written or composed," it is sufficient against demurrer. Henderson v Tompkins (1894, CC Mass) 60 F 758.

Person doing business under conventional or fictitious firm name may secure copyright. Scribner v Henry G. Allen Co. (1892, CC NY) 49 F 854; Werckmeister v Springer Lithographing Co. (1894, CC NY) 63 F 808.

"Authorship" presumptively connotes "originality." Remick Music Corp. v Interstate Hotel Co. (1944, DC Neb) 58 F Supp 523, 63 USPQ 327, affd (CA8 Neb) 157 F2d 744, 71 USPQ 138, cert den 329 US 809, 91 L Ed 691, 67 S Ct 622, reh den 330 US 854, 91 L Ed 1296, 67 S Ct 769.

Property right exists with respect to combination of ideas evolved into radio program, as distinguished from rights to particular scripts. Cole v Phillips H. Lord, Inc. (1941) 262 App Div 116, 28 NYS2d 404, 50 USPQ 490.

Copyright is right which is available only to author or proprietor of literary property; its purpose is to secure to such author or proprietor exclusive right to that property. McClintic v Sheldon (1943) 182 Misc 32, 43 NYS2d 695, 59 USPQ 41, revd on other grounds 269 App Div 356, 55 NYS2d 879, affd without opinion 295 NY 682, 65 NE2d 328.

5. —Of compilations

Plaintiff who had entered into contract with reporter and other state officials to publish certain decisions could not be considered owners of volume prepared by reporter after his term of office had expired. Little v Hall (1856) 59 US 165, 15 L Ed 328.

Reporter of volume of law reports can obtain copyright that will cover parts of book of which he is author. Callaghan v Myers (1888) 128 US 617, 32 L Ed 547, 9 S Ct 177.

Person compiling statutes of state and annotating, has right to obtain copyright on volumes, as the author. Howell v Miller (1898, CA6 Mich) 91 F 129.

Person who obtains facts and puts them together in pamphlet showing different size piston rings for different makes of motor vehicles is author of it. No-Leak-O Piston Ring Co. v Norris (1921, CA4 Md) 277 F 951.

Compiler is "author" within meaning of Constitution and copyright laws. Bullinger v Mackey, (1879, CC NY) F Cas No 2127.

One compiling, editing, and publishing catalogue for another advertising other's products is entitled to copyright same although there is no contract provision therefor. R. R. Donnelley & Sons Co. v Haber (1942, DC NY) 43 F Supp 456, 52 USPQ 445.

6. —Of derivative works

To constitute one author, he must, by his own intellectual labor applied to materials of his composition, produce arrangement or compilation new in itself. Atwill v Ferrett (1846, CC NY) F Cas No 640.

Author of translation of play, copyrighted with permission of holder of copyright of original play, is entitled to protection of Copyright Act with respect to such translation, same as if it had been original story. Shook v Rankin (1875, CC Ill) F Cas No 12804.

Trust upon translator's copyright will not be implied in favor of author. Rolland v Henry Holt & Co. (1957, DC NY) 152 F Supp 167, 113 USPQ 253.

Predecessor statute does not recognize any right of performing artist in his interpretative rendition of musical composition or in acting of play composed by another. Waring v WDAS Broadcasting Station, Inc. (1937) 327 Pa 433, 194 A 631, 35 USPQ 272.

7. Co-authors

Consent of coauthor to take out copyright in name of one does not destroy his interest therein, although legal title vests in person taking out copyright; where one person holds legal title to copyright in trust for other joint owners, he cannot appropriate it exclusively to himself so as to impair its worth as to others. Maurel v Smith (1921, CA2 NY) 271 F 211.

Composer transferred all his rights, including renewal rights, in music to publisher which, thereafter, employed another to write lyric for music; publisher then copyrighted resulting song; song is "joint" work, not "composite" of music and lyric; test is consent, to collaboration of second author, by one who holds copyright on product of first author. Shapiro, Berstein & Co. v Jerry Vogel Music Co. (1955, CA2 NY) 221 F2d 569, 105 USPQ 178, adhered to (CA2 NY) 223 F2d 252, 105 USPQ 460.

Person may claim copyright on his part of production, although others also contributed to work; to entitle one to copyright it is unnecessary that he be sole creator of work for which protection is claimed. Schuberth v Shaw (1879, CC Pa) F Cas No 12482.

Where two companies prior to printing of directory enter into contract whereby they agree to jointly take canvass of inhabitants, and to jointly do compiling, typesetting, and proofreading, one cannot, by virtue of having obtained copyright on the directory, restrain other party from distributing their directory. Maloney v Foote (1900, CC Ga) 101 F 264.

Canadian soldier composed music for popular ballad, and United States citizen wrote words; there was joint authorship. G. Ricordi & Co. v Columbia Graphophone Co. (1919, DC NY) 258 F 72.

Where author of lyrics sends them to composer, either directly or through producer or publisher, to have composer write music for lyrics, so that two are united into one composition, author and composer are coauthors and statutory copyright of composition is owned jointly; same is true if composer submits music to lyric writer; coauthor copyrighting composition in own name is constructive trustee for other coauthor; copyright protects both words and music. Edward B. Marks Music Corp. v Jerry Vogel Music Co. (1942, DC NY) 42 F Supp 859, 52 USPQ 219.

On original copy of song on file in copyright office, names of T and S appear on inside page, below title and above music, but on outside cover and 1910 certificate of copyright T claimed sole authorship; S worked for T from prior to 1910 to 1925; S was given credit for coauthorship of other songs; during T's life, S never asserted formal claim of coauthorship; from 1910 to 1938, T or assignee published nine editions in all of which T was indicated as sole author; in 1937, T renewed copyright as sole author; S was not coauthor. Forster Music Publishers, Inc. v Jerry Vogel Music Co. (DC NY) 62 USPQ 142, (CA2 NY) 147 F2d 614, 64 USPQ 417, cert den 325 US 880, 89 L Ed 1996, 65 S Ct 1573.

To prove coauthorship of song nearly 30 years before, alleged coauthor must prove case by clear and satisfactory evidence; evidence should be scrutinized with great care and perhaps even with suspicion; copyright by one coauthor of song in own name was copyright on joint work which he held with trust for benefit of other coauthor. Edward B. Marks Music Corp. v Wonnell (1945, DC NY) 61 F Supp 722, 65 USPQ 456.

Joint authorship gives rise to joint ownership of a copyright. Picture Music, Inc. v Bourne, Inc. (1970, DC NY) 314 F Supp 640, 167 USPQ 348, affd (CA2 NY) 457 F2d 1213, cert den 409 US 997, 34 L Ed 2d 262, 93 S Ct 320.

Co-ownership in copyright is tenancy in common; in dealing with rights of co-owners, courts have relied largely on general principles governing tenancies in common; it is noteworthy that in such cases involving literary property courts have restricted remedy of co-owner to accounting and have denied injunctive relief. Noble v D. Van Nostrand Co. (1960) 63 NJ Super 534, 164 A2d 834, 128 USPQ 100.

Writing need not be work of one individual, for author to be entitled to protection afforded to writers of unpublished manuscripts. French v Maguire (NY) 55 How Pr 471.

Person cannot assert his rights as co-owner of copyright, against other person holding interest in copyright, when such action is violation of contract between them. Gould v Banks & Gould (NY) 8 Wend 562.

Co-owners of copyrighted work are accountable to each other for profits derived from licensing third party to use work. Jerry Vogel Music Co. v Miller Music, Inc. (1947) 272 App Div 571, 74 NYS2d 425, 75 USPQ 205, affd 299 NY 782, 87 NE2d 681, 82 USPQ 458.

Where parties are equal owners of copyrighted work, in absence of agreement governing their rights in exploitation of work, they are accountable to each other for such exploitation; they are held to standard of dealing befitting their mutual interest in work. Kapplow v Abelard Schuman, Ltd. (1959) 21 Misc 2d 306, 193 NYS2d 931, 124 USPQ 58.

It is not necessary, to establish property rights in intellectual or artistic productions, that entire ultimate product should be work of single creator; such rights may be acquired by one who perfects original work or substantially adds to it in some manner. Waring v WDAS Broadcasting Station, Inc. (1937) 327 Pa 433, 194 A 631, 35 USPQ 272.

8. Photographers

Photographer is entitled to copyright photographs which were taken gratuitously and for his own benefit. Lumiere v Pathe Exchange, Inc. (1921, CA2 NY) 275 F 428; Yardley v Houghton Mifflin Co. (1939, CA2 NY) 108 F2d 28, 44 USPQ 1, cert den 309 US 686, 84 L Ed 1029, 60 S Ct 891.

One who arranges pose and lighting of photograph is to be treated as author thereof and is entitled to copyright of his photographs. Falk v Gast Lithograph & Engraving Co. (1891, CC NY) 48 F 262, affd (CA2 NY) 54 F 890.

Photographist producing artistic photograph may secure copyright. Falk v Donaldson (1893, CC NY) 57 F 32.

Photographer who took picture of hotel with consent of owner and developed and printed it at his own expense for his own benefit had sole proprietary right therein and was entitled to copyright. Cory v Physical Culture Hotel, Inc. (1936, DC NY) 14 F Supp 977, 30 USPQ 353, affd (CA2 NY) 88 F2d 411, 33 USPQ 58.

Rights of person in his dog's photograph are dependent on his contract with photographer; if latter takes photograph on own initiative, without arrangement or payment by dog's owner, proprietary interest in photograph, including right to copyright, is in photographer; if photograph is taken at owner's request and owner pays photographer, all interest, including right to copyright, is in owner. Lawrence v Ylla (1945) 184 Misc 807, 55 NYS2d 343, 65 USPQ 342.

9. Publishers and printers

American publisher of production which has been copyrighted in England, but not in United States may not, by taking out copyright in United States, secure benefits of the copyright statute. Ferris v Frohman (1912) 223 US 424, 56 L Ed 492, 32 S Ct 263.

Publisher may obtain copyright on behalf of himself and author, which would protect interests of both, and publisher would become trustee of copyright on behalf of both. Mifflin v Dutton (1902, CA1 Mass) 112 F 1004, affd 190 US 265, 47 L Ed 1043, 23 S Ct 771.

Copyright of periodical containing articles and pictures, authors of which have not transferred their rights to publisher, affords publisher no protection as to such articles or pictures. Mail & Express Co. v Life Pub. Co. (1911, CA2 NY) 192 F 899.

Airlines, preparing material which was furnished to publisher of airline guides, do not part with all interest in such material, where airlines paid for publication and publisher's contribution was limited to editorial revision, and airlines may use such material in another publication. Official Aviation Guide Co. v American Aviation Associates (1945, CA7 Ill) 150 F2d 173, 65 USPQ 553, cert den 326 US 776, 90 L Ed 469, 66 S Ct 267, reh den 326 US 811, 90 L Ed 495, 66 S Ct 335.

Where contract made no present grant of title to future drawings, but contemplated that publisher's title should not attach until drawings were furnished to it, publisher has no title to artist's drawings never furnished to publisher. Esquire, Inc. v Varga Enterprises, Inc. (1950, CA7 Ill) 185 F2d 14, 87 USPQ 342.

When, with knowledge and acquiescence of author, copyright is obtained by publisher, author loses all rights to publish such work. Pulte v Derby (1852, CC Ohio) F Cas No 11465.

Copyright of story by foreign author in publisher's and author's name under contract so providing gave valid copyright to publisher and author. Harper & Bros. v M. A. Donohue & Co. (1905, CC Ill) 144 F 491, affd (CA7 Ill) 146 F 1023.

Copyright taken out by publisher for protection of itself and general owner is valid. Quinn-Brown Pub. Corp. v Chilton Co. (1936, DC NY) 15 F Supp 213, 30 USPQ 373.

Right in printer to reproduce copyrighted material, upon order of copyright proprietor, was license by proprietor to printer for that express purpose and did not constitute transfer of legal title of copyrighted right of reproduction. Hiawatha Card Co. v Colourpicture Publishers, Inc. (1966, DC Mich) 255 F Supp 1015, 149 USPQ 603.

One not proprietor of manuscript, but merely printer thereof, is not entitled to obtain copyright to protect that interest only. Koppel v Downing (1897) 11 App DC 93.

Authority granted by artist to publisher to copyright cartoons drawn by artist does not give publisher right to copyright drama based on cartoons. Outcault v Lamar (1909) 135 App Div 110, 119 NYS 930.

Publisher, who publishes book under agreement to pay author and holder of copyright 7½ cents for each copy, has not exclusive right to publish such book. Willis v Tibbals (1871) 33 NY Super Ct 220.

II. WORKS MADE FOR HIRE [17 USCS § 201(b)]

A. In General

10. Generally

Employer is author of works for hire. National Cloak & Suit Co. v Kaufman (1911, CC Pa) 189 F 215; Vitaphone Corp. v Hutchinson Amusement Co. (1939, DC Mass) 28 F Supp 526, 42 USPQ 431; Dan Kasoff, Inc. v Palmer Jewelry Mfg. Co. (1959, DC NY) 171 F Supp 603, 120 USPQ 445; Peter Pan Fabrics, Inc. v Acadia Co. (1959, DC NY) 173 F Supp 292, 121 USPQ 81, affd (CA2 NY) 274 F2d 487, 124 USPQ 154; Tobani v Carl Fischer (DC NY) 36 USPQ 97, mod on other grounds (CA2 NY) 98 F2d 57, 38 USPQ 198, cert den 305 US 650, 83 L Ed 420, 59 S Ct 243.

Under predecessor statute, no power exists in agent to copyright anything. Societe Des Films Menchen v Vitagraph Co. (1918, CA2 NY) 251 F 258.

Presumption of copyright ownership runs in favor of employer where intention of parties cannot be determined. Brattleboro Publishing Co. v Winmill Publishing Corp. (1966, CA2 Vt) 369 F2d 565, 151 USPQ 666, 5 ALR Fed 617.

Employee hired to compile, prepare, and revise materials may not claim copyright therein, for products of his labors become property of his employer. Colliery Engineer Co. v United Correspondence Schools Co. (1899, CC NY) 94 F 152.

Annotations:

Application of "works for hire" doctrine under Federal Copyright Act (17 USCS §§ 1 et seq.). 11 ALR Fed 457.

11. As affected by contract of employment

Where owner of all but five shares of stock of publishing company contracted for writing of book, stockholder and author were "proprietors," and copyright taken out in name of corporation was void, there being no assignment, and no elements of estoppel present as against defendant in infringement suit. Public Ledger Co. v Post Printing & Publishing Co. (1923, CA8 Mo) 294 F 430.

Author in general employ of another will not be deemed to have parted with his right to copyright and transferred it to his employer, in absence of valid agreement to that effect. Boucicault v Fox (1862, CC NY) F Cas No 1691.

Plaintiff seeks to restrain defendant from distributing and exhibiting motion picture unless she receives credit; contract providing that defendant would be deemed author of literary property created by plaintiff during employment divested plaintiff of all rights generally known as moral rights of authors, which rights include right to credit as author of work. Harris v Twentieth Century-Fox Film Corp. (1940, DC NY) 35 F Supp 153, 47 USPQ 11.

B. Particular Works

12. Advertising materials

Absent agreement between advertiser and newspaper, advertiser who commissioned design and creation of advertisement was entitled to copyright on that advertisement. Brattleboro Publishing Co. v Winmill Publishing Corp. (1966, CA2 Vt) 369 F2d 565, 151 USPQ 666, 5 ALR Fed 617.

M employed S to put advertising on radio and S employed B to "build" program and direct it; B concocted jingle for theme song to old music and it was used continuously without protest on part of B; case falls within rule that where employee creates something as part of duties, thing created is property of employer and copyright belongs to S in trust for M. Brown v Molle Co. (1937, DC NY) 20 F Supp 135, 35 USPQ 183.

13. Art works; designs

If artist is solicited by patron to execute commission for pay, presumption should be that patron desires to control publication of copies and that the artist consents; mural was painted for city high school and copyright belonged to city although artist marked it with notice of copyright in his name and registered claim to copyright, but there is no evidence of city's observation of notice or approval by city. Yardley v Houghton Mifflin Co. (1939, CA2 NY) 108 F2d 28, 44 USPQ 1, cert den 309 US 686, 84 L Ed 1029, 60 S Ct 891.

Small painting, design of which president of corporation originated and directed to be painted by hired artist was properly copyrightable in corporation's name. Schumacher v Schwencke (1885, CC NY) 25 F 466.

In general, when artist is commissioned to execute work of art not in existence he may not retain or be entitled to copyright therein. Dielman v White (1900, CC Mass) 102 F 892.

Where independent contractor created textile design for employer, and no contrary intent was shown to rebut presumption of copyright ownership by employer, employer could properly have registered design as an author under predecessor section. Irving J. Dorfman Co., Inc. v Borlan Industries, Inc. (1969, DC NY) 309 F Supp 21.

14. Books

Person who is employed to write book, is author of such book when his name appears on title page, although suggestions may have been offered by his employer. Pierpont v Fowle (1846, CC Mass) F Cas No 11152.

It is not necessary for corporation to show that it is author of book in order to assert its rights under copyright, but it is sufficient to show that work is result of intellectual labor of editors and compilers employed by it. Edward Thompson Co. v American Law Book Co. (1902, CC NY) 119 F 217.

15. Dramas

Play was literary property of plaintiff, although he wrote it while in employ of another; author who wrote play while employed as actor and received half of profits therefrom as compensation for his work did not part with right to obtain copyright upon play. Boucicault v Fox (1862, CC NY) F Cas No 1691.

Copyright on drama was properly taken out by its author, as against contention that author's employer had right thereto. Roberts v Myers (1860, CC Mass) F Cas No 11906.

16. Lectures

In absence of evidence to contrary, teacher rather than university owns copyright to his lectures. Williams v Weisser (1969) 273 Cal App 2d 726, 78 Cal Rptr 542, 38 ALR3d 761, 163 USPQ 42.

17. Musical compositions

"Work for hire" doctrine applies to both employees and independent contractors, and television producers have right to own copyrights to musical compositions they commissioned, and refusal to give up ownership of copyrights is not contrary to antitrust or other laws or evidence of illegal conspiracy in restraint of trade. Bernstein v Universal Pictures, Inc. (1974, DC NY) 379 F Supp 933, 183 USPQ 422, revd on other grounds (CA2 NY) 517 F2d 976.

Employee's services as conductor and musician in connection with motion pictures were rendered without any reservation as to use employer might make of them or as to manner in which completed films might be exploited; employee was in same position as other musicians; as conductor, he had same rights; having been paid for his services, all rights to product of those services passed to employer; rule applies that, where employee creates something as part of his duties under employer, thing created is employer's property unless, by appropriate agreement, employee retains some right in it. Zahler v Columbia Pictures Corp. (1960) 180 Cal App 2d 582, 4 Cal Rptr 612, 125 USPQ 462.

18. Photographs

Person employing photographer to take picture has right to copyright picture and not photographer. Lumiere v Pathe Exchange, Inc. (1921, CA2 NY) 275 F 428; Lumiere v Robertson-Cole Distributing Corp. (1922, CA2 NY) 280 F 550, 24 ALR 1317, cert den 259 US 583, 66 L Ed 1075, 42 S Ct 586; Yardley v Houghton Mifflin Co. (1939, CA2 NY) 108 F2d 28, 44 USPQ 1, cert den 309 US 686, 84 L Ed 1029, 60 S Ct 891.

All rights to delivered picture are in client who hired photographer to take picture; rule applies to commercial photography as well as to portrait photography; evidence of custom and usage cannot be offered to alter rule; however, contract governs if it provides for retention of rights in photographer. Avedon v Exstein (1956, DC NY) 141 F Supp 278, 109 USPQ 376.

19. Others

Where employee secures copyright on treatise relating to use of product of his employer's business, employee holds copyright in trust for employer. United States Ozone Co. v United States Ozone Co. (1932, CA7 Ill) 62 F2d 881, 16 USPQ 233.

Where radio program is written and developed by employee during course of employment for employer radio station, using employer's radio facilities, without any special agreement as to ownership, ownership vests in employer. Storer Broadcasting Co. v Jack (1952, DC Mich) 107 F Supp 988, 95 USPQ 11.

III. CONTRIBUTIONS TO COLLECTIVE WORKS [17 USCS § 201(c)]

20. Generally

Sale of story to magazine company was absolute sale without reservation, including right to dramatize it. Dam v Kirk La Shelle Co. (1910, CA2 NY) 175 F 902 (ovrld on other grounds Sheldon v Metro-Goldwyn Pictures (CA2 NY) 106 F2d 45, affd 309 US 390, 84 L Ed 825, 60 S Ct 681).

Gratuitous contributions to proprietor of book vested such title to contributions in proprietor as might be copyrighted by her. Lawrence v Dana (1869, CC Mass) F Cas No 8136.

21. Advertisements

Absent contrary agreement, advertisements cannot be copyrighted by newspaper, and it is irrelevant that newspaper complied with notice requirements necessary to protect all copyrightable material in newspaper. Brattleboro Publishing Co. v Winmill Publishing Corp. (1966, CA2 Vt) 369 F2d 565, 151 USPQ 666, 5 ALR Fed 617.

Copyright in classified advertisement belongs to advertiser who is original writer of advertisement, and publisher is licensee to publish advertisement. Jacobs v Robitaille (1976, DC NH) 406 F Supp 1145, 189 USPQ 601.

22. Cartoons

If all rights in artist's cartoons were not assigned to magazine publisher, publisher's copyright upon entire issues of magazine does not cover cartoons; it would then follow that cartoons would be in public domain because they were published without a separate copyright; this result would transpire because a work can be copyrighted only by its author or proprietor; proprietor can be assignee but not licensee of right to use work; to be assignee, one must have been assigned all rights in work. Geisel v Poynter Products, Inc. (1968, DC NY) 295 F Supp 331, 160 USPQ 590.

IV. TRANSFER OF OWNERSHIP, GENERALLY [17 USCS § 201(d)(1)]

A. In General

23. Generally

Copyrights can be mortgaged only under federal copyright law. Re Leslie-Judge Co. (1921, CA2 NY) 272 F 886, cert den 256 US 704, 65 L Ed 1180, 41 S Ct 625.

Copyright proprietor may transfer legal title to copyright only in totality; copyright may not be split up and partially assigned as to various rights encompassed therein. Hirshon v United Artists Corp. (1957) 100 App DC 217, 243 F2d 640, 113 USPQ 110.

Compact between state and state reporter, by which latter relinquishes and former assumes copyright in court reports was not inconsistent with laws of United States. Little v Gould (1851, CC NY) F Cas No 8394.

Literary work of author is property and is subject to disposal. Tobani v Carl Fischer, Inc. (DC NY) 36 USPQ 97, mod on other grounds (CA2 NY) 98 F2d 57, 38 USPQ 198, cert den 305 US 650, 83 L Ed 420, 59 S Ct 243.

Transfer of rights sufficient under predecessor section to entitle someone to obtain copyright is not necessarily "an assignment of the copyright," condition precedent to recordation requirement. Davis v E. I. Du Pont De Nemours & Co. (1965, DC NY) 240 F Supp 612, 145 USPQ 258.

24. Right to transfer, generally

Mere possession of manuscript of play by playbroker is not of itself sufficient to give him authority to make contract for sale of copyright. Stodart v Mutual Film Corp. (1917, DC NY) 249 F 507, affd (CA2 NY) 249 F 513.

25. —Co-owners' rights

In absence of existing agreement to contrary, co-owner of copyright has right to give permission to third party to publish copyrighted book. Meredith v Smith (1944, CA9 Cal) 145 F2d 620, 63 USPQ 216.

Where rights in dramatic production belong jointly to two persons, either one may license another to produce such drama on stage or in motion pictures, but such person will be obliged to account to other. Klein v Beach (1916, DC NY) 232 F 240, affd (CA2 NY) 239 F 108.

In action by owner of quarter of motion-picture rights of play to obtain accounting from another quarter owner of profits from making motion picture, copyright proprietors, who assigned half of motion-picture rights to predecessor of both plaintiff and defendant, need not be made parties since complaint does not present question whether action by proprietors has defeated claim for relief and plaintiff claims no more rights than those assigned to predecessor. Crosney v Edward Small Productions, Inc. (1942, DC NY) 52 F Supp 559, 59 USPQ 193.

Although parties stipulate that S and G were joint composers of musical composition, S having written music and S and G together having written lyrics, S's assignee is entitled to one half, not three fourths, interest in renewal copyright, since there are no facts in evidence indicating that ownership was intended as other than as undivided one half interest for each coauthor; assignment, providing for royalties to be paid to S and G, had stated that royalties were to be divided equally; by analogy, coauthors were tenants in common. Sweet Music, Inc. v Melrose Music Corp. (1960, DC Cal) 189 F Supp 655, 127 USPQ 513.

Where contract is entered into between two co-owners of copyright and third person, giving such person right to publish copyrighted work, and providing for payment of $2,000 to such person upon termination of contract by copyright owners, such sum must be paid upon termination although such assignee still retains right to publish work through purchase of rights of one co-owner. Holt v Silver (1897) 169 Mass 435, 48 NE 837.

Generally with respect to problems of co-owners of literary or creative productions in copyright field, courts have held (1) such co-owners are tenants in common, (2) one co-owner may use or license use of production without other's consent, being liable only to account for profits, (3) tendency of courts is to oppose judicial action which discourages collaboration in literary or creative productions or bars publication of creative work, (4) neither co-owner has superior right in literary or creative work, and (5) injunction or action for accounting will not lie against licensee of one co-owner by the other. Noble v D. Van Nostrand Co. (1960) 63 NJ Super 534, 164 A2d 834, 128 USPQ 100.

All co-owners of copyrighted material having joined in granting exclusive motion picture rights to third person, one co-owner alone is unable to procure rescission of contract; also, co-owner may not have partial rescission as to his interest alone since he thereby would acquire right to grant nonexclusive license to produce picture with result that third person's license would become nonexclusive, thus significantly altering position of third person and other co-owners; all co-owners must join to obtain rescission. Denker v Twentieth Century-Fox Film Corp. (1961) 10 NY2d 339, 223 NYS2d 193, 179 NE2d 336, 132 USPQ 82, 3 ALR3d 1292.

Co-owner of copyright may grant license for use of such copyright. Herbert v Fields (1915, Sup) 152 NYS 487.

Where two persons collaborate in writing play upon agreement that each should have interest therein, and one person completes play after death of other, such person completing play cannot receive royalties from licensing of play to exclusion of deceased person's administrator. Ongley v Marcin (1925) 214 App Div 455, 212 NYS 690.

Co-owners of copyrighted material are considered tenants in common; either co-owner has power, acting alone, to grant nonexclusive motion picture rights to third persons but exclusive rights to copyright may be effected only by grant in which all co-owners join. Denker v Twentieth Century-Fox Film Corp. (1961) 10 NY2d 339, 223 NYS2d 193, 179 NE2d 336, 132 USPQ 82, 3 ALR3d 1292.

26. —Renewal rights

In action by first assignee of copyright renewal right against second assignee from common assignor to obtain assignment of renewal procured by second assignee, summary judgment for plaintiff should not be granted without considering issues of fraud and failure of consideration in first assignment although issues were not raised by affirmative defenses. Rossiter v Vogel (1943, CA2 NY) 134 F2d 908, 57 USPQ 161.

Previous judgment that all rights in copyright of Superman Comics belong to publisher includes renewal rights so that creators of comic cannot relitigate title. Siegel v National Periodical Publications, Inc. (1974, CA2 NY) 508 F2d 909, 184 USPQ 257.

Fact that renewal statute gives no right of renewal to legatee does not require holding that legatee of copyright proprietor has no title to original copyright as right and property of copyright owner may be bequeathed by will. Stuff v La Budde Feed & Grain Co. (1941, DC Wis) 42 F Supp 493, 52 USPQ 23.

Widow, who assigned renewal, is not entitled to keep all stipulated royalties against rights (not known when assignment was made) coauthor has in renewal; assignee was to have sole and exclusive right for which it was to pay royalty to widow who succeeded to husband's interest; this interest is impressed with trust in favor of husband's coauthor, with whom widow must share royalties. Edward B. Marks Music Corp. v Wonnell (1945, DC NY) 61 F Supp 722, 65 USPQ 456.

Title to renewal rights in copyrighted musical composition may be established by action for declaratory judgment; where both composer and publisher claim title, there is justiciable issue concerning renewal rights for songs whose original copyright terms have already expired; fact that composer might sue for coercive relief is no bar to this action; justiciable controversy also exists as to unexpired copyrights; fact that 11 unexpired copyright terms will expire at intervals within next seven years confirmed court's opinion that it ought to entertain single action now, rather than to require multiplicity of future suits. Carmichael v Mills Music, Inc. (1954, DC NY) 121 F Supp 43, 101 USPQ 279.

Assignment of expectancy of renewal of copyright must remain in full force where, despite fact that assignee paid large royalties for 30 years, assignors offer no evidence of adjustments necessary to accomplish a complete rescission; it will not do to deprive assignee of copyright as renewed without any adjustment; assignee is entitled to all rights for which he bargained or, if assignors are entitled to relief, to have the bargain completely rescinded. Rose v Bourne, Inc. (1959, DC NY) 176 F Supp 605, 123 USPQ 29, affd (CA2 NY) 279 F2d 79, 125 USPQ 509, cert den 364 US 880, 5 L Ed 2d 103, 81 S Ct 170.

Assignment of individual defendant's copyright renewal rights to corporate defendant acknowledge existence of dispute between individual defendant and plaintiff as to their ownership and provided that corporate defendant acquired no rights until court declared that individual defendant was owner. T. B. Harms Co. v Eliscu (1964, DC NY) 226 F Supp 337, 141 USPQ 11, affd (CA2 NY) 339 F2d 823, 144 USPQ 46, cert den 381 US 915, 14 L Ed 2d 435, 85 S Ct 1534.

Purchase of copyright on condition of also securing renewal copyright is not illegal tie-in invalidating assignment, and purchase of renewal rights together with original copyright for single lump sum payment without allocation does not make assignment unenforceable as to renewal rights. Landon v Twentieth Century-Fox Film Corp. (1974, DC NY) 384 F Supp 450, 185 USPQ 221, (disapproved on other grounds Imperial Point Colonnades Condominium, Inc. v Mangurian (CA5 Fla) 549 F2d 1029, reh den (CA5 Fla) 552 F2d 369).

Assignment by widow of rights in deceased spouse's estate is not effective to convey renewal rights vesting separately in widow upon death of composer spouse. Hill & Range Songs, Inc. v Fred Rose Music, Inc. (1975, DC Tenn) 403 F Supp 420, 189 USPQ 233, motion den (DC Tenn) 413 F Supp 967.

27. Territorial matters

Where license to use copyrighted advertisements is limited to one city, licensee infringes where he publishes advertisements in another city. Local Trademarks, Inc. v Grantham (1957, DC Neb) 166 F Supp 494, 177 USPQ 335.

Plaintiff granted defendant exclusive license to sell plaintiff's copyrighted works of art in specific area which did not include Florida; three days after termination of license, defendant sold one of such works of art in Florida; such sale was infringement of copyright, making defendant liable for statutory damages; also, defendant is ordered to tender to plaintiff all of plaintiff's copyrighted works of art in defendant's possession; plaintiff shall thereupon refund to defendant the cost of such works. Creative Arts, Inc. v Abady & Sultan, Inc. (DC Fla) 134 USPQ 388.

B. Particular Transfers

28. Assignments, generally

Copyright may be assigned, and rights of assignee will be protected same as those of author. Wheaton v Peters (1834) 33 US 591, 8 L Ed 1055; Ager v Murray (1882) 105 US 126, 26 L Ed 942; American Tobacco Co. v Werckmeister (1907) 207 US 284, 52 L Ed 208, 28 S Ct 72.

Contract made by reporter of court of appeals, assigning his copyright rights to volumes of opinions of court, to publisher, does not give publisher any right to volume which reporter compiled after his term of office had expired. Little v Hall (1856) 59 US 165, 15 L Ed 328.

State could not claim title to copyright upon law reports as assignee thereof, where assignor, court reporter, had obtained copyright upon judicial decisions of which he was not author. Banks v Manchester (1888) 128 US 244, 32 L Ed 425, 9 S Ct 36.

Author must have right to copyright in order to make assignment. Bong v Alfred S. Campbell Art Co. (1909) 214 US 236, 53 L Ed 979, 29 S Ct 628.

One other than author or proprietor must have assignment in order to procure copyright. Public Ledger Co. v Post Printing & Publishing Co. (1923, CA8 Mo) 294 F 430.

Author's assignment to wife of half interest in unpublished and uncopyrighted story was ineffective for income tax purposes since assignment lacked economic reality. Wodehouse v Commissioner (1949, CA4) 178 F2d 987, 84 USPQ 162.

It is contrary to public interest to permit anyone to buy up copyright to anything written about himself and to use copyright ownership to restrain others from publishing biographical material concerning him. Rosemont Enterprises, Inc. v Random House, Inc. (1966, CA2 NY) 366 F2d 303, 150 USPQ 715, 23 ALR3d 122, cert den 385 US 1009, 17 L Ed 2d 546, 87 S Ct 714.

Where plaintiff is assignee of copyright, it must have received all of assignor's rights in copyright by valid assignment, and assignor (which took out copyright) must have had authority to take out copyright in its own name and to assign copyright free and clear of any liabilities which would interfere with assignee's title. Machaty v Astra Pictures, Inc. (1952, CA2 NY) 197 F2d 138, 93 USPQ 51, cert den 334 US 827, 97 L Ed 644, 73 S Ct 29.

Assignee, of work from alien author, cannot obtain protection of copyright law. Keene v Wheatley (1861, CC Pa) F Cas No 7644.

Assignment of copyright refers to what is in existence, not to any future contingency, and to what is personal to author. Pierpont v Fowle (1846, CC Mass) F Cas No 11152.

Where person assigns his rights in copyright to another, reserving for himself percentage of profits, he loses all right to copyright. Mackaye v Mallory (1882, CC NY) 12 F 328.

Nonresident foreigner may take and hold by assignment copyright granted to citizen of United States. Carte v Evans (1886, CC Mass) 27 F 861.

Rights of assignee of copyright are measured by those of his assignor. Davies v Bowes (1913, DC NY) 209 F 53, affd (CA2 NY) 219 F 178.

Owners of copyright cannot claim infringement against one using copyrighted matter in advertisements under contract made with copyright holder prior to award of copyright. Industrial R. & Locomotive Works, Inc. v Cagney Bros. (1932, DC NJ) 1 F Supp 970, 15 USPQ 263.

Assignee may not acquire copyright if artist himself, because of domicil and citizenship, could not claim benefit of Copyright Act. Gross v Twentieth Century Fox Film Corp. (DC NY) 38 USPQ 399.

Employee for hire has no rights which can be assigned to third party. Von Tilzer v Jerry Vogel Music Co. (1943, DC NY) 53 F Supp 191, 59 USPQ 292, affd (CA2 NY) 158 F2d 516.

Assignee of copyright takes no more than assignor had at time of assignment. Detective Comics, Inc. v Fawcett Publications, Inc. (1944, DC NY) 4 FRD 237, 64 USPQ 116.

Officers of association, who were authorized to negotiate with composers for permission to publish their songs in compilation, had authority to carry out any proper condition, even if only implied, that composer's rights to be protected; their later assignment of song to composer, who had permitted use of his song without charge, was within scope of their authority; it was fair thing to do; it deprived no member of association of anything to which it was rightfully entitled. Mills Music, Inc. v Cromwell Music, Inc. (1954, DC NY) 126 F Supp 54, 103 USPQ 84.

Only "proprietor" of work may copyright it; person to whom right to copyright is assigned is proprietor; mere licensee cannot copyright work. Morse v Fields (1954, DC NY) 127 F Supp 63, 104 USPQ 54.

Copyright holder who was not author of the pin in question failed to prove an assignment of the pin by the author since there was no exclusive use or an employer-contractor relationship, and therefore did not prove ownership of the copyright. Van Cleef & Arpels, Inc. v Schechter (1969, DC NY) 308 F Supp 674, 164 USPQ 540.

By merely taking assignment, assignee does not become party to private agreements between proprietor and author; when liable to author at all, assignee is liable on theory of equitable lien, not on theory of contract. Gay v Robbins Music Corp. (1942, Sup) 38 NYS2d 337, 55 USPQ 461.

29. —Construction of assignments

Copyright taken out by author will inure to benefit of publisher if contract provides that publisher is to have all rights of copyright; person who assigns his rights to work under contract which provides that assignees "shall have the copyright of said reports to them, their heirs and assigns forever," parts with all his interests in such copyright, and his executors cannot bring suit for infringement. Paige v Banks (1872) 80 US 608, 20 L Ed 709.

Instrument reading "I hereby transfer the copyright in my picture" when read in light of other circumstances, is construed as assignment of all rights and not mere license. American Tobacco Co. v Werckmeister (1907) 207 US 284, 52 L Ed 208, 28 S Ct 72.

Contract wherein foreign author agrees to have play copyrighted "prior to its appearance in the book trade" does not convey author's title or right to copyright in United States. Saake v Lederer (1909, CA3 Pa) 174 F 135.

Royalties are due under contract for assignment of copyright in song rather than rescission of contract where assignee paid portion of royalties due, and breach of contract by withholding portion of royalties did not amount to fraud requiring rescission. Nolan v Sam Fox Publishing Co. (1974, CA2 NY) 499 F2d 1394, 182 USPQ 513.

Assignment of copyright of play by publisher to author conveyed only statutory play right and not copyright. Fitch v Young (1911, DC NY) 230 F 743, affd (CA2 NY) 239 F 1021.

Where composer objected to unauthorized use of his song in connection with radio program and applied for copyright in 1930, such facts show that composer did not completely assign song to third party by allowing him to include such song in song book which had been published in 1921. Egner v E. C. Schirmer Music Co. (1942, DC Mass) 48 F Supp 187, 56 USPQ 214, affd (CA1 Mass) 139 F2d 398, 60 USPQ 74 cert den 322 US 730, 88 L Ed 1565, 64 S Ct 947.

Combination of members of American Society of Composers, Authors, and Publishers in transferring to American Society of Composers, Authors, and Publishers all their nondramatic performing rights in their copyrighted musical works is combination in restraint of interstate commerce prohibited by Antitrust Laws [15 USCS §§ 1 et seq.], especially since American Society of Composers, Authors, and Publishers has power to fix prices. Alden-Rochelle, Inc. v American Soc. of Composers, Authors & Publishers (1948, DC NY) 80 F Supp 888, 78 USPQ 197.

Unless assignment of copyright grants assignee right to sue for infringements antedating assignment, no such right is conferred. Group Publishers, Inc. v Winchell (1949, DC NY) 86 F Supp 573, 83 USPQ 461.

Music publishers to whom writers transfer their compositions with right to secure copyright, but with obligation to pay royalties, are obligated to exploit them in good faith for benefit of writers, as well as for themselves. Schwartz v Broadcast Music, Inc. (1959, DC NY) 180 F Supp 322, 124 USPQ 34.

Only copyright owner at time of infringement is entitled to bring actions for infringement in absence of express provision in copyright assignment conferring cause of action on assignee; rule applies although assignor and assignee are corporations having same directors, officers, and stockholders. DeSilva Constr. Corp. v Herrald (1962, DC Fla) 213 F Supp 184, 137 USPQ 96.

Copyright claimants' assignment of interest in musical composition "subject to our ownership hereto," merely reserves claimants' right on any copies which might have been previously published without incurring liability, and does not reserve prospective ownership rights; assignee's earlier assignment to third party of interest in copyrighted composition transfers to third party assignee's title acquired under subsequent assignment from copyright claimants. Rosette v Rainbo Record Mfg. Corp. (1973, DC NY) 354 F Supp 1183, affd (CA2 NY) 546 F2d 461.

In contract granting factor exclusive right to place creator's indorsement upon designs, and granting him right to take out any copyrights as may be necessary, and providing for accounting of profits each month, implies promise on part of factor to use reasonable efforts to bring profits into existence. Wood v Lucy, Lady Duff-Gordon

(1917) 222 NY 88, 118 NE 214, reh den 222 NY 643, 118 NE 1082.

30. —Form of assignments

Transfer by author of his manuscript for sum of money "in full payment for story" vested purchaser with proprietory rights therein. Dam v Kirk La Shelle Co. (1910, CA2 NY) 175 F 902 (ovrld on other grounds Sheldon v Metro-Goldwyn Pictures (CA2 NY) 106 F2d 45, affd 309 US 390, 84 L Ed 825, 60 S Ct 681).

Acquiescence in publication of author's manuscript or in republication of his printed book would authorize presumption of assignment. Bartlett v Crittenden (1849, CC Ohio) F Cas No 1076.

Plaintiff's possession of manuscript is evidence of his ownership and is sufficient against defendants who had no rights therein; since authors of musical composition did not take out copyright, there was no need for formal assignment from them to plaintiff who obtained copyright. Freudenthal v Hebrew Pub. Co. (1942, DC NY) 44 F Supp 754, 53 USPQ 466.

Where copyright owner transferred all its assets under general assignment and assets were insufficient to pay creditors, assignment included copyright although not specifically mentioned, and subsequent assignment of copyright by original owner gave no title. Kaplan v Fox Film Corp. (DC NY) 37 USPQ 248.

Copyright of book and movie rights therein are rights of literary property incapable of manual delivery; affidavit filed in copyright office after death of copyright proprietor, claiming that he had conveyed all rights in copyrighted book to affiant, was insufficient. Snook v Blank (1948, DC Mont) 92 F Supp 518, 87 USPQ 201.

Where artist authorized publisher to reproduce painting once in its magazine but did not assign copyright on painting, it is doubtful whether artist succeeds to copyright by virtue of assignment from publisher, where assignment purports to convey not copyright on reproduction, but copyright on original painting. Leigh v Barnhart (1951, DC NJ) 96 F Supp 194, 89 USPQ 307.

Though informal and unrecorded, written assignment of copyrighted song is sufficient as between parties to pass to assignee all rights of assignors in copyright and song. Klasmer v Baltimore Football, Inc. (1961, DC Md) 200 F Supp 255, 132 USPQ 36.

Sheriff's sale of items including copyright certificates is not effective to transfer copyright, because certificate is not copyright and certificate possessor is not ipso facto copyright owner, and copyright assignment requires instrument in writing, but motions for summary judgment are denied to resolve disputed facts at trial. Kingsrow Enterprises, Inc. v Metromedia, Inc. (1975, DC NY) 397 F Supp 879, 189 USPQ 90.

If motion-picture producer is not commercially soliciting, and is not willing to accept obligation to pay for, valuable ideas, or compositions adapting them, which ideas are offered to be conveyed only upon assumption of such obligation, he does not need to read manuscripts, which he knows are submitted on those terms, and then use them. Desny v Wilder (1956) 46 Cal 2d 715, 299 P2d 257, 110 USPQ 433.

Fact that actor expressly accepted literary material submitted by author and invited submission of further material indicates that express contract to pay for material if used could be reasonably implied; only item unexpressed is amount or rate of compensation. Yadkoe v Fields (1944) 66 Cal App 2d 150, 151 P2d 906, 63 USPQ 103.

Fact that cartoonist by sale of legal title fully divested himself of all rights in his drawings and characters is evidenced by fact that on several occasions he asked for and obtained express permission from owner to use drawings and characters for his own benefit. Segar v King Features Syndicate, Inc. (1940) 175 Misc 25, 22 NYS2d 790, 47 USPQ 46 mod on other grounds 262 App Div 221, 28 NYS2d 542, 50 USPQ 399, reh den 262 App Div 993, 30 NYS2d 811 and affd without opinion 289 NY 579, 43 NE2d 717, reh den 289 NY 643, 44 NE2d 617.

31. —Restrictive conditions

Restrictions not to resell, rent, or export attached to sale of uncopyrighted motion-picture film were invalid. Universal Film Mfg. Co. v Copperman (1914, CA2 NY) 218 F 577, cert den 235 US 704, 59 L Ed 433, 35 S Ct 209.

Contract provided that artist convey to publisher all title to paintings and also right to use artist's name therewith; condition is not implied into contract that publisher cannot publish paintings without accrediting them to artist. Vargas v Esquire, Inc. (1947, CA7 Ill) 164 F2d 522, 75 USPQ 304.

Art work is personal property, transferrable by sale and delivery; there is no distinction in that respect between it and any other property; paintings are no exception to general rule; if in transfer there is any limitation for artist's benefit, it must be expressed and clearly imposed; otherwise it is not presumed; burden of showing limitation is on artist. Grant v Kellogg Co. (1944, DC NY) 58 F Supp 48, 63 USPQ 173, affd (CA2 NY) 154 F2d 59, 75 USPQ 301.

Owner of patent right, copyright, or trademark, having exclusive right to manufacture and sell article, may impose upon his assignee such restrictions as he may see proper, and to which his assignee will agree, including price and territory within which article may be sold. Coca-Cola Co. v State (1920, Tex Civ App) 225 SW 791.

32. Bequests; intestate succession

On intestate death of copyright proprietor, title to copyright was vested in heirs at law by Illinois statute of descent and distribution; assignment of copyright by heirs is valid and passes title to assignee. Forster Music Publishers, Inc. v Jerry Vogel Music Co. (DC NY) 62 USPQ 142, aff'd (CA2 NY) 147 F2d 614, 64 USPQ 417, cert den 325 US 880, 89 L Ed 1996, 65 S Ct 1573.

Bequest transferring copyright separate from provisions of will establishing trust show testator's intent to transfer title to copyright and not merely income from copyright. Bell v Combined Registry Co. (1975, DC Ill) 188 USPQ 707.

33. Gift of ownership

Author may, through knowledge and acquiescence, give publisher of his work right to copyright. Pulte v Derby (1852, CC Ohio) F Cas No 11465.

Corporation owned exclusive license to produce musical play and motion picture based on licensor's play; individual, who owned 98% of corporation's shares, wrote letter to his secretary, stating that he gave her stated percentage of his "shares of profits" of musical play and motion picture; delivery of letter constituted valid, complete, present gift of share in royalties when and if collected from musical play and motion picture and transferred to secretary enforcible right to such share of royalties to accrue to stockholder on production of musical play and motion picture even though, at time of delivery of letter, musical play and motion picture were not in existence. Speelman v Pascal (1961) 10 NY2d 313, 222 NYS2d 324, 178 NE2d 723, 131 USPQ 489.

34. Licenses, generally

In action on infringement of copyright, defendant cannot use as defense alleged written contract of license, when such contract is not produced or satisfactorily accounted for. Historical Pub. Co. v Jones Bros. Pub. Co. (1916, CA3 Pa) 231 F 638.

License from coholder of copyright immunizes licensee from liability to other coholder for copyright infringement. McKay v Columbia Broadcasting System, Inc. (1963, CA2 NY) 324 F2d 762, 139 USPQ 400.

Assignment by foreign author of his proprietory right to play for United States operated as mere license, under which assignee, though she had no rights under copyright law, would receive equitable protection in her license rights. Keene v Wheatley (1861, CC Pa) F Cas No 7644.

Oral agreement between foreign company and author regarding former's use of author's article was but license, and copyright was properly taken in author's name. Black v Henry G. Allen Co. (1893, CC NY) 56 F 764.

When copyrighted book is sold without agreement concerning such sale, notice in book that "no dealer is licensed to sell it at a less price" than that stated, reserves no right to seller and does not constitute buyer licensee. Bobbs-Merrill Co. v Straus (1905, CC NY) 139 F 155, affd (CA2 NY) 147 F 15, affd 210 US 339, 52 L Ed 1086, 28 S Ct 722.

Evidence that author sold rights to perform play on stage after selling rights of publication to plaintiff and that check from plaintiff to author was indorsed "For all serial rights," showed license and not assignment to plaintiff. New Fiction Pub. Co. v Star Co. (1915, DC NY) 220 F 994

Burden of proving license is on persons claiming it. Schellberg v Empringham (1929, DC NY) 36 F2d 991.

Mere license to publish is not proprietorship. Quinn-Brown Pub. Corp. v Chilton Co. (1936, DC NY) 15 F Supp 213, 30 USPQ 373.

Where complainants were in receivership in state court at time notices of alleged cancellation were mailed, it is incumbent on plaintiff to show that such action was with permission of state court; failing in this, court holds licenses not cancelled. Buck v Trianon Co. (1939, DC Wash) 26 F Supp 96, 40 USPQ 425.

Holders of domestic copyrights may refrain from licensing at all. Paine v Electrical Research Products, Inc. (1939, DC NY) 27 F Supp 780, 41 USPQ 575.

Any limitation or conditions which parties insert are binding and may be enforced except where they are contrary to public policy or in violation of law; thus, it is proper for license to fix release date of moving picture upon basis of time of closing of stage play. Inge v Twentieth Century-Fox Film Corp. (1956, DC NY) 143 F Supp 294, 11 USPQ 153.

To be effective as a transfer of ownership in copyright, transfer must convey all ownership rights; legal title to copyright may be transferred only in totality; when rights are split up and partially assigned either as to time, place, or particular rights, limited grant of exclusive rights operates merely as a license, not an assignment of ownership of copyright. First Financial Marketing Services Group, Inc. v Field Promotions,

Inc. (1968, DC NY) 286 F Supp 295, 159 USPQ 572.

35. —Construction of licenses

Contract for license for "sole and exclusive use of advance sheets" conveys only qualified interest, and does not entitle licensee to right to copyright. Fraser v Uack (1902, CA7 Ill) 116 F 285.

One licensing use of copyrighted song in compilation consented to its use in subsequent editions. Gabriel v McCabe (1896, CC Ill) 74 F 743.

Giving license to publish copyrighted material under licensee's own copyright without insertion of original copyright notice is abandonment. West Publishing Co. v Edward Thompson Co. (1909, CC NY) 169 F 833, mod on other grounds (CA2 NY) 176 F 833.

License to produce copyrighted play on spoken stage may well be perpetual license when agreement is silent as to duration of licensee's rights. Fitch v Shubert (1937, DC NY) 20 F Supp 314, 35 USPQ 245.

Copyright license clauses are interpreted as seems most reasonable to accomplish purposes and as interpreted by parties. Paine v Electrical Research Products, Inc. (1939, DC NY) 27 F Supp 780, 41 USPQ 575.

Nonexclusive license to defendant to use some of music of plaintiff's opera in moving picture does not preclude plaintiff from granting to another right to make motion picture of opera. G. Ricordi & Co. v Paramount Pictures, Inc. (1950, DC NY) 92 F Supp 537, 86 USPQ 452, mod on other grounds (CA2 NY) 189 F2d 469, 89 USPQ 289, cert den 342 US 849, 96 L Ed 641, 72 S Ct 77.

Grant to another of exclusive right to sell, lease, license, or exhibit positive prints made from licensor's negatives excludes licensor from so dealing with positive prints. Weiss v Hollywood Film Enterprises, Inc. (Cal Sup Ct) 81 USPQ 570.

Where defendant fails to comply with terms of contract of license within time limit specified, and plaintiff declares contract terminated, state court may issue temporary injunction against defendant, preventing him from acting under license until question as to whether license is terminated is adjudicated. Bobbs-Merrill Co. v Universal Film Mfg. Co. (1916, Sup) 160 NYS 37.

36. —Restraint of trade; anti-trust matters

Although object of copyright law is to secure monopoly, contracts made by owners of copyrights whereby, in order to maintain price of books, through publishers and booksellers associations, any dealer who sells his books below prescribed price is blacklisted and prevented from buying more books, may be in violation of the Anti-Trust Laws [15 USCS §§ 1 et seq.]. Straus & Straus v American Publishers' Asso. (1913) 231 US 222, 58 L Ed 192, 34 S Ct 84.

Contract, by which first-run motion-picture exhibitor required distributor and holder of copyrights to impose restrictions as to price and character of exhibition by subsequent run exhibitors, was not protected by such copyrights. Interstate Circuit, Inc. v United States (1939) 306 US 208, 83 L Ed 610, 59 S Ct 467, 40 USPQ 299.

Distributor of trade-marked articles may not lawfully limit by agreement, express or implied, price at which or persons to whom its purchaser may resell, except as seller moves along route marked by Miller-Tydings Act [15 USCS § 1]; even additional protection of copyright or patent adds nothing to distributor's power to control prices of resale by purchaser; same is true as to restriction of customers. United States v Bausch & Lomb Optical Co. (1944) 321 US 707, 88 L Ed 1024, 64 S Ct 805, 61 USPQ 61.

Irrespective of amount of trade or commerce, contracts providing for sharing of revenues from licensing of musical performance rights constitute unlawful restraint of trade under § 1 of Sherman Antitrust Act [15 USCS § 1]; although defendant's contracts with publishers, whereby it obtains exclusive performance rights in copyrighted music, violate Antitrust Acts [15 USCS §§ 1 et seq.], plaintiff does not show injury entitling it to treble damages since plaintiff is not publisher but rival which seeks to have publishers enter into contracts with it rather than with defendant. Affiliated Music Enterprises, Inc. v Sesac, Inc. (1959, CA2 NY) 268 F2d 13, cert den 361 US 831, 4 L Ed 2d 74, 80 S Ct 82.

It is not unlawful for copyright owners merely to pool their compositions for one royalty for them as pooled and no valid exercise of police power can limit it; so long as combination is not to unlawfully fix prices there is no offense in mere pooling. Buck v Gibbs (1940, DC Fla) 34 F Supp 510, 46 USPQ 455, mod on other grounds 313 US 387, 85 L Ed 1416, 61 S Ct 962, 49 USPQ 468, 136 ALR 1426.

Provision in exclusive license requiring licensee to get prints of copyrighted motion pictures exclusively from licensor is no abuse of lawful copyright monopoly; licensor, as copyright proprietor, could license exhibition of pictures and could license or retain right to process and reproduce its own films. Cardinal Films, Inc. v Republic Pictures Corp. (1957, DC NY) 148 F Supp 156, 112 USPQ 292.

Contract, granting license to print copyrighted prayer book and containing provisions that such books shall not be sold below specified price, is not agreement in violation of Antitrust Laws [15 USCS §§ 1 et seq.]. Murphy v Christian Press Ass'n Pub. Co. (1899) 38 App Div 426, 56 NYS 597.

37. —Royalty matters

Licensee's failure to pay royalties stipulated by license for manufacture of records of musical composition makes it liable to triple damages because of incorporation of statutory provision in license and authorizes licensor to repudiate license. Edward B. Marks Music Corp. v Foullon (1949, CA2 NY) 171 F2d 905, 80 USPQ 56.

Agreement to pay royalties, including advance of $200, is adequate consideration for copyright assignment. Edward B. Marks Music Corp. v Charles K. Harris Music Publishing Co. (1958, CA2 NY) 255 F2d 518, 117 USPQ 308, cert den 358 US 831, 3 L Ed 2d 69, 79 S Ct 51.

One who acquires copyright from trustee in bankruptcy who has notice of agreement for payment of royalty to author is required to fulfill agreement of bankrupt concerning payment of royalty. Cohan v Richmond (1936, DC NY) 19 F Supp 771, 35 USPQ 80.

In action on contract licensing recordation and reproduction of musical compositions, it was decided that each time defendant exported and used in foreign country recordations of compositions on which plaintiffs principals held domestic or Canadian copyrights, and which were in public domain, defendant became obligated to pay stipulated compensation for such use as was made of compositions. Paine v Electrical Research Products, Inc. (1939, DC NY) 27 F Supp 780, 41 USPQ 575.

Plaintiff's failure to pay royalties on folios is not breach of contract to pay royalties on each printed copy of song sold since in music publishing industry "printed copy" applies to sheet music only and does not include copy in folio. Von Tilzer v Jerry Vogel Music Co. (1943, DC NY) 53 F Supp 191, 59 USPQ 292, affd (CA2 NY) 158 F2d 516, 71 USPQ 285.

If licensee fails to pay royalties, licensor, copyright owner, may terminate license and sue former licensee as infringer for publication of copyrighted work after cancellation of license. King v Edward B. Marks Music Corp. (1944, DC NY) 56 F Supp 446, 62 USPQ 249.

Whether royalty payments specified in copyright assignment are fair or unfair must be decided by parties to assignment and cannot be decided by court in absence of fraud or overreaching. Fisher v Edwin H. Morris & Co. (DC NY) 113 USPQ 251.

Agreement to pay royalties on certain uses of musical composition constitutes valid consideration for assignment of composition. Rose v Bourne, Inc. (1959, DC NY) 176 F Supp 605, 123 USPQ 29, affd (CA2 NY) 279 F2d 79, 125 USPQ 509, cert den 364 US 880, 5 L Ed 2d 103, 81 S Ct 170.

Person, granted license to perform musical compositions, upon payment of specified amount each month, must pay such amount whether or not such performances were for profit. Maxwell v Faust Co. (1915) 90 Misc 702, 154 NYS 224.

Where person by contract agrees to pay royalty for each week musical sketch is produced, he is not obligated to pay any royalties when he does not produce sketch. Kennedy v Rolfe (1916) 174 App Div 10, 160 NYS 93.

Under contract granting defendant right to produce play in motion pictures with provision that sum of money equal to twenty per cent of gross sales derived by defendant should be paid to plaintiff, defendant is bound only to pay twenty per cent of money received by him and not to pay percentage upon moneys received by exhibitor. Arden v Lubin (1916) 173 App Div 782, 160 NYS 109.

Where plaintiff licenses defendant to produce play for period of three years, and such contract provides for payment of percentage of profits to plaintiff at end of each season and that plaintiff is not responsible for losses, defendant cannot, where there was loss first season and profit second, deduct such losses from plaintiff's percentage of second season's profits. West End Theatre Syndicate, Ltd. v Shubert (1917) 180 App Div 310, 167 NYS 250.

Royalties must be recovered by action at law, and not by way of accounting. Danks v Gordon (1922) 119 Misc 571, 197 NYS 648.

Contract licensing defendant to make motion-picture plays of certain plays owned by plaintiff, for period of eight years, may be rescinded by plaintiff after six months when royalties required by contract are no longer paid, and there is likelihood that default will continue. De Mille Co. v Casey (1923) 121 Misc 78, 201 NYS 20.

Where plaintiff assigns all his right, title, and interest to right of copyright of song, contract assigning such right providing for certain payment of royalties to plaintiff, suit for accounting in equity cannot be had when such royalties are not paid, since relationship existing between plaintiff and assignee is that of debtor and creditor. Ehrlich v Jack Mills, Inc. (1925) 215 App Div 116, 213 NYS 395, affd 248 NY 598, 162 NE 539.

One who undertakes to work property, such as copyright on royalty arrangement, is obligated to work it in good faith and for benefit of recipient of royalties, as well as for own avail; if he fails so to do, and thereby destroys essential object of royalty contract, rescission may be decreed. Broadcast Music, Inc. v Taylor (1945) 10 Misc 2d 9, 55 NYS2d 94, 65 USPQ 503.

38. —Transfers by licensees

Licensee may sell unbound copyright book, which any purchaser may bind and sell. Kipling v G. P. Putnam's Sons (1903, CA2 NY) 120 F 631.

Person licensed to use uncopyrighted manuscript of play for specific purpose cannot assign right to copyright such work to publisher. Koppel v Downing (1897) 11 App DC 93.

Contract licensing newspaper publishing company to print certain copyrighted articles is assignable when there is no express provision to contrary, and rights under such contract will devolve upon anyone purchasing assets of such company from receiver. Meyer v Washington Times Co. (1935) 64 App DC 218, 76 F2d 988, cert den 295 US 734, 79 L Ed 1682, 55 S Ct 646.

Copyright owner in authorizing partnership, of which he is member, to publish and sell his copyrighted maps does not authorize such partnership or any member of partnership, other than himself, right to license others to print such map. Sauer v Detroit Times Co. (1917, DC Mich) 247 F 687.

Bare licensee authorized to publish story in magazine has no right to authorize another to publish story in book; that licensee copyrighted magazine gives it no right to authorize publication in book; blanket copyright on issue of periodical does not give any rights to particular article unless such rights had been previously assigned to publisher. Ilyin v Avon Publications, Inc. (1956, DC NY) 144 F Supp 368, 110 USPQ 356.

Composer licensed another to record song; license was silent as to licensee's right to assign license; it was unassignable without express provision to that effect since down payment paid composer was nominal, with composer to be paid percentage of sales, and since license involved relationship of personal credit and confidence; therefore, acts of licensee's assignee, who made and sold recordings without copyright notice, cannot be charged to composer. Mills Music, Inc. v Cromwell Music, Inc. (1954, DC NY) 126 F Supp 54, 103 USPQ 84.

Licensee who has received from author right of dramatic reproduction is liable to author, if, without authority, he grants rights to produce play in motion picture. Underhill v Schenck (1924) 238 NY 7, 143 NE 773, 33 ALR 303.

V. TRANSFER OF OWNERSHIP OF PARTICULAR RIGHTS [17 USCS § 201(d)(2)]

39. Generally

Copyright owner can assign separately one or more of sum of separable rights making up copyright property, but when he splits off rights by assignment, assignee does not become owner of copyright and acquires only lesser rights granted by assignment; it does not matter whether he is called assignee in instrument or whether it is called assignment; if he gets only rights of licensee, so-called assignment amounts only to license. Goldsmith v Commissioner (1944, CA2) 143 F2d 466, 62 USPQ 112, cert den 323 US 774, 89 L Ed 619, 65 S Ct 135.

Exclusive and perpetual grant of any one of "bundle of rights" which go to make up copyright is "sale" of personal property, rather than mere "license." Herwig v United States (1952) 122 Ct Cl 493, 105 F Supp 384, 93 USPQ 421.

Publisher may make valid transfer of copyright on one picture in periodical, keeping for himself copyright on all other contents of periodical. Kaplan v Fox Film Corp. (1937, DC NY) 19 F Supp 780, 33 USPQ 469.

Owner of copyrighted property may grant license to use or exercise some or all of rights in and to such property, or he may make full and complete disposition or sale of property and his rights with respect thereto. Cory v Commissioner (1955) 23 TC 775(A), 104 USPQ 209, affd (CA2) 230 F2d 941, 109 USPQ 1, cert den 352 US 828, 1 L Ed 2d 50, 77 S Ct 43.

40. Right to reproduce copies (as specified in 17 USCS § 106(1))

Assignment of certain rights of reproduction of painting by foreign author not entitled to secure copyright here was ineffectual as basis upon which United States copyright could be properly granted. Bong v Alfred S. Campbell Art Co. (1907, CA2 NY) 155 F 116, affd 214 US 236, 53 L Ed 979, 29 S Ct 628.

Sale of painting with right of reproduction reserved did not vest purchaser with rights of "proprietor." Werckmeister v Springer Lithographing Co. (1894, CC NY) 63 F 808.

41. Right to make derivative work (as specified in 17 USCS § 106(2))

Where publishing company copyrighted song under royalty agreement with composer and later with author's consent copyrighted orchestral arrangement of song; then, to settle dispute concerning song, transferred copyright of song to author, such transfer did not affect rights of publishers to copyright of orchestral score. Edmonds v Stern (1918, CA2 NY) 248 F 897.

License released licensee from consequence of any infringement in composing "arrangement" of musical composition and consented to its future use in manufacturing records; when licensor excepted from licensee's rights any "use" without its consent of song in "medley," only reasonable implication was that other "arrangements" did not need its consent, for medley is "arrangement"; negotiations between parties support same conclusion. Edward B. Marks Music Corp. v Foullon (1949, CA2 NY) 171 F2d 905, 80 USPQ 56.

Defendant employed composer to record composer's new arrangement of musical composition owned by third party; later, composer assigned new arrangement to plaintiff, who copyrighted it; prior to such copyrighting, defendant had sold 4,000 records; composer of new arrangement was vested with right to grant valid licenses; this was vested property right which he could assign; plaintiff's application for copyright did not do away with rights which defendant had acquired before that time. Biltmore Music Corp. v Kittinger (1956, CA9 Cal) 238 F2d 373, 111 USPQ 228, cert den 352 US 954, 1 L Ed 2d 243, 77 S Ct 327.

Renewal copyright for novel does not affect copyright in derivative motion picture based on novel and made and copyrighted before death of author who specifically granted derivative rights under renewal copyright. Rohauer v Killiam Shows, Inc. (1977, CA2) 192 USPQ 545.

Licensee of popular song has right so to alter copyrighted work as to suit his own style and interpretation. Stratchborneo v Arc Music Corp. (1973, DC NY) 357 F Supp 1393.

42. Right to publish or distribute, generally (as specified in 17 USCS § 106(3))

Contract for publication of foreign book in United States which did not expressly assign author's rights and which contained provision that "the said William Meyer Foster [author] agrees to have the within-named play in order to have the protection of the American law copyrighted prior to its appearance in the book trade," did not convey author's title. Saake v Lederer (1909, CA3 Pa) 174 F 135.

Licensee with permission to publish song in compilation is neither assignee nor proprietor and cannot copyright song when he copyrights combination. Egner v E. C. Schirmer Music Co. (1943, CA1 Mass) 139 F2d 398, 60 USPQ 74, cert den 322 US 730, 88 L Ed 1565, 64 S Ct 947.

Mere contract authorizing publication of story in magazine does not imply sale of copyright.

Ford v Charles E. Blaney Amusement Co. (1906, CC NY) 148 F 642.

Contract granting exclusive right to publish plaintiff's book for period of ten years and providing that publisher shall advertise book during such period, and otherwise promote its sale, implies that publisher shall not publish another book concerning which statements are made which depreciate value of plaintiff's book. Foster v Callaghan & Co. (1918, DC NY) 248 F 944.

Contract by foreign newspaper, granting certain facilities and rights of republication of news matter to American newspaper did not constitute latter "proprietor" within meaning of predecessor section. Public Ledger v New York Times (1921, DC NY) 275 F 562, affd (CA2 NY) 279 F 747, cert den 258 US 627, 66 L Ed 798, 42 S Ct 383.

Where contract granting exclusive publication rights to defendant by plaintiff and deceased provided that contract could not be cancelled except by mutual consent of authors, or in event of death of one of authors by mutual consent of executor of estate and remaining author, son of deceased author was necessary party to cancellation even though mother had consented to cancellation, and son had requested payment of royalties to mother. Anderson v Educational Publishers, Inc. (DC Minn) 87 USPQ 149.

Conveyance of "exclusive right of publication" of copyrighted books cannot be construed as withholding right of paperback publication even though contract provides that "the general format shall be consistent with the educational purposes for which the material is intended" since publication in paperback form is not inconsistent with such purposes; moreover, provision for minimum royalties cannot be construed as limiting exclusive right of publication to books with hard covers; also, author is not entitled to rescind contract so far as it grants paperback rights, on ground that publisher failed to exploit such rights, since there was no market for paperbacks at time contract was signed and later it was author's contention that publisher did not have such rights. Dolch v Garrard Publishing Co. (1968, DC NY) 289 F Supp 687, 159 USPQ 480.

Plaintiff granted to defendant right to publish music which had been assigned by authors to plaintiff; defendant copyrighted music; after obtaining copyright, defendant held it in trust for plaintiff to extent that plaintiff reserved all rights except music publication rights. April Productions, Inc. v G. Schirmer, Inc. (1955) 308 NY 366, 126 NE2d 283, 105 USPQ 286, 69 ALR2d 1305.

43. —Phonorecords

License to use musical composition in manufacture of sound records does not include right to inclose words on printed slips in boxes containing such records. Standard Music Roll Co. v Mills (1917, CA3 NJ) 241 F 360.

Where one is licensed to manufacture and sell records, license covers another's share in manufacture and its delivery of finished product to licensee for sale; only liability is that of licensee. Edward B. Marks Music Corp. v Foullon (1949, CA2 NY) 171 F2d 905, 80 USPQ 56.

German granted to defendant's predecessor the right to make and vend phonograph records in Czechoslovakia, but not in United States; German granted to plaintiff right to make and vend same records in United States; since owner of literary property may, by negative covenant, subject use of such property to restrictions in hands of remote assignee, defendant cannot claim rights to make and vend records outside of Czechoslovakia. Capitol Records, Inc. v Mercury Records Corp. (1955, CA2 NY) 221 F2d 657, 105 USPQ 163.

Composer's authorization that recording be made of his song is broad enough to include license to distribute records. Royal v Radio Corp. of America (DC NY) 107 USPQ 173.

44. Right to perform, generally (as specified in 17 USCS § 106(4))

License to perform nondramatic renditions of musical compositions excludes therefrom "oratorios, choral, operatic or dramatico-musical works (including plays with music, reviews and ballets) in their entirety"; this is clear indication of intent that permission to play and sing all songs included in some work of another character does not give right to perform over-all work; same conclusion is reached from exclusion of "songs or other excerpts from operas or musical plays accompanied either by words, pantomime, dance, or visual representation of the work from which the music is taken"; provision that "fragments of instrumental selections from such works may be instrumentally rendered without words, dialogue, costume accompanying dramatic action or scenic accessory, and unaccompanied by any stage action or visual representation of the work of which such music forms a part" prohibits addition to instrumental rendition of instrumental selections of any words and dialogue; license is construed to permit rendition of noninstrumental compositions with "words, dialogue, costume accompanying dramatic action or scenic accessory" without such rendition getting into dramatic class; thus, songs may be sung in intermission between acts of nonrelated dramatic performance. April Productions, Inc. v

Strand Enterprises, Inc. (1955, CA2 NY) 221 F2d 292, 105 USPQ 83.

Giving of professional copies of copyrighted musical composition does not constitute license to publicly perform such composition. Harms v Cohen (1922, DC Pa) 279 F 276.

Fact that licensee of copyrighted musical compositions, having right to give performances for profits, gave no performances for profit did not affect his liability for agreed compensation. Maxwell v Faust Co. (1915) 90 Misc 702, 154 NYS 224.

Constitution of membership corporation of music composers and publishers provides that members shall, as condition of becoming such, assign performing rights to corporation; formal assignment is prerequisite to corporation's acquisition of rights in members' compositions and where member never gave assignment, but refused to give one when belatedly requested to do so, corporation never acquired any rights in member's compositions. Kubik v American Composers Alliance, Inc. (1945, Sup) 54 NYS2d 764, 65 USPQ 62.

Five-year assignments of public performing rights by publisher to American Society of Composers, Authors, and Publishers were modus operandi for effectuating basic purpose of parties as American Society of Composers, Authors, and Publishers members; it is breach of contract and trust for publisher to attempt to cut off rights of other members of American Society of Composers, Authors, and Publishers by licensing society's competitor without their consent and without paying them part of consideration from competitor; American Society of Composers, Authors, and Publishers remains beneficial owner of public performance rights with sole right to grant licenses as to songs composed by composer members. Broadcast Music, Inc. v Taylor (1945) 10 Misc 2d 9, 55 NYS2d 94, 65 USPQ 503.

45. —Dramatic works

Owner of copyright of book may give person sole right of performing particular copyrighted drama based upon book, and give another right of performing different dramatic composition of same story. Harper & Bros. v Kalem Co. (1909, CA2 NY) 169 F 61, affd 222 US 55, 56 L Ed 92, 32 S Ct 20.

Right of dramatization is included in sale of story appearing in and covered by copyright of periodical in which it appears. Dam v Kirk La Shelle Co. (1910, CA2 NY) 175 F 902 (ovrld on other grounds Sheldon v Metro-Goldwyn Pictures (CA2 NY) 106 F2d 45, affd 309 US 390, 84 L Ed 825, 60 S Ct 681).

In contract granting plaintiff license to produce exclusively copyrighted play upon living stage, expressly reserving motion-picture rights to owners of copyright, law does not imply negative covenant that copyright owners cannot grant right to produce talking motion pictures which may come in competition with plaintiff's stage productions. MacLoon v Vitagraph, Inc. (1929, CA2 NY) 30 F2d 634.

Script writer does not infringe copyrighted novel by making dramatization thereof under contract with party to whom copyright owner had assigned right to dramatize. Szekely v Eagle Lion Films, Inc. (1957, CA2 NY) 242 F2d 266, 113 USPQ 98, cert den 354 US 922, 1 L Ed 2d 1437, 77 S Ct 1382.

Contract providing that "the party of the first part secures the exclusive dramatic rights including moving picture rights" and "the party of the first part has exclusive leasing of the play" and that contract will not terminate upon death, but is to be carried out by heirs, executors, or assigns of parties, creates assignment and not license; holder of copyright of book may sell right to dramatize story to one person and right to make motion-picture play to another. Photo Drama Motion Picture Co. v Social Uplift Film Corp. (1914, DC NY) 213 F 374, affd (CA2 NY) 220 F 448.

Playright and copyright are distinct, and although printed publication may forfeit both, author may reserve his playright from assignment to publishing company of right to print play in story form. Fitch v Young (1911, DC NY) 230 F 743, affd (CA2 NY) 239 F 1021.

Where motion-picture rights remain in grantee, under contract made while motion-picture industry was in its infancy, granting licensee right to produce drama on stage, such grantee cannot use such picture rights to detriment of any rights of licensees. Harper Bros. v Klaw (1916, DC NY) 232 F 609.

Less evidence to prove licensor's title to drama is required where licensee of motion-picture rights to drama has acted under his license. Hart v Fox (1917, Sup) 166 NYS 793.

Grant of "stage rights" to play is license to present play on stage with living actors; grant of "motion picture rights" is license to use material in production and exhibition of photoplay; each grant involves only right to use and exploit literary work of another; right is separate and distinct from right of ownership in work itself. McClintic v Sheldon (1943) 182 Misc 32, 43 NYS2d 695, 59 USPQ 41, revd on other grounds 269 App Div 356, 55 NYS2d 879, affd without opinion 295 NY 682, 65 NE2d 328.

46. —Motion pictures

Contract granting "the sale and exclusive li-

cense and liberty to produce, perform, and represent the said play" does not grant right to represent play in moving pictures. Manners v Morosco (1920) 252 US 317, 64 L Ed 590, 40 S Ct 335.

Contract made after motion pictures have become common and granting "the sole and exclusive right to dramatize the said book for presentation on the stage," does not grant motion-picture rights. Klein v Beach (1917, CA2 NY) 239 F 108.

Owners of copyright on book or play own right to represent on screen photographs telling copyrighted story, and when right to represent it on screen is assigned, assignee has all lawful rights in regard to such production. National Picture Theatres, Inc. v Foundation Film Corp. (1920, CA2 NY) 266 F 208.

Assignment of motion-picture rights of book did not convey any copyright of book, but only right upon which assignee might obtain copyright on motion-picture photoplay of book. Goldwyn Pictures Corp. v Howells Sales Co. (1922, CA2 NY) 282 F 9.

Author's assignment of "exclusive motion-picture rights," of novel to publisher included not only silent pictures of date of contract but talking pictures subsequently developed entitling publisher to restrain talking picture filmed by company with notice of publisher's rights but which negotiated only with author. L. C. Page & Co. v Fox Film Corp. (1936, CA2 NY) 83 F2d 196, 29 USPQ 386.

In copyright contract "complete and entire motion picture rights" includes right to production of dialogue. Murphy v Warner Bros. Pictures, Inc. (1940, CA9 Cal) 112 F2d 746.

Plaintiff produced opera, which was copyrighted, and renewed as result of original contract with author of play and author of novel, and thereafter granted defendant limited right to use certain selections from opera in production of movie based on assignment of rights of author who renewed copyright on novel, and on assignment of rights by playright, who did not renew his copyright, plaintiff had exclusive rights to movie based solely on opera less limited rights previously granted defendant to use certain selections, and defendant had right to produce movie based on novel and play plus limited rights to use certain operatic selections. G. Ricordi & Co. v Paramount Pictures, Inc. (1951, CA2 NY) 189 F2d 469, 89 USPQ 289, 89 USPQ 564, cert den 342 US 849, 96 L Ed 641, 72 S Ct 77.

Motion-picture producer prepared contract whereby author assigned to it motion-picture, radio, and television rights in copyrighted story;

since use of characters and character names are nowhere specifically mentioned in contract, while other items, including title, are specifically mentioned as being granted, contract is construed as not granting exclusive right to use characters and their names. Warner Bros. Pictures, Inc. v Columbia Broadcasting System, Inc. (1954, CA9 Cal) 216 F2d 945, 104 USPQ 103, cert den 348 US 971, 99 L Ed 756, 75 S Ct 532.

Contract granting "exclusive right of producing such dramatic version on the stage" and limiting such right to production in certain manner, and only in cities of certain size, does not give such licensee motion-picture rights. Harper Bros. v Klaw (1916, DC NY) 232 F 609.

When contract through which defendant acquired motion-picture rights contained provision that no alterations, eliminations, or additions could be made without approval of author, such author could enjoin production of motion picture when there is substantial deviation from locus of play or sequence of development of plot. Manners v Famous Players-Lasky Corp. (1919, DC NY) 262 F 811.

Author of play assigned original copyright and right to renewal to plaintiff which subsequently conveyed motion-picture rights to third party; shortly before expiration of original copyright, author, his wife, and son conveyed motion-picture rights under original and renewal to same third party; by assignment from author, plaintiff has total rights pertaining to play, third party took nothing by latter conveyance, and plaintiff was not injured thereby; therefore, plaintiff, under original assignment, was not entitled to sum received by defendant for conveyance of motion-picture rights. Selwyn & Co. v Veiller (1942, DC NY) 43 F Supp 491, 52 USPQ 630.

Author of copyrighted novel transferred motion-picture rights thereto to motion-picture producer; agreement contained reversionary clause providing that rights transferred should revert to author if "production of a feature length photoplay is not completed" within specified time; although court finds that motion picture is not completed upon completion of principal photography, it finds that picture is completed when major photography and editing are done and picture awaits only those technical steps which may be necessary to put it in distribution; instant picture was completed by required date although thereafter new background music was substituted for stock music, two lines of dialogue were added, five minutes of film were deleted, and credit acknowledging cooperation was removed; it was not necessary for completion of picture that prints be made for final distribution to exhibitors. Mailer v RKO Teleradio Pictures, Inc. (1963, DC NY) 213 F Supp 294, 136 USPQ

300, affd (CA2 NY) 332 F2d 747, 141 USPQ 462.

Owner of French motion picture partially based on novel, under which author had granted license expiring in 1945, sold to producer right to remake picture (with exception of material from novel and excepting owner's right to exploit French picture) in English, granted producer option to purchase owner's rights in novel, and agreed to assist producer in obtaining extension of rights in novel; later, third party acquired rights in novel; later, third party acquired rights in novel after 1945 and sold same to producer; as between producer and owner, latter is not entitled to exhibit French picture after 1945; producer dealt fairly and honestly with owner and had no obligation under contract to do nothing when third party acquired rights in novel, but was free to secure such rights. Quader-Kino A. G. v Nebenzal (1950) 35 Cal 2d 287, 217 P2d 650, 85 USPQ 320.

Defendant, owner of copyrighted book, granted to plaintiff's predecessor, for term of ten years, sole and exclusive motion-picture rights and motion-picture copyright; contract provided that, upon expiration of ten years, all rights should revert to defendant unless predecessor elected to pay additional sum, in which event predecessor would acquire all rights in perpetuity; predecessor did not exercise option; hence, upon termination of ten-year period, all rights, including copyright on motion picture made by predecessor, reverted to defendant. Sunset Secur. Co. v Coward McCann, Inc. (1957) 47 Cal 2d 907, 306 P2d 777, 112 USPQ 449.

Contract which sells and assigns "exclusive right to produce said play" in United States and Canada, and which was entered into before motion pictures became known, will prevent grantor from producing play in motion pictures. Frohman v Fitch (1914) 164 App Div 231, 149 NYS 633.

Contract granting exclusive license for term of 24 years "to play, perform, and produce or cause to be played, performed and produced, said play or drama," carries with it right of production of moving pictures. Lipzin v Gordin (1915, Sup) 166 NYS 792.

Licensee of motion-picture rights to drama may not, in action by licensor to recover license fee, impeach his licensor's title. Hart v Fox (1917, Sup) 166 NYS 793.

Contract granting right "to translate and adapt into the English language and to perform or cause to be performed in such language" copyrighted drama does not confer motion-picture rights. Underhill v Schenck (1921) 114 Misc 520, 187 NYS 589, mod on other grounds 201

App Div 46, 193 NYS 745, mod on other grounds 238 NY 7, 143 NE 773, 33 ALR 303.

47. —Television

Plaintiff, owner of two motion pictures, exclusively licensed defendant to exploit such films for reissue purposes and through television; defendant agreed to use its best efforts to exploit films; license provided that it could not be assigned without plaintiff's consent; defendant did not violate license by entering into agreement constituting a third party its exclusive agent for television distribution of films; defendant did not technically assign license, but merely delegated a part of its duties; defendant did not divest itself of its ultimate responsibility to plaintiff since it reserved adequate supervisory powers over third party. Arnold Productions, Inc. v Favorite Films Corp. (1962, CA2 NY) 298 F2d 540, 133 USPQ 56.

Broad assignment by experienced businessman of right "to copyright, vend, license and exhibit such motion picture photoplays throughout the world" includes right to "license" broadcaster to "exhibit" copyrighted motion picture by a telecast without further grant by copyright owner. Bartsch v Metro-Goldwyn-Mayer, Inc. (1968, CA2 NY) 391 F2d 150, 157 USPQ 65, cert den 393 US 826, 21 L Ed 2d 96, 89 S Ct 86.

Plaintiffs' consent to use, in defendants' radio show, of copyrighted material from plaintiffs' motion picture does not impart consent to defendants' subsequent use of such material in television show. Loew's, Inc. v Columbia Broadcasting System, Inc. (1955, DC Cal) 131 F Supp 165, 105 USPQ 302, affd (CA9 Cal) 239 F2d 532, 112 USPQ 11, affd 356 US 43, 2 L Ed 2d 583, 78 S Ct 667, 116 USPQ 479, reh den 356 US 934, 2 L Ed 2d 764, 78 S Ct 770.

Assignment clause relative to foreign distribution of TV series is valid against attacks of producer of series who was aware of assignment clause, and actions of producer to prevent effectiveness of assignment clause are interference with contract. Viacom International, Inc. v Tandem Productions, Inc. (1974, DC NY) 368 F Supp 1264, 181 USPQ 749, affd (CA2 NY) 526 F2d 593.

1930 conveyance of motion-picture rights, whereby transferee was authorized "to project, transmit and otherwise reproduce the said musical play," granted to transferee right to exhibit motion picture on television; such exhibition comes within words of conveyance, "by the art of cinematography or any process analogous thereto." Bartsch v Metro-Goldwyn-Mayer, Inc. (1967, DC NY) 270 F Supp 896, 154 USPQ 616.

Assignment of motion-picture and television rights making some specific exceptions but not excepting right to television series based on work grants assignee right to make and exhibit TV series so that copyright infringement claim is summarily dismissed; producing TV series "based on" serious literary novel does not damage author's privacy or reputation, because TV series was not falsely attributed to author and was truthfully presented as "based on" work of author, especially where assignee had full right to modify work. Landon v Twentieth Century-Fox Film Corp. (1974, DC NY) 384 F Supp 450, 185 USPQ 221 (disapproved on other grounds Imperial Point Colonnades Condominium, Inc. v Mangurian (CA5 Fla) 549 F2d 1029, reh den (CA5 Fla) 552 F2d 369).

Plaintiff granted to defendant exclusive right to make, sell, exploit, lease, license, rent, and exhibit positive prints made from negatives, "nontheatrical only," owned by plaintiff; defendant has no television rights and cannot sell or lease such rights; television is in theatrical field. Weiss v Hollywood Film Enterprises, Inc. (Cal Sup Ct) 81 USPQ 570.

48. Right to display or exhibit (as specified in 17 USCS § 106(5))

Where license to exhibit uncopyrighted motion-picture film had been sold in England prior to copyright of film in United States, rights under such license could not be repudiated, nor assignees thereof treated as infringers. Universal Film Mfg. Co. v Copperman (1914, CA2 NY) 218 F 577, cert den 235 US 704, 59 L Ed 433, 35 S Ct 209.

Contract between plaintiff (copyright proprietor) and third party expressly provides that plaintiff "licenses" third party to do certain things, thereby precluding construction that there was assignment; moreover, third party was licensed to make reproductions of copyrighted silent motion picture film "and to license the use thereof," thereby precluding construction that plaintiff gave third party right to sell reproductions; if it be assumed that contract was assignment and that third party was given power to sell reproductions, such power was restricted with third party merely to license use thereof "for strictly nontheatrical exhibitions"; while third party may have purported to unconditionally sell positive print to defendant, third party's only authority from plaintiff was to reproduce miniature prints and license them for nontheatrical use; hence, defendant's commercial exhibition of film was not authorized by plaintiff. Hampton v Paramount Pictures Corp. (1960, CA9 Cal) 279 F2d 100, 125 USPQ 623, 84 ALR2d 454, cert den 364 US 882, 5 L Ed 2d 103, 81 S Ct 170.

VI. INVOLUNTARY TRANSFER [17 USCS § 201(e)]

49. Generally

No creditor can reach copyright unless some special provision of law is made on subject. Dart v Woodhouse (1879) 40 Mich 399.

Author's rights may be acquired by adverse possession or claim of ownership by another. O'Neill v General Film Co. (1916) 171 App Div 854, 157 NYS 1028.

50. Death of copyright owner

Court is not persuaded that copyright may not descend under laws of decedent's foreign domicile; it does not follow that, because proprietor under Copyright Act is given no rights against infringing foreign publication his rights of ownership may not descend by law of foreign domi-

cile. Brecht v Bentley (1960, DC NY) 185 F Supp 890, 126 USPQ 356.

51. Execution or seizure by creditor

While copyright is not subject to seizure and sale on execution it may be reached by creditor's bill. Stephens v Cady (1853) 55 US 528, 14 L Ed 528.

Copyright may be subjected on creditor's bill to payment of debts. Ager v Murray (1882) 105 US 126, 26 L Ed 942.

Author's manuscripts cannot be seized by his creditors as property under common law. Bartlett v Crittenden (1849, CC Ohio) F Cas No 1076.

Unpublished literary work is not subject to execution. Dart v Woodhouse (1879) 40 Mich 399.

§ 202. Ownership of copyright as distinct from ownership of material object

Ownership of a copyright, or of any of the exclusive rights under a copyright, is distinct from ownership of any material object in which the work is embodied. Transfer of ownership of any material object, including the copy or phonorecord in which the work is first fixed, does not of itself convey any rights in the copyrighted work embodied in the object; nor, in the absence of an agreement, does transfer of ownership of a copyright or of any exclusive rights under a copyright convey property rights in any material object.

(Added Oct. 19, 1976, P. L. 94-553, Title I, § 101, 90 Stat. 2568.)

HISTORY; ANCILLARY LAWS AND DIRECTIVES

Effective date of section:

Section 102 of Act Oct. 19, 1976, P. L. 94-553, 90 Stat. 2598 provided that this section "becomes effective on January 1, 1978".

CROSS REFERENCES

Validity of transfer of copyright ownership, 17 USCS § 204(a).
Preemption with respect to other laws, 17 USCS § 301.

RESEARCH GUIDE

Am Jur:

18 Am Jur 2d, Copyright and Literary Property § 18.

INTERPRETIVE NOTES AND DECISIONS

1. Generally
2. Right to transfer material object
3. Transfer of material object as distinct from copyright

4. Transfer of copyright as distinct from material object

1. Generally

Copyright does not give its owner any property in thing copyrighted, but simply gives him protection against anybody else copying it. Taylor v Commissioner (1931, CA3) 51 F2d 915, cert den 284 US 689, 76 L Ed 581, 52 S Ct 265.

Copyright is intangible, incorporeal right in nature of privilege or franchise and is independent of any material substance such as manuscript or plate used for printing. Local Trademarks, Inc. v Price (1948, CA5 Ala) 170 F2d 715, 79 USPQ 344.

Artist may sell picture and copyright to picture separately. Werckmeister v American Lithographic Co. (1905, CC NY) 142 F 827.

2. Right to transfer material object

Purchaser of book, sold by authority of copyright owner without agreement, may dispose of such book in whatever manner he chooses, regardless of any notice as to price contained therein. Bobbs-Merrill Co. v Straus (1908) 210 US 339, 52 L Ed 1086, 28 S Ct 722.

Purchaser of unbound copyrighted volumes, sold with authority of copyright owner, has right to bind and resell them. Kipling v G. P. Putnam's Sons (1903, CA2 NY) 120 F 631.

Dealer, in absence of knowledge of limitation of authority of publisher's agents from whom he purchased, may sell book for any price he may see fit. Clemens v Estes (1885, CC Mass) 22 F 899.

Purchaser of copyrighted books, having knowledge of restrictions placed upon sales, receives only such title as agents of author are authorized to give, and notice of conditions of resale is binding upon him. Authors & Newspapers Asso. v O'Gorman Co. (1906, CC RI) 147 F 616.

Copyright proprietor is not empowered, merely by virtue of copyright, to control sales of published copies after they have come into lawful ownership of first purchaser; pivotal issue is whether title to particular copy has been retained by proprietor or passed to first purchaser; if title has been retained, copy remains under protection of copyright law, and infringement proceedings may be had against all subsequent purchasers of copy who interfere with proprietor's exclusive right to vend copyrighted work; if title passed to first purchaser, copy loses protection of copyright law. United States v Wells (1959, DC Tex) 176 F Supp 630, 123 USPQ 65 (disapproved on other grounds United States v Wise (CA9 Cal) 550 F2d 1180).

Copyright proprietor was granted restrictive license to use musical compositions on records which were to be used only as premium in connection with sale of shampoo; defendant purchased records with shampoo and resold records separately; infringement action is dismissed under "first sale" doctrine. Burke & Van Heusen, Inc. v Arrow Drug, Inc. (1964, DC Pa) 233 F Supp 881, 143 USPQ 17.

Motion picture dealer's sale and lease of copyrighted movies infringes copyrights of proprietors and is not excused as transfer of copy lawfully obtained, because evidence falls far short of showing that copies purchased from individuals in other states were lawfully obtained, and plaintiffs' evidence shows elaborate system to protect copyright in movie distribution activities. Avco Embassy Pictures Corp. v Korshnak (1974, DC Pa) 189 USPQ 303.

Plaintiffs' evidence of general policy against sale of 16mm prints of motion pictures, compared with defendant's evidence of many transfers of such films by plaintiffs, fails to meet burden of proof that films purchased and resold by defendant were not authorized under first sale doctrine; "first sale" doctrine gives copyright proprietor exclusive right to first sale of any one copy, but no right to restrict future sale of that particular copy, and copyright proprietors have burden of proving that 16mm motion pictures sold by defendant were not originally sold by copyright proprietors. American International Pictures, Inc. v Foreman (1975, DC Ala) 400 F Supp 928, 188 USPQ 249.

Owner of article protected by copyright, when he has manufactured and sold same, cannot impose restrictions upon his vendee as to future sale of same. Coca-Cola Co. v State (1920, Tex Civ App) 225 SW 791.

3. Transfer of material object as distinct from copyright

Copperplate engraving of copyrighted map is property which may be sold upon execution, but such sale does not give buyer right to print map, since copyright remains in the author, who may restrain such buyer from infringing his copyright. Stephens v Cady (1853) 55 US 528, 14 L Ed 528.

When copyrighted book is sold ownership of book is in buyer and he has right to maintain book as nearly as possible in its original condition, so far, at least, as cover and binding of book is concerned. Doan v American Book Co. (1901, CA7 Ill) 105 F 772.

Manufacturer of copyrighted goods under contract with copyright proprietor obtains no right to sell goods solely by virtue of its title to materials of which goods are made; assuming that manufacturer had title to undelivered goods and that this title had not passed to proprietor, this type of title is not superior, for purpose of alienating rights from proprietor, to title acquired by buying from proprietor's agent who had apparent but not acutal authority to sell or by buying in good faith from someone who bought from such agent; copyright protection should not turn on which party (manufacturer or proprietor) furnished physical stuff to which copyrighted conception is affixed, with protection lost if author does not assume role of manufacturer. Platt & Munk Co. v Republic Graphics, Inc. (1963, CA2 NY) 315 F2d 847, 137 USPQ 268.

Predecessor statute is not unconstitutionally vague because judicial construction has consistently viewed section as requiring transfer of rights rather than mere possession of copyrighted material to convey copyrights to holder. United States v Wise (1977, CA9) 194 USPQ 59.

Sale of uncopyrighted painting carries with it right to copy it without author's consent. Parton v Prang (1872, CC Mass) F Cas No 10784.

Author may sell his painting and retain right to copyright in himself. Werckmeister v Springer Lithographing Co. (1894, CC NY) 63 F 808.

Sale of type plates and impression sheets for copyrighted book to satisfy judgment is not sale of copyright, so as to give purchaser thereof right to publish copyrighted work. Patterson v J. S. Ogilvie Pub. Co. (1902, CC NY) 119 F 451.

Sale of author's manuscript of copyrighted play by playbroker without power to so do does not transfer title to copyright. Stodart v Mutual Film Corp. (1917, DC NY) 249 F 507, affd (CA2 NY) 249 F 513.

Giving of professional copies of musical composition to musicians does not authorize them to publicly perform it for profit. Harms v Cohen (1922, DC Pa) 279 F 276.

Purchaser of telegraphic code was not entitled to copy code, copyright of which was owned by seller. Hartfield v Herzfeld (1932, DC NY) 60 F2d 599.

Assignment of literary product after publication with notice did not carry copyright. Davenport Quigley Expedition, Inc. v Century Productions, Inc. (1937, DC NY) 18 F Supp 974, 32 USPQ 608.

By publishing and selling to public, musical manuscripts in way of sheet music or more detailed orchestrations of copyrighted musical composition, copyright proprietor does not confer on purchasing public right publicly to perform compositions sold without liability for infringement. Remick Music Corp. v Interstate Hotel Co. (1944, DC Neb) 58 F Supp 523, 63 USPQ 327, affd (CA8 Neb) 157 F2d 744, 71 USPQ 138, cert den 329 US 809, 91 L Ed 691, 67 S Ct 622, reh den 330 US 854, 91 L Ed 1296, 67 S Ct 769.

Sheriff's sale of items including copyright certificates is not effective to transfer copyright, because certificate is not copyright and certificate possessor is not ipso facto copyright owner, and copyright assignment requires instrument in writing, but motions for summary judgment are denied to resolve disputed facts at trial. Kingsrow Enterprises, Inc. v Metromedia, Inc. (1975, DC NY) 397 F Supp 879, 189 USPQ 90.

Separate copyright, or control of right to reproduce, belongs to artist or author until disposed of by him, and will be protected by courts; since author never intended that it be published, purchaser of manuscript from third party could not have bought publication rights. Chamberlain v Feldman (1949) 300 NY 135, 89 NE2d 863, 84 USPQ 148.

4. Transfer of copyright as distinct from material object

Right to copyright painting may be assigned without sale of painting itself and assignee may secure copyright as "proprietor." American Tobacco Co. v Werckmeister (1907) 207 US 284, 52 L Ed 208, 28 S Ct 72.

Copyright may be assigned without transfer of article. Werckmeister v American Lithographic Co. (1905, CC NY) 142 F 827.

Defendant employed plaintiff to paint gnomes for use in defendant's advertisements; artist sold what his conception was as executed in what he sold; he could not hold unexecuted conception of gnome, or what that conception might be inferred to be from what he had executed; he sold all that could be drawn, depicted, or used from what he had sold; when he sold executed conception, he sold conception; he claims to have retained conception of gnome in other settings, dress, or occupations, but he cannot retain those except in his mind either in choate or inchoate form, conceived or to be conceived, or as present or future ideas; as such they are not property. Grant v Kellogg Co. (1944, DC NY) 58 F Supp 48, 63 USPQ 173, affd (CA2 NY) 154 F2d 59, 75 USPQ 301.

Action brought in equity for damages and for assignment of copyright in book is improperly dismissed as seeking remedies available at law and is remanded to chancery because both common law and statutory copyright are distinct from matter copyrighted and require equity jurisdiction for copyright transfer. Hughes Tool Co. v Fawcett Publications, Inc. (1974, Del Sup Ct) 181 USPQ 525.

Copyright is distinct from property copyrighted, and its assignment will no more effect transfer of property than sale of property will effect assignment of copyright. McClintic v Sheldon (1943) 182 Misc 32, 43 NYS2d 695, 59 USPQ 41, revd on other grounds 269 App Div 356, 55 NYS2d 879, affd 295 NY 682, 65 NE2d 328.

§ 203. Termination of transfers and licenses granted by the author

(a) Conditions for termination. In the case of any work other than a work made for hire, the exclusive or nonexclusive grant of a transfer or license of copyright or of any right under a copyright, executed by the author on or after January 1, 1978, otherwise than by will, is subject to termination under the following conditions:

(1) In the case of a grant executed by one author, termination of the grant may be effected by that author or, if the author is dead, by the person or persons who, under clause (2) of this subsection, own and are entitled to exercise a total of more than one-half of that author's termination interest. In the case of a grant executed by two or more authors of a joint work, termination of the grant may be effected by a majority of the authors who executed it; if any of such authors is dead, the termination interest of any such author may be exercised as a unit by the person or persons who, under clause (2) of this subsection, own and are entitled to exercise a total of more than one-half of that author's interest.

(2) Where an author is dead, his or her termination interest is owned, and may be exercised, by his widow or her widower and his or her children or grandchildren as follows:

(A) the widow or widower owns the author's entire termination interest unless there are any surviving children or grandchildren of the author, in which case the widow or widower owns one-half of the author's interest;

(B) the author's surviving children, and the surviving children of any dead child of the author, own the author's entire termination interest unless there is a widow or widower, in which case the ownership of one-half of the author's interest is divided among them;

(C) the rights of the author's children and grandchildren are in all cases divided among them and exercised on a per stirpes basis according to the number of such author's children represented; the share of the children of a dead child in a termination interest can be exercised only by the action of a majority of them.

(3) Termination of the grant may be effected at any time during a period of five years beginning at the end of thirty-five years from the date of execution of the grant; or, if the grant covers the right of publication of the work, the period begins at the end of thirty-five years from the date of publication of the work under the grant or at the end of forty years from the date of execution of the grant, whichever term ends earlier.

(4) The termination shall be effected by serving an advance notice in writing, signed by the number and proportion of owners of termination interests required under clauses (1) and (2) of this subsection, or by their duly authorized agents, upon the grantee or the grantee's successor in title.

(A) The notice shall state the effective date of the termination, which shall fall within the five-year period specified by clause (3) of this subsection, and the notice shall be served not less than two or more than ten years before that date. A copy of the notice shall be recorded in the Copyright Office before the effective date of termination, as a condition to its taking effect.

(B) The notice shall comply, in form, content, and manner of service, with requirements that the Register of Copyrights shall prescribe by regulation.

(5) Termination of the grant may be effected notwithstanding any agreement to the contrary, including an agreement to make a will or to make any future grant.

(b) Effect of termination. Upon the effective date of termination, all rights under this title [17 USCS §§ 101 et seq.] that were covered by the terminated grants revert to the author, authors, and other persons owning termination interests under clauses (1) and (2) of subsection (a), including those owners who did not join in signing the notice of termination under clause (4) of subsection (a), but with the following limitations:

(1) A derivative work prepared under authority of the grant before its termination may continue to be utilized under the terms of the grant after its termination, but this privilege does not extend to the preparation after the termination of other derivative works based upon the copyrighted work covered by the terminated grant.

(2) The future rights that will revert upon termination of the grant become vested on the date the notice of termination has been served as provided by clause (4) of subsection (a). The rights vest in the author, authors, and other persons named in, and in the proportionate shares provided by, clauses (1) and (2) of subsection (a).

(3) Subject to the provisions of clause (4) of this subsection, a further grant, or agreement to make a further grant, of any right covered by a terminated grant is valid only if it is signed by the same number and proportion of the owners, in whom the right has vested under clause (2) of this subsection, as are required to terminate the grant under clauses (1) and (2) of subsection (a). Such further grant or agreement is effective with respect to all of the persons in whom the right it covers has vested under clause (2) of this subsection, including those who did not join in signing it. If any person dies after rights under a terminated grant have vested in him or her, that person's legal representatives, legatees, or heirs at law represent him or her for purposes of this clause.

(4) A further grant, or agreement to make a further grant, of any right covered by a terminated grant is valid only if it is made after the effective date of the termination. As an exception, however, an agreement for such a further grant may be made between the persons provided by clause (3) of this subsection and the original grantee or such grantee's successor in title, after the notice of termination has been served as provided by clause (4) of subsection (a).

(5) Termination of a grant under this section affects only those rights covered by the grants that arise under this title [17 USCS §§ 101 et seq.], and in no way affects rights arising under any other Federal, State, or foreign laws.

(6) Unless and until termination is effected under this section, the grant, if it does not provide otherwise, continues in effect for the term of copyright provided by this title [17 USCS §§ 101 et seq.].

(Added Oct. 19, 1976, P. L. 94-553, Title I, § 101, 90 Stat. 2569.)

HISTORY; ANCILLARY LAWS AND DIRECTIVES

Effective date of section:
Section 102 of Act Oct. 19, 1976, P. L. 94-553, 90 Stat. 2598 provided that this section "becomes effective on January 1, 1978".

CROSS REFERENCES

"Transfer of copyright ownership" defined, 17 USCS § 101.
"Works for hire" defined, 17 USCS § 101.

RESEARCH GUIDE

Law Review Articles:
Melniker and Melniker, Termination of Transfers and Licenses Under The New Copyright Law. 22 New York Law School Law Rev 589.

§ 204. Execution of transfers of copyright ownership

(a) A transfer of copyright ownership, other than by operation of law, is not valid unless an instrument of conveyance, or a note or memorandum of the transfer, is in writing and signed by the owner of the rights conveyed or such owner's duly authorized agent.

(b) A certificate of acknowledgement is not required for the validity of a transfer, but is prima facie evidence of the execution of the transfer if—

(1) in the case of a transfer executed in the United States, the certificate is issued by a person authorized to administer oaths within the United States; or

(2) in the case of a transfer executed in a foreign country, the certificate is issued by a diplomatic or consular officer of the United States, or by a person authorized to administer oaths whose authority is proved by a certificate of such an officer.

(Added Oct. 19, 1976, P. L. 94-553, Title I, § 101, 90 Stat. 2570.)

HISTORY; ANCILLARY LAWS AND DIRECTIVES

Effective date of section:
Section 102 of Act Oct. 19, 1976, P. L. 94-553, 90 Stat. 2598 provided that this section "becomes effective on January 1, 1978".

CROSS REFERENCES

"Copyright owner" defined, 17 USCS § 101.

RESEARCH GUIDE

Am Jur:

6 Am Jur 2d, Assignments §§ 75, 89, 90.

18 Am Jur 2d, Copyright and Literary Property § 90.

Forms:

6 Federal Procedural Forms L Ed, Copyrights §§ 17:96, 17:102.

INTERPRETIVE NOTES AND DECISIONS

1. Generally
2. Validity of oral transfers
3. Writing and signing requirement [17 USCS § 204(a)]
4. Acknowledgement of transfer [17 USCS § 204(b)]

1. Generally

Author made verbal assignment in Trinidad in 1943 to plaintiff who obtained Trinidad copyright which conferred on plaintiff status of copyright owner and was adequate to support his June, 1945, copyright registration in United States, although author did not assign in writing until April, 1945, and even though applicable English statute requires written assignment; written assignment is deemed to have been established as of 1943, since author stated that to be his purpose and both parties acted in accordance with that understanding. Khan v Leo Feist, Inc. (1947, DC NY) 70 F Supp 450, 73 USPQ 104, affd (CA2 NY) 165 F2d 188, 76 USPQ 27.

2. Validity of oral transfers

Rights in manuscript before copyright has been taken out may be transferred by parol. Callaghan v Myers (1888) 128 US 617, 32 L Ed 547, 9 S Ct 177.

Legislative committee contracted with plaintiff to furnish to state copy of index which plaintiff was providing for its own annotated statutes and attorney general orally agreed with plaintiff that copyright of index should remain in plaintiff; plaintiff was entitled to copyright in index as against third persons. W. H. Anderson Co. v Baldwin Law Pub. Co. (1928, CA6 Ohio) 27 F2d 82.

Oral sale of painting subsequently followed by delivery transferred entire property in painting, so that purchaser thereof would be entitled to copyright and publish print-copies of painting. Parton v Prang (1872, CC Mass) F Cas No 10784.

Assignment of copyright, though not in writing, is valid as between parties. Webb v Powers (1897, CC Mass) F Cas No 17323.

Inchoate right to copyright may, prior to taking of copyright, be transferred by parol. Black v Henry G. Allen Co. (1890, CC NY) 42 F 618.

Assignment by owner to one who takes out copyright in his own name may be by parol. M. Witmark & Sons v Calloway (1927, DC Tenn) 22 F2d 412.

Oral claim that assignment was merely for life of assignee is not accepted. Arnstein v American Soc. of Composers, etc. (1939, DC NY) 29 F Supp 388, 42 USPQ 581.

Oral license of copyrighted material gives no greater right to use than does written license. Loew's, Inc. v Columbia Broadcasting System, Inc. (1955, DC Cal) 131 F Supp 165, 105 USPQ 302, affd (CA9 Cal) 239 F2d 532, 112 USPQ 11, affd 356 US 43, 2 L Ed 2d 583, 78 S Ct 667, 116 USPQ 479, reh den 356 US 934, 2 L Ed 2d 764, 78 S Ct 770.

3. Writing and signing requirement [17 USCS § 204(a)]

Author of political article may deliver same to magazine for publication with intention that title shall vest, and formal bill of sale is not essential. Atlantic Monthly Co. v Post Pub. Co. (1928, DC Mass) 27 F2d 556.

Oral assignment of copyright in series of magazine articles later collected into books is ineffective to transfer title to copyright, which requires written instrument signed by proprietor of copyright. Gardner v Nizer (1975, DC NY) 391 F Supp 940, 185 USPQ 485 mod on other grounds (DC NY) 396 F Supp 63.

Person may make valid contract by parol for assignment of copyright, although assignment itself must be in writing. Gould v Banks & Gould (NY) 8 Wend 562.

4. Acknowledgement of transfer [17 USCS § 204(b)]

Assignment of copyright executed in Germany was not acknowledged before consular officer and signed only in firm name and not also in name of officer of corporation; possible failure to observe all formalities of signing or acknowledging is at most only matter of form going to proof of due execution which may be supplied, as here, by affidavits in evidence; whatever lack of signatures there may be according to German law assignment satisfies our requirements. Houghton Mifflin Co. v Stackpole Sons, Inc. (1939, CA2 NY) 104 F2d 306, 42 USPQ 96, cert den 308 US 597, 84 L Ed 499, 60 S Ct 131.

§ 205. Recordation of transfers and other documents

(a) Conditions for recordation. Any transfer of copyright ownership or other document pertaining to a copyright may be recorded in the Copyright Office if the document filed for recordation bears the actual signature of the person who executed it, or if it is accompanied by a sworn or official certification that it is a true copy of the original, signed document.

(b) Certificate of recordation. The Register of Copyrights shall, upon receipt of a document as provided by subsection (a) and of the fee provided by section 708 [17 USCS § 708], record the document and return it with a certificate of recordation.

(c) Recordation as constructive notice. Recordation of a document in the Copyright Office gives all persons constructive notice of the facts stated in the recorded document, but only if—

(1) the document, or material attached to it, specifically identifies the work to which it pertains so that, after the document is indexed by the Register of Copyrights, it would be revealed by a reasonable search under the title or registration number of the work; and

(2) registration has been made for the work.

(d) Recordation as prerequisite to infringement suit. No person claiming by virtue of a transfer to be the owner of copyright or of any exclusive right under a copyright is entitled to institute an infringement action under this title [17 USCS §§ 101 et seq.] until the instrument of transfer under which such person claims has been recorded in the Copyright Office, but suit may be instituted after such recordation on a cause of action that arose before recordation.

(e) Priority between conflicting transfers. As between two conflicting transfers, the one executed first prevails if it is recorded, in the manner required to give constructive notice under subsection (c), within one month after its execution in the United States or within two months after its execution outside the United States, or at any time before recordation in such manner of the later transfer. Otherwise the later transfer prevails if recorded first in such manner, and if taken in good faith, for valuable consideration or on the basis of a binding promise to pay royalties, and without notice of the earlier transfer.

(f) Priority between conflicting transfer of ownership and nonexclusive license. A nonexclusive license, whether recorded or not, prevails over a conflicting transfer of copyright ownership if the license is evidenced by a written instrument signed by the owner of the rights licensed or such owner's duly authorized agent, and if—

(1) the license was taken before execution of the transfer; or

(2) the license was taken in good faith before recordation of the transfer and without notice of it.

(Added Oct. 19, 1976, P. L. 94-553, Title I, § 101, 90 Stat. 2571.)

HISTORY; ANCILLARY LAWS AND DIRECTIVES

Effective date of section:

Section 102 of Act Oct. 19, 1976, P. L. 94-553, 90 Stat. 2598 provided that this section "becomes effective on January 1, 1978".

Other provisions:

Registration of claims received before January 1, 1978. Act Oct. 19, 1976, P. L. 94-553, Title I, § 109, 90 Stat. 2600, provided: "The registration of claims to copyright for which the required deposit, application, and fee were received in the Copyright Office before January 1, 1978, and the recordation of assignments of copyright or other instruments received in the Copyright Office before January 1, 1978, shall be made in accordance with title 17 [former 17 USCS §§ 1 et seq.] as it existed on December 31, 1977."

CROSS REFERENCES

Copyright Office's indexing and search reports, 17 USCS § 705.
This section referred to in 17 USCS §§ 501, 708.

RESEARCH GUIDE

Am Jur:

18 Am Jur 2d, Copyright and Literary Property § 91.

68 Am Jur 2d, Secured Transactions § 30.

69 Am Jur 2d, Secured Transactions § 353.

Forms:

5 Am Jur Legal Forms 2d, Copyright and Literary and Artistic Property § 72:66.

INTERPRETIVE NOTES AND DECISIONS

1. Generally
2. Conditions for recordation [17 USCS § 205(a)]
3. Certificate of recordation [17 USCS § 205(b)]
4. Recordation as constructive notice, generally [17 USCS § 205(c)]
5. —Effect of actual notice
6. Recordation as prerequisite to infringement [17 USCS § 205(d)]
7. Priority between conflicting transfers [17 USCS § 205(e, f)]

1. Generally

Assignments of copyrights must be recorded in office of Register of Copyrights. Fred Fisher Music Co. v M. Witmark & Sons (1943) 318 US 643, 87 L Ed 1055, 63 S Ct 773, 57 USPQ 50.

Plaintiff's failure to record copyright assignment within three months of its execution vests no rights in defendant, who was not subsequent purchaser without notice; it matters little that plaintiff might have had notice of defendant's invalid claim. Edward B. Marks Music Corp. v

Charles K. Harris Music Publishing Co. (1958, CA2 NY) 255 F2d 518, 117 USPQ 308, cert den 358 US 831, 3 L Ed 2d 69, 79 S Ct 51.

Assignments which are not recorded are valid as between parties and as to others not claiming under assignors. Webb v Powers (1897, CC Mass) F Cas No 17323.

Predecessor section protects subsequent purchasers or mortgagees for value and is akin in principle to filing or recording acts, which relate to bills of sale or chattel mortgages. New Fiction Pub. Co. v Star Co. (1915, DC NY) 220 F 994.

Failure to record assignment of copyright in copyright office does not invalidate assignment as between parties and is not available as defense to infringer; being real party in interest, assignee may bring infringement action; assignor is not indispensable party thereto. DeSilva Constr. Corp. v Herrald (1962, DC Fla) 213 F Supp 184, 137 USPQ 96.

Transfer of rights sufficient to entitle someone to obtain copyright is not necessarily "an assignment of the copyright," condition precedent to recordation requirement of predecessor section. Davis v E. I. Du Pont De Nemours & Co. (1965, DC NY) 240 F Supp 612, 145 USPQ 258.

2. Conditions for recordation [17 USCS § 205(a)]

Assignment of expectancy (renewal right) is as recordable as any other assignment. Rossiter v Vogel (1943, CA2 NY) 134 F2d 908, 57 USPQ 161.

While assignee of expectancy of renewal of copyright may, under predecessor section, record assignment, recordation is not essential to his title although, if made within prescribed period after its execution, it will protect recording assignee against subsequent assignee. Rose v Bourne, Inc. (1959, DC NY) 176 F Supp 605, 123 USPQ 29, affd (CA2 NY) 279 F2d 79, 125 USPQ 509, cert den 364 US 880, 5 L Ed 2d 103, 81 S Ct 170.

Although assignee of expectancy of renewal of copyright can, under predecessor section, record assignment in copyright office, recordation does not create legal ownership that did not exist already; if made within prescribed period, it simply serves to protect recording assignee against bona fide purchaser. Tobias v Joy Music, Inc. (1962, DC NY) 204 F Supp 556, 133 USPQ 181.

3. Certificate of recordation [17 USCS § 205(b)]

Title is recorded when received by Librarian of Congress, rather than when it is actually written in record book. Edward Thompson Co. v American Law Book Co. (1902, CC NY) 119 F 217.

4. Recordation as constructive notice, generally [17 USCS § 205(c)]

Where formal transfer of copyright is recorded in compliance with copyright law, such record operates as notice. Little v Hall (1856) 59 US 165, 15 L Ed 328.

5. —Effect of actual notice

Although promise to pay future royalties, coupled with notice of prior claim before payment, might deprive subsequent purchaser of status of bona fide purchaser, doctrine has no application to prior purchaser. Edward B. Marks Music Corp. v Charles K. Harris Music Publishing Co. (1958, CA2 NY) 255 F2d 518, 117 USPQ 308, cert den 358 US 831, 3 L Ed 2d 69, 79 S Ct 51.

Failure to record trust agreement is no defense to infringer who had actual knowledge of such agreement. Brady v Reliance Motion Picture Corp. (1916, DC NY) 232 F 259.

Although assignment to defendants of renewal rights by author was not recorded, plaintiff took from author with full knowledge of prior assignment; hence, author's post renewal assignment to plaintiff is of no legal effect. Sweet Music, Inc. v Melrose Music Corp. (1960, DC Cal) 189 F Supp 655, 127 USPQ 513.

6. Recordation as prerequisite to infringement [17 USCS § 205(d)]

It is no defense to infringement suit that assignment of copyright to plaintiff was not filed within three months of its execution since predecessor section does not invalidate assignee's title as against infringers. Machaty v Astra Pictures, Inc. (1952, CA2 NY) 197 F2d 138, 93 USPQ 51, cert den 334 US 827, 97 L Ed 644, 73 S Ct 29.

Failure to record one assignment in chain of title has no bearing as between parties to infringement suit. Deward & Rich, Inc. v Bristol Sav. & Loan Corp. (1940, DC Va) 34 F Supp 345, 47 USPQ 128, affd (CA4 Va) 120 F2d 537, 50 USPQ 1.

Infringer cannot escape liability on ground that plaintiff executed a security assignment of its copyright since assignment was to effectuate a transfer of ownership only in event of default, which has not occurred, and since assignee consents to plaintiff's enforcement of copyright; plaintiff continues as real party in interest and is entitled, as both equitable owner and copyright proprietor, to maintain infringement suit; purpose of recordation of assignment pursuant to this section was to put subsequent purchasers or mortgagees on notice; it did not destroy plaintiff's status as copyright proprietor. Pantone, Inc.

v A. I. Friedman, Inc. (1968, DC NY) 294 F Supp 545, 160 USPQ 530.

Defendants who did not record their purported assignment of copyright thereby violate recording requirement and are not entitled to defense on ground that plaintiff did not record copyright assignment. Kenya Music, Inc. v Warner Bros., Inc. (1975, DC NY) 391 F Supp 1228, 188 USPQ 605.

7. Priority between conflicting transfers [17 USCS § 205(e,f)]

Unrecorded assignment of dramatic rights to play was void as against later assignment recorded by assignee of motion-picture rights without actual notice of prior assignment. Photo-Drama Motion Picture Co. v Social Uplift Film Corp. (1915, CA2 NY) 220 F 448.

Purchaser of exclusive stage rights for copyrighted play was not entitled to injunction against subsequent bona fide purchaser on theory of negative covenant, his contract not having been recorded in copyright office. MacLoon v Vitagraph, Inc. (1929, CA2 NY) 30 F2d 634.

Assignment not recorded is void as against subsequent purchasers or mortgagees without notice. Brady v Reliance Motion Picture Corp. (1916, DC NY) 232 F 259.

Though 1911 assignment, in consideration of promise to pay one cent for every printed copy sold, was not recorded until 1938, it is good as against 1938 assignment because 1938 assignee paid nothing for assignment and is not purchaser for valuable consideration and without notice, mere promise to pay consideration not constituting valuable consideration within recording act. Von Tilzer v Jerry Vogel Music Co. (1943, DC NY) 53 F Supp 191, 59 USPQ 292, affd (CA2 NY) 158 F2d 516, 71 USPQ 285.

Despite fact that 1940 contract concerning literary work and 1940 assignment thereof were capable of being recorded in copyright office, they were not so recorded until after plaintiff had entered into 1954 contract concerning such rights and had recorded such contract in copyright office; plaintiff had no knowledge of 1940 contract and assignment and it is not shown that plaintiff knew of newspaper reports and gossip items concerning rights in literary work; hence, plaintiff has rights granted to it by 1954 contract. Vidor v Serlin (Misc) 119 USPQ 104, mod on other grounds 7 App Div 2d 978, 184 NYS2d 482, affd 7 NY2d 502, 199 NYS2d 669, 166 NE2d 680, 125 USPQ 364.

CHAPTER 3. DURATION OF COPYRIGHT

§ 301. Preemption with respect to other laws

(a) On and after January 1, 1978, all legal or equitable rights that are equivalent to any of the exclusive rights within the general scope of copyright as specified by section 106 [17 USCS § 106] in works of authorship that are fixed in a tangible medium of expression and come within the subject matter of copyright as specified by sections 102 and 103 [17 USCS §§ 102 and 103], whether created before or after that date and whether published or unpublished, are governed exclusively by this title [17 USCS §§ 101 et seq.]. Thereafter, no person is entitled to any such right or equivalent right in any such work under the common law or statutes of any State.

(b) Nothing in this title [17 USCS §§ 101 et seq.] annuls or limits any rights or remedies under the common law or statutes of any State with respect to—

(1) subject matter that does not come within the subject matter of copyright as specified by sections 102 and 103 [17 USCS §§ 102 and 103], including works of authorship not fixed in any tangible medium of expression; or

(2) any cause of action arising from undertakings commenced before January 1, 1978; or

(3) activities violating legal or equitable rights that are not equivalent to any of the exclusive rights within the general scope of copyright as specified by section 106 [17 USCS § 106].

(c) With respect to sound recordings fixed before February 15, 1972, any rights or remedies under the common law or statutes of any State shall not be annulled or limited by this title [17 USCS §§ 101 et seq.] until February 15, 2047. The preemptive provisions of subsection (a) shall apply to any such rights and remedies pertaining to any cause of action arising from undertakings commenced on and after February 15, 2047. Notwithstanding the provisions of section 303 [17 USCS § 303], no sound recording fixed before February 15, 1972, shall be subject to copyright under this title [17 USCS §§ 101 et seq.] before, on, or after February 15, 2047.

(d) Nothing in this title [17 USCS §§ 101 et seq.] annuls or limits any rights or remedies under any other Federal statute.
(Added Oct. 19, 1976, P. L. 94-553, Title I, § 101, 90 Stat. 2572.)

HISTORY; ANCILLARY LAWS AND DIRECTIVES

Effective date of section:
Section 102 of Act Oct. 19, 1976, P. L. 94-553, 90 Stat. 2598 provided that this section "becomes effective on January 1, 1978".

CROSS REFERENCES

General subject matter categories of copyrightable works, 17 USCS § 102.
Compilations and derivative works, 17 USCS § 103.
Exclusive rights in copyrighted works, 17 USCS § 106.
Exclusive jurisdiction of federal courts, 28 USCS § 1338.

RESEARCH GUIDE

Am Jur:
18 Am Jur 2d, Copyright and Literary Property §§ 19, 98, 127, 131, 135.

Forms:
1 Am Jur Pl & Pr Forms (Rev ed), Advertising, Form 10.

Annotations:
Unfair competition by direct reproduction of literary, artistic, or musical property. 40 ALR3d 566.
What constitutes publication of architectural plans, drawings, or designs, so as to result in loss of common-law copyright. 77 ALR2d 1048.

Law Review Articles:
Copyright Symposium, 22 New York Law School Law Review 193.

INTERPRETIVE NOTES AND DECISIONS

1. Generally
2. Common-law rights [17 USCS § 301(a)]
3. State law rights [17 USCS § 301(a)]
4. Subject matter not within copyright statute [17 USCS § 301(b)(1)]
5. Causes of action arising from undertakings commenced before January 1, 1978 [17 USCS § 301(b)(2)]
6. Rights not protected by copyright [17 USCS § 301(b)(3)]
7. Sound recordings fixed before February 15, 1972 [17 USCS § 301(c)]
8. Rights or remedies under other federal statutes [17 USCS § 301(d)]

1. Generally

Copyright property under federal law is wholly statutory and depends upon right created under Acts of Congress passed in pursuance of authority conferred under § 8, clause 8 of Article I of Constitution. Bobbs-Merrill Co. v Straus (1908) 210 US 339, 52 L Ed 1086, 28 S Ct 722.

Copyright statute provides comprehensive system of rights and remedies, and however inadequate latter may be no others can be resorted to. Globe Newspaper Co. v Walker (1908) 210 US 356, 52 L Ed 1096, 28 S Ct 726.

State criminal statute forbidding individuals from "pirating" or appropriating sound recordings of others at any time after release is not void as creating copyright of unlimited duration in violation of provision in copyright clause (Article 1, § 8, cl 8) of Constitution that copyrights may only be granted for "limited" times, since such durational limitation applies only to Congress and the reasons for such limitation are not applicable to state copyrights. Goldstein v California (1973) 412 US 546, 37 L Ed 2d 163, 93 S Ct 2303, reh den 414 US 883, 38 L Ed 2d 131, 94 S Ct 27.

Copyright property under federal law is wholly statutory. Metro-Goldwyn-Mayer Distributing Corp. v Bijou Theatre Co. (1932, CA1 Mass) 59 F2d 70, 13 USPQ 147.

Copyright has no extraterritorial effect. Capitol Records, Inc. v Mercury Records Corp. (1955, CA2 NY) 221 F2d 657, 105 USPQ 163.

Copyright Act did not give any form of relief which did not previously exist in federal or state courts. Pierpont v Fowle (1846, CC Mass) F Cas No 11152.

Copyright is wholly statutory. Shapiro, Bernstein & Co. v Bryan (1939, DC NY) 27 F Supp 11, 41 USPQ 134; Tobani v Carl Fischer, Inc., (DC NY) 36 USPQ 97, mod on other grounds (CA2 NY) 98 F2d 57, 38 USPQ 198, cert den 305 US 650, 83 L Ed 420, 59 S Ct 243.

State courts have no jurisdiction of action for infringement of registered copyright. Avon Periodicals, Inc. v Ziff-Davis Pub. Co. (1952) 27 Misc 2d 160, 113 NYS2d 737, 93 USPQ 235, mod on other grounds 282 App Div 200, 122 NYS2d 92.

Rights incident to registered copyrights are for determination of federal court, not state court. Stowe v Croy (1953, Sup) 124 NYS2d 291, 97 USPQ 581, mod on other grounds 284 App Div 302, 130 NYS2d 848, 101 USPQ 500.

State court refuses relief since plaintiff has not established any rights based upon common-law copyright; whatever rights plaintiff may have under federal copyright statute must be vindicated in federal court. Hill & Range Songs, Inc. v London Records, Inc. (Misc) 105 USPQ 302.

2. Common-law rights [17 USCS § 301(a)]

Copyright laws of one country have no extra-territorial operation, unless otherwise provided. Ferris v Frohman (1912) 223 US 424, 56 L Ed 492, 32 S Ct 263.

There is no common-law design copyright, and statute does not permit procuring of design copyright. Chas. D. Briddell, Inc. v Alglobe Trading Corp. (1952, CA2 NY) 194 F2d 416, 92 USPQ 100.

Author has at common law property in his unpublished works, which he may assign, and which equity will protect until its publication. Parton v Prang (1872, CC Mass) F Cas No 10784.

Broadly speaking, statutory copyright operates to divest party of common-law right, but this does not mean that author is divested of all legal rights incident to authorship other than those

expressly protected by copyright statutes. Warner Bros. Pictures, Inc. v Columbia Broadcasting System, Inc. (1951, DC Cal) 102 F Supp 141, 92 USPQ 54, affd in part and revd in part on other grounds (CA9 Cal) 216 F2d 945, 104 USPQ 103, cert den 348 US 971, 99 L Ed 756, 75 S Ct 532.

British composer's common-law rights in his work are recognized in United States even though in Britain those rights appear to have merged in statutory copyright. Mills Music, Inc. v Cromwell Music, Inc. (1954, DC NY) 126 F Supp 54, 103 USPQ 84.

Federal court does not have jurisdiction over cases in which copyright laws are involved or over controversies about copyrighted material; jurisdiction is present only if case arises under act of Congress relating to copyright; instant case does not arise under copyright laws where issue presented is one of title to copyright with resolution of question depending on rules of common law and interpretation of contract and not on any statute of United States; plaintiff was not author of copyright material, it is alleged that copyright was secured in violation of his rights, and contract assigned to plaintiff no rights in copyrighted material but only gave him right to secure copyright. Gorham v Edwards (1958, DC NY) 164 F Supp 781, 118 USPQ 532.

Absent basis for claim of infringement, case presenting claim of equitable ownership of copyright with prayer for assignment and accounting does not arise under copyright law; claim of federally protected interest forms part of plaintiff's legal position, but, unlike suit for infringement, federal legislation relating to copyrights does not confer specific right of action sought to be enforced; sources of obligations to assign and account are equitable doctrines relating to unjust enrichment and general principles of law governing rights of co-owners, not remedial provisions of copyright law. Harrington v Mure (1960, DC NY) 186 F Supp 655, 126 USPQ 506.

Common law prohibits unauthorized use of unpublished manuscript; author has exclusive right to possess, use, and dispose of this literary property. Cantor v Mankiewicz (1960, Sup) 203 NYS2d 626, 125 USPQ 598.

Annotations:

What constitutes publication of architectural plans, drawings, or designs, so as to result in loss of common-law copyright. 77 ALR2d 1048.

3. State law rights [17 USCS § 301(a)]

Copyright, although derived from federal government, is property of individual, and copyright or income derived from it may be taxed by state. Fox Film Corp. v Doyal (1932) 286 US 123, 76 L Ed 1010, 52 S Ct 546.

In suit to enjoin enforcement of state statute against copyright pool, issue is right of copyright owners in association to conduct business of licensing public performances for profit. Gibbs v Buck (1939) 307 US 66, 83 L Ed 1111, 59 S Ct 725, 41 USPQ 162.

State law prohibiting activities of unlawful combinations controlling performing rights of copyrighted music did not contravene copyright laws. Watson v Buck (1941) 313 US 387, 85 L Ed 1416, 61 S Ct 962, 49 USPQ 468, 136 ALR 1426.

State statute setting up complete scheme for regulation of combinations controlling performing rights in copyrighted music was not unconstitutional. Marsh v Buck (1941) 313 US 406, 85 L Ed 1426, 61 S Ct 969, 49 USPQ 474, 136 ALR 1434.

Insofar as predecessor statute provides that owner of musical copyright, after recording or permitting recording of copyright work, must be paid a royalty on recordings manufactured by others, state statutes that operate to diminish number of recordings produced by others—such as criminal statutes prohibiting "piracy" of sound recordings, or tax statutes raising cost of producing or selling records—are not in such direct conflict as to render them invalid under supremacy clause (Article 6, cl 2) of Constitution. Goldstein v California (1973) 412 US 546, 37 L Ed 2d 163, 93 S Ct 2303, reh den 414 US 883, 38 L Ed 2d 131, 94 S Ct 27.

Copyright by state of its judicial reports does not preclude others from publishing opinions of judges contained therein, work of reporter being only portion entitled to protection. Banks & Bros. v West Pub. Co. (1886, CC Minn) 27 F 50.

Tennessee statute providing for compulsory licensing of copyrighted musical compositions at prices to be stated in advance, for complicated reports to state officials and prohibiting blanket licensing is unconstitutional; it is class legislation; it is improper exercise of police power as it was enacted, not in public interest, but for benefit of group of users of music; it deprives copyright owners of exclusive rights under Copyright Act; it contravenes treaties relating to copyrights; it impairs obligation of contract; it deprives copyright owners of right of free access to federal courts to maintain infringement suits. Buck v Harton (1940, DC Tenn) 33 F Supp 1014, 47 USPQ 18.

American Society of Composers, Authors, and Publishers has power to fix prices for right to publicly perform copyrighted musical compositions for profit and has restricted substantially all competition in sale of such right since it has substantially all such rights; neither it, nor members composing it, are entitled to decree for its benefit holding unconstitutional Washington state statute prohibiting pooling of copyrights in order to issue blanket licenses and to collect fees except on per piece system and enjoining its enforcement against them. Buck v Gallagher (1940, DC Wash) 36 F Supp 405, 48 USPQ 316, app dismd 315 US 780, 86 L Ed 1187, 62 S Ct 579.

Congress did not reserve to federal courts all questions relating to copyright titles; instead, it provided for exclusive federal jurisdiction of "copyright cases," those in which federal legislation defines substance of claim and relief to be secured; Congress left considerable residue of power in state courts to pass on "copyright questions," among them, questions arising in contract and title disputes. Harrington v Mure (1960, DC NY) 186 F Supp 655, 126 USPQ 506.

Maryland statute which makes it a misdemeanor for anyone to reproduce, for the purpose of sale for profit, tax maps produced and sold by Maryland department of assessments and taxation, thereby creating a monopoly for the state, is in conflict with federal copyright law and, hence, is invalid; however, state is free to seek relief against unfair competition in equity courts. State's Attorney for Prince George's County v Sekuler (1968) 249 Md 499, 240 A2d 608, 158 USPQ 231.

4. Subject matter not within copyright statute [17 USCS § 301(b)(1)]

Provisions stating that works for which copyrights may be secured include all "writings" of author, and provisions stating that specifications of categories of protected works contained therein shall not be held to limit subject matter of copyright, do not indicate that Congress intended to exercise its authority over all works to which copyright clause (Article 1, § 8, cl 8) of Constitution might apply, and thus Congress, under copyright laws has not so occupied field of copyright protection as to pre-empt all comparable state action. Goldstein v California (1973) 412 US 546, 37 L Ed 2d 163, 93 S Ct 2303, reh den 414 US 883, 38 L Ed 2d 131, 94 S Ct 27.

Author's right in fruits of his intellectual labor is broader than that which he has under copyright law. Stanley v Columbia Broadcasting System, Inc. (1949, Cal) 208 P2d 9, 82 USPQ 123, subsequent op on reh 35 Cal 2d 653, 221 P2d 73, 86 USPQ 520, 23 ALR2d 216.

Video tape of TV performance is motion picture, and electronic impressions on tape for reproducing sound are within meaning of copyright statute so that only federal court has jurisdiction, and action to enjoin use of sound from video tape is dismissed. Trophy Productions, Inc. v Telebrity, Inc. (1975, NY Sup Ct) 185 USPQ 830.

At common law, rights in literary or artistic work were recognized on substantially same basis as title to other property; rights given by statute supersede those of common law so far as statute applies, but common-law rights in regard to any field of literary or artistic production which does not fall within purview of copyright statute are not affected thereby. Waring v WDAS Broadcasting Station, Inc. (1937) 327 Pa 433, 194 A 631, 35 USPQ 272.

Annotations:

Unfair competition by direct reproduction of literary, artistic, or musical property. 40 ALR3d 566.

5. Causes of action arising from undertakings commenced before January 1, 1978 [17 USCS § 301(b)(2)]

Writings which may eventually be the subject of federal copyright may be protected under state law prior to publication. Goldstein v California (1973) 412 US 546, 37 L Ed 2d 163, 93 S Ct 2303, reh den 414 US 883, 38 L Ed 2d 131, 94 S Ct 27.

6. Rights not protected by copyright [17 USCS § 301(b)(3)]

Suit for infringement of copyright against defendants who had purchased copyrighted books from dealers under retail price agreement and sold them for less than fixed price constituted suit independent of complainant's statutory copyright rights. Scribner v Straus (1908) 210 US 352, 52 L Ed 1094, 28 S Ct 735.

Suit for appropriation of literary property is separate from suit under copyright laws. Newport Industries, Inc. v Crosby Naval Stores, Inc. (1944, CA5 Miss) 139 F2d 611, 60 USPQ 219.

Unfair competition and trade-mark and copyright infringements involve similar issues; they are phases of overzealous competition or evident lack of ethical ideals in business transactions which call for judicial correction. Soy Food Mills, Inc. v Pillsbury Mills, Inc. (1947, CA7 Ill) 161 F2d 22, 73 USPQ 141, cert den 332 US 766, 92 L Ed 351, 68 S Ct 73.

Where copyright upon dictionary has expired anyone may reprint work and use original title thereon. Merriam v Famous Shoe & Clothing Co. (1891, CC Mo) 47 F 411.

Owner of a copyright is not entitled to equitable relief against another publication solely because writer of other publication may have saved some stenographic labor or manual handwriting by cutting or copying words of citations, which include no literary ability. West Publishing Co. v

Edward Thompson Co. (1909, CC NY) 169 F 833, mod on other grounds (CA2 NY) 176 F 833.

By intrusting films to defendant with contract to show on certain days only, plaintiff did not waive right to sue in tort under copyright law and was not relegated to suit on contract. Twentieth Century-Fox Film Corp. v Peoples Theatres of Alabama, Inc. (1938, DC Ala) 24 F Supp 793, 39 USPQ 469.

If it should appear that in broadcasts defendant has appropriated without plaintiff's consent plot and principal characters of plaintiff's copyrighted novel and that use being made injured reputation of author and of work, and amounts to deception upon public, it may be proper to afford relief by applying principles of unfair competition. Prouty v National Broadcasting Co. (1939, DC Mass) 26 F Supp 265, 40 USPQ 331.

Illegal combination of copyrights and pooling of proceeds derived from licensing of copyrights through illegal combination renders unenforceable rights granted under Copyright Act, at least while illegal combination continues. Alden-Rochelle, Inc. v American Soc. of Composers, Authors & Publishers (1948, DC NY) 80 F Supp 900, 79 USPQ 402.

Federal copyright law pre-empts state unfair competition law so that preliminary injunction that is unavailable for copying under federal copyright law is also unavailable under unfair competition theory. Triangle Publications, Inc. v Sports Eye, Inc. (1976, DC Pa) 193 USPQ 50.

Complaint alleging unfair competition and avoiding reference to "copyright" or "infringement" is nevertheless based on federal copyright law and involves rights under copyrights in motion pictures so that state court action is dismissed. Janus Films, Inc. v Budget Films, Inc. (1976, Cal App) 193 USPQ 123.

In absence of copyright or design patent, dress designs are not protected by common-law copyright, for design copyrights do not exist at common law; there is no protection against style piracy. A. J. Sandy, Inc. v Junior City, Inc. (1962) 17 App Div 2d 407, 234 NYS2d 508, 136 USPQ 144.

7. Sound recordings fixed before February 15, 1972 [17 USCS § 301(c)]

State criminal statute prohibiting "piracy" of sound recordings by copying, without permission, records or tapes of another, with intent to sell duplicate recordings thus made—insofar as such statute is applied with regard to pirating of recordings made before February 15, 1972, the effective date of the 1971 amendments of the federal copyright law which extend copyright protection to recordings—is not invalid as being beyond state powers in violation of copyright clause (Article 1 § 8, cl 8) of Constitution; nor is such state statute, as so applied, invalid as being in conflict with federal copyright law and thus violative of supremacy clause (Article 6, cl 2) of Constitution, since Congress has not pre-empted area of protection of recordings made prior to February 15, 1972, indicating neither that it wishes to protect, nor to free from protection, such recordings. Goldstein v California (1973) 412 US 546, 37 L Ed 2d 163, 93 S Ct 2303, reh den 414 US 883, 38 L Ed 2d 131, 94 S Ct 27.

8. Rights or remedies under other federal statutes [17 USCS § 301(d)]

Authorization in 28 USCS § 1498 as to suits against United States for infringement of work protected under federal copyright laws, does not authorize recovery by widow of alleged presidential assassin for government's alleged infringement of common-law copyright interests in assassin's writings by government's publication of writings in investigative report of assassination. Porter v United States (1973, CA5 Tex) 473 F2d 1329.

Copyright laws do not grant to copyright owners privilege of combining in violation of otherwise valid federal laws. Alfred Bell & Co. v Catalda Fine Arts, Inc. (1947, DC NY) 74 F Supp 973, 75 USPQ 66.

Annotations:

Unfair competition by direct reproduction of literary, artistic, or musical property. 40 ALR3d 566.

§ 302. Duration of copyright: Works created on or after January 1, 1978

(a) In general. Copyright in a work created on or after January 1, 1978, subsists from its creation and, except as provided by the following subsections, endures for a term consisting of the life of the author and fifty years after the author's death.

(b) Joint works. In the case of a joint work prepared by two or more authors who did not work for hire, the copyright endures for a term consisting of the life of the last surviving author and fifty years after such last surviving author's death.

(c) Anonymous works, pseudonymous works, and works made for hire. In the case of an anonymous work, a pseudonymous work, or a work made for hire, the copyright endures for a term of seventy-five years from the year of its first publication, or a term of one hundred years from the year of its creation, whichever expires first. If, before the end of such term, the identity of one or more of the authors of an anonymous or pseudonymous work is revealed in the records of a registration made for that work under subsections (a) or (d) of section 408 [17 USCS § 408], or in the records provided by this subsection, the copyright in the work endures for the term specified by subsection (a) or (b), based on the life of the author or authors whose identity has been revealed. Any person having an interest in the copyright in an anonymous or pseudonymous work may at any time record, in records to be maintained by the Copyright Office for that purpose, a statement identifying one or more authors of the work; the statement shall also identify the person filing it, the nature of that person's interest, the source of the information recorded, and the particular work affected, and shall comply in form and content with requirements that the Register of Copyrights shall prescribe by regulation.

(d) Records relating to death of authors. Any person having an interest in a copyright may at any time record in the Copyright Office a statement of the date of death of the author of the copyrighted work, or a statement that the author is still living on a particular date. The statement shall identify the person filing it, the nature of that person's interest, and the source of the information recorded, and shall comply in form and content with requirements that the Register of Copyrights shall prescribe by regulation. The Register shall maintain current records of information relating to the death of authors of copyrighted works, based on such recorded statements and, to the extent the Register considers practicable, on data contained in any of the records of the Copyright Office or in other reference sources.

(e) Presumption as to author's death. After a period of seventy-five years from the year of first publication of a work, or a period of one hundred years from the year of its creation, whichever expires first, any person who obtains from the Copyright Office a certified report that the records provided by subsection (d) disclose nothing to indicate that the author of the work is living, or died less than fifty years before, is entitled to the benefit of a presumption that the author has been dead for at least fifty years. Reliance in good faith upon this presumption shall be a complete defense to any action for infringement under this title [17 USCS §§ 101 et seq.].
(Added Oct. 19, 1976, P. L. 94-553, Title I, § 101, 90 Stat. 2572.)

HISTORY; ANCILLARY LAWS AND DIRECTIVES

Effective date of section:
Section 102 of Act Oct. 19, 1976, P. L. 94-553, 90 Stat. 2598 provided that this section "becomes effective on January 1, 1978".

Other provisions:
Extension until December 31, 1965, of renewal terms expiring prior to such date. Act Sept. 19, 1962, P. L. 87-668, 76 Stat. 555, provided that in any case in which the renewal term of a copyright subsisting in any work on Sept. 19, 1962, would expire prior to Dec. 31, 1965, such term was continued until Dec. 31, 1965.

Extension until December 31, 1967, of renewal terms expiring prior to such date. Act Aug. 28, 1965, P. L. 89-142, 79 Stat. 581, provided that in any case in which the renewal term of a copyright subsisting in any work on Aug. 28, 1965, or the term thereof as extended by Act Sept. 19, 1962 [set out as a note under this section], would expire prior to Dec. 31, 1967, such term was continued until Dec. 31, 1967.

Extension until December 31, 1968, of renewal terms expiring prior to such date. Act P. L. 90-141, Nov. 16, 1967, 81 Stat. 464, provided that in any case in which the renewal term of a copyright subsisting in any work on Nov. 16, 1967, or the term thereof as extended by Act Sept. 19, 1962 or by Act Aug. 28, 1965 (or by either or both of said laws) [set out as notes under this section], would expire prior to Dec. 31, 1968, such term was continued until Dec. 31, 1968.

Extension until December 31, 1969, of renewal terms expiring prior to such date. Act July 23, 1968, P. L. 90-416, 82 Stat. 397, provided that in any case in which the renewal term of a copyright subsisting in any work on July 23, 1968, or the term thereof as extended by Act Sept. 19, 1962, by Act Aug. 28, 1965 or by Act Nov. 16, 1967 (or by all or certain of said laws) [set out as notes under this section], would expire prior to Dec. 31, 1969, such term was continued until Dec. 31, 1969.

Extension until December 31, 1970, of renewal terms expiring prior to such date. Act Dec. 16, 1969, P. L. 91-147, 83 Stat. 360, provided that in any case in which the renewal term of a copyright subsisting in any work on Dec. 16, 1969, or the term thereof as extended by Act Sept. 19, 1962, by Act Aug. 28, 1965, by Act Nov. 16, 1967, or by Act July 23, 1968 (or by all or certain of said laws) [set out as notes under this section], would expire prior to Dec. 31, 1970, such term was continued until Dec. 31, 1970.

Extension until December 31, 1971, of renewal terms expiring prior to such date. Act Dec. 17, 1970, P. L. 91-555, 84 Stat. 1441, provided that in any case in which the renewal term of a copyright subsisting in any work on Dec. 17, 1970, or the term thereof as extended by Act Sept. 19, 1962, by Act Aug. 28, 1965, by Act Nov. 16, 1967, by Act July 23, 1968, or by Act Dec. 16, 1969, (or by all or certain of said laws) [set out as notes under this section], would expire prior to Dec. 31, 1971, such term was continued until Dec. 31, 1971.

Extension until December 31, 1972, of renewal terms expiring prior to such date. Act Nov. 24, 1971, P. L. 92-170, 85 Stat. 490, provided that in any case in which the renewal term of a copyright subsisting in any work on Nov. 24, 1971, or the term thereof as extended by Act Sept. 19, 1962, by Act Aug. 28, 1965, by Act Nov. 16, 1967, by Act July 23, 1968, by Act Dec. 16, 1969, or by Act Dec. 17, 1970 (or by all or certain of said laws), would expire prior to Dec. 31, 1972, such term was continued until Dec. 31, 1972.

Extension until December 31, 1974, of renewal terms expiring prior to such date. Act Oct. 25, 1972, P. L. 92-566, § 1, 86 Stat. 1181, provided that in any case in which the renewal term of a copyright subsisting in any work on Oct. 25, 1972, or the term thereof as extended by Act Sept. 19, 1962, by Act Aug. 28, 1965, by Act Nov. 16, 1967, by Act July 23, 1968, by Act Dec. 16, 1969, by Act Dec. 17, 1970, or by Act Nov. 24, 1971 (or by all or certain of said laws) [set out as notes under this section], would expire prior to Dec. 31, 1974, such term was continued until Dec. 31, 1974.

Extension until December 31, 1976, of renewal terms expiring prior to such date. Act Dec. 31, 1974, P. L. 93-573, Title I, § 104, 88 Stat. 1873, provided that in any case in which the renewal term of a copyright subsisting in any work on Dec. 31, 1974, or the term thereof as extended by Act Sept. 19, 1962, by Act Aug. 28, 1965, by Act Nov.

16, 1967, by Act July 23, 1968, by Act Dec. 16, 1969, by Act Dec. 17, 1970, by Act Nov. 24, 1971, or by Act Oct. 25, 1972 (or by all or certain of said laws) [set out as notes under this section], would expire prior to Dec. 31, 1976, such term was continued until Dec. 31, 1976.

CROSS REFERENCES

"Anonymous work" defined, 17 USCS § 101.
"Created" defined, 17 USCS § 101.
"Fixed" defined, 17 USCS § 101.
"Joint work" defined, 17 USCS § 101.
"Pseudonymous work" defined, 17 USCS § 101.
Records of Register of Copyrights as to death of author, 17 USCS § 705.
This section referred to in 17 USCS §§ 303, 305, 406, 708.

RESEARCH GUIDE

Am Jur:
18 Am Jur 2d, Copyright and Literary Property §§ 66–72.

Annotations:
Persons entitled to renewal of copyright following author's death. 100 L Ed 1430; 4 L Ed 2d 2069.

§ 303.   Duration of copyright: Works created but not published or copyrighted before January 1, 1978

Copyright in a work created before January 1, 1978, but not theretofore in the public domain or copyrighted, subsists from January 1, 1978, and endures for the term provided by section 302 [17 USCS § 302]. In no case, however, shall the term of copyright in such a work expire before December 31, 2002; and, if the work is published on or before December 31, 2002, the term of copyright shall not expire before December 31, 2027. (Added Oct. 19, 1976, P. L. 94-553, Title I, § 101, 90 Stat. 2573.)

HISTORY; ANCILLARY LAWS AND DIRECTIVES

Effective date of section:
Section 102 of Act Oct. 19, 1976, P. L. 94-553, 90 Stat. 2598 provided that this section "becomes effective on January 1, 1978".

CROSS REFERENCES

·Original work of authorship, 17 USCS § 102.
This section referred to in 17 USCS §§ 301, 305.

RESEARCH GUIDE

Am Jur:
18 Am Jur 2d, Copyright and Literary Property §§ 66–72.

§ 304. Duration of copyright: Subsisting copyrights

(a) Copyrights in their first term on January 1, 1978. Any copyright, the first term of which is subsisting on January 1, 1978, shall endure for twenty-eight years from the date it was originally secured: *Provided,* That in the case of any posthumous work or of any periodical, cyclopedic, or other composite work upon which the copyright was originally secured by the proprietor thereof, or of any work copyrighted by a corporate body (otherwise than as assignee or licensee of the individual author) or by an employer for whom such work is made for hire, the proprietor of such copyright shall be entitled to a renewal and extension of the copyright in such work for the further term of forty-seven years when application for such renewal and extension shall have been made to the Copyright Office and duly registered therein within one year prior to the expiration of the original term of copyright: *And provided further,* That in the case of any other copyrighted work, including a contribution by an individual author to a periodical or to a cyclopedic or other composite work, the author of such work, if still living, or the widow, widower, or children of the author, if the author be not living, or if such author, widow, widower, or children be not living, then the author's executors, or in the absence of a will, his or her next of kin shall be entitled to a renewal and extension of the copyright in such work for a further term of forty-seven years when application for such renewal and extension shall have been made to the Copyright Office and duly registered therein within one year prior to the expiration of the original term of copyright: *And provided further,* That in default of the registration of such application for renewal and extension, the copyright in any work shall terminate at the expiration of twenty-eight years from the date copyright was originally secured.

(b) Copyrights in their renewal term or registered for renewal before January 1, 1978. The duration of any copyright, the renewal term of which is subsisting at any time between December 31, 1976, and December 31, 1977, inclusive, or for which renewal registration is made between December 31, 1976, and December 31, 1977, inclusive, is extended to endure for a term of seventy-five years from the date copyright was originally secured.

(c) Termination of transfers and licenses covering extended renewal term. In the case of any copyright subsisting in either its first or renewal term on January 1, 1978, other than a copyright in a work made for hire, the exclusive or nonexclusive grant of a transfer or license of the renewal copyright or any right under it, executed before January 1, 1978, by any of the persons designated by the second proviso of subsection (a) of this section, otherwise than by will, is subject to termination under the following conditions:

(1) In the case of a grant executed by a person or persons other than the author, termination of the grant may be effected by the surviving person or persons who executed it. In the case of a grant executed by one or more of the authors of the work, termination of the grant may be

effected, to the extent of a particular author's share in the ownership of the renewal copyright, by the author who executed it or, if such author is dead, by the person or persons who, under clause (2) of this subsection, own and are entitled to exercise a total of more than one-half of that author's termination interest.

(2) Where an author is dead, his or her termination interest is owned, and may be exercised, by his widow or her widower and his or her children or grandchildren as follows:

(A) the widow or widower owns the author's entire termination interest unless there are any surviving children or grandchildren of the author, in which case the widow or widower owns one-half of the author's interest;

(B) the author's surviving children, and the surviving children of any dead child of the author, own the author's entire termination interest unless there is a widow or widower, in which case the ownership of one-half of the author's interest is divided among them;

(C) the rights of the author's children and grandchildren are in all cases divided among them and exercised on a per stirpes basis according to the number of such author's children represented; the share of the children of a dead child in a termination interest can be exercised only by the action of a majority of them.

(3) Termination of the grant may be effected at any time during a period of five years beginning at the end of fifty-six years from the date copyright was originally secured, or beginning on January 1, 1978, whichever is later.

(4) The termination shall be effected by serving an advance notice in writing upon the grantee or the grantee's successor in title. In the case of a grant executed by a person or persons other than the author, the notice shall be signed by all of those entitled to terminate the grant under clause (1) of this subsection, or by their duly authorized agents. In the case of a grant executed by one or more of the authors of the work, the notice as to any one author's share shall be signed by that author or his or her duly authorized agent or, if that author is dead, by the number and proportion of the owners of his or her termination interest required under clauses (1) and (2) of this subsection, or by their duly authorized agents.

(A) The notice shall state the effective date of the termination, which shall fall within the five-year period specified by clause (3) of this subsection, and the notice shall be served not less than two or more than ten years before that date. A copy of the notice shall be recorded in the Copyright Office before the effective date of termination, as a condition to its taking effect.

(B) The notice shall comply, in form, content, and manner of service, with requirements that the Register of Copyrights shall prescribe by regulation.

175

(5) Termination of the grant may be effected notwithstanding any agreement to the contrary, including an agreement to make a will or to make any future grant.

(6) In the case of a grant executed by a person or persons other than the author, all rights under this title [17 USCS §§ 101 et seq.] that were covered by the terminated grant revert, upon the effective date of termination, to all of those entitled to terminate the grant under clause (1) of this subsection. In the case of a grant executed by one or more of the authors of the work, all of a particular author's rights under this title that were covered by the terminated grant revert, upon the effective date of termination, to that author or, if that author is dead, to the persons owning his or her termination interest under clause (2) of this subsection, including those owners who did not join in signing the notice of termination under clause (4) of this subsection. In all cases the reversion of rights is subject to the following limitations:

(A) A derivative work prepared under authority of the grant before its termination may continue to be utilized under the terms of the grant after its termination, but this privilege does not extend to the preparation after the termination of other derivative works based upon the copyrighted work covered by the terminated grant.

(B) The future rights that will revert upon termination of the grant become vested on the date the notice of termination has been served as provided by clause (4) of this subsection.

(C) Where the author's rights revert to two or more persons under clause (2) of this subsection, they shall vest in those persons in the proportionate shares provided by that clause. In such a case, and subject to the provisions of subclause (D) of this clause, a further grant, or agreement to make a further grant, of a particular author's share with respect to any right covered by a terminated grant is valid only if it is signed by the same number and proportion of the owners, in whom the right has vested under this clause, as are required to terminate the grant under clause (2) of this subsection. Such further grant or agreement is effective with respect to all of the persons in whom the right it covers has vested under this subclause, including those who did not join in signing it. If any person dies after rights under a terminated grant have vested in him or her, that person's legal representatives, legatees, or heirs at law represent him or her for purposes of this subclause.

(D) A further grant, or agreement to make a further grant, of any right covered by a terminated grant is valid only if it is made after the effective date of the termination. As an exception, however, an agreement for such a further grant may be made between the author or any of the persons provided by the first sentence of clause (6) of this subsection, or between the persons provided by subclause (C) of this clause, and the original grantee or such grantee's successor in title, after the notice of termination has been served as provided by clause (4) of this subsection.

(E) Termination of a grant under this subsection affects only those rights covered by the grant that arise under this title [17 USCS §§ 101 et seq.], and in no way affects rights arising under any other Federal, State, or foreign laws.

(F) Unless and until termination is effected under this subsection, the grant, if it does not provide otherwise, continues in effect for the remainder of the extended renewal term.

(Added Oct. 19, 1976, P. L. 94-553, Title I, § 101, 90 Stat. 2573.)

HISTORY; ANCILLARY LAWS AND DIRECTIVES

Effective date of section:

Section 102 of Act Oct. 19, 1976, P. L. 94-553, 90 Stat. 2598 provided that this section "becomes effective on January 1, 1978", except that subsec. (b) shall take "effect upon enactment of this Act [enacted Oct. 19, 1976]."

Other provisions:

Ad interim copyright subsisting on December 31, 1977. Act Oct. 19, 1976, P. L. 94-553, Title I, § 107, 90 Stat. 2600, provided: "In the case of any work in which an ad interim copyright is subsisting or is capable of being secured on December 31, 1977, under section 22 of title 17 [former 17 USCS § 22] as it existed on that date, copyright protection is hereby extended to endure for the term or terms provided by section 304 of title 17 [17 USCS § 304] as amended by the first section of this Act [section 101 of Act Oct. 19, 1976, which appears as 17 USCS §§ 101 et seq.]"

CROSS REFERENCES

Termination of transfers and licenses granted by author, 17 USCS § 203.
This section referred to in 17 USCS §§ 101 note, 304 note, 305, 408, 708.

RESEARCH GUIDE

Am Jur:

18 Am Jur 2d, Copyright and Literary Property §§ 66–72.

Annotations:

Persons entitled to renewal of copyright following author's death. 100 L Ed 1430; 4 L Ed 2d 2069.

INTERPRETIVE NOTES AND DECISIONS

I. IN GENERAL

1. Generally
2. First-term copyright
3. Expiration of copyright

II. RENEWAL TERM

4. Generally

5. Purpose
6. Accrual of right to renew, generally
7. —As affected by assignment
8. Co-authors
9. Composite works
10. Non-authors entitled to renew, generally

11. —Widows, widowers, or children
12. —Executors, administrators, legatees, or next of kin
13. Termination of transfer under renewal, generally
14. —Derivative works
15. Works made for hire

I. IN GENERAL

1. Generally

"Date of publication" in predecessor statute limiting duration of copyright refers to date of deposit under this section of works of which copies are not reproduced for sale notwithstanding other definition of "date of publication" of published work to mean earliest date when copies are placed on sale, sold, or publicly distributed. Shilkret v Musicraft Records, Inc. (1942, CA2 NY) 131 F2d 929, 55 USPQ 469, cert den 319 US 742, 87 L Ed 1699, 63 S Ct 1030; Loew's, Inc. v Superior Court of Los Angeles County (1941) 18 Cal 2d 419, 115 P2d 983, 50 USPQ 641.

Where date of publication was advertised, but books were actually placed in mail three days prior to such date, advertised date will be taken as date of publication in absence of proof that any of subscribers received books prior to that date. Black v Henry G. Allen Co. (1893, CC NY) 56 F 764.

2. First-term copyright

Term of copyright cannot be extended by filing of second or amended application for copyright. Caliga v Inter Ocean Newspaper Co. (1909) 215 US 182, 54 L Ed 150, 30 S Ct 38.

Antedating of copyright merely shortens its duration. Southern Music Pub. Co. v Bibo-Lang, Inc. (1935, DC NY) 10 F Supp 972, 26 USPQ 321.

3. Expiration of copyright

After expiration of copyright, name by which publication was known and sold under copyright becomes public property. G. & C. Merriam Co. v Syndicate Publishing Co. (1915) 237 US 618, 59 L Ed 1148, 35 S Ct 708.

Upon expiration of copyright, right to use copyrighted name goes out to public subject to certain and well-understood limitation or condition, namely, that public right to use shall be so exercised as not to deceive members of public and lead them into belief that they are buying particular or identical thing which was produced under copyright. G. & C. Merriman Co. v Ogilvie (1908, CA1 Mass) 159 F 638, cert den 209 US 551, 52 L Ed 922, 28 S Ct 761.

Upon expiration of term of copyright of novel any person may make any use of novel which he may see fit, whether by copying, publishing or dramatizing. Atlas Mfg. Co. v Street & Smith (1913, CA8 Mo) 204 F 398, app dismd 231 US 348, 58 L Ed 262, 34 S Ct 73.

Expiration of copyright of novel does not affect copyright of so much of opera based thereon as was new work and entitled to be independently copyrighted as such. G. Ricordi & Co. v Paramount Pictures, Inc. (1951, CA2 NY) 189 F2d 469, 89 USPQ 289, 564, cert den 342 US 849, 96 L Ed 641, 72 S Ct 77.

Failure to renew copyright in motion pictures based on novels does not amount to abandonment of renewal copyrights in novels. Filmvideo Releasing Corp. v Hastings (1976, DC NY) 426 F Supp 690, 193 USPQ 305.

When statutory copyright expires without being renewed, common-law rights are not revived. Tams-Witmark Music Library, Inc. v New Opera Co. (1948) 298 NY 163, 81 NE2d 70, 78 USPQ 298.

All copyrighted compositions enter public domain at expiration of copyrights, and thereafter, anyone has right to use them freely. Taylor v State (1948) 29 Wash 2d 638, 188 P2d 671, 76 USPQ 275.

II. RENEWAL TERM

4. Generally

Renewal of copyright does not grant any other or greater rights than existed in original term. Wheaton v Peters (1834) 33 US 591, 8 L Ed 1055.

Right to obtain renewal copyright and renewal copyright itself exists only by reason of statute and are derived solely and directly from statute. Miller Music Corp. v Daniels (1960) 362 US 373, 4 L Ed 2d 804, 80 S Ct 792.

Predecessor section is applicable primarily to original copyrights, wherein author and proprietor stand on equal footing, and does not give proprietor same right as author to renewal. White-Smith Music Pub. Co. v Goff (1910, CC RI) 180 F 256, affd (CA1 RI) 187 F 247.

Right of renewal is new grant and not extension of original term. Southern Music Pub. Co. v Bibo-Lang, Inc. (1935, DC NY) 10 F Supp 975, 26 USPQ 324; Shapiro, Bernstein & Co. v Bryan (1939, DC NY) 27 F Supp 11, 41 USPQ 134; April Productions, Inc. v G. Schirmer, Inc. (1955) 308 NY 366, 126 NE2d 283, 105 USPQ 286, 69 ALR2d 1305.

Grant obtained through renewal of copyright is new estate, one which is acquired free and clear of all rights, interests, or licenses granted under original copyright. Shapiro, Bernstein & Co. v Jerry Vogel Music Co. (1953, DC NY) 115 F Supp 754, 98 USPQ 438, 99 USPQ 381, revd on other grounds (CA2 NY) 221 F2d 569, 105 USPQ 178, adhered to (CA2 NY) 223 F2d 252.

Unlike original copyright, renewal is created, not by publication with claim of copyright, but by registration of application for renewal in copyright office; such application cannot be validly made until last year of original term of copyright so that, until that time, no one can have anything more than right to secure renewal. Rose v Bourne, Inc. (1959, DC NY) 176 F Supp 605, 123 USPQ 29, affd (CA2 NY) 279 F2d 79, 125 USPQ 509, cert den 364 US 880, 5 L Ed 2d 103, 81 S Ct 170.

Where renewal application for registration of proprietor's claim to copyright, predicated on renewal rights accorded under predecessor statute asserts in same application mutually exclusive claims as "proprietor of copyright in composite work" and as "employer of work made for hire," Register of Copyrights, in proper exercise of his discretion, may refuse to register application which relies upon both of these mutually exclusive grounds. 43 OAG No. 2.

5. Purpose

Basic consideration of policy underlying renewal provisions is to enable author to sell copyright without losing his renewal interest. Fred Fisher Music Co. v M. Witmark & Sons (1943) 318 US 643, 87 L Ed 1055, 63 S Ct 773, 57 USPQ 50.

Purpose of renewal provisions is to enable composer to sell copyright without losing renewal interest which passes to family of composer, and fact that assignment of copyright occurred during composer's lifetime, during which work was performed publicly, but delayed publication of score did not occur until after death of composer, does not make work "posthumous" or defeat congressional intent that family of composer should own renewal rights. Bartok v Boosey & Hawkes, Inc. (1975, CA2 NY) 523 F2d 941, 187 USPQ 529.

Main purpose of predecessor section is to protect interest of author. Shapiro, Bernstein & Co. v Bryan (1939, DC NY) 27 F Supp 11, 41 USPQ 134.

Congressional purposes in enacting predecessor section were to protect author against his own improvident conduct in surrendering renewal rights during original term, to set up statutory scheme of priority in renewal rights for benefit of those naturally dependent upon, and properly expectant of, author's bounty, and to permit author who had no wife or children to bequeath by will right to apply for renewal. Gibran v Alfred A. Knopf, Inc. (1957, DC NY) 153 F Supp 854, 115 USPQ 214, affd (CA2 NY)

255 F2d 121, 117 USPQ 218, cert den 358 US 828, 3 L Ed 2d 67, 79 S Ct 47.

Basic purpose of renewal provisions of copyright statutes is to give reward to author rather than bookseller. Miller Music Corp. v Charles N. Daniels, Inc. (1957, DC NY) 158 F Supp 188, 116 USPQ 92, affd without opinion (CA2 NY) 265 F2d 925, affd 362 US 373, 4 L Ed 2d 804, 80 S Ct 792.

6. Accrual of right to renew, generally

Author cannot, prior to beginning of 28th year, devise right to renewal; renewal of copyright which is afforded author, his relatives, or executors does not extend to another's work, although author was associated in same book. Harris v Coca-Cola Co. (1934, CA5 Ga) 73 F2d 370, 23 USPQ 182, cert den 294 US 709, 79 L Ed 1243, 55 S Ct 406.

Right to renew copyright accrues and can be exercised only during one-year period prior to expiration of existing term. Tobani v Carl Fischer, Inc. (1938, CA2 NY) 98 F2d 57, 38 USPQ 198, cert den 305 US 650, 83 L Ed 420, 59 S Ct 243; Shapiro, Bernstein & Co. v Bryan (1941, CA2 NY) 123 F2d 697, 51 USPQ 422; M. Witmark & Sons v Fred Fisher Music Co. (1942, CA2 NY) 125 F2d 949, 52 USPQ 385, affd 318 US 643, 87 L Ed 1055, 63 S Ct 773, 57 USPQ 50.

Previous judgment that all rights in copyright of Superman Comics belong to publisher includes renewal rights so that creators of comic cannot relitigate title. Siegel v National Periodical Publications, Inc. (1974, CA2 NY) 508 F2d 909, 184 USPQ 257.

Original registration of copyright in photoplay by corporation, without any evidence that individual creator of photoplay and controller of corporation was employee of corporation or made work for hire, indicates that original corporation acquired rights by license or assignment from creator so that subsequent assignment to other corporation could not convey renewal rights of creator. Epoch Producing Corp. v Killiam Shows, Inc. (1975, CA2 NY) 522 F2d 737, 187 USPQ 270, cert den 424 US 955, 47 L Ed 2d 360, 96 S Ct 1429.

Composition assigned during lifetime of author is not "posthumous" because of publication and copyrighting after death of author, so that widow and children of composer are entitled to renewal rights. Bartok v Boosey & Hawkes, Inc. (1975, CA2 NY) 523 F2d 941, 187 USPQ 529.

Publisher registered song with copyright office as unpublished work on March 22, 1929, and registered it as published song on June 1, 1929; renewal of copyright could be secured only during twenty-eighth year of original copyright term, that is, within period of one year commencing March 22, 1956. Tobias v Joy Music, Inc. (1962, DC NY) 204 F Supp 556, 133 USPQ 181.

Right accrues on application during last year of original term of copyright and is limited to those persons enumerated. Tobani v Carl Fischer, Inc. (1942) 263 App Div 503, 33 NYS2d 294, 52 USPQ 640, affd without opinion 289 NY 727, 46 NE2d 347.

7. —As affected by assignment

Author can assign original copyright and, after he has secured it, renewal copyright as well. Fred Fisher Music Co. v M. Witmark & Sons (1943) 318 US 643, 87 L Ed 1055, 63 S Ct 773, 57 USPQ 50.

Renewal or additional term of copyright vests in author if living, but he may divest himself of right thus reserved by parting absolutely with entire interest in work or by agreement to convey copyright for additional term when it shall be secured. Tobani v Carl Fischer, Inc. (1938, CA2 NY) 98 F2d 57, 38 USPQ 198, cert den 305 US 650, 83 L Ed 420, 59 S Ct 243.

"Bill of sale," signed 11 years before time for renewal, selling "all copyright renewals" is construed as immediate and outright transfer and assignment of expectancy; assignment, signed at about time renewal application was filed, granting "exclusive right for entire period of renewal copyright" is assignment of expectancy since it contains unmistakable language denoting intention to grant presently transferable right, although at its execution application had not been filed for renewal; renewal right does not strictly accrue until filing of application in twenty-eighth year of original term and renewal does not become effective until first day of twenty-ninth year. Rossiter v Vogel (1943, CA2 NY) 134 F2d 908, 57 USPQ 161.

While general assignment of copyright does not assign right to renew, yet fact that alleged coauthor made no legal or formal claim to copyright during almost entire 28 years of its original term is circumstance to be considered on issue of coauthorship; if he had no interest in original term, he had no right to apply for and receive renewal certificate. Jerry Vogel Music Co. v Forster Music Publishers, Inc. (1945, CA2 NY) 147 F2d 614, 64 USPQ 417, cert den 325 US 880, 89 L Ed 1996, 65 S Ct 1573.

General transfer by author of original copyright without mention of renewal rights conveys no interest in renewal rights without proof of contrary intention; such intent is not shown by author's silence in response to assignee's ambiguous statement that renewals belonged to assignee. Edward B. Marks Music Corp. v Charles K.

Harris Music Publishing Co. (1958, CA2 NY) 255 F2d 518, 117 USPQ 308, cert den 358 US 831, 3 L Ed 2d 69, 79 S Ct 51.

Power of attorney to apply for copyright renewal rights is implied from fact of assignment of such rights; prior to copyright renewal period, author's interest in renewal rights is only expectancy which can be defeated by his death prior to commencement of period; author may assign expectancy, and assignment is valid against world if author is alive at commencement of renewal period; however, author may challenge validity of assignment if consideration therefor was inadequate. Rose v Bourne, Inc. (1960, CA2 NY) 279 F2d 79, 125 USPQ 509, cert den 364 US 880, 5 L Ed 2d 103, 81 S Ct 170.

Assignment of copyright in photoplay by corporation controlled by creator of photoplay is analogous to transfer from individual author and is construed under rule that favors author's retention of renewal rights, and assignments did not transfer renewal rights where they did not mention renewal rights and one of them mentioned 28 years. Epoch Producing Corp. v Killiam Shows, Inc. (1975, CA2 NY) 522 F2d 737, 187 USPQ 270, cert den 424 US 955, 47 L Ed 2d 360, 96 S Ct 1429.

Assignment by author of copyright in composition performed during composer's lifetime, but without publication of score until after death of composer, does not make work "posthumous," and renewal rights belong to heirs of composer. Bartok v Boosey & Hawkes, Inc. (1975, CA2 NY) 523 F2d 941, 187 USPQ 529.

Statement by author that he had intended to convey all his interest in copyrighted work, after first term of copyright had expired, will prevent legal representatives of author from claiming that rights of assignee existed only during first term of copyright. Cowen v Banks (1862, DC NY) F Cas No 3295.

Assignment of copyright during initial term confers on assignee no right to renewal of copyright, notwithstanding usage among booksellers to contrary. Pierpont v Fowle (1846, CC Mass) F Cas No 11152.

Right to further extension of life of any particular copyright, through refiling or registering, has been confined to author "or his widow or children if he be dead" and does not extend to assignee. West Publishing Co. v Edward Thompson Co. (1909, CC NY) 169 F 833, mod on other grounds (CA2 NY) 176 F 833.

Where corporation assigned copyright to one of joint authors, renewal on latter's application was proper. Southern Music Pub. Co. v Bibo-Lang, Inc. (1935, DC NY) 10 F Supp 972, 26 USPQ 321.

Renewal copyright obtained by author is property of author's assignee under assignment executed 15 years before whereby author assigned copyright and renewal and authorized assignee "to apply for and receive renewals and extensions." Selwyn & Co. v Veiller (1942, DC NY) 43 F Supp 491, 52 USPQ 630.

Since assignment of all of author's right, title, and interest in song did not expressly provide for renewal of copyright by assignee in author's name, assignee has no right to apply for renewal in author's name; composer of music was entitled to renewal, which he holds for benefit of himself and author or his assignee. Von Tilzer v Jerry Vogel Music Co. (1943, DC NY) 53 F Supp 191, 57 USPQ 292, affd (CA2 NY) 158 F2d 516, 71 USPQ 285.

Assignment of expectancy operating as executory contract to transfer renewal rights when they accrue in last year of copyright, if without consideration, is unenforceable. Rossiter v Vogel (DC NY) 61 USPQ 514, affd (CA2 NY) 148 F2d 292, 65 USPQ 72.

Predecessor section creates only expectancy as to renewal copyright; author must be alive on first day of twenty-eighth year to obtain renewal; author's assignment of expectancy, likewise resting on author's survival is valid and is not against public policy, but such assignment does not cut off rights of renewal extended to widow and others if author dies prior to renewal period. Carmichael v Mills Music, Inc. (1954, DC NY) 121 F Supp 43, 101 USPQ 279; Miller Music Corp. v Charles N. Daniels, Inc. (1957, DC NY) 158 F Supp 188, 116 USPQ 92 affd without opinion (CA2 NY) 265 F2d 925, affd 362 US 373, 4 L Ed 2d 804, 80 S Ct 792.

Authors, by agreement, sold and assigned to publisher certain specific rights in song, including "all copyrights and the rights to secure copyrights and extensions and renewals of the copyrights"; agreement effectively conveyed renewal rights to publisher since it conveyed all rights to original copyright and expectancy in renewal copyright; exercise of publisher-assignee's renewal rights is not contingent upon authors' assistance; although application for renewal must be in authors' names, assignment of expectancy implies power of attorney in assignee to apply for renewal in authors' names; hence, assignee's use of authors' names in applying for renewal is proper and cannot deprive assignee of any renewal rights. Tobias v Joy Music, Inc. (1962, DC NY) 204 F Supp 556, 133 USPQ 181.

Author may assign his expectant interest in copyright renewal rights; widow has like capacity to assign her expectancy; rights of adult children of author to assign their expectancies do not differ from those of author or of his widow who succeeds to right of renewal only as member of class which includes children; there is no basis for contention that there are restrictions upon child's capacity to assign her expectant interest in father's original copyrights or that she is not proprietor entitled to assign; predecessor statute does not so provide and does not express any policy imposing such restrictions. Cresci v Music Publishers Holding Corp. (1962, DC NY) 210 F Supp 253, 135 USPQ 189.

An assignment of the renewal expectancy entitles an assignee to the renewal copyright, absent circumstances rendering the assignment unconscionable. Picture Music, Inc. v Bourne, Inc. (1970, DC NY) 314 F Supp 640, 167 USPQ 348, affd (CA2 NY) 457 F2d 1213, cert den 409 US 997, 34 L Ed 2d 262, 93 S Ct 320.

General assignment of rights under estate of deceased composer is not effective assignment of renewal expectancies of widow, because renewal rights are separate property already vested in widow upon death of composer spouse. Hill & Range Songs, Inc. v Fred Rose Music, Inc. (1975, DC Tenn) 403 F Supp 420, 189 USPQ 233, motion den (DC Tenn) 413 F Supp 967.

Defendant conveyed musical compositions to plaintiff under contract which also conveyed in future renewal term of copyright; subsequently, defendant obtained renewal but refused to convey to plaintiff; complaint in state court seeking specific performance of contract by assignment of renewal, which defendant had conveyed to another defendant with knowledge of contract, states cause of action and is not dismissed on motion; contract is valid and enforcible. G. Schirmer, Inc. v Robbins Music Corp. (1941) 176 Misc 578, 28 NYS2d 699, 49 USPQ 467, affd without opinion 267 App Div 751, 45 NYS2d 924.

8. Co-authors

Assignee of renewal obtained by author of words of musical composition, being joint work, holds legal title in trust for composer of music and his assignee and cannot forbid composer's assignee from exploiting subject matter. Edward B. Marks Music Corp. v Jerry Vogel Music Co. (1944, CA2 NY) 140 F2d 266, 60 USPQ 257.

Composer assigned all rights, including renewal rights, in music to publisher, which employed author to write lyric; publisher copyrighted resulting song as joint work; as publisher's assignee, plaintiff later acquired all renewal rights in music and renewal copyrights therein; plaintiff also obtained renewal copyright on joint work; although plaintiff had not acquired author's renewal rights to joint work, it had status as composer's assignee to apply for renewal of joint work; having obtained renewal copyright on joint work, plaintiff holds it as constructive trustee for benefit of coauthors or their assignees. Shapiro, Berstein & Co. v Jerry Vogel Music Co. (1955, CA2 NY) 221 F2d 569, 105 USPQ 178, adhered to (CA2 NY) 223 F2d 252, 105 USPQ 460.

Registration of original copyright of coauthors in proprietor's name gives him no right to renewal. Edward B. Marks Music Corp. v Jerry Vogel Music Co. (1942, DC NY) 42 F Supp 859, 52 USPQ 219.

Renewal by coauthor of joint work (musical composition) enures to benefit of his coauthor or those entitled to renewal if that coauthor is dead. Von Tilzer v Jerry Vogel Music Co. (1943, DC NY) 53 F Supp 191, 59 USPQ 292 affd (CA2 NY) 158 F2d 516, 71 USPQ 285.

When renewal copyright issues, one coauthor, or his assignee, cannot exclude other coauthors from beneficial rights therein. Edward B. Marks Music Corp. v Jerry Vogel Music Co. (1943, DC NY) 49 F Supp 135, 57 USPQ 37, affd (CA2 NY) 140 F2d 270, 60 USPQ 259.

Widow who obtained renewal is not entitled to keep all royalties resulting from assignment by widow of such renewal, where there was coauthor of work although unknown at time of renewal, and widow's interest in royalties is impressed with trust in favor of coauthor with whom she must share. Edward B. Marks Music Corp. v Wonnell (1945, DC NY) 61 F Supp 722, 65 USPQ 456.

Each co-owner must account to other for his transactions in renewal. Shapiro, Bernstein & Co. v Jerry Vogel Music Co. (1947, DC NY) 73 F Supp 165, 74 USPQ 264.

Renewal provisions of predecessor section were designed to protect only classes of persons specifically designated therein, and not surviving coauthor. Sweet Music, Inc. v Melrose Music Corp. (1960, DC Cal) 189 F Supp 655, 127 USPQ 513.

9. Composite works

Copyright of book did not extend to illustrations furnished by person other than author of book; and latter's widow, by renewal of copyright, could not sue for infringement of illustrations. Harris v Coca-Cola Co. (1934, CA5 Ga) 73 F2d 370, 23 USPQ 182, cert den 294 US 709, 79 L Ed 1243, 55 S Ct 406.

"Composite works" are those to which number of authors have contributed distinguishable parts not separately registered but included by proprietor in one copyright. Shapiro, Bernstein & Co. v Bryan (1941, CA2 NY) 123 F2d 697, 51 USPQ 422.

Author wrote words as words for song and sold them to third party, who engaged composer (without knowledge of author) to compose music for words; author was not entitled to renew words alone since song is not "composite" work and had to be renewed as whole, or not at all, it being indivisible product of "joint authors." Edward B. Marks Music Corp. v Jerry Vogel Music Co. (1944, CA2 NY) 140 F2d 266, 60 USPQ 257.

Renewal of "subsisting" copyright in musical composition comprises music and lyrics together, not either alone. Edward B. Marks Music Corp. v Jerry Vogel Music Co. (1942, DC NY) 42 F Supp 859, 52 USPQ 219.

Song being composite work, not joint work, all that author of lyric can assign is his renewal interest in lyric; neither author nor assignee, after assignee's renewal of copyright in song, has right to publish music in connection with lyric. Shapiro Bernstein & Co. v Jerry Vogel Music Co. (1953, DC NY) 115 F Supp 754, 98 USPQ 438, 99 USPQ 381, revd on other grounds (CA2 NY) 221 F2d 569, 105 USPQ 178, adhered to (CA2 NY) 223 F2d 252.

Composite works involve contributions by several authors and are mutually exclusive of works done for hire where employer is sole "author" so that Register of Copyrights properly refuses renewal registration claiming contradictory rights under both composite work and work done for hire in comic books. Opinion of Atty. Gen. of United States (1974) 183 USPQ 624.

10. Non-authors entitled to renew, generally

Defendant argues that unless conveying instrument expressly states that renewal rights have been conveyed, courts will find that parties did not intend to transfer them; this rule reflects policy of statutory copyright law which is not applicable in instant infringement action wherein none of parties are within class of persons given special statutory consideration; by requiring express mention of renewal rights in such transfers, thus avoiding inadvertent or unintended transfer of such rights, courts have found means of carrying out statutory policy of protecting copyright interests of original authors and certain of their heirs; scope of factual examination to determine intent of parties to instant assignment to plaintiff's predecessor is not limited; language of agreement in general, as well as circumstances surrounding its execution, may also serve to indicate intent of parties; where there is evidence which shows intention to transfer renewal rights, fact that they were not expressly mentioned in assignment of original copyright will not preclude their passing with copyright. Rohauer v Friedman (1962, CA9 Cal) 306 F2d 933, 134 USPQ 384, 2 ALR3d 1395.

Only persons who may obtain renewals are

those specified in statutes. Shapiro, Bernstein & Co. v Bryan (1939, DC NY) 27 F Supp 11, 41 USPQ 134.

Renewal of copyright by person not entitled thereto is void and cannot be cured by ratification by person entitled to renew. Von Tilzer v Jerry Vogel Music Co. (1943, DC NY) 53 F Supp 191, 59 USPQ 292, affd (CA2 NY) 158 F2d 516, 71 USPQ 285.

Right of renewal does not belong to author's estate by right of succession, but to person designated in statute. Miller Music Corp. v Charles N. Daniels, Inc. (1957, DC NY) 158 F Supp 188, 116 USPQ 92, affd without opinion (CA2 NY) 265 F2d 925, affd 362 US 373, 4 L Ed 2d 804, 80 S Ct 792.

Right of renewal of copyright is in nature of expectancy; consequently, if author dies before time for renewal, any inter vivos assignment of renewal rights by deceased author is of no force and right to renew devolves upon those classes of persons designated in predecessor section; however, assignment of renewal rights is valid where assignor survives fruition of expectancy; to hold that entire assignment is of no force, merely because part of otherwise valid assignment fails due to death of one coauthor assignor would be to ignore policy expressed in predecessor statute; circumstance that two coauthors joined in same assignment, instead of executing separate assignments, does not change result; in either case, surviving coauthor is bound by assignment. Sweet Music, Inc. v Melrose Music Corp. (1960, DC Cal) 189 F Supp 655, 127 USPQ 513.

Ordinarily, only proprietor of initial term copyright is entitled to renew; this includes corporate proprietor of works written or composed by its employee in course of employment; however, only composer of author may renew copyrights secured by copyright proprietor as assignee or licensee of author or composer. Austin v Steiner (1962, DC Ill) 207 F Supp 776, 134 USPQ 561.

Under scheme prescribed by Congress in predecessor section, renewal right is severed from right to original copyright; renewal right does not accrue until filing of application in 28th year of original term; application may be filed by persons designated by statute only if appropriate circumstances provided by statute then prevail; until then rights of author, widow, widower, or children of author, or his next of kin, remain merely expectancies. Cresci v Music Publishers Holding Corp. (1962, DC NY) 210 F Supp 253, 135 USPQ 189.

11. —Widows, widowers, or children

On death of author, widow and children of author succeed to right of renewal as class and are each entitled to share in renewal term of copyright. De Sylva v Ballentine (1956) 351 US 570, 100 L Ed 1415, 76 S Ct 974, 109 USPQ 431, reh den 352 US 859, 1 L Ed 2d 69, 77 S Ct 22 and reh den 362 US 907, 4 L Ed 2d 558, 80 S Ct 608.

Prior assignment by author cannot bar renewal rights of widow, widower, and children for they are among those to whom predecessor section grants renewal right, irrespective of whether author in his lifetime has or has not made any assignment of it; also, where author dies intestate prior to renewal period leaving no widow, widower, or children, next of kin obtain renewal copyright free of any claim founded upon assignment made by author in his lifetime; these results follow not because testator's assignment is invalid but because he had only expectancy to assign, and his death, prior to renewal period, terminates his interest in renewal which by predecessor section vests in named classes; right to obtain renewal copyright and renewal copyright itself exist only by reason of copyright statute and are derived solely and directly from it. Miller Music Corp. v Charles N. Daniels, Inc. (1960) 362 US 373, 4 L Ed 2d 804, 80 S Ct 792, 125 USPQ 147.

Assignee of author's widow having obtained renewal copyright without knowledge that author was survived by illegitimate child. Court refused to determine nineteen years later that child's assignee had a share in the renewal copyright. Jerry Vogel Music Co., Inc. v Edward B. Marks Music Corp. (1969, CA2) 425 F2d 834, 164 USPQ 33.

Widow and children of composer are entitled to renewal rights of composition assigned by composer and publicly performed during composer's lifetime, even though score was not published or copyrighted until after death of composer. Bartok v Boosey & Hawkes, Inc. (1975, CA2 NY) 523 F2d 941, 187 USPQ 529.

Author's widow does not, by remarriage, lose rights to renew copyright; it is significant that author's brother, who had filed earlier renewal application, did not protest renewal to alleged widow; that her signature on assignment differs from her writing in letter to assignee does not overcome presumption of validity attaching to assignment since apparently she was largely illiterate and letter could have been written for her by another. Edward B. Marks Music Corp. v Borst Music Pub. Co. (1953, DC NJ) 110 F Supp 913, 97 USPQ 394.

Widow and children of author succeed to author's right of renewal of copyright as class. Fisher v Edwin H. Morris & Co. (DC NY) 113 USPQ 251.

Common law wife and putative wife qualify as "widow" entitled to renewal of copyright of spouse, and "widow" status referrs to woman who is married to man at time of his death so that widow status is not lost by remarriage of woman after death of spouse; nor is general assignment of rights under estate of spouse effective to assign renewal expectancies, which are separate property of widow. Hill & Range Songs, Inc. v Fred Rose Music, Inc. (1975, DC Tenn) 403 F Supp 420, 189 USPQ 233, motion den (DC Tenn) 413 F Supp 967.

Inasmuch as there is exclusive federal jurisdiction, state court has no jurisdiction of action to determine whether under state law defendants are "children" of composer so as to qualify as claimants for renewal of copyright. Ross Jungnickel, Inc. v Joy Music, Inc. (Misc) 129 USPQ 373.

Widow and children share, as a class, author's right to renew copyright; author's widow conveyed to bank right to apply for any copyright renewal that might accrue to widow; although it was not clear at time of conveyance that anyone other than widow would have right to renew, author's children ratified conveyance; thereafter, while law still was unclear, bank assigned renewal right to defendant; assignment bore consent of widow and children; defendant renewed copyright and, after widow's death, children sued defendant, alleging that they owned renewal; court holds that renewal had been assigned to defendant. Easton v Universal Pictures Co., Inc. (1968) 56 Misc 2d 406, 288 NYS2d 776, 158 USPQ 301.

Annotations:

Persons entitled to renewal of copyright following author's death. 100 L Ed 1430; 4 L Ed 2d 2069.

12. —Executors, administrators, legatees, or next of kin

Intent of predecessor section is that, if there is no widow or child of author, executor may exercise power that testator might have exercised if he had been alive; death of author before beginning of one year next prior to expiration of existing term does not prevent renewal by his executor. Fox Film Corp. v Knowles (1923) 261 US 326, 67 L Ed 680, 43 S Ct 365.

Author's executors do not succeed to renewal interest under predecessor section unless all named persons (author, widow, widower, and children) are dead. De Sylva v Ballentine (1956) 351 US 570, 100 L Ed 1415, 76 S Ct 974, 109 USPQ 431, reh den 352 US 859, 1 L Ed 2d 69, 77 S Ct 22 and reh den 362 US 907, 4 L Ed 2d 558, 80 S Ct 608.

Right of executor to renew copyright of composer who died unmarried and without children prior to one-year renewal period was not defeated by composer's inter vivos assignment of his renewal right; assignment by author of renewal rights made before original copyright expires is valid against world if author is alive at commencement of renewal period; all questions of assignment apart, renewal rights go by statute to executor, absent widow or child. Miller Music Corp. v Charles N. Daniels, Inc. (1960) 362 US 373, 4 L Ed 2d 804, 80 S Ct 792, 125 USPQ 147.

Administrator of estate of author has no right to renew copyright obtained by author. Danks v Gordon (1921, CA2 NY) 272 F 821.

It is not necessary for all of next of kin to join in application for renewal; renewal granted on application by only part of next of kin in their own names inures to benefit of all. Silverman v Sunrise Pictures Corp. (1921, CA2 NY) 273 F 909, 19 ALR 289 (disapproved on other grounds Silverman v Sunrise Pictures Corp. (CA2 NY) 290 F 804, cert den 262 US 758, 67 L Ed 1219, 43 S Ct 705).

If, prior to commencement of one year prior to expiration of term of copyright, executor of owner of copyright has been discharged, and there is then no executor in existence, renewal right is not extinguished, but may be exercised by next of kin, there being no surviving widow or children. Silverman v Sunrise Pictures Corp. (1923, CA2 NY) 290 F 804, cert den 262 US 758, 67 L Ed 1219, 43 S Ct 705.

Author died prior to end of term of copyright, leaving no widow or child and no will; plaintiff was next of kin and made application for renewal within one year before initial term expired; plaintiff thus acquired new and independent right in copyright free and clear of any rights, interests, or licenses attached to copyright for original term. Fitch v Shubert (1937, DC NY) 20 F Supp 314, 35 USPQ 245.

After death of artist, copyright expired, and while executor was still acting, sister applied as next of kin for renewal of copyright; she was only one of several surviving sisters and did not have any right to secure renewal, and such renewal was ineffective. Yardley v Houghton Mifflin Co. (1938, DC NY) 25 F Supp 361, 40 USPQ 234, affd (CA2 NY) 108 F2d 28, 44 USPQ 1, cert den 309 US 686, 84 L Ed 1029, 60 S Ct 891.

In suit by brothers as next of kin of author for adjudication of renewal rights, finding in prior suit that author had been married was not material in present suit where complaint alleged that author left no widow, children, or will, since question is whom did author leave when he died. Jerry Vogel Music Co. v Edward B. Marks Music Corp. (1944, DC NY) 56 F Supp 779, 63 USPQ 1.

Fact that brother of deceased author applied for renewal of copyright prior to widow's application therefor does not impair widow's right to renewal, since rights of next of kin are nonexistent if widow lives. Edward B. Marks Music Corp. v Borst Music Pub. Co. (1953, DC NJ) 110 F Supp 913, 97 USPQ 394.

Administrator c. t. a. appointed to administer provisions of author's will, which has been admitted to probate, stands in shoes of executor and is entitled to exercise right of renewal of copyright; his right is superior to that of next of kin; however, in exercising right of renewal, he does so on behalf of those entitled to receive royalties. Gibran v Alfred A. Knopf, Inc. (1957, DC NY) 153 F Supp 854, 115 USPQ 214, affd (CA2 NY) 255 F2d 121, 117 USPQ 218, cert den 358 US 828, 3 L Ed 2d 67, 79 S Ct 47.

Executor has same rights under predecessor section as widow and children and next of kin; fact that author assigned inchoate renewal rights to third party would not bar widow or children, if any, from exercising their statutory renewal rights; since executor's rights are no less than that of widow and children or next of kin, they cannot be defeated by author's assignment. Miller Music Corp. v Charles N. Daniels, Inc. (1957, DC NY) 158 F Supp 188, 116 USPQ 92, affd without opinion (CA2 NY) 265 F2d 925, affd 362 US 373, 4 L Ed 2d 804, 80 S Ct 792.

Annotations:

Persons entitled to renewal of copyright following author's death. 100 L Ed 1430; 4 L Ed 2d 2069.

13. Termination of transfer under renewal, generally

Inability of author to carry out promise to effect renewal of copyright because of author's death prior to renewal date does not terminate right of holder of derivative copyright in motion picture to continue to publish derivative work copyrighted before author's death on which copyright in novel was thereafter renewed, so that exhibition of motion picture does not infringe renewal copyright in novel. Rohauer v Killiam Shows, Inc. (1977, CA2) 192 USPQ 545.

Rescission of assignment of expectancy of renewal of copyright is barred by laches where changes, upon which are based contention that assignment should be rescinded, occurred in 1927, 1930, and 1932, but contention was not raised until 1953. Rose v Bourne, Inc. (1959, DC NY) 176 F Supp 605, 123 USPQ 29, affd (CA2 NY) 279 F2d 79, 125 USPQ 509, cert den 364 US 880, 5 L Ed 2d 103, 81 S Ct 170.

14. —Derivative works

Assignment of motion-picture rights in novel is limited to term of copyright unless assignment includes right of renewal. G. Ricordi & Co. v Paramount Pictures, Inc. (1951, CA2 NY) 189 F2d 469, 89 USPQ 289, 89 USPQ 564, cert den 342 US 849, 96 L Ed 641, 72 S Ct 77.

Copyright in derivative motion picture based on novel under assignment from author specifically granting derivative right under renewal copyright does not expire with original copyright, and motion picture does not infringe renewal copyright in novel made by child of author. Rohauer v Killiam Shows, Inc. (1977, CA2) 192 USPQ 545.

Play, which dramatizes novel, is copyrightable as new work; copyright on play exists and protects all new matter therein, independently of ownership of original or renewal copyrights on novel. Davis v E. I. Du Pont De Nemours & Co. (1965, DC NY) 240 F Supp 612, 145 USPQ 258.

15. Works made for hire

Only author and persons named have right of renewal, and it does not extend to proprietor, except on composite work originally copyrighted by proprietor himself. White-Smith Music Pub. Co. v Goff (1911, CA1 RI) 187 F 247.

Plaintiff's predecessor having obtained copyright of song written and composed by defendants as employees "for hire" of predecessor, plaintiff, and not defendants, is entitled to renewal copyright. Shapiro, Bernstein & Co. v Bryan (1941, CA2 NY) 123 F2d 697, 51 USPQ 422.

Songwriter was not employee for hire of corporation for which he composed songs and in which he had dominant role since drawing account provided in contract was not equivalent of salary but constituted loan which, to extent drawings exceeded royalty earnings, had to be repaid; corporation had no power to control or supervise songwriter's performance. Songwriter was free to engage in profitable outside activities without sharing proceeds with corporation. Donaldson Publishing Co. v Bregman, Vocco & Conn, Inc. (1967, CA2 NY) 375 F2d 639, 153 USPQ 149, cert den 389 US 1036, 19 L Ed 2d 823, 88 S Ct 768.

Evidence that revisions directed by defendants were simply to accommodate Superman comic strip to magazine format was not sufficient to create presumption that comic strip was work for hire. Siegel v National Periodical Publications, Inc. (1974, CA2 NY) 508 F2d 909.

Evidence is insufficient to show that photoplay was made for hire allowing assignee to renew copyrights, where there is no showing of payment to, contract with, or supervision of work of photoplay creator, assignee corporation was formed after photoplay was made, and contracts with others do not establish any work for hire. Epoch Producing Corp. v Killiam Shows, Inc. (1975, CA2 NY) 522 F2d 737, 187 USPQ 270, cert den 424 US 955, 47 L Ed 2d 360, 96 S Ct 1429.

"Author" includes employer in case of works made for hire; employer in case of works made for hire is person entitled to renewal. Tobani v Carl Fischer (DC NY) 36 USPQ 97, mod on other grounds (CA2 NY) 98 F2d 57, 38 USPQ 198, cert den 305 US 650, 83 L Ed 420, 59 S Ct 243.

Proprietor who may obtain renewal of copyright of work by employee for hire is proprietor at time of renewal and not at time of original copyright; employee for hire, who has parted with his entire property in work, has no interest left to protect and he need not be considered in connection with renewal, and right of renewal is not cut off when transfer takes place, but instead rights of renewal reserved to proprietors are assignable along with copyright itself. Shapiro, Bernstein & Co. v Bryan (1939, DC NY) 27 F Supp 11, 41 USPQ 134.

Where employee for hire wrote part or all of lyrics of copyrighted song for employer, employer alone is entitled to copyright and renewal; employee's widow cannot give another right to publish song or right to money collected by employer on theory that since renewal employer held part of proceeds received by it in trust for widow. Von Tilzer v Jerry Vogel Music Co. (1943, DC NY) 53 F Supp 191, 59 USPQ 292, affd (CA2 NY) 158 F2d 516, 71 USPQ 285.

Composer agreed to write songs for music publisher, who agreed to pay composer salary; contract created relationship of employer and employee; publisher assigned all assets to defendant; composer continued to work for defendant and acquiesced and ratified assignment; while in defendant's employ, composer wrote song which

defendant copyrighted; defendant as employer alone is entitled to renewal rights in copyrighted song whether or not contract was assignable or actually assigned. Fred Fisher Music Co. v Leo Feist, Inc. (1944, DC NY) 55 F Supp 359, 61 USPQ 229.

Author of lyric sold to publisher right to copyright lyric for use with another's music, but, since author was not publisher's employee for hire, publisher had no renewal interest in lyric. Shapiro Bernstein & Co. v Jerry Vogel Music Co. (1953, DC NY) 115 F Supp 754, 98 USPQ 438, 99 USPQ 381, revd on other grounds (CA2 NY) 221 F2d 569, 105 USPQ 178, adhered to (CA2 NY) 223 F2d 252, 105 USPQ 460.

Despite fact that author also had outside employment, he was employee for hire, and his corporate employer which had become proprietor of original copyright was entitled to renewal rights. Donaldson Publishing Co. v Bregman, Vocco & Conn, Inc. (DC NY) 147 USPQ 409.

Proprietor of work composed for hire, and not author, is entitled to renewal copyright; Whether works were composed in course of employment involves inquiry into nature of relationship between author and employer including extent of employer's right to exert supervision and control over composer's efforts. Rytvoc, Inc. v Robbins Music Corp. (1967, DC NY) 289 F Supp 136, 157 USPQ 612.

If the relationship is one of employment, then the renewal rights vest in the employer or his successor in interest, absent any contrary agreement and provided the particular work was made pursuant to the relationship and not as a special assignment outside the regular scope of employment; On the other hand, the rights vest in the author, not the proprietor, if the author was a commissioned independent contractor, or if any of the ingredients of the employment relationship are lacking. Picture Music, Inc. v Bourne, Inc. (1970, DC NY) 314 F Supp 640, 167 USPQ 348, affd (CA2) 457 F2d 1213, cert den 409 US 997, 34 L Ed 2d 262, 93 S Ct 320.

§ 305.   Duration of copyright: Terminal date

All terms of copyright provided by sections 302 through 304 [17 USCS §§ 302–304] run to the end of the calendar year in which they would otherwise expire.

(Added Oct. 19, 1976, P. L. 94-553, Title I, § 101, 90 Stat. 2576.)

HISTORY; ANCILLARY LAWS AND DIRECTIVES

Effective date of section:

Section 102 of Act Oct. 19, 1976, P. L. 94-553, 90 Stat. 2598 provided that this section "becomes effective on January 1, 1978".

CROSS REFERENCES

Duration of copyright, 17 USCS §§ 302–304.

CHAPTER 4. COPYRIGHT NOTICE, DEPOSIT, AND REGISTRATION

§ 401. Notice of copyright: Visually perceptible copies

(a) General requirement. Whenever a work protected under this title [17 USCS §§ 101 et seq.] is published in the United States or elsewhere by authority of the copyright owner, a notice of copyright as provided by this section shall be placed on all publicly distributed copies from which the work can be visually perceived, either directly or with the aid of a machine or device.

(b) Form of notice. The notice appearing on the copies shall consist of the following three elements:

(1) the symbol © (the letter C in a circle), or the word "Copyright", or the abbreviation "Copr."; and

(2) the year of first publication of the work; in the case of compilations or derivative works incorporating previously published material, the year date of first publication of the compilation or derivative work is sufficient. The year date may be omitted where a pictorial, graphic, or sculptural work, with accompanying text matter, if any, is reproduced in or on greeting cards, postcards, stationery, jewelry, dolls, toys, or any useful articles; and

(3) the name of the owner of copyright in the work, or an abbreviation by which the name can be recognized, or a generally known alternative designation of the owner.

(c) Position of notice. The notice shall be affixed to the copies in such manner and location as to give reasonable notice of the claim of copyright.

The Register of Copyrights shall prescribe by regulation, as examples, specific methods of affixation and positions of the notice on various types of works that will satisfy this requirement, but these specifications shall not be considered exhaustive.

(Added Oct. 19, 1976, P. L. 94-553, Title I, § 101, 90 Stat. 2576.)

HISTORY; ANCILLARY LAWS AND DIRECTIVES

Effective date of section:
Section 102 of Act Oct. 19, 1976, P. L. 94-553, 90 Stat. 2598 provided that this section "becomes effective on January 1, 1978".

Other provisions:
Work published before January 1, 1978. Act Oct. 19, 1976, P. L. 94-553, Title I, § 108, 90 Stat. 2600, provided: "The notice provisions of sections 401 through 403 of title 17 [17 USCS §§ 401-403] as amended by the first section of this Act [section 101 of Act Oct. 19, 1976, which appears as 17 USCS §§ 101 et seq.] apply to all copies or phonorecords publicly distributed on or after January 1, 1978. However, in the case of a work published before January 1, 1978, compliance with the notice provisions of title 17 [17 USCS] either as it existed on December 31, 1977, or as amended by the first section of this Act [section 101 of Act Oct. 19, 1976, which appears as 17 USCS §§ 101 et seq.] is adequate with respect to copies publicly distributed after December 31, 1977."

CROSS REFERENCES

Notice requirements for phonorecords of sound recording, 17 USCS § 402. Application for registration covering compilation or derivative work, 17 USCS § 409.
Regulations promulgated by Copyright Office, 17 USCS § 702.
This section referred to in 17 USCS §§ 401 note, 403-405.

RESEARCH GUIDE

Am Jur:
18 Am Jur 2d, Copyright and Literary Property §§ 56–59, 156.

Forms:
5 Am Jur Legal Forms 2d, Copyright and Literary and Artistic Property §§ 72:32, 72:35–72:45.

Annotations:
Copyright notice where work is in several parts. 59 L Ed 113.
Fabric and dress designs as protected by copyright under Federal Copyright Act. 26 ALR Fed 408.

Law Review Articles:
Copyright Symposium, 22 New York Law School Law Review 193.

INTERPRETIVE NOTES AND DECISIONS

I. IN GENERAL [17 USCS § 401(a)]

1. Generally
2. Purpose
3. Legibility of notice
4. Necessity of notice, generally
5. —Publication as requiring notice
6. Notice on composite works or component parts

II. FORM OF NOTICE [17 USCS § 401(b)]

7. Generally
8. Symbol for copyright [17 USCS § 401(b)(1)]
9. Year of first publication [17 USCS § 401(b)(2)]
10. Name of owner [17 USCS § 401(b)(3)]

III. POSITION OF NOTICE [17 USCS § 401(c)]

11. Generally
12. Artistic works; photography and sculpture, generally
13. —Removable or separable notice
14. Fabric designs, generally
15. —Removable or separable notice
16. Literary works
17. Motion pictures and audiovisual works
18. Musical works

I. IN GENERAL [17 USCS § 401(a)]

1. Generally

All conditions are important, and law requires them to be performed, and their performance is essential to perfect copyright. Wheaton v Peters (1834) 33 US 591, 8 L Ed 1055.

Conditions prescribed by statute are conditions precedent to perfection of copyright. Callaghan v Myers (1888) 128 US 617, 32 L Ed 547, 9 S Ct 177.

Owner of copyright is not responsible for changes made on particular copy when same bore proper statutory notice of copyright when it left owner's hands. Falk v Gast Lithograph & Engraving Co. (1893, CA2 NY) 54 F 890.

Copyright is secured on published material by accompanying its publication with copyright notice at place and in form required by statute; subsequent registration under provisions of statute does not create copyright but only records it; publication without proper notice is ineffective to secure copyright. Krafft v Cohen (1941, CA3 Pa) 117 F2d 579, 48 USPQ 401.

Publication with notice is sufficient to copyright whatever may be copyrighted at all. United States v Backer (1943, CA2 NY) 134 F2d 533, 57 USPQ 133.

Where book dealer buys books contrary to agreement between holder of copyright and sales agents, he may be restrained from selling such books although he had no notice of agreement, since notice of copyright on book was sufficient to put him upon inquiry as to any agreement concerning its sale. Henry Bill Pub. Co. v Smythe (1886, CC Ohio) 27 F 914.

Compliance with predecessor section must be pleaded and proved. Falk v Gast Lith. & Eng. Co. (1889, CC NY) 40 F 168.

All articles can only be protected on publication by affixing the notice of copyright as is required by predecessor section. Universal Film Mfg. Co. v Copperman (1914, DC NY) 212 F 301, affd (CA2 NY) 218 F 577, cert den 235 US 704, 59 L Ed 433, 35 S Ct 209.

Statutory marking is of essence to preservation of copyright monopoly. Basevi v Edward O'Toole Co. (1939, DC NY) 26 F Supp 41, 40 USPQ 333.

After copyright notice has been published everyone is under duty to learn facts and copies at his peril. Chappell & Co. v Costa (1942, DC NY) 45 F Supp 554, 53 USPQ 674.

2. Purpose

It was object of predecessor statute to require inscription of copyright notice, not upon original painting, map, photograph, drawing, but upon those published copies concerning which it is designed to convey information to public which shall limit use and circumscribe rights of purchaser. American Tobacco Co. v Werckmeister (1907) 207 US 284, 52 L Ed 208, 28 S Ct 72.

Purpose of notice of copyright is to inform public of existence of copyright, time of commencement, by whom claimed, and to prevent innocent persons, who are unaware of existence of copyright, from suffering by making use of material. Harry Alter Co. v Graves Refrigeration, Inc. (1951, DC Ga) 101 F Supp 703, 91 USPQ 236.

Purpose of requiring that copyright notice be affixed to copyrighted article is to advise public of claim of copyright proprietor and to prevent innocent persons from incurring infringement penalties. Stecher Lithographic Co. v Dunston Lithograph Co. (1916, DC NY) 233 F 601; Trifari, Krussman & Fishel, Inc. v B. Steinberg-Kaslo Co. (1956, DC NY) 144 F Supp 577, 110 USPQ 487.

There must be substantial compliance with predecessor section in order that copyright be preserved; purpose of notice is to inform public of copyright and warn against republication. Inter-City Press, Inc. v Siegfried (1958, DC Mo) 172 F Supp 37, 118 USPQ 446.

Purpose of predecessor section is to afford to those, who might otherwise innocently infringe, notice that copyright is claimed and by whom; predecessor section does not establish what degree of proximity must exist between two to satisfy requirement that symbol be "accompanied by" name; placement of symbol and name is left wholly to taste or discretion so long as purpose of statute is fulfilled by so placing them in relation to each other as to give reasonable notice of claim of copyright and of claimant's identity. Glenco Refrigeration Corp. v Raetone Commercial Refrigerator Corp. (1957, DC Pa) 149 F Supp 691, 113 USPQ 155.

Copyright notice serves as warning to public that work is protected by copyright and protects innocent persons from copying copyrighted work; notice also serves further purpose of informing public of date of first publication, which, in turn, determines duration of monopoly granted to copyright proprietor. De Silva Constr. Corp. v Herrald (1962, DC Fla) 213 F Supp 184, 137 USPQ 96.

3. Legibility of notice

Section of predecessor Act which protects component parts of work copyrighted, does not protect plaintiff which deliberately made notice of copyright on mats furnished to purchasers of copyrighted material illegible to lead reading public to think that matter published was original with advertiser. Deward & Rich v Bristol Savings & Loan Corp. (1941, CA4 Va) 120 F2d 537, 50 USPQ 1.

Copyright notice, consisting of letter C inclosed within circle, if so badly indistinct and blurred as to be illegible, is insufficient. Strauss v Penn Printing & Pub. Co. (1915, DC Pa) 220 F 977.

Fact that notice is blurred and indistinct does not invalidate copyright, but damages cannot be recovered in suit for infringement. Strauss v Penn Printing & Pub. Co. (1915, DC Pa) 220 F 977.

Symbol of initials with "c" in circle in scroll, impossible to identify with naked eye and without close scrutiny with magnifying glass, does not comply with copyright statute. Alfred Decker Cohn Co. v Etchison Hat Co. (1914, DC Va) 225 F 135; Smith v Wilkinson (1937, DC NH) 19 F Supp 841, 35 USPQ 113, affd (CA1 NH) 97 F2d 506, 38 USPQ 1.

Notice of copyright on picture, illegible without artificial aid to eye, and without proprietor's name, was insufficient and precluded restraint of infringement. Goes Lithographing Co. v Apt Lithographic Co. (1936, DC NY) 14 F Supp 620, 30 USPQ 119.

Defense that copyright notice was in such

small type that it was difficult to decipher even under reading glass and that consequently defendant read "1911" for "1931" did not justify inclusion of reproduction of copyrighted matter in copyright secured by defendant on complete issue of its magazine. Zenn v National Golf Review (1939, DC NY) 27 F Supp 732, 41 USPQ 535.

Microscopic print is not sufficient to comply with statutory requirement of copyright notice. Deward & Rich, Inc. v Bristol Sav. & Loan Corp. (1939, DC Va) 29 F Supp 777, 44 USPQ 26.

Although illegible copyright notice is insufficient, as matter of law, to charge with knowledge of copyright infringer who had no actual notice, it may be sufficient to charge with knowledge infringer who had deciphered it. Trifari, Krussman & Fishel, Inc. v B. Steinberg-Kaslo Co. (1956, DC NY) 144 F Supp 577, 110 USPQ 487.

Newspaper's copyright notice is sufficient to reasonably inform intelligent person that newspaper is copyrighted since, despite fact that it is in smaller type than rest of newsprint, it is legible to naked eye. Inter-City Press, Inc. v Siegfried (1958, DC Mo) 172 F Supp 37, 118 USPQ 446.

Difficulty in discerning copyright notice on leaf of copyrighted artificial flower should not of itself prevent granting of preliminary injunction, if plaintiff is otherwise entitled to it, since plaintiff makes prima facie case that defendant had actual notice of copyright before engaging in sale of alleged infringement. Prestige Floral, Societe Anonyme v California Artificial Flower Co. (1962, DC NY) 201 F Supp 287, 132 USPQ 350.

Notice is sufficient where it is discernible to unaided eye although some scrutiny is required to locate it and it is in small type. Ted Arnold, Ltd. v Silvercraft Co. (1966, DC NY) 259 F Supp 733, 151 USPQ 286.

4. Necessity of notice, generally

General testimony as to inscription of statutory copyright notice on copies published is sufficient to establish compliance with predecessor section. Burrow-Giles Lithographic Co. v Sarony (1884) 111 US 53, 28 L Ed 349, 4 S Ct 279.

Printing of required notice in copyrighted book is condition precedent to perfection of copyright. Thompson v Hubbard (1889) 131 US 123, 33 L Ed 76, 9 S Ct 710.

American copyright notice is not required on editions of books simultaneously published and sold abroad; original maps, charts, and pictures may and usually do remain in possession of original makers, and there is no necessity of any notice upon them. American Tobacco Co. v Werckmeister (1907) 207 US 284, 52 L Ed 208, 28 S Ct 72.

Every reproduction of copyrighted work must bear statutory notice. Dejonge & Co. v Breuker & Kessler Co. (1914) 235 US 33, 59 L Ed 113, 35 S Ct 6.

Printing of notice of copyright is one of necessary steps to be taken before obtaining copyright. Jollie v Jaques (1850, CC NY) F Cas No 7437.

Compliance with requirement of notice must be pleaded and proved as prerequisite to maintenance of action for infringement of copyright; it is not necessary that complainant show separate, distinct, and specific proof of notice on each one of his copies, general testimony is sufficient to establish prima facie case. Falk v Gast Lith. & Eng. Co. (1889, CC NY) 40 F 168.

Copyright notice which does not comply in substance with predecessor statute is legally ineffective; such notice is not rendered legally effective as to a particular infringer because he had actual knowledge of copyright or circumstances were such as to direct his attention to sources from which information as to copyright might be obtained. Metro Associated Services, Inc. v Webster City Graphic, Inc. (1953, DC Iowa) 117 F Supp 224, 100 USPQ 88.

Fact that defendant knew that there was copyright will not prevent work from falling into public domain if there is substantial variation in form of notice or if there is no notice. Ross Products, Inc. v New York Merchandise Co. (1964, DC NY) 233 F Supp 260, 141 USPQ 652.

5. —Publication as requiring notice

Requirement as to copyright notice extends to editions published by assignee of copyright. Thompson v Hubbard (1889) 131 US 123, 33 L Ed 76, 9 S Ct 710.

Sample advertisement, from which dealers might place orders for calendars mounting copyrighted picture, does not require notice. Gerlach-Barklow Co. v Morris & Bendien, Inc. (1927, CA2 NY) 23 F2d 159.

Reproductions in trade journals do not result in loss of copyright where each copyright object is properly labeled to comply with notice requirements of predecessor section. Rushton v Vitale (1955, CA2 NY) 218 F2d 434, 104 USPQ 158.

Date of publication of book used for promotion and advertising purposes in jewelry trade is when shipments were made to jewelers, not when copies were distributed to public by jewelers. Advisers, Inc. v Wiesen-Hart, Inc. (1956, CA6 Ohio) 238 F2d 706, 111 USPQ 318, cert den 353 US 949, 1 L Ed 2d 858, 77 S Ct 861.

Printed copies of song copyrighted under predecessor section are required to bear notice of copyright only if (1) they were reproduced for sale or published or offered for sale, and (2) such reproduction, publication, or offering was by authority of copyright proprietor. Hirshon v United Artists Corp. (1957) 100 App DC 217, 243 F2d 640, 113 USPQ 110.

Use of improper copyright notice on small set of copyrighted cards by another company does not invalidate plaintiff's copyright inasmuch as interests of two companies were precisely same (having same officers, employees, agents, directors, and shareholders), especially since defendants were not prejudiced by reliance on such notice; during development of infringing cards, defendants had before them plaintiff's cards containing a proper notice. Gelles-Widmer Co. v Milton Bradley Co. (1963, CA7 Ill) 313 F2d 143, 136 USPQ 240, cert den 373 US 913, 10 L Ed 2d 414, 83 S Ct 1303.

Learning that dress manufacturers possessed garments, and fabric cut up for garments, made of fabric bearing design infringing copyrighted design, copyright proprietor acquiesced in sale of such garments to avoid hardship to manufacturers; such sale of garments not bearing copyright notice did not forfeit copyright since sales were not "authorized" by proprietor within statutory meaning of term; predecessor section does not impose upon proprietors duty of policing distribution of pirated works; only goods sold by authority of proprietor are required to carry notice; normally, proprietor discharges his obligation by seeing that each copy of protected work has notice affixed to it when it leaves his control; therefore, fact that unmarked copies of work have come into possession of alleged infringer will not, without more, justify denial of injunction; hence, as proprietor has no affirmative duty to police subsequent distributions of his own products, he has no affirmative duty as to subsequent distribution of unauthorized copies. H. M. Kolbe Co. v Armgus Textile Co. (1963, CA2 NY) 315 F2d 70, 137 USPQ 9, 99 ALR2d 390.

Plaintiff furnished defendant under contract matrices of advertisements bearing improper copyright notice; having permitted publication without statutory notice, plaintiff released advertisements for use to general public, including defendant whose use after termination of contract is lawful. Advertisers Exchange, Inc. v Anderson (1943, DC Iowa) 52 F Supp 809, 59 USPQ 391, affd (CA8 Iowa) 144 F2d 907, 63 USPQ 39.

Fact that owner of copyrighted label distributed advertising placards, picturing cans bearing label without copyright symbol on them, did not constitute a publication and dedication to public so as to void copyright; cited cases involving matrices, mats and other newspaper material, and mezzotints are distinguished in that in each of them it was the product sold, whereas instant product sold was not the label, that is, copyrighted thing, but contents of can upon which label appeared. S. C. Johnson & Son, Inc. v Drop Dead Co. (1961, DC Cal) 201 F Supp 442, 132 USPQ 309.

General publication of copyrighted work without adequate copyright notice dedicates work to public; even if publication was not by plaintiff, but by manufacturers of work, plaintiff cannot prevail since a party is not free to present its allegedly unique work to a manufacturer, impose no legal or otherwise effective restraints upon manufacturer, permit work to be copied and sold in quantity with inadequate copyright notice, and then seek to reverse the flood by a grossly tardy copyright registration. Florabelle Flowers, Inc. v Joseph Markovits, Inc. (1968, DC NY) 296 F Supp 304, 160 USPQ 611.

6. Notice on composite works or component parts

Mere notice of copyright in each book was insufficient to identify or distinguish parts of book in which complainants claimed copyright. Flint v Jones (1875, CC Pa) F Cas No 4872.

One proper notice of copyright on book protects all contents of book. Deward & Rich, Inc. v Bristol Sav. & Loan Corp. (1939, DC Va) 29 F Supp 777, 44 USPQ 26.

When manual containing advertisements was copyrighted as book, plaintiff does not comply with predecessor statute in preserving copyright by furnishing under contract matrices of advertisements not bearing copyright notice required for book but bearing notice specified for works of art, there having been no attempt to register advertisements as works of art. Advertisers Exchange, Inc. v Anderson (1943, DC Iowa) 52 F Supp 809, 59 USPQ 391, affd (CA8 Iowa) 144 F2d 907, 63 USPQ 39.

Annotations:

Copyright notice where work is in several parts. 59 L Ed 113.

II. FORM OF NOTICE [17 USCS § 401(b)]

7. Generally

Statement upon label that it had been registered in patent office was not notice required by Copyright Act. Higgins v Keuffel (1891) 140 US 428, 35 L Ed 470, 11 S Ct 731.

It is incorrect to say that any form of notice is good which calls attention to person of whom inquiry can be made and information obtained, since, right to copyright being purely statutory,

public may justly demand that statutory method of securing it be observed. Mifflin v R. H. White Co. (1903) 190 US 260, 47 L Ed 1040, 23 S Ct 769.

Slight variance in words, or in order of words, if matter is substantially same, will not invalidate copyright notice. Bentley v Tibbals (1915, CA2 NY) 223 F 247.

While some slight literal variance from form of notice prescribed may perhaps not necessarily be fatal, there can be no general or substantial deviation; use of special form and designation is limited to specified classes as matter of law and its use as to copyright for which general form and designation are required is not sufficient notice. Advertisers Exchange, Inc. v Anderson (1944, CA8 Iowa) 144 F2d 907, 63 USPQ 39.

Slight variation from form of notice may not be fatal, but there must be no substantial deviation. Booth v Haggard (1950, CA8 Iowa) 184 F2d 470, 87 USPQ 141.

Continuous attempt to publish comic strips with some sort of copyright notice affixed, however imperfect, is conclusive evidence of wish to claim copyright, and precludes holding of abandonment; publication of certain "Superman" comic strips with improper copyright notice does not result in abandonment of right to copyright all pictorial portrayals of exploits of "Superman." National Comics Publications, Inc. v Fawcett Publications, Inc. (1951, CA2 NY) 191 F2d 594, 90 USPQ 274.

Residence of party is not required to be stated in copyright notice. Werckmeister v Springer Lithographing Co. (1894, CC NY) 63 F 808.

"Copyright Notice. This work is copyrighted, as prescribed by the laws of the United States and anyone duplicating or causing to be duplicated the whole or a part of the same without written permission from [copyright proprietor] will be prosecuted to the fullest extent. October 22, 1931. ©" substantially complies with predecessor section. Deward & Rich, Inc. v Bristol Sav. & Loan Corp. (1940, DC Va) 34 F Supp 345, 47 USPQ 128, affd (CA4 Va) 120 F2d 537, 50 USPQ 1.

Strict compliance with statutory requirements is essential to perfection of copyright, and failure fully to conform to form of notice prescribed by statute results in abandonment of right and dedication of work to public. Group Publishers, Inc. v Winchell (1949, DC NY) 86 F Supp 573, 83 USPQ 461.

Copyright notice on catalogue reads "All Prices F. O. B. Chicago—Keep These Prices Confidential" in line one, "Copyright, 1948. The

H. A. Co. Printed in U. S. A." in line two, then solid line, and then "The Harry Alter Co., Inc." in line four; notice is sufficient. Harry Alter Co. v Graves Refrigeration, Inc. (1951, DC Ga) 101 F Supp 703, 91 USPQ 236.

Insubstantial variations from notice prescribed by predecessor statute do not destroy proprietor's rights so long as innocent persons are not thereby misled. Trifari, Krussman & Fishel, Inc. v B. Steinberg-Kaslo Co. (1956, DC NY) 144 F Supp 577, 110 USPQ 487.

Court is not obligated to look beyond face of copyright notice to determine its sufficiency. Inter-City Press, Inc. v Siegfried (1958, DC Mo) 172 F Supp 37, 118 USPQ 446.

Courts are liberal in saving copyright where deviation from notice requirements of predecessor section is formal and not substantial. Peter Pan Fabrics, Inc. v Acadia Co. (1959, DC NY) 173 F Supp 292, 121 USPQ 81, affd (CA2 NY) 274 F2d 487, 124 USPQ 154.

If copyright notice is insufficient, copyright is forfeited and article is in public domain where it may be freely copied; once inadequate copyright notice has placed article in public domain, forfeited copyright cannot be revived by notice of its former existence. American Fabrics Co. v Lace Art, Inc., (1968, DC NY) 291 F Supp 589, 160 USPQ 366.

8. Symbol for copyright [17 USCS § 401(b)(1)]

Where copyright as book was obtained for book containing illustrations and text for advertisements, furnishing of matrices for publication without proper copyright notice for book, but merely "C" in circle, released those parts from copyright to general public. Advertisers Exchange, Inc. v Anderson (1944, CA8 Iowa) 144 F2d 907, 63 USPQ 39.

Costume jewelry sold to wholesalers bore plaintiff's registered trade-mark and "C" in circle stamped thereon; this constituted proper "publication" of copyrights as required by predecessor section. Dan Kasoff, Inc. v Palmer Jewelry Mfg. Co. (1959, DC NY) 171 F Supp 603, 120 USPQ 445.

If formalities of notice required by Universal Copyright Convention are complied with, copyright has protection in all contracting states even if state in which protection is sought has different requirements; work is so protected if notice contains "c" in circle, together with date and name of proprietor. Ross Products, Inc. v New York Merchandise Co. (1964, DC NY) 233 F Supp 260, 141 USPQ 652.

9. Year of first publication [17 USCS § 401(b)(2)]

Second or subsequent edition without altera-

tions or additions should have date of original copyright, but second or subsequent editions with notes or other improvements should have date of entry of improved edition, and no reference need be made to original entry. West Pub. Co. v Edward Thompson Co. (1910, CA2 NY) 176 F 833.

Original copyright notice may be inserted in another edition published in different number of volumes, without impairing copyright. Dwight v Appleton (1843, CC NY) F Cas No 4215.

10. Name of owner [17 USCS § 401(b)(3)]

Notice given under trade name is effective. Bleistein v Donaldson Lithographing Co. (1903) 188 US 239, 47 L Ed 460, 23 S Ct 298.

It is not sufficient that copies of works of art be marked with letter "C" in circle accompanied by initials of copyright proprietor, since predecessor section also provides that proprietor's name shall appear on back, base, or pedestal of substance on which copy is mounted. E. I. Horsman & Aetna Doll Co. v Kaufman (1922, CA2 NY) 286 F 372, cert den 261 US 615, 67 L Ed 828, 43 S Ct 361.

Predecessor section requires that notice of copyright appearing on copies of published musical work must correctly state name of registered copyright proprietor and year of copyright. Hirshon v United Artists Corp. (1957) 100 App DC 217, 243 F2d 640, 113 USPQ 110.

In a civil action for the infringement of copyrights, although the trademark of the copyright proprietor was printed on all statuettes, where the proprietary name was printed illegibly on some statuettes and was completely absent from others, such markings did not constitute a notice of copyright, and the deficiency was not cured by the fact that the defendants had actual notice of the identity of the copyright proprietor. Puddu v Buonamici Statuary, Inc. (1971, CA2 NY) 450 F2d 401.

Use of two names does not invalidate copyright provided proprietor has right to use either and he may use any name both in applying for registration and in making his notice of copyright; but names which he uses must be legal where he uses them, else they cannot be called his names at all. Haas v Leo Feist (1916, DC NY) 234 F 105.

Notice of copyright not disclosing identity of proprietor was insufficient. W. S. Bessett, Inc. v Germain (1937, DC Mass) 18 F Supp 249, 32 USPQ 550.

Notice in book is printed in three lines as follows: "Published and Printed by" above "'Ziegelheim', New York" above "Printed in U.S.A. Copyright 1943"; notice sufficiently states name of copyright owner, since "Copyright 1943" appears directly below and in close proximity to "'Ziegelheim,' New York," and since proof is clear that there was only one "Ziegelheim" in publishing business in New York. Ziegelheim v Flohr (1954, DC NY) 119 F Supp 324, 100 USPQ 189.

III. POSITION OF NOTICE [17 USCS § 401(c)]

11. Generally

Predecessor section is culmination of long history of increasing liberalization of restriction on placement of notice of copyright; in case of books and musical compositions, placement of notice has always been rigidly and narrowly confined, but, in case of other items, series of revisions has steadily expanded permissible locations of notice. Coventry Ware, Inc. v Reliance Picture Frame Co. (1961, CA2 NY) 288 F2d 193, 129 USPQ 83, cert den 368 US 818, 7 L Ed 2d 24, 82 S Ct 34, reh den 368 US 908, 7 L Ed 2d 101, 82 S Ct 171.

Substantial compliance with Copyright Act is all that is required, but when Act requires notice at particular place in work, court may not dispense with requirement and say that notice appearing somewhere else is enough. J. A. Richards, Inc. v New York Post, Inc. (1938, DC NY) 23 F Supp 619, 38 USPQ 475.

Copyright notice complies with predecessor section where "© 1955 G.R.C. Printed in U.S.A." appears in small letters on lower left portion of title page, one inch above which and three inches to right of which appears "Glenco Refrigeration Corp. Philadelphia 34, Pa." in larger letters. Glenco Refrigeration Corp. v Raetone Commercial Refrigerator Corp. (1957, DC Pa) 149 F Supp 691, 113 USPQ 155.

Copyright notice that has been permanently covered so that it cannot be seen without tearing article apart is considered defective notice by copyright office. Peter Pan Fabrics, Inc. v Acadia Co. (1959, DC NY) 173 F Supp 292, 121 USPQ 81, affd (CA2 NY) 274 F2d 487, 124 USPQ 154.

12. Artistic works; photography and sculpture, generally

Where cut is published in copyrighted newspaper, cut is not copyrighted when notice does not appear upon cut itself. Bennett v Boston Traveler Co. (1900, CA1 Mass) 101 F 445.

Copyright notice is sufficient where it appears on only one integral part of necklace; because earrings may be used singly does not mean that they are separate works of art; although some of defendants' earrings are sold singly for use as dress ornament or clip, plaintiff invariably sells them in pairs, each pair being considered as a unit; copyright notice on only one earring of each of plaintiff's pairs is sufficient under Copyright Act. Boucher v Du Boyes, Inc. (1958, CA2 NY) 253 F2d 948, 117 USPQ 156, cert den 357 US 936, 2 L Ed 2d 1550, 78 S Ct 1384.

Predecessor section places no limitation on possible location of notice of copyright in case of works of art and kindred items, provided that notice complies with general requirement that notice be affixed to each copy. Coventry Ware, Inc. v Reliance Picture Frame Co. (1961, CA2 NY) 288 F2d 193, 129 USPQ 83, cert den 368 US 818, 7 L Ed 2d 24, 82 S Ct 34, reh den 368 US 908, 7 L Ed 2d 101, 82 S Ct 171.

Plaintiff's copyrighted doll bears copyright notice on head and between shoulder blades; doll's body previously had been published without notice on shoulder blades; court rejects contention that extra copyright notice on shoulder blades bars plaintiff from access to equity court on theory that such notice was attempt to extend copyright protection to doll's torso as distinguished from entire doll and demonstrates intent to defraud public. Ideal Toy Corp. v J-Cey Doll Co. (1961, CA2 NY) 290 F2d 710, 129 USPQ 241.

Abbreviation "U. D. Co. Inc. © 1965," which appears on sole of foot of 3½ inch plastic doll, when read in conjunction with legend "© Uneeda Doll Co., Inc. 1966" printed on cardboard display package with three-sided transparent plastic window in which dolls are sold, satisfied predecessor section. Uneeda Doll Co. v Goldgarb Novelty Co. (1967, CA2 NY) 373 F2d 851, 153 USPQ 88, cert dismd 389 US 801, 19 L Ed 2d 56, 88 S Ct 9.

Notice is proper for model airplane kits when placed on boxes containing kits, and copyright notice on each piece of kit is not necessary. Monogram Models, Inc. v Industro Motive Corp. (1974, CA6 Mich) 492 F2d 1281, 181 USPQ 425, cert den 419 US 843, 42 L Ed 2d 71, 95 S Ct 76.

Engraving has sufficient notice of copyright, when, on prints made from it, notice is in position that would not ordinarily be covered with frame. Rossiter v Hall (1866, CC NY) F Cas No 12082.

When group of pictures is copyrighted as book, copyright cannot be maintained by having form of copyright notice put on individual pictures, which is required for reproduction of works of art, and when photograph embodying artistic conception taken from copyrighted catalogue is sold, it should have printed on it notice of copyright which will identify owner of copyright to anyone who purchases photograph. Basevi v Edward O'Toole Co. (1939, DC NY) 26 F Supp 41, 40 USPQ 333.

Notice of copyright on costume jewelry consists of "c" in circle with name of copyright owner; it is located at place where, according to industry usage, name of maker of article usually appears; it is legible although it is in small letters and close examination is required to locate it; nature of article is such that area in which notice may be placed is necessarily limited; however, it is so located as to apprise anyone, seeking to copy article, of existence of copyright; therefore, it is sufficient to satisfy statutory requirements. Trifari, Krussman & Fishel, Inc. v Charel Co. (1955, DC NY) 134 F Supp 551, 107 USPQ 48.

Predecessor section requires that copyright notice appear on some portion of copyrighted article itself; although copyright notice is placed only on hood of copyrighted Santa Claus figure and not on other two components thereof, notice is not defective since it appears on accessible portion of figure, especially since all three components are sold as unit and cannot be used separately. Doran v Sunset House Distributing Corp. (1961, DC Cal) 197 F Supp 940, 131 USPQ 94, affd (CA9 Cal) 304 F2d 251, 134 USPQ 4, and (disapproved on other grounds L. Batlin & Son, Inc. v Snyder (CA2 NY) 536 F2d 486, cert den 429 US 857, 50 L Ed 2d 135, 97 S Ct 156).

Fact that copyright notice is on underside of leaf of copyrighted artificial flower does not of itself seem objectionable; size of notice is sufficient since it can be seen by naked eye even though close examination is required to locate it. Prestige Floral, Societe Anonyme v California Artificial Flower Co. (1962, DC NY) 201 F Supp 287, 132 USPQ 350.

Copyright notice is defective where it is placed on box in which is packed figure sought to be protected. Ross Products, Inc. v New York Merchandise Co. (1964, DC NY) 233 F Supp 260, 141 USPQ 652.

Copyright legends on three dimensional copies of work of art are always noticable, although in some cases partially unclear. Even where copyright notice is partially unclear, copyright notice

symbol can be distinguished; hence, copyright has not been lost by abandonment, dedication to public, or forfeiture. Copyright notice on work of art need not include the year. Florence Art Co. v Quartite Creative Corp. (1968, DC Ill) 158 USPQ 382.

Although Copyright Act is silent as to where copyright notice should appear on works of art, its purpose is to apprise anyone, seeking to copy article of existence of copyright; this purpose is frustrated where notice is placed on large statue in such a place that it cannot be seen by anyone standing on the ground. Scherr v Universal Match Corp. (1967, DC NY) 297 F Supp 107, 160 USPQ 216, affd (CA2 NY) 417 F2d 497, 164 USPQ 225, 11 ALR Fed 447, cert den 397 US 936, 25 L Ed 2d 116, 90 S Ct 945.

Under literal reading of prior law, date is not required on notice on doll which is work of art. Uneeda Doll Co. v Regent Baby Products Corp. (1972, DC NY) 355 F Supp 438.

13. —Removable or separable notice

Copyright notice is affixed to work of art within meaning of predecessor section although notice is on gummed label pasted on work of art. Coventry Ware, Inc. v Reliance Picture Frame Co. (1961, CA2 NY) 288 F2d 193, 129 USPQ 83, cert den 368 US 818, 7 L Ed 2d 24, 82 S Ct 34, reh den 368 US 908, 7 L Ed 2d 101, 82 S Ct 171.

Courts have protected copyrights when notice appears on one of two or more separate or detachable parts of single item. Uneeda Doll Co. v Goldgarb Novelty Co. (1967, CA2 NY) 373 F2d 851, 153 USPQ 88, cert dismd 389 US 801, 19 L Ed 2d 56, 88 S Ct 9.

Copyright notice on tags attached to copyrighted pin does not meet requirement of predecessor section. Trifari, Krussman & Fishel, Inc. v B. Steinberg-Kaslo Co. (1956, DC NY) 144 F Supp 577, 110 USPQ 487.

Copyright notice affixed to removable disc which fits securely into hole on bottom of toy bank satisfies requirements of predecessor section since disc is essential part of bank and without it bank would not serve its purpose; bank is sold with disc securely inserted; disc is so placed as to give adequate notice of existence of copyright to anyone seeking to copy bank. Royalty Designs, Inc. v Thrifticheck Service Corp. (1962, DC NY) 204 F Supp 702, 133 USPQ 148.

While under predecessor section word "copyright" is sufficient notice, name of proprietor or his trade-mark must be indicated; also, efficacy of notice affixed to easily removable hangtag is doubtful. Ross Products, Inc. v New York Merchandise Co. (1964, DC NY) 233 F Supp 260, 141 USPQ 652.

Copyright notices which appear on paper tags attached to articles do not meet requirement of affixation in predecessor section. Gardenia Flowers, Inc. v Joseph Markovits, Inc. (1968, DC NY) 280 F Supp 776, 157 USPQ 685.

Since deck of playing cards is single commercial unit, copyright notice on ace of spades is sufficient. Freedman v Grolier Enterprises, Inc. (1973, DC NY) 179 USPQ 476.

Copyright notice on removable plug that closes bottom opening in coin bank is distinguishable from copyright notice on detachable tag and is adequate notice of copyright where clear enough to be legible. Goldman-Morgen, Inc. v Dan Brechner & Co. (1976, DC NY) 190 USPQ 478.

14. Fabric designs, generally

Copyright notice repeated every 16 inches throughout length of fabric bearing continuous textile design is sufficient where design is printed by master roller which repeats basic pattern every 16 inches; as copyright notice is itself printed by master roller, it appears at least once for every repetition of basic design. H. M. Kolbe Co. v Armgus Textile Co. (1963, CA2 NY) 315 F2d 70, 137 USPQ 9, 99 ALR2d 390.

Printing of copyright notice on selvage of fabric is sufficient. Loomskill, Inc. v Slifka (1964, CA2 NY) 330 F2d 952, 141 USPQ 318.

Requirement of predecessor section as to affixation of notice to each copy of copyrighted work should be given realistic and liberal interpretation, consonant with business practices, that will reasonably protect both copyright owner and innocent copyist; accordingly, where copyrighted work is repetitive design, imprinted on sheet or continuous strip or roll of material (dress fabric), and when notice is imprinted at least once for every repeat of design on edge of material, copyright proprietor, having done all that is reasonably within his power to imprint notice of material without marring appearance of work, has satisfied notice requirements of statute; any subsequent removal, destruction, or obliteration of notice by others (dress manufacturers) over whom proprietor has no control may serve to mitigate relief awarded against innocent infringer, without resulting in loss forever of rights given by copyright; copyright is not forfeited. Peter Pan Fabrics, Inc. v Acadia Co. (1959, DC NY) 173 F Supp 292, 121 USPQ 81, affd (CA2 NY) 274 F2d 487, 124 USPQ 154.

Only one copyright notice need appear on blouse bearing two separate imprints of same design. Scarves by Vera, Inc. v United Merchants & Mfrs., Inc. (1959, DC NY) 173 F Supp 625, 121 USPQ 578.

Requirement of predecessor section is met where copyrighted work is repetitive design printed on continuous roll of material with notice being printed on edge at least once for every repeat of design. Peter Pan Fabrics, Inc. v Candy Frocks, Inc. (1960, DC NY) 187 F Supp 334, 126 USPQ 171.

Copyright notice printed on selvage of cloth is adequate since it is not shown that there is any other feasible location for placing notice; placement of notice in middle of design would make cloth unusuable for garments since garments having such notice on their face would be unsaleable. Peter Pan Fabrics, Inc. v Dixon Textile Corp. (1960, DC NY) 188 F Supp 235, 127 USPQ 329.

Printing copyright notice on selvage of cloth bearing copyrighted design is adequate method of giving notice of copyright to dress manufacturers. Peter Pan Fabrics, Inc. v Puritan Dress Co. (1962, DC NY) 207 F Supp 563, 133 USPQ 678.

Copyright notice is sufficient where it is engraved on printing rollers and is mechanically printed on selvage of each and every repeat of copyrighted fabric design; alleged infringers have burden of proving that copyright notice could have been incorporated in body of design, instead of selvage, without impairing market value of fabric; burden is not sustained where evidence demonstrates that placement of notice in body of design would make fabric unusable for garments, since garments having such notice on their face would be unusable; placing copyright notice on selvage, when no other location is feasible, constitutes adequate notice. Cortley Fabrics Co. v Slifka (DC NY) 138 USPQ 110.

Copyright notice complies with predecessor section where copyrighted design bears notice printed on selvage of every yard of fabric. John Wolf Textiles Inc. v Andris Fabrics, Inc. (DC NY) 139 USPQ 365.

Copyright notice repeated on selvage of copyrighted fabric complies with predecessor section in absence of showing that notice could have been embodied in design itself without impairing its market value. United Merchants & Mfrs., Inc. v Sarne Co. (1967, DC NY) 278 F Supp 162, 157 USPQ 331.

Placing of copyright notice on selvage of copyrighted fabric constitutes adequate notice. United Merchants & Mfrs., Inc. v K. Gimbel Accessories, Inc. (1968, DC NY) 294 F Supp 151, 161 USPQ 147.

Placement of one copyright notice at beginning of spools of lace 100 to 500 yards long raises question of adequacy of copyright notice and precludes preliminary injunction where authorities indicate that notice must be repeated at least every 38 inches. Kauber Bros., Inc. v Westchester Lace Work, Inc. (1974, DC NY) 181 USPQ 523.

Annotations:

Fabric and dress designs as protected by copyright under Federal Copyright Act. 26 ALR Fed 408.

15. —Removable or separable notice

Copyright notice on cardboard hangtag attached to blouse bearing copyrighted design does not comply with predecessor section; however, copyright notice on woven label sewed into side seam adjacent to bottom of garment complies with statute; fact that label is sewed into side seam rather than on neck or some more obvious place is no basis for copier to argue that he was entrapped; label is not hidden and is located in sufficiently obvious place to apprise anyone seeking to copy design of existence of copyright. Scarves by Vera, Inc. v United Merchants & Mfrs., Inc. (1959, DC NY) 173 F Supp 625, 121 USPQ 578.

Court rejects infringer's contention that copyright notice could be affixed by way of hang tag to dresses made of cloth embodying copyrighted design; this method of notice does not meet burden of showing that notice could have been embodied in design, and requirement of predecessor section that notice "be affixed to each copy thereof" would not be satisfied in this manner. Peter Pan Fabrics, Inc. v Dixon Textile Corp. (1960, DC NY) 188 F Supp 235, 127 USPQ 329.

Defendant, which manufactures handbags from towels bearing plaintiff's copyrighted design, affixes hang tags thereto reading, "the design on the cover of this handbag is the copyrighted design of" plaintiff; tags do not meet requirement of predecessor section. Scarves by Vera, Inc. v American Handbags, Inc. (1960, DC NY) 188 F Supp 255, 127 USPQ 47.

Although selvage bearing copyright notice was cut from fabric bearing copyrighted design before fabric was made into dresses, and although defendant alleges that it copied design after examining purchased dress, notice was adequate; if defendant had no actual notice of copyright, this can be shown as defense to claim for damages; however, defendant made some sales after it had actual notice. Loomskill, Inc. v Slifka (1963, DC NY) 223 F Supp 845, 139 USPQ 476, affd (CA2 NY) 330 F2d 952, 141 USPQ 318.

16. Literary works

Notice of copyright appearing on back cover only is defective. Krafft v Cohen (1941, CA3 Pa) 117 F2d 579, 48 USPQ 401; W. S. Bessett, Inc.

v Germain (1937, DC Mass) 18 F Supp 249, 32 USPQ 550; J. A. Richards, Inc. v New York Post, Inc. (1938, DC NY) 23 F Supp 619, 38 USPQ 475.

Manual containing instructions as to playing of organ bears title of publication on first page (cover), second page is blank, third page contains text, and fourth page is first page of music; under predecessor section, copyright notice can be placed on cover or on fourth page if work is musical composition or on cover or second page if work is book; third page cannot be deemed to be title page which contains title; in construing statutory language "page immediately following," court states that it would be reasonable to conclude that page immediately following title page could be third page, because that is first page on first leaf, or could be inside front cover (second page); however, court limits opinion to peculiar circumstances of case, in which title appears only on cover and in which cover is of harder and less malleable material than leaves within, and holds that notice on third page is sufficient. Neal v Thomas Organ Co. (1963, CA9 Cal) 325 F2d 978, 140 USPQ 103, cert den 379 US 828, 13 L Ed 2d 37, 85 S Ct 55.

Copyright notice of page three of newspaper did not comply with predecessor section since third page was not title page in that it did not carry complete title and had no volume or issue number. OA Business Publications, Inc. v Davidson Publishing Co. (1964, CA7 Ill) 334 F2d 432, 142 USPQ 119.

Notice in proper form on instruction sheet and on boxes containing model airplane kits is proper, and notice need not appear on each part of kit. Monogram Models, Inc. v Industro Motive Corp. (1974, CA6 Mich) 492 F2d 1281, 181 USPQ 425, cert den 419 US 843, 42 L Ed 2d 71, 95 S Ct 76.

Under former copyright law, insertion of notice on page next following title page of first volume of set of books composed of four volumes was sufficient. Dwight v Appleton (1843, CC NY) F Cas No 4215.

Notice was sufficient where affixed to title page, though not on cover page which contained advertisements. Blume v Spear (1887, CC NY) 30 F 629.

Where advance sheets of publication are copyrighted separately, book containing all these sheets in one volume without change must indicate copyrights of advance sheets. West Publishing Co. v Edward Thompson Co. (1909, CC NY) 169 F 833, mod on other grounds (CA2 NY) 176 F 833.

Copyright notice in periodical appearing on editorial page which was not first page of text is not compliance. Freeman v The Trade Register (1909, CC Wash) 173 F 419.

Fact that book has advertising pages preceding title page and notice of copyright does not constitute failure to comply with statute. American Travel & Hotel Directory Co. v Gehring Publishing Co. (1925, DC NY) 4 F2d 415.

Copyright notice on last page is insufficient. United Thrift Plan, Inc. v National Thrift Plan, Inc. (1929, DC NY) 34 F2d 300, 2 USPQ 345.

Placing of copyright notice on page other than that provided for was not accident or mistake within predecessor section. W. S. Bessett, Inc. v Germain (1937, DC Mass) 18 F Supp 249, 32 USPQ 550.

Plaintiff's bound volume of advertisements intended to be used separately bears title and proper copyright notice on front cover; on inside of front cover appears another copyright notice substantially complying with predecessor section; volume has no other title page; plaintiff's front cover was properly used as title page and copyright was valid as either notice was sufficient. Deward & Rich, Inc. v Bristol Sav. & Loan Corp. (1940, DC Va) 34 F Supp 345, 47 USPQ 128, affd (CA4 Va) 120 F2d 537, 50 USPQ 1.

Copyright notice need not appear upon cover of pamphlet or on page immediately following, since cover is not part of published matter and has no connection with it other than that of cover to protect printed matter of text, hence notice appearing on reverse of first page following cover leaf is proper. Powell v Stransky (1951, DC SD) 98 F Supp 434, 89 USPQ 310.

Catalogue is composed of loose leaf sheets including paper backing sheet; sheets are held together by paper fasteners; first sheet identifies catalogue as to contents, manufacturer, and manufacturer's address; it contains no illustrations; second, third, and fourth sheets contain illustrations and descriptions of goods, as does fifth sheet; in addition, fifth sheet carries copyright notice; copyright is invalid since first sheet is title page, which does not bear copyright notice. Siewek Tool Co. v Morton (1954, DC Mich) 128 F Supp 71, 105 USPQ 60.

Brochures made of single sheets of paper folded to produce pages and titled or identified only on front cover page have proper copyright notice where notice appears on reverse face of cover page but improper copyright notice where notice appears on page following reverse face of cover page. Foreign Car Parts, Inc. v Auto World, Inc. (1973, DC Pa) 366 F Supp 977, 181 USPQ 162.

Construing this section together with requirements for compilations, court finds that copyright notices on each page of looseleaf supplement pages inserted at back of uncopyrighted catalog are valid notices of copyright for material in supplemental pages, even though no notice appears on title page of basic catalog. L & L White Metal Casting Corp. v Joseph (1975, DC NY) 387 F Supp 1349, 185 USPQ 269.

17. Motion pictures and audiovisual works

Copyright Act does not expressly require notice upon each reel of multiple reel motion picture. Patterson v Century Productions, Inc. (1937, CA2 NY) 93 F2d 489, 35 USPQ 471, cert den 303 US 655, 82 L Ed 1114, 58 S Ct 759.

Inasmuch as copyright proprietor's assertion of copyright was clearly printed on print of film (purchased by defendant) in strict accordance with statutory requirements, proprietor had right to assume that assertion provided ample notice to defendant of proprietor's interest in film; being charged with this notice, defendant could ascertain facts by inquiring of proprietor. Hampton v Paramount Pictures Corp. (1960, CA9 Cal) 279 F2d 100, 125 USPQ 623, 84 ALR2d 454, cert den 364 US 882, 5 L Ed 2d 103, 81 S Ct 170.

No notice is necessary on a motion-picture film with sound in order to protect song. Famous Music Corp. v Melz (1939, DC La) 28 F Supp 767, 42 USPQ 573.

18. Musical works

Notice of copyright in musical work must appear upon its title page or first page of music; purpose of notice is to prevent innocent persons, in ignorance of existence of copyright, from using copyrighted article. Tempo Music, Inc. v Myers (1969, CA4 NC) 407 F2d 503, 160 USPQ 707.

Copyright notice on musical composition may be printed below music on first page on which music is printed. Blume v Spear (1887, CC NY) 30 F 629.

§ 402.   Notice of copyright: Phonorecords of sound recordings

(a) General requirement. Whenever a sound recording protected under this title [17 USCS §§ 101 et seq.] is published in the United States or elsewhere by authority of the copyright owner, a notice of copyright as provided by this section shall be placed on all publicly distributed phonorecords of the sound recording.

(b) Form of notice. The notice appearing on the phonorecords shall consist of the following three elements:

(1) the symbol ® (the letter P in a circle); and

(2) the year of first publication of the sound recording; and

(3) the name of the owner of copyright in the sound recording, or an abbreviation by which the name can be recognized, or a generally known alternative designation of the owner; if the producer of the sound recording is named on the phonorecord labels or containers, and if no other name appears in conjunction with the notice, the producer's name shall be considered a part of the notice.

(c) Position of notice. The notice shall be placed on the surface of the phonorecord, or on the phonorecord label or container, in such manner and location as to give reasonable notice of the claim of copyright.
(Added Oct. 19, 1976, P. L. 94-553, Title I, § 101, 90 Stat. 2577.)

HISTORY; ANCILLARY LAWS AND DIRECTIVES

Effective date of section:
Section 102 of Act Oct. 19, 1976, P. L. 94-553, 90 Stat. 2598 provided that this section "becomes effective on January 1, 1978".

CROSS REFERENCES

"Copies" defined, 17 USCS § 101.
"Phonorecords" defined, 17 USCS § 101.
Notice of copyright for visually perceptible works, 17 USCS § 401.
This section referred to in 17 USCS §§ 401 note, 403–405.

RESEARCH GUIDE

Am Jur:
18 Am Jur 2d, Copyright and Literary Property §§ 57–59.

INTERPRETIVE NOTES AND DECISIONS

Copyright Act is not invalid as failing to give fair notice of what is copyrighted, even though single copyright notice on album may cover both protected and unprotected songs, because certificate of registration is available and gives adequate information of coverage of copyright. United States v Taxe (1976, CA9 Cal) 540 F2d 961, 192 USPQ 204.

§ 403. Notice of copyright: Publications incorporating United States Government works

Whenever a work is published in copies or phonorecords consisting preponderantly of one or more works of the United States Government, the notice of copyright provided by sections 401 or 402 [17 USCS §§ 401 or 402] shall also include a statement identifying, either affirmatively or negatively, those portions of the copies or phonorecords embodying any work or works protected under this title [17 USCS §§ 101 et seq.]. (Added Oct. 19, 1976, P. L. 94-553, Title I, § 101, 90 Stat. 2577.)

HISTORY; ANCILLARY LAWS AND DIRECTIVES

Effective date of section:
Section 102 of Act Oct. 19, 1976, P. L. 94-553, 90 Stat. 2598 provided that this section "becomes effective on January 1, 1978".

CROSS REFERENCES

"Work of United States Government" defined, 17 USCS § 101.
Consequences of omission of notice, 17 USCS § 405.
This section referred to in 17 USCS §§ 401 note, 404, 405.

§ 404. Notice of copyright: Contributions to collective works

(a) A separate contribution to a collective work may bear its own notice of copyright, as provided by sections 401 through 403 [17 USCS §§ 401–403]. However, a single notice applicable to the collective work as a whole is sufficient to satisfy the requirements of sections 401 through 403 [17 USCS §§ 401–403] with respect to the separate contributions it contains (not including advertisements inserted on behalf of persons other than the owner of copyright in the collective work), regardless of the ownership of copyright in the contributions and whether or not they have been previously published.

(b) Where the person named in a single notice applicable to a collective work as a whole is not the owner of copyright in a separate contribution that does not bear its own notice, the case is governed by the provisions of section 406(a) [17 USCS § 406(a)].
(Added Oct. 19, 1976, P. L. 94-553, Title I, § 101, 90 Stat. 2577.)

HISTORY; ANCILLARY LAWS AND DIRECTIVES

Effective date of section:
Section 102 of Act Oct. 19, 1976, P. L. 94-553, 90 Stat. 2598 provided that this section "becomes effective on January 1, 1978".

CROSS REFERENCES

Contributions to collective works, 17 USCS § 201(c).
Error in name in copyright notice, 17 USCS § 406(a).

INTERPRETIVE NOTES AND DECISIONS

Copyright entry of magazine will not validate author's subsequent entry under different title of article appearing therein. Mifflin v R. H. White Co. (1903) 190 US 260, 47 L Ed 1040, 23 S Ct 769.

Notice of copyright of magazine protected story contained therein, including dramatic rights. Dam v Kirk La Shelle Co. (1910, CA2 NY) 175 F 902 (ovrld on other grounds Sheldon v Metro-Goldwyn Pictures (CA2 NY) 106 F2d 45, affd 309 US 390, 84 L Ed 825, 60 S Ct 681).

Copyright notice on title page of "Woodman's

Minnetonka Map-Directory" covers map found in pocket of book. Woodman v Lydiard-Peterson Co. (1912, CC Minn) 192 F 67, affd (CA8 Minn) 204 F 921, reh den (CA8 Minn) 205 F 900.

Copyrighted advertisement for motion picture

first published in newspaper without special copyright notice is protected by copyright notice for newspaper. Warner Bros., Inc. v Film Ventures International (1975, DC Cal) 403 F Supp 522, 189 USPQ 591.

§ 405. Notice of copyright: Omission of notice

(a) **Effect of omission on copyright.** The omission of the copyright notice prescribed by sections 401 through 403 [17 USCS §§ 401–403] from copies or phonorecords publicly distributed by authority of the copyright owner does not invalidate the copyright in a work if—

(1) the notice has been omitted from no more than a relatively small number of copies or phonorecords distributed to the public; or

(2) registration for the work has been made before or is made within five years after the publication without notice, and a reasonable effort is made to add notice to all copies or phonorecords that are distributed to the public in the United States after the omission has been discovered; or

(3) the notice has been omitted in violation of an express requirement in writing that, as a condition of the copyright owner's authorization of the public distribution of copies or phonorecords, they bear the prescribed notice.

(b) **Effect of omission on innocent infringers.** Any person who innocently infringes a copyright, in reliance upon an authorized copy or phonorecord from which the copyright notice has been omitted, incurs no liability for actual or statutory damages under section 504 [17 USCS § 504] for any infringing acts committed before receiving actual notice that registration for the work has been made under section 408 [17 USCS § 408], if such person proves that he or she was misled by the omission of notice. In a suit for infringement in such a case the court may allow or disallow recovery of any of the infringer's profits attributable to the infringement, and may enjoin the continuation of the infringing undertaking or may require, as a condition or permitting the continuation of the infringing undertaking, that the infringer pay the copyright owner a reasonable license fee in an amount and on terms fixed by the court.

(c) **Removal of notice.** Protection under this title [17 USCS §§ 101 et seq.] is not affected by the removal, destruction, or obliteration of the notice, without the authorization of the copyright owner, from any publicly distributed copies or phonorecords.

(Added Oct. 19, 1976, P. L. 94-553, Title I, § 101, 90 Stat. 2578.)

HISTORY; ANCILLARY LAWS AND DIRECTIVES

Effective date of section:
Section 102 of Act Oct. 19, 1976, P. L. 94-553, 90 Stat. 2598 provided that this section "becomes effective on January 1, 1978".

CROSS REFERENCES

Basic notice requirements, 17 USCS §§ 401(a), 402(a).
Certificate of registration within five years of first publication, 17 USCS § 410(c).
Copyright Office registration records, 17 USCS § 705.
This section referred to in 17 USCS §§ 406, 408.

RESEARCH GUIDE

Am Jur:

18 Am Jur 2d, Copyright and Literary Property §§ 57, 87, 106, 128, 129, 134, 137.

Forms:

6 Federal Procedural Forms L Ed, Copyrights § 17:93.

Annotations:

Abandonment of statutory copyright. 84 ALR2d 462.

INTERPRETIVE NOTES AND DECISIONS

1. Generally
2. Actual notice
3. Authorization to publish without notice
4. Extent of publication or distribution without notice, generally
5. —Derivative publication or use
6. —Foreign publication
7. —Subsequent publication
8. Intent of party omitting notice
9. Innocent infringers [17 USCS § 405(b)]
10. Removal of notice [17 USCS § 405(c)]

1. Generally

Prior to enactment of predecessor section, accidental omission of copyright notice by licensee did not result in loss to proprietor of any of his rights under copyright laws. American Press Asso. v Daily Story Pub. Co. (1902, CA7 Ill) 120 F 766, app dismd 193 US 675, 48 L Ed 842, 24 S Ct 852.

Publication with notice of copyright is essence of compliance with statute, and publication without such notice amounts to dedication to public sufficient to defeat all subsequent efforts at copyright protection. Universal Film Mfg. Co. v Copperman (1914, CA2 NY) 218 F 577, cert den 235 US 704, 59 L Ed 433, 35 S Ct 209.

Accidental omission of copyright notice in law book used by infringer was immaterial and no defense to infringer. W. H. Anderson Co. v Baldwin Law Pub. Co. (1928, CA6 Ohio) 27 F2d 82.

Omission of date is fatal. King v Force (1820, CC Dist Col) F Cas No 7791.

Where, by accident or mistake, notice of copyright has been omitted from some published copies, copyright is not thereby invalidated, and recovery for infringement may be had from any person who is not misled by such copies. Stecher Lithographic Co. v Dunston Lithograph Co. (1916, DC NY) 233 F 601.

Publication of portion of copyrighted wrapper bearing no copyright notice did not justify infringer in appropriating whole wrapper. Hoague-Sprague Corp. v Frank C. Meyer Co. (1929, DC NY) 31 F2d 583.

Predecessor section cures omission of copyright notice on particular copies where due to accident or mistake, but has no application when notice in all copies is defective. J. A. Richards, Inc. v New York Post, Inc. (1938, DC NY) 23 F Supp 619, 38 USPQ 475.

Publication of score cards without notice required by copyright statute amounts to dedication to public sufficient to defeat all subsequent effort for copyright protection of score cards containing similar information. Penn Sportservice, Inc. v Goldstein (DC Pa) 46 USPQ 477.

When the statutory notice is not affixed to an article which is then passed into the stream of commerce, the copyright holder abandons his rights under the copyright and the article may be freely copied by others. Irving J. Dorfman Co., Inc. v Borlan Industries, Inc. (1969, DC NY) 309 F Supp 21.

Annotations:

Abandonment of statutory copyright. 84 ALR2d 462.

2. Actual notice

Omission in copyright notice of year or name debars proprietor from maintaining action for infringement even against former proprietor, his grantor, who had full knowledge of the facts. Thompson v Hubbard (1889) 131 US 123, 33 L Ed 76, 9 S Ct 710.

Newspaper printing advertisement from matrices furnished to it by advertiser, which matrices contained no notice of copyright, was not liable for infringement, it having no knowledge of copyright. Wilkes-Barre Record Co. v Standard Advertising Co. (1933, CA3 Pa) 63 F2d 99, 16 USPQ 346.

Lack of copyright notice upon article will not protect infringer who has actual notice. Schellberg v Empringham (1929, DC NY) 36 F2d 991.

Defendants cannot avoid infringement of 1916 copyright on ground that 1930 copyright of reissued book contained no notice of 1916 copyright since defendants were not misled, having copied from 1916 edition. Harris v Miller (DC NY) 50 USPQ 306, mod on other grounds 50 USPQ 625.

3. Authorization to publish without notice

Publication, by state, of index to statutes, which plaintiff had copyrighted, does not constitute abandonment of copyright, although no notice of copyright was printed on such state publications. W. H. Anderson Co. v Baldwin Law Pub. Co. (1928, CA6 Ohio) 27 F2d 82.

Fact that defendant first secured copyrighted book from plaintiff through contract, paying plaintiff for use, does not change rule that every reproduction of copyrighted work must bear statutory notice. Deward & Rich v Bristol Savings & Loan Corp. (1941, CA4 Va) 120 F2d 537, 50 USPQ 1.

If owner gives another unconditional license to publish comic strips, their publication without required notice is by authority of proprietor and has same effect upon copyrights that similar publication by owner would have. National Comics Publications, Inc. v Fawcett Publications, Inc. (1951, CA2 NY) 191 F2d 594, 90 USPQ 274.

Findings that great volume of nearly identical prints appeared over long period and that copyright proprietor was derelict in preventing others from infringing copyright support inference that proprietor authorized or acquiesced in wide circulation of copies without copyright notice; print was dedicated to public, barring suit for infringement. Stuff v E. C. Publications, Inc. (1965, CA2 NY) 342 F2d 143, 144 USPQ 560, cert den 382 US 822, 15 L Ed 2d 68, 86 S Ct 50.

Publication of book by licensee without proper notice of copyright is dedication to public. West Publishing Co. v Edward Thompson Co. (1909, CC NY) 169 F 833, mod on other grounds (CA2 NY) 176 F 833.

Where owner of copyright of song licenses manufacturer to reproduce song as part of motion picture it is not necessary to put notice of copyright of song on motion-picture film; no notice of copyright could be imprinted because there was no license from copyright owner to manufacturer of reel or to producer of the film authorizing use of reel for public performance. Famous Music Corp. v Melz (1939, DC La) 28 F Supp 767, 42 USPQ 573.

Defendant, which contracts for use for specific time of duly-copyrighted book of advertisements bearing notice of copyright and then continues to use material without authorization beyond time specified in contract, after having in sense recognized validity of copyright by paying for use of material, cannot, when sued for infringement, set up as valid defense mere fact that copyright owner furnished for defendant's convenience mats for printing separate advertisements from book without copyright notice on mats so that material, when printed from mats, also contained no copyright notice. Deward & Rich, Inc. v Bristol Sav. & Loan Corp. (1939, DC Va) 29 F Supp 777, 44 USPQ 26.

Author of unpublished work does not lose right to obtain statutory copyright by reason of unauthorized publication of work; he does not lose that right if person, with whom he contracts for publication of work, breaches condition of contract requiring him to comply with copyright law; he does not forfeit statutory copyright already obtained where publisher breaches provision of contract requiring him to affix appropriate copyright notice to each copy of published work. Mills Music, Inc. v Cromwell Music, Inc. (1954, DC NY) 126 F Supp 54, 103 USPQ 84.

Plaintiff granted third party permission to reprint plaintiff's catalogue on condition that proper notice of plaintiff's copyright be inserted; thereafter, plaintiff discovered that reprints omitted notice; if permission had been given without this condition, plaintiff might have forfeited its rights; however, violation of condition by third party places reprints in category of infringements. Perkins Marine Lamp & Hardware Corp. v Long Island Marine Supply Corp. (1960, DC NY) 185 F Supp 353, 126 USPQ 169.

Summary judgment based on dedication of cartoon figure to public is granted on evidence showing copyright proprietor granted permission for publication of cartoon figure on thousands of business cards without copyright notice. Crumb v A. A. Sales, Inc. (1975, DC Cal) 188 USPQ 445.

4. Extent of publication or distribution without notice, generally

Giving miniature samples of copyrighted photographs to dealers to use in taking orders, where samples did not contain notice of copyright, was not publication destroying copyright. Falk v Gast Lithograph & Engraving Co. (1893, CA2 NY) 54 F 890.

General circulation by copyright proprietor of copyrighted picture without copyright notice thereon estops proprietor from complaining about anything defendant, who used copy of picture without copyright notice as reference for his picture, did up to date of trial. Lucas v Nattrass-Schenck, Inc. (DC NY) 44 USPQ 344.

Half-tone reproduction of mezzotint engravings appeared without notice of copyright in widely circulated catalogues, but this was done only for advertising purposes and did not mislead defendants and did not result in abandonment of copyright protection of engravings. Alfred Bell & Co. v Catalda Fine Arts, Inc. (1947, DC NY) 74 F Supp 973, 75 USPQ 66.

Precise number of "particular" copies with respect to which notice may be mistakenly omitted has not been judicially determined, although some courts hold that it applies only in case of very few copies; omission from only 2 per cent might bring case within coverage of predecessor section. Kramer Jewelry Creations, Inc. v Capri Jewelry, Inc. (1956, DC NY) 143 F Supp 120, 111 USPQ 151.

Copies not bearing copyright notice were distributed to limited group causing forfeiture of copyright since interest in copies was confined to such group and anyone interested could have obtained copy. Continental Cas. Co. v Beardsley (1957, DC NY) 151 F Supp 28, 113 USPQ 181, mod on other grounds (CA2 NY) 253 F2d 702, 117 USPQ 1, cert den 358 US 816, 3 L Ed 2d 58, 79 S Ct 25.

Plaintiff deposited three copies of his thesis, which he alleges bore copyright notice, in university library; defendant borrowed from library copy, which he alleges bore no copyright notice; even if copy did not bear notice, this would not invalidate copyright in view of predecessor section. Christie v Raddock (1959, DC NY) 169 F Supp 48, 120 USPQ 76.

Publication of author's articles, pursuant to agreement with author, in trade publications, without any notice of restriction of reservation of rights in author, extinguished any right to first publication which author may have had or retained in articles, since right to first publication terminated as of date of first publication. Settel v Office Appliance Co. (DC Ill) 122 USPQ 123.

Public distribution of copies of copyrighted work not bearing copyright notice amounts to general publication of work and results in dedication or forfeiture where it is without any limitation as to use and is made with knowledge and express or implied approval of copyright owners. Klasmer v Baltimore Football, Inc. (1961, DC Md) 200 F Supp 255, 132 USPQ 36.

Abandonment of copyright in architectural plans is shown where (1) owner of plans applied for building permit for construction of home as his private residence, (2) plans were freely circulated among subcontractors, who were not warned that plans were protected by copyright, (3) public was invited to view completed house freely without any restriction as to taking of measurements, and (4) newspaper advertisement depicting house and floor plan thereof did not show notice of copyright. De Silva Constr. Corp. v Herrald (1962, DC Fla) 213 F Supp 184, 137 USPQ 96.

Omission of copyright notice from very small percentage of copyrighted fabric constitutes omission by accident or mistake within meaning of predecessor does not grant absolute immunity to innocent infringers; it merely provides immunity from damage claims against those misled by omission of copyright notice; furthermore, predecessor section contemplates prospect of permanent injunction against innocent infringer. United Merchants & Mfrs., Inc. v Sarne Co. (1967, DC NY) 278 F Supp 162, 157 USPQ 331.

Defendant's allegations that some of plaintiff's copyrighted lace is sold to jobbers without copyright notice raises question of validity and precludes preliminary injunction. Kauber Bros., Inc. v Westchester Lace Work, Inc. (1974, DC NY) 181 USPQ 523.

Plaintiff's wide distribution of portions of copyrighted catalog without copyright notice on portions probably invalidates copyright in distributed portions, but questions of fact remain for jury whether plaintiff thereby abandoned copyright. Rexnord, Inc. v Modern Handling Systems, Inc. (1974, DC Del) 379 F Supp 1190, 183 USPQ 413.

Limited publication of zodiac pins to persons whose criticism was sought without using copyright notice does not defeat claim to copyright. Jerry De Nicola, Inc. v Genesco, Pakula & Co. (1974, DC NY) 188 USPQ 304.

Doctrine of dedication is intended to protect persons from liability for reproducing material that does not indicate it is protected by copyright law so that summary judgment is affirmed on reconsideration because of distribution of several thousand business cards bearing representation of cartoon figure without copyright notice, and fact that cards were distributed only to printers does not overcome dedication. Crumb v A. A. Sales, Inc. (1975, DC Cal) 188 USPQ 447.

Distribution of many copies of poem to servicemen during World War II and to friends at Christmas time without including copyright notice shows invalidation of copyright by both forfeiture and intentional abandonment. Bell v Combined Registry Co. (1975, DC Ill) 188 USPQ 707.

5. —Derivative publication or use

Fact that roll music had no notice of copyright upon it, and that the manufacturers of roll music had permission of owner of copyright, is no defense to action for infringement of right to perform copyright work publicly for profit. Lutz v Buck (1930, CA5 Tex) 40 F2d 501, cert den 282 US 880, 75 L Ed 776, 51 S Ct 83.

Orchestra conductor's common-law property in his performances ended with sale of records and legend on records that they could not be used except on phonographs in homes did not save it; even if such restriction did save it, records themselves could not be clogged with servitude. RCA Mfg. Co. v Whiteman (1940, CA2 NY) 114 F2d 86, 46 USPQ 324, cert den 311 US 712, 85 L Ed 463, 61 S Ct 393 and cert den 311 US 712, 85 L Ed 463, 61 S Ct 394.

Crayon sketch of painting printed without copyright notice in catalogue of salon where painting was exhibited was not such publication as would work forfeiture of right of copyright. Werckmeister v Springer Lithographing Co. (1894, CC NY) 63 F 808.

Defense that no notice of copyright appeared on phonograph record played on victrola in cafe was without merit. Buck v Heretis (1928, DC SC) 24 F2d 876.

Defense that no notice of copyright appeared on perforated roll used on player piano at theatre was without merit. Buck v Lester (1928, DC SC) 24 F2d 877.

Even if design printed on fabric from which dresses are manufactured were copyrightable, copyright was lost by failure to publish proper copyright notice on fabric and dresses. Verney Corp. v Rose Fabric Converters Corp. (1949, DC NY) 87 F Supp 802, 83 USPQ 386.

Lack of copyright notices on plaintiff's Christmas tree ornaments is of no moment in action alleging infringement through copying not from ornaments themselves but from plaintiff's copyrighted catalogues. Walco Products, Inc. v Kittay & Blitz, Inc. (1972, DC NY) 354 F Supp 121.

Uncopyrighted advertisements illustrating copyrighted compilation of executive desk calendar do not invalidate copyright on overall arrangement of work. Baldwin Cooke Co. v Keith Clark, Inc. (1974, DC Ill) 383 F Supp 650, 183 USPQ 209, affd without opinion (CA7 Ill) 505 F2d 1250 and supp op (DC Ill) 420 F Supp 404.

6. —Foreign publication

Omission of American copyright notice on work published abroad and sold there does not destroy rights of copyright holder. United Dictionary Co. v G. & C. Merriam Co. (1908) 208 US 260, 52 L Ed 478, 28 S Ct 290.

Acts of abandonment by author in permitting publication of her work in England and America without notice of copyright did not deprive American proprietors of their copyright. Harper & Bros. v M. A. Donohue & Co. (1905, CC Ill) 144 F 491, affd (CA7 Ill) 146 F 1023.

Notice, on publication of song in foreign country, that it cannot be used for stage performances except with consent of their agents, although lawful in country where published, does not protect it in this country without compliance with our copyright laws. Savage v Hoffmann (1908, CC NY) 159 F 584.

Since United States does not belong to Berne Union, it is required in order to secure copyright here that any publication in foreign country must contain notice of United States copyright. Basevi v Edward O'Toole Co. (1939, DC NY) 26 F Supp 41, 40 USPQ 333.

7. —Subsequent publication

Publication of leaflet without proper copyright notice results in loss of rights of copyright unless predecessor section saves them; predecessor section applies only where notice is omitted from one or perhaps a very few copies, but does not apply where statutory notice is omitted from all copies published, as was case with all first published by plaintiff although those subsequently published bore proper notice. Krafft v Cohen (1941, CA3 Pa) 117 F2d 579, 48 USPQ 401.

Publication of part or parts of author's works serially without statutory notice of copyright makes such work public property even though copyright covering entire work had previously been taken out. Deward & Rich v Bristol Savings & Loan Corp. (1941, CA4 Va) 120 F2d 537, 50 USPQ 1.

Predecessor section does not excuse omission of prescribed copyright notice upon all subsequent copies, even though notice on first published copy was proper. National Comics Publications, Inc. v Fawcett Publications, Inc. (1951, CA2 NY) 191 F2d 594, 90 USPQ 274.

Copyright was abandoned by failure to repeat notice when copyrighted matter was republished. Record & Guide Co. v Bromley (1909, CC Pa) 175 F 156.

Copyrights were lost by plaintiff publishing same subject matter in later editions without copyright notice. Landis Machine Co. v Chaso Tool Co. (DC Mich) 53 USPQ 200, affd (CA6 Mich) 141 F2d 800, 61 USPQ 164, cert den 323 US 720, 89 L Ed 579, 65 S Ct 52.

Defendants did not copy design of plaintiff's copyrighted labels but only directions for use which appeared on plaintiff's earlier uncopyrighted labels; publication and use for several months prior to application for copyright and without notice thereof dedicated to public directions for use and prevented maintenance of infringement action predicated only on use of directions. Superfine Products, Inc. v Denny (1943, DC Ga) 54 F Supp 148, 60 USPQ 126.

Copyright on advertisements is invalidated where proprietor subsequently published them without giving required statutory notice. Davis-Robertson Agency v Duke (1953, DC Va) 119 F Supp 931, 100 USPQ 211.

Advertisements in suit differ sufficiently from previous uncopyrighted advertisements so that copyright in later advertisements is valid, but mailing coupon substantially the same as mailing coupons of prior uncopyrighted advertisements and welcoming letter substantially the same as previous uncopyrighted welcoming letter are public domain. G. R. I. Corp. v Golden Fifty Pharmaceutical Co. (1975, DC Ill) 185 USPQ 674.

8. Intent of party omitting notice

Deliberate use of copyright notice which fails to meet requirements of predecessor is not omission by accident or mistake. Advertisers Exchange, Inc. v Anderson (1944, CA8 Iowa) 144 F2d 907, 63 USPQ 39.

It is no defense in copyright infringement action that plaintiff's copyrighted advertisements appeared, without required copyright notice, in two newspapers, since defendant did not sustain burden to prove that plaintiff was at fault for absence of notice. Modern Aids, Inc. v R. H. Macy & Co. (1959, CA2 NY) 264 F2d 93, 120 USPQ 470.

Predecessor section is applicable only where notice of copyright has been accidentally omitted, not where omission is done with knowledge. Smith v Bartlett (1937, DC Me) 18 F Supp 35, 32 USPQ 287.

Predecessor section saves rights in copyright only if omission of notice was by accident or mistake and not if it was due to neglect and oversight. Sieff v Continental Auto Supply, Inc. (1941, DC Minn) 39 F Supp 683, 50 USPQ 19.

After distribution of 15,000 copies of first printing of its catalogue, plaintiff ordered abbreviated second edition of 1,000 copies; in ordering second printing, plaintiff made no reference to any change in copyright notice that had been affixed to original printing; after 25 copies of second printing had been distributed, it was noted that catalogue began with page eight and remaining 975 copies were destroyed; although second printing did not bear copyright notice, plaintiff had sought to comply with notice provisions of Copyright Act, there is no evidence that plaintiff was at fault for absence of notice; on motion for preliminary injunction, defendant has burden upon issue of invalidation; same may be said concerning appearance of copyright notice on sixth page of first printing instead of upon title page or page immediately following; although evidence may warrant different result on the trial, sufficient has been presented to justify preliminary injunction. Perkins Marine Lamp & Hardware Corp. v Long Island Marine Supply Corp. (1960, DC NY) 185 F Supp 353, 126 USPQ 169.

Predecessor section does not apply when defect in copyright notice is result of mistake of law, neither does it excuse defective forms of notice which were deliberately selected and used. Gardenia Flowers, Inc. v Joseph Markovits, Inc. (1968, DC NY) 280 F Supp 776, 157 USPQ 685.

Deliberate deletion of copyright notice by assignee of copyright forfeits copyright so that no infringement occurs after reassignment to assignor. Walker v University Books, Inc. (1977, DC Cal) 193 USPQ 596.

9. Innocent infringers [17 USCS § 405(b)]

Infringer who had actual knowledge of existence of copyright will be enjoined, even though copies of work have inadvertently been published without notice. Gerlach-Barklow Co. v Morris & Bendien, Inc. (1927, CA2 NY) 23 F2d 159.

Profits made by innocent infringer are recoverable. Strauss v Penn Printing & Pub. Co. (1915, DC Pa) 220 F 977.

Profits made by defendant who innocently infringed on account of defective or accidentally omitted copyright notice are recoverable. Alfred Decker Cohn Co. v Etchison Hat Co. (1914, DC Va) 225 F 135.

Where copyright proprietor has sought to comply with respect to notice, omission by accident or mistake of such notice from particular copies does not invalidate copyright, or prevent recovery for infringement after actual notice of copyright, but no damages are recoverable against innocent infringer who has been misled by omission of notice. Stecher Lithographic Co. v Dunston Lithograph Co. (1916, DC NY) 233 F 601.

Plaintiffs owning copyrighted advertising material forfeited and waived their right to obtain relief from defendant, who innocently used one of their figures, where they had permitted the figure to be used without sufficient notice of copyright. Smith v Bartlett (1937, DC Me) 18 F Supp 35, 32 USPQ 287.

Effect of predecessor section is that, where one copies copyrighted article and, because of unintentional omission of copyright notice from original, is unaware of copyright, he cannot be treated as infringer except with respect to things done after he learns of copyright; however, if he is aware of copyright, omission of notice or defect in notice will not protect him. Trifari, Kurssman & Fishel, Inc. v B. Steinberg-Kaslo Co. (1956, DC NY) 144 F Supp 577, 110 USPQ 487.

10. Removal of notice [17 USCS § 405(c)]

It is no defense to suit for injunction for infringement of copyright, that defendant has in his possession pictures without notice of copyright, when it cannot be shown that pictures left plaintiff's possession without notice. Gerlach-Barklow Co. v Morris & Bendien, Inc. (1927, CA2 NY) 23 F2d 159.

§ 406.   Notice of copyright: Error in name or date

(a) Error in name. Where the person named in the copyright notice on copies or phonorecords publicly distributed by authority of the copyright owner is not the owner of copyright, the validity and ownership of the copyright are not affected. In such a case, however, any person who innocently begins an undertaking that infringes the copyright has a complete defense to any action for such infringement if such person proves that he or she was misled by the notice and began the undertaking in good faith under a purported transfer or license from the person named therein, unless before the undertaking was begun—

(1) registration for the work had been made in the name of the owner of copyright; or

(2) a document executed by the person named in the notice and showing the ownership of the copyright had been recorded.

The person named in the notice is liable to account to the copyright owner for all receipts from transfers or licenses purportedly made under the copyright by the person named in the notice.

(b) Error in date. When the year date in the notice on copies or phonorecords distributed by authority of the copyright owner is earlier than the year in which publication first occurred, any period computed from the year of first publication under section 302 [17 USCS § 302] is to be computed from the year in the notice. Where the year date is more than one year later than the year in which publication first occurred, the work is considered to have been published without any notice and is governed by the provisions of section 405 [17 USCS § 405].

(c) Omission of name or date. Where copies or phonorecords publicly distributed by authority of the copyright owner.contain no name or no date that could reasonably be considered a part of the notice, the work is considered to have been published without any notice and is governed by the provisions of section 405 [17 USCS § 405].

(Added Oct. 19, 1976, P. L. 94-553, Title I, § 101, 90 Stat. 2578.)

HISTORY; ANCILLARY LAWS AND DIRECTIVES

Effective date of section:

Section 102 of Act Oct. 19, 1976, P. L. 94-553, 90 Stat. 2598 provided that this section "becomes effective on January 1, 1978".

CROSS REFERENCES

Duration of copyright for works created on or after 1 January 1978, 17 USCS § 302.
Omission of notice, 17 USCS § 405.
Copyright Office records, 17 USCS § 705.
This section referred to in 17 USCS § 404.

RESEARCH GUIDE

Forms:

6 Federal Procedural Forms L Ed, Copyrights § 17:94.

Annotations:

Abandonment of statutory copyright. 84 ALR2d 462.

INTERPRETIVE NOTES AND DECISIONS

1. Generally
2. Error in name, generally [17 USCS § 406(a)]
3. —Name of transferee
4. —Trade name
5. Error in date [17 USCS § 406(b)]
6. Omission of name or date [17 USCS § 406(c)]

1. Generally

Use of Roman numerals, instead of Arabic, is sufficient. Stern v Jerome H. Remick & Co. (1910, CC NY) 175 F 282.

Annotations:

Abandonment of statutory copyright. 84 ALR2d 462.

2. Error in name, generally [17 USCS § 406(a)]

Notice on plaintiff's doll " 'Betty Boop' des. and Copyrighted by Fleischer Studios" was sufficient despite failure to add "Inc." to proprietor's name. Fleischer Studios, Inc. v Ralph A. Freundlich, Inc. (1934, CA2 NY) 73 F2d 276, 23 USPQ 295, cert den 294 US 717, 79 L Ed 1250, 55 S Ct 516.

Copyright is not forfeited, although copyright notice gives as name of proprietor name of wholly-owned subsidiary corporation of proprietor, if corporations have same officers, directors, and shareholders and subsidiary is promotional agency. National Comics Publications, Inc. v Fawcett Publications, Inc. (1951, CA2 NY) 191 F2d 594, 90 USPQ 274.

Copyright owner's true name need not be used on copyright notice so long as a name with which it is identified is used and no innocent persons are misled. Tennessee Fabricating Co. v Moultrie Mfg. Co. (1970, CA5 Ga) 421 F2d 279, 164 USPQ 481, cert den 398 US 928, 26 L Ed 2d 91, 90 S Ct 1819.

Where copyright notice in weekly periodicals contained trade name of copyrighter, notice of copyright in annual volume which combined weekly issues, containing different trade name of copyrighter, vitiated copyright. Record & Guide Co. v Bromley (1909, CC Pa) 175 F 156.

Person, who, in his notice of copyright, uses fictitious name which is unlawful for him to use, cannot bring suit to protect articles containing such notice. Haas v Leo Feist (1916, DC NY) 234 F 105.

Fact that copyright was secured in name of person who was not composer does not invalidate copyright. Sebring Pottery Co. v Steubenville Pottery Co. (1932, DC Ohio) 9 F Supp 383, 14 USPQ 46.

Valid copyright is not obtained where music as published gives fictitious name for that of composer, although publisher knew that third party had composed music and had not assigned same to publisher. Mills Music, Inc. v Cromwell Music, Inc. (1954, DC NY) 126 F Supp 54, 103 USPQ 84.

Copyright notice wherein copyright proprietor is identified as "Vera" is sufficient since "Vera" is dominant part of proprietor's full name (Scarves by Vera, Inc.), is proprietor's registered trade-mark, and is name by which proprietor is known throughout the industry; no innocent person could be misled. Scarves by Vera, Inc. v United Merchants & Mfrs., Inc. (1959, DC NY) 173 F Supp 625, 121 USPQ 578.

Copyright notices are sufficient since no innocent person could be misled by "Vera" accompanied by encircled "C", nor by encircled "C" followed by "Scarves by Vera"; notices disclose identity of proprietor, Scarves by Vera, Inc.; "Vera" is commonly used as abbreviated form of proprietor's name and has been registered as proprietor's trademark. Fabrex Corp. v Scarves by Vera, Inc. (DC NY) 129 USPQ 392.

Copyright notice is inadequate because "Denmark" appearing in notice is not name of copyright proprietor but identifies country of origin. Scandia House Enterprises, Inc. v Dam Things Establishment (1965, DC Dist Col) 243 F Supp 450, 146 USPQ 342.

Copyright notice using initials of proprietor is valid because proprietor is widely known by initials and has registered to do business under initials, and copyright notices on each page of loose-leaf supplements at back of uncopyrighted catalog are valid even though no notice appears on title page of catalog. L & L White Metal Casting Corp. v Joseph (1975, DC NY) 387 F Supp 1349, 185 USPQ 269.

Art design can use abbreviated copyright notice in form of initials on face of design providing full name appears elsewhere on article, and copyright notice in name of well-recognized subsidiary is permissible. American Greetings Corp. v Kleinfab Corp. (1975, DC NY) 400 F Supp 228, 188 USPQ 297.

Copyright notice abbreviating proprietor's name to "Cyn" mark consistently used and applied for registration as trademark is adequate notice of copyright. Cynthia Designs, Inc. v Robert Zentall, Inc. (1976, DC NY) 416 F Supp 510, 191 USPQ 35.

3. —Name of transferee

Where circumstances show consent by copyright proprietor, publication of work by mere licensee with licensee's name in notice of copyright may work forfeiture; consent is not shown, although proprietor acquiesced in form of notice, since proprietor questioned it and licensee said that it was normal procedure; predecessor section permits substitution of name of assignee as proprietor in copyright notice only if assignment has been recorded. Hirshon v United Artists Corp. (1957) 100 App DC 217, 243 F2d 640, 113 USPQ 110.

Notice need give only date and owner of copyright in derivative work, leaving reader to his own devices in ferreting out information as to original; copyright notice on published piano arrangement was proper although it bore only assignee's name and although assignment was not recorded in copyright office until later date. Nom Music, Inc. v Kaslin (1965, CA2 NY) 343 F2d 198, 145 USPQ 237.

Substitution of assignee's name in notice of copyright prior to recordation of assignment results in abandonment of copyright and dedication of work to public; Congressional policy is that notice of copyright shall contain, as proprietor, name of holder of record. Group Publishers, Inc. v Winchell (1949, DC NY) 86 F Supp 573, 83 USPQ 461.

If story published and copyrighted by magazine publisher in 1944 had been republished and copyrighted alone and without change by author in 1948 with no mention of 1944 copyright, it would have fallen into public domain, because substitution of name of assignee in notice of copyright prior to recordation of assignment from publisher results in abandonment of copyright and because recital of date later than actual copyright date invalidates copyright, but 1948 copyright is valid where author's revision of story was so substantial as to constitute new work. Wrench v Universal Pictures Co. (1952, DC NY) 104 F Supp 374, 92 USPQ 350.

Copyright notice reading "Copyright 1947, by The Baltimore Colts, Jo Lombardi and Benjamin Klasmer" is defective since there is no showing of assignment to Colts of any interest in copyright from owners Lombardi and Klasmer. Klasmer v Baltimore Football, Inc. (1961, DC Md) 200 F Supp 255, 132 USPQ 36.

If copyright owner publishes copyrighted material with defective notice of copyright, he abandons copyright and dedicates material to public; thus, owner of copyrighted map abandoned copyright and dedicated map to public by publication of substantially similar map bearing name of another party as copyright proprietor inasmuch as there is no evidence that valid, registered assignment of copyright was made by owner to other party prior to latter publication; therefore, notice did not contain name of proprietor of record. Carter v Hawaii Transp. Co. (1961, DC Hawaii) 201 F Supp 301, 133 USPQ 65.

Copyright is invalid if name of assignee was inserted in notice of copyright prior to recordation of assignment in copyright office; such insertion would be tantamount to dedication of copyrighted work to public; such dedication would vitiate statutory copyright. DeSilva Constr. Corp. v Herrald (1962, DC Fla) 213 F Supp 184, 137 USPQ 96.

Predecessor section is not violated where

names of assignor and assignee appear in copyright notice. Davis v E. I. Du Pont De Nemours & Co. (1965, DC NY) 240 F Supp 612, 145 USPQ 258.

Substitution of assignee's name in notice of copyright before recording assignment results in abandonment of copyright and dedication of work to public and raises issue of fact precluding preliminary injunction for copyright infringement of lace where defendant raises such issue. Kauber Bros., Inc. v Westchester Lace Work, Inc. (1974, DC NY) 181 USPQ 523.

Copyright on teddy bears is not defeated by use of name of unincorporated division of parent company in copyright notice, because basic notification requirements of statute are met, even though plaintiff's did not observe statutory requirements relative to assignment of copyright from one entity to another. Kuddle Toy, Inc. v Pussycat-Toy Co. (1974, DC NY) 183 USPQ 642.

4. —Trade name

Notice given under trade name is effective. Bleistein v Donaldson Lithographing Co. (1903) 188 US 239, 47 L Ed 460, 23 S Ct 298.

Even if copyright notice might not be sufficient for some purposes, because it used proprietor's trade-mark rather than its name, willful infringers wholly aware of existence of copyright are in no position to assert insufficiency of notice. Dan Kasoff, Inc. v Novelty Jewelry Co. (1962, CA2 NY) 309 F2d 745, 135 USPQ 234.

Plaintiff filed certificate that he was doing business as "T. W. Allen Company" but registered copyright in name of "The Thornton Allen Company"; difference in name in certificate and name on copyright was but slight variance and not material; name on copyright notice gave sufficient notice to public of name of owner of composition on which copyright was claimed and date when this right was obtained and this is all that predecessor statute requires. Allen v Walt Disney Productions, Ltd. (1941, DC NY) 41 F Supp 134, 50 USPQ 365.

Copyright is not void although name of proprietor in copyright notice is proprietor's trade name and although proprietor also uses other trade names. Powell v Stransky (1951, DC SD) 98 F Supp 434, 89 USPQ 310.

Copyright notice on jewelry is not defective although it merely gives proprietor's trade name; notice reveals proprietor's corporate identity inasmuch as trade name has been in widespread use by plaintiff for period of years. Hollywood Jewelry Mfg. Co. v Dushkin (1955, DC NY) 136 F Supp 738, 107 USPQ 354.

Copyright notice which only sets forth trade name of proprietor and fails to include corporate name is sufficient compliance with identification requirement of predecessor section; however, copyright symbol must also appear thereon. Kramer Jewelry Creations, Inc. v Capri Jewelry, Inc. (1956, DC NY) 143 F Supp 120, 111 USPQ 151.

Predecessor section is substantially complied with where copyright notice identifies proprietor as "Trifari"; proprietor is Trifari, Krussman & Fishel, Inc., which owns "Trifari" trade-mark registered in patent office; also "Trifari" is trade name adopted by proprietor's founders to do business at same address as proprietor. Trifari, Krussman & Fishel, Inc. v B. Steinberg-Kaslo Co. (1956, DC NY) 144 F Supp 577, 110 USPQ 487.

Purpose of notice requirement in predecessor section is to advise public of copyright proprietor's claim and to prevent innocent persons, unaware of copyright, from incurring infringement penalties; proprietor's name is sufficient in form if it gives notice of copyright to one who is looking for truth and desires to avoid infringement; thus, whether proprietor uses present trade name "Plasti-Personalities" in copyright notice or original trade name "Plastic Personalities," either designation gives notice of copyright to interested persons and is sufficient to lead them to proprietor. Doran v Sunset House Distributing Corp. (1961, DC Cal) 197 F Supp 940, 131 USPQ 94, affd (CA9 Cal) 304 F2d 251, 134 USPQ 4, and (disapproved on other grounds L. Batlin & Son, Inc. v Snyder (CA2 NY) 536 F2d 486, cert den 429 US 857, 50 L Ed 2d 135, 97 S Ct 156).

Copyright notice properly identifies proprietor where it bears word which has been registered as proprietor's trademark and which has been extensively advertised so that it has become known in trade as indicative of proprietor. Dan Kasoff, Inc. v Gresco Jewelry Co. (1962, DC NY) 204 F Supp 694, 133 USPQ 438, affd (CA2 NY) 308 F2d 806, 135 USPQ 209.

Copyrighted catalog did not fall into public domain even though it also was published by proprietor, under different trade name, and by corporation owned and controlled by same proprietor, and although such latter publications, respectively, as copyright proprietors, since such company and corporation constituted merely alter ego for proprietor; it is noteworthy that infringer, who deliberately copied from catalog in which copyright notice contained proprietor's name, was not aware of latter publications at that time and was not prejudiced thereby. B & B Auto Supply, Inc. v Plesser (1962, DC NY) 205 F Supp 36, 133 USPQ 247.

5. Error in date [17 USCS § 406(b)]

Where title was deposited in 1867 and copyright notice was dated 1866, variance was immaterial. Callaghan v Myers (1888) 128 US 617, 32 L Ed 547, 9 S Ct 177.

Where essential steps have been taken to secure copyright of unpublished song, slight variance in dates does not destroy proof of copyright. Turner & Dahnken v Crowley (1918, CA9 Cal) 252 F 749.

Fact that book published in 1915, carried copyright notice of 1914, which was year in which printing was begun, is of no consequence, since error is in favor of public, notice claiming year less than Copyright Act allows. American Code Co. v Bensinger (1922, CA2 NY) 282 F 829.

Innocent misstatement or clerical error, alleging date of publication later than actual date, in affidavit and certificate of registration, unaccompanied by fraud or intent to extend statutory period of copyright protection, does not invalidate copyright, and it is not thereby rendered incapable of supporting infringement action. Advisers, Inc. v Wiesen-Hart, Inc. (1956, CA6 Ohio) 238 F2d 706, 111 USPQ 318, cert den 353 US 949, 1 L Ed 2d 858, 77 S Ct 861.

Where notice of copyright gave date as 1847 when in fact date was 1846, title does not comply with predecessor statute. Baker v Taylor (1848, CC NY) F Cas No 782.

It is doubtful whether insertion of wrong year in notice of copyright, through mistake, is fatal to action for infringement. Schumacher v Wogram (1888, CC NY) 35 F 210.

Copyright secured in name of person other than composer was valid although mistake was made as to date of publication in affidavit attached to application. Sebring Pottery Co. v Steubenville Pottery Co. (1932, DC Ohio) 9 F Supp 383, 14 USPQ 46.

Where sheet music bears date, in notice of copyright, that is prior to time that actual copyright was obtained, error does not affect validity of copyright, but merely shortens duration of copyright period. Southern Music Pub. Co. v Bibo-Lang, Inc. (1935, DC NY) 10 F Supp 972, 26 USPQ 321.

Fact that application for copyright registration claims date of publication few days prior to actual publication does not invalidate copyright as it is mistake in favor of public; although copyright time runs against copyright owner, he cannot recover for infringement during period prior to actual publication. Basevi v Edward O'Toole Co. (1939, DC NY) 26 F Supp 41, 40 USPQ 333.

Although apparently no date was necessary on copyrighted artificial flower, copyright notice on stem contained 1961 date despite fact that publication date was 1959; however, flower also bore on leaf another copyright notice which correctly gave date as 1959; since notices differ as to date, this may be confusing, but notice is not thereby rendered so affirmatively misleading as to justify invalidating copyright. Prestige Floral, Societe Anonyme v California Artificial Flower Co. (1962, DC NY) 201 F Supp 287, 132 USPQ 350.

If catalog published in 1957 were merely republication of previously copyrighted catalog, recital of 1957 date in notice of copyright would render copyright invalid as attempt to extend copyright protection beyond statutory period; however, copyright is not invalidated inasmuch as 1957 catalog contained changes which are substantial and sufficient enough to constitute 1957 catalog new work subject to copyright; such material as is newly or additionally presented in 1957 catalog must be regarded as newly copyrighted, while at same time subsisting copyrights on repeated matter in catalog remain valid, but without any extension in their scope or duration. B & B Auto Supply, Inc. v Plesser (1962, DC NY) 205 F Supp 36, 133 USPQ 247.

In absence of any suggestion of prejudicial reliance, variance of 27 days between copyright date and notice date does not invalidate copyright. Davis v E. I. Du Pont De Nemours & Co. (1965, DC NY) 240 F Supp 612, 145 USPQ 258.

Since misdating (1961 instead of 1963) of copyright notice was in favor of public, error does not result in abandonment of copyright into the public domain. Frederick Chusid & Co. v Marshall Leeman & Co. (1968, DC NY) 279 F Supp 913, 158 USPQ 188.

Innocent use of later date of reprinting of copyrighted map instead of earlier date of publication of map in copyright notice on map does not invalidate copyright. Newton v Voris (1973, DC Or) 364 F Supp 562, 180 USPQ 262.

6. Omission of name or date [17 USCS § 406(c)]

Owner of copyright of picture who omitted his name from all copies thereof could not obtain relief under predecessor section as this section applied only where omission is on limited number of copies. Goes Lithographing Co. v Apt Lithographic Co. (1936, DC NY) 14 F Supp 620, 30 USPQ 119.

§ 407. Deposit of copies or phonorecords for Library of Congress

(a) Except as provided by subsection (c), and subject to the provisions of subsection (e), the owner of copyright or of the exclusive right of publication in a work published with notice of copyright in the United States shall deposit, within three months after the date of such publication—

(1) two complete copies of the best edition; or

(2) if the work is a sound recording, two complete phonorecords of the best edition, together with any printed or other visually perceptible material published with such phonorecords.

Neither the deposit requirements of this subsection nor the acquisition provisions of subsection (e) are conditions of copyright protection.

(b) The required copies or phonorecords shall be deposited in the Copyright Office for the use or disposition of the Library of Congress. The Register of Copyrights shall, when requested by the depositor and upon payment of the fee prescribed by section 708 [17 USCS § 708], issue a receipt for the deposit.

(c) The Register of Copyrights may be regulation exempt any categories of material from the deposit requirements of this section, or require deposit of only one copy or phonorecord with respect to any categories. Such regulations shall provide either for complete exemption from the deposit requirements of this section, or for alternative forms of deposit aimed at providing a satisfactory archival record of a work without imposing practical or financial hardships on the depositor, where the individual author is the owner of copyright in a pictorial, graphic, or sculptural work and (i) less than five copies of the work have been published, or (ii) the work has been published in a limited edition consisting of numbered copies, the monetary value of which would make the mandatory deposit of two copies of the best edition of the work burdensome, unfair, or unreasonable.

(d) At any time after publication of a work as provided by subsection (a), the Register of Copyrights may make written demand for the required deposit on any of the persons obligated to make the deposit under subsection (a). Unless deposit is made within three months after the demand is received, the person or persons on whom the demand was made are liable—

(1) to a fine of not more than $250 for each work; and

(2) to pay into a specially designated fund in the Library of Congress the total retail price of the copies or phonorecords demanded, or, if no retail price has been fixed, the reasonable cost of the Library of Congress of acquiring them; and

(3) to pay a fine of $2,500, in addition to any fine or liability imposed under clauses (1) and (2), if such person willfully or repeatedly fails or refuses to comply with such a demand.

(e) With respect to transmission programs that have been fixed and transmitted to the public in the United States but have not been published, the Register of Copyrights shall, after consulting with the Librarian of Congress and other interested organizations and officials, establish regulations governing the acquisition, through deposit or otherwise, of copies or phonorecords of such programs for the collections of the Library of Congress.

(1) The Librarian of Congress shall be permitted, under the standards and conditions set forth in such regulations, to make a fixation of a transmission program directly from a transmission to the public, and to reproduce one copy or phonorecord from such fixation for archival purposes.

(2) Such regulations shall also provide standards and procedures by which the Register of Copyrights may make written demand, upon the owner of the right of transmission in the United States, for the deposit of a copy or phonorecord of a specific transmission program. Such deposit may, at the option of the owner of the right of transmission in the United States, be accomplished by gift, by loan for purposes of reproduction, or by sale at a price not to exceed the cost of reproducing and supplying the copy or phonorecord. The regulations established under this clause shall provide reasonable periods of not less than three months for compliance with a demand, and shall allow for extensions of such periods and adjustments in the scope of the demand or the methods for fulfilling it, as reasonably warranted by the circumstances. Willful failure or refusal to comply with the conditions prescribed by such regulations shall subject the owner of the right of transmission in the United States to liability for an amount, not to exceed the cost of reproducing and supplying the copy or phonorecord in question, to be paid into a specially designated fund in the Library of Congress.

(3) Nothing in this subsection shall be construed to require the making or retention, for purposes of deposit, of any copy or phonorecord of an unpublished transmission program, the transmission of which occurs before the receipt of a specific written demand as provided by clause (2).

(4) No activity undertaken in compliance with regulations prescribed under clauses (1) or (2) of this subsection shall result in liability if intended solely to assist in the acquisition of copies or phonorecords under this subsection.

(Added Oct. 19, 1976, P. L. 94-553, Title I, § 101, 90 Stat. 2579.)

HISTORY; ANCILLARY LAWS AND DIRECTIVES

Effective date of section:
Section 102 of Act Oct. 19, 1976, P. L. 94-553, 90 Stat. 2598 provided that this section "becomes effective on January 1, 1978".

Other provisions:
Copyright secured by publication before December 31, 1977. Act Oct. 19, 1976, P. L. 94-553, Title I, § 110, 90 Stat. 2600, provided: "The

demand and penalty provisions of section 14 of title 17 [former 17 USCS § 14] as it existed on December 31, 1977, apply to any work in which copyright has been secured by publication with notice of copyright on or before that date, but any deposit and registration made after that date in response to a demand under that section shall be made in accordance with the provisions of title 17 [17 USCS] as amended by the first section of this Act [section 101 of Act Oct. 19, 1976, which appears as 17 USCS §§ 101 et seq.]."

CROSS REFERENCES

"Best edition" defined, 17 USCS § 101.
"Copies" defined, 17 USCS § 101.
"Copyright owner" defined, 17 USCS § 101.
Retention and disposition of articles deposited in Copyright Office, 17 USCS § 704.
This section referred to in 17 USCS §§ 408, 704, 708.

RESEARCH GUIDE

Am Jur:
18 Am Jur 2d, Copyright and Literary Property §§ 55, 63, 128, 156.

Forms:
6 Federal Procedural Forms L Ed, Copyrights § 17:95.

Annotations:
Requirements as to deposit of copies of work in copyright office under § 13 of Federal Copyright Act (17 USCS § 13) as prerequisite to infringement action. 16 ALR Fed 595.

INTERPRETIVE NOTES AND DECISIONS

1. Generally
2. Deposit as condition of copyright
3. Proof or allegation of deposit
4. Time of deposit

1. Generally

There is no predecessor statutory provision for second filing of photograph or description, or for filing any amendments thereto. Caliga v Inter Ocean Newspaper Co. (1909) 215 US 182, 54 L Ed 150, 30 S Ct 38.

Prompt deposit when deemed necessary should be enforced through actual notice by register. Washingtonian Publishing Co. v Pearson (1939) 306 US 30, 83 L Ed 470, 59 S Ct 397, reh den 306 US 668, 83 L Ed 1063, 59 S Ct 588.

Requirement of prior statute for deposit of description and photograph of painting was not fulfilled by deposit of photograph only with title "Four-in-Hand." Bennett v Carr (1899, CA2 NY) 96 F 213.

Predecessor section is complied with by depositing complete episode, not summary or outline, which is intended to constitute first of series of connected episodes, that being only one which authors had written. Marx v United States (1938, CA9 Cal) 96 F2d 204, 37 USPQ 380.

Where only one edition of book has been published, copies thereof deposited with register of copyrights are of best edition although book might not be suitable for inclusion in "library" collection for public use. Bouve v Twentieth Century-Fox Film Corp. (1941) 74 App DC 271, 122 F2d 51, 50 USPQ 338.

Where company had samples of an object and placed photographs in a catalogue to advertise, company was not required to submit to the register of copyrights copies of the object, because there was no sale and no other reproduction for sale or publication for sale, since the company was not in a position to realize any benefits from such action. Hub Floral Corp. v Royal Brass Corp. (1972, CA2 NY) 454 F2d 1226, 172 USPQ 418, 16 ALR Fed 588.

Mailing of copies after printing and before formal publication is sufficient. Chapman v Ferry (1883, CC Or) 18 F 539.

Copies may be both delivered and mailed. Scribner v Henry G. Allen Co. (1890, CC NY) 43 F 680.

Cutting out and depositing pages containing article in bound volume of encyclopedia is sufficient compliance with "best edition" provision of predecessor statute. Black v Henry G. Allen Co. (1893, CC NY) 56 F 764.

Ignorance of recent change of law in reference to deposit of copies is no excuse for noncompliance therewith. Osgood v A. S. Aloe Instrument Co. (1897, CC Mo) 83 F 470.

Deposit of two copies of song with Librarian of Congress, was "publication." Stern v Jerome H. Remick & Co. (1910, CC NY) 175 F 282.

Book consisting of comic strips was published with proper copyright notice; publication of certain or all of its parts in newspapers, under authority of copyright proprietor subsequent to initial publication in book, constitutes mere republication of parts and proprietor should not be required to deposit copies of newspapers or to apply for special registration in respect to re-published parts. King Features Syndicate, Inc. v Bouve (DC DC) 48 USPQ 237.

Complaint for copyright infringement is dismissed where it merely alleges proper deposit of two copies of work, but admits that certificate of registration has not been obtained. Algonquin Music, Inc. v Mills Music, Inc. (1950, DC NY) 93 F Supp 268, 86 USPQ 481.

Annotations:

Requirements as to deposit of copies of work in copyright office under § 13 of Federal Copyright Act (17 USCS § 13) as prerequisite to infringement action. 16 ALR Fed 595.

2. Deposit as condition of copyright

It is unnecessary to deposit anything to secure copyright of published work; it is only necessary to publish with notice of copyright; deposit of copies is not required primarily in order to insure complete permanent collection of all copyrighted works open to public. Washington Publishing Co. v Pearson (1939) 306 US 30, 83 L Ed 470, 59 S Ct 397, 40 USPQ 190, reh den 306 US 668, 83 L Ed 1063, 59 S Ct 588.

Where domestic and foreign editions of book were published and copyright was obtained on domestic edition by compliance with copyright law, failure to file copies of foreign edition did not affect its copyright. G. & C. Merriam Co. v United Dictionary Co. (1906, CA7 Ill) 146 F 354, affd 208 US 260, 52 L Ed 478, 28 S Ct 290.

Predecessor section implies that copyright is secured by publication other than deposit with copyright office. American Visuals Corp. v Holland (1956, CA2 NY) 239 F2d 740, 111 USPQ 288.

Deposit of copies after publication was not required as prerequisite to title to copyright. Jollie v Jaques (1850, CC NY) F Cas No 7437.

To secure copyright in photograph it is not necessary that copies should be mailed after publication. Falk v Donaldson (1893, CC NY) 57 F 32.

Copyright proprietor, having complied with predecessor section, court holds that demands and notices by register of copyrights, purporting to be pursuant to predecessor section, that proprietor should deposit copies of newspapers in which copyrighted matter was republished and should apply for special registration as to each item so republished, should be vacated and set aside. King Features Syndicate, Inc. v Bouve (DC DC) 48 USPQ 237.

Failure to promptly file copies of copyrighted editions of newspaper does not invalidate copyright. Massapequa Publishing Co. v Observer, Inc. (DC NY) 126 USPQ 229.

Annotations:

Requirements as to deposit of copies of work in copyright office under § 13 of Federal Copyright Act (17 USCS § 13) as prerequisite to infringement action. 16 ALR Fed 595.

3. Proof or allegation of deposit

Memorandum endorsed on bottom of certificate of Librarian of Congress is not part of certificate and is not admissible to prove that copies of book were deposited. Merrell v Tice (1882) 104 US 557, 26 L Ed 854.

Certificate of clerk of district court is prima facie evidence of deposit of title; signed memorandum on same paper as certificate is prima facie evidence of deposit. Callaghan v Myers (1888) 128 US 617, 32 L Ed 547, 9 S Ct 177.

In suit for infringement, bill alleging compliance with predecessor section by deposit of "two copies of the best edition" was sufficient. Gerlach-Barklow Co. v Morris & Bendien, Inc. (1927, CA2 NY) 23 F2d 159.

Oral proof of deposit of copies and production of librarian's receipt is sufficient evidence. Blume v Spear (1887, CC NY) 30 F 629.

Bill that alleges that author deposited within 10 days after publication, in office of Library of Congress at Washington, two copies of book, is sufficient against demurrer although it does not allege all prior steps. Scribner v Henry G. Allen Co. (1892, CC NY) 49 F 854.

Averment in bill that "your orator did all the things required by law to be done in order to secure to himself the full enjoyment of all rights and privileges granted by the laws of the land governing copyrights," is not sufficient to show that plaintiff has filed two copies after publication. Burnell v Chown (1895, CC Ohio) 69 F 993.

Evidence by complainant that he personally inclosed two copies of his book in package addressed to Librarian of Congress and deposited same in mail constituted sufficient proof of mailing of copies, though register of copyrights certified that he had made search and could find no copies of book on file. Patterson v J. S. Ogilvie Pub. Co. (1902, CC NY) 119 F 451.

Certificate showing that two copies of book were deposited is competent evidence of such fact in action for infringement of copyright of book, but certificate does not per se establish copyright. Huebsch v Arthur H. Crist Co. (1914, DC NY) 209 F 885.

Uncontradicted testimony as to depositing of copyright books in mail addressed to register of copyrights was sufficient evidence as to compliance with predecessor statute. Maddux v Grey (1930, DC Cal) 43 F2d 441.

Findings of fact and conclusions of law as to publication and deposit of copies made by register of copyrights may be reviewed by court in suit against register and are neither conclusive nor binding on court; if erroneous, they may be rectified by court. King Features Syndicate, Inc. v Bouve (DC DC) 48 USPQ 237.

4. Time of deposit

Where copies are not filed within proper time after publication, there can be no copyright. Wheaton v Peters (1834) 33 US 591, 8 L Ed 1055.

Deposit of copies one day before publication instead of within ten days thereafter was substantial compliance. Belford v Scribner (1892) 144 US 488, 36 L Ed 514, 12 S Ct 734.

Mere delay in making deposit of copies of copyrighted material is not enough to cause forfeiture of copyright distinctly granted on publication with notice; lapse of 14 months between publication with notice and deposit in copyright office did not vitiate retroactive right of recovery for unauthorized use ad interim. Washingtonian

Publishing Co. v Pearson (1939) 306 US 30, 83 L Ed 470, 59 S Ct 397, 40 USPQ 190, reh den 306 US 668, 83 L Ed 1063, 59 S Ct 588.

Where plaintiff deposited copies same day 50 copies were received from printer, such copies being retained by plaintiff or sent to branch offices although no general distribution was made until two days later, there was sufficient publication to comply with predecessor statute. No-Leak-O Piston Ring Co. v Norris (1921, CA4 Md) 277 F 951.

Where work consists of series of volumes, delivery of first volume within required time and others before piracy has been committed or action begun is sufficient compliance. Dwight v Appleton (1843, CC NY) F Cas No 4215.

Direct proof to show seasonable deposit of copies of publication for purposes of predecessor copyright statute is not required where it is beyond doubt that such copies were forwarded so early that defendant could not possibly have been prejudiced by any delay. Ladd v Oxnard (1896, CC Mass) 75 F 703.

Deposit of copies with register two weeks before publication does not defeat copyright where such deposit continued after publication; owner who fails to deposit promptly may do so without prejudice after delinquency. Joe Mittenthal, Inc. v Irving Berlin, Inc. (1923, DC NY) 291 F 714.

Where there was publication with notice of copyright in January and deposit in March the delay did not prejudice rights. Freedman v Milnag Leasing Corp. (1937, DC NY) 20 F Supp 802, 35 USPQ 184.

Acquisition of federal copyright requires (1) publication of work with notice and (2) prompt deposit in copyright office or in mail of two complete copies of best edition of publication; delay of 13 years in making deposit does not invalidate copyright; so far as institution of civil action is concerned, delay merely means that no action can be maintained until deposit has been made. Silvers v Russell (1953, DC Cal) 113 F Supp 119, 98 USPQ 376.

Copyright may be completed by depositing two copies after publication at any time, when book had not previously been published by anyone else. 1 OAG 532.

§ 408. Copyright registration in general

(a) Registration permissive. At any time during the subsistence of copyright in any published or unpublished work, the owner of copyright or of any exclusive right in the work may obtain registration of the copyright claim by delivering to the Copyright Office the deposit specified by this section, together with the application and fee specified by sections 409 and 708 [17 USCS §§ 409 and 708]. Subject to the provisions of section 405(a) [17 USCS § 405(a)], such registration is not a condition of copyright protection.

(b) Deposit for copyright registration. Except as provided by subsection (c), the material deposited for registration shall include—

(1) in the case of an unpublished work, one complete copy or phonorecord;

(2) in the case of a published work, two complete copies or phonorecords of the best edition;

(3) in the case of a work first published outside the United States, one complete copy or phonorecord as so published;

(4) in the case of a contribution to a collective work, one complete copy or phonorecord of the best edition of the collective work.

Copies or phonorecords deposited for the Library of Congress under section 407 [17 USCS § 407] may be used to satisfy the deposit provisions of this section, if they are accompanied by the prescribed application and fee, and by any additional identifying material that the Register may, by regulation, require. The Register shall also prescribe regulations establishing requirements under which copies or phonorecords acquired for the Library of Congress under subsection (e) of section 407 [17 USCS § 407(e)], otherwise than by deposit, may be used to satisfy the deposit provisions of this section.

(c) Administrative classification and optional deposit. (1) The Register of Copyrights is authorized to specify by regulation the administrative classes into which works are to be placed for purposes of deposit and registration, and the nature of the copies or phonorecords to be deposited in the various classes specified. The regulations may require or permit, for particular classes, the deposit of identifying material instead of copies or phonorecords, the deposit of only one copy or phonorecord where two would normally be required, or a single registration for a group of related works. This administrative classification of works has no significance with respect to the subject matter of copyright or the exclusive rights provided by this title [17 USCS § 408].

(2) Without prejudice to the general authority provided under clause (1), the Register of Copyrights shall establish regulations specifically permitting a single registration for a group of works by the same individual author, all first published as contributions to periodicals, including newspapers, within a twelve-month period, on the basis of a single deposit, application, and registration fee, under all of the following conditions—

(A) if each of the works as first published bore a separate copyright notice, and the name of the owner of copyright in the work, or an abbreviation by which the name can be recognized, or a generally known alternative designation of the owner was the same in each notice; and

(B) if the deposit consists of one copy of the entire issue of the periodical, or of the entire section in the case of a newspaper, in which each contribution was first published; and

(C) if the application identifies each work separately, including the periodical containing it and its date of first publication.

(3) As an alternative to separate renewal registrations under subsection (a) of section 304 [17 USCS § 304(a)], a single renewal registration may be made for a group of works by the same individual author, all first published as contributions to periodicals, including newspapers, upon the filing of a single application and fee, under all of the following conditions:

(A) the renewal claimant or claimants, and the basis of claim or claims under section 304(a) [17 USCS § 304(a)], is the same for each of the works; and

(B) the works were all copyrighted upon their first publication, either through separate copyright notice and registration or by virtue of a general copyright notice in the periodical issue as a whole; and

(C) the renewal application and fee are received not more than twenty-eight or less than twenty-seven years after the thirty-first day of December of the calendar year in which all of the works were first published; and

(D) the renewal application identifies each work separately, including the periodical containing it and its date of first publication.

(d) Corrections and amplifications. The Register may also establish, by regulation, formal procedures for the filing of an application for supplementary registration, to correct an error in a copyright registration or to amplify the information given in a registration. Such application shall be accompanied by the fee provided by section 708 [17 USCS § 708], and shall clearly identify the registration to be corrected or amplified. The information contained in a supplementary registration augments but does not supersede that contained in the earlier registration.

(e) Published edition of previously registered work. Registration for the first published edition of a work previously registered in unpublished form may be made even though the work as published is substantially the same as the unpublished version.

(Added Oct. 19, 1976, P. L. 94-553, Title I, § 101, 90 Stat. 2580.)

HISTORY; ANCILLARY LAWS AND DIRECTIVES

Effective date of section:
Section 102 of Act Oct. 19, 1976, P. L. 94-553, 90 Stat. 2598 provided that this section "becomes effective on January 1, 1978".

CROSS REFERENCES

"Copies" defined, 17 USCS § 101.
"Phonorecords" defined, 17 USCS § 101.
Compilations and derivative works, 17 USCS § 103.
Effect of omission of notice of copyright, 17 USCS § 405(a).
Deposit of copies or phonorecords for Library of Congress, 17 USCS § 407.
Notification of filing and determination of actions, 17 USCS § 508.
Copyright Office regulations, 17 USCS § 702.
This section referred to in 17 USCS §§ 302, 405, 601, 704, 708, 710.

RESEARCH GUIDE

Am Jur:
18 Am Jur 2d, Copyright and Literary Property §§ 55, 63, 128.

Annotations:
Requirements as to deposit of copies of work in copyright office under § 13 of Federal Copyright Act (17 USCS § 13) as prerequisite to infringement action. 16 ALR Fed 595.

INTERPRETIVE NOTES AND DECISIONS

1. Generally [17 USCS § 408(a)]
2. Deposit for copyright registration [17 USCS § 408(b)]
3. Administrative classification and optional deposit [17 USCS § 408(c)]
4. Corrections and amplifications [17 USCS § 408(d)]

1. Generally

Subsequent registration of work of art published as element in manufactured article is not misuse of copyright. Mazer v Stein (1954) 347 US 201, 98 L Ed 630, 74 S Ct 460, 100 USPQ 325, reh den 347 US 949, 98 L Ed 1096, 74 S Ct 637.

Register of copyrights has no power to refuse or deny registration of claim of copyright which is entitled to registration under Copyright Act; whether applicant or claimant has complied with law so that his claim is entitled to registration raises questions of fact and law to be decided by court; register has no power to decide such questions, especially where deposit of copies and application filed, when read together as they should be, are in apparent compliance with predecessor Act. King Features Syndicate, Inc. v Bouve (DC DC) 48 USPQ 237.

Copyright is not destroyed because assignee applied for copyright registration before it filed with copyright office assignment pursuant to power of attorney. Mills Music, Inc. v Cromwell Music, Inc. (1954, DC NY) 126 F Supp 54, 103 USPQ 84.

Inconsequential differences between marketed coin bank and coin bank shown in copyright registration are insufficient to invalidate registration. Goldman-Morgen, Inc. v Dan Brechner & Co. (1976, DC NY) 190 USPQ 478.

2. Deposit for copyright registration [17 USCS § 408(b)]

Depositing printed copy, instead of typewritten or manuscript copy as specified in office rule was sufficient for unpublished song. Turner & Dahnken v Crowley (1918, CA9 Cal) 252 F 749.

Copy of continuous textile design deposited with register of copyrights sets no more than outer limit within which published copies must bear statutory notice. H. M. Kolbe Co. v Armgus Textile Co. (1963, CA2 NY) 315 F2d 70, 99 ALR2d 390, 137 USPQ 9.

Register of copyrights had no power to refuse to register copyright on ground that writing sought to be copyrighted consisted merely of "page proof" of contribution to newspaper; book in question consisted of sheets printed on one side only, each sheet bearing copyright notice; fact that it was apparent from face of book that purpose was to have it published in installments in periodicals does not prevent registration of whole as book. United States ex rel. Twentieth Century-Fox Film Corp. v Bouve (1940, DC Dist Col) 33 F Supp 462, 45 USPQ 411, affd 74 App DC 271, 122 F2d 51, 50 USPQ 338.

One carbon copy of intended radio talk with

statutory fee deposited with register of copyrights procures copyright. Vinick v Charm Publications, Inc. (DC NY) 46 USPQ 510.

By depositing in copyright office or in mail addressed thereto two copies of best editions of books then published together with applications for registration of claims to copyright in books, same being on duly completed copyright office forms, accompanied by payment or tender of fee of $2 for registration as to each volume of books, predecessor section was duly complied with not only in respect to books but also as to every copyrightable component part thereof. King Features Syndicate, Inc. v Bouve (DC DC) 48 USPQ 237.

Annotations:

Requirements as to deposit of copies of work in copyright office under § 13 of Federal Copyright Act (17 USCS § 13) as prerequisite to infringement action. 16 ALR Fed 595.

3. Administrative classification and optional deposit [17 USCS § 408(c)]

Where poem was registered as periodical within classification of "books" and not as "dramatic or dramatico-musical composition," despite provision of predecessor statute that errors in classification shall not invalidate or impair copyright protection, doubt may exist whether copyright proprietor is permitted in infringement suit to say that his work belongs in class other than that in which it was actually registered. Corcoran v Montgomery Ward & Co. (1941, CA9 Cal) 121 F2d 572, 50 USPQ 274, cert den 314 US 687, 86 L Ed 550, 62 S Ct 300.

Register may refuse to issue certificate until required fee is paid and other formal requisites of act have been satisfied, but he has no power to exercise uncontrolled discretion in refusing registration of material which is subject to copyright, merely because he disagrees with author as to how it should be classified. Bouve v Twentieth Century-Fox Film Corp. (1941) 74 App DC 271, 122 F2d 51, 50 USPQ 338.

It is not error for copyright proprietor to fail to specify proper classification of copyrighted model airplane kits where classifications are not accurate descriptions of subject matter to be copyrighted, and any error in classification should not invalidate or impair copyright. Monogram Models, Inc. v Industro Motive Corp. (1974, CA6 Mich) 492 F2d 1281, 181 USPQ 425, cert den 419 US 843, 42 L Ed 2d 71, 95 S Ct 76.

Fact that sketch is improperly classified as dramatic composition rather than dramatico-musical composition would not affect its validity. Green v Luby (1909, CC NY) 177 F 287.

Classification of copyrights as books or dramatic compositions is not absolutely rigid and is provided partly for convenience of register's office. Seltzer v Sunbrock (1938, DC Cal) 22 F Supp 621, 37 USPQ 491.

Design or exact copy of it can be copyrighted as work of art; consequently, its classification as a reproduction of a work of art is mere error and does not impair copyright protection. Peter Pan Fabrics, Inc. v Dan River Mills, Inc. (1969, DC NY) 295 F Supp 1366, 161 USPQ 119, affd (CA2 NY) 415 F2d 1007, 163 USPQ 670.

Classification of motion picture as "other than photoplay" for registration purposes does not invalidate copyright, even if erroneous, especially in absence of evidence of intentional or fraudulent deception. Mitchell Bros. Film Group v Cinema Adult Theater (1976, DC Tex) 192 USPQ 138.

Existence of separate classifications for copyrighted works does not mean that works copyrighted under one subject matter class cannot infringe copyrights secured under another, so that motion picture can infringe copyright in novel, even though motion picture has become public domain. Filmvideo Releasing Corp. v Hastings (1976, DC NY) 426 F Supp 690, 193 USPQ 305.

4. Corrections and amplifications [17 USCS § 408(d)]

Certificate of registration may be corrected by copyright office. Advisers, Inc. v Wiesen-Hart, Inc. (1956, CA6 Ohio) 238 F2d 706, 111 USPQ 318, cert den 353 US 949, 1 L Ed 2d 858, 77 S Ct 861.

Although book was published and distributed early in 1943, affidavit accompanying application for copyright registration erroneously stated that December 20, 1943, was date of publication; all copies of book contained notice of copyright; inaccuracy as to date of publication, standing alone, did not affect validity of copyright. Ziegelheim v Flohr (1954, DC NY) 119 F Supp 324, 100 USPQ 189.

In absence of prejudice, innocent clerical error in application and certificate of copyright registration, unaccompanied by fraud, does not invalidate copyright or render it incapable of supporting infringement action. Alart Associates, Inc. v Aptaker (1968, DC NY) 279 F Supp 268, 156 USPQ 559, app dismd (CA2 NY) 402 F2d 779.

§ 409. Application for copyright registration

The application for copyright registration shall be made on a form prescribed by the Register of Copyrights and shall include—

(1) the name and address of the copyright claimant;

(2) in the case of a work other than an anonymous or pseudonymous work, the name and nationality or domicile of the author or authors, and, if one or more of the authors is dead, the dates of their deaths;

(3) if the work is anonymous or pseudonymous, the nationality or domicile of the author or authors;

(4) in the case of a work made for hire, a statement to this effect;

(5) if the copyright claimant is not the author, a brief statement of how the claimant obtained ownership of the copyright;

(6) the title of the work, together with any previous or alternative titles under which the work can be identified;

(7) the year in which creation of the work was completed;

(8) if the work has been published, the date and nation of its first publication;

(9) in the case of a compilation or derivative work, an identification of any preexisting work or works that it is based on or incorporates, and a brief, general statement of the additional material covered by the copyright claim being registered;

(10) in the case of a published work containing material of which copies are required by section 601 [17 USCS § 601] to be manufactured in the United States, the names of the persons or organizations who performed the processes specified by subsection (c) of section 601 [17 USCS § 601(c)] with respect to that material, and the places where those processes were performed; and

(11) any other information regarded by the Register of Copyrights as bearing upon the preparation or identification of the work or the existence, ownership, or duration of the copyright.

(Added Oct. 19, 1976, P. L. 94-553, Title I, § 101, 90 Stat. 2582.)

HISTORY; ANCILLARY LAWS AND DIRECTIVES

Effective date of section:
Section 102 of Act Oct. 19, 1976, P. L. 94-553, 90 Stat. 2598 provided that this section "becomes effective on January 1, 1978".

CROSS REFERENCES

"Anonymous work" defined, 17 USCS § 101.
"Compilation" defined, 17 USCS § 101.
"Derivative work" defined, 17 USCS § 101.
"Pseudonymous work" defined, 17 USCS § 101.
"Publication" defined, 17 USCS § 101.
"Work made for hire" defined, 17 USCS § 101.
Manufacturing requirement, 17 USCS § 601.
This section referred to in 17 USCS §§ 408, 506.

INTERPRETIVE NOTES AND DECISIONS

Registration is valid, although on application made before there was publication with copyright notice or deposit of copies in copyright office, since application was not acted on until after publication with copyright notice and deposit of copies. United States v Backer (1943, CA2 NY) 134 F2d 533, 57 USPQ 133.

Affidavit of agent of proprietor of foreign copyright made pursuant to predecessor section did not invalidate United States copyright, though agent did not actually see type set or binding of book, but employed printer to do printing and furnished him copy. Meccano, Ltd.

v Wagner (1916, DC Ohio) 234 F 912, mod (CA6 Ohio) 246 F 603.

Copyright is not defective because author's application for copyright registration erroneously failed to state that book was new edition. Wrench v Universal Pictures Co. (1952, DC NY) 104 F Supp 374, 92 USPQ 350.

Register of copyrights is vested with some discretionary powers of investigation and may require satisfactory showing of compliance with plain conditions prescribed by copyright law. 30 OAG 422.

§ 410. Registration of claim and issuance of certificate

(a) When, after examination, the Register of Copyrights determines that, in accordance with the provisions of this title [17 USCS §§ 101 et seq.], the material deposited constitutes copyrightable subject matter and that the other legal and formal requirements of this title [17 USCS §§ 101 et seq.] have been met, the Register shall register the claim and issue to the applicant a certificate of registration under the seal of the Copyright Office. The certificate shall contain the information given in the application, together with the number and effective date of the registration.

(b) In any case in which the Register of Copyrights determines that, in accordance with the provisions of this title [17 USCS §§ 101 et seq.], the material deposited does not constitute copyrightable subject matter or that the claim is invalid for any other reason, the Register shall refuse registration and shall notify the applicant in writing of the reasons for such refusal.

(c) In any judicial proceedings the certificate of a registration made before or within five years after first publication of the work shall constitute prima facie evidence of the validity of the copyright and of the facts stated in the certificate. The evidentiary weight to be accorded the certificate of a registration made thereafter shall be within the discretion of the court.

(d) The effective date of a copyright registration is the day on which an application, deposit, and fee, which are later determined by the Register of Copyrights or by a court of competent jurisdiction to be acceptable for registration, have all been received in the Copyright Office.
(Added Oct. 19, 1976, P. L. 94-553, Title I, § 101, 90 Stat. 2582.)

HISTORY; ANCILLARY LAWS AND DIRECTIVES

Effective date of section:
Section 102 of Act Oct. 19, 1976, P. L. 94-553, 90 Stat. 2598 provided that this section "becomes effective on January 1, 1978".

Other provisions:

Registration of claims received before January 1, 1978. Act Oct. 19, 1976, P. L. 94-563, Title I, § 109, 90 Stat. 2600, provided: "The registration of claims to copyright for which the required deposit, application, and fee were received in the Copyright Office before January 1, 1978, and the recordation of assignments of copyright or other instruments received in the Copyright Office before January 1, 1978, shall be made in accordance with title 17 [former 17 USCS §§ 1 et seq.] as it existed on December 31, 1977."

CROSS REFERENCES

Register of Copyrights, 17 USCS § 701(a).
This section referred to in 17 USCS § 708.

RESEARCH GUIDE

Am Jur:
18 Am Jur 2d, Copyright and Literary Property §§ 63, 65, 151.

INTERPRETIVE NOTES AND DECISIONS

1. Generally
2. Issuance of certificate [17 USCS § 410(a)]
3. Refusal of registration [17 USCS § 410(b)]
4. Certificate as evidence, generally [17 USCS § 410(c)]
5. —Prima facie evidence of validity of copyright
6. —Prima facie evidence of facts stated
7. —Prima facie evidence of deposit

1. Generally

Where copies of copyrighted photograph have been sold, no action can be brought for infringement of copyright unless certificate of registration shows date of publication. Lumiere v Pathe Exchange, Inc. (1921, CA2 NY) 275 F 428.

Since registration of copyright is essentially ministerial action, proper remedy for refusal of registration is mandamus. Eltra Corp. v Ringer (1976, DC Va) 194 USPQ 198.

2. Issuance of certificate [17 USCS § 410(a)]

Predecessor statute imposes duty on Librarian of Congress to give certificate of deposit of title. Huebsch v Arthur H. Crist Co. (1914, DC NY) 209 F 885.

Librarian does not issue certificate until he learns date of publication. Joe Mittenthal, Inc. v Irving Berlin, Inc. (1923, DC NY) 291 F 714.

While Register of Copyrights is not required to issue certificate which, because it states conflicting claims, is prima facie defective, Register may issue separate certificates, each asserting only single, albeit conflicting, claim; certificates do not establish copyright ownership and any conflict may thereafter be judicially resolved. 43 OAG No. 2.

3. Refusal of registration [17 USCS § 410(b)]

Discretion of register of copyrights, in refusing to accept objects for deposit and registration, is not uncontrolled, but is subject to judicial review. Bailie v Fisher (1958) 103 App DC 331, 258 F2d 425, 117 USPQ 334.

Register of copyrights has no discretionary power to refuse to register any copyright entitled to registration under law; it is question of fact whether applicant has complied with law and if he has he is entitled to registration; any finding of fact or conclusion of law on part of register is not binding on court; mandamus issues to force register to accept deposit and register claim of copyright. United States ex rel. Twentieth Century-Fox Film Corp. v Bouve (1940, DC Dist Col) 33 F Supp 462, 45 USPQ 411, affd 74 App DC 271, 122 F2d 51, 50 USPQ 338.

No statute or regulation authorizes appeal to Librarian of Congress from decision of copyright office refusing copyright registration. 40 OAG 27, 48 USPQ 439.

It is unclear whether register of copyrights has authority to deny registration of claim to copyright in work which, while it meets all formal requirements for registration, contains seditious, libellous, obscene, or other matter which may be illegal or opposed to public policy; Copyright

Act imposes no duty upon register to deny registration of such claims to copyright; it confers discretion upon him to accept for registration works which courts may ultimately deprive of copyright protection. 41 OAG 395.

4. Certificate as evidence, generally [17 USCS § 410(c)]

Issuance of certificate of registration of copyright is prima facie proof of authorship and copyrightability. Edward B. Marks Music Corp. v Stasny Music Corp. (1941, DC NY) 1 FRD 720, 49 USPQ 553.

Predecessor section does not dispense with necessity of alleging facts showing title in action for infringement. Foreign & Domestic Music Corp. v Twentieth Century-Fox Film Corp. (1936, DC NY) 19 F Supp 769, 34 USPQ 109.

Certificates of copyright registration constitute prima facie evidence of title, validity, and facts therein stated; their introduction in evidence shifts to alleged infringer burden of going forward with evidence to overcome prima facie case. Hedeman Products Corp. v Tap-Rite Products Corp. (1964, DC NJ) 228 F Supp 630, 141 USPQ 381.

Introduction of certificate of copyright raises presumption of authorship of lyrics and music of copyrighted musical composition, and of their originality and of validity of copyright, although denied in answer; presumption is sufficient basis for decree in absence of proof by defendant attacking validity. Remick Music Corp. v Interstate Hotel Co. (1944, DC Neb) 58 F Supp 523, 63 USPQ 327, affd (CA8 Neb) 157 F2d 744, 71 USPQ 138, cert den 329 US 809, 91 L Ed 691, 67 S Ct 622, reh den 330 US 854, 91 L Ed 1296, 67 S Ct 769.

Plaintiff, in copyright infringement action based on statutory copyright, is entitled to prima facie presumption of originality, since among facts to be set forth in certificate is statement of author of work, and authorship presumptively connotes originality. Blazon, Inc. v Deluxe Game Corp. (1965, DC NY) 268 F Supp 416, 156 USPQ 195.

Certificates of registration in Copyright Office are prima facie proof of originality; upon introduction into evidence of certificate in infringement action, burden of going forward shifts to alleged infringer, who must prove work was not original. Stratchborneo v Arc Music Corp. (1973, DC NY) 357 F Supp 1393.

5. —Prima facie evidence of validity of copyright

When suit for infringement is brought, certificate of copyright does not per se establish copyright, but burden rests on plaintiff to show compliance with statutory requirements. Saake v Lederer (1909, CA3 Pa) 174 F 135.

Certificate of copyright registration is prima facie evidence of validity of copyright; burden of proof is on alleged infringer to overcome this prima facie presumption of validity. Wihtol v Wells (1956, CA7 Ill) 231 F2d 550, 109 USPQ 200.

Predecessor law confers exclusive rights in respect to songs on which copyright has been obtained by persons entitled thereto and to extent of provisions of predecessor section author loses right of control over his work; it is not presumed that copyrights duly registered were fraudulently obtained; on contrary, predecessor section makes certificate of register of copyrights prima facie evidence in any court of facts stated therein. Vance v American Soc. of Composers, etc. (1959, CA8 Mo) 271 F2d 204, 123 USPQ 296, cert den 361 US 933, 4 L Ed 2d 355, 80 S Ct 373.

Presumption of validity applies only to original certificates of copyright and not to renewal certificates, and even if presumption applied to renewal, it is rebutted by proof that material statements in renewal certificate were false. Epoch Producing Corp. v Killiam Shows, Inc. (1975, CA2 NY) 522 F2d 737, 187 USPQ 270, cert den 424 US 955, 47 L Ed 2d 360, 96 S Ct 1429.

Where there is nothing to contradict facts stated in certificate of copyright, such certificate is sufficient proof to establish valid copyright in owner. M. Witmark & Sons v Calloway (1927, DC Tenn) 22 F2d 412.

Action for copyright infringement is not dismissed on motion for failure of declaration to sufficiently contain allegations that plaintiff has complied with predecessor section since not only does plaintiff allege that he has complied with predecessor section and all other laws governing copyright but he also annexes to declaration copy of certificate of registration issued by register of copyrights, which carries with it presumption of regularity. Pizzano v Knowles & Co. (1941, DC Mass) 37 F Supp 118, 49 USPQ 140.

Certificate of copyright registration issued to plaintiff is prima facie evidence of validity of copyright and that plaintiff is proprietor thereof and has title thereto. Home Art, Inc. v Glensder Textile Corp. (1948, DC NY) 81 F Supp 551, 79 USPQ 12.

Trade-mark and label copyright certificates demonstrate prima facie right to registered symbol, but this is not necessarily determinative of question of validity of mark or copyright. Northmont Hosiery Corp. v True Mfg. Co. (1951, DC Wis) 100 F Supp 909, 91 USPQ 3.

Registered copyrights are prima facie valid; at end of plaintiff's presentation of its case, court cannot consider defendant's assertion as to invalidity or as to plaintiff's failure to secure copyright protection by required publication of notice of copyright. Marcal Paper Mills, Inc. v Scott Paper Co. (1968, DC NJ) 290 F Supp 43, 160 USPQ 147.

In absence of proof that plaintiffs' design was either copied or in the public domain, defendant must fail in his effort to overcome the presumption that the copyright is valid. Covington Fabrics Corp. v Artel Products, Inc. (1971, DC NY) 328 F Supp 202.

Certificate of copyright registration makes out prima facie case of originality and validity, and court will not take judicial notice of lack of originality of material in advertising brochure copyrighted by distributor of automotive lamps and lighting equipment. Foreign Car Parts, Inc. v Auto World, Inc. (1973, DC Pa) 366 F Supp 977, 181 USPQ 162.

Where certificate of copyright shows different title than article involved in suit, such certificate is not evidence that article involved in suit was copyrighted. McMurty v Popham (1887) 8 Ky LR (abstract) 704.

6. —Prima facie evidence of facts stated

Certificate is prima facie evidence of facts stated therein. Gerlach-Barklow Co. v Morris & Bendien, Inc. (1927, CA2 NY) 23 F2d 159; Nutt v National Institute, Inc. for Improv. of Memory (1929, CA2 Conn) 31 F2d 236. Rohauer v Friedman (1962, CA9 Cal) 306 F2d 933, 134 USPQ 384, 2 ALR3d 1395; Tennessee Fabricating Co. v Moultrie Mfg. Co. (1970, CA5 Ga) 421 F2d 279, 164 USPQ 418, cert den 398 US 928, 26 L Ed 2d 91, 90 S Ct 1819; Monogram Models, Inc. v Industro Motive Corp. (1971, CA6 Mich) 448 F2d 284, later app (CA6 Mich) 492 F2d 1281, cert den 419 US 843, 42 L Ed 2d 71, 95 S Ct 76.

To determine whether plaintiff proved prima facie case, affidavits and exhibits, as well as bill, must be examined, and certificate of registration of copyright, filed as exhibit, establishes authorship of copyrighted work. Gerlach-Barklow Co. v Morris & Bendien, Inc. (1927, CA2 NY) 23 F2d 159.

Certificate of registration is prima facie evidence of facts stated therein but this does not mean that certificate establishes that publication bore correct copyright notice; certificate does not say so, and there is nothing in predecessor statute, reason of matter, or circumstances to indicate that it should be so; certificate cannot be prima facie evidence of anything more than it

says. Krafft v Cohen (1941, CA3 Pa) 117 F2d 579, 48 USPQ 401.

Registration certificate is prima facie evidence of all that appears on its face and is not limited to facts within personal knowledge of register; this includes more than that proprietor filed two copies of song and that copyright had issued. Jerry Vogel Music Co. v Forster Music Publishers, Inc. (1945, CA2 NY) 147 F2d 614, 64 USPQ 417, cert den 325 US 880, 89 L Ed 1996, 65 S Ct 1573.

Certificate of copyright is prima facie evidence of dates of fixation of copyrighted songs, even though certificate is hearsay evidence as to proof of dates, and certificate should be deemed prima facie accurate until contrary evidence is introduced. United States v Taxe (1976, CA9 Cal) 540 F2d 961, 192 USPQ 204.

Certificate of registration was prima facie proof of authorship. Fred Fisher, Inc. v Dillingham (1924, DC NY) 298 F 145.

Fact that defendants applied for copyright registration of same arrangement does not estop defendants from denying that plaintiff's arrangement of defendants' song was original and substantial; certificate of registration is only prima facie evidence of facts therein stated; such facts may be controverted by defendants as well as by plaintiff; likewise, in order to claim estoppel, one must show detrimental reliance; plaintiff has failed to do this. McIntyre v Double-A Music Corp. (1958, DC Cal) 166 F Supp 681, 119 USPQ 106, motion den (DC Cal) 179 F Supp 160.

Although certificate of copyright registration is prima facie evidence of facts stated therein, presumption is dispelled where it is shown that work is uncopyrightable. Grove Press, Inc. v Collectors Publication, Inc. (1967, DC Cal) 264 F Supp 603, 152 USPQ 787.

Certificate of registration of copyright in executive desk calendar is prima facie evidence of facts stated in certificate, and misstatements in registration certificate, if unaccompanied by fraud, do not invalidate copyright or render certificate incapable of supporting infringement action, and evidence shows copyright is valid. Baldwin Cooke Co. v Keith Clark, Inc. (1974, DC Ill) 383 F Supp 650, 183 USPQ 209, affd without opinion (CA7 Ill) 505 F2d 1250 and supp op (DC Ill) 420 F Supp 404.

Plaintiff sustains burden of showing ownership of copyright upon proof of certificate of registration and wills and assignments in chain of title leading to plaintiff, especially in view of prior court holding on validity of plaintiff's title, and fact that original copyright notice used company name not registered under Indiana law does not invalidate federal copyright, but evidence of distribution of copies without copyright notice to friends at Christmas time and to servicemen during World War II shows both forfeiture and abandonment of copyright. Bell v Combined Registry Co. (1975, DC Ill) 188 USPQ 707.

Copyright registration certificate establishes prima facie validity and prima facie validity of facts stated therein, and registration is not defective because fabric design is registered and only garment including fabric design is published. Nik-Nik Industries, Inc. v Walt Disney Productions, Inc. (1976, DC NY) 194 USPQ 108.

Compliance with Copyright Act to secure exclusive performance of unpublished dramatic work serves as constructive notice of exclusive right and affords prima facie evidence of facts stated in certificate of registration. Loew's Inc. v Superior Court of Los Angeles County (1941) 18 Cal 2d 419, 115 P2d 983, 50 USPQ 641.

7. —Prima facie evidence of deposit

In suit for infringement of copyright, certificate of Librarian of Congress attesting to deposit of title of book was incompetent evidence as to proof of deposit of the copies of the book. Merrell v Tice (1882) 104 US 557, 26 L Ed 854.

Certificate of Librarian of Congress acknowledging receipt of two copies of book was competent evidence of deposit of such book, although certificate was not under seal. Belford v Scribner (1892) 144 US 488, 36 L Ed 514, 12 S Ct 734.

Certificate of register of copyrights indicates that copies were received in attempted compliance with copyright statute, on date set out, but does not determine whether or not deposit was made in time. Davies v Bowes (1914, CA2 NY) 219 F 178.

Certificate of librarian is competent evidence to prove that books were deposited. Huebsch v Arthur H. Crist Co. (1914, DC NY) 209 F 885.

§ 411.   Registration as prerequisite to infringement suit

(a) Subject to the provisions of subsection (b), no action for infringement of the copyright in any work shall be instituted until registration of the copyright claim has been made in accordance with this title [17 USCS §§ 101 et seq.]. In any case, however, where the deposit, application, and fee required for registration have been delivered to the Copyright Office in proper form and registration has been refused, the applicant is entitled to institute an action for infringement if notice thereof, with a copy of the complaint, is served on the Register of Copyrights. The Register may, at his or her option, become a party to the action with respect to the issue of registrability of the copyright claim by entering an appearance within sixty days after such service, but the Register's failure to become a party shall not deprive the court of jurisdiction to determine that issue.

(b) In the case of a work consisting of sounds, images, or both, the first fixation of which is made simultaneously with its transmission, the copyright owner may, either before or after such fixation takes place, institute an action for infringement under section 501 [17 USCS § 501], fully subject to the remedies provided by sections 502 through 506 and sections 509 and 510 [17 USCS §§ 502–506, 509, 510], if, in accordance with requirements that the Register of Copyrights shall prescribe by regulation, the copyright owner—

(1) serves notice upon the infringer, not less than ten or more than thirty days before such fixation, identifying the work and the specific time and source of its first transmission, and declaring an intention to secure copyright in the work; and

(2) makes registration for the work within three months after its first transmission.

(Added Oct. 19, 1976, P. L. 94-553, Title I, § 101, 90 Stat. 2583.)

HISTORY; ANCILLARY LAWS AND DIRECTIVES

Effective date of section:

Section 102 of Act Oct. 19, 1976, P. L. 94-553, 90 Stat. 2598 provided that this section "becomes effective on January 1, 1978".

CROSS REFERENCES

Register of Copyrights, 17 USCS § 701(a).
Copyright Office regulations, 17 USCS § 702.
This section referred to in 17 USCS §§ 412, 501.

RESEARCH GUIDE

Am Jur:

18 Am Jur 2d, Copyright and Literary Property § 65.

Annotations:

Requirements as to deposit of copies of work in copyright office under § 13 of Federal Copyright Act (17 USCS § 13) as prerequisite to infringement action. 16 ALR Fed 595.

INTERPRETIVE NOTES AND DECISIONS

1. Generally [17 USCS § 411(a)]
2. Time of registration [17 USCS § 411(b)]

1. Generally [17 USCS § 411(a)]

Predecessor provision prohibiting maintaining of action for infringement of copyright until certain provisions are complied with applies to equity action for injunction and accounting, since such action is action for infringement of copyright. New York Times Co. v Sun Printing & Publishing Assn. (1913, CA2 NY) 204 F 586, cert den 234 US 758, 58 L Ed 1579, 34 S Ct 676.

Plaintiff must show compliance with copyright statutes to be entitled to maintain suit for infringement of copyright. Davies v Bowes (1914, CA2 NY) 219 F 178.

Where photographs were registered as not to be reproduced for sale, but they had been reproduced for sale, action for infringement could not be maintained until registration requirements had been complied with. Lumiere v Pathe Exchange, Inc. (1921, CA2 NY) 275 F 428.

Where motion picture was copyrighted as motion picture other than photoplay by depositing one copy and title, and several copies were made in different sizes and shown to employees and others and were sent to many organizations to be shown without charge, so that motion picture was exhibited to many thousands of people; this was not publication requiring deposit of two copies, and owner could sue infringer

without further deposits. Patterson v Century Productions, Inc. (1937, CA2 NY) 93 F2d 489, 35 USPQ 471, cert den 303 US 655, 82 L Ed 1114, 58 S Ct 759.

Predecessor section makes compliance with provisions of Copyright Act as to deposit of copies and registration condition precedent to maintaining infringement action; "action" in this setting includes criminal as well as civil action. United States v Backer (1943, CA2 NY) 134 F2d 533, 57 USPQ 133.

Predecessor section forbids action for copyright infringement where register of copyrights had refused to accept watch as copyrightable work of art. Vacheron & Constantin-Le Coultre Watches, Inc. v Benrus Watch Co. (1958, CA2 NY) 260 F2d 637, 119 USPQ 189.

Copyright Act gives no remedy for infringement of work on which no copyright is alleged to have issued, and without diversity, federal courts lack jurisdiction over common law copyright claim. Simon & Flynn, Inc. v Time, Inc. (1975, CA2 NY) 513 F2d 832, 185 USPQ 325.

Injunction against infringement issued prior to deposit is premature and has no binding force; prohibition in predecessor section respecting maintenance of actions for infringement of copyright goes to jurisdiction of courts. New York Times Co. v Star Co. (1912, CC NY) 195 F 110.

Essence of copyright is publication with notice of copyright; registration is merely means of perfecting it, no specific time for such registration being provided for, though registration is essential to maintaining action for infringement. Davenport Quigley Expedition, Inc. v Century Productions, Inc. (1937, DC NY) 18 F Supp 974.

Deposit of copies of work and registration are conditions precedent to right to maintain action for copyright infringement after publication for sale; it is immaterial that plaintiff holds proper certificate of registration covering work of art not to be reproduced for sale. Rosedale v News Syndicate Co. (1941, DC NY) 39 F Supp 357, 50 USPQ 27.

Where complaint alleges fictitious date and number of certificate of copyright action and is dismissed for failure to make deposit in copyright office before action was commenced, federal court has no jurisdiction of claim for breach of printer's implied contract not to reproduce customer's material for own purpose. Rudolf Lesch Fine Arts, Inc. v Metal (1943, DC NY) 51 F Supp 69, 58 USPQ 668.

Predecessor section does not authorize maintenance of infringement action without registration but merely on publication with copyright notice, since it deals with right, not remedy. G. P. Putnam's Sons v Lancer Books, Inc. (1966, DC NY) 251 F Supp 210, 148 USPQ 596.

Copyright infringement action is dismissed, although plaintiff deposited two copies of copyrighted work with copyright office and placed copyright notice on each work, since registration certificate has not been received from copyright office; in order to complete registration, it is necessary that certificate be obtained; since certificate has not been obtained, copyright has not been registered in manner required for maintenance of action. Loomskill, Inc. v Rubin Levine & Co. (1968, DC NY) 159 USPQ 676.

Complaint failing to allege compliance with deposit requirements is dismissed without prejudice to filing amended or supplemental complaint showing compliance, where such action does not prejudice defendants. Charron v Meaux (1973, DC NY) 60 FRD 619, 180 USPQ 645.

Cause of action for copyright infringement is dismissed where subject matter is not protected by copyright registration and registration has been refused, registration being indispensable to maintenance of cause of action. Imperial Toy Corp. v Ben Cooper, Inc. (1975, DC Cal) 185 USPQ 453.

Annotations:

Requirements as to deposit of copies of work in copyright office under § 13 of Federal Copyright Act (17 USCS § 13) as prerequisite to infringement action. 16 ALR Fed 595.

2. Time of registration [17 USCS § 411(b)]

While no action for infringement can be maintained before copies are actually deposited, mere delay, in this case fourteen months, will not destroy right to sue. Washingtonian Publishing Co. v Pearson (1939) 306 US 30, 83 L Ed 470, 59 S Ct 397, 40 USPQ 190, reh den 306 US 668, 83 L Ed 1063, 59 S Ct 588.

Although first registration of a copyright may not have been valid, second registration obtained by filing two copies after publication may be made basis of suit. Turner & Dahnken v Crowley (1918, CA9 Cal) 252 F 749.

District court had jurisdiction of action for infringement of copyright where the action was filed on the same day that the copyright claimant had placed revised applications in the mail to the copyright office where they were received two days later. Roth Greeting Cards v United Card Co. (1970, CA9 Cal) 429 F2d 1106, 166 USPQ 291.

Complaint is dismissed under predecessor section where copyright proprietor made no deposit in copyright office until several months after action was commenced, although before trial. Rudolf Lesch Fine Arts, Inc. v Metal (1943, DC NY) 51 F Supp 69, 58 USPQ 668.

Although certificate of registration shows that copyright on catalogue was secured by publication in 1942, catalogue displays notice "copyrighted 1942, 1943" and evidence shows that some material was added to original edition of catalogue; since no evidence is adduced to show that subsequent altered edition was deposited in copyright office and since, therefore, office does not have on deposit two complete copies of catalogue, predecessor section bars plaintiffs from maintaining copyright infringement action. Unistrut Corp. v Power (1958, DC Mass) 175 F Supp 294, 121 USPQ 381, affd in part and vacated in part on other grounds (CA1 Mass) 280 F2d 18, 126 USPQ 82.

Delay in registering claim for copyright until after initiation of copyright infringement action does not bar action for infringement of copyright in map. Newton v Voris (1973, DC Or) 364 F Supp 562, 180 USPQ 262.

Under registration and deposit of copies as condition precedent to bringing of infringement action, and where all copyright certificates in question were received by copyright office before suit was filed, registration was timely and plaintiff has right to maintain action. G. R. I. Corp. v Golden Fifty Pharmaceutical Co. (1975, DC Ill) 185 USPQ 674.

§ 412. Registration as prerequisite to certain remedies for infringement

In any action under this title [17 USCS §§ 101 et seq.], other than an action instituted under section 411(b) [17 USCS § 411(b)], no award of statutory damages or of attorney's fees, as provided by sections 504 and 505 [17 USCS §§ 504 and 505], shall be made for—

(1) any infringement of copyright in an unpublished work commenced before the effective date of its registration; or

(2) any infringement of copyright commenced after first publication of the work and before the effective date of its registration, unless such registration is made within three months after the first publication of the work.

(Added Oct. 19, 1976, P. L. 94-553, Title I, § 101, 90 Stat. 2583.)

HISTORY; ANCILLARY LAWS AND DIRECTIVES

Effective date of section:

Section 102 of Act Oct. 19, 1976, P. L. 94-553, 90 Stat. 2598 provided that this section "becomes effective on January 1, 1978".

CROSS REFERENCES

Statutory damages for infringement, 17 USCS § 504(c).

Costs and attorney's fees as element of damages for infringement, 17 USCS § 505.

RESEARCH GUIDE

Annotations:

Requirements as to deposit of copies of work in copyright office under § 13 of Federal Copyright Act (17 USCS § 13) as prerequisite to infringement action. 16 ALR Fed 595.

CHAPTER 5.   COPYRIGHT INFRINGEMENT AND REMEDIES

---

§ 501.   Infringement of copyright

(a) Anyone who violates any of the exclusive rights of the copyright owner as provided by sections 106 through 118 [17 USCS §§ 106–118], or who imports copies or phonorecords into the United States in violation of section 602 [17 USCS § 602], is an infringer of the copyright.

(b) The legal or beneficial owner of an exclusive right under a copyright is entitled, subject to the requirements of sections 205(d) and 411 [17 USCS §§ 205(d) and 411], to institute an action for any infringement of that particular right committed while he or she is the owner of it. The court may require such owner to serve written notice of the action with a copy of the complaint upon any person shown, by the records of the Copyright Office or otherwise, to have or claim an interest in the copyright, and shall require that such notice be served upon any person whose interest is likely to be affected by a decision in the case. The court may require the joinder, and shall permit the intervention, of any person having or claiming an interest in the copyright.

(c) For any secondary transmission by a cable system that embodies a performance or a display of a work which is actionable as an act of infringement under subsection (c) of section 111 [17 USCS § 111(c)], a television broadcast station holding a copyright or other license to transmit or perform the same version of that work shall, for purposes of subsection (b) of this section, be treated as a legal or beneficial owner if such secondary transmission occurs within the local service area of that television station.

(d) For any secondary transmission by a cable system that is actionable as an act of infringement pursuant to section 111(c)(3) [17 USCS § 111(c)(3)], the following shall also have standing to sue: (i) the primary transmitter

whose transmission has been altered by the cable system; and (ii) any broadcast station within whose local service area the secondary transmission occurs.
(Added Oct. 19, 1976, P. L. 94-553, Title I, § 101, 90 Stat. 2584.)

HISTORY; ANCILLARY LAWS AND DIRECTIVES

Effective date of section:
Section 102 of Act Oct. 19, 1976, P. L. 94-553, 90 Stat. 2598 provided that this section "becomes effective on January 1, 1978".

Other provisions:
Causes of actions arising before January 1, 1978. Act Oct. 19, 1976, P. L. 94-553, Title I, § 112, 90 Stat. 2600, provided: "All causes of action that arose under title 17 [former 17 USCS §§ 1 et seq.] before January 1, 1978, shall be governed by title 17 [former 17 USCS §§ 1 et seq.] as it existed when the cause of action arose."

CROSS REFERENCES

Exclusive rights of copyright owner, 17 USCS §§ 106–118.
Nonsimultaneous secondary transmissions by cable systems, 17 USCS § 111(e).
Principle of divisibility of copyright ownership, 17 USCS § 201(d).
Remedies for alteration of programming by cable systems, 17 USCS § 510.
   This section referred to in 17 USCS §§ 111, 115, 116, 411, 510, 602.

RESEARCH GUIDE

Am Jur:
18 Am Jur 2d, Copyright and Literary Property §§ 97, 98, 104, 134, 137–141, 144, 146, 147, 150, 154.
58 Am Jur 2d, Newspapers, Periodicals, and Press Associations § 35.

Am Jur Trials:
Copyright Infringement Litigation, 9 Am Jur Trials, p. 293.

Forms:
6 Federal Procedural Forms L Ed, Copyrights §§ 17:51–17:54, 17:119.

Annotations:
Liability as "Vicarious" or "Contributory" infringer under Federal Copyright Act. 14 ALR Fed 825.

Law Review Articles:
Copyright Symposium, 22 New York Law School Law Review 193.

INTERPRETIVE NOTES AND DECISIONS

I. IN GENERAL (notes 1–7)
II. WHAT CONSTITUTES INFRINGE-
       MENT [17 USCS § 501(a)]
   A. In General (notes 8–12)

B. Reproduction of Copies (as specified in 17 USCS § 106(1))
   1. In General (notes 13–25)
   2. Similarity (notes 26–40)

I. IN GENERAL

1. Generally

In order to be entitled to relief for infringement of copyright it is essential that copyright shall exist, and that copying shall have taken place. Davies v Bowes (1913, DC NY) 209 F 53, affd (CA2 NY) 219 F 178.

Finding of unfair use by defendants means infringement of copyright and entitles plaintiff to injunction, costs, and damages and profits. Detective Comics, Inc. v Bruns Publications, Inc. (1939, DC NY) 28 F Supp 399, 41 USPQ 182, mod on other grounds (CA2 NY) 111 F2d 432, 45 USPQ 291.

Originality is essential as basis for infringement action; copyright cannot prevent others from using old material. Chamberlin v Uris Sales Corp. (1944, DC NY) 56 F Supp 987, 62 USPQ 375, affd (CA2 NY) 150 F2d 512, 65 USPQ 544.

If stranger exploits copyrighted work and deprives creator of right to its exclusive enjoyment, infringement action will lie; however, if co-author, one who cannot be charged with infringement, authorizes exploitation of work and exclusion of his collaborator, access may not be had to federal court. Harrington v Mure (1960, DC NY) 186 F Supp 655, 126 USPQ 506.

Elements of infringement action are essentially same whether alleged infringement is of uncopyrighted, unpublished material or of published material protected by statutory copyright. Smith v Little, Brown & Co. (1965, DC NY) 245 F Supp 451, affd (CA2 NY) 360 F2d 928, 149 USPQ 799, on remand (DC NY) 273 F Supp 870, affd (CA2 NY) 396 F2d 150.

In determining infringement, each case must be determined on own facts. Stanley v Columbia Broadcasting System, Inc. (1949, Cal) 208 P2d 9, 82 USPQ 123, subsequent op on reh 35 Cal 2d 653, 221 P2d 73, 86 USPQ 520, 23 ALR2d 216.

2. Federal law applicability

Person cannot maintain action for infringement of his copyright unless he has complied with all provisions of law. Bennett v Boston Traveler Co. (1900, CA1 Mass) 101 F 445.

In determining infringement it must be kept in mind that applicable law is purely statutory and that Copyright Act has little elasticity or flexibility. Wihtol v Crow (1962, CA8 Iowa) 309 F2d 777, 135 USPQ 385.

Statutory requirements must be carefully observed before right to sue for infringement accrues to author or owner of copyright. Record & Guide Co. v Bromley (1909, CC Pa) 175 F 156.

Congress has full power to restrict actions for infringement of copyrights. New York Times Co. v Star Co. (1912, CC NY) 195 F 110.

Rights of owner of copyright depend upon statute in force at time of infringement of copyright. Davies v Bowes (1913, DC NY) 209 F 53, affd (CA2 NY) 219 F 178.

Remedies which copyright proprietor may obtain in event of infringement are statutory remedies enumerated in this chapter; measure of his rights and liabilities must be found from its language. Miller v Goody (1954, DC NY) 125 F Supp 348, 103 USPQ 292.

Common-law right to prevent copying, publication, or use of unpublished musical composition without consent of owner or author has not been restricted by statute. McCarter v Barton Music Corp. (NY, Sup Ct) 115 USPQ 299.

3. State law applicability

State statute requiring owner of copyright to obtain license before collecting royalties or fees did not preclude such owner without license from bringing infringement suit. Leo Feist, Inc. v Demarie (1935, DC La) 16 F Supp 827, 32 USPQ 122.

State court judgment adjudging assignments of copyright as valid involved parties bringing infringement suit, or their privies, leaving them with no standing to prosecute infringement suit. Dorf v Denton (1937, DC NY) 17 F Supp 531, 33 USPQ 24.

Nebraska statute endeavors to free anyone purchasing sheet music or orchestral arrangements of copyrighted music in Nebraska and using or rendering music in Nebraska from liability in infringement suit for damages by copyright proprietor in any court in state; since, under Copyright Act, federal courts alone possess jurisdiction in such suits, statute is directed at Nebraska federal court only and is unconstitutional. Remick Music Corp. v Interstate Hotel Co. (1944, DC Neb) 58 F Supp 523, 63 USPQ 327, affd (CA8 Neb) 157 F2d 744, 71 USPQ 138, cert den 329 US 809, 91 L Ed 691, 67 S Ct 622, reh den 330 US 854, 91 L Ed 1296, 67 S Ct 769.

4. Equity considerations

Copyright Act permits actions for its violation either at law or in equity; plaintiff can elect whether to sue at law or in equity. Arnstein v Twentieth Century Fox Film Corp. (1943, DC NY) 3 FRD 58, 56 USPQ 511.

In suit for infringement demand for accounting of profits renders case one for relief in a court of equity. Sheldon v Moredall Realty Corp. (1937, DC NY) 22 F Supp 91, 37 USPQ 254, mod on other grounds (CA2 NY) 95 F2d 48, 37 USPQ 286.

5. Jurisdictional considerations

Lack of jurisdiction in court of claims over actions against United States for patent infringement was changed by 28 USCS § 1498; this legislation, however, was restricted to actions for patent infringement and did not change law as to copyright infringement; since court of claims has no jurisdiction over actions against United States for copyright infringement, jurisdiction in district court under 28 USCS § 1346(a)(2) is also lacking. Turton v United States (1954, CA6 Ky) 212 F2d 354, 101 USPQ 164.

Complaint alleging infringement of registered copyright for layout of historical map supports federal jurisdiction, even though case involves contract questions between parties as to preparation of work. Hughey v Palographics Co. (1976, DC Colo) 189 USPQ 527.

State court has no jurisdiction if main purpose of action, whatever its form, is to establish patent or to enjoin its infringement or to recover damages therefor; same rule applies where subject matter of action is protected by copyright; there, too, sole remedy is in federal courts for infringement of owner's rights under copyright. Ideal Toy Corp. v Newman Priemier Corp. (1961) 29 Misc 2d 192, 217 NYS2d 664, 129 USPQ 437.

6. Relationship to other causes of action, generally

Where copyrighted book contains notice of certain conditions concerning resale, owner of copyright cannot bring suit for violation of notice, if he bases his action on infringement of his copyright. Authors & Newspapers Asso. v O'Gorman Co. (1906, CC RI) 147 F 616.

Copyright owner cannot sue one contracting for use of copyright for infringement amounting to breach of contract. Metro-Goldwyn-Mayer Distributing Corp. v Bijou Theatre Co. (1931, DC Mass) 50 F2d 908, revd on other grounds (CA1 Mass) 59 F2d 70, 13 USPQ 147.

Infringement of copyright is merely wrongful interference with statutory right of copyright proprietor and will not support action for trover and conversion. Local Trademarks, Inc. v Rogers (1947, DC Ala) 73 F Supp 907, 75 USPQ 336.

Action for copyright infringement is not action for conversion; infringement and conversion are inconsistent with each other; by conversion, title is taken; by infringement, title remains in original owner but is damaged by infringer. Pickford Corp. v De Luxe Laboratories, Inc. (1958, DC Cal) 169 F Supp 118, 120 USPQ 521.

7. —Copyright infringement as tort

Infringement of copyright is tort, and all persons concerned therein are jointly and severally liable as such joint tort-feasors. Ted Browne Music Co. v Fowler (1923, CA2 NY) 290 F 751.

Infringement of copyright, whether common law or statutory, constitutes tort. Porter v United States (1973, CA5 Tex) 473 F2d 1329.

Copyright infringement is tort. Buck v Cecere (1942, DC NY) 45 F Supp 441, 53 USPQ 519.

Courts have not defined "infringement," standing by itself, as referring only to tort; definition consistently has been that "infringement of copyright" connotes tort; although "infringement" is most commonly applied to actions for unlawful appropriation of copyright, trademark, or patent, its usage is not limited solely to such actions. Weitzenkorn v Lesser (1953) 40 Cal 2d 778, 256 P2d 947, 97 USPQ 545.

II. WHAT CONSTITUTES INFRINGEMENT [17 USCS § 501(a)]

A. In General

8. Generally

Although person obtains his copyright after depositing two copies as provided for, he must prove, in suit for infringement, facts of originality, of intellectual production, and of thought and conception on part of author. Burrow-Giles Lithographic Co. v Sarony (1884) 111 US 53, 28 L Ed 349, 4 S Ct 279.

Copyright Act does not give copyright holder control over all uses of copyrighted work; instead, it enumerates several "rights" that are made "exclusive" to copyright holder; if a person, without authorization from copyright holder, puts copyrighted work to a use within scope of one of these "exclusive rights," he infringes copyright; if he puts work to a use not enumerated, he does not infringe. Fortnightly Corp. v United Artists Television, Inc. (1968) 392 US 390, 20 L Ed 2d 1176, 88 S Ct 2084, reh den 393 US 902, 21 L Ed 2d 190, 89 S Ct 65.

Although Copyright Act does not contain explicit definition of infringement, unauthorized use of copyrighted material inconsistent with "exclusive rights" constitutes copyright infringement; use of copyrighted material not in conflict with rights secured however, no matter how widespread, is not copyright infringement and the fundamental is that "use" is not identical with "infringement", and use short of infringement is to be encouraged. Teleprompter Corp. v Columbia Broadcasting System, Inc. (1974) 415 US 394, 39 L Ed 2d 415, 94 S Ct 1129.

Marketability of unlawful reproductions of copyrighted work has no bearing on question of infringement. Fishel v Lueckel (1892, CC NY) 53 F 499.

Article that is not subject to copyright cannot

be made subject of suit for infringement. Amberg File & Index Co. v Shea Smith & Co. (1896, CC Ill) 78 F 479, affd (CA7 Ill) 82 F 314.

Fraudulent use of book with knowledge of restrictions as to use was infringement. Produce Reporter Co. v Fruit Produce Rating Agency (1924, DC Ill) 1 F2d 58.

Since advertisement is not copyrightable by newspaper, copyright is not infringed by another who, at advertiser's request, reproduces advertisement in another newspaper. Brattleboro Publishing Co. v Winmill Publishing Corp. (1966, DC Vt) 250 F Supp 215, 149 USPQ 41, affd (CA2 Vt) 369 F2d 565, 5 ALR Fed 617.

It is copyright infringement if defendant makes unauthorized offering of identical films and sound tracks for sale with "100% of all rights" which would include right to make positives therefrom and to exhibit positives to public, in violation of plaintiff's common-law copyright. Independent Film Distributors, Ltd. v Chesapeake Industries, Inc. (1958, CA2 NY) 250 F2d 951, 116 USPQ 28.

9. Intent to infringe

Intent is not element of infringement. Johns & Johns Printing Co. v Paull-Pioneer Music Corp. (1939, CA8 Mo) 102 F2d 282, 41 USPQ 3.

One copying part of copyrighted composition even subconsciously is liable. Fred Fisher, Inc. v Dillingham (1924, DC NY) 298 F 145.

Only permissible test of unconscious and unintentional copying is similarity to ordinary reader of book and observer of motion picture. Cain v Universal Pictures Co. (1942, DC Cal) 47 F Supp 1013, 56 USPQ 8.

Infringement does not depend upon intent but upon the fact of copying copyrighted matter. Carter v Hawaii Transportation Co. (1961, DC Hawaii) 201 F Supp 301, 133 USPQ 65.

10. Loss of remuneration as infringement consideration

Among criteria for ascertaining infringement are whether so much has been taken as would sensibly diminish value of original or whether labors of party entitled to copyright are substantially to injurious extent appropriated by another. Mathews Conveyer Co. v Palmer-Bee Co. (1943, CA6 Mich) 135 F2d 73, 57 USPQ 219.

Rendering work less remunerative infringes author's exclusive right; complainant's exclusive right to put his own book, as his own, upon market was violated by defendants who represented their book as and for complainant's. Estes v Williams (1884, CC NY) 21 F 189.

Test of infringement is whether or not appropriated portions, as used, are likely to injure sale of original work. Harper v Shoppell (1886, CC NY) 26 F 519.

Bill for infringement which alleged that many people had been induced to buy defendant's copies in belief that they were complainant's disclosed adequate cause for complaint and entitled complainants to some form of equitable relief. Merriam v Famous Shoe & Clothing Co. (1891, CC Mo) 47 F 411.

Criticism of original work, which tends to lessen its money value by showing that it is not worth seeing or hearing, may not form basis for charge of infringement of copyright. Hill v Whalen & Martell (1914, DC NY) 220 F 359.

Fact that defendant's dahlia is causing plaintiff to lose customers and sales is not determinative of whether defendant's dahlia infringes plaintiff's copyrighted artificial dahlia; any competitive product will normally have some effect on sales of others, but copyright on reproduction of natural object does not foreclose others from copying that natural object also. Prestige Floral, Societe Anonyme v Zunino-Altman, Inc. (1962, DC NY) 203 F Supp 649, 133 USPQ 75, affd (CA2 NY) 301 F2d 286, 133 USPQ 58.

It may be that defendant's doll competes in market in which copyrighted doll has been selling, and buyers may choose defendant's doll in place of copyrighted doll, but that does not necessarily mean that there has been infringement of protected rights. Uneeda Doll Co. v P & M Doll Co. (1965, DC NY) 241 F Supp 675, 145 USPQ 326, affd (CA2 NY) 353 F2d 788, 148 USPQ 7.

11. Separate or multiple infringements

Where defendants' two catalogues each copied nine items from copyrighted catalogue, there was total of 18 infringements. Markham v A. E. Borden Co. (1953, CA1 Mass) 206 F2d 199, 98 USPQ 346.

Where several distinct passages from one copyrighted work are unlawfully reproduced in one publication there is only one infringement. Journal of Commerce & Commercial Bulletin v Boston Transcript Co. (1923, DC Mass) 292 F 311.

Where obsolete sheet infringing publication was replaced by another containing infringing matter there was not new and distinct infringement. Cravens v Retail Credit Men's Asso. (1924, DC Tenn) 26 F2d 833.

Reprintings separated by eight months are separate infringements of copyright. Eliot v Geare-Marston, Inc. (1939, DC Pa) 30 F Supp 301, 43 USPQ 249.

Ordinarily each separate publication constitutes infringement; however, it is plaintiff's practice to authorize reprint of copyrighted contest during particular contest and to charge commissions on basis of sales during contest only, rather than by publication; therefore, one or more publications during same contest constitutes but one infringement. Gordon v Weir (1953, DC Mich) 111 F Supp 117, 97 USPQ 387, affd (CA6 Mich) 216 F2d 508, 104 USPQ 40.

Where copied item appeared in several copyrighted catalogues, court did not consider that catalogue in which it first appeared was one which was copied and that it was copyright on that catalogue which was infringed; it would be unrealistic to suppose that defendant went through whole series of plaintiff's catalogues to select first appearance of each item as one to be copied; logical assumption is that defendant turned to current catalogue as its source when it wished to copy plaintiff's material. Harry Alter Co. v A. E. Borden Co. (1954, DC Mass) 121 F Supp 941, 102 USPQ 2.

Fact that defendant copied one of plaintiff's dresses is no evidence that it copied another of plaintiff's dresses. Richard J. Cole, Inc. v Manhattan Modes Co. (NY, Sup Ct) 109 USPQ 370, affd 2 App Div 2d 593, 157 NYS2d 259, 112 USPQ 193.

12. Threatened infringement

Where evidence shows that defendant is threatening to infringe copyright, plaintiff is entitled to protection although no actual infringement has yet taken place. Historical Pub. Co. v Jones Bros. Pub. Co. (1916, CA3 Pa) 231 F 638.

Complaint does not sufficiently charge threatened infringement of plaintiff's copyright where it merely alleges that defendant has represented and asserted that it has right to use and authorize use of plaintiff's copyrighted song; mere assertion in general terms of claimed right without accompanying act or threatened act to implement asserted right is not sufficient to state charge of threatened copyright infringement; until some action or conduct based upon asserted right is threatened, there is no enforceable claim for relief under Copyright Act; in order to sustain claim for threatened infringement, it must appear that one is about to infringe or take some action prejudicial to rights of copyright owner. Southern Music Publishing Co. v C & C Films, Inc. (1959, DC NY) 171 F Supp 832, 121 USPQ 450.

B. Reproduction of copies (as specified in 17 USCS § 106(1))

1. In General

13. Generally

To infringe copyright of map substantial copy must be reproduced, and map of Philadelphia cannot infringe map of New York City, although same system of signs are used on both maps. Perris v Hexamer (1879) 99 US 674, 25 L Ed 308.

Without copying there can be no infringement. Mazer v Stein (1954) 347 US 201, 98 L Ed 630, 74 S Ct 460, 100 USPQ 325, reh den 347 US 949, 98 L Ed 1096, 74 S Ct 637; C. M. Paula Co. v Logan (1973, DC Tex) 355 F Supp 189.

When defendants made negatives from plaintiff's positive film of wild animals, and positive film from negative, they copied and infringed, and when film was shown, defendant thereby made enlarged copy of picture, which though temporary, was still copy while it lasted, and was infringement. Patterson v Century Productions, Inc. (1937, CA2 NY) 93 F2d 489, 35 USPQ 471, cert den 303 US 655, 82 L Ed 1114, 58 S Ct 759.

Infringement is shown by picking at random several quotations from plaintiff's book and by comparing them with defendant's analogous quotations. Adventures in Good Eating, Inc. v Best Places to Eat, Inc. (1942, CA7 Ill) 131 F2d 809, 56 USPQ 242.

Affidavit of defendant's president states that he instructed advertising agent to employ original material in preparing defendant's catalogue; agent's affidavit states that he followed president's instructions; however, careful omission from affidavits of any denial that copying took place suggests that there was copying of plaintiff's copyrighted catalogue. Joshua Meier Co. v Albany Novelty Mfg. Co. (1956, CA2 NY) 236 F2d 144, 111 USPQ 197.

In determining whether defendant made substantial copy of plaintiff's copyrighted books, court must keep in mind that copying is not necessarily literal or exact reproduction. Eisenschiml v Fawcett Publications, Inc. (1957, CA7 Ill) 246 F2d 598, 114 USPQ 199, cert den 355 US 907, 2 L Ed 2d 262, 78 S Ct 334.

Defendant is not liable to charge of infringement unless proofs justify conclusion that he has copied another's work; to infringe copyright defendant must have actually copied or "pirated" production of plaintiff, and not merely, while ignorant of it, have made something similar. S. S. White Dental Co. v Sibley (1889, CC Pa) 38 F 751.

Copying from infringing works is itself infringement. Gilmore v Anderson (1889, CC NY) 38 F 846.

Dramatic composition, copied from book printed in France containing copyrighted dramatic composition is infringement of copyrighted drama. Hervieu v J. S. Ogilvie Pub. Co. (1909, CC NY) 169 F 978.

Appropriation of alterations and additions

original with translator of foreign production constitutes infringement. Stevenson v Fox (1915, DC NY) 226 F 990.

To constitute infringement there must be actual copying; whether willful or unintentional, made possible by defendant's access to plaintiff's copyrighted material. Seltzer v Sunbrock (1938, DC Cal) 22 F Supp 621, 37 USPQ 491.

Test of infringement is whether work claimed to infringe is independent production or copy of copyrighted work. Mathews Conveyor Co. v Palmer Bee Co. (1941, DC Mich) 41 F Supp 401, 51 USPQ 286, affd (CA6 Mich) 135 F2d 73, 57 USPQ 219.

Copying or printing copyrighted work is infringement although there is no sale or profits made from sale of copies. Chappell & Co. v Costa (1942, DC NY) 45 F Supp 554, 53 USPQ 674.

There may be three-dimensional infringement of copyrighted picture or perhaps of literary composition, but use of knowledge derived from written exposition of idea of purely utilitarian character is not infringement. Clair v Philadelphia Storage Battery Co. (1941, DC Pa) 43 F Supp 286, 52 USPQ 176.

Although there can be no copyright infringement without access and similarity, converse does not follow that, simply because there was access and there are similarities, such are result of copying. Warshawsky v Carter (1955, DC Dist Col) 132 F Supp 758, 107 USPQ 80.

Mere printing or copying of copyrighted work, without proof of sales thereof is infringement. Greenbie v Noble (1957, DC NY) 151 F Supp 45, 113 USPQ 115.

Copying involves use of original copyrighted work so as to produce a work so near to original as to give to every person seeing it the idea created by original. Richards v Columbia Broadcasting System, Inc. (1958, DC Dist Col) 161 F Supp 516, 17 USPQ 174.

Prose poem "Desiderata" is infringed by copying poem in full on several posters. Bell v Pro Arts, Inc. (1973, DC Ohio) 366 F Supp 474, 180 USPQ 517, affd (CA6 Ohio) 511 F2d 451, cert den 423 US 829, 46 L Ed 2d 46, 96 S Ct 47.

Copyright infringement is proved by showing federal registration of copyright in manual on stopping smoking and copying of manual by former employee starting competing program. SmokEnders, Inc. v Smoke No More, Inc. (1974, DC Fla) 184 USPQ 309.

Mail order tool catalog is infringed by direct copying in competitor's tool catalog. Bliss & Laughlin Industries, Inc. v Starvaggi (1975, DC NY) 188 USPQ 89.

Copying requires tangible reproduction of

work and not mere blueprint preliminary to production, and plaintiff has no cause of action for copying by making tangible reproductions only after assignment of copyright by plaintiff to third party. Walker v University Books, Inc. (1977, DC Cal) 193 USPQ 596.

Publishing series of pamphlets copied either totally or largely from copyrighted book amounts to infringement. Urantia Foundation v King (1977, DC Cal) 194 USPQ 171.

As construed in law of plagiarism, copying is not confined to literary repetition, but includes various ways in which matter in any publication may be adopted, imitated, or transferred, with more or less colorable alterations to disguise piracy; no matter how different portion of work may be from plagiarized product, it is enough if substantial parts were lifted. Cantor v Mankiewicz (1960, Sup) 203 NYS2d 626, 125 USPQ 598.

14. Access as relevant to copying

Granting of motion to dismiss copyright infringement suit without taking testimony but upon reading of play and viewing motion picture was error, since such reading admits access and use which is tantamount to presumption of piracy and denial of good faith; with access admitted, similarity of incident rests on high degree of probability of copying and low degree of probability of independent creation. Shipman v R. K. O. Radio Pictures, Inc. (1938, CA2 NY) 100 F2d 533, 40 USPQ 211.

Access and palpable and significant similarities justify conclusion of infringement. Twentieth Century-Fox Film Corp. v Stonesifer (1944, CA9 Cal) 140 F2d 579, 60 USPQ 392.

Where neither of authors, who could, directly or indirectly, have contributed to defendants' motion picture, had any acquaintance with, or access to, plaintiff's play, infringement is not found. Shurr v Warner Bros. Pictures, Inc. (1944, CA2 NY) 144 F2d 200, 62 USPQ 60.

Asserted inverse ratio rule, under which stronger evidence is as to access, less proof of similarity is required, is not found in federal law of copyright; access shown either directly or indirectly is element of plaintiff's case, and it is not unnatural step in inference of fact for ease of access to suggest deduction of copying when similarity is found, but access will not supply its lack, and undue stress upon that one feature can only confuse and even conceal this basic requirement; however, inference of copying may arise when there is proof of access coupled with showing of similarity. Arc Music Corp. v Lee (1961, CA2 NY) 296 F2d 186, 131 USPQ 338.

Lack of substantial similarities between two works means that no amount of evidence of access can prove copying. Reyher v Children's Television Workshop (1976, CA2 NY) 533 F2d 87, 190 USPQ 387.

To establish infringement there must be proof of defendant's access to plaintiff's book. Lewys v O'Neill (1931, DC NY) 49 F2d 603, 9 USPQ 465.

Where musical composition alleged to be infringement is only similar in parts which are not continuous or extended, it is not sufficient proof of infringement to show that defendant had plaintiff's composition in his possession for several months, when evidence of defendant tends to show that he never read or played it. Arnstein v Edward B. Marks Music Corp. (1935, DC NY) 11 F Supp 535, 27 USPQ 127, affd (CA2 NY) 82 F2d 275, 28 USPQ 426.

Where defendant had constant access to plaintiff's chart since date of copyright and was fully familiar with it and apparently copied subject matter of plaintiff's chart, in some instances changing words, but retaining their meanings, infringement was clear and deliberate. Deutsch v Felton (1939, DC NY) 27 F Supp 895, 41 USPQ 616.

Where access is not proven, and experts differ as to similarity, court holds that there is no such similarity as indicates copying. Arnstein v American Soc. of Composers, etc. (1939, DC NY) 29 F Supp 388, 42 USPQ 581.

In infringement cases involving musical compositions, plaintiff must prove access and identity; access alone is not important but, if there is identity, access may determine infringement claim; time element is helpful in determining access. Carew v R. K. O. Radio Pictures, Inc. (1942, DC Cal) 43 F Supp 199, 53 USPQ 152.

In second circuit, first question for determination in case of alleged literary larceny is whether there is direct evidence of access to plaintiff's book; possible access does not require speculation that there was actual access. Sarkadi v Wiman (1942, DC NY) 43 F Supp 778, affd (CA2 NY) 135 F2d 1002, 57 USPQ 361.

Despite similarities between plays, court accepts defendant author's testimony that he did not read plaintiff's play although plaintiff submitted it to him and defendant, after his secretary had read play and orally reported, declined to produce it; it is significant that after such rejection there was no production or publication of plaintiff's play; two years elapsed before defendant began writing play; origin of defendant's play is plausibly explained. McConnor v Kaufman (1943, DC NY) 49 F Supp 738, 57 USPQ 80, affd (CA2 NY) 139 F2d 116, 60 USPQ 356.

Defense of nonaccess is sustained although corporate defendant had access to plaintiff's composition for day or two before completion of script of defendant's motion picture, since none of its employees, connected immediately or remotely with conception of picture, its production, direction, or making changes in it, had access thereto and no similarity sustains suspicion of plagiarism. Stein v RKO Radio Pictures, Inc. (DC NY) 57 USPQ 102.

There can be no copying in absence of access. Arnstein v Twentieth Century Fox Film Corp. (1943, DC NY) 52 F Supp 114, 59 USPQ 21.

Protection afforded literary or musical property by copyright law differs substantially from that afforded patentee under patent law; originator of patentable article is protected against infringements even as against subsequent originator who had no notice of patented article; in realm of copyrights, however, each originator has property right in his artistic achievement and plaintiff must establish that defendant was guilty of plagiarism; access to plaintiff's work must be shown. Edward B. Marks Music Corp. v Borst Music Pub. Co., Inc. (1953, DC NJ) 110 F Supp 913, 97 USPQ 394.

Access together with similarity between defendant's and plaintiff's copyrighted works warrants inference that defendant copied copyrighted work. Advisers Inc. v Wiesen-Hart Inc. (1958, DC Ohio) 161 F Supp 831, 117 USPQ 330.

In addition to requiring showing of copying, some cases state that alleged infringer's access to copyrighted article must be proved in order to establish infringement; however, since there can be no copying unless infringer is familiar with copyrighted work, and since there is no infringement if two authors independently create similar works, access is but a means of eliminating coincidence or independent effort as an explanation for likeness between copyrighted and infringing articles. Doran v Sunset House Distributing Corp. (1961, DC Cal) 197 F Supp 940, 131 USPQ 94, affd (CA9 Cal) 304 F2d 251, 134 USPQ 4, and (disapproved on other grounds L. Batlin & Son, Inc. v Snyder (CA2 NY) 536 F2d 486, cert den 429 US 857, 50 L Ed 2d 135, 97 S Ct 156).

Proof of access establishes no more than opportunity to copy, not actual copying; inference of copying may arise when there is proof of access coupled with showing of similarity; where there is strong evidence of access, less proof of similarity may suffice; if evidence of access is uncertain, strong proof of similarity should be shown before inference of copying may be indulged. Golding v R. K. O. Pictures, Inc. (1949, Cal) 208 P2d 1, 82 USPQ 136, subsequent op on reh 35 Cal 2d 690, 221 P2d 95, 86 USPQ 537.

When two individuals write concerning same

subject matter it is not unnatural to find common features, particularly if purpose and treatment of subject run in same channel; unless it is clearly established that alleged plagiarist had access to story of other, plagiarism cannot be predicated. Tamas v 20th Century Fox Film Corp. (1941, Sup) 25 NYS2d 899, 48 USPQ 573.

To sustain charge of copying musical composition, more than similarity and identity must be shown; inference of copying may arise when there is proof of access coupled with showing of similarity; with access and identity assumed, ultimate offense to be established is tortious copying; however, explanation of origin of material allegedly plagiarized is sufficient to defeat plaintiff even where access is proved; one cannot infer access from identity and then, based upon inference of access, infer that tortious appropriation occurred, since this is improper founding of one inference upon another inference; also, before inference of access from identity may even be considered, it is incumbent upon plaintiff to prove priority of his composition. Smith v Berlin (1955) 207 Misc 862, 141 NYS2d 110, 105 USPQ 296.

15. Amount copied as affecting infringement, generally

Business information and credit rating book was infringed, but to such slight extent that equity would refuse any remedy. Dun v Lumbermen's Credit Asso. (1908) 209 US 20, 52 L Ed 663, 28 S Ct 335.

To constitute infringement there must be copying of substantial or material part of work. Hirsch v Paramount Pictures, Inc. (1937, DC Cal) 17 F Supp 816, 32 USPQ 233; De Montijo v 20th Century Fox Film Corp. (1941, DC Cal) 40 F Supp 133, 50 USPQ 440; Solomon v R. K. O. Radio Pictures, Inc. (1942, DC NY) 44 F Supp 780, 53 USPQ 468; Christianson v West Pub. Co. (1944, DC Cal) 53 F Supp 454, 60 USPQ 279, affd (CA9 Cal) 149 F2d 202, 65 USPQ 263; Silvers v Russell (1953, DC Cal) 113 F Supp 119, 98 USPQ 376; Loew's, Inc. v Columbia Broadcasting System, Inc. (1955, DC Cal) 131 F Supp 165, 105 USPQ 302, affd (CA9 Cal) 239 F2d 532, 112 USPQ 11, affd 356 US 43, 2 L Ed 2d 583, 78 S Ct 667, 116 USPQ 479, reh den 356 US 934, 2 L Ed 2d 764, 78 S Ct 770; Ansehl v Puritan Pharmaceutical Co. (1932, CA8 Mo) 61 F2d 131, 15 USPQ 38, cert den 287 US 666, 77 L Ed 574, 53 S Ct 224; Reed v Holliday (1884, CC Pa) 19 F 325.

Appropriation of but part of copyright constitutes infringement of whole of copyright. Brady v Daly (1897, CA2 NY) 83 F 1007, affd 175 US 148, 44 L Ed 109, 20 S Ct 62.

Infringement of copyright consists in copying

of some substantial and material part thereof, and it is not necessary to compare in detail copyrighted and infringing articles. Wilson v Haber Bros., Inc. (1921, CA2 NY) 275 F 346; Dymow v Bolton (1926, CA2 NY) 11 F2d 690.

Appropriation of idea, form, or perspective of two cuts from hundreds in catalogue is unsubstantial infringement. Mathews Conveyer Co. v Palmer-Bee Co. (1943, CA6 Mich) 135 F2d 73, 57 USPQ 219.

Fact that common fictional matter is only small and early part of life of historical character, and only portion of defendant's biography, may affect amount of recovery, but does not prevent liability for copying from plaintiff's uncopyrighted screen play; same is true as to magazine publisher which reprinted only small portion of defendant's work; particularly in view of importance of love interest to movie trade, copying cannot be considered insignificant. De Acosta v Brown (1944, CA2 NY) 146 F2d 408, 63 USPQ 311, cert den 325 US 862, 89 L Ed 1983, 65 S Ct 1197 and cert den 325 US 862, 89 L Ed 1983, 65 S Ct 1198.

Test of material and substantial infringement has no application to catalogues; defendants infringe despite fact that they copied only nine of hundreds of items in copyrighted catalogues. Markham v A. E. Borden Co. (1953, CA1 Mass) 206 F2d 199, 98 USPQ 346.

Differences between copyrighted work and accused production do not negative infringement, which exists where there is copying of substantial portion of copyrighted work. Wihtol v Wells (1956, CA7 Ill) 231 F2d 550, 109 USPQ 200.

To constitute invasion of copyright, it is not necessary that whole of work be copied or even large portion of it in form or substance, but it is sufficient to constitute infringement if so much is taken that value of original is sensibly diminished, or labors of original author are substantially, to injurious extent, appropriated by another; test of infringement is whether work is recognizable by ordinary observance as having been taken from copyrighted source; slight differences and variations will not serve as defense. Bradbury v Columbia Broadcasting System, Inc. (1961, CA9 Cal) 287 F2d 478, 128 USPQ 376, cert dismd 368 US 801, 7 L Ed 2d 15, 82 S Ct 19.

Copying and publishing of substantial part of author's manuscript subjects appropriator to liability for fraudulent use of another's property. Bartlett v Crittenden (CC Ohio) F Cas No 1076.

Though author's works may not be complete for publication, piracy of material portions thereof constitutes infringement. Bartlett v Crittenden (CC Ohio) F Cas No 1082.

Infringement is not predicated upon quantity of material pirated. Gray v Russell (CC Mass) F Cas No 5728.

Although new work has some similarities and shows evidence of copying small parts of copyrighted work, it does not amount to infringement when work is dictionary or almanac. Webb v Powers (CC Mass) F Cas No 17323.

It is no defense, in action for infringement of musical composition, that playing consisted only of short excerpts. Harms v Cohen (1922, DC Pa) 279 F 276.

If so much is taken that value of original is diminished, or labors of original author are substantially appropriated by another, that is sufficient to constitute infringement. National Institute, Inc. v Nutt (1928, DC Conn) 28 F2d 132, affd (CA2 Conn) 31 F2d 236.

Where, in advertising pamphlet defendant copied three sentences, although not exactly, from plaintiff's copyrighted book, which constituted only small part of book, and about one-twentieth of pamphlet, this constituted infringement and although defendant acknowledged source, this did not relieve it from liability. Henry Holt & Co. v Liggett & Myers Tobacco Co. (1938, DC Pa) 23 F Supp 302, 37 USPQ 449.

By contract which did not mention copyright, plaintiff gave defendant mats for printing in its newspaper; after termination of contract defendant printed one cut inadvertently; this was not copyright infringement since on notice all mats were returned to plaintiff. Norm Co. v John A. Brown Co. (1939, DC Okla) 26 F Supp 707, 40 USPQ 419.

Defendant infringed copyrighted telephone directories published periodically by publishing directories copied from telephone directories. Southern Bell Tel. & Tel. Co. v Donnelly (1940, DC Fla) 35 F Supp 425, 48 USPQ 11.

Fact that diagrams on only 11 pages are infringements does not in itself prevent securing relief limited to 11 infringing pages although book has 254 pages. Colonial Book Co. v Amsco School Publications, Inc. (1941, DC NY) 41 F Supp 156, 51 USPQ 33.

It is not necessary to exactly duplicate another's literary work to be liable for plagiarism, it being sufficient if unfair use is made by lifting substantial portion of it, but even exact counterpart does not constitute plagiarism if it was arrived at independently and without resort to other's work, or even if some changes in defendant's story were suggested by plaintiff's work. O'Rourke v RKO Radio Pictures, Inc. (1942, DC Mass) 44 F Supp 480, 53 USPQ 95.

After termination of contract for use in advertising by defendant of plaintiff's matrices, defendant infringes by using such matrices in newspaper advertising although advertisements were used without defendant's approval, defendant paying for such advertisements; where only small part of matrix is used, there is no liability. Advertisers Exch., Inc. v Bayless Drug Store, Inc. (1943, DC NJ) 50 F Supp 169, 57 USPQ 273.

Rule of de minimis non curat lex does not apply although defendant used only small amount of copyrighted material, since portion taken was important. Advertisers Exchange, Inc. v Hinkley (1951, DC Mo) 101 F Supp 801, 92 USPQ 313, affd (CA8 Mo) 199 F2d 313, 95 USPQ 124, cert den 344 US 921, 97 L Ed 710, 73 S Ct 388.

Fact that portion of plaintiff's manuscript copied in defendant's book constitutes only relatively small part of book is not test of infringement; question is whether material and substantial portion was copied. Smith v Little, Brown & Co. (1965, DC NY) 245 F Supp 451, 146 USPQ 540, affd (CA2 NY) 360 F2d 928, 149 USPQ 799, on remand (DC NY) 273 F Supp 870, affd (CA2 NY) 396 F2d 150.

Copyright in telephone directory is infringed by extracting portions of directory to form smaller directory for town included in larger directory and copying advertising art work from directory. Southwestern Bell Tel. Co. v Nationwide Independent Directory Service, Inc. (1974, DC Ark) 371 F Supp 900, 182 USPQ 193.

Copying of only insubstantial phrases or sentences relating to historical facts and events in biographical work on Rosenbergs is insufficient for infringement by work differing in nearly every other respect. Gardner v Nizer (1975, DC NY) 391 F Supp 940, 185 USPQ 485, mod on other grounds (DC NY) 396 F Supp 63.

If such similarities exist as to justify inference of copying of protectible material from plaintiff's unpublished, uncopyrighted play, it is necessary to prove only that substantial part of play was copied. Golding v R. K. O. Pictures, Inc. (1949, Cal) 208 P2d 1, 82 USPQ 136, subsequent op on reh 35 Cal 2d 690, 221 P2d 95, 86 USPQ 537.

16. —Motion pictures

Motion picture is infringed where defendant deliberately lifted almost bodily 57 consecutive scenes constituting 20 per cent of picture; whole motion picture need not be copied to constitute infringement; copying of major sequence is sufficient; slight differences are no defense. Universal Pictures Co. v Harold Lloyd Corp. (1947, CA9 Cal) 162 F2d 354, 73 USPQ 317.

While access is sine qua non in copyright cause, fact that defendant had, by hypothesis, access to plaintiff's work is not fatal to defense, for additional question is always whether defendant has made unfair use of sufficient amount of plaintiff's copyrightable matter to justify holding of infringement. Shipman v R. K. O. Radio Pictures, Inc. (1937, DC NY) 20 F Supp 249, 35 USPQ 242, affd (CA2 NY) 100 F2d 533, 40 USPQ 211.

17. —Musical works

Copying chorus only of song is infringement. Johns & Johns Printing Co. v Paull-Pioneer Music Corp. (1939, CA8 Mo) 102 F2d 282, 41 USPQ 3.

Song written for score of movie is properly held not to infringe copyrighted song in spite of identity of first four notes, where evidence shows four note sequence is common to many songs and that alleged infringement differs in some respects and was written without knowledge of copyrighted song. Granite Music Corp. v United Artists Corp. (1976, CA9 Cal) 532 F2d 718, 189 USPQ 406.

Piracy of song is committed if that portion which is whole meritorious part of song is incorporated in another song, without any material alteration in sequence of bars. Northern Music Corp. v King Record Distributing Co. (1952, DC NY) 105 F Supp 393, 93 USPQ 512.

Since there are only three notes involved in sequences which are common to two songs, it cannot be said that there is sufficiency of musical concept in either to rise to dignity of motif; coincidence of concept could account for sequences; infringement is not found since plaintiff does not prove access. Lampert v Hollis Music, Inc. (1956, DC NY) 138 F Supp 505, 109 USPQ 242.

Only two lines are claimed to have been appropriated from plaintiffs' copyrighted lyric, one of which is from source in public domain; however, this does not prevent finding of infringement if lines appropriated constitute important and vital part of two compositions rather than being merely incidental or trivial. Whitney v Ross Jungnickel, Inc. (1960, DC NY) 179 F Supp 751, 124 USPQ 219.

18. Common source material, generally

Pamphlet, consisting of official report of World War by General Pershing, poems, and drawings was not infringed by defendant's pamphlet which contained same report, but different drawings. Eggers v Sun Sales Corp. (1920, CA2 NY) 263 F 373.

In the case of compilation, if it were demonstrated that any portions which A copied were taken by B from prior sources available to both parties, former would still be infringer; fact that such prior sources were shown to exist could

have no bearing except on question whether A copied from these sources rather than from B's code. Hartfield v Peterson (1937, CA2 NY) 91 F2d 998, 34 USPQ 305.

Similarity of make-up usually signifies same source. Time, Inc. v Ultem Publications, Inc. (1938, CA2 NY) 96 F2d 164, 37 USPQ 559.

One work does not violate copyright in another simply because of similarity resulting from fact that both deal with same subject or have same common source. Dorsey v Old Surety Life Ins. Co. (1938, CA10 Okla) 98 F2d 872, 39 USPQ 92, 119 ALR 1250.

Question is not whether defendant could have obtained same information by going to same source as did plaintiff, but whether she did go to same sources and do her own independent research. Toksvig v Bruce Pub. Co. (1950, CA7 Wis) 181 F2d 664, 85 USPQ 339.

Lack of substantial similarities between copyrighted book and magazine article both based on same folk legend requires finding of no infringement. Reyher v Children's Television Workshop (1976, CA2 NY) 533 F2d 87, 190 USPQ 387.

Similarity of background does not give rise to infringement; piracy is not shown by resemblances expected of authors writing of common topic. Chrisite v Harris (1942, DC NY) 47 F Supp 39, 54 USPQ 360, affd (CA2 NY) 154 F2d 827, 69 USPQ 198, cert den 329 US 734, 91 L Ed 634, 67 S Ct 97.

Availability to defendant of common sources for obtaining names for inclusion in its directory is no defense to action for copyright infringement if defendant actually copied names from plaintiff's directory; ultimate probandum is copying; existence of common sources is merely evidence negating copying. Caldwell-Clements, Inc. v Cowan Publishing Corp. (1955, DC NY) 130 F Supp 326, 105 USPQ 116.

Similarities of incidents alone are not infringement, especially when both works are based on common sources and concern events in life of historic figure. Greenbie v Noble (1957, DC NY) 151 F Supp 45, 113 USPQ 115.

Copying of names and addresses of suppliers of gardening materials from copyrighted compilation does not infringe because some of lists are in public domain or were copied from other copyrighted works, and since descriptive material was not copied, copyright does not extend to names, addresses, and subject matter headings that are generally available from other sources. Schroeder v William Morrow & Co. (1976, DC Ill) 194 USPQ 37.

Fact that defendant could have obtained similar story from prior works is of no consequence if it copied plaintiffs' story. Golding v R. K. O.

Pictures, Inc. (1949, Cal) 208 P2d 1, 82 USPQ 136, subsequent op on reh 35 Cal 2d 690, 221 P2d 95, 86 USPQ 537.

19. —Art works

There is no infringement where both parties, independently, went to common sources for their maps, using coloring always associated with maps, and novelty in plaintiff's map, such as state grouping, originated with defendant. Christianson v West Pub. Co. (1944, DC Cal) 53 F Supp 454, 60 USPQ 279, affd (CA9 Cal) 149 F2d 202, 65 USPQ 263.

Inspiration for plaintiffs' and defendants' miniature religious shrines was specific shrine; by reason of such resemblance, infringement may not be assumed because principal elements of both designs are taken from common source. Allegrini v De Angelis (1944, DC Pa) 59 F Supp 248, 64 USPQ 165, affd (CA3 Pa) 149 F2d 815, 65 USPQ 589.

Even though alleged infringer may get idea for his work from copyrighted work, there is no infringement unless copyrighted work was copied; this is especially true where allegedly infringing material is limited to pictorial representation of commonly known vegetable which is attached as label upon containers in which vegetable is packed. Rochelle Asparagus Co. v Princeville Canning Co. (1959, DC Ill) 170 F Supp 809, 121 USPQ 78.

Jeweled turtle pin resembling natural turtle and differing in many minor details from copyrighted turtle pin does not infringe, because copyright does not prevent others from copying natural turtles. Herbert Rosenthal Jewelry Corp. v Honora Jewelry Co. (1974, DC NY) 378 F Supp 485, 183 USPQ 97, affd (CA2 NY) 509 F2d 64.

20. —Musical works

With relatively few existing musical intervals and vast amount of music in public domain, it is rash to infer that sequence in melody is copied from any particular song containing same sequence. Arnstein v Broadcast Music, Inc. (1943, CA2 NY) 137 F2d 410, 58 USPQ 451.

Similarities of rhythm plainly attributable to words and phrases of common "lyric" (Lincoln's Gettysburg Address) constitute no indication of improper copying or wrongful appropriation of music; just as text of address is in public domain, so is natural rhythm of words in which its thoughts are articulated. O'Brien v Thall (1960, CA2 Conn) 283 F2d 741, 127 USPQ 296.

Trial court properly admitted evidence showing that several other songs use same four note sequence of copyrighted song as common musical phrase as tending to show likelihood of alleged infringer using same four note sequence without copying, and judgment of noninfringement is affirmed. Granite Music Corp. v United Artists Corp. (1976, CA9 Cal) 532 F2d 718, 189 USPQ 406.

Where use of eight notes in sequence in chorus of respondent's composition is similar to eight notes contained and used in prior copyrighted works by previous masters, melody of plaintiff's copyrighted musical number is not entirely original and there is no infringement. Darrell v Joe Morris Music Co. (DC NY) 37 USPQ 446, affd (CA2 NY) 113 F2d 80, 46 USPQ 167.

There is no plagiarism where it is obvious that source of lyrics of two songs was old rhyme or ditty. Newcomb v Young (1942, DC NY) 43 F Supp 744, 52 USPQ 373.

Court considers technical details of notes in composition; since same sequence of notes appeared in prior compositions, its use by defendant does not establish that defendant copied plaintiff's song; similarity may be coincidental; defendant's song may have been derived from source other than plaintiff. Perlman v Remick Music Corp. (DC NY) 61 USPQ 227.

Words in specific lines of songs are practically identical, but language is repetition of title of songs, which plaintiff concedes was not original with herself; hence, element of similarity has no significance. Gingg v Twentieth Century-Fox Film Corp. (1944, DC Cal) 56 F Supp 701, 62 USPQ 121.

Fact that remainder of lyrics, music, and themes of two songs are entirely different strengthens conclusion that similar first two lines of lyrics were created independently from common source in public domain. Whitney v Ross Jungnickel, Inc. (1960, DC NY) 179 F Supp 751, 124 USPQ 219.

21. Independent creations

Copyrighted directory is not infringed by similar directory which is product of independent work. Mazer v Stein (1954) 347 US 201, 98 L Ed 630, 74 S Ct 460, 100 USPQ 325, reh den 347 US 949, 98 L Ed 1096, 74 S Ct 637.

Mere similarity or even identity of two works independently produced does not of itself constitute infringement, there being no actual copying. Harold Lloyd Corp. v Witwer (1933, CA9 Cal) 65 F2d 1, cert dismd (US) 78 L Ed 1507, 54 S Ct 94; Twentieth Century-Fox Film Corp. v Stonesifer (1944, CA9 Cal) 140 F2d 579, 60 USPQ 392; Christianson v West Pub. Co. (1944, DC Cal) 53 F Supp 454, 60 USPQ 279, affd (CA9 Cal) 149 F2d 202, 65 USPQ 263.

Plagiarism, but not independent reproduction of copyrighted musical work, is infringement.

Arnstein v Edward B. Marks Music Corp. (1936, CA2 NY) 82 F2d 275, 28 USPQ 426.

Evidence was properly admitted showing use of same four note musical phrase in songs other than copyrighted song to support testimony that alleged infringer independently used same phrase and did not copy or have access to copyrighted song. Granite Music Corp. v United Artists Corp. (1976, CA9 Cal) 532 F2d 718, 189 USPQ 406.

Copyright of painting, features of which were originated by prospective purchaser thereof, was not infringed by later painting made independently of former, but having same essential features. McCarthy v L. Adler Bros. & Co. (1915, DC NY) 227 F 630.

To arrive independently upon precise material copyrighted, without copying, does not constitute infringement. Fred Fisher, Inc. v Dillingham (1924, DC NY) 298 F 145.

Test of infringement is whether second work is original treatment of subject open to treatment by all, or is but copy of first work. Pellegrini v Allegrini (1924, DC Pa) 2 F2d 610.

Independent reproduction of copyrighted work is not infringement; similarities or identities must do more than engender suspicion of piracy; they must establish piracy with reasonable certainty; defendant's play must be so like plaintiff's that one may reasonably infer that it was copied therefrom. Chrisite v Harris (1942, DC NY) 47 F Supp 39, 54 USPQ 360, affd (CA2 NY) 154 F2d 827, 69 USPQ 198, cert den 329 US 734, 91 L Ed 634, 67 S Ct 97.

Although defendant's books contain considerable data as to estate taxes contained in plaintiff's copyrighted books, there is no infringement; comparison of books discloses considerable difference between them; defendant's books were independent conception of its employee without knowledge of data in plaintiff's books; defendant did not copy plaintiff's books but published only that which it believed original with itself. Carpenter v Peoples-Pittsburgh Trust Co. (1943, DC Pa) 49 F Supp 597, 57 USPQ 141.

Had defendant created his material in exact form as plaintiff's, but without knowledge of existence of plaintiff's material and without copying it, there could be no infringement since there would have been no copying. Gordon v Weir (1953, DC Mich) 111 F Supp 117, 97 USPQ 387, affd (CA6 Mich) 216 F2d 508, 104 USPQ 40.

Fact that plaintiff, although he had known of accused map for many years, never challenged right of owner thereof to use it lends support to thought that plaintiff considered that map was independent production entitled to copyright and not map plagiarized from his map. Hayden v Chalfant Press, Inc. (1959, DC Cal) 177 F Supp 303, 123 USPQ 475, affd (CA9 Cal) 281 F2d 543, 126 USPQ 483.

If two works were result of independent intellectual effort of two authors and are derived from common sources available to all, there can be no copyright infringement even if works resemble each other, since there was no copying. Barton Candy Corp. v Tell Chocolate Novelties Corp. (1959, DC NY) 178 F Supp 577, 123 USPQ 425.

There can be no infringement of copyright without copying; thus, there is no infringement where defendant did not copy plaintiff's copyrighted star, but conceived and developed star independently of plaintiff's work. Elekes v Bradford Novelty Co. (1960, DC Mass) 183 F Supp 730, 125 USPQ 166.

When alleged infringer did his own independent research and based his work on that research, there can be no copyright infringement of another's work regardless of degree of similarity between publications. Holdredge v Knight Publishing Corp. (1963, DC Cal) 214 F Supp 921, 136 USPQ 615.

Proof of copying is basic to any claim of infringement; identical works may, if independently created, each receive statutory copyright protection, and each withstand charges, by the other, of infringement. Stratchborneo v Arc Music Corp. (1973, DC NY) 357 F Supp 1393.

22. Memorized material

If thing covered by copyright has become familiar to mind's eye, and one produces it from memory and writes it down, he copies just same, and this may be done without conscious plagiarism. Edwards & Deutsch Lithographing Co. v Boorman (1926, CA7 Ill) 15 F2d 35, cert den 273 US 738, 71 L Ed 867, 47 S Ct 247.

Although defendant did not have plaintiff's song before him when he composed his song, he was acquainted with words and music of plaintiff's song; infringement exists, since one may copy from memory. Wihtol v Wells (1956, CA7 Ill) 231 F2d 550, 109 USPQ 200.

Copying from memory would be infringement. Freudenthal v Hebrew Pub. Co. (1942, DC NY) 44 F Supp 754, 53 USPQ 466.

23. Phonorecord reproduction

Owner of unpublished musical composition copyrighted under this title and not later reproduced in copies for sale, can maintain infringement action against one making and selling phonographic records of composition. Shilkret v Musicraft Records, Inc. (1942, CA2 NY) 131

F2d 929, 55 USPQ 469, cert den 319 US 742, 87 L Ed 1699, 63 S Ct 1030.

Motion-picture producer infringes if he sells sound tracks which reproduce copyrighted song, but vendee to whom he sells is not infringer until he in turn sells or uses same in public performance for profit. Foreign & Domestic Music Corp. v Licht (1952, CA2 NY) 196 F2d 627, 93 USPQ 272.

Unauthorized manufacture of set of records is infringement of each copyright, and unauthorized sale of some or all of that set is separate infringement. Shapiro, Bernstein & Co. v Goody (1957, CA2 NY) 248 F2d 260, 115 USPQ 36, cert den 355 US 952, 2 L Ed 2d 529, 78 S Ct 536.

Even though some individual songs of album may not be protectible, copyright claimed for album is infringed by unauthorized duplication of any copyrightable component part. United States v Taxe (1976, CA9 Cal) 540 F2d 961, 192 USPQ 204.

Record produced from one manufactured by plaintiff, so that it will produce same song with same voice as plaintiff's record, cannot be made subject of infringement suit unless song was copyrighted. Fonotipia, Ltd. v Bradley (1909, CC NY) 171 F 951 (ovrld on other grounds G. Ricordi & Co. v Haendler (CA2 NY) 194 F2d 914).

Fact that mechanical music roll can produce tune alone and not words does not negative infringement of copyright of both music and lyric. M. Witmark & Sons v Calloway (1927, DC Tenn) 22 F2d 412.

Musical composition is infringed by (1) causing copies of sheet music of infringing composition to be printed and by purporting to license phonograph records and broadcasting of infringing composition, (2) offering to sell and selling copies of sheet music of infringing composition, and (3) making and selling phonograph records of infringing composition. Northern Music Corp. v King Record Distributing Co. (1952, DC NY) 105 F Supp 393, 93 USPQ 512.

Ordinarily, authorized recorder of copyrighted music cannot sue for copyright infringement although, in addition to payment of royalties to copyright owner and to recording artists, he may be required, as condition of recording, to make payments to trust funds for benefit of musicians. Persons who sell and distribute records of pirated songs are liable in independant action under copyright law. Harms, Inc. v F. W. Woolworth Co. (1958, DC Cal) 163 F Supp 484, 118 USPQ 436.

Unauthorized recordings and tape copies of recordings of copyrighted music infringe proprietor's exclusive rights to record, copy and manufacture tape recordings of its musical compositions. Mills Music, Inc. v Arizona (1975, DC Ariz) 187 USPQ 22.

Duplication of phonorecords onto magnetic tapes and leasing magnetic tapes to commercial establishments for use as background music constitutes copyright infringement and is subject to full remedies under copyright act. Polylok Corp. v Steinberg & Neumann, Inc. (1976, DC NY) 194 USPQ 87.

24. Public domain material

Card carrying new and old matter is infringed only by copying new matter. Jackson v Quickslip Co. (1940, CA2 NY) 110 F2d 731, 45 USPQ 6.

Irrespective of sources from which author may derive material which he uses, picture or writing which is his own production cannot be copied; prior art is only relevant as bearing on question whether alleged infringer has copied author or has taken his material directly from prior art. Detective Comics, Inc. v Bruns Publications, Inc. (1940, CA2 NY) 111 F2d 432, 45 USPQ 291.

Court need not determine whether, if basic design had been original with plaintiff, defendants' might not be sufficiently imitative to infringe plaintiff's copyright; inasmuch as basic design is in public domain, plaintiff is entitled to relief only if defendants copied its expression; whatever their intent, defendants did not succeed in copying expression; hence, there was no infringement. Millworth Converting Corp. v Slifka (1960, CA2 NY) 276 F2d 443, 125 USPQ 506.

Even though source of material in plaintiff's copyrighted newsreel film was in public domain, this does not permit defendant to directly copy plaintiff's film; defendant can use copy of original films which were part of public domain, but he cannot copy plaintiff's copy thereof. Axelbank v Rony (1960, CA9 Cal) 277 F2d 314, 125 USPQ 262.

Author in writing second book does not infringe copyright of former book written by him, although same historical facts are brought out and there is some similarity of expression, provided it is not merely reproduction of former book. Kennerley v Simonds (1917, DC NY) 247 F 822.

Plaintiff may offer information in possession of defendant as to whether matter is in public domain abroad and as to whether defendant has proceeded on such assumption. Paine v Electrical Research Products, Inc. (1939, DC NY) 30 F Supp 260, 43 USPQ 240.

After showing of access, strong proof is required that defendant's material came from independent source, but when dates, records, and story drafts showing independent source appear to be authentic, to nullify their effect plaintiff must show that defendant fraudulently falsified them. O'Rourke v RKO Radio Pictures, Inc. (1942, DC Mass) 44 F Supp 480, 53 USPQ 95.

There is no infringement of plaintiff's means of expression if similarities result from common subjects and sources within public domain of common knowledge and property. Crume v Pacific Mut. Life Ins. Co. (DC Ill) 55 USPQ 267, affd (CA7 Ill) 140 F2d 182, 60 USPQ 359, cert den 322 US 755, 88 L Ed 1584, 64 S Ct 1265.

Use of ideas of others in producing motion pictures does not render one liable for infringement; most stories are based upon knowledge of facts about people, places, and things, and knowledge is acquired largely by learning what others have learned. Funkhouser v Loew's, Inc. (1952, DC Mo) 108 F Supp 476, 96 USPQ 115, affd (CA8 Mo) 208 F2d 185, 99 USPQ 448, reh den 348 US 890, 99 L Ed 700, 75 S Ct 209 and cert den 348 US 843, 99 L Ed 664, 75 S Ct 64.

In order to establish that defendant's novel infringes upon plaintiff's biography, plaintiff must show that defendant copied from biography rather than resorted to original sources available to all. Greenbie v Noble (1957, DC NY) 151 F Supp 45, 113 USPQ 115.

Test as to copyright infringement is not test of mere likeness, but claimed infringement must be copy, more or less servile, of copyrighted work and not original treatment of subject open alike to treatment by copyright holder and others; where principal elements of design of plaintiff's copyrighted work and of defendant's allegedly infringing article are taken, as common source, from object in public domain, mere resemblance will not justify finding of infringement; publication of identical works cannot be enjoined if defendant's is result of independent research; one work does not violate copyright in another simply because there is similarity between two, if similarity results from fact that both deal with same subject or have same source; however, availability of common source, is no defense if defendant actually copied plaintiff's work. Alva Studios, Inc. v Winninger (1959, DC NY) 177 F Supp 265, 123 USPQ 487.

Originality in map making is confined to original designation of mountains, lakes, rivers, trails, and roads and other contours and configurations of the territory, and of their names, which are not found in maps prepared by others; hence, claim of infringement must be confined to "lifting" of these novel additions; cartographer is limited to what, by expenditure of labor and money, he was able to discover in territory and note on his maps which was not noted on basic

official or other maps. Hayden v Chalfant Press, Inc. (1959, DC Cal) 177 F Supp 303, 123 USPQ 475, affd (CA9 Cal) 281 F2d 543, 126 USPQ 483.

Fact that materials used in making plaintiff's copyrighted map were in public domain is important on issue of infringement, since later comers are entitled to use not only all that has gone before but even plaintiff's contribution if they draw from it only more general pattern, that is, if they keep clear of its expression. C. S. Hammond & Co. v International College Globe, Inc. (1962, DC NY) 210 F Supp 206, 135 USPQ 56.

Material that is in public domain can be used by an author; in infringement action, substantial similarity between works is not established by mere appearance of such material in accused work. Stratchborneo v Arc Music Corp. (1973, DC NY) 357 F Supp 1393.

Fact that plaintiff submitted and offered to sell to defendant synopsis containing public domain material and that, thereafter, defendant used same material does not support inference that defendant promised to pay for synopsis or for idea of using material; however, fact that plaintiff used public domain material does not justify defendant in appropriating plaintiff's synopsis. Desny v Wilder (1956) 46 Cal 2d 715, 299 P2d 257, 110 USPQ 433.

Reading and comparison of books can best dispose of claim of infringement; infringement is not shown by similarities in historical facts in public domain, easily available to anyone interested in pursuing the subject. Turner v Century House Publishing Co. (1968, NY Sup Ct) 159 USPQ 699.

25. Reprints

Reprinting in this country of English edition of dictionary, when American edition was properly copyrighted in this country, is infringement of American edition. G. & C. Merriam Co. v United Dictionary Co. (1906, CA7 Ill) 146 F 354, affd 208 US 260, 52 L Ed 478, 28 S Ct 290.

Reprint of foreign book, not protectible by copyright, is infringement of American author's copyrighted book, forming part thereof. Black v Henry G. Allen Co. (1890, CC NY) 42 F 618.

Reproduction, retracing, or relithographing of any material part of map is infringement. Sanborn Map & Pub. Co. v Dakin Pub. Co. (1889, CC Cal) 39 F 266.

Copyright of statistical atlas containing maps, tables, and printed text was infringed by unauthorized reprinting of eight maps therefrom. Black v Henry G. Allen Co. (1890, CC NY) 42 F 618.

Reprinting and replacing missing pages of copyrighted book is infringement. Purchaser of second-hand copyrighted schoolbook, cannot copy map or small portion of the text of original publication, which may be missing from such book, and resell it with its replaced parts without infringing copyright. Ginn & Co. v Apollo Pub. Co. (1914, DC Pa) 215 F 772.

Making of reproductions in part of copyrighted map constituted infringement whether defendants acted in good faith and by mistake or by design; neither absence of key to map nor reduction in size, so that some of symbols could be used only with difficulty, makes difference. Towle v Ross (1940, DC Or) 32 F Supp 125, 45 USPQ 143.

Defendant infringes where, instead of making his own corrections in accents and cantillation marks in Books of Moses, which were in public domain (in which case there would have been no infringement), he photographed plaintiff's books and published them as his own work. Shulsinger v Grossman (1954, DC NY) 119 F Supp 691.

2. Similarity

26. Generally

Copying is essence of plagiarism; direct proof of copying is often impossible to procure; hence, access to original plus similarity between original and accused works frequently do duty for proof of copying, and sometimes similarity alone does duty for both; but opportunity plus inclination are insufficient to establish plagiarism unless there be similarity between works. Millstein v Leland Hayward, Inc. (1950, DC NY) 10 FRD 198, 85 USPQ 448.

Availability of plaintiff's work in magazine of national circulation is merely some circumstantial evidence of access; also, access is merely circumstantial evidence of copying; against this double circumstantial evidence, defendant's denial that he ever saw plaintiff's work must be weighed; with evidence so posited, plaintiff is entitled to little benefit from "inverse ratio" rule to effect that, when access is established, lesser degree of similarity is required. Morse v Fields (1954, DC NY) 127 F Supp 63, 104 USPQ 54.

Plaintiffs must establish that actual copying occurred in order to make out case of copyright infringement; mere coincidental similarity, absent copying, is not enough; since direct proof of copying is virtually impossible to adduce, evidence of copying must necessarily be circumstantial and is ordinarily based on proof of access and similarity; if copying occurred, it does not matter if it was done unconsciously and without intent to appropriate plaintiffs' work; bad faith is not necessary ingredient of plaintiffs' proof.

Whitney v Ross Jungnickel, Inc. (1960, DC NY) 179 F Supp 751, 124 USPQ 219.

To prove copyright infringement, plaintiff must establish copying going so far as to constitute improper appropriation; evidence of copying may consist of admission by defendant that it copied or circumstantial evidence; circumstantial evidence showing copying may consist of sufficiently strong showings of combination of access by defendant to plaintiff's work and strong similarity between works. Marcal Paper Mills, Inc. v Scott Paper Co. (1968, DC NJ) 290 F Supp 43, 160 USPQ 147.

In determining plagiarism where there is no direct evidence, trier of fact must rely upon circumstantial evidence and reasonable inferences drawn therefrom. Golding v R. K. O. Pictures, Inc. (1949, Cal) 208 P2d 1, 82 USPQ 136, subsequent op on reh 35 Cal 2d 690, 221 P2d 95, 86 USPQ 537.

27. Error reproduction

Proof of errors and blunders common to plaintiff's work and their reproduction in defendant's production creates prima facie case of infringement. Jeweler's Circular Pub. Co. v Keystone Pub. Co. (1922, CA2 NY) 281 F 83, 26 ALR 571, cert den 259 US 581, 66 L Ed 1074, 42 S Ct 464.

Copying of errors is evidence of infringement. Investment Service Co. v Fitch Pub. Co. (1923, CA7 Ill) 291 F 1010; W. H. Anderson Co. v Baldwin Law Pub. Co. (1928, CA6 Ohio) 27 F2d 82.

Common errors and similarities in selection of roads, peculiarities of road meandering and classification, selection of towns and location of symbols therefor, population errors, and river and shore boundaries, together with other evidence pointed to copying from plaintiff's map. General Drafting Co. v Andrews (1930, CA2 NY) 37 F2d 54, 4 USPQ 72.

Although both parties went to state university's list of French words as source for their word lists, defendant, who admitted owning copies of plaintiff's copyrighted books at time he arranged his own list, so copied from plaintiff's list as to infringe; infringement was shown by omission by both of same common words from state list, by treatment of same words as nouns or adjectives where they could be properly used as either, by choice, sometimes erroneous, of same articles to prefix same nouns, and by choice of identical translations. College Entrance Book Co. v Amsco Book Co. (1941, CA2 NY) 119 F2d 874, 49 USPQ 517.

Copying of substantial error should be decisive in determining infringement. Ricker v General

Electric Co. (1947, CA2 NY) 162 F2d 141, 73 USPQ 458.

Proof of common peculiarities may warrant inference of copying copyrighted work. Schultz v Holmes (1959, CA9 Cal) 264 F2d 942, 121 USPQ 117.

Similarity of errors and peculiarities is strong proof of copying; reproduction of clerical and typographical errors proves piracy. Lawrence v Dana (CC Mass) F Cas No 8136.

Society directory was infringed by similar publication which was shown to contain many errors common to original directory. List Pub. Co. v Keller (1887, CC NY) 30 F 772.

Listing of same nonexistent hotels in defendant's hotel director, as appeared in plaintiff's directory was evidence of copying. American Travel & Hotel Directory Co. v Gehring Publishing Co. (1925, DC NY) 4 F2d 415.

One of most significant evidences of infringement is identity of errors; immediately on discovery of similar errors in both books, burden falls heavily on defendant, whose publication was later in time, to explain their presence. Sammons v Larkin (1940, DC Mass) 38 F Supp 649, 49 USPQ 350, mod on other grounds (CA1 Mass) 126 F2d 341, 53 USPQ 71.

In suit for infringement, showing of reproduction of considerable number of errors common to complainant's publication in defendant's works constitutes evidence of copying. Colonial Book Co. v Amsco School Publications, Inc. (1941, DC NY) 41 F Supp 156, 51 USPQ 33; R. R. Donnelley & Sons Co. v Haber (1942, DC NY) 43 F Supp 456, 52 USPQ 445.

Where plaintiff inserted list of fictitious names for purpose of detecting infringement, inclusion of same by defendant indicates that they were copied from plaintiff's directory, and might lead to inference that other names were copied, but evidence standing alone will not compel finding of infringement, if other evidence negatives inference of substantial copying. R. L. Polk & Co. v Musser (1952, DC Pa) 105 F Supp 351, 92 USPQ 124, affd (CA3 Pa) 196 F2d 1020, 93 USPQ 468.

In dealing with materials like maps, which are purely descriptive of terrains, courts have, at times, looked not only for similarities but for identity of errors, either in names or other data, as indicating access to copyrighted material. Hayden v Chalfant Press, Inc. (1959, DC Cal) 177 F Supp 303, 123 USPQ 475, affd (CA9 Cal) 281 F2d 543, 126 USPQ 483.

Mere similarity with respect to angle, curvatures, and positioning of place names on maps does not prove copying; in this crowded area, there is little room for variety; likewise, mere similarity of selection of places to be shown does not prove copying where selection seems to be what almost anyone would make; also, inclusion or exclusion of other towns does not prove copying since inclusion or exclusion is as consistent with independent research of common sources as it is with copying; moreover, use of noticeably different spelling of names of other towns is not consistent with mere copying; fact that maps have same errors does not show copying since they also appear in earlier map available to both parties; difference in number of towns named in one country makes maps significantly different; copying is not shown by inclusion of unimportant town where its exclusion would leave empty space on map. C. S. Hammond & Co. v International College Globe, Inc. (1962, DC NY) 210 F Supp 206, 135 USPQ 56.

Copying of copyrighted telephone directory is shown by corresponding mistakes in infringing directory and proof of actual copying. Southwestern Bell Tel. Co. v Nationwide Independent Directory Service, Inc. (1974, DC Ark) 371 F Supp 900, 182 USPQ 193.

Evidence showing access, extensive similarity, and duplication of errors in defendant's catalog of equipment similar to plaintiff's shows probability of copying, but ordinary observers might disagree about "substantial and material similarity" so that questions of fact remain for jury, and summary judgment is denied. Rexnord, Inc. v Modern Handling Systems, Inc. (1974, DC Del) 379 F Supp 1190, 183 USPQ 413.

Considering opportunities for access and only trivial variations between infringement and original, virtual identity of copy shows both access and copying to support infringement judgment. Goldman-Morgen, Inc. v Dan Brechner & Co. (1976, DC NY) 190 USPQ 478.

Strongest evidence of copying is that of common errors in both books; such common mistakes most frequently occur in directories; however, in historical works it is natural to find common errors repeated in other books on same subject; thus, unsubstantial errors traceable to common sources are not probative of copying. Turner v Century House Publishing Co. (1968, NY Sup Ct) 159 USPQ 699.

28. Ordinary observation or impression as measure of similarity, generally

Copy is that which comes so near to original as to give to every person seeing it idea created by original. Carr v National Capital Press, Inc. (1934) 63 App DC 210, 71 F2d 220, 21 USPQ 408.

To establish copyright infringement, copyright holder must prove that infringer copied protected work and show substantial similarity between two works, test being response of ordinary lay person. Universal Athletic Sales Co. v Salkeld (1975, CA3 Pa) 511 F2d 904, 185 USPQ 76, cert den 423 US 863, 46 L Ed 2d 92, 96 S Ct 122.

Summary judgment of noninfringement is reversed, because even casual examination of copyrighted and accused luggage retrieval labels reveals marked similarity, and since ordinary reasonable person would fail to differentiate between 2 labels, case is remanded for trial. International Luggage Registry v Avery Products Corp. (1976, CA9) 192 USPQ 426.

Comparison of minute details of plays is frowned upon as method of proving identity; infringement of work of imagination is determined by result of comparative reading, on imagination of reader, not by dissection of sentences and incidents. Chrisite v Harris (1942, DC NY) 47 F Supp 39, 54 USPQ 360, affd (CA2 NY) 154 F2d 827, 69 USPQ 198, cert den 329 US 734, 91 L Ed 634, 67 S Ct 97.

Copy is that which ordinary observation would cause to be recognized as having been taken from another work or reproduction of another work. Allegrini v De Angelis (1944, DC Pa) 59 F Supp 248, 64 USPQ 165, affd (CA3 Pa) 149 F2d 815, 65 USPQ 589.

Test of infringement is whether there is such similarity in theme, development of theme, means used, climax of story, and denouement to carry impression to court, not as judge or as person familiar with literature, but as average person who reads scenario and sees play, that they are same. Schwarz v Universal Pictures Co. (1945, DC Cal) 85 F Supp 270, 83 USPQ 153.

Copying must be of means of expression; if that means be words, there must be copying of words; if means be some other method, copying must conform to some pattern, so that it is clear to ordinary reader that there is a copying. Lewis v Kroger Co. (1952, DC W Va) 109 F Supp 484, 95 USPQ 359.

Basic test of plagiarism is whether resemblance between works could be recognized by ordinary observation and not by fine analysis or by argument and dissection by experts. Greenbie v Noble (1957, DC NY) 151 F Supp 45, 113 USPQ 115.

To constitute infringement, there need not be verbatim copying of plaintiff's work or any part thereof, but defendant must have appropriated substantial or material part of protected work, and alleged copy must come so near to original as to give to every person seeing it the idea created by original; copying may be inferred where there was access and similarities between works raise reasonable inference of copying, but similarity must be recognizable by ordinary ob-

servation, and test is not whether by some hypercritical dissection of sentences and incidents seeming similarities are shown to exist. Costello v Loew's, Inc. (1958, DC Dist Col) 159 F Supp 782, 116 USPQ 372.

Where dissection, rather than observation, is required to discern any resemblance, there has been no copying. Barton Candy Corp. v Tell Chocolate Novelties Corp. (1959, DC NY) 178 F Supp 577, 123 USPQ 425.

To constitute copyright infringement, copying need not be of every detail so long as copy is substantially similar to copyrighted work; copy, such as will constitute infringement, is that which ordinary observation would cause to be recognized as having been appropriated from or patterned after copyrighted work. Doran v Sunset House Distributing Corp. (1961, DC Cal) 197 F Supp 940, 131 USPQ 94, affd (CA9 Cal) 304 F2d 251, 134 USPQ 4, and (disapproved on other grounds L. Batlin & Son, Inc. v Snyder (CA2 NY) 536 F2d 486, cert den 429 US 857, 50 L Ed 2d 135, 97 S Ct 156).

Problem of similarity between two compositions, whether literary, musical, or dramatic, is question of fact to be determined ultimately by comparison of works upon basis of opinion of average individual possessing practical understanding of subject; same test applies whether plaintiff's work is copyrighted or, as in instant case, is idea for radio program. Stanley v Columbia Broadcasting System, Inc. (1949, Cal) 208 P2d 9, 82 USPQ 123, subsequent op on reh 35 Cal 2d 653, 221 P2d 73, 23 ALR2d 216, 86 USPQ 520.

In determining whether similarity is due to copying, common knowledge of average reader, observer, spectator, or listener is standard of judgment which must be used. Heywood v Jericho Co. (1948) 193 Misc 905, 85 NYS2d 464, 79 USPQ 450.

Test of plagiarism is not whether expert could so dissect the two works as to be able to demonstrate, by virtue of his peculiar knowledge, that there are similarities prohibited by law; similarity must be one apparent upon ordinary observation. Cantor v Mankiewicz (1960, Sup) 203 NYS2d 626, 125 USPQ 598.

29. —Literary works

Infringement of copyrighted book by another book is to be determined by reading and comparison of books themselves without fine analysis or argument and dissection of expert. Wiren v Shubert Theatre Corp. (1933, DC NY) 5 F Supp 358, affd (CA2 NY) 70 F2d 1023, cert den 293 US 591, 79 L Ed 685, 55 S Ct 105, reh den 293 US 631, 79 L Ed 716, 55 S Ct 140.

There is no plagiarism when it requires dissection rather than observation to discern resemblance between literary works; critical analysis is not test; test is pragmatic. Bradbury v Columbia Broadcasting System, Inc. (1959, DC Cal) 174 F Supp 733, 123 USPQ 10, revd on other grounds (CA9 Cal) 287 F2d 478, 128 USPQ 376, cert dismd 368 US 801, 7 L Ed 2d 15, 82 S Ct 19.

Although California state court will dissect literary production to determine what portion thereof is protectible, it will not dissect protectible portion to discover isolated similarities as to each segment of the whole; instead, upon issue of similarity, standard of ordinary observer should be applied and comparison of protectible portions should be made without dissection and without expert or elaborate analysis. Burtis v Universal Pictures Co. (1953) 40 Cal 2d 823, 256 P2d 933, 97 USPQ 567.

Test of infringement is impression received by average reasonable man upon comparative reading of two works, not by dissection of sentences and incidents. Stanley v Columbia Broadcasting System, Inc. (1949, Cal) 208 P2d 9, 82 USPQ 123, subsequent op on reh 35 Cal 2d 653, 221 P2d 73, 23 ALR2d 216, 86 USPQ 520.

30. —Musical works

There is no infringement where similarities between songs cannot be readily detected by lay ear, or by effect of composition as whole, but only by dissection. Arnstein v Broadcast Music, Inc. (1943, CA2 NY) 137 F2d 410, 58 USPQ 451.

Musical composition infringes another only when similarity is substantially copy, so that to ear of average person two melodies sound to be same. Hein v Harris (1910, CC NY) 175 F 875, affd (CA2 NY) 183 F 107.

Similarity is question of fact to be determined by comparison of two works, and, while expert testimony is helpful, especially in matters involving musical composition, test is resemblance noticeable to average hearer. Hirsch v Paramount Pictures, Inc. (1937, DC Cal) 17 F Supp 816, 32 USPQ 233.

Similarity in motive alone is not enough to prove infringement and use of two or three notes in reverse order not carrying idea of similarity to ear of court is not enough to prove infringement. Carew v R. K. O. Radio Pictures, Inc. (1942, DC Cal) 43 F Supp 199, 53 USPQ 152.

Rather than attempting to resolve different interpretations by analysts trained in music, court must determine question of confusion between two recorded arrangements of same song by placing itself in position of average person who would listen to records and determining whether such person would confuse one with the other. Supreme Records, Inc. v Decca Records, Inc. (1950, DC Cal) 90 F Supp 904, 85 USPQ 405.

Conflicting expert testimony as to similarity of songs is of some help, but judge relies on only other test available to musical layman, namely, whether there is resemblance noticeable to average hearer. Northern Music Corp. v King Record Distributing Co. (1952, DC NY) 105 F Supp 393, 93 USPQ 512.

31. —Visual works

Underlying test for infringement of fabric design is whether average lay observer would find substantial similarity in designs, and good eyes and common sense are used for this. Soptra Fabrics Corp. v Stafford Knitting Mills, Inc. (1974, CA2 NY) 490 F2d 1092, 26 ALR Fed 402, 180 USPQ 545.

Test of copyright infringement is whether similarity between products would lead average lay observer to recognize alleged copy as having been appropriated from copyrighted work, and unlike patents, copyrights give no exclusive right to art disclosed and protection is given only to expression of idea—not idea itself. Herbert Rosenthal Jewelry Corp. v Hondra Jewelry Co. (1974, CA2 NY) 509 F2d 64, 184 USPQ 264.

Wall chart for exercise machine similar to copyrighted chart only in use of stick figures, and dissimilar in many other respects including color, arrangement, drawing of other figures, and use of legends, is not so similar to copyrighted chart in view of ordinary lay person as to be infringement, especially because copyright does not protect basic idea, but only expression of idea. Universal Athletic Sales Co. v Salkeld (1975, CA3 Pa) 511 F2d 904, 185 USPQ 76, cert den 423 US 863, 46 L Ed 2d 92, 96 S Ct 122.

Plaintiff's "Betty Boop" doll was infringed by defendant's doll, two dolls being substantially same and creating same impression. Fleischer Studios, Inc. v Ralph A. Freundlich, Inc. (1934, DC NY) 5 F Supp 808, 21 USPQ 216, affd (CA2 NY) 73 F2d 276, 23 USPQ 295, cert den 294 US 717, 79 L Ed 1250, 55 S Ct 516.

Examination of two designs for miniature religious shrines gives clear impression that they are both of same original shrine, that figures are of same character, and that medals and inscriptions are identical; figures and symbols, or their combination into shrine, are not copyrightable because in public domain, and infringement must be of other elements entering into plaintiffs' composite design; inspection of designs distinguishes them; although of same general shape, they are different in every detail, positions and forms of elements are different; there is no infringement since ordinary reasonable person would not fail to differentiate between works and would consider them dissimilar by reasonable observation. Allegrini v De Angelis (1944, DC Pa) 59 F Supp 248, 64 USPQ 165, affd (CA3 Pa) 149 F2d 815, 65 USPQ 589.

Although it is arguable that none of differences between plaintiff's copyrighted artificial dahlia and defendant's dahlia when taken alone would be conclusive in establishing that there has been no copying, when taken together result is that dahlias create different impressions on court in its role as inexpert observer; there is no infringement. Prestige Floral, Societe Anonyme v Zunino-Altman, Inc. (1962, DC NY) 203 F Supp 649, 133 USPQ 75, affd (CA2 NY) 301 F2d 286, 133 USPQ 58.

Test of copying of copyrighted design is whether ordinary observer who does not set out to detect the disparities would be disposed to overlook them and regard aesthetic appearances as same. Cortley Fabrics Co. v Slifka (DC NY) 138 USPQ 110.

Test of copying of design is whether ordinary observer who does not set out to detect disparities would be disposed to overlook them and regard aesthetic appearances as same. John Wolf Textiles, Inc. v Andris Fabrics, Inc. (DC NY) 139 USPQ 365.

Test to determine if copyrighted design has been copied is whether ordinary observer, who is not attempting to discover disparities, would be disposed to overlook them and regard aesthetic appeal as the same. United Merchants & Mfrs., Inc. v Sutton (1967, DC NY) 282 F Supp 588, 157 USPQ 487.

Plaintiff's copyrighted doll is infringed by defendant's doll where observer would conclude that defendant's doll had been drawn from plaintiff's through purposive combination of features characterizing body of doll and comprising considerable part of its character and appeal, notwithstanding that defendant adopted clear-cut modifications of detail and used different head. Uneeda Doll Co. v Regent Baby Products Corp. (1972, DC NY) 355 F Supp 438.

Test for infringement of copyrighted dolls is whether average lay observer would find substantial similarity between copyrighted dolls and alleged copies, and comparison of dolls, and especially facial features and eyes of dolls, compels conclusion that average lay observer would find substantial similarity and results in infringement holding. Fisher-Price Toys, Div. of Quaker Oats Co. v My-Toy Co. (1974, DC NY) 385 F Supp 218, 184 USPQ 376.

Test of infringement of copyright on turtle doll is whether average lay observer would find substantial similarity, and test is met where

differences between copyrighted turtle and alleged infringing turtle are not sufficient to make average layman believe that turtles came from different sources. Samet & Wells, Inc. v Shalom Toy Co. (1975, DC NY) 185 USPQ 36.

32. Paraphrasing

Paraphrasing or copying with evasion is infringement of copyright holders' rights, even though there may be little or no conceivable identity between two. Nutt v National Institute, Inc. for Improv. of Memory (1929, CA2 Conn) 31 F2d 236.

Paraphrasing constitutes infringement of copyright as well as copying of copyrighted matter. Ansehl v Puritan Pharmaceutical Co. (1932, CA8 Mo) 61 F2d 131, 15 USPQ 38, cert den 287 US 666, 77 L Ed 574, 53 S Ct 224.

Infringement exists when study of two writings indicates that one of them is not in fact creation of putative author, but instead was copied in substantial part exactly or in transparent rephrasing to produce essentially story of other writing. Warner Bros. Pictures, Inc. v Columbia Broadcasting System, Inc. (1954, CA9 Cal) 216 F2d 945, 104 USPQ 103, cert den 348 US 971, 99 L Ed 756, 75 S Ct 532.

In some instances, language in defendant's catalogue is same as that in plaintiff's copyrighted catalogue except for inversion of certain words or substitution of one word for another; this crude effort to give appearance of dissimilarity is evidence of copying, even though parties are describing similar items in simple nontechnical words and although substantial similarity in language would not necessarily indicate copying. Joshua Meier Co. v Albany Novelty Mfg. Co. (1956, CA2 NY) 236 F2d 144, 111 USPQ 197.

Copyright infringement is not confined to literal and exact reproduction; it includes various modes in which work may be adopted, imitated, transferred, or reproduced, with more or less colorable alterations to disguise piracy; paraphrasing is copying and infringement, if carried to sufficient extent. Eisenschiml v Fawcett Publications, Inc. (1957, CA7 Ill) 246 F2d 598, 114 USPQ 199, cert den 355 US 907, 2 L Ed 2d 262, 78 S Ct 334.

In order to infringe copyright it is not necessary that whole or even large portion of book shall have been copied; it is sufficient if material and substantial part shall have been copied even though it be but small part of whole; reproduction need not be literal or exact; and it is piracy if it appears that copyrighted matter is copied although altered or paraphrased. Henry Holt & Co. v Liggett & Myers Tobacco Co. (1938, DC Pa) 23 F Supp 302, 37 USPQ 440.

Several instances of almost identical phrasing alone probably are not enough to support claim of copyright infringement; however, there may be infringement although compositions are not identical, since paraphrasing is infringement. Holdredge v Knight Publishing Corp. (1963, DC Cal) 214 F Supp 921, 136 USPQ 615.

33. Similarity to copyrighted work as affecting infringement, generally

Publication of noncopyrighted matter with accompanying embellishments, similar to, but not identical with, those accompanying its previous publication registered by another publisher was not infringement. Eggers v Sun Sales Corp. (1920, CA2 NY) 263 F 373.

If there is access, probability that similarities are result of copying, intentional or unintentional, is so high that there is only one pertinent question: are there similarities of matters which justify infringement claimed? Shipman v R. K. O. Radio Pictures, Inc. (1938, CA2 NY) 100 F2d 533, 40 USPQ 211.

Points of similarity are continuous and striking in booklets; almost every idea and means of expression has been copied in its essence; it is no defense that infringing booklet is more attractive and salable. American Visuals Corp. v Holland (CA2) 110 USPQ 482.

Copying need not be of every detail so long as copy is substantially similar to copyrighted work; test of infringement is whether one charged with infringement made independent production or substantial and unfair use of copyrighted work. Comptone Co. v Rayex Corp. (1958, CA2 NY) 251 F2d 487, 116 USPQ 105.

Test of copyright infringement differs from standard of copyrightability which is extended to any work promoting progress, even though there may be infringement because of substantial similarity with other work. L. Batlin & Son, Inc. v Snyder (1975, CA2) 187 USPQ 721.

Lack of similarity in works supports finding of no infringement between book and magazine article each based on same folk legend. Reyher v Children's Television Workshop (1976, CA2 NY) 533 F2d 87, 190 USPQ 387.

Identity existing between original and subsequent work, in absence of positive evidence to contrary, warrants conclusion that original work has been copied. Brightley v Littleton (1888, CC Pa) 37 F 103; Woodman v Lydiard-Peterson Co. (1912, CC Minn) 192 F 67, affd (CA8 Minn) 204 F 921, reh den (CA8 Minn) 205 F 900.

Substantial similarity due to mere coincidence and not to actual copying was not infringement. Moore v Ford Motor Co. (1928, DC NY) 28 F2d 529, affd (CA2 NY) 43 F2d 685.

Similarities between 1939 and 1940 maps are so striking and complete that they point unmistakably to copying; infringement is shown by internal evidence of copying in 1940 map such as arbitrarily abrupt road endings not on defendant's base maps, town not on defendant's base maps, and same distortion of portion of map. Crocker v General Drafting Co. (1943, DC NY) 50 F Supp 634, 58 USPQ 60.

Copying is not confined to literary repetition; infringement of copyright is not avoided by taking substance or idea and producing it through different medium and picturing in shape and details in sufficient imitation to make it true copy of subject thought of by originator of copyrighted work; copy, constituting infringement, is that which comes so near to original as to give every person seeing it the idea created by original. Gordon v Weir (1953, DC Mich) 111 F Supp 117, 97 USPQ 387, affd (CA6 Mich) 216 F2d 508, 104 USPQ 40.

Copying of copyrighted story may be proven by similarity between both the protected and unprotected parts of plaintiff's and defendant's works; court should reach problem of eliminating from consideration the unprotected part of plaintiff's work only if and when it finds that defendant has copied and the issue of improper appropriation, substantially or materially, is property before it. Morse v Fields (1954, DC NY) 127 F Supp 63, 104 USPQ 54.

It is significant as showing dissimilarity that, when plaintiff first wrote to defendant, after having seen defendant's motion picture, she made no claim of plagiarism. Buckler v Paramount Pictures, Inc. (1955, DC NY) 133 F Supp 223, 106 USPQ 256.

In determining whether defendants copied substantial part of plaintiff's copyrighted chart, test is not quantity but quality of what was copied. Nikanov v Simon & Schuster, Inc. (1956, DC NY) 144 F Supp 375, 110 USPQ 491, affd (CA2 NY) 246 F2d 501, 114 USPQ 89.

In determining existence of plagiarism, court must discuss both similarities and dissimilarities; although copying of single sequence may amount to plagiarism if it is important, when similitude is sought to be established between two works, points of essential difference may so far outnumber points of similarity that it is difficult to understand how anyone could persuade himself that one was borrowed from the other. Bradbury v Columbia Broadcasting System, Inc. (1959, DC Cal) 174 F Supp 733, 123 USPQ 10, revd on other grounds (CA9 Cal) 287 F2d 478, 128 USPQ 376, cert dismd 368 US 801, 7 L Ed 2d 15, 82 S Ct 19.

Infringement of plaintiff's copyrighted law book by defendant's subsequent law book is shown by (1) defendant's adoption of plaintiff's unique analysis of the subject, (2) many instances of almost verbatim identity of language, (3) use of same hypothetical illustration without supporting legal authority, (4) use of same striking words, (5) defendant's apparent adoption of statements from plaintiff's work without independent research, although such research would have disclosed pertinent legal decisions reported after publication of plaintiff's book, (6) common error as to rulings in certain decisions, and (7) fact that, when books are read together in continuity the content is so similar in arrangement, language, and substance that conclusion is inescapable that defendant took unfair advantage of his access to plaintiff's book. Orgel v Clark Boardman Co. (CA2 NY) 301 F2d 119, 2 ALR3d 1203, 133 USPQ 94, cert den 371 US 817, 9 L Ed 2d 58, 83 S Ct 31.

Court considers complete text of both plays, including any matter unprotected by statute, as evidence on issue of copying. Burnett v Lambino (1962, DC NY) 204 F Supp 327, 133 USPQ 325.

Copyright is not infringed where comparison of defendants' scripts and plaintiff's copyrighted play evidences fact that points of essential difference so far outnumber points of similarity that it does not appear that anyone could persuade himself that one was borrowed from the other. Dugan v American Broadcasting Corp. (1963, DC Cal) 216 F Supp 763, 137 USPQ 238.

Copying need not be of every detail so long as copy is substantially similar to copyrighted work. United Merchants & Mfrs., Inc. v K. Gimbel Accessories, Inc. (1968, DC NY) 294 F Supp 151, 161 USPQ 147.

Applying average lay observer test of substantial similarity and noting that identity is not required, court finds that some lamp base castings made from modified versions of copyright proprietor's molds are sufficiently changed to not infringe, but other lamp base casting retains substantial similarity and infringes. L & L White Metal Casting Corp. v Joseph (1975, DC NY) 387 F Supp 1349, 185 USPQ 269.

Copying of copyrighted layout for historical map is shown by completion of work by other artists, many similarities in infringement, and copying of several errors in infringing work, and court in applying average lay observer test finds that observable similarities affect overall appearance more than differences. Hughey v Palographics Co. (1976, DC Colo) 189 USPQ 527.

Motion picture advertisement similar to copyrighted advertisement infringes and is enjoined. Warner Bros., Inc. v Film Ventures International (1975, DC Cal) 403 F Supp 522, 189 USPQ 591.

Access and inclination to copy being admitted by demurrer, issues of similarity and copying are to be determined by trier of fact if it may be said that some substantial similarity between radio programs reasonably could be found; having both programs before it upon demurrer in accordance with California Code of Civil Procedure, court may determine whether there is substantial similarity between them; if, as matter of law, there is no such similarity, then there is no question of fact and demurrer must be sustained. Kurlan v Columbia Broadcasting System, Inc. (1953) 40 Cal 2d 799, 256 P2d 962, 97 USPQ 556.

For evidence to be sufficient to support finding of similarity, and thus of copying, two works must present substantial similarity insofar as plaintiff's property in his work is concerned. Burtis v Universal Pictures Co. (1953) 40 Cal 2d 823, 256 P2d 933, 97 USPQ 567.

34. —Jewelry

Copyright on jeweled turtle pin does not exclude all others from manufacturing jeweled turtle pins on ground that they are substantially similar in appearance, and others have right to imitate turtles in making jeweled pins so that minor differences between alleged infringing pin and copyrighted pin support finding of noninfringement. Herbert Rosenthal Jewelry Corp. v Honora Jewelry Co. (1974, CA2 NY) 509 F2d 64, 184 USPQ 264.

Although there is no direct proof of access or copying of copyrighted jewelry, similarities between items pass bounds of accident and are beyond explanation by coincidence; burden of proving copying is on plaintiff, but, when he makes strong prima facie case by pointing out convincing number of similarities, burden of going forward with evidence explaining similarities is on defendant; defendant made no attempt to meet burden; hence, court concludes that defendant copied plaintiff's jewelry. Hollywood Jewelry Mfg. Co. v Dushkin (1955, DC NY) 136 F Supp 738, 107 USPQ 354.

Finding of infringement of plaintiff's copyrighted pin requires only that pins be observably similar; since there is no doubt that defendants copied plaintiff's pin, it is not necessary that defendants' pin be "Chinese copy" of plaintiff's. Trifari, Krussman & Fishel, Inc. v B. Steinberg-Kaslo Co. (1956, DC NY) 144 F Supp 577, 110 USPQ 487.

Substitution by defendant of artificial pearls in its bracelet in place of glass stones in plaintiff's copyrighted bracelet, while using same metal designs and settings, constitutes infringement. Dan Kasoff, Inc. v Palmer Jewelry Mfg. Co. (1959, DC NY) 171 F Supp 603, 120 USPQ 445.

Copyright on motif of red apple bearing words "I Like You" protects expression of idea and not basic idea of "I Like You" used in conjunction with apples or fruit, and copyright is infringed by jewelry using apple, cherry, and strawberry with "I Like You" to achieve same overall aesthetic effect, but is not infringed by jewelry using pear, orange, and cluster of grapes with "I Like You" because of differences in color and shape changing overall appearance. PPS, Inc. v Jewelry Sales Representatives, Inc. (1975, DC NY) 392 F Supp 375, 185 USPQ 374.

35. —Labels or prints

There is infringement of copyrighted label when there is general resemblance in size, arrangement of printed matter, and color and pictures although there are differences in detail of infringing label. Nekritz v Duberstein (1921, DC NY) 271 F 17.

In alleged infringing label defendant did not copy design and details of plaintiff's label; inspection reveals different arrangement both as to text as well as well-known illustration or medallion or vignette; scrolls •re different; both employed long used texts and well-known pictures; infringement is not confined to literal and exact registration or reproduction but here each product was but variation of familiar and frequently reproduced labels of stock nature. Bobrecker v Denebeim (1939, DC Mo) 28 F Supp 383, 42 USPQ 194.

Carton bearing "C.J.'S Combined Herbs" and cut of dancing Indian does not infringe carton bearing "O.G.'S United Herbs" and larger cut of head and shoulders of Indian. Needham v Becker (DC Ohio) 62 USPQ 434.

Label with elk's head does not infringe label with deer's head. Griesedieck Western Brewery Co. v Peoples Brewing Co. (1944, DC Minn) 56 F Supp 600, 63 USPQ 74, affd (CA8 Minn) 149 F2d 1019, 66 USPQ 1.

Manufacturer's copyrighted label is infringed by unauthorized use of label on garments made from woolen piece goods purchased as surplus material from government that were originally manufactured by owner of copyrighted label. Forstmann Woolen Co. v J. W. Mays, Inc. (1950, DC NY) 89 F Supp 964, 85 USPQ 200.

Luggage registration label is not substantially similar to copyrighted label and does not infringe by using inherent necessities of luggage identification labels and differing in artistic ornament and design. International Luggage Registry v Avery Products Corp. (1974, DC Cal) 184 USPQ 66.

36. —Musical works

While there are enormous numbers of possible permutations of musical notes, only few are pleasing, and much fewer suit demands of popular ear; recurrence is not inevitable badge of plagiarism. Darrell v Joe Morris Music Co. (1940, CA2 NY) 113 F2d 80, 46 USPQ 167.

Same short musical sequences recur spontaneously; reappearance in later composition is feeble proof of plagiarism and it is as unfair to impute imitation to second comer as it would be to impute it to author. Brodsky v Universal Pictures Co. (1945, CA2 NY) 149 F2d 600, 65 USPQ 385.

Common-law copyright of song was infringed by defendant's song, portions of which were similar to plaintiff's original composition. Wilkie v Santly Bros., Inc. (1935, DC NY) 13 F Supp 136, 28 USPQ 452, affd (CA2 NY) 91 F2d 978, adhered to (CA2 NY) 94 F2d 1023, 37 USPQ 839, and cert den 302 US 735, 82 L Ed 568, 58 S Ct 120.

In the case of musical composition, similarity may arise out of grouping of notes, similarity of bars, accent, harmony, or melody. Hirsch v Paramount Pictures, Inc. (1937, DC Cal) 17 F Supp 816, 32 USPQ 233.

Test of infringement has not been met where, having heard both plaintiff's song and alleged infringing one, layman did not notice claimed similarity; slight resemblance in progression of few bars in both compositions is something which occurs frequently but which is not enough to make out piracy. Davilla v Harms, Inc. (1940, DC NY) 36 F Supp 843, 48 USPQ 103.

Fact that plaintiff's and defendant's songs are written in same key is not significant on question of plagiarism, each having been originally in different key but changed by publishers. Allen v Walt Disney Productions, Ltd. (1941, DC NY) 41 F Supp 134, 50 USPQ 365.

March in two-quarter time which makes lively rhythm is not infringed by composition designed to accompany song. McMahon v Harms, Inc. (1942, DC NY) 42 F Supp 779, 52 USPQ 321.

Criterion of similarity of songs is not dissection under microscopic eye of musician but impression song or phrase carries to average ear. Carew v R. K. O. Radio Pictures, Inc. (1942, DC Cal) 43 F Supp 199, 53 USPQ 152.

To recover for infringement of copyrighted music, plaintiff must prove identity of compositions and access by alleged infringer. Heim v Universal Pictures Co. (1943, DC NY) 51 F Supp 233, 58 USPQ 314, affd (CA2 NY) 154 F2d 480, 68 USPQ 303.

Unpublished copyrighted song is not infringed by defendant's song; although there are slight similarities, there are enough important differences to indicate that there was no copying. Rizzi v Robbins Music Corp. (DC NY) 58 USPQ 315.

Similarities do not establish copying where prior popular songs have same similarities; similarity of musical compositions is not established by manipulation of plaintiff's composition; plaintiff transfers notes from accompaniment in bass to melody in treble, omits and changes notes and rhythm of some phrases, and separates parts of some phrases and places them in different parts of composition; where two compositions do not sound alike when played as written, melodies, harmonies, accent, and rhythm are different, and one was written as vocal quartet and burlesque on grand opera and other as popular song, one is not copy of other. Arnstein v Twentieth Century Fox Film Corp. (1943, DC NY) 52 F Supp 114, 59 USPQ 21.

To show infringement of copyrighted song, plaintiff must establish not only that ideas of both compositions and form of expressing ideas are similar, but also that this was not mere coincidence and was accomplished with previous knowledge of plaintiff's composition, and plaintiff must prove this by evidence to show that plaintiff's work was completed prior to defendant's work and that there was contact between plaintiff's work and defendant either through public medium or privately. Northern Music Corp. v King Record Distributing Co. (1952, DC NY) 105 F Supp 393, 93 USPQ 512.

Plaintiff must prove that there was copying of his copyrighted work by defendant and that portions copied were sufficiently substantial and unfair to constitute unlawful appropriation; copying may be shown by proof of access and showing that, on an analysis and dissection of defendant's composition, sufficient similarity in use of chords, chord progression, devices used for tone color, key changes, rhythm, melody, and like, to those used in plaintiff's composition in phrase by phrase comparison as reasonably to support inference that defendant must have copied from plaintiff; if there are no similarities, evidence of access will not prove copying. O'Brien v Thall (DC Conn) 127 USPQ 325, affd (CA2 Conn) 283 F2d 741, 127 USPQ 296.

Evidence amply supported conclusion that defendant's song was copied from plaintiff's song, where profusion of melodic similarities coupled with close similarity between lyrics, and accompanied by direct proof of access created overpowering inference of copying. Nom Music, Inc. v Kaslin (1964, DC NY) 227 F Supp 922, 141 USPQ 22, affd (CA2 NY) 343 F2d 198, 145 USPQ 237.

In action for infringement of plaintiff's copyrighted popular song, entitled "Mojo Workout," wherein defendants counterclaimed for infringe-

ment of copyrighted song "I've Got My Mojo Working," there is no infringement by either party, and both parties are entitled to produce their respective works, where (1) "Mojo" concept, as used in lyrics of both songs, was so commonplace as to be substantially within public domain, (2) aside from some similarities in opening passages, which conveyed different moods, works sounded quite different to non-professional customer's ear, and (3) lyrics varied, except as to similarity relating to "Mojo" concept, which could not be appropriated by either party. Stratchborneo v Arc Music Corp. (1973, DC NY) 357 F Supp 1393.

Musical composition copyright is infringed, if there is substantial similarity due to sizeable quantity copied or due to quality and value because essential, material, or important part is copied. Navara v M. Witmark & Sons (1959) 17 Misc 2d 174, 185 NYS2d 563, 121 USPQ 107.

37. Similarity in works as relating to similar subject matter, generally

In case of works dealing with same period in history, subject matter is of necessity what events have made it and order of treatment whether that be chronological or topical is fixed by facts; it follows that infringement is not established by showing that same thing has been said on same subject in different words. Oxford Book Co. v College Entrance Book Co. (1938, CA2 NY) 98 F2d 688, 39 USPQ 7.

To constitute infringement of copyrighted form of insurance contract, showing of appropriation in exact or substantially exact form of copyrighted material is required since, where same contractual provision is to be made, there will necessarily be similarity of language. Dorsey v Old Surety Life Ins. Co. (1938, CA10 Okla) 98 F2d 872, 119 ALR 1250, 39 USPQ 92.

Where access is proved, or assumed, likeness between copyrighted work and putative piracy may give rise to inference of plagiarism, but inference is weakened when similarities relate to expression of scientific principles which must be stated in stereotyped language. Ricker v General Electric Co. (1947, CA2 NY) 162 F2d 141, 73 USPQ 458.

Subsequently compiled shippers' guide book did not infringe prior compilation based on same subject matter. Bullinger v Mackey (CC NY) F Cas No 2127.

Horse racing year book was infringed in part by publication consisting of list of trotting and pacing horses and information concerning them. American Trotting Register Asso. v Gocher (1895, CC Ohio) 70 F 237.

Copyright of algebra book was not infringed by subsequent work of like character compiled from authorities used as basis for original book. Colliery Engineer Co. v Ewald (1903, CC NY) 126 F 843.

Racing charts are not infringed by use solely to find clue as to where and when horse raced, and then using clue to locate and copy defendants' own material. Triangle Publications, Inc. v New England Newspaper Pub. Co. (1942, DC Mass) 46 F Supp 198, 54 USPQ 171.

Since specific similarities between works treating with same subject are unavoidable, they do not support finding of infringement even if access is established. Alexander v Irving Trust Co. (1955, DC NY) 132 F Supp 364, 106 USPQ 74, affd (CA2 NY) 228 F2d 221, 108 USPQ 24, cert den 350 US 996, 100 L Ed 860, 76 S Ct 545.

Generally, defendant's access to plaintiff's book, and strong similarity or identity between works, creates inference of copying; defendant may rebut inference by proof that material came from independent sources; inference does not exist where similarity arises because of nature of subject matter and fact that both authors used materials available to all. Greenbie v Noble (1957, DC NY) 151 F Supp 45, 113 USPQ 115.

As between plaintiff's and defendant's scripts, many words are same because they are both quiz programs about motion pictures, but there is no copyright infringement since style and arrangement of words present no substantial similarity to ordinary observer; with respect to radio and television broadcasts, it is perhaps more significant to compare in detail sequence of episodes which taken together make up program as whole and which form concrete manner of expressing basic idea; method is similar when there is comparison of stage plays. Richards v Columbia Broadcasting System, Inc. (1958, DC Dist Col) 161 F Supp 516, 117 USPQ 174.

No action for copyright infringement lies where similarities in advertisements are inherent in product advertised rather than result of outright copying. Remington Research, Inc. v Modern Aids, Inc. (1959, DC NY) 170 F Supp 7, 120 USPQ 289.

If historian copyrights history, it would be infringement for another historian to publish history rewritten from first historian's book without independent research; also city directory, which publishes nothing but facts, cannot be copied without infringing copyright; second historian or directory publisher cannot bodily appropriate predecessor's research. Huie v National Broadcasting Co. (1960, DC NY) 184 F Supp 198, 125 USPQ 226.

Copyright on printing of point count values on playing cards requires such an invariable stereotype that infringement is avoided by small differ-

ences in mode of expression of same idea, such as different size and style of numbers. Freedman v Grolier Enterprises, Inc. (1973, DC NY) 179 USPQ 476.

Copying of portions of 6 copyrighted manuals for computers and related components is not excused from infringement liability by fact that manuals contained simple directions dictated by functional considerations, and presence of noninfringing material does not exonerate infringement by copying substantial portions of manuals. Telex Corp. v International Business Machines Corp. (1973, DC Okla) 367 F Supp 258, 179 USPQ 777, affd in part and revd in part on other grounds (CA10 Okla) 510 F2d 894, cert dismd 423 US 802, 46 L Ed 2d 244, 96 S Ct 8.

Copyright in biographical work on Rosenbergs does not protect historical facts and events and requires considerable copying for infringement. Gardner v Nizer (1975, DC NY) 391 F Supp 940, 185 USPQ 485, mod on other grounds (DC NY) 396 F Supp 63.

Applying test of substantial similarity between plaintiff's copyrighted ads and defendant's ads, and noting that copyright protects manner of expression and not basic idea, court finds that defendant's ads are similar only in basic idea of using models and illustrating cosmetics and otherwise differ from plaintiff's ads using different models, picture, and explanations, and substantial similarity in mailing coupon does not result in infringement, because same mailing coupon was used by plaintiff in previous uncopyrighted ads and is public domain. G. R. I. Corp. v Golden Fifty Pharmaceutical Co. (1975, DC Ill) 185 USPQ 674.

38. —Legal publications

Copyright upon law reporters was infringed by subsequent legal publications containing materials copied from prior work. Callaghan v Myers (1888) 128 US 617, 32 L Ed 547, 9 S Ct 177.

Law reporters were infringed by law digest. West Pub. Co. v Lawyers' Co-op. Pub. Co. (1897, CA2 NY) 79 F 756.

Appropriation by publisher of annotated statute of work of competitor in making page to page search of reports and selecting and classifying material for annotations constituted infringement, though with citations thus obtained he went to original source and wrote up material; if defendant in such case had gathered his own material by the same processes employed by competitor, and had merely checked accuracy of his work from competitor's list of cases there would have been no infringement. W. H. Anderson Co. v Baldwin Law Pub. Co. (1928, CA6 Ohio) 27 F2d 82.

Book of court rules was infringed by later work which contained like index and rules. Banks v McDivitt (CC NY) F Cas No 961.

Notes of copyrighted law book were infringed by similar work. Lawrence v Dana (CC Mass) F Cas No 8136.

Taking of authorities from original book and inserting them in subsequent competing publication was no infringement. Mead v West Pub. Co. (1896, CC Minn) 80 F 380.

Exclusive rights in law encyclopedia were not infringed by later work containing citations copied from original work, but examined for their applicability. Edward Thompson Co. v American Lawbook Co. (1904, CC NY) 130 F 639, affd (CA2 NY) 157 F 1003.

Cutting or copying citations from digests, where no literary ability is appropriated, does not constitute infringement. West Publishing Co. v Edward Thompson Co. (1909, CC NY) 169 F 833, mod (CA2 NY) 176 F 833.

Rights in law reporter and digest system were infringed by legal encyclopedia. West Pub. Co. v Edward Thompson Co. (1911, CC NY) 184 F 749.

Legal textbooks were infringed in part by subsequent book pertaining to same subject matter; it is not infringement for author to use and copy citations of another, providing he examines and verifies cases before using them. White v Bender (1911, CC NY) 185 F 921.

39. —Plans, systems and ideas

System of spelling words by less than usual number of letters, known as "Steno-Short-Type System," was not infringed as to its description of system. Brief English Systems, Inc. v Owen (1931, CA2 NY) 48 F2d 555, 9 USPQ 20, cert den 283 US 858, 75 L Ed 1464, 51 S Ct 650.

Even if all material for plaintiff's stories had been gathered through his own efforts and no information was obtained from third parties, still plaintiff published his material as facts, and law is clear that this same material could be used by another author if he so substantially changed incidents of story that literally compositions bear no real resemblance to each other. Funkhouser v Loew's Inc. (1953, CA8 Mo) 208 F2d 185, 99 USPQ 448, cert den 348 US 843, 99 L Ed 664, 75 S Ct 64, reh den 348 US 890, 99 L Ed 700, 75 S Ct 209.

Use by defendant of plaintiff's map for purpose of correcting and bringing to date map previously published by defendant, was, on the evidence, not actionable infringement. Chamberlin v Bekins Van & Storage Co. (1928, DC Cal) 23 F2d 541.

Newspaper's published solution to bridge problems did not infringe publication "Rapid Contract Bridge," duly copyrighted. Russell v Northeastern Pub. Co. (1934, DC Mass) 7 F Supp 571, 23 USPQ 123.

Where there does not appear to be any identity of language, phraseology, or literary style, arrangement or form although there may be similarity in plan and purpose of insurance and method of operation advanced to effectuate the plan, there is no infringement of copyright. Long v Jordan (1939, DC Cal) 29 F Supp 287, 43 USPQ 176.

Copyright of drawing showing novel bridge approach does not prevent others from using and applying system set forth. Muller v Triborough Bridge Authority (1942, DC NY) 43 F Supp 298, 52 USPQ 227.

Public cannot use invention described in patent but can use information (including forms) in copyrighted book about any system, art, or manufacture described; such use is consideration public receives for grant of copyright. Aldrich v Remington Rand, Inc. (1942, DC Tex) 52 F Supp 732, 59 USPQ 210.

There can be no infringement by appropriating idea, which, once it is expressed, becomes public property; however, copyright protects method of expressing idea. Lewis v Kroger Co. (1952, DC W Va) 109 F Supp 484, 95 USPQ 359.

There is no copyright infringement where only ideas are copied. Condotti, Inc. v Slifka (1963, DC NY) 223 F Supp 412.

40. Trivial variations

Slight differences between pictures, observable by close scrutiny, do not avoid infringement. Gerlach-Barklow Co. v Morris & Bendien, Inc. (1927, CA2 NY) 23 F2d 159.

Copyrighted sculpture of dog is infringed although defendant's expert dog breeder and fancier may be able to distinguish between dogs for technical reasons, since average reasonable observer would not distinguish. Contemporary Arts, Inc. v F. W. Woolworth Co. (1950, DC Mass) 93 F Supp 739, 86 USPQ 476, affd (CA1 Mass) 193 F2d 162, 92 USPQ 4, affd 344 US 228, 97 L Ed 276, 73 S Ct 222, 95 USPQ 396, motion den 350 US 810, 100 L Ed 727, 76 S Ct 37.

Infringement of insignia is not avoided by fact that defendant copied with variations. Nash v Alaska Airlines, Inc. (1950, DC NY) 94 F Supp 428, 88 USPQ 85.

Considering opportunities for access and only trivial variations between infringement and original, virtual identity of copy shows both access and copying to support infringement judgment. Goldman-Morgen, Inc. v Dan Brechner & Co. (1976, DC NY) 190 USPQ 478.

To establish infringement, plaintiff must prove

unauthorized copying of whole or substantial part of his play; trivial similarities are of no legal import; part taken must be substantial and material part of play. Heywood v Jericho Co. (1948) 193 Misc 905, 85 NYS2d 464, 79 USPQ 450.

3. Reproduction of Particular Features

41. Generally

Defendant's use of same stock number, "LE-2," as that used in plaintiff's copyrighted catalogue is hard to explain on any hypothesis other than copying, especially since neither party designates any of its products "LE-1"; defendant's choice of "2" can only be result of imitation. Joshua Meier Co. v Albany Novelty Mfg. Co. (1956, CA2 NY) 236 F2d 144, 111 USPQ 197.

Copyright of grammer book was infringed by subsequent publication of like character. Greene v Bishop (CC Mass) F Cas No 5763.

Grammar book was infringed by key manual made to aid in teaching from infringed book. Reed v Holliday (1884, CC Pa) 19 F 325.

Physiognomy book was not infringed by later work of same sort. Simms v Stanton (1896, CC Cal) 75 F 6.

Play entitled "The Cohens and Kellys" did not infringe play "Abie's Irish Rose," though depicting same emotions. Nichols v Universal Pictures Corp. (1929, DC NY) 34 F2d 145, 2 USPQ 139, affd (CA2 NY) 45 F2d 119, 7 USPQ 84, cert den 282 US 902, 75 L Ed 795, 51 S Ct 216.

Meaning or interpretation which author gives to his literary efforts cannot be accepted as deciding test of infringement. Wiren v Shubert Theatre Corp. (1933, DC NY) 5 F Supp 358, affd (CA2 NY) 70 F2d 1023, cert den 293 US 591, 79 L Ed 685, 55 S Ct 105, reh den 293 US 631, 79 L Ed 716, 55 S Ct 140.

Copyrighted catalogue containing photographs of uncopyrighted and unpatented articles is not infringed by catalogue containing photographs of imitative articles. Kashins v Lightmakers, Inc. (1956, DC NY) 155 F Supp 202, 115 USPQ 325.

42. Characterization

It is infringement to take substance or idea and produce it through different medium such as picturing its shape and details in sufficient imitation to make it true copy of character thought of by owner; manufacturing of horse as figure doll which is named "Sparky" or "Spark Plug," and fashioned from figure of horse in copyrighted cartoon strip which horse is known as "Spark Plug," constitutes infringement of cartoon. King Features Syndicate v Fleischer (1924, CA2 NY) 299 F 533.

Defendants do not avoid copyright by arguing that various attributes of plaintiff's fictional character find prototypes or analogies among heroes of literature and mythology; if plaintiff's production involves more than presentation of general type he may copyright it. Detective Comics, Inc. v Bruns Publications, Inc. (1940, CA2 NY) 111 F2d 432, 45 USPQ 291.

Copyright of "Mutt" and "Jeff" cartoons was infringed by similar appearing cartoon characters "Nut" and "Giff." Hill v Whalen & Martell, Inc. (1914, DC NY) 220 Fed 359.

Test of infringement in cases dealing with incidents and stock characters is whether association and grouping of characters and incidents is such as to make new conception or novel arrangement. Simonton v Gordon (1924, DC NY) 297 Fed 625.

Where there has been no copying of plaintiff's manuscript, and characters therein are without such distinctive qualities as would be sine qua non of their copyrightability and incidents in both copyrighted manuscript and alleged infringement are, with one exception, familiar to all readers of type of stories, there is no infringement. Caruthers v R. K. O. Radio Pictures, Inc. (1937, DC NY) 20 F Supp 906, 35 USPQ 115, 35 USPQ 542.

"Tiny Tim," "Florence Nightingale," and "Lord Fauntleroy," when used as rhetorical personifications, though they might predicate access, are not copyrightable, and their adoption in totally different settings falls short of copying. McConnor v Kaufman (1943, DC NY) 49 F Supp 738, 57 USPQ 80, affd (CA2 NY) 139 F2d 116, 60 USPQ 356.

Locale of plays, dominant theme, characters, detailed description of characters, parts they take and words they speak, scenes, and dramatic effect are so similar that they preclude possibility of coincidence and conclusively establish access and substantial copying. Select Theatres Corp. v Ronzoni Macaroni Co. (DC NY) 59 USPQ 288.

Right of author or his licensee to use characters of copyrighted work does not protect against action for copyright infringement, brought by assignee of copyrighted work, if characters are so employed in subsequent works as to invade copyright monopoly. Warner Bros. Pictures, Inc. v Columbia Broadcasting System, Inc. (1951, DC Cal) 102 F Supp 141, 92 USPQ 54, affd in part and revd in part on other grounds (CA9 Cal) 216 F2d 945, 104 USPQ 103, cert den 348 US 971, 99 L Ed 756, 75 S Ct 532.

43. Design features

On comparison of fabric design with copyrighted design court considers overall affect including color combinations and black and white reproductions and finds infringement where differences are insubstantial and not practically discernible in dresses made from fabrics. Soptra Fabrics Corp. v Stafford Knitting Mills, Inc. (1974, CA2 NY) 490 F2d 1092, 26 ALR Fed 402, 180 USPQ 545.

Copyrighted design of top and side of parachute with irregular curved lines painted upon parachute is not infringed by parachutes employing such design. Fulmer v United States (1952) 122 Ct Cl 195, 103 F Supp 1021, 93 USPQ 102.

Billiard table design, not novel in itself, was not infringed by similar design. Collender v Griffiths (1873, CC NY) F Cas No 3000.

Cursory comparison of plaintiffs' copyrighted design and defendant's fabric evokes impression that designs are identical; closer scrutiny reveals that each minor detail of plaintiffs' design has been altered in defendant's copy; copyright is infringed; physical facts of copying become virtually incontestable in light of (1) one defendant's admission that it had examined dress made of plaintiffs' copyrighted fabric and, after some minor changes, ordered rollers, and (2) second defendant's admission that its designer prepared infringing pattern while having before him a dress made of plaintiffs' copyrighted fabric. Peter Pan Fabrics, Inc. v Acadia Co. (1959, DC NY) 173 F Supp 292, 121 USPQ 81, affd (CA2 NY) 274 F2d 487, 124 USPQ 154.

Although accused designs are not Chinese copies of copyrighted designs, they infringe, since cursory comparison reveals such striking and pronounced similarity as to give rise to strong inference of copying; since designs involve commonplace subject matter, substantial similarity would not necessarily indicate copying, but dissimilarities obviously were result of studied effort to make minor distinctions; this effort is itself evidence of copying; final and overwhelming clue is that, while it is not alleged that copying of color constitutes infringement, use of colors in accused designs is devastating indication that plaintiff's designs were source of defendants'. Scarves by Vera, Inc. v United Merchants & Mfrs., Inc. (1959, DC NY) 173 F Supp 625, 121 USPQ 578.

Butterfly designs of parties involve commonplace subject matter, so substantial similarity would not necessarily indicate copying; however, copying is shown since dissimilarities appear obviously to be result of studied effort to make minor distinctions, and similarities in general appearance and overall design, identity, and arrangement of parts are striking; moreover, while it is not alleged, that copying of color constitutes infringement, use of same colors is indication that copyrighted design was source of accused design; viewing designs side by side,

copying cannot be denied. Fabrex Corp. v Scarves by Vera, Inc. (DC NY) 129 USPQ 392.

Copyrighted designs are not infringed by designs which contain enough variants to give them different over-all appearance and aesthetic appeal when fabrics are made into garments. Condotti Inc. v Slifka (1963, DC NY) 223 F Supp 412, 139 USPQ 373.

Although plaintiff's copyrighted design inspired defendants' design, and although three of the various color schemes of fabrics bearing defendants' design were deliberately copied from plaintiff's design, there is no infringement since color schemes in plaintiff's design are not copyrighted and defendants did not copy plaintiff's design as well as plaintiff's colors; defendants have not gone past permissible appropriation of idea and reached point of forbidden appropriation of its expression. Clarion Textile Corp. v Slifka (DC NY) 139 USPQ 340.

Infringement of copyrighted design is not shown where total aesthetic appeal of each design is different. Prestige Fabrics, Inc. v Universal Mfg. Corp. (1969, DC NY) 304 F Supp 903, 163 USPQ 669.

44. Format or arrangement

Similarity in analysis of statute annotations and identity of numbering of chapters in body of the statute was not convincing evidence of infringement. W. H. Anderson Co. v Baldwin Law Pub. Co. (1928, CA6 Ohio) 27 F2d 82.

Where general correspondence in form and close correspondence in detail were found to exist when compared with copyrighted chart for analyzing handwriting, infringement was shown although defendant omitted specimens shown by plaintiff. Deutsch v Arnold (1938, CA2 NY) 98 F2d 686, 39 USPQ 5.

Comparison of plaintiff's and defendants' airline guides shows that much information is same, but that sequence and arrangement are not identical; they are not similar enough to warrant infringement; resemblance in internal arrangement arises largely from adherence to form sanctioned by custom, usage, and general practice in presenting railway and airline timetables and fare tables. Official Aviation Guide Co. v American Aviation Associates (1945, CA7 Ill) 150 F2d 173, 65 USPQ 553, cert den 326 US 776, 90 L Ed 469, 66 S Ct 267, reh den 326 US 811, 90 L Ed 495, 66 S Ct 335.

In fields of insurance and commerce, use of specific language in forms and documents may be so essential to accomplish desired result and so integrated with use of legal or commercial conception that proper standard of infringement is one which will protect as far as possible copyrighted language and yet allow free use of thought beneath language; there is no infringement of copyrighted insurance forms since use of language of forms is only incidental to use of underlying idea. Continental Casualty Co. v Beardsley (1958, CA2 NY) 253 F2d 702, 117 USPQ 1, cert den 358 US 816, 3 L Ed 2d 58, 79 S Ct 25.

Where subsequent author appropriates essential parts of another's plan, arrangement, examples, and table of arithmetic book he is guilty of infringement. Emerson v Davies (CC Mass) F Cas No 4436.

Where, in suit for infringement of copyright upon legal case book, it appears that author of later case book has not cited other cases which have been decided on same points as those contained in cases cited in prior case book, or noted cases which have been overruled or reversed, such showing constitutes evidence of copying. White v Bender (1911, CC NY) 185 F 921.

Placing of roads and other physical entities within township and section lines in the same manner as they appear on plaintiff's copyrighted map, where no other source of material or information is clearly shown, justifies inference that plaintiff's map was used and copied in making defendant's map. Blackburn v Southern California Gas Co. (1936, DC Cal) 14 F Supp 553, 29 USPQ 437.

In copyright infringement action there may be comparison of pages to show they are substantially identical as to arrangement, style and layout even to point of copying common errors. Burndy Engineering Co. v Penn-Union Electric Corp. (1938, DC Pa) 25 F Supp 507, 39 USPQ 321.

Copyrighted insurance policies are not infringed where there is no similarity in arrangement of words of plaintiff's and defendant's policies and where defendant has not appropriated copyrighted material, either substantially or in exact form. Miner v Employers Mut. Liability Ins. Co. (DC DC) 105 USPQ 357, affd 97 App DC 152, 229 F2d 35, 108 USPQ 100.

Expression of business form is not infringed unless one descends so far into what is concrete as to invade expression. First Financial Marketing Services Group, Inc. v Field Promotions, Inc. (1968, DC NY) 286 F Supp 295, 150 USPQ 572.

Photographer who collaborated with writer as coauthor of book and co-owner of copyright cannot be liable for copyright infringement for producing other books having similar format, and contributions of coauthors are not separated by court for application of rule. Donna v Dodd, Mead & Co. (1974, DC NY) 183 USPQ 166, 374 F Supp 429.

Copyright on compilation and arrangement of executive desk calendar is infringed by desk calendar having substantially identical compilation and arrangement of art work, including many identical pages, and differing only in few minor respects. Baldwin Cooke Co. v Keith Clark, Inc. (1974, DC Ill) 383 F Supp 650, 183 USPQ 209, affd without opinion (CA7 Ill) 505 F2d 1250 and supp op (DC Ill) 420 F Supp 404.

Copying is shown by proof of access coupled with similarity of content, format, sequence in presentation of various educational skills in preschool reading skills kits. Grolier, Inc. v Educational Reading Aids Corp. (1976, DC NY) 193 USPQ 632.

Copyright on compilation of suppliers of gardening material covers selection, arrangement, and combinations of information, but is not infringed by copying of names and addresses of suppliers and headings or categories of suppliers without copying descriptive material, because some of lists are in public domain or were copied from other copyrighted sources, and considering circumstances of case, copyright does not extend to names and addresses copied. Schroeder v William Morrow & Co. (1976, DC Ill) 194 USPQ 37.

45. Graphics or illustrations

Where print, otherwise uncopyrighted, was copyrighted as part of newspaper, suit for infringement for wrongful publishing of print must be based upon infringement of newspaper and not on infringement of print. Bennett v Boston Traveler Co. (1900, CA1 Mass) 101 F 445.

Trade-mark directory was infringed by similar publication containing illustrations obtained from plaintiff's work. Jeweler's Circular Pub. Co. v Keystone Pub. Co. (1922, CA2 NY) 281 F 83, 26 ALR 571, cert den 259 US 581, 66 L Ed 1074, 42 S Ct 464.

Copyrighted card of Gilbert Stuart's portrait of George Washington with eagle standing on United States shield in upper left of the card was not infringed. Carr v National Capital Press, Inc. (1934) 63 App DC 210, 71 F2d 220, 21 USPQ 408.

Drawing and cartoons in history book were found to infringe those appearing in another book on same subject, access having been established. Oxford Book Co. v College Entrance Book Co. (1938, CA2 NY) 98 F2d 688, 39 USPQ 7.

Sketches do not infringe copyrighted photographs of bearings; while photographs were used, in part, as models, sketches were made from defendant's own detail drawings, are at different angle with different shading, and depict bearings different in important detail of design. Mathews Conveyer Co. v Palmer-Bee Co. (1943, CA6 Mich) 135 F2d 73, 57 USPQ 219.

Copyright of playing card design was infringed by similar design used upon defendant's cards. Richardson v Miller (CC Mass) F Cas No 11791.

Sale of chromos designed from picture in foreign publication circulated here before plaintiff took out copyright was not infringement. Johnson v Donaldson (1880, CC NY) 3 F 22.

Unauthorized reproduction and sale of copy of cut of picture published in copyrighted illustrated newspaper is not infringement of copyright. Harper v Schoppell (1886, CC NY) 26 F 519.

Illustrative engravings of church furniture contained in copyrighted book and price list were not infringed by similar illustrations in book of like character. Lamb v Grand Rapids School Furniture Co. (1889, CC Mich) 39 F 474.

Picture accompanying complainant's copyrighted stories was not infringed by picture which accompanied defendant's stories. Munro v Smith (1890, CC NY) 42 F 266.

Copyright of photograph was infringed by one who used original photograph to produce copies thereof. Falk v Brett Lithographing Co. (1891, CC NY) 48 F 678.

Partially completed reproductions of copyrighted picture are infringement whether in marketable state or not. Fishel v Lueckel (1892, CC NY) 53 F 499.

Copyright may be infringed when retail seller of manufactured articles of plaintiff inserts in his advertisement reproduction of copyrighted picture of plaintiffs without their permission. Golden Rule, Inc. v B. V. D. Co. (1917, CA8 Minn) 242 F 929.

Diagrammatic instruction sheet accompanying crude model of steamship, parts of which are to be assembled according to instructions, is infringed by similar model and instruction sheet issued by defendant. Ideal Aeroplane & Supply Co. v Brooks (1936, DC NY) 18 F Supp 936, 33 USPQ 193.

Defendant's copyright picture both in idea it conveys and in illustrations used to convey idea is entirely dissimilar and unlike plaintiff's copyrighted pictures; there is no infringement. Lucas v Nattrass-Schenck, Inc. (DC NY) 44 USPQ 344.

Copyright on card having its corners marked off by four black lines forming square or box, even if valid, is not infringed by card having corners marked off by two red lines forming angle. Kessler v Schreiber (1941, DC NY) 39 F Supp 655, 49 USPQ 610.

Plaintiff submitted design for advertising insignia under understanding that plaintiff would be compensated if design were used, defendant's retention of design until after defendant's use of similar design in advertising creates inference that defendant used and infringed plaintiff's design. Nash v Alaska Airlines, Inc. (1950, DC NY) 94 F Supp 428, 88 USPQ 85.

Copyright covering cover of fashion magazine is infringed by reproduction of cover in catalogue advertising school of fashion modelling. Conde Nast Publications, Inc. v Vogue School of Fashion Modelling, Inc. (1952, DC NY) 105 F Supp 325, 94 USPQ 101.

Plaintiff's copyright is infringed since defendant took substantial part of plaintiff's execution for his own; infringement is not negatived by fact that art work and composition of defendant's pamphlet are better than in plaintiff's pamphlet. American Visuals Corp. v Holland (1957, DC NY) 162 F Supp 14, 117 USPQ 180, affd (CA2 NY) 261 F2d 652, 119 USPQ 482.

Graphic plagiarism is committed when copyist preserves structural and material characteristics of original, notwithstanding deliberate and systematic variation of each subordinate detail. Peter Pan Fabrics, Inc. v Acadia Co. (1959, DC NY) 173 F Supp 292, 121 USPQ 81, affd (CA2 NY) 274 F2d 487, 124 USPQ 154.

Material and substantial test is not applied to entire copyrighted catalog but only to each component part which has been infringed; thus, test is satisfied where certain illustrations from catalog have been almost exactly, if not identically, reproduced. Hedeman Products Corp. v Tap-Rite Products Corp. (1964, DC NJ) 228 F Supp 630, 141 USPQ 381.

Photographs, diagrams and text from brochures on automotive lamps and lighting equipment copied in competitor's brochures is copyright infringement. Foreign Car Parts, Inc. v Auto World, Inc. (1973, DC Pa) 366 F Supp 977, 181 USPQ 162.

Illustration for story about reunion of mother and child is not infringement of previous illustration of same story where ordinary lay observer can see many distinctions in style and form. Reyher v Children's Television Workshop (1975, DC NY) 387 F Supp 869, 185 USPQ 277, affd (CA2 NY) 533 F2d 87.

46. Incidents or episodes

Railroad scene from play "Under The Gaslight" was infringed by scene in defendant's play representing same material elements. Daly v Webster (1893, CA2 NY) 56 F 483.

C assisted plaintiff to revise his copyrighted play; thereafter C went to work for defendant and wrote play about same theme; court is bound in common sense to scrutinize C's play closely for evidence of copying; there is no correspondence in plot, characters, or impressions but merely in reform school background and touch of similarity of few incidents and few points of dialogue of trifling importance; C's play is more like original story of another which he bought; there is no infringement. Bein v Warner Bros. Pictures, Inc. (1939, CA2 NY) 105 F2d 969, 42 USPQ 395.

Author of copyrighted dramatic composition is protected against piracy of even single scene of his work; "railroad scene" in author's composition was infringed by similar scene in another composition. Daly v Palmer (CC NY) F Cas No 3552.

To constitute infringement of copyright of "gag" monologue it must be established that such "gags" were original with complainant. Hoffman v Le Traunik (1913, DC NY) 209 F 375.

Book or play is not infringed, simply because there is found in another later story, some of same incidents, when those incidents are familiar in life or fiction. Stevenson v Harris (1917, DC NY) 238 F 432.

Infringement of play may consist of plagiarism of language, incident, or plot. Frankel v Irwin (1918, DC NY) 34 F2d 142.

Plaintiffs gave defendants option to purchase play to be written; in suit for infringement of common-law copyright plaintiffs' contention that they suggested to defendant additional ideas which defendants later used is not proven as description of ideas is too vague and last conversation with defendant was four months before plaintiffs' play was finished so it is probable that play represented full story. Rapp v Harold Lloyd Corp. (1940, DC NY) 33 F Supp 47, 45 USPQ 225.

Denials of copying by defendant author, who had access, dissolve in presence of internal evidence so overwhelming as to exclude coincidence almost to mathematical certainty; coincidence cannot explain use of fictional names and incidents invented by plaintiff in her uncopyrighted and unpublished play based on life of historical character; fact that defendant author mistook plaintiff's fiction for fact is no excuse; since intentions of defendant author's assistants, who did research, must be ascribed to author, author intended to copy. De Acosta v Brown (1943, DC NY) 50 F Supp 615, 58 USPQ 596, affd (CA2 NY) 146 F2d 408, 63 USPQ 311, cert den 325 US 862, 89 L Ed 1983, 65 S Ct 1197 and cert den 325 US 862, 89 L Ed 1983, 65 S Ct 1198.

There is no infringement by movie where details, sequences, and raiment of idea are ut-

terly different; touch of similarity in few incidents and few points of dialogue are unimportant. Shurr v Warner Bros. Pictures, Inc. (DC NY) 59 USPQ 49, affd (CA2 NY) 144 F2d 200, 62 USPQ 60.

Fact that defendants' book on reckless driving uses certain episodes which are typical of dangers of such driving is not, in and of itself, sufficient to indicate on motion for preliminary injunction that book infringes plaintiff's copyrighted book on reckless driving. American Visuals Corp. v Holland (1954, DC NY) 126 F Supp 513, 103 USPQ 139, affd (CA2 NY) 219 F2d 223, 104 USPQ 222.

Presentation of parallel incidents in combination with similar phraseology, when considered in light of admitted access, is evidence of copying. Greenbie v Noble (1957, DC NY) 151 F Supp 45, 113 USPQ 115.

47. Literary style

While news as such is not subject to copyright and mere statement of news disclosed in copyrighted article will not constitute infringement of copyrighted article, where literary quality and style, other than bare recital of facts, is copied, it is infringement. Chicago Record-Herald Co. v Tribune Asso. (1921, CA7 Ill) 275 F 797.

Racing charts are infringed by copying symbols, notations, and cryptic expressions therefrom and also by stating same information in equivalent words. Triangle Publications, Inc. v New England Newspaper Pub. Co. (1942, DC Mass), 46 F Supp 198, 54 USPQ 171.

48. Name or title

Use of well-known proper name in both works may signify little under many circumstances, but in others it may assist to conclusive demonstration of copying otherwise indicated. De Acosta v Brown (1944, CA2 NY) 146 F2d 408, 63 USPQ 311, cert den 325 US 862, 89 L Ed 1983, 65 S Ct 1197 and cert den 325 US 862, 89 L Ed 1983, 65 S Ct 1198.

Mere use of name as title of play presenting none of scenes, incidents, plot, or dialogue of copyrighted book of same name is not infringement. Harper v Ranous (1895, CC NY) 67 F 904.

Copyright of "Social Register" was infringed by "Newport Social Index." Social Register Ass'n v Murphy (1904, CC RI) 128 F 116.

Copyright of play "Threads of Destiny" was not infringed by later play "At Bay." Vernon v Sam S. & Lee Shubert (1915, DC NY) 220 F 694.

Although title of plaintiff's copyrightable story is not protected, it is considered by court on issue of copying. Morse v Fields (1954, DC NY) 127 F Supp 63, 104 USPQ 54.

By giving names to unnamed lakes, creeks, trails, hills, and peaks, proprietor of copyrighted map did not acquire exclusive right of having maps with such names on them; by giving names, he granted to everyone right of having names used; presence of names in subsequent maps, if they appeared too soon after his map, might indicate that they may have been taken from his map, but this would be merely evidence of copying, not of plagiarism; subsequent cartographers may use same names without infringing first cartographer's copyright. Hayden v Chalfant Press, Inc. (1959, DC Cal) 177 F Supp 303, 123 USPQ 475, affd (CA9 Cal) 281 F2d 543, 126 USPQ 483.

49. Plans, ideas, or subject matter

Sales plan, not new or revolutionary, was not infringed. Moore v Ford Motor Co. (1930, CA2 NY) 43 F2d 685.

Fact that directions as to use of stamp plan by one merchant would be similar to those of another merchant would be expected; to express directions and to comment upon plan is right of every concern exploiting plan; however, he must use right in manner to avoid encroaching upon authorship of another who is holding his writings under copyright; if he deliberately copies or by chance gets so close to copyright matter that it is practically the same, he has infringed. Cash Dividend Check Corp. v Davis (1957, CA9 Cal) 247 F2d 458, 114 USPQ 32.

While copyrighted plans may not have been intended to place model home before general public, this was purpose of copyrighted booklet; since booklet was copyrighted to preserve its value as advertising medium, and not to give plaintiff exclusive right to copy plans depicted therein, complaint does not support claim of infringement based upon alleged copying of plans and construction of house therefrom. Scholz Homes, Inc. v Maddox (1967, CA6 Ky) 379 F2d 84, 3 ALR Fed 787, 154 USPQ 197.

Copyright on rule book for playing games does not cover rules, which are in public domain, and because of simplicity of rules, is entitled to very narrow scope, so that although defendant used and copied portions of plaintiff's rule book, defendant did not infringe, because copying was not slavish, and considerable changes were made to clarify rules. Affiliated Hospital Products, Inc. v Merdel Game Mfg. Co. (1975, CA2 NY) 513 F2d 1183, 185 USPQ 321.

Pamphlet consisting of advertisements of merchants and containing explanation of redeemable coupon system was not infringed by similar system explained in folded paper. Mutual Advertising Co. v Refo (1896, CC SC) 76 F 961.

Restatement by defendant, in his own language, of rules of game, was not infringement. Whist Club v Foster (1929, DC NY) 42 F2d 782.

Mere use without publication of copyrighted plan for increasing circulation of newspapers was not infringement. Taylor v Commissioner (1931, CA3) 51 F2d 915, cert den 284 US 689, 76 L Ed 581, 52 S Ct 265.

Applying name "Big Bank Night" to pin ball game is not infringement of copyright on various written materials plaintiff uses in promulgating instructions and promoting plan of bank night prize awards at motion-picture theaters. Affiliated Enterprises, Inc. v Rock-Ola Mfg. Corp. (1937, DC Ill) 23 F Supp 3, 38 USPQ 35.

Building of structure from copyrighted architectural plans is not infringement of plans. DeSilva Constr. Corp. v Herrald (1962, DC Fla) 213 F Supp 184, 137 USPQ 96.

Admitted copying of copyrighted abridged floor plans derived from copyrighted architectural drawings is copyright infringement although building of house similar to plans is not in itself infringement, and infringement by copying floor plans is not excused by fact that plans appeared in advertising brochure indicating that plans were copyrighted. Herman Frankel Organization v Tegman (1973, DC Mich) 367 F Supp 1051, 181 USPQ 317.

Unauthorized taking and copying of architectural plans for house and starting to build house according to plans is copyright infringement by home buyers, home builder, and person performing copying. Herman Frankel Organization, Inc. v Wolfe (1974, DC Mich) 184 USPQ 819.

Owing to difficulties of enforcing such rights, courts have uniformly refused to protect property in ideas that have not been reduced to concrete form; paragraph in complaint alleging that defendants wrongfully appropriated plaintiff's advertising idea and plan without paying plaintiff fair and reasonable compensation therefor is insufficient in law and is stricken on motion. Stone v Liggett & Myers Tobacco Co. (1940) 260 App Div 450, 23 NYS2d 210, 47 USPQ 529, app den 260 App Div 1006, 24 NYS2d 994.

50. Plot or theme

Play entitled "Estelle" was not infringed by subsequently composed "After Many Days" embodying same motif as prior composition. Bachman v Belasco (1915, CA2 NY) 224 F 817.

One play will not infringe another, although fundamental plot is same, when plot had become common property long before either was written.

London v Biograph Co. (1916, CA2 NY) 231 F 696.

Where dramatic composition uses what is called "fundamental plot" or "old story," author can devise and use his own way of expressing that plot and will not infringe. Dymow v Bolton (1926, CA2 NY) 11 F2d 690.

Play may be pirated without using dialogue. Sheldon v Metro-Goldwyn Pictures Corp. (1936, CA2 NY) 81 F2d 49, 28 USPQ 330, cert den 298 US 669, 80 L Ed 1392, 56 S Ct 835.

In deciding whether play has been infringed, it is necessary to determine whether fundamental theme has been appropriated. Underhill v Belasco (1918, DC NY) 254 F 838.

Fact that two productions display the trend of emotions is not enough to show plagiarism. Nichols v Universal Pictures Corp. (1929, DC NY) 34 F2d 145, 2 USPQ 139, affd (CA2 NY) 45 F2d 119, 7 USPQ 84, cert den 282 US 902, 75 L Ed 795, 51 S Ct 216.

Autobiography, entitled "Border and the Buffalo" was not infringed by love story, entitled "The Thundering Herd," theme of which is set in buffalo hunting. Maddux v Grey (1930, DC Cal) 43 F2d 441.

In order to infringe, production on stage must obviously tell same story as copyrighted drama, and if it tells another story or enacts another sequence of events, it is outside protection afforded the registered work. Seltzer v Sunbrock (1938, DC Cal) 22 F Supp 621, 37 USPQ 491.

There is no infringement of plaintiff's uncopyrighted play where plots, scenes, and incidents differ substantially and plaintiffs do not claim that dialogue has been copied. Rapp v Harold Lloyd Corp. (1940, DC NY) 33 F Supp 47, 45 USPQ 225.

Claim of plagiarism is quite fantastic since plays differ in plot, in character interest, in background, in general purpose and intent, and in substantially all points of reader or theater interest. Rose v Connelly (1941, DC NY) 38 F Supp 54, 49 USPQ 170, 49 USPQ 497.

Gross dissimilarities in all other important aspects of plays, particularly in theme, dialogue, setting, and sequence, defeat charge of substantial copying; ordinary reader would find no connection between plays; ordinary observer rule is accepted test. McConnor v Kaufman (1943, DC NY) 49 F Supp 738, 57 USPQ 80, affd (CA2 NY) 139 F2d 116, 60 USPQ 356.

There is no infringement simply because one writes and publishes story upon same theme previously used by another, even though copyrighted; to be infringement, there must be copying, intentional or unintentional, of other's work, and this does not occur simply by writing on same subject or theme; similarity can occur from copying, but it may also occur by reason of subject matter and setting with which both stories deal. Warshawsky v Carter (1955, DC Dist Col) 132 F Supp 758, 107 USPQ 80.

To determine whether there is copying in play, court places itself in position of ordinary observer and asks whether he would see similarity, not in idea, but in incidents, sequence of events, development and interplay of characters, and the denouement; law protects not general pattern, but its expression. Bradbury v Columbia Broadcasting System, Inc. (1959, DC Cal) 174 F Supp 733, 123 USPQ 10, revd on other grounds (CA9 Cal) 287 F2d 478, 128 USPQ 376, cert dismd 368 US 801, 7 L Ed 2d 15, 82 S Ct 19.

Copyright in motion picture is not infringed by other motion picture based on similar theme of exorcising evil spirits, where story and characters are different, and infringement cannot be based on light and sound effects and theatrical tricks generally known in art. Warner Bros., Inc. v Film Ventures International (1975, DC Cal) 403 F Supp 522, 189 USPQ 591.

C. Derivative Works (as specified in 17 USCS § 106(2))

51. Generally

Publication of index to accompany copyrighted volumes of author's works, though containing words and phrases found in text, does not constitute infringement of copyright. Kipling v G. P. Putnam's Sons (1903, CA2 NY) 120 F 631.

Biography was infringed by popular fiction book. Gilmore v Anderson (1889, CC NY) 38 F 846.

Novelization of copyrighted play is not infringement unless it is copy. Fitch v Young (1911, DC NY) 230 F 743, affd (CA2 NY) 239 F 1021.

Story does not infringe play since differences outweigh similarities; novel character of story has no counterpart in play; both have detectives but detectives are old dramatic props; no author has monopoly on maids and cooks. West v Hatch (1943, DC NY) 49 F Supp 307, 57 USPQ 64.

Copyright by artist on layout of historical map is valid, and work is infringed by defendant who hired other artist to complete map; and repudiated contract between parties does not give defendant ownership of map when plaintiff was not paid for work. Hughey v Palographics Co. (1976, DC Colo) 189 USPQ 527.

Where contract between owner of foreign play and American theatrical company, provides that theatrical company shall produce play in English and interpolations for such play are to be written by owner, but that when such interpolations are not satisfactorily furnished, theatrical company may have them produced elsewhere, and further provision provides that it applies only to numbers of owner of songs and interpolations that belong to him; he has no right to interpolations furnished by theatrical company and cannot sue for infringement. Karczag Pub. Co. v Shubert Theatrical Co. (1918) 181 App Div 529, 169 NYS 1.

52. Art work reproductions

Painting is infringed by picture having same essential features. Gerlach-Barklow Co. v Morris & Bendien, Inc. (1927, CA2 NY) 23 F2d 159.

Copyrights of statuettes are valid even though proprietor intended primarily to use statuettes in form of lamp bases and did so use them; copyrights are infringed by defendants, who minutely copied statuettes in form of bases for lamps. Stein v Mazer (1953, CA4 Md) 204 F2d 472, 97 USPQ 310, affd 347 US 201, 98 L Ed 630, 74 S Ct 460, 100 USPQ 325, reh den 347 US 949, 98 L Ed 1096, 74 S Ct 637.

Engraving "The Home of Washington" was infringed by photographic prints thereof. Rossiter v Hall (1866, CC NY) F Cas No 12082.

Copyright of painting may be infringed by lithographic prints thereof. Schumacher v Schwencke (1887, CC NY) 30 F 690.

Copyright of artistic photograph may be infringed by stamping design on leather intended for bottom or back of chair. Falk v T. P. Howell & Co. (1888, CC NY) 37 F 202.

Photograph of actress was infringed by lithographic reproduction of material parts thereof. Falk v Donaldson (1893, CC NY) 57 F 32.

Infringement of copyrights of photographs of dancer was not shown by illustrations in newspaper of certain poses of such dancer. Falk v City Item Printing Co. (1897, CC La) 79 F 321.

Copyright of piece of statuary may be infringed by photograph thereof. Bracken v Rosenthal (1907, CC Ill) 151 F 136.

Although defendants could have photographed old masters in public domain, it is infringement where they make lithographs of copyrighted mezzotint engravings of old masters. Alfred Bell & Co. v Catalda Fine Arts, Inc. (1947, DC NY) 74 F Supp 973, 75 USPQ 66.

Artist has no cause of action against one, who, innocently and without notice, publishes reproductions of painting copied from magazine. Leigh v Barnhart (1951, DC NJ) 96 F Supp 194, 89 USPQ 307.

Copyright for engraving can be infringed by reproducing copy of it by photographic process;

photograph of copyrighted piece of sculpture infringes; also, there can be infringement by making three dimensional doll of two dimensional copyrighted cartoon; therefore, three dimensional copyrighted plaque is infringed by making sketch thereof. M. J. Golden & Co. Inc. v Pittsburgh Brewing Co. (1956, DC Pa) 137 F Supp 455, 108 USPQ 250.

Copyrighted photographs are infringed by artist's charcoal copies thereof. Time, Inc. v Bernard Geis Associates (1968, DC NY) 293 F Supp 130, 159 USPQ 663.

Defendant's process of purchasing at retail plaintiff's greeting cards and stationery containing copyrighted pictorial art work, making decals of such art work from each item purchased, and using decals to transfer art work to ceramic plaques which were sold by defendant—an individual piece of plaintiff's art work being purchased for each decal and plaque produced by defendant—does not constitute "copying" of plaintiff's work, but defendant will be required to indicate on its products that art work is copyrighted design of plaintiff and that plaintiff is not connected with defendant. C. M. Paula Co. v Logan (1973, DC Tex) 355 F Supp 189.

Turtle doll made from design supplied by person who previously sold same design to copyright proprietor amounts to copying and infringes copyright. Samet & Wells, Inc. v Shalom Toy Co. (1975, DC NY) 185 USPQ 36.

53. Burlesque, parody, or satire

Fact that it has been defendant's custom for many years to present his burlesqued version of various dramatic works is no defense to action for copyright infringement; defendant cannot copy and present another's dramatic work without consent of copyright owner; Presentation of burlesque is not literary or dramatic criticism of dramatic work; it is subject to action for copyright infringement. Benny v Loew's, Inc. (1956, CA9 Cal) 239 F2d 532, 112 USPQ 11, affd 356 US 43, 2 L Ed 2d 583, 78 S Ct 667, 116 USPQ 479, reh den 356 US 934, 2 L Ed 2d 764, 78 S Ct 770.

Parody lyrics do not infringe in view of disparities in theme, content, and style between original copyrighted lyrics and parody lyrics; humorous effect achieved when familiar line is interposed in incongruous setting is not substantial taking; parody having neither intent nor effect of fulfilling demand for original, and parodist not having appropriated greater amount of original work than necessary to recall or conjure up object of his satire, finding of infringement was improper. Berlin v E. C. Publications, Inc. (1964, CA2 NY) 329 F2d 541, 9 ALR3d 612,

141 USPQ 1, cert den 379 US 822, 13 L Ed 2d 33, 85 S Ct 46.

Operatic tragedy called "U. S. A. with music," was not infringed by musical satire burlesquing politics and called "Of Thee I Sing." Lowenfels v Nathan (1932, DC NY) 2 F Supp 73, 16 USPQ 421.

54. Dramatizations, generally

Copyright of play based on murder trial was infringed by motion picture based on same murder trial. Sheldon v Metro-Goldwyn Pictures Corp. (1936, CA2 NY) 81 F2d 49, 28 USPQ 330, cert den 298 US 669, 80 L Ed 1392, 56 S Ct 835.

Suit for infringement of copyright and literary property by moving picture should be dismissed where, even though defendants took from play all those matters in which film resembled it, they were within their rights in doing so. Dellar v Samuel Goldwyn, Inc. (1939, CA2 NY) 104 F2d 661, 42 USPQ 164.

Motion picture contains incidents similar to some in copyrighted book which is series of stories, and court must assume copying of parts common to both where case comes up on motion to dismiss, but such assumption would not justify legal conclusion that copyright had been infringed since, judging from cutting continuity alone, language of book is not used and events in book purport to represent real occurrences which aside from expression are not protected by Copyright Act. Collins v Metro-Goldwyn Pictures Corp. (1939, CA2 NY) 106 F2d 83, 42 USPQ 553.

There is no infringement where defendant did not use plaintiff's book and comparison of works disproves access or copying, especially since defendant did not adopt identical title until after its story was fully written. Becker v Loew's, Inc. (1943, CA7 Ill) 133 F2d 889, 56 USPQ 455, cert den 319 US 772, 87 L Ed 1720, 63 S Ct 1438, reh den 320 US 811, 88 L Ed 490, 64 S Ct 30.

Motion-picture producer infringes insofar as it copies details of copyrighted comic strips, but plaintiff must point out exploits which defendant reproduced and must prove that reproduction was sufficiently close in detail. National Comics Publications, Inc. v Fawcett Publications, Inc. (1951, CA2 NY) 191 F2d 594, 90 USPQ 274.

Attempt to show similarities by comparing word or phrase taken from plaintiff's story with word or words appearing in lyrics of defendant's motion picture is not in conformity with approved test of infringement; test of infringement of story by motion picture is whether ordinary observation of picture would cause it to be recognized as picturization of story, and not whether by some hypercritical dissection of sentences and incidents seeming similarities are shown to exist. Funkhouser v Loew's Inc. (1953, CA8 Mo) 208 F2d 185, 99 USPQ 448, cert den 348 US 843, 99 L Ed 664, 75 S Ct 64, reh den 348 US 890, 99 L Ed 700, 75 S Ct 209.

Infringement exists where ordinary person, after reading plaintiff's copyrighted works and viewing defendant's teleplay, might well believe that defendant copied plaintiff's works to which he had access; similarities which exist are novel in plaintiff's story; defendant not only copies theme and ideas of plaintiff's works but also their expression. Bradbury v Columbia Broadcasting System, Inc. (1961, CA9 Cal) 287 F2d 478, 128 USPQ 376, cert dismd 368 US 801, 7 L Ed 2d 15, 82 S Ct 19.

Owner of copyright upon episode printed as news, but which in fact was fiction, was denied relief from infringement against producer of play based on said episode. Davies v Bowes (1913, DC NY) 209 F 53, affd (CA2 NY) 219 F 178.

Contract granting right to produce dramatic version of novel on stage, or to perform dramatic version, does not grant motion-picture right, and person holding dramatic right through such contract would infringe upon novel if he was to produce photoplay. Harper Bros. v Klaw (1916, DC NY) 232 F 609.

Play may infringe book if substantial number of incidents, scenes, and episodes are in detail, arrangement, and combination, so nearly identical with those in book as to exclude reasonable possibility of chance coincidence. Simonton v Gordon (1925, DC NY) 12 F2d 116.

Motion picture featuring wild horse cannot be said to infringe novel which features wild horse unless public would be deceived so as to believe that films are picturization of novel. Roe-Lawton v Hal E. Roach Studios (1927, DC Cal) 18 F2d 126.

There is no infringement of copyrightable subject matter in use of motion picture of automobile salesroom and selling of car in which principles set out in plaintiff's books "How to Win an Argument," "Sales Argument," are used in dialogue. Borden v General Motors Corp. (1939, DC NY) 28 F Supp 330, 42 USPQ 117.

Where it is shown that plaintiffs' scenario was derived from magazine article about motion picture in question, there was no infringement. Sheets v Twentieth Century Fox Film Corp. (1940, DC Dist Col) 33 F Supp 389, 46 USPQ 120.

Since theme in public domain is not copyrightable, in infringement suit question is whether expression or treatment of idea in defendant's motion picture, characters and dialogue, infringe plaintiff's treatment in his play. Gropper v Warner Bros. Pictures, Inc. (1941, DC NY) 38 F Supp 329, 49 USPQ 17.

Test applied in determining whether motion picture infringes play is net impression picture makes on average person. Solomon v R. K. O. Radio Pictures, Inc. (1942, DC NY) 44 F Supp 780, 53 USPQ 468.

Infringement of book by motion picture consists (1) of copying part of plaintiff's work and its inclusion in scenario for (2) incorporation into picture (3) for exhibition purposes; writer's wrong consists of (1) deliberate copying and delivery to others for (2) inclusion in finished picture and (3) exhibition to public; continuous exhibition of picture being one aim of composition of scenario, writer is chargeable not only with act of composing screen play but is also participant in its incorporation into picture and its subsequent exhibition. Cain v Universal Pictures Co. (1942, DC Cal) 47 F Supp 1013, 56 USPQ 8.

Motion picture has advantage over play in ability to present outdoor scenes but that play has been elaborated on with this advantage does not relieve picture from charge of plagiarism if story or theme, central idea or plot, treatment and development are so similar that one, seeing or reading play, and seeing picture, would recognize at once that picture had been taken from play; test is conclusion of ordinary observer; it is not matter of cold analysis but impressions of similarity or actual copying; striking similarities must have been result of copying. Stonesifer v Twentieth Century-Fox Film Corp. (1942, DC Cal) 48 F Supp 196, 56 USPQ 94, affd (CA9 Cal) 140 F2d 579, 60 USPQ 392.

Infringement is not shown where there is no similarity between plaintiff's copyrighted unpublished play and defendant's motion pictures that would not be result of coincidence; court finds that defendant never had access to play since unpublished copyrights are not open to public, and there is no evidence of any other possibility of access. Brody v Columbia Pictures Corp. (1950, DC Mass) 90 F Supp 711, 85 USPQ 158.

After motion picture producer had acquired screen rights to plaintiff's copyrighted play, producer entered into agreement with author to adapt play for screen; before author published alleged infringing novel, producer advised author and book publisher that it could not give clearance for publication of novel without plaintiff's consent; hence, producer has not infringed copyright even if author and publisher have done so. Gethers v Blatty (1968, DC Cal) 283 F Supp 303, 157 USPQ 297.

Test of whether substantial part of play is used in motion picture is whether ordinary person spontaneously detects literary piracy. Gold-

ing v RKO Radio Pictures, Inc. (1948, Cal App) 193 P2d 153, 77 USPQ 415, superseded (Cal) 208 P2d 1, 83 USPQ 136, subsequent op on reh 35 Cal 2d 690, 221 P2d 95, 86 USPQ 537.

Where German play is adapted for American stage by one party and others, and plaintiffs write lyrics and music for purpose of using it as musical comedy, but one adapting play and plaintiffs, did not collaborate, motion picture of play without music does not infringe upon plaintiff's rights. Herbert v Fields (1915, Sup) 152 NYS 487.

55. —Plot or theme appropriation

Exhibition of series of photographs of persons or things, arranged on film as moving pictures and so depicting principal scenes of author's work as to tell story, is dramatization of such work, and person producing films and offering them for sale for exhibition, even if not himself exhibiting them, infringes copyright of author. Atlas Mfg. Co. v Street & Smith (1913, CA8 Mo) 204 F 398, app dismd 231 US 348, 58 L Ed 262, 34 S Ct 73.

There is no infringement of copyrighted story by photoplay unless picturization appears to ordinary observer as being taken from story. Harold Lloyd Corp. v Witwer (1933, CA9 Cal) 65 F2d 1, cert dismd (US) 78 L Ed 1507, 54 S Ct 94; Kustoff v Chaplin (1941, CA9 Cal) 120 F2d 551, 49 USPQ 580.

Another can use theme so long as mode of expression is not plagiarized; where book is not development of theme but abstract discussion in essay form of economic and social problems without plot, dialogue, or characters and could not be dramatized without being rewritten so thoroughly as to make it another book, defendant's motion picture of romantic story did not appropriate material portions of book, no scene or dialogue being plagiarized from book. Becker v Loew's, Inc. (1943, CA7 Ill) 133 F2d 889, 56 USPQ 455, cert den 319 US 772, 87 L Ed 1720, 63 S Ct 1438, reh den 320 US 811, 88 L Ed 490, 64 S Ct 30.

"Woodsman," copyrighted play was infringed by motion-picture drama having same plot as play. Stodart v Mutual Film Corp. (1917, DC NY) 249 F 507, affd (CA2 NY) 249 F 513.

Motion picture does not infringe novel unless same emotions are excited in same sequence and order. Curwood v Affiliated Distributors, Inc. (1922, DC NY) 283 F 223.

Where both authors made use of common fundamental plot, but told their stories differently, copyrighted play "Woman" was not infringed by motion picture "Blonde Venus." Ornstein v Paramount Productions, Inc. (1935, DC NY) 9 F Supp 896, 25 USPQ 242.

Comparison of theme and its development in synopsis of literary composition entitled "Nulias Filias" and motion picture "Across the Pacific" did not show infringement of former by latter. Echevarria v Warner Bros. Pictures, Inc. (1935, DC Cal) 12 F Supp 632, 28 USPQ 213.

In action for infringement of common-law copyright of story, plaintiff must establish that there was, in movie, substantial and material part of his story that was so appropriated; theme of plaintiff's story is not found in defendants' play and there is difference in plot, action, and treatment; plaintiff's rights have not been invaded. Lynch v Warner Bros. Pictures, Inc. (1940, DC NY) 32 F Supp 575, 45 USPQ 273.

Where book based on story heard from another is deemed to be derivative work, copyright on book is not infringed by TV production and magazine articles retelling same story in new forms. Reyher v Children's Television Workshop (1975, DC NY) 387 F Supp 869, affd (CA2 NY) 533 F2d 87.

Infringement of play by motion picture is apparent if similar emotions are portrayed by sequence of events presented in like manner, expression, and form. Golding v RKO Radio Pictures, Inc. (1948, Cal App) 193 P2d 153, 77 USPQ 415, superseded (Cal) 208 P2d 1, 82 USPQ 136, subsequent op on reh 35 Cal 2d 690, 221 P2d 95, 86 USPQ 537.

56. Musical work arrangements

If defendant's copying of plaintiff's copyrighted song was infringement of both of plaintiff's copyrights thereon, defendant would be liable for two infringements; thus, defendant is liable for two infringements where his new arrangement of song included music and lyrics of 1935 copyrighted version as well as changes in music and lyrics included in 1944 copyrighted version, inasmuch as each version of song is covered by a separate valid copyright. Wihtol v Crow (1962, CA8 Iowa) 309 F2d 777, 135 USPQ 385.

New arrangement or adaptation of original musical composition is infringement if it incorporates such parts and portions of original as may interfere with rights of its composer. Jollie v Jaques (1850, CC NY) F Cas No 7437.

Defendants infringe copyright in musical composition by making arrangements and distributing printed copies to performers for promoting and commercializing Arizona State Fair. Mills Music, Inc. v Arizona (1975, DC Ariz) 187 USPQ 22.

57. Synopsis or outline

Brief synopsis of opera did not infringe author's copyright. G. Ricordi & Co. v Mason (1911, CC NY) 201 F 182, later app (DC NY) 201 F 184, affd (CA2 NY) 210 F 277.

Typewritten or mimeographed "outlines" taken from copyrighted book and furnished by teacher to his students constituted "versions" of substantial portions of book and were infringement. Macmillan Co. v King (1914, DC Mass) 223 F 862.

58. Translations

Prose translation of copyrighted prose romance, when translation does not paraphrase original work, does not infringe upon rights of author of original; German translation of "Uncle Tom's Cabin" did not infringe copyright of American authoress. Stowe v Thomas (1863, CC Pa) F Cas No 13514.

D. Distributions (as specified in 17 USCS § 106(3))

59. Generally

Dealer's sale of book at cut price in disregard of notice therein that such sale would be considered infringement was not infringement. Bobbs-Merrill Co. v Straus (1908) 210 US 339, 52 L Ed 1086, 28 S Ct 722.

Vendor of infringing book is liable as infringer. Greene v Bishop (1858, CC Mass) F Cas No 5763.

Distributor of infringing toy dolls, even though innocent purchaser, is infringer by virtue of its supplier's infringement. Uneeda Doll Co. v Regent Baby Products Corp. (1972, DC NY) 355 F Supp 438.

Actual copying by another company of copyrighted manuals on computer components is not defense to copyright infringement claim against party solely distributing infringing manuals and having sole right to sell equipment relating to manuals. Telex Corp. v International Business Machines Corp. (1973, DC Okla) 367 F Supp 258, 179 USPQ 777, affd in part and revd in part on other grounds (CA10 Okla) 510 F2d 894, cert dismd 423 US 802, 46 L Ed 2d 244, 96 S Ct 8.

60. Distribution of phonorecords

Seller of unauthorized records of copyrighted music, although having no connection with manufacturer, is infringer. Shapiro, Bernstein & Co. v Goody (1957, CA2 NY) 248 F2d 260, 115 USPQ 36, cert den 355 US 952, 2 L Ed 2d 529, 78 S Ct 536.

61. Restoration, rebinding, and repair

Rebinding of copyrighted book in exact imitation of original set is not infringement. Doan v American Book Co. (1901, CA7 Ill) 105 F 772.

Author's copyrights are not infringed by defendants who purchase unbound volumes of his works from his licensed publishers and subsequently bind and sell them. Kipling v G. P. Putnam's Sons (1903, CA2 NY) 120 F 631.

Sale of reconstructed secondhand books, copyrighted by plaintiff, as and for plaintiff's new books would constitute unfair competition, but not infringement of copyright. Bureau of Nat. Literature v Sells (1914, DC Wash) 211 F 379.

Plaintiff published and copyrighted magazine and books largely compiled from magazine; defendant purchased secondhand copies of magazines and broke them down and rearranged and assembled matter in bound books and sold them; this constituted infringement of copyright; right of the owner thereof to restore secondhand book to original condition so far as cover and binding are concerned is established; but this right does not extend to printing or replacing pages lost or mutilated, and compiling of articles from copyrighted magazine in book or pamphlet form and sale of them infringes copyright. National Geographic Soc. v Classified Geographic, Inc. (1939, DC Mass) 27 F Supp 655, 41 USPQ 719.

Defendant does not infringe by binding secondhand copies of plaintiff's copyrighted magazine, together with publications of third parties, within cover copyrighted by defendant and selling same; defendant has not copied, reprinted or rearranged copyrighted material or any of its component parts and has not removed plaintiff's copyright notice. Fawcett Publications, Inc. v Elliot Pub. Co. (1942, DC NY) 46 F Supp 717, 54 USPQ 137.

62. Transfers, generally

Producers of infringing motion-picture film are liable for infringement after sale of film to others with knowledge of its intended illegal use. Kalem Co. v Harper Bros. (1911) 222 US 55, 56 L Ed 92, 32 S Ct 20.

Licensee's sale or use of maps without copyright notice constituted infringement; it is error to award licensor as damages reasonable market value of copyright less consideration received for license; court should take into consideration extent to which fair market value was affected by rights granted to licensee. County of Ventura v Blackburn (1966, CA9 Cal) 362 F2d 515, 150 USPQ 160, 4 ALR Fed 454.

Sale of infringing dramatic composition renders seller liable for representation thereof by his vendee. Daly v Palmer (1868, CC NY) F Cas No 3552.

Defendant who sold copy of original cut, which plaintiffs had not copyrighted independently, but as part of their newspaper, was not liable for infringement, where purchasers of cut later used it unlawfully. Harper v Schoppell (1886, CC NY) 26 F 519.

Where infringing copies of photograph have all passed from possession of defendant, and plaintiff has recovered their value, defendant may not subsequently be subjected to liability respecting infringement of copyrights. Sarony v Ehrich (1886, CC NY) 28 F 79.

Defendant's mere filing of application for renewal copyright to which he was not entitled did not constitute infringement of plaintiff's renewal copyright; defendant did not copy composition; at most he is charged with having represented to copyright office that he had right to copy; he did not publish composition other than by his incorporation of earlier deposited copies by reference; that is not publication; therefore, it is not infringement. Austin v Steiner (1962, DC Ill) 207 F Supp 776, 134 USPQ 561.

Neither institution of declaratory judgment action to determine ownership of copyright renewal rights, demands for payment of royalties based upon claim of title, nor filing with register of copyrights of assignment resting upon alleged retention of renewal rights infringes upon or violates copyrighted material. T. B. Harms Co. v Eliscu (1964, DC NY) 226 F Supp 337, 141 USPQ 11, aff'd (CA2 NY) 339 F2d 823, 144 USPQ 46, cert den 381 US 915, 14 L Ed 2d 435, 85 S Ct 1534.

63. —As affected by independent agreements

There is no infringement by publication of copyrighted pictures without copyright notice, although copies of pictures sent by licensor to licensee bore on their backs condition that copyright notice be used, since licensor later orally waived condition; copyright owner who might elect to publish without copyright notice and thereby forego whatever protection that would give can also authorize licensee so to publish. Swift v Collegian Press, Inc. (1942, CA2 NY) 131 F2d 900, 55 USPQ 472.

It is no defense in action to enjoin book dealer from selling copyrighted books contrary to sales agreement, that he had no notice of such agreement. Henry Bill Pub. Co. v Smythe (1886, CC Ohio) 27 F 914.

Rights in training and operational manuals for employment agency are infringed by defendants' use without permission in violation of agreement not to disclose contents. Snelling & Snelling, Inc. v Armel, Inc. (1973, DC La) 360 F Supp 1319.

E. Performance (as specified in 17 USCS § 106(4))

64. Generally

Each publication of same copyrighted matter

at different times is separate infringement; all component parts of copyrighted work are protected by copyright and performance of single scene from one act of play with very little dialogue is infringement; each performance or broadcast of different scene of play on different occasions is separate infringement. Select Theatres Corp. v Ronzoni Macaroni Co. (DC NY) 59 USPQ 288.

65. Dramatic works

Where labors of author are substantially and injuriously appropriated by another, infringement occurs, as where basic situation of drama, development of idea and manner of expression are markedly similar in broadcast over radio. Marx v United States (1938, CA9 Cal) 96 F2d 204, 37 USPQ 380.

Canadian performances of rock opera are not infringements of US copyrights in drama or music, and steps preliminary to Canadian performances are not "manufacture" or "recordings" from which Canadian performances could be reproduced. Robert Stigwood Group, Ltd. v O'Reilly (1976, CA2 Conn) 530 F2d 1096, 189 USPQ 453, cert den 429 US 848, 50 L Ed 2d 121, 97 S Ct 135.

Plaintiffs licensed manufacturers of motion pictures but did not give them right to license for public performance and did not license defendant to perform publicly; defendant purchased copyrighted motion-picture films containing songs which were copyrighted by plaintiffs; exhibition of these films publicly for profit was infringement of plaintiffs' copyright. Famous Music Corp. v Melz (1939, DC La) 28 F Supp 767, 42 USPQ 573.

Radio station, which was made defendant by amendment to complaint alleging separate and independent cause of action solely against it, is separately and independently liable for copyright infringement by retransmitting infringing play telephoned to it by infringing originating radio station. Select Theatres Corp. v Ronzoni Macaroni Co. (DC NY) 59 USPQ 288.

Unauthorized public performance of dramatic work by means of moving picture is infringement. Inge v Twentieth Century-Fox Film Corp. (1956, DC NY) 143 F Supp 294, 111 USPQ 153.

Television play based on lives of gangster and woman does not infringe copyrighted manuscript submitted to network before play was broadcast, because even assuming network writers copied from submitted script, only similarities involved are matters of historical fact and treatment and emphasis is entirely different in play as broad-

cast. Fuld v National Broadcasting Co. (1975, DC NY) 390 F Supp 877, 185 USPQ 460.

66. Musical works, generally

Playing of copyrighted music in restaurant for entertainment of guests during meal time was public performance for profit and infringement. Herbert v Shanley Co. (1917) 242 US 591, 61 L Ed 511, 37 S Ct 232.

Unauthorized public performance of copyrighted musical composition in dance hall to which admission is charged, is infringement. Irving Berlin, Inc. v Daigle (1929, CA5 La) 31 F2d 832.

Playing of roll music which had no notice of copyright thereon created liability for infringement. Lutz v Buck (1930, CA5 Tex) 40 F2d 501, 5 USPQ 452, cert den 282 US 880, 75 L Ed 776, 51 S Ct 83.

Singing chorus of copyrighted song on stage in mimicking song voice and actions of an actress was not infringement. Bloom & Hamlin v Nixon (1903, CC Pa) 125 F 977; Green v Minzensheimer (1909, CC NY) 177 F 286.

Impersonator who sings whole of copyrighted song, in mimicking its singer, infringes such copyright. Green v Luby (1909, CC NY) 177 F 287.

It was not necessary that musicians have music before them to infringe copyrighted compositions. Leo Feist, Inc. v Demarie (1935, DC La) 16 F Supp 827, 32 USPQ 122.

Plaintiffs proved writing several letters to defendant, proprietor of restaurant, about license so he cannot claim he was in ignorance of need for license to have orchestra play copyrighted music; such playing was not accidental or due to ignorance but was infringement. Buck v Lisa (1939, DC NY) 28 F Supp 379, 42 USPQ 116.

Choruses played by orchestra constituted material and substantial portions of copyrighted pieces; this is infringement. Buck v Crescent Gardens Operating Co. (1939, DC Mass) 28 F Supp 576, 42 USPQ 435.

Hotel orchestra playing copyrighted musical composition without permission infringes copyrights although no admission is charged. Buck v Coe (1940, DC Pa) 32 F Supp 829, 45 USPQ 230.

Contention that defendant's orchestra played plaintiff's copyrighted music is not proved by inconclusive, vague, and discrepant testimony of plaintiff's two investigators, in view of direct denial, expert explanation, and direct straight forward presentation by defendant's witnesses.

Buck v Roman (1943, DC NY) 49 F Supp 23, 56 USPQ 310.

Elements of copyright infringement are (a) authorship of lyric and music of composition, (b) originality, (c) taking of steps required by law as to copyright registration, (d) title of plaintiff, composition's copyright, and right of public performance for profit, and (e) defendant's public performance for profit without license or consent from plaintiff. Remick Music Corp. v Interstate Hotel Co. (1944, DC Neb) 58 F Supp 523, 63 USPQ 327, affd (CA8 Neb) 157 F2d 744, 71 USPQ 138, cert den 329 US 809, 91 L Ed 691, 67 S Ct 622, reh den 330 US 854, 91 L Ed 1296, 67 S Ct 769.

There is infringement where copyrighted musical compositions are played on transcription discs and transmitted by leased telephone wires to customers who purchase such music service, and who amplify music on loudspeakers in their places of business without permission of copyright owners. Harms, Inc. v Sansom House Enterprises, Inc. (1958, DC Pa) 162 F Supp 129, 117 USPQ 272, affd (CA3 Pa) 267 F2d 494.

Unauthorized public performance of copyrighted music in restaurant for entertainment of patrons was performance for profit and constituted infringement. Bourne v Fouche (1965, DC SC) 238 F Supp 745, 145 USPQ 340.

Artists Management Corporation which organized, supervised, and controlled community concert association, and which provided concert artists, was liable in copyright infringement action for publicly performing music at concerts without copyright owner's permission and without payment of either license fees or royalties. Gershwin Publishing Corp. v Columbia Artists Management, Inc. (1970, DC NY) 312 F Supp 581, 165 USPQ 543, affd (CA2 NY) 443 F2d 1159, 14 ALR Fed 819.

Performance of copyrighted songs in club operated for profit and open to public is copyright infringement regardless of local licensing of club as "private." Broadcast Music, Inc. v Walters (1973, DC Okla) 181 USPQ 327.

67. —Transmission or broadcast

Broadcasting of copyrighted musical composition by radio is infringement of statutory copyright. Jerome H. Remick & Co. v American Auto. Accessories Co. (1925, CA6 Ohio) 5 F2d 411, 40 ALR 1511, cert den 269 US 556, 70 L Ed 409, 46 S Ct 19.

Defendant did not broadcast music directly to public, but sent it by private telephone wire to restaurant for purpose of having it played to restaurant's customers as and when restaurant wished to so entertain them; rendition of musical composition under these circumstances is public performance for profit by defendant as well as restaurant. Leo Feist, Inc. v Lew Tendler Tavern, Inc. (1959, CA3 Pa) 267 F2d 494, 121 USPQ 545.

Unauthorized broadcasting by radio of musical composition may constitute infringement, but broadcasting performance of one having such authority is not unlawful under copyright. Jerome H. Remick & Co. v General Electric Co. (1924, DC NY) 4 F2d 160.

One who by means of microphone "picks up" another's unauthorized performance of copyrighted musical composition and transmits it by radio is liable for infringement. Jerome H. Remick & Co. v General Electric Co. (1926, DC NY) 16 F2d 829.

Unlicensed broadcast of copyrighted musical composition on noncommercial sustaining program of nonprofit radio station, devoting third of its time to commercial broadcasts, is performance for profit and infringement; such broadcast on sustaining program of commercial station is infringement. Associated Music Publishers, Inc. v Debs Memorial Radio Fund, Inc. (1942, DC NY) 46 F Supp 829, 54 USPQ 461, affd (CA2 NY) 141 F2d 852, 61 USPQ 161, cert den 323 US 766, 89 L Ed 613, 65 S Ct 120.

Company infringes copyright by purporting to license broadcasting stations and others to perform infringing musical composition. Northern Music Corp. v King Record Distributing Co. (1952, DC NY) 105 F Supp 393, 93 USPQ 512.

It is infringement to publicly perform for profit, or to authorize public performance for profit, on radio and television of commercial announcements containing music substantially copied from plaintiff's copyrighted musical composition. Robertson v Batten, Barton, Durstine & Osborn, Inc. (1956, DC Cal) 146 F Supp 795, 111 USPQ 251.

Copyrighted musical composition is infringed by (1) printing, reprinting, publishing, and vending copies of infringing musical composition, (2) licensing public performance for profit of infringing composition on radio, television, and elsewhere, (3) licensing manufacture of phonograph records using infringing composition, and (4) publicly performing infringing composition for profit. Dorchester Music Corp. v National Broadcasting Co. (1959, DC Cal) 171 F Supp 580, 120 USPQ 429.

Infringement by broadcast of copyrighted music at racetrack is not excused by use of independent contractor to provide music or by failure of ASCAP to provide editing and repertory information not requested by defendant. Famous Music Corp. v Bay State Harness Horse Racing

& Breeding Asso., Inc. (1977, CA1) 194 USPQ 177.

F. Display (as specified in 17 USCS § 106(5))

68. Generally

Still pictures used for display which were reproductions of some of pictures that went to make up motion-picture film constituted infringement of cover of copyrighted magazine of which they were copies; projecting on screen reproduction of those pictures was infringement of copyright, and the films themselves, positive and negative, were infringement. Kaplan v Fox Film Corp. (DC NY) 37 USPQ 248.

69. Motion picture

Unlicensed exhibition of copyrighted motion picture of dramatic composition is infringement. Metro-Goldwyn-Mayer Distributing Corp. v Bijou Theatre Co. (1932, CA1 Mass) 59 F2d 70, 13 USPQ 147.

Motion-picture company selling unmutilated films to defendant was not entitled to recover for unlicensed exhibitions where evidence failed to show defendant had breached its agreement with plaintiff. Pathe Exchange, Inc. v Emile Snyder, Inc. (1936, CA3 NJ) 84 F2d 566, 29 USPQ 559.

It is infringement for one without permission of owner to exhibit or perform motion-picture photoplay. Tiffany Productions, Inc. v Dewing (1931, DC Md) 50 F2d 911, 9 USPQ 545.

Plaintiff leased copyrighted motion-picture "shorts" to C which runs theater under same management as defendant; without license from plaintiff, defendant borrowed them from C and exhibited in its theater; this is infringement of copyright. Vitaphone Corp. v Hutchinson Amusement Co. (1939, DC Mass) 28 F Supp 526, 42 USPQ 431.

70. Television

Defendant is not liable as infringer since it did not exhibit motion picture and did not participate in co-defendant's exhibition thereof on television; co-defendant is liable as infringer. Pickford Corp. v De Luxe Laboratories, Inc. (1958, DC Cal) 169 F Supp 118, 120 USPQ 521.

Television sponsor and advertising agency were liable for copyright infringement as they had power to determine content of program and stood to benefit from program. Davis v E. I. Du Pont De Nemours & Co. (1965, DC NY) 240 F Supp 612, 145 USPQ 258.

Television showing of motion pictures now in public domain and originally made under agreement with author of novels on which motion pictures were based infringe renewal copyright in novels if substantially similar to novels so that

summary judgment is refused. Filmvideo Releasing Corp. v Hastings (1976, DC NY) 426 F Supp 690, 193 USPQ 305.

G. Importation (as specified in 17 USCS § 602)

71. Generally

License to import recordings of copyrighted music from United States or Canada into any other country is really license to export from United States or Canada, and royalty must be paid with respect to exports although the music may be in public domain and not copyrightable in foreign country. Paine v Electrical Research Products, Inc. (1939, DC NY) 27 F Supp 780, 41 USPQ 575.

Importer whose luggage is covered with infringing fabric is liable to manufacturer of copyrighted fabric for sale to luggage manufacturers. United Merchants & Mfrs., Inc. v K. Gimbel Accessories, Inc. (1968, DC NY) 294 F Supp 151, 161 USPQ 147.

III. CABLE TELEVISION [17 USCS § 501(b)]

72. Generally

Mere quantitative contribution to television viewing cannot be proper test to determine copyright liability in context of television broadcasting; rather resolution of issue of copyright violation by CATV systems depends upon determination of function that CATV plays in total process of television broadcasting and reception. Teleprompter Corp. v Columbia Broadcasting System, Inc. (1974) 415 US 394, 39 L Ed 2d 415, 94 S Ct 1129.

IV. DEFENSES [17 USCS § 501(b)]

73. Generally

Fact that compilation of statutes was authorized by legislature does not justify infringement of plaintiff's rights under copyright laws. Howell v Miller (1898, CA6 Mich) 91 F 129.

Fact that defendants acknowledged source from which infringing passages were taken does not excuse infringement. Toksvig v Bruce Pub. Co. (1950, CA7 Wis) 181 F2d 664, 85 USPQ 339.

Previous infringement by others is not defense; purpose of invasion, or previous unlawful appropriation of parts of author's writing by others is no justification or defense to suit for infringement; though appropriator of another's work enclose such portions as he takes within quotations, he is not thereby relieved from liability for infringement. Gilmore v Anderson (1889, CC NY) 38 F 846.

Failure to prosecute other suits to final hearing did not justify defendants in going ahead with infringement. Black v Henry G. Allen Co. (1893, CC NY) 56 F 764.

It is no defense, in action for infringement of musical composition by broadcasting it on radio, that song was advertised by so doing. M. Witmark & Sons v L. Bamberger & Co. (1923, DC NJ) 291 F 776.

Any action growing out of infringement of copyright is not affected by artistic merit of work. Pellegrini v Allegrini (1924, DC Pa) 2 F2d 610.

Publication of part of plaintiff's book in magazine copyrighted by publisher thereof was no defense to infringement by copying directly from plaintiff's book. Warren v White & Wyckoff Mfg. Co. (1930, DC NY) 39 F2d 922.

In action for infringement of copyright, plaintiff was not bound to accept defendant's offer of apology and proposal to print retraction. Zenn v National Golf Review (1939, DC NY) 27 F Supp 732, 41 USPQ 535.

In suit for copyright infringement, defendants set up defense that suit is brought without authority in plaintiff's name by association, that association is engaged as common barrator, and that association is engaged in unlawful practice of law; defenses are urged as grounds for abatement and could not be availed of as justification for alleged tort. Vitaphone Corp. v Hutchinson Amusement Co. (1939, DC Mass) 28 F Supp 526, 42 USPQ 431.

Issuance of copyright certificate to defendant on plagiarized material does not relieve him from liability for infringement; copyright office, by accepting his material as copyrightable, does not thereby determine his rights under copyright laws. Gordon v Weir (1953, DC Mich) 111 F Supp 117, 97 USPQ 387, affd (CA6 Mich) 216 F2d 508, 104 USPQ 40.

Fact that defendant burlesqued other plays or motion pictures is no defense to instant action for copyright infringement based upon burlesque of plaintiff's motion picture. Loew's, Inc. v Columbia Broadcasting System, Inc. (1955, DC Cal) 131 F Supp 165, 105 USPQ 302, affd (CA9 Cal) 239 F2d 532, 112 USPQ 11, affd 356 US 43, 2 L Ed 2d 583, 78 S Ct 667, 116 USPQ 479, reh den 356 US 934, 2 L Ed 2d 764, 78 S Ct 770.

Claim that involved songs are trite and commonplace is no defense in copyright infringement action where proof of access is direct and uncontroverted and proof of copying is compelling. Nom Music, Inc. v Kaslin (1964, DC NY) 227 F Supp 922, 141 USPQ 22, affd (CA2 NY) 343 F2d 198, 145 USPQ 237.

In action wherein defendant reasonably contended that plaintiff's failure to file timely notice

of use constituted complete defense, court refrained from penalizing defendant prior to decision rejecting such defense. Norbay Music, Inc. v King Records, Inc. (1966, DC NY) 249 F Supp 285, 148 USPQ 420.

Even though third party's work was published with defective notice of copyright, it is no defense in infringement suit that source of defendant's work was in public domain if that source was unknown to defendant and was not used by it. Stanley v Columbia Broadcasting System, Inc. (1948, Cal App) 192 P2d 495, 77 USPQ 404, superseded (Cal) 208 P2d 9, 82 USPQ 123, subsequent op on reh 35 Cal 2d 653, 221 P2d 73, 23 ALR2d 216, 86 USPQ 520.

Solution of question of whether proof of absence of copying establishes defense is governed by same principle whether action be one for infringement of statutory or common-law copyright; in both types of action, there is no liability where there was no copying. Teich v General Mills, Inc. (1959) 170 Cal App 2d 791, 339 P2d 627, 121 USPQ 639.

74. Estoppel

Where, in consent decree, defendant had agreed that copyright was valid, he will be held to his agreement and is estopped from later contesting validity of copyright. Wilson v Haber Bros., Inc. (1921, CA2 NY) 275 F 346.

Performing rights society generally offering repertory information is not estopped to sue for infringement by broadcast of copyrighted music at racetrack relative to defendant who did not request repertory information. Famous Music Corp. v Bay State Harness Horse Racing & Breeding Asso., Inc. (1977, CA1) 194 USPQ 177.

Although English and instant United States copyright infringement actions involve same musical compositions and although English court entered judgment for defendants on ground that there was no copying, there is no res judicata since actions were brought under different statutes for different infringements; nevertheless, summary judgment was entered for defendants on basis of collateral estoppel since plaintiff was estopped to contend that its composition was copied, and under both English and United States law, either conscious or subconscious copying is required to support action for copyright infringement; if no copying occurs, there can be no recovery for a coincidental similarity even though substantial. Leo Feist Co. v Debmar Publishing Co. (1964, DC Pa) 232 F Supp 623, 141 USPQ 729.

Prior adjudication of validity and infringement of copyright in poem does not create collateral estoppel against challenge of copyright validity by different defendant, especially where new grounds of attack on copyright are raised. Bell v Combined Registry Co. (1975, DC Ill) 188 USPQ 707.

75. Innocent or unintentional infringement, generally

Unconscious plagiarism is actionable as much as deliberate plagiarism. Sheldon v Metro-Goldwyn Pictures Corp. (1936, CA2 NY) 81 F2d 49, 28 USPQ 330, cert den 298 US 669, 80 L Ed 1392, 56 S Ct 835.

One who copies from plagiarist is himself necessarily plagiarist, however innocent he may be. Barry v Hughes (1939, CA2 NY) 103 F2d 427, 41 USPQ 340, cert den 308 US 604, 84 L Ed 505, 60 S Ct 141.

Innocent copying by newspapers and magazines is not protection against infringement suit. De Acosta v Brown (1944, CA2 NY) 146 F2d 408, 63 USPQ 311, cert den 325 US 862, 89 L Ed 1983, 65 S Ct 1197 and cert den 325 US 862, 89 L Ed 1983, 65 S Ct 1198.

Absence of intent to infringe is not defense. Toksvig v Bruce Pub. Co. (1950, CA7 Wis) 181 F2d 664, 85 USPQ 339; Wihtol v Crow (1962, CA8 Iowa) 309 F2d 777, 135 USPQ 385.

If landlord lets his premises without knowledge of impending copyright infringement by tenant, exercises no supervision over him, charges fixed rental, receives no other benefit from infringement, and contributes in no way to it, landlord is not liable for tenant's infringement; however, dance hall proprietor is liable for copyright infringement resulting from performance of musical composition by band whose activities provide proprietor with source of customers and enhanced income; proprietor is liable whether bandleader is employee or independent contractor and whether proprietor has knowledge of compositions to be played or any control over their selection. Shapiro, Bernstein & Co. v H. L. Green Co. (1963, CA2 NY) 316 F2d 304, 137 USPQ 275.

Innocent intent with which the person acted who is charged with infringement is not defense where it appears that party setting it up has invaded copyright. Lawrence v Dana (1869, CC Mass) F Cas No 8136.

Lack of knowledge as to infringing character is no defense. Gilmore v Anderson (1889, CC NY) 38 F 846.

Since recovery provided for in suit for infringement of copyright, is penalty, it is defense that servants or agents of master acted without his knowledge or consent. McDonald v Hearst (1899, DC Cal) 95 F 656.

Ignorance of copyright, or honest intention, is no defense to action for infringement. Altman v New Haven Union Co. (1918, DC Conn) 254 F 113.

One who innocently copies list which infringes upon copyright of another is also guilty of infringement. Norris v No-Leak-O Piston Rings Co. (1921, DC Md) 271 F 536, affd (CA4 Md) 277 F 951.

Contention of defendant that no directions were given to orchestra and no designations made as to what orchestra should or should not play cannot be upheld in copyright infringement suit. Buck v Levin (DC Mass) 40 USPQ 27.

When notice of copyright is published, duty is on all to know the fact concerning it and innocence of intent to invade that right is no excuse for actually doing so. Sammons v Larkin (1940, DC Mass) 38 F Supp 649, 49 USPQ 350, mod on other grounds (CA1 Mass) 126 F2d 341, 53 USPQ 71.

It is no defense in infringement suit that use of plaintiff's copyrighted music in defendant's restaurant was without defendant's consent and contrary to his orders. Buck v Cecere (1942, DC NY) 45 F Supp 441, 53 USPQ 519.

Those who, with knowledge of copyright, commit acts which they believe do not constitute infringements may be liable. Chappell & Co. v Costa (1942, DC NY) 45 F Supp 554, 53 USPQ 674.

It is no defense that orchestra leader agreed with defendant not to play nonlicensed American Society of Composers, Authors, and Publishers' music and that defendant posted prominent notices objecting to playing such music. Shapiro, Bernstein & Co. v Veltin (1942, DC La) 47 F Supp 648, 55 USPQ 335.

It is no answer that defendant in making map was acting on instruction from third party who in previous years had his maps made by plaintiffs, since plaintiffs alone, and not third party, held copyright. Crocker v General Drafting Co. (1943, DC NY) 50 F Supp 634, 58 USPQ 60.

Fact that infringement was in ignorance and without dishonest intention is no defense to copyright infringement action, but is considered in determining damages. Phillips v Constitution Publishing Co. (DC Ga) 72 USPQ 69.

One who innocently copies from infringing copy is liable as infringer to owner whose unpublished work was infringed. Leigh v Gerber (1949, DC NY) 86 F Supp 320, 82 USPQ 271.

It is immaterial whether party is innocent infringer; infringer of valid copyright copies at his peril and intent to infringe is not essential in determining liability; also, knowledge to infringe is not essential element. Massapequa Publishing Co. v Observer, Inc. (1961, DC NY) 191 F Supp 261, 128 USPQ 418.

Fact that defendant was innocent does not excuse infringement; infringer of valid copyright copies at his peril and intent to infringe and knowledge to infringe are not essential in determining liability. John Wolf Textiles, Inc. v Andris Fabrics, Inc. (DC NY) 139 USPQ 365.

It is no defense that restaurant proprietor had no intent to infringe and did not know of infringing performance, that musicians were independent contractors, and that performance was contrary to proprietor's instructions. Bourne v Fouche (1965, DC SC) 238 F Supp 745, 145 USPQ 340.

That copying of copyrighted material was unintentional is no excuse, since it is result and not intention that determines question of infringement. Walco Products, Inc. v Kittay & Blitz, Inc. (1972, DC NY) 354 F Supp 121.

Any copy of copyrighted article made or found in possession of infringer after notice is separate infringement, and innocence of intention to infringe is no defense. Bell v Pro Arts, Inc. (1973, DC Ohio) 366 F Supp 474, 180 USPQ 517, affd (CA6 Ohio) 511 F2d 451, cert den 423 US 829, 46 L Ed 2d 46, 96 S Ct 47.

Defendant's trust in printer supplied with plaintiff's catalog of equipment to make noninfringing catalog not copied from plaintiff's is no defense to copyright infringement action if defendant's catalog infringes. Rexnord, Inc. v Modern Handling Systems, Inc. (1974, DC Del) 379 F Supp 1190, 183 USPQ 413.

Copying of portions of copyrighted technical brochures is copyright infringement and is not excused by salesmen's unauthorized grant of permission, but lack of wilfulness of infringement results in award of statutory minimum damages of $250 per infringement. USAchem, Inc. v Sands (1975, DC NM) 185 USPQ 387.

76. —Lack of knowledge of copyright

Lack of knowledge of copyrighted musical composition was no defense to a suit to enjoin. Hein v Harris (1910, CA2 NY) 183 F 107.

Where agent, acting in course of his employment, finds that article is copyrighted, such knowledge is imputed to principal, and principal may be sued for infringement whether he had actual knowledge or not. Christian v American Druggist Syndicate (1922, CA2 NY) 285 F 359.

Evidence that appellant had knowledge that its artists included copyrighted compositions in their performances, that appellant created an audience as a market for these artists, and that it participated in the formation and direction of the association of artists and its programming of compositions presented amply supported district court's finding that it "caused this copyright

infringement" and was liable as a "contributory" infringer; evidence that although appellant had no formal power to control either the local association or the artists for whom it served as agent, the local association did depend upon appellant for direction in matters such as this, that appellant was in a position to police the infringing conduct of its artists, that it derived substantial financial benefit from the actions of the primary infringers, that appellant knew that copyrighted works were being performed at the concert and that neither the local association nor the performing artists would secure copyright license, supported district court's finding that it was responsible for, and vicariously liable as a result of, the infringement of those primary infringers. Gershwin Publishing Corp. v Columbia Artists Management, Inc. (1971, CA2 NY) 443 F2d 1159, 14 ALR Fed 819.

If copyright has been infringed, person who has caused injury is liable whether he knew of copyright or not. Millett v Snowden (1844, CC NY) F Cas No 9600.

It is no defense, in action for infringement, that defendant had, without knowledge of plaintiff's copyright, copied his work from magazine which had wrongfully reprinted plaintiff's work. Norris v No-Leak-O Piston Rings Co. (1921, DC Md) 271 F 536, affd (CA4 Md) 277 F 951.

It is no defense, in suit on infringement of copyright, that there were no copyright notices appearing on articles, when defendant had actual knowledge of copyright. Schellberg v Empringham (1929, DC NY) 36 F2d 991.

Infringement is not avoided by lack of knowledge of copyright; also, lack of intent to violate it does not excuse one from liability. Metro Associated Services, Inc. v Webster City Graphic, Inc. (1953, DC Iowa) 117 F Supp 224, 100 USPQ 88.

One is not deliberate pirate where he copies another's work without knowledge that work is claimed to have been copyrighted. Christie v Raddock (1959, DC NY) 169 F Supp 48, 120 USPQ 76.

Infringer of valid copyright copies at his peril; intent to infringe is not essential; infringer's lack of knowledge of copyright is immaterial; thus, he infringes if he copies from copyrighted work that does not bear copyright notice and although he is without knowledge of fact that work had been copyrighted. Peter Pan Fabrics, Inc. v Acadia Co. (1959, DC NY) 173 F Supp 292, 121 USPQ 81, affd (CA2 NY) 274 F2d 487, 124 USPQ 154.

Copyright notice on all coin banks sold in United States precludes defense of innocent infringement from acquisition of infringing copy in Japan without copyright notice. Goldman-Morgen, Inc. v Dan Brechner & Co. (1976, DC NY) 190 USPQ 478.

Publication of copyright notice is not necessary where party infringing has actual notice of copyright. Nichols v Ruggles (Conn) 3 Day 145.

77. Invalidity of copyright

It is no defense, in action for infringement of copyright, brought by author and proprietor of copyright, that licensee of author had wrongfully printed story without copyright notice. American Press Asso. v Daily Story Pub. Co. (1902, CA7 Ill) 120 F 766, app dismd 193 US 675, 48 L Ed 842, 24 S Ct 852.

It is no defense, in action for infringement of copyright, that complainant had published English edition of copyrighted work, without notice of American copyright, when in fact English edition was copyrighted under laws of England and not of United States. G. & C. Merriam Co. v United Dictionary Co. (1906, CA7 Ill) 146 F 354, affd 208 US 260, 52 L Ed 478, 28 S Ct 290.

If what alleged infringer took was not copyrightable, copyright owner may not complain although his work may have directly inspired work of infringer. Chamberlin v Uris Sales Corp. (1945, CA2 NY) 150 F2d 512, 65 USPQ 544.

No suit can be maintained for infringement of work that is not subject to copyright even though all requirements of copyright law were complied with and certificate of copyright issued. Bleistein v Donaldson Lithographing Co. (1899, CC Ky) 98 F 608.

Lack of originality and musical merit of complainants' "rag-time" song did not constitute good defense to action for infringement. Hein v Harris (1910, CC NY) 175 F 875, affd (CA2 NY) 183 F 107.

Defendant's objection that there is no proof that copyrighted matter is original dramatic work is overcome by long acquiescence in paying royalty for many years which creates presumption of validity of copyright in absence of proof to contrary. Fitch v Shubert (1937, DC NY) 20 F Supp 314, 35 USPQ 245.

Bill for copyright infringement will be dismissed when plaintiff negligently and consistently fails properly to mark for copyright purposes photographs of subjects taken from copyrighted catalogue. Basevi v Edward O'Toole Co. (1939, DC NY) 26 F Supp 41, 40 USPQ 333.

Even if proprietor had valid copyright on advertisements, infringement of valid copyright is not shown where wording of advertisements was changed each time they were published, with no effort being made to have varied publications copyrighted. Davis-Robertson Agency v Duke (1953, DC Va) 119 F Supp 931, 100 USPQ 211.

There is no copyright infringement inasmuch as copyright proprietor had republished copyrighted catalogue illustrations in form of advertising without carrying copyright notice. S. A. Hirsh Mfg. Co. v Childs (DC Pa) 113 USPQ 331.

Plaintiff satisfies burden of proof by showing validity of original copyright and transfers in chain of title to plaintiff, but copyright is invalid as forfeited and abandoned by distribution of many copies of poem without copyright notice. Bell v Combined Registry Co. (1975, DC Ill) 188 USPQ 707.

Adequate copyright notice on all coin banks sold in United States supports validity of copyright so that virtually identical copies derived from Japanese copy are infringements. Goldman-Morgen, Inc. v Dan Brechner & Co. (1976, DC NY) 190 USPQ 478.

Counterclaims or affirmative defenses based on fraudulent procurement and invalidity of 64 copyrights on greeting cards in addition to 6 copyrights alleged to be infringed by plaintiff are dismissed as not presenting justiciable controversy, because plaintiff is not allowed to bring piecemeal suits on repeated groups of cards and defendant need not challenge validity of copyrights of cards not asserted by plaintiff. United Card Co. v Joli Greeting Card Co. (1976, DC Ill) 192 USPQ 667.

It is no defense to copyright infringement action that copyrighted preschool reading skills kit is made up of public domain material, unless public domain also includes similar kits having similar content, format, sequence, and similar arrangement of skills presented. Grolier, Inc. v Educational Reading Aids, Inc. (1976, DC NY) 193 USPQ 632.

78. Laches or delay

Registration of copyright in fabric design after publication of infringing copies of design is no defense to infringement action. Primcot Fabrics, Dept. of Prismatic Fabrics, Inc. v Kleinfab Corp. (1974, DC NY) 368 F Supp 482, 181 USPQ 443.

79. License or assignment of rights

Third party licensed to use copyrighted work by one co-owner is not liable for infringement to other co-owners who gave no consent; copyrights are similar in purpose to patents, and patent law protects licensee of joint owner from suit by another joint owner. Piantadosi v Loew's Inc. (1943, CA9 Cal) 137 F2d 534, 59 USPQ 174.

Copyright proprietor loaned book of illustrations to advertising agency with intent that illustrations be extracted for use at royalty of one dollar each; agency incorporated illustrations in advertisement which was published before payment of royalty; although book contains one sentence indicating that cash prepayment is required, it contains other statements susceptible to construction that prepayment is not required; proprietor having employed ambiguous and uncertain terminology in stating reproduction terms, agency was in substantial compliance with proffered license when it construed it to require only that payment of one dollar use fee be made after ultimate use of material; therefore, infringement complaint is dismissed. Stivers v Sir Francis Drake Hotel Co. (1953, CA9 Cal) 205 F2d 4, 98 USPQ 7.

Exemption in defendant's license of non-dramatic musical performances did not apply to defendant's concert, in which singers entered and exited, maintained specific roles and occasionally made gestures, and in which the story line of plaintiff's original copyrighted musical play was preserved by performing all but one of the songs in identical sequence; lack of costumes and scenery did not render concert non-dramatic. Robert Stigwood Group Ltd. v Sperber (1972, CA2 NY) 457 F2d 50, 173 USPQ 258.

Where defendants by contract were permitted to advertise certain patented "product" in their sales literature, plaintiff cannot complain that defendants use cuts made from photographs of "product" which were copyrighted after such agreement. Industrial R. & Locomotive Works, Inc. v Cagney Bros. (1932, DC NJ) 1 F Supp 970, 15 USPQ 263.

Where defendant used advertising material from plaintiff's copyrighted scheme after expiration of contract between them, defense that plaintiff's only remedy was for breach of contract was not good in infringement suit. Doll v Libin (1936, DC Mont) 17 F Supp 546, 33 USPQ 17.

Defendant had used supply of copyrighted cards under license from plaintiff and later bought from another printer and used card which differs slightly in wording but is substantial copy of copyrighted card; infringement is certain but not especially willful. Druley v Thompson (DC Pa) 44 USPQ 284.

Assignment of motion picture and television rights making some specific exceptions but not excepting right to television series based on work grants assignee right to make and exhibit TV series so that copyright infringement claim is summarily dismissed. Landon v Twentieth Century-Fox Film Corp. (1974, DC NY) 384 F Supp 450, 185 USPQ 221 (disapproved on other grounds Imperial Point Colonnades Condominium, Inc. v Mangurian (CA5 Fla) 549 F2d 1029, reh den (CA5 Fla) 552 F2d 369).

Copying of portions of copyrighted technical brochures is copyright infringement and is not excused by salesmen's unauthorized grant of permission, but lack of wilfulness of infringement results in award of statutory minimum damages of $250 per infringement. USAchem, Inc. v Sands (1975, DC NM) 185 USPQ 387.

Contract for performing rights in song is complete bar to action against television stations for broadcast use of song in commercial. Jackson v Stone & Simon Advertising, Inc. (1974, DC Mich) 188 USPQ 564.

Singer who assigned all rights in sound recordings to third party and reserved no rights to himself has no standing to sue for copyright infringement for playing of recordings by steamship line. Bertolino v Italian Line (1976, DC NY) 193 USPQ 743.

80. Misuse of copyright, generally

It is not actionable wrong for one to assert in good faith that he intends to enforce what he conceives to be his legal rights, even if he is mistaken as to what such rights are; one who claims that his patent has been infringed may communicate infringement claim to customers of alleged infringer and may even threaten them with suit, provided he acts in good faith; there is no reason why rule should be limited to patent infringement cases or why it should not apply to copyright infringement cases; however such assertions of legal rights must be kept within proper bounds; thus, if another's customers are threatened, intimidated, or harassed, equity court will enjoin such conduct; same result follows where infringement claims against another's customers or threats of suit are made in bad faith. Remington Research, Inc. v Modern Aids, Inc. (1959, DC NY) 170 F Supp 7, 120 USPQ 289.

Tie-in sales and allegations of antitrust violations are not defense to copyright infringement action if factually unsubstantiated. Foreign Car Parts, Inc. v Auto World, Inc. (1973, DC Pa) 366 F Supp 977, 181 USPQ 162.

ASCAP and BMI do not misuse copyrights by granting blanket licenses to CBS where evidence fails to show that direct licensing for each composition to be performed is impractical or that ASCAP or BMI would refuse direct licensing. Columbia Broadcasting System, Inc. v American Soc. of Composers (1975, DC NY) 400 F Supp 737, 187 USPQ 431.

81. —Use in violation of law

Defense to copyright infringement action is not made out by contention that American Society of Composers, Authors, and Publishers was authorized by antitrust judgment to issue blanket performance licenses which might be contrary to Washington statute, since there is no evidence that defendant applied for license and could obtain only blanket license. K-91, Inc. v Gershwin Publishing Corp. (1967, CA9 Wash) 372 F2d 1, 152 USPQ 375, cert den 389 US 1045, 19 L Ed 2d 838, 88 S Ct 761.

Antitrust decree placed upon ASCAP duty to advise of its obligation to inform prospective users whether specified musical compositions were in ASCAP's repertory of copyrighted compositions, and to advise that such service was available upon request, when a communication was made to ASCAP by supper club proprietor which could have been fairly interpreted as request for aid in avoiding infringement; as ASCAP failed to comply with proprietor's request for listing of ASCAP compositions and also failed to offer editing service contemplated by decree, it would be inequitable to permit recovery for infringement which occurred and which was caused and brought about, in part at least, by dereliction of ASCAP in failing to facilitate proprietor's expressed intention of avoiding infringement. Plaintiffs, ASCAP's members, are estopped to assert infringement. Tempo Music, Inc. v Myers (1969, CA4 NC) 407 F2d 503, 160 USPQ 707.

In suit for infringement of copyright, exceptions to clauses in answers which set up state and federal antitrust statutes were good. Scribner v Straus (1904, CC NY) 130 F 389.

It is no defense, to action for infringement of copyright, that plaintiff is engaged in conspiracy in restraint of trade in violation of Sherman Antitrust Act [15 USCS §§ 1–7, 15 note]. Harms v Cohen (1922, DC Pa) 279 F 276; Buck v Hillsgrove Country Club, Inc. (1937, DC RI) 17 F Supp 643, 33 USPQ 134; Buck v Del Papa (1937, DC RI) 17 F Supp 645; Buck v Newsreel, Inc. (1938, DC Mass) 25 F Supp 787, 40 USPQ 20; Buck v Spanish Gables, Inc. (1938, DC Mass) 26 F Supp 36, 40 USPQ 19; Society of European Stage Authors & Composers, Inc. v WCAU Broadcasting Co. (1940, DC Pa) 35 F Supp 460, 47 USPQ 310; Buck v Cecere (1942, DC NY) 45 F Supp 441, 53 USPQ 519; Buck v Repertory Theatre (DC Mass) 40 USPQ 23; Buck v Holyoke Theatre (DC Mass) 40 USPQ 24; Buck v Wrentham Show Boat (DC Mass) 40 USPQ 25.

Although American Society of Composers, Authors, and Publishers is outlawed in Nebraska, it is lawful society elsewhere, and fact that plaintiffs in copyright infringement suits in Nebraska federal court, in dealings exclusively beyond Nebraska, adhere to American Society of Composers, Authors, and Publishers' membership, does not subject them to imputation of wrongdoing, make them violators of Nebraska laws, or bar doors of Nebraska courts to them.

Remick Music Corp. v Interstate Hotel Co. (1944, DC Neb) 58 F Supp 523, 63 USPQ 327, affd (CA8 Neb) 157 F2d 744, 71 USPQ 138, cert den 329 US 809, 91 L Ed 691, 67 S Ct 622, reh den 330 US 854, 91 L Ed 1296, 67 S Ct 769.

It is no defense to copyright infringement suit that English copyright proprietor and other Guild members violated Antitrust Acts [15 USCS §§ 1 et seq.] by agreeing to limit production of copyrighted engravings and to maintain minimum prices. Alfred Bell & Co. v Catalda Fine Arts, Inc. (1947, DC NY) 74 F Supp 973, 75 USPQ 66.

It is not permissible defense in copyright infringement action to allege that copyright proprietors and others have effectuated conspiracy to monopolize entire field of musical compositions in violation of Antitrust Acts [15 USCS §§ 1 et seq.] and have been guilty of discrimination to defendants' damage. Harms, Inc. v Sansom House Enterprises, Inc. (1958, DC Pa) 162 F Supp 129, 117 USPQ 272, affd (CA3 Pa) 267 F2d 494.

Generally, it is no defense to copyright infringement action that plaintiff is violating antitrust statutes by combination or conspiracy in restraint of trade; although equity court will withhold relief against even stranger to misuse, where patentee is using patent privilege contrary to public interest, it is substantial question whether like rule, invokable in same manner, is applicable to copyright infringement action; motion to strike misuse defense is denied without prejudice in copyright infringement action since insufficiency of defense is not clearly apparent and since determination of effect of alleged misuse on plaintiff's action requires delicate balancing of competing public policies in area of law that is yet evolving. United Artists Associated, Inc. v NWL Corp. (1961, DC NY) 198 F Supp 953, 132 USPQ 248.

Defendants performing copyrighted music for profit are not excused from infringement by failure of performing rights society to provide complete list of songs proprietary to society, where society, on at least two occasions, advised defendants of editing service and availability of song list for public inspection in New York City. Big Sky Music v Todd (1974, DC Ga) 388 F Supp 498, 184 USPQ 286.

Pendency of appeal on Federal District Court judgment of no misuse of copyright or violation of antitrust law is sufficient grounds for temporarily enjoining litigation of same issues in state court action on contract for performing rights royalties, especially considering balance of equities and likelihood of injury to plaintiff from allowing complex technical issues to be relitigated. Broadcast Music, Inc. v CBS Inc. (1976, DC NY) 193 USPQ 501.

82. Res judicata

State court judgment dismissing complaint for unfair competition, by use in magazines of titles to copyrighted songs, is not res judicata in federal court copyright infringement suit; even if, in earlier action, court had made adverse finding of fact essential to support judgment in copyright action, finding would bar latter action; but state court made no such finding; it rested decision on finding that purchasers would not be misled, fact unimportant in copyright action. Leo Feist, Inc. v Song Parodies, Inc. (1944, CA2 NY) 146 F2d 400, 64 USPQ 92.

Plaintiff brought tort action for copyright infringement but never returned writ and declaration into court; instead, instant action was started day after return day of writ; failure of plaintiff to enter his first writ and declaration on return day operated as complete abandonment of that suit and there is no danger of defendant being annoyed by having to respond to it; therefore, there are no adequate grounds for staying or abating instant action. Pizzano v Knowles & Co. (1941, DC Mass) 37 F Supp 118, 49 USPQ 140.

Suit for infringing broadcast of motion picture is not barred by res judicata relative to previous suit on same copyright but for different infringement, especially where previous suit was not tried on merits but dismissed for procedural failure. Rohauer v Killiam Shows, Inc. (1974, DC NY) 379 F Supp 723, 183 USPQ 592, revd on other grounds (CA2 NY) 551 F2d 484.

Decisions of courts of appeals reversing district courts on finding of literary piracy in equity cases have no value in state appellate court on appeal from judgment on jury's verdict. Golding v RKO Radio Pictures, Inc. (1948, Cal App) 193 P2d 153, 77 USPQ 415, superseded (Cal) 208 P2d 1, 82 USPQ 136, subsequent op on reh 35 Cal 2d 690, 221 P2d 95, 86 USPQ 537.

Judgment of United States court in action on infringement of copyright, is res judicata in another suit involving same facts in state court. Kirke La Shelle Co. v Armstrong (1916) 173 App Div 232, 159 NYS 363, affd 224 NY 582, 120 NE 866.

83. Title of copyright proprietor

It is no defense to action for infringement of copyright that plaintiff is not owner, his assignor being married woman who had no right to assign it. Belford v Scribner (1892) 144 US 488, 36 L Ed 514, 12 S Ct 734.

Copy of mural in high school is published in text book with legend "Copyright, Courtesy New York Board of Education"; this tends to support inference that author had received consent, although after lapse of years he cannot remember to what official he applied for permission; fact board gave consent indicated board did not understand artist owned copyright. Yardley v Houghton Mifflin Co. (1939, CA2 NY) 108 F2d 28, 44 USPQ 1, cert den 309 US 686, 84 L Ed 1029, 60 S Ct 891.

Copyright infringement suit is dismissed where plaintiff is assignee of renewal obtained by composer of music of song and defendant is assignee of renewals obtained by authors of words of song. Edward B. Marks Music Corp. v Jerry Vogel Music Co. (1944, CA2 NY) 140 F2d 270, 60 USPQ 259.

It is unnecessary to consider whether defendant infringed where plaintiff's rights in copyrighted map are held in trust for government, his employer. Sawyer v Crowell Publishing Co. (1944, CA2 NY) 142 F2d 497, 61 USPQ 389, cert den 323 US 735, 89 L Ed 589, 65 S Ct 74.

Infringing broadcast of motion picture is not excused by assertion that attorneys securing renewal copyright were not agents of next of kin of author or that agreement assigning motion picture rights under renewal copyright was invalid because of motion picture rights assignment made by author under original copyright terms. Rohauer v Killiam Shows, Inc. (1974, DC NY) 379 F Supp 723, 183 USPQ 592, revd on other grounds (CA2 NY) 551 F2d 484.

Copying of classified advertisements is not violation of copyright in classified advertisement weekly, because copyright in ads belongs to advertisers and is not assigned to publisher without express agreement. Jacobs v Robitaille (1976, DC NH) 406 F Supp 1145, 189 USPQ 601.

Plaintiff has no cause of action for infringement occurring only after assignment of copyright by plaintiff to third party not joined in suit, and publication of work without copyright notice by third party forfeits copyright so that plaintiff has no rights for infringement occurring after reassignment of copyright back to plaintiff. Walker v University Books, Inc. (1977, DC Cal) 193 USPQ 596.

84. Unclean hands

In suit for infringement of copyright where defendant shows that complainant is also guilty of piracy, equity may refuse relief to complainant. Edward Thompson Co. v American Law Book Co. (1903, CA2 NY) 122 F 922.

Copyright proprietor, suing for infringement in Wisconsin federal court, does not have unclean hands because it has not complied with Wisconsin statutes requiring license from state to issue copyright licenses or to use threats to procure licenses. Leo Feist, Inc. v Young (1943, CA7 Wis) 138 F2d 972, 59 USPQ 450.

Copyright infringers are in poor position to question plaintiffs' motives and character when infringers are guilty of wrongfully appropriating plaintiffs' property. Interstate Hotel Co. v Remick Music Corp. (1946, CA8 Neb) 157 F2d 744, 71 USPQ 138, cert den 329 US 809, 91 L Ed 691, 67 S Ct 622, reh den 330 US 854, 91 L Ed 1296, 67 S Ct 769.

Plaintiff cannot recover in action for copyright infringement and unfair competition since its copyrighted cards are sold for purpose of being used in lottery known as "Banko" or "Bank-Night." Kessler v Schreiber (1941, DC NY) 39 F Supp 655, 49 USPQ 610.

Even if biographer uses matter in public domain and matter copyrighted by others without objection by them, defendants may not avoid infringement by means of doctrine of unclean hands since what they took from biography was original with biographer and was not something biographer had taken from some one else. Harris v Miller (DC NY) 50 USPQ 306, mod on other ground 50 USPQ 625.

Copyright infringement suit was dismissed for unclean hands where plaintiff had notice that defendant's employee, while secretly stockholder, director, and editor of plaintiff's predecessor, obtained ideas for textbook originated by defendant and used ideas in preparing predecessor's copyrighted textbook. Colonial Book Co. v Oxford Book Co. (1942, DC NY) 45 F Supp 551, 53 USPQ 599, affd (CA2 NY) 135 F2d 463, 57 USPQ 569.

It is not unclean hands that different plaintiff's contemporaneously brought 11 instant infringement suits, and few others, against different defendants; if rights asserted exist, court has no concern whether they are vindicated in concurrent or successive proceedings. Remick Music Corp. v Interstate Hotel Co. (1944, DC Neb) 58 F Supp 523, 63 USPQ 327, affd (CA8 Neb) 157 F2d 744, 71 USPQ 138, cert den 329 US 809, 91 L Ed 691, 67 S Ct 622, reh den 330 US 854, 91 L Ed 1296, 67 S Ct 769.

Copyright infringement is not justifiable on grounds of unclean hands of copyright proprietor for publishing original book without copyright and copyrighting supplements to keep book up to date without notifying users of public domain status of original book. Neal v Glickman (1975, DC Tex) 391 F Supp 1088, 185 USPQ 549.

V. PRACTICE AND PROCEDURE

A. In General

85. Generally

In suit for infringement of copyright, rights of plaintiff will also be determined. Binns v Woodruff (1821, CC Pa) F Cas No 1424.

Fact that bill for infringement shows existence of license contract is not conclusive as to election of remedy for breach of contract precluding suit for infringement where defendant may have trespassed on plaintiff's monopoly beyond terms of contract. Metro-Goldwyn-Mayer Distributing Corp. v Bijou Theatre Co. (1933, DC Mass) 3 F Supp 66, 17 USPQ 124.

Where question of infringement was not referred to master (on reference for accounting), his finding that copying was deliberate was not necessary to his decision and defendant's exception to such finding was sustained. Jones Brothers Co. v Underkoffler (DC Pa) 35 USPQ 448.

86. Jurisdiction

Action in federal court for infringement of uncopyrighted and unpublished play, jurisdiction being founded on diversity of citizenship, is governed by state law, which in New York is like federal copyright law. De Acosta v Brown (1943, DC NY) 50 F Supp 615, 58 USPQ 596, affd (CA2 NY) 146 F2d 408, 63 USPQ 311, cert den 325 US 862, 89 L Ed 1983, 65 S Ct 1197 and cert den 325 US 862, 89 L Ed 1983, 65 S Ct 1198.

Test for determining whether nonresident corporation or its agent is "found" within district, within meaning of 28 USCS § 1400(a) is same as that for determining whether corporation is amenable to suit in jurisdiction other than that in which it is incorporated. Geo-Physical Maps, Inc. v Toycraft Corp. (1958, DC NY) 162 F Supp 141, 117 USPQ 316.

Suit by California resident in California District Court against New York defendant for copyright infringement is not dismissable under California long-arm statute where alleged tort of defendant affects California resident. Walker v University Books, Inc. (1974, DC Cal) 382 F Supp 126, 184 USPQ 10.

Complaint alleging infringement of registered copyright for layout of historical map supports federal jurisdiction, even though case involves contract questions between parties as to preparation of work. Hughey v Palographics Co. (1976, DC Colo) 189 USPQ 527.

Jurisdiction and venue are proper relative to defendants involved in selling within district via allegedly infringing catalog, especially when defendants operate sufficiently within district to be subject to long-arm statute. Precision Universal Joint Corp. v Republic Gear Co. (1976, DC Ill) 193 USPQ 26.

Venue improperly placed and service under long-arm statute result in no personal jurisdiction over defendant. Mode Art Jewelers Co. v Expansion Jewelry, Ltd. (1976, DC NY) 409 F Supp 921, 193 USPQ 48.

87. Settlement attempts

Refusal to arbitrate does not bar infringement suit and grant of license is not election to sue in assumpsit. Tiffany Productions, Inc. v Dewing (1931, DC Md) 50 F2d 911, 9 USPQ 545.

Plaintiff's offer to settle with defendant for breach of contract to use plaintiff's advertising scheme, had no bearing upon plaintiff's right to sue for infringements after expiration of contract. Doll v Libin (1936, DC Mont) 17 F Supp 546, 33 USPQ 17.

Settlement of copyright infringement action cannot be proof of defendant's acquiescence in merits of plaintiff's claims. Continental Cas. Co. v Beardsley (1957, DC NY) 151 F Supp 28, 113 USPQ 181, mod on other grounds (CA2 NY) 253 F2d 702, 117 USPQ 1, cert den 358 US 816, 3 L Ed 2d 58, 79 S Ct 25.

B. Parties

1. Plaintiffs

88. Generally

Action to determine rights in copyright can be maintained against copyright owner even though person named as author in copyright is not party to suit. Machaty v Astra Pictures, Inc. (1952, CA2 NY) 197 F2d 138, 93 USPQ 51, cert den 334 US 827, 97 L Ed 644, 73 S Ct 29.

Person who has never completed his copyright cannot give another person right to complete such copyright 16 years later, so as to enable such person to sue for infringement. Koppel v Downing (1897) 11 App DC 93.

In a suit to restrain infringement demurrer for want of proper parties will be overruled where it cannot be sustained as to whole bill, and defendant has not pointed out specifically parts objected to. Empire City Amusement Co. v Wilton (1903, CC Mass) 134 F 132.

Although cases hold that unauthorized person, who takes out copyright and claims to be owner thereof, acts as trustee for true owner and copyright is held in trust for owner, court cannot hold that alleged trustee is not true owner since, although present in court, he is not party to infringement suit and has not assigned copyright to plaintiff. Machaty v Astra Pictures, Inc. (DC NY) 89 USPQ 539, affd (CA2 NY) 197 F2d 138, 93 USPQ 51, cert den 334 US 827, 97 L Ed 644, 73 S Ct 29.

German citizen who has strictly complied with provisions of Copyright Act at any time between July 1, 1909, the date upon which Act became effective, and date of proclamation of President declaring that citizens of Germany were entitled to general copyright privileges, is not only vested with copyright in his work, but may maintain action for any infringement which occurred between said dates. 29 OAG 64.

89. Agents, trustees, and representatives

Author holding legal title to copyright of pamphlet for benefit of another was entitled to sue for its infringement. Hanson v Jaccard Jewelry Co. (1887, CC Mo) 32 F 202.

Foreign administrator, not taking out ancillary letters, cannot maintain suit for infringement. Black v Henry G. Allen Co. (1890, CC NY) 42 F 618.

Proprietor of copyrighted publication may sue for infringement of article in publication copyrighted for benefit of author of article. Schellberg v Empringham (1929, DC NY) 36 F2d 991.

Suit for infringement of copyright brought by copyright protective bureau in name of copyright owner for such owner's benefit was not barratrous. Vitaphone Corp. v Hutchinson Amusement Co. (1937, DC Mass) 19 F Supp 359, 33 USPQ 422.

Copyright protective bureau organized by plaintiff and other motion-picture producers to find, prosecute, and settle infringements was authorized to bring action since plaintiff's sales manager asked bureau to look into infringement and plaintiff was notified of suit and helped with prosecution. Vitaphone Corp. v Hutchinson Amusement Co. (1939, DC Mass) 28 F Supp 526, 42 USPQ 431.

90. Assignees as plaintiffs

Where author made assignment of all his musical compositions to be written during five-year period, and later made assignment of one of his compositions and assignee secured copyright thereon, assignee stood in same position as author and could not restrain infringement on copyright by original assignee. T. B. Harms & Francis, Day & Hunter v Stern (1916, CA2 NY) 231 F 645.

Assignee of motion-picture rights of copyrighted book without any copyright of his motion-picture photoplay could not maintain suit for infringement of his rights under assignment. Goldwin Pictures Corp. v Howells Sales Co. (1922, CA2 NY) 282 F 9.

Plaintiff, as composer's assignee, is real party in interest entitled to sue in own behalf in copyright infringement action; nonjoinder of deceased author's successors is not fatal since they are not indispensable within Rule 19(b) of Federal Rules of Civil Procedure because their rights can be reserved in judgment. Edward B. Marks Music Corp. v Jerry Vogel Music Co. (1944, CA2 NY) 140 F2d 268, 60 USPQ 256.

Assignee of exclusive right of performing a play in all places throughout United States, excepting in five principal cities, for term of one year had sufficient interest in copyright to be able to maintain suit for infringement. Roberts v Myers (1860, CC Mass) F Cas No 11906.

Assignees of owner of copyrighted translation of French play were entitled to maintain suit for infringement of translation. Shook v Rankin (1875, CC Ill) F Cas No 12804.

Assignees of exclusive right to print and sell series of juvenile books were proper parties to sue for its infringement. Estes v Williams (1884, CC NY) 21 F 189.

Arrangement whereby composer authorized copyrighting of his song in name of complainant prior to its delivery to complainant constituted in fact such assignment of song before copyrighting as to permit complainant to sue subsequently for infringement. White-Smith Music Pub. Co. v Apollo Co. (1905, CC NY) 139 F 427, affd (CA2 NY) 147 F 226, affd 209 US 1, 52 L Ed 655, 28 S Ct 319.

As against defendant who knows that title under which play was copyrighted has been changed, and another title adopted, assignee of copyright may maintain an action for infringement of such play. Collier v Imp Films Co. (1913, DC NY) 214 F 272.

E wrote, and sold to C, all rights in article which was published and copyrighted by C who assigned to E all rights except American serial rights (including, right to republish in various publications including trade papers or others not competitive with first class magazine); C therefore retained right to republish in such trade or other papers including lesser right to grant permission to others to so republish; E was mere licensee and not proper party plaintiff to sue for infringement by publication in house organ, but since C is joined as plaintiff, suit is not dismissed but is proceeded with under Rule 21 of Federal Rules of Civil Procedure. Eliot v Geare-Marston, Inc. (1939, DC Pa) 30 F Supp 301, 43 USPQ 249.

Outright sale of song by author in consideration that purchaser pay royalties is absolute assignment passing absolute ownership and right to apply for copyright; subsequent release to author of all purchaser's right, title, and interest in song, which purchaser had copyrighted, does not carry right to sue for infringement occurring during purchaser's ownership. Kriger v MacFadden Publications, Inc. (1941, DC NY) 43 F Supp 170, 52 USPQ 217.

Author has no right to sue where article was accepted by publisher for exclusive publication in magazine; copyright was secured by publisher in its name; there was no contract between publisher and author, and author does not allude to any reservation of rights when she gave publisher authority to publish article. Alexander v Irving Trust Co. (1955, DC NY) 132 F Supp 364, 106 USPQ 74, affd (CA2 NY) 228 F2d 221, 108 USPQ 24, cert den 350 US 996, 100 L Ed 860, 76 S Ct 545.

Sale of copyright does not prevent owner at time of infringement from suing for damages sustained while it was owner. M. J. Golden & Co. v Pittsburgh Brewing Co. (1956, DC Pa) 137 F Supp 455, 108 USPQ 250.

Copyright Act gives only copyright proprietors the right to sue for infringement; "proprietor" is either author of work or his assignee; party bringing suit must not only be proprietor in this sense but also copyright proprietor, in other words, he must have owned copyright at time of infringement; transfer of copyright owner's right, title, and interest ordinarily does not vest in assignee cause of action for prior infringement, and assignor cannot maintain such action if infringement took place subsequent to assignment, or unless it took place before transfer; however, legal title to copyright may be in one person and equitable title in another; thus, one may be proprietor of copyright if he holds legal title, though equitable title may be in another either expressly or as trustee ex malificio; in such case, courts treat equitable owner as copyright proprietor and permit him to maintain infringement action. Manning v Miller Music Corp. (1959, DC NY) 174 F Supp 192, 121 USPQ 600.

Motion for judgment on pleadings on ground that plaintiff lacks standing to sue as licensee rather than assignee is denied, and agreement granting rights to plaintiff and reserving rights against earlier infringers and right to license under same terms as granted to others by plaintiff in future is assignment giving plaintiff standing to sue, especially where no purpose would be served in bringing assignor into suit. Ed Brawley, Inc. v Gaffney (1975, DC Cal) 399 F Supp 115, 188 USPQ 648.

91. Co-owners of copyright

Complaint charging defendant with infringement by public performance of copyrighted musical compositions owned by two of three plaintiffs, third plaintiff having exclusive rights of publicly presenting compositions, should not have been dismissed for multifariousness and misjoinder, but court could have ordered separate trials if it decided convenience required two trials. Buck v Elm Lodge, Inc. (1936, CA2 NY) 83 F2d 201, 29 USPQ 390.

Contracts between coauthors and publisher provide for payment of royalties to coauthors in designated proportions; one coauthor sues publisher to determine whether specific sales are subject to royalties; other coauthor is joined as party since, although not indispensable party (inasmuch as each coauthor could maintain action to recover royalties), he is necessary party if subsequent suit against publisher on similar claim is to be avoided; advantage of his presence outweights any disadvantage resulting from court's loss of diversity jurisdiction. Curtis v American Book Co. (1955, DC NY) 17 FRD 504, 107 USPQ 116.

Joint proprietors of copyright may sue jointly for its infringement; thus, author and owner of right to produce copyrighted play on stage may maintain action against one to whom they granted right to make moving picture. Inge v Twentieth Century-Fox Film Corp. (1956, DC NY) 143 F Supp 294, 111 USPQ 153.

Co-author cannot bring infringement action against other co-authors, their assignees, or licensees; proper balance between interest of excluded co-author and that of public is achieved by allowing each co-author to exploit work, but subject to duty to account to his collaborators. Harrington v Mure (1960, DC NY) 186 F Supp 655, 126 USPQ 506.

92. Joinder of separate plaintiffs

Four separate plaintiffs cannot join in one suit against defendant on ground that their demands are similar, against same defendant, and upon same kind of cause of action, when causes of action grow out of different facts, and none of plaintiffs has interest in copyright of others. Desylva, Brown & Henderson, Inc. v Weyman (1934, DC La) 7 F Supp 725, 23 USPQ 172.

Where copyrights of several separate compositions are infringed simultaneously by same defendant, proprietors may not join together in one bill and sue for infringement. Buck v Kloeppel (1935, DC Fla) 10 F Supp 345, 26 USPQ 9.

Two plaintiffs and their separate claims are properly joined in copyright infringement action since their separate claims for copyright infringement arose out of same series of occurrences and questions of fact and law establishing infringements are common to both claims. Edwin H. Morris & Co. v Munn (1964, DC SC) 233 F Supp 71, 142 USPQ 440.

Four proprietors of different copyrighted musical compositions are properly joined as plaintiffs in infringement action against operator of cafe in which such compositions were performed. Harm's, Inc. v Theodosiades (1965, DC Pa) 246 F Supp 799, 148 USPQ 147.

Failure to join third party assignee of copyright during period in which alleged infringement occurred results in summary judgment against assignor of copyright. Walker v University Books, Inc. (1977, DC Cal) 193 USPQ 596.

93. Legal or beneficial owner of rights infringed, generally

Where the plaintiff has no authority to copyright, he can maintain no action for infringement. Public Ledger Co. v New York Times Co. (1922, CA2 NY) 279 F 747, cert den 258 US 627, 66 L Ed 798, 42 S Ct 383.

Equitable owner of copyright may sue for infringement. Bisel v Ladner (1924, CA3 Pa) 1 F2d 436.

Copyright Act gives right to sue for infringement to copyright proprietor; plaintiff, publisher member of the American Society of Composers, Authors, and Publishers, is proprietor and may sue. Leo Feist, Inc. v Young (1943, CA7 Wis) 138 F2d 972, 59 USPQ 450.

Holder of legal title to copyright may sue for copyright infringement without joining others having equitable interest. Edward B. Marks Music Corp. v Jerry Vogel Music Co. (1944, CA2 NY) 140 F2d 268, 60 USPQ 256.

Person, giving events of his life to another for purpose of preparing book, is not author, and therefore person receiving his title under him cannot sue for infringement. De Witt v Brooks (CC NY) F Cas No 3851.

Proprietors of copyright on law reports were entitled to sue to restrain infringement without resorting to suit at law to establish their right to copyright. Gould v Hastings (1840, CC NY) F Cas No 5639.

Complainants who had by contract been given exclusive right to publish copyrighted judicial opinions of a state's courts, as was permitted by state's laws had such rights and title in reports as would enable them to maintain suit for infringement. Little v Gould (1851, CC NY) F Cas No 8394; Little v Gould (1852, CC NY) F Cas No 8395.

When all legal and equitable owners of copyright are joined it is not necessary to state formalities or mode of conveyance by which equitable interests became vested in cocomplainants. Black v Henry G. Allen Co. (1890, CC NY) 42 F 618.

Person doing business under conventional or fictitious firm name may sue for infringement of copyright without alleging compliance with state law requiring filing of certificate. Scribner v Henry G. Allen Co. (1892, CC NY) 49 F 854.

Proof showing that complainant took out copyright of infringed edition of book in company name under which he then conducted his business entitled him to subsequently maintain suit for infringement of copyright of book in his own name. Scribner v Clark (1888, CC Ill) 50 F 473, affd 144 US 488, 36 L Ed 514, 12 S Ct 734.

Sale on execution of plates used to print copyrighted book did not estop owner of copyright on book from enforcing his statutory rights as against subsequent purchaser of plates. Patterson v J. S. Ogilvie Pub. Co. (1902, CC NY) 119 F 451.

Where person publishes picture which had been copied from a copyrighted photograph, which, in turn, had been taken from copyrighted painting, owner of copyright of the photograph is entitled to sue and not owner of painting. Champney v Haag (1903, CC Pa) 121 F 944.

Composer cannot maintain copyright infringement suit where another is owner of copyright and composer only has right to receive royalties, although copyright owner is added as party defendant because it refuses to sue for alleged infringement. Stringfield v Warner Bros. Pictures, Inc. (1943, DC NY) 51 F Supp 746, 58 USPQ 59.

Authors and composers pleading facts on which equitable interest in copyright can be predicated are proper parties entitled to bring infringement suit, although legal title to copyright is in another. Hoffman v Santly-Joy, Inc. (1943, DC NY) 51 F Supp 778, 58 USPQ 526.

Copyright law does not permit action for damages for infringement to be brought by any party other than copyright proprietor. Local Trademarks, Inc. v Rogers (1947, DC Ala) 73 F Supp 907, 75 USPQ 336.

Author of biography is proper party to sue for copyright infringement arising from biographical novel, although assignment to publisher conveyed sole right to publish in book form, inasmuch as assignment provided that copyright be taken out in author's name and be her sole property and since assignment did not purport to convey all rights secured by copyright, author having retained right to make another version by novelizing work. Greenbie v Noble (1957, DC NY) 151 F Supp 45, 113 USPQ 115.

It is proper for wholly-owned corporate subsidiary to be proprietor of copyright, while its corporate parent causes original work of art to be reproduced, published, and copyrighted; both subsidiary and parent are proper parties plaintiff in infringement action. Peter Pan Fabrics, Inc. v Acadia Co. (1959, DC NY) 173 F Supp 292, 121 USPQ 81, affd (CA2 NY) 274 F2d 487, 124 USPQ 154.

Equitable owner of copyright may sue for infringement in federal court where complaint sets forth facts showing validity of copyright, basis of his ownership interest, and infringement by defendant; foundation of suit is alleged infringement; incidental power to decide title claim, as to which court lacks original jurisdiction, depends upon specifically conferred power to adjudicate infringement claim; absent such ancillary jurisdiction, plaintiff whose citizenship is same as his adversary's would be forced to look to state court in first instance; state forum could declare plaintiff's status as equitable owner but could not go on to consider claim or infringement because exclusive jurisdiction of that matter resides in federal court. Harrington v Mure (1960, DC NY) 186 F Supp 655, 126 USPQ 506.

Where orchestra is corporation and leader owns substantially all of stock, equity regards leader and corporation as identical and recognizes leader as true party in interest; although corporation should have been named as party plaintiff, jurisdiction was retained. Waring v WDAS Broadcasting Station, Inc. (1937) 327 Pa 433, 194 A 631, 35 USPQ 272.

94. —Joinder of owners of other rights

In a suit by owner of equitable title, owner of the legal title must ordinarily be joined as party. Ted Browne Music Co. v Fowler (1923, CA2 NY) 290 F 751.

In action by publisher of book, copyright of which stood in name of author, which publisher was exclusive licensee of motion-picture rights, to restrain distribution of unauthorized motion picture, joinder of author as nominal party plaintiff was proper and necessary. L. C. Page & Co. v Fox Film Corp. (1936, CA2 NY) 83 F2d 196, 29 USPQ 386.

Where renewal of copyright, taken out by son after his father's death, was held for benefit of his living children, such children are proper parties plaintiff to infringement suit. Tobani v Carl Fischer, Inc. (1938, CA2 NY) 98 F2d 57, 38 USPQ 198, cert den 305 US 650, 83 L Ed 420, 59 S Ct 243.

Federal Rules of Civil Procedure relating to parties, evidence general purpose of Federal Rules of Civil Procedure to eliminate old restrictive and inflexible rules of joinder and to allow joinder of interested parties liberally to end that unnecessary multiplicity of action can be avoided; joinder by supplemental bill of owners of copyrights exclusively licensed to original plaintiff, and whose infringement is alleged by supplemental bill, is permitted although they have no interest in original cause of action. Society of European Stage Authors & Composers, Inc. v WCAU Broadcasting Co. (1940, DC Pa) 1 FRD 264, 46 USPQ 198.

Lessor of copyright did not part with title and is necessary and proper party in suit for infringement. Gaumont Co. v Hatch (1913, DC Pa) 208 F 378.

Licensee was entitled to join licensor as co-plaintiff in suit for infringement, and suit was not collusive, though licensee paid licensor sum of money to induce him to come into case and has agreed to hold him harmless from expense of suit. Stephens v Howells Sales Co. (1926, DC NY) 16 F2d 805.

Holder of the legal title to copyrights and beneficial owner may join as plaintiffs in action for infringement of each and all of six different copyrights. Society of European Stage Authors & Composers, Inc. v WCAU Broadcasting Co. (1938, DC Pa) 25 F Supp 385, 39 USPQ 261.

Owner of legal title to copyright is necessary party to infringement suit by owners of equitable interest; since owner of legal title was improperly made involuntary plaintiff and is not bound by process, complaint is dismissed on motion. Hoffman v Santly-Joy, Inc. (1943, DC NY) 51 F Supp 779, 58 USPQ 537.

Nonresident author is proper defendant to copyright infringement suit brought against alleged infringer by exclusive licensee where author sets up as cross-claim against alleged infringer essentially the same claim as that alleged by plaintiff, alleging that author's rights and claims against alleged infringer are superior to those of plaintiff. Field v True Comics, Inc. (1950, DC NY) 89 F Supp 611, 84 USPQ 358.

Even sole and exclusive licensee may not sue for copyright infringement without joining owner of copyright; where exclusive licensee is unable to join foreign copyright owner, complaint is dismissed for failure to join indispensable party, but decree is left open to enable licensee to request owner to join. Ilyin v Avon Publications, Inc. (1956, DC NY) 144 F Supp 368, 110 USPQ 356.

Authors assigned musical composition with right to obtain copyright thereon to publisher by agreement reserving substantial rights to participate in proceeds of exploitation and providing that, if publisher should refuse to sue infringers, authors could institute such action; because of fiduciary relationship, imposing equitable obligations upon publisher beyond those ordinarily imposed by law upon those dealing fully at arms' length, authors may sue infringers, upon publisher's refusal to sue, provided that publisher is joined as defendant. Manning v Miller Music Corp. (1959, DC NY) 174 F Supp 192, 121 USPQ 600.

Since validity of W's copyright would be affected adversely to W in his exclusive licensee's suit to obtain declaratory judgment that copyrighted work does not infringe defendant's copyright, W is an indispensable party to suit; test of infringement of defendant's copyright necessarily tests copyright owned by W; if W refuses to join voluntarily and cannot be served, he may be joined as involuntary plaintiff; doctrine permitting such joinder is limited to patent and copyright cases. First Financial Marketing Services Group, Inc. v Field Promotions, Inc. (1968, DC NY) 286 F Supp 295, 159 USPQ 572.

Party in position as first assignee in chain of assignments of copyright is necessary but not indispensable party where dispute between other parties can be resolved without prejudicing missing party, but missing party is indispensable to claim involving missing party's remaining interest in copyright. Charron v Meaux (1973, DC NY) 60 FRD 619, 180 USPQ 645.

Equitable owners of either total or partial rights under patents and copyrights can enforce rights even where patentee or copyright proprietor is infringer, and even where they must join owner of legal title as plaintiff without his consent and against his will. Gay v Robbins Music Corp. (1942, Sup) 38 NYS2d 337, 55 USPQ 461.

95. Licensees as plaintiffs

While it is general rule that mere licensee cannot sue in its own name strangers who infringe, yet complainant with full equitable title to copyright may sue legal titleholder for infringement. Wooster v Crane & Co. (1906, CA8 Kan) 147 F 515.

Mere licensee of American stage rights, who undertook to obtain American copyright, could not maintain action for infringement. Saake v Lederer (1909, CA3 Pa) 174 F 135.

Licensee of right to mechanically reproduce copyrighted composition and to make rolls therefrom was entitled to sue for infringing copying and duplication of his roll. Aeolian Co. v Royal Music Roll Co. (1912, DC NY) 196 F 926.

License of serial rights to copyrighted story vests no right to sue for infringement. New Fiction Pub. Co. v Star Co. (1915, DC NY) 220 F 994.

Rights of licensee under copyright do not depend on legal title and he has no right to sue in own name for infringement but must join as plaintiff owner of copyright who holds title in trust for licensee. Buck v Virgo (1938, DC NY) 22 F Supp 156, 37 USPQ 325.

Copyright owner granted plaintiff exclusive right to use copyrighted newspaper advertisements, plaintiff to acquire full title on payment of $400; plaintiff gave defendant right to use for year, but defendant continued use after year;

plaintiff's copyright infringement suit is dismissed on motion; license under copyright is same as under patent insofar as it concerns right to sue; since there is no averment in complaint of payment of $400, plaintiff is mere licensee; plaintiff must join copyright owner in order that suit may be properly brought under Copyright Act since maintenance of action alone would oust court of jurisdiction for being mere licensee; jurisdiction of court would have to depend on diversity of citizenship which is not shown by complaint. Local Trademarks, Inc. v Powers (1944, DC Pa) 56 F Supp 751, 62 USPQ 149.

Exclusive licensee of right to publish copyrighted work in book form cannot maintain infringement suit against one publishing work in other than book form. Field v True Comics, Inc. (1950, DC NY) 89 F Supp 611, 84 USPQ 358.

Bare licensee, who published previously copyrighted story in magazine, is not even proper party, let alone indispensable one, in copyright infringement action. Ilyin v Avon Publications, Inc. (1956, DC NY) 144 F Supp 368, 110 USPQ 356.

Publisher having exclusive license of copyright is entitled to sue along with copyright proprietor for infringement of copyright. Droke House Publishers, Inc. v Aladdin Distributing Corp. (1973, DC Ga) 360 F Supp 311, 179 USPQ 467.

Licensee may maintain infringement suit against purchaser of his proprietor's copyright who, with knowledge, is violating lawful contract made by licensee and former proprietor regarding use of copyright. Murphy v Christian Press Ass'n Pub. Co. (1899) 38 App Div 426, 56 NYS 597.

96. Performing rights societies

Copyright proprietor, being principal, and American Society of Composers, Authors, and Publishers, in whom was vested nondramatic public performing rights, being agent, copyright proprietor was proper party plaintiff in suit for infringement by playing of music. Leo Feist, Inc. v Young (1943, CA7 Wis) 138 F2d 972, 59 USPQ 450.

Since plaintiff, copyright proprietor, transferred to American Society of Composers, Authors, and Publishers only one (public performance) of nine rights obtained under copyright American Society of Composers, Authors, and Publishers was not assignee, but licensee, and cannot maintain infringement suit alone, but can do so only by joining copyright proprietor as plaintiff; hence, in instant suit by copyright proprietor alone, defendant being fully protected from second suit for same infringement (public performance), there is no necessity for joining American Society of Composers, Authors, and Publishers

as plaintiff. Widenski v Shapiro, Bernstein & Co. (1945, CA1 RI) 147 F2d 909, 64 USPQ 448.

Chapter 138, Nebraska Laws of 1937, does not bar copyright owners from maintaining copyright infringement suit, although owners are members of American Society of Composers, Authors, and Publishers, alleged to be illegal price-fixing combination, since American Society of Composers, Authors, and Publishers is not party to suit, has no interest in copyrights, and does not do business in Nebraska. Interstate Hotel Co. v Remick Music Corp. (1946, CA8 Neb) 157 F2d 744, 71 USPQ 138, cert den 329 US 809, 91 L Ed 691, 67 S Ct 622, reh den 330 US 854, 91 L Ed 1296, 67 S Ct 769.

Licensee of stage rights is not proper party in suit for infringement of copyrighted drama by production of motion-picture photoplay. Tully v Triangle Film Corp. (1916, DC NY) 229 F 297.

Members of American Society of Composers, Authors, and Publishers may maintain copyright infringement suit despite consent decree in antitrust suit. Shapiro, Bernstein & Co. v Veltin (1942, DC La) 47 F Supp 648, 55 USPQ 335.

In copyright infringement suit in which defendant counterclaims for declaratory judgment of title to copyrights, defendant may not file third-party complaint against American Society of Composers, Authors, and Publishers, to whom plaintiff assigned nondramatic public performance rights; society is not, and may not be, liable for any part of plaintiff's claim against defendant; defendant may join Society as defendant under Rule 13(h) of Federal Rules of Civil Procedure since Society's presence is required for granting complete relief on counterclaim; fact that defendant and Society are both domiciled in state of suit does not oust jurisdiction since federal courts have jurisdiction to determine title to copyright in musical composition and to decide suit involving copyright, although person asserting claim has interest in copyright less than full title. King v Edward B. Marks Music Corp. (1944, DC NY) 56 F Supp 446, 62 USPQ 249.

Plaintiff, publisher members of American Society of Composers, Authors and Publishers, is proper party in interest in action for infringement of plaintiff's copyrighted musical composition; American Society of Composers, Authors and Publishers is not proper party. Dorchester Music Corp. v National Broadcasting Co. (1959, DC Cal) 171 F Supp 580, 120 USPQ 429.

2. Defendants

97. Generally

All who unite in infringement are liable for damages resulting from infringement, but only those who profit thereby are liable for profits.

Gross v Van Dyk Gravure Co. (1916, CA2 NY) 230 F 412.

Motion-picture producer is liable where its agents, acting within scope of agency and employment, willfully incorporated into picture material which they knew to be patterned after another's copyrighted picture; corporation is chargeable with knowledge and notice of matters becoming known to its agents and employees within course and scope of agency and employment. Universal Pictures Co. v Harold Lloyd Corp. (1947, CA9 Cal) 162 F2d 354, 73 USPQ 317.

It makes little difference in infringement liability whether defendant copied from plaintiff's song or whether defendant copied from third party who copied from plaintiff. Wihtol v Wells (1956, CA7 Ill) 231 F2d 550, 109 USPQ 200.

Not only cannot copyright infringement action be maintained against state, but it cannot be maintained against public school district, which is instrumentality of state. Wihtol v Crow (1962, CA8 Iowa) 309 F2d 777, 135 USPQ 385.

One who avails himself in whole or in part of the materials and labors of another is guilty of infringement. Blunt v Patten (1828, CC NY) F Cas No 1579; Blunt v Patten (1828, CC NY) F Cas No 1580.

Though subject matter of author's work is open to all, another may not, in order to avoid expense and labor, appropriate portions of original work without becoming liable for infringement. Farmer v Calvert Lithographing & M. Pub Co. (1872, CC Mich) F Cas No 4651.

Director and sole stockholder of defendant corporation is individually liable, in addition to corporation, for copyright and trade-mark infringement and unfair competition if, in addition to corporate capacity, she acted in individual capacity and for her personal gain in authorizing and personally participating in infringing acts. Conde Nast Publications, Inc. v Vogue School of Fashion Modeling, Inc. (1952, DC NY) 105 F Supp 325, 94 USPQ 101.

98. Contributory infringers

Evidence that appellant had knowledge that its artists included copyrighted compositions in their performances, that appellant created an audience as a market for these artists, and that it participated in the formation and direction of the association of artists and its programming of compositions presented amply supported district court's finding that it "caused this copyright infringement" and was liable as a "contributory" infringer; evidence that although appellant had no formal power to control either the local association or the artists for whom it served as agent, the local association did depend upon

appellant for direction in matters such as this, that appellant was in a position to police the infringing conduct of its artists, and that it derived substantial financial benefit from the actions of the primary infringers, that appellant knew that copyrighted works were being performed at the concert and that neither the local association nor the performing artists would secure copyright license, supported district court's finding that it was responsible for, and vicariously liable as a result of, the infringement of those primary infringers. Gershwin Publishing Corp. v Columbia Artists Management, Inc. (1971, CA2 NY) 443 F2d 1159, 14 ALR Fed 819, 170 USPQ 182.

Television broadcaster and party furnishing print of infringing motion picture are liable for infringing renewal copyright, but individual not shown to control party furnishing print is not liable as contributory infringer, and bank sponsoring broadcast but not shown to control subject matter or to have knowledge of infringement is not liable. Rohauer v Killiam Shows, Inc. (1974, DC NY) 379 F Supp 723, 183 USPQ 592, revd on other grounds (CA2 NY) 551 F2d 484.

"Participate" does not embrace every person having connection with television program which allegedly infringes plaintiff's literary property; to be liable, it must be shown that defendant not only contributed to production but to infringement; such activities would be appropriating material from original presentation, issuing licenses to reproduce it, and like activity; bridge expert, who appeared in both plaintiff's pilot film and allegedly infringing television program, is not infringer since he did not contribute to infringement; purpose of his selection for both programs was his reputation and that he would supply his own material, but he had nothing to do with formulating original idea or making possible its alleged pirating; he was not only expert who could perform role he was retained for, so he was not responsible for infringement in sense that it could not have resulted without his participation; moreover, plaintiff, not expert, revealed format of pilot film to corporate defendant. Gordon v Goren (1962) 17 App Div 2d 381, 235 NYS2d 314, 136 USPQ 148.

99. Employees of infringer

Employee of firm, who had infringing labels under his charge, but who did not have complete control thereover, was not liable in suit for infringement for penalties of one dollar for each infringing label "found in his possession." Thornton v Schreiber (1888) 124 US 612, 31 L Ed 577, 8 S Ct 618.

President of corporation infringing copyright is personally liable for infringement since he organized corporation, paid for nearly all stock, lent it substantial sums, gave employee who wrote infringing book material with which to begin book, showed employee copy of plaintiff's book, passed on part of original copy of infringing book, and made numerous calls on employee relative to book. Adventures in Good Eating, Inc. v Best Places to Eat, Inc. (1942, CA7 Ill) 131 F2d 809, 56 USPQ 242.

Corporation was formed to publish book including infringing composition prepared by defendant; defendant was dominant influence in corporation and ran its affairs; he personally applied for copyright on infringing song in his own name; no other individual was of any consequence in planning and carrying out infringement; defendant is liable for corporation's acts. Wihtol v Wells (1956, CA7 Ill) 231 F2d 550, 109 USPQ 200.

General rule imposing liability upon directors, officers, and stockholders in connection with patent infringement, which is pertinent to copyright cases, is that they are not personally liable for damages resulting from infringement unless they have inflicted wrong otherwise than through usual relations between officer and corporation, that is to say, infringement by officers must be as individuals before they can be held personally liable. Buck v Newsreel, Inc. (1938, DC Mass) 25 F Supp 787, 40 USPQ 20; Buck v Spanish Gables, Inc. (1938, DC Mass) 26 F Supp 36, 40 USPQ 19; Buck v Sunbeam (DC Mass) 40 USPQ 18.

Managing agent of corporation who hired orchestra and who controlled operation and who by control of lease could turn corporation out at any time was responsible for infringement. Buck v Crescent Gardens Operating Co. (1939, DC Mass) 28 F Supp 576, 42 USPQ 435.

Individual defendant is not personally liable where he was neither dominant nor controlling stockholder and was not in control of corporate defendant at time of alleged infringement. Edward B. Marks Music Corp. v Bank (DC NY) 76 USPQ 217.

Copyright infringement action was dismissed as to individual defendants who had no connection with infringing publication other than being officers, directors, or stockholders of defendant corporation, but was not dismissed as against corporation's president who knew of and took part in copying of plaintiff's catalogues. Harry Alter Co. v A. E. Borden Co. (1954, DC Mass) 121 F Supp 941, 102 USPQ 2.

Officer of corporation is personally liable where he was personally involved in arranging and directing production of infringing design even if he was acting within normal scope of his authority, and it is immaterial that officer re-

ceived no personal gain from infringement. H. M. Kolbe Co. v Shaff (1965, DC NY) 240 F Supp 588, 145 USPQ 77, affd in part and app dismd in part (CA2 NY) 352 F2d 285, 147 USPQ 336.

100. Joinder of separate defendants

Printer may be equally liable with publisher for infringement. Belford v Scribner (1892) 144 US 488, 36 L Ed 514, 12 S Ct 734.

Infringement is tort and persons concerned therein are jointly and severally liable, but if they do not act in concert they cannot be joined in same suit. Ted Browne Music Co. v Fowler (1923, CA2 NY) 290 F 751.

Where parties have acted severally in infringement of copyright, and not jointly or in concert, they cannot be sued jointly. Ted Browne Music Co. v Fowler (1923, CA2 NY) 290 F 751.

Infringing printer and publisher may be joined as codefendants in copyright infringement suit. Sammons v Colonial Press, Inc. (1942, CA1 Mass) 126 F2d 341, 53 USPQ 71.

Author is liable for damages as contributory and participating infringer and joint tort-feasor where he deliberately chose material which he knew had been used in plaintiff's copyrighted motion picture; fact that author received no profits does not relieve him from liability for damages. Universal Pictures Co. v Harold Lloyd Corp. (1947, CA9 Cal) 162 F2d 354, 73 USPQ 317.

Church is jointly liable with choir director for copyright infringement where infringing song was performed in church by church choir since, in selecting and arranging infringing song for such use, choir director was engaged in course and scope of his employment by church. Wihtol v Crow (1962, CA8 Iowa) 309 F2d 777, 135 USPQ 385.

Manufacturer of cut taken from copyrighted newspaper, selling same with knowledge that it will be used in infringing article, is joint tortfeasor and is guilty of infringement. Harper v Shoppell (1886, CC NY) 28 F 613.

Parties procuring infringing act to be done are liable as joint tort-feasors. Fishel v Lueckel (1892, CC NY) 53 F 499.

Where all defendants were united in infringement, all were responsible for damages resulting. Fleischer Studios, Inc. v Ralph A. Freundlich, Inc. (1936, DC NY) 14 F Supp 401, 30 USPQ 125.

Parties agreed it would be economical and satisfactory and court fixes damages and profits at $1500; defendant news dealers are only secondarily liable in case defendant publisher cannot answer therefor; in such event they shall be jointly and severally liable as joint and several infringers. Detective Comics, Inc. v Bruns Publications, Inc. (1939, DC NY) 28 F Supp 399, 41 USPQ 182, mod on other grounds (CA2 NY) 111 F2d 432, 45 USPQ 291.

Although printer and author are properly sued jointly and severally in same copyright infringement suit, plaintiffs have suffered no recoverable damage for which both defendants are jointly and severally liable as joint tort-feasors; printer is not liable for profits received by author; fact that printer and author opened joint bank account is not too significant since this was merely attempt by printer to protect its bill for work done. Sammons v Larkin (1940, DC Mass) 38 F Supp 649, 49 USPQ 350, mod on other grounds (CA1 Mass) 126 F2d 341, 53 USPQ 71.

Where sponsor engaged producer and radio time to broadcast play on radio; sponsor, producer, and radio station were jointly and severally liable for infringement. Select Theatres Corp. v Ronzoni Macaroni Co. (DC NY) 59 USPQ 288.

Where party causes or procures independent contractor to print or copy copyrighted work, party is equally liable with contractor as joint tort-feasor. Greenbie v Noble (1957, DC NY) 151 F Supp 45, 113 USPQ 115.

Second Circuit holds that infringement of copyright is tort and that all persons concerned therein are jointly and severally liable; likewise, First Circuit holds that all persons uniting in infringement are jointly and severally liable for damages resulting therefrom; principle is applicable to action for mechanical recording of copyrighted song in that copyright infringement is involved; thus, since S manufactured or pressed and shipped to Canadian copies of infringing record from master made by C, and since C's function was master acetates shipped (at direction of first Canadian) to another Canadian in Canada plus mastering and processing of two units shipped to first Canadian, S and C are joint tortfeasors with first Canadian and infringe copyrighted music even though S denies that it is manufacturer. Reeve Music Co. v Crest Records, Inc. (1959, DC NY) 190 F Supp 272, 128 USPQ 37, affd in part and app dismd in part (CA2 NY) 285 F2d 546, 128 USPQ 24.

Basic common-law doctrine that one who knowingly participates in or furthers tortious act is jointly and severally liable with prime tortfeasor is applicable in suits arising under Copyright Act. Screen Gems-Columbia Music, Inc. v Mark-Fi Records, Inc. (1966, DC NY) 256 F Supp 399, 150 USPQ 523.

Copyright infringement is tort in which all participants are jointly and severally liable; individual, who is president, major stockholder, and director of corporation which infringed copyrights, is joint tort-feasor with corporation since he caused whole process of infringement; his knowledge, or lack of knowledge, of infringement does not alter that fact; copyright proprietor's filing of claim against corporation in bankruptcy is no barrier to recovery from individual. Chappell & Co. v Frankel (1968, DC NY) 285 F Supp 798, 157 USPQ 693.

Participation in tort of copyright infringement makes each participant jointly and severally liable; thus, individuals who ran corporate infringer, who participated in editing, manufacturing, and sale of infringements, and, who, upon dissolution of corporation shared corporation's profits or losses between them, are liable as infringers; however, corporate officers, who performed mere ministerial functions and who never functioned as corporate executives, are not personally liable. Pickwick Music Corp. v Record Productions, Inc. (1968, DC NY) 292 F Supp 39, 159 USPQ 228.

Copyright infringement is a tort and all infringers may be held jointly and severally liable for damages occasioned by the infringement; accordingly plaintiff may sue such infringers as he chooses. Celestial Arts, Inc. v Neylor Color-Lith Co. (1971, DC Wis) 339 F Supp 1018.

Owner of nightclub who contracted with codefendant for dinner dance show in which copyrighted music was performed without license is jointly and severally liable with codefendant, and it is not significant that codefendant planned event and nightclub owner had no voice in selection of music. Italian Book Corp. v Palms Sheepshead Country Club, Inc. (1975, DC NY) 186 USPQ 326.

Annotations:

Liability as "Vicarious" or "Contributory" infringer under Federal Copyright Act. 14 ALR Fed 825.

101. Premises owner or operator as defendant

Company having copyrighted map in their office is not liable for infringement of map by person over whom they have no control, even though 500 copies of infringing map were sent to company when these copies were not given to public. Morris County Traction Co. v Hence (1922, CA3 NJ) 281 F 820.

Hotel company using radio to entertain guests was liable for infringement of copyrighted song. Buck v Jewell-Lasalle Realty Co. (1931, CA8 Mo) 51 F2d 726, 10 USPQ 70; Buck v Jewell-La Salle Realty Co. (1931, CA8 Mo) 51 F2d 730, 10 USPQ 101.

Something more than relation of landlord and tenant must exist to give rise to cause of action against landlord for infringement of copyright which took place on demised premises. Deutsch v Arnold (1938, CA2 NY) 98 F2d 686, 39 USPQ 5.

Store owner is liable for copyright infringement where concessionaire in store sold phonograph records infringing plaintiff's copyrights, although concessionaire purchased records to be sold by its employees, since owner retained ultimate right of supervision over conduct for concession and its employees and owner reserved for itself stated percentage of concession's sales. Shapiro, Bernstein & Co. v H. L. Green Co. (1963, CA2 NY) 316 F2d 304, 137 USPQ 275.

Where owner of concert hall has no notice that copyrighted composition is to be performed, at time he executes lease for hall, he is not liable for any infringement by lessees. Fromont v Aeolian Co. (1918, DC NY) 254 F 592.

Although musician in theater was independent contractor and was given permission to play whatever he thought appropriate to accompany motion picture, operator of theater by giving such permission, was responsible for infringement of copyright of a musical composition. Harms v Cohen (1922, DC Pa) 279 F 276.

Theater owner was liable for use of copyrighted music roll by operator of player piano in theater, to which admission was charged, though use was without his knowledge and against his orders. M. Witmark & Sons v Calloway (1927, DC Tenn) 22 F2d 412.

Owner of hotel who gave consent to photographer to take aerial picture of property and then appropriated copyrighted print was liable for infringement. Cory v Physical Culture Hotel, Inc. (1936, DC NY) 14 F Supp 977, 30 USPQ 353, affd (CA2 NY) 88 F2d 411, 33 USPQ 58.

Where orchestra received space in defendant's restaurant but no remuneration, and defendant had control over what they should play, he was liable for infringement by unauthorized playing of copyrighted music. Donaldson, Douglas & Gumble, Inc. v Terris (DC Pa) 37 USPQ 39.

Notwithstanding booking agency furnished stage show, musicians, and orchestra, owner of theatre was guilty of infringement where copyrighted music was played and sung. Buck v Newsreel, Inc. (1938, DC Mass) 25 F Supp 787, 40 USPQ 20.

Hotel orchestra which played copyrighted musical compositions without permission infringed copyrights although no admission was charged and hotel proprietor was liable therefore even if wrongful acts were committed without his authority and against his orders. Buck v Coe (1940, DC Pa) 32 F Supp 829, 45 USPQ 230; Buck v Pettijohn (1940, DC Tenn) 34 F Supp

968, 46 USPQ 514; Edwin H. Morris & Co. v Kaufman (DC Pa) 59 USPQ 393.

Proprietor of establishment cannot escape liability for copyright violation on ground that person furnishing musical performance is independent contractor who selects compositions to be played. M. Witmark & Sons v Tremont Social & Athletic Club (1960, DC Mass) 188 F Supp 787, 127 USPQ 447.

Hotel in which is located club wherein copyright infringement occurred is liable as a coin-fringer with club since club is operator of facility of hotel. Porter v Marriott Motor Hotels, Inc. (DC Tex) 137 USPQ 473.

Operator of cafe wherein copyrighted musical compositions were publicly performed for profit is liable for infringement whether or not operator paid performers. Harm's, Inc. v Theodosiades (1965, DC Pa) 246 F Supp 799, 148 USPQ 147.

102. Printer or publisher as defendant

One who prints infringing work is infringer, as is also publisher and vendor. American Code Co. v Bensinger (1922, CA2 NY) 282 F 829.

Newspaper printing advertisement from matrices furnished to it by advertiser, which matrices contained no notice of copyright, was not liable for infringement, it having no knowledge of copyright. Wilkes-Barre Record Co. v Standard Advertising Co. (1933, CA3 Pa) 63 F2d 99, 16 USPQ 346.

Publisher cannot maintain infringement action against competing publisher whose magazine carries identical advertisement or listing, where advertising and listing copy were furnished by advertiser or lister, who retained right to alter arrangement, and where both publishers are paid standard space rate by advertiser. Official Aviation Guide Co. v American Aviation Associates (1945, CA7 Ill) 150 F2d 173, 65 USPQ 553, cert den 326 US 776, 90 L Ed 469, 66 S Ct 247, reh den 326 US 811, 90 L Ed 495, 66 S Ct 335.

Publisher aiding infringer was liable. Schellberg v Empringham (1929, DC NY) 36 F2d 991.

Plaintiff's publicity agent did not authorize defendant to publish material from plaintiff's copyrighted articles until after termination of agent's employment; defendant is infringer by publication thereafter. Vinick v Charm Publications, Inc. (DC NY) 46 USPQ 510.

Printer of infringing book is infringer. Sammons v Larkin (1940, DC Mass) 38 F Supp 649, 49 USPQ 350, mod on other grounds (CA1 Mass) 126 F2d 341, 53 USPQ 71.

Magazine publisher, which published digest of infringing author's book, also infringes since smaller quantity of material copied is not different in kind; innocence of publisher is no excuse. De Acosta v Brown (1943, DC NY) 50 F Supp

615, 58 USPQ 596, affd (CA2 NY) 146 F2d 408, 63 USPQ 311, cert den 325 US 862, 89 L Ed 1983, 65 S Ct 1197 and cert den 325 US 862, 89 L Ed 1983, 65 S Ct 1198.

Printer becomes liable to copyright owner moment he prints infringing work. Maloney v Stone (1959, DC Mass) 171 F Supp 29, 121 USPQ 257.

Employee's knowledge that book contained plagiarized material binds publisher; but, even if publisher were innocent infringer, and had published work which none of its employees knew contained copied material, it would still be liable for infringement. Smith v Little, Brown & Co. (1965, DC NY) 245 F Supp 451, 146 USPQ 540, affd (CA2 NY) 360 F2d 928, 149 USPQ 799, on remand (DC NY) 273 F Supp 870, affd (CA2 NY) 396 F2d 150.

If defendant composer wrongfully appropriated plaintiff's melody, and thus infringed plaintiff's common-law copyright, defendant motion-picture producer (whose motion picture contains infringing song) and defendant music publisher (who published infringing song) are liable to plaintiff regardless of whether they had knowledge of wrongful appropriation. Navara v M. Witmark & Sons (1959) 17 Misc 2d 174, 185 NYS2d 563, 121 USPQ 107.

C. Pleadings

103. Generally

Where passages that constitute infringement are recited in declaration, they cannot be expunged on ground that they are evidential. Journal of Commerce & Commercial Bulletin v Boston Transcript Co. (1923, DC Mass) 292 F 311.

There being no infringement, allegation of conspiracy to infringe adds no support to claim for damages. Shurr v Warner Bros. Pictures, Inc. (DC NY) 59 USPQ 49, affd (CA2 NY) 144 F2d 200, 62 USPQ 60.

104. Amended and supplemental pleadings

Filing of supplemental bill is proper way in which to introduce alleged additional copyright infringements occurring after filing of bill; instant supplemental bill alleges infringement of copyrights exclusively licensed to plaintiff but owned by parties added as plaintiffs by supplemental bill. Society of European Stage Authors & Composers, Inc. v WCAU Broadcasting Co. (1940, DC Pa) 1 FRD 264, 46 USPQ 198.

Nearly two years after answering, court permits defendant to amend answer by denying that copyrighted song has always borne proper copyright notice; pleaded defense had been title, but, since case has been marked off calendar by

stipulation with leave to either party to move for trial on notice, plaintiff will not be prejudiced in preparing to meet new defense. Forster Music Publisher, Inc. v Fred Fisher Music Co. (1944, DC NY) 6 FRD 314, 63 USPQ 60, 63 USPQ 112.

Where, subsequent to filing of original bill for infringement, defendant commits other separate infringements of separate copyrights, complainant may file supplemental bill. Banks Law Pub. Co. v Lawyers' Co-op. Pub. Co. (1905, CC NY) 139 F 701.

Payment of certain expenses as condition of amending bill for infringement, where inaccurate copy of alleged infringed work has been presented to court, should be dealt with on trial of suit. Tully v Triangle Film Corp. (1916, DC NY) 229 F 297.

Amended bill was not open to objection that it did not allege any material facts not set forth in original bill. Metro-Goldwyn-Mayer Distributing Corp. v Bijou Theatre Co. (1933, DC Mass) 3 F Supp 66, 17 USPQ 124.

Cause of action for alleged violation of author's right of privacy involves new and different cause based on different ground of jurisdiction from suit for copyright infringement, and infringement bill cannot be amended to include first-mentioned cause. Henry Holt & Co. v Liggett & Myers Tobacco Co. (1938, DC Pa) 23 F Supp 302, 37 USPQ 449.

105. Copies accompanying pleadings

Complaint should be accompanied by copy of infringing work and copy of work alleged to have been infringed, with certain exceptions; failure to comply with requirements must be satisfactorily explained in complaint or pleading is defective. Cole v Allen (1942, DC NY) 3 FRD 236, 58 USPQ 56.

Plaintiff must annex to complaint copy of copyrighted musical composition alleged to be infringed. Machtenberg v Sterner (1948, DC NY) 8 FRD 169, 77 USPQ 463.

In infringement suit, where profert of copyrighted article is made in bill, article will be regarded as part of bill and may be examined on demurrer. American Mutoscope & Biograph Co. v Edison Mfg. Co. (1905, CC NJ) 137 F 262.

Defendant was entitled to have copy of alleged infringement of copyright, if made, and copy of work alleged to be infringed, as provided by rule of practice of July 1, 1909, where absence of such exhibits from complainant's petition was not explained and record did not show copyrighted article to be sculpture, or other similar work. Lesser v Feorge Borgfeldt & Co. (1911, CC NY) 188 F 864.

Copy of work should accompany complaint; where copy of work infringed does not accompany complaint, as provided by Supreme Court rule, satisfactory reasons for its absence must be presented. Tully v Triangle Film Corp. (1916, DC NY) 229 F 297.

Declaration containing 525 counts alleging infringements in 90 issues of defendant's publication infringing matter copyrighted in 196 issues of plaintiff's paper presented case within exception to requirement of rule as to copies of infringing and infringed publications. Journal of Commerce & Commercial Bulletin v Boston Transcript Co. (1923, DC Mass) 292 F 311.

Annexation of two books in controversy to bill of complaint was proper. Lowenfels v Nathan (1932, DC NY) 2 F Supp 73, 16 USPQ 421.

Since copyrighted musical play alleged to be infringed is dramatico-musical composition, copies of play and of alleged infringement need not be annexed to complaint. April Productions, Inc. v Strand Enterprises, Inc. (1948, DC NY) 79 F Supp 515, 77 USPQ 155.

Copyright infringement complaint is deficient where no copy of copyrighted composition containing copyright notice or certificate of copyright registration forms part thereof. Lampert v Hollis Music, Inc. (1952, DC NY) 105 F Supp 3, 94 USPQ 226.

Copyright infringement complaint to which plaintiff attached copyrighted business forms specifically alleged to be infringed is not stricken on motion for failure to attach all copyrighted forms involved since defendant can easily procure copies of or access to other forms by discovery and hence has not been prejudicially harmed by failure to attach all subject matter of copyrights. Norton Printing Co. v Augustana Hospital (1967, DC Ill) 155 USPQ 133.

Federal courts consistently have held that failure to attach copies of infringed and infringing compositions, or to explain such failure, renders complaint for copyright infringement defective. Weitzenkorn v Lesser (1953) 40 Cal 2d 778, 256 P2d 947, 97 USPQ 545.

106. Complaint, generally

Where two motion-picture photoplays had been adapted from same copyrighted stage play, bill, brought by owner of copyright of motion picture, must allege infringement of such copyright and not infringement of play. Societe Des Films Menchen v Vitagraph Co. (1918, CA2 NY) 251 F 258.

Where plaintiff charges that defendants copied his advertisement it must be assumed that allegation is true unless two advertisements are so dissimilar as to negative completely theory of infringement. Ansehl v Puritan Pharmaceutical Co. (1932, CA8 Mo) 61 F2d 131, 15 USPQ 38, cert den 287 US 666, 77 L Ed 574, 53 S Ct 224.

Allegation that language in defendants' publications "is substantially identical in all material respects with language in plaintiff's copyrighted publications" was insufficient. Affiliated Enterprises, Inc. v Gruber (1936, CA1 Mass) 86 F2d 958, 32 USPQ 94.

Since person who is neither citizen nor subject of any government can take out copyright, citizenship of author is not material issue and it is not of least consequence that complaint alleged that author was citizen of state with whom United States had reciprocal relations. Houghton Mifflin Co. v Stackpole Sons, Inc. (1940, CA2 NY) 113 F2d 627, 46 USPQ 296.

If plaintiffs allege that they are citizens of United States, which is not denied, fact must be considered as admitted. Webb v Powers (1847, CC Mass) F Cas No 17323.

Bill for infringement of copyright which merely alleged that copyright was taken out previous to publication thereof, "in full accordance with the requirements of the laws of the United States," was insufficient. Trow City Directory Co. v Curtin (1888, CC NY) 36 F 829.

Where all parts of copyrighted matter, taken together, constitute, in use, single implement, bill alleging infringement of 30 different copyrights relating to it is not subject to demurrer on ground that bill is multifarious. Amberg File & Index Co. v Shea Smith & Co. (1896, CC Ill) 78 F 479, affd (CA7 Ill) 82 F 314.

Demurrer will not be sustained to bill on ground of multifariousness, unless several copyrights alleged to be infringed relate to such diverse subjects that they cannot be conveniently considered together. Harper v Holman (1897, CC Pa) 84 F 222.

If bill for infringement of copyright states a cause of action, demurrer to it which does not specifically state what parts of bill are demurred to, should not be sustained. Empire City Amusement Co. v Wilton (1903, CC Mass) 134 F 132.

Bill for infringement which did not contain specific allegations, but general allegation that all conditions and requisites to obtain copyright, as required by laws of the United States, were complied with, was insufficient on demurrer. Ford v Charles E. Blaney Amusement Co. (1906, CC NY) 148 F 642.

Specific acts necessary to constitute compliance with copyright laws must be alleged in complaint. Ohman v New York (1909, CC NY) 168 F 953.

In suit for infringement complainant must show that his work is copyrightable work.

Crown Feature Film Co. v Levy (1912, DC NY) 202 F 805.

Where complainant, seeking damages for infringement of copyright, alleges that photograph was his own original conception, to which he gave visible form by selecting position and time at which to take picture, it is allegation of fact and is not subject to demurrer on ground that complaint does not show that photograph was copyrightable. Pagano v Chas. Beseler Co. (1916, DC NY) 234 F 963.

It is not necessary to allege, in bill, that musical composition was written for purpose of public performance for profit, since it will be inferred that he had written work for purpose of securing all rights attainable under Copyright Act. Hubbell v Royal Pastime Amusement Co. (1917, DC NY) 242 F 1002.

Plaintiff in suit for infringement may set forth one cause of action in several different counts when it is good pleading in state practice. Journal of Commerce & Commercial Bulletin v Boston Transcript Co. (1923, DC Mass) 292 F 311.

Complaint setting forth works involved did not show on its face infringement of copyrighted song, "What are Your Intentions?" Park v Warner Bros. (1934, DC NY) 8 F Supp 37, 23 USPQ 202.

Bill for copyright infringement of label need not aver originality and copyrightability of label. Bobrecker v Denebeim (1938, DC Mo) 25 F Supp 208, 39 USPQ 336.

Complaint sets forth claim sufficiently by alleging ownership, compliance with statute, and infringement. April Productions, Inc. v Strand Enterprises, Inc. (1948, DC NY) 79 F Supp 515, 77 USPQ 155.

If there are two or more separate and distinct claims of copyright infringement, they should be separately stated and numbered; also, allegations of palming off and unfair competition should be eliminated from association therewith. Kashins v Keystone Lamp Mfg. Corp. (1955, DC NY) 135 F Supp 681, 107 USPQ 137.

On motion to dismiss copyright infringement complaint for failure to state claim on which relief can be granted, court may assume validity of copyright and, comparing literary products incorporated into complaint, determine as matter of law whether copyright has been infringed. Lake v Columbia Broadcasting System, Inc. (1956, DC Cal) 140 F Supp 707, 110 USPQ 173.

Complaint alleges that defendant breached contract by use of plaintiff's book in defendant's motion picture; cause of action in contract is not stated since substantial similarity between ideas embodied in book and picture is not shown.

Sutton v Walt Disney Productions (1953) 118 Cal App 2d 598, 258 P2d 519, 98 USPQ 198.

In order for complaint to state cause of action for plagiarism, there must be some substantial similarity between defendants' motion picture and protectible portions of plaintiff's literary composition; however, question of protectibility need not be considered as to cause of action for breach of contract (express or implied in fact) not to use idea of composition without paying for same, since, even if not original, idea may be subject of contract provided it is valuable; yet, no cause of action is stated for use of idea if there is no similarity whatsoever between productions. Weitzenkorn v Lesser (1953) 40 Cal 2d 778, 256 P2d 947, 97 USPQ 545.

In action by licensor of motion picture against his licensee to recover contract price of drama rights, it is not essential that plaintiff allege facts with same particularity and detail as is necessary in case where defendant is proceeded against by author of play for infringement of copyright. Hart v Fox (1917, Sup) 166 NYS 793.

107. —Authorship or ownership allegation

Assignee, suing for infringement, must show authorship in his assignor and nonpublication prior to copyright. Bosselman v Richardson (1909, CA2 NY) 174 F 622.

In action for infringement complainant must show his title not merely by allegation that he is proprietor, but by setting forth facts which show how he became proprietor, and why he has right to bring action. Danks v Gordon (1921, CA2 NY) 272 F 821.

Where bill alleges title in complainant and that complainant is still owner of copyright it is sufficient; it is not necessary to allege various steps by which he became proprietor of work. American Code Co. v Bensinger (1922, CA2 NY) 282 F 829.

Where copyright is not obtained in plaintiff's name, plaintiff must connect himself with it by proper averments, showing assignment or transfer of it to him, or license under it sufficient to entitle him to sue. Ted Browne Music Co. v Fowler (1923, CA2 NY) 290 F 751.

Averment of ownership was sufficient, in view of prima facie presumption arising from possession. Gerlach-Barklow Co. v Morris & Bendien, Inc. (1927, CA2 NY) 23 F2d 159.

Allegations of bill for infringement were set forth and were sufficiently explicit to amount to assertion of authorship, and to constitute perfect title at law. Atwill v Ferrett (1846, CC NY) F Cas No 640.

Demurrer to bill of infringement, wherein plaintiff has merely alleged that he is proprietor of copyright, but does not state how he became proprietor, or aver compliance with copyright statutes, should be sustained. Chicago Music Co. v J. W. Butler Paper Co. (1884, CC Ill) 19 F 758.

It is not necessary, when all legal and equitable owners of copyright are joined as complainants, to state formalities or mode of conveyance by which equitable interests become vested in co-complainants. Black v Henry G. Allen Co. (1890, CC NY) 42 F 618.

It is not necessary in copyright cases to allege preliminary steps and procedures adopted in producing or composing work; allegation that "your orator, at all times hereafter stated, was and still is a citizen of the United States and a resident therein" is sufficient against demurrer on ground that bill does not show that complainant was citizen of the United States at time he produced allegedly infringing photograph. Falk v Schumacher (1891, CC NY) 48 F 222.

Bill for infringement which fails to allege authorship except by implication arising from statute words "written" and "composed" required court to presume that these words impart originality of defendant's dramatic composition in absence of specific objection on that account. Henderson v Tompkins (1894, CC Mass) 60 F 758.

Complainant must allege and prove existence of facts of originality, of intellectual production, of thought and conception, on part of author. Falk v City Item Printing Co. (1897, CC La) 79 F 321.

It is not necessary in bill for infringement of copyright that complainant set forth his claim of title; complainants' averment in bill for infringement that they were proprietors of book prior to time of securing copyright was sufficient. Lillard v Sun Printing & Pub. Asso. (1898, CC NY) 87 F 213.

Fact of recording of title should be alleged in bill in suit for infringement; corporation proprietor suing for infringement of work need not set forth in its bill names of editors and compilers. Edward Thompson Co. v American Law Book Co. (1902, CC NY) 119 F 217.

Plaintiff must show title by setting forth facts which indicate how he became copyright proprietor; bill for infringement filed by publisher of article read at meeting of association, showing right given by association but not showing transfer from author, was insufficient to show title in plaintiff entitling it to bring suit. Quinn-Brown Pub. Corp. v Chilton Co. (1936, DC NY) 15 F Supp 213, 30 USPQ 373.

Rule 8 of Federal Rules of Civil Procedure provides what contents of petition shall be, whether in law or equity, and it is sufficient if

bill for copyright infringement alleges that plaintiff is owner and proprietor of registered label and that it has been infringed by defendant and will not be dismissed for either failure to show derivation of ownership or to set out copy of label. Bobrecker v Denebeim (1938, DC Mo) 25 F Supp 208, 39 USPQ 336.

In infringement suit by authors and composers alleging equitable interest in copyright whose legal title is in another, it is proper for plaintiffs to allege substance of agreement with other; agreement that other will secure copyright and hold it for benefit of plaintiffs and itself subject to payment of royalties and reversion to plaintiffs on default or termination, probably sufficiently alleges title in plaintiffs. Hoffman v Santly-Joy, Inc. (1943, DC NY) 51 F Supp 779, 58 USPQ 537.

Where part owner sues for infringement, complaint is bad if it does not expressly negative possibility that one of plaintiff's cotenants may have licensed defendant. Crosney v Edward Small Productions, Inc. (1942, DC NY) 52 F Supp 559, 59 USPQ 193.

Complaint must allege facts and not bare conclusions showing plaintiff's equity title to copyright, and facts may appear not solely from allegations of complaint but from contracts attached to and made part of complaint. Southern Music Pub. Co. v Walt Disney Productions (1947, DC NY) 73 F Supp 580, 74 USPQ 145.

Under theory of misappropriation of literary property and infringement of common-law copyright, which sounds in tort, plaintiff is required to allege ownership of protectible property interest, unauthorized copying by defendant, and damage resulting to plaintiff through unauthorized copying; it is necessary for plaintiff, in order to show ownership of protectible property interest, to show originality of idea and format, and that protectible portions of plaintiff's material and defendant's material are similar. Glane v General Mills, Inc. (1956, Cal App) 298 P2d 626, 110 USPQ 391, hear gr by sup ct, app dismd.

108. —Notice allegation

In suit for infringement of work of art, complainant must allege and prove that copies bore name of copyright proprietor. E. I. Horsman & Aetna Doll Co. v Kaufman (1922, CA2 NY) 286 F 372, cert den 261 US 615, 67 L Ed 828, 43 S Ct 361.

In copyright infringement case, letters giving notice of infringement attached to complaint are not stricken since such notice is part of plaintiff's case; although criticism might be made because plaintiff has pleaded evidence to allow them to remain part of pleading will not harm defendant.

Parts Mfg. Corp. v Weinberg (1940, DC NY) 1 FRD 329, 46 USPQ 509.

Demurrer to bill on ground that it contained no allegation that notice had been printed in all foreign editions was overruled. Haggard v Waverly Pub. Co. (1895, CC NJ) 144 F 490.

109. —Registration or deposit allegation

Where bill alleged deposit of "two copies of the best edition of said picture," objection that "complete" was omitted before "copies" and words "thereof then published" were also omitted was without merit. Gerlach-Barklow Co. v Morris & Bendien, Inc. (1927, CA2 NY) 23 F2d 159.

Allegations of bill for infringement that "complainant has complied in all respects with the requirements of the Revised Statutes" amounted to allegation that complainant had deposited copy of his title page, and that he had never published his work. Boucicault v Hart (1875, CC NY) F Cas No 1692.

Bill for infringement which contained no specific allegations of deposit of title and copies and of proper copyright notice was insufficient on demurrer. Parkinson v Laselle (1875, CC Cal) F Cas No 10762.

Averment that complainant delivered copies at office of Librarian of Congress "or" deposited copies in mail was alternative pleading and was insufficient. Falk v Howell (1888, CC NY) 34 F 739.

Complainant's allegation, that he "delivered at the office of the librarian of Congress," and "deposited in the mail, addressed to the librarian of Congress" title and copies of his book, is proper and requires no amendments or election by complainant where it appears that both acts were done. Scribner v Henry G. Allen Co. (1890, CC NY) 43 F 680.

Inasmuch as copyright vests upon publication with notice, no allegation as to registration or entry "in form and manner, etc.," is necessary in bill of complaint. National Cloak & Suit Co. v Kaufman (1911, CC Pa) 189 F 215.

Bill for infringement which merely alleges that "two complete copies of said photographs" were filed was not sufficient to state cause of action. Crown Feature Film Co. v Levy (1912, DC NY) 202 F 805.

Complaint alleging, that motion-picture photograph or photoplay not having been reproduced in copies for sale claims for copyright, title and description, and prints from each scene or act were deposited with register of copyrights, and complainant received the certificate of registration, was sufficient. Gaumont Co. v Hatch (1913, DC Pa) 208 F 378.

Complaint need not contain an allegation that label registered contains copyrighted subject matter or is original work. Hoague-Sprague Corp. v Frank C. Meyer Co. (1928, DC NY) 27 F2d 176.

Infringement suit must be dismissed where plaintiff states that he has no certificates of registration of copyrights covering exhibits attached to complaint, such exhibits being alleged in complaint to be basis of plaintiff's right. Guild v Thompson's Industries, Inc. (DC Mass) 84 USPQ 224.

110. —Other allegations

Averments that one defendant printed labels and that other defendants used them on their products in pursuance of common plan, sufficiently averred conspiracy between defendants. Premier Malt Products Co. v G. A. Ackerman Printing Co. (1927, CA7 Ill) 24 F2d 89.

In copyright infringement case, paragraph in complaint alleging financial irresponsibility of defendant corporation is not stricken since financial responsibility of corporation may be relevant to liability of individual defendants. Parts Mfg. Corp. v Weinberg (1940, DC NY) 1 FRD 329, 46 USPQ 509.

Complaint alleging that plaintiff is owner of radio program "Double or Nothing," that it broadcast such program on certain date and that defendants infringed copyright by broadcasting radio program "Take It or Leave It" merely pleads conclusions, allegations being insufficient to set forth cause of action for copyright infringement; it is not alleged in what respect defendants infringe. American Broadcasting Co. v Wahl Co. (1940, DC NY) 36 F Supp 167, 47 USPQ 338, revd on other grounds (CA2 NY) 121 F2d 412, 50 USPQ 156.

Complaint for copyright infringement, to which is annexed exhibit evidencing compliance with Copyright Act, alleges that defendant enclosed with circular letter, without authorization, copy of title, editorial page masthead, and leading editorial published in plaintiff's copyrighted newspaper; defendant's motion for summary judgment is denied since complaint states good cause of action on its face. New York Tribune, Inc. v Otis & Co. (1941, DC NY) 39 F Supp 67, 49 USPQ 361.

Copyright infringement complaint and plaintiff's affidavit in support of motion for receiver of defendants' property used in infringing copyright do not make out prima facie case, since there is no prima facie assumption of burden of proof to show identity in form of expression adopted to clothe idea as between parties' compositions. Lampert v Hollis Music, Inc. (1952, DC NY) 105 F Supp 3, 94 USPQ 226.

111. Answer, generally

From practical standpoint burden on plaintiff is same whether answer merely denies plaintiff's allegation of proper copyright notice, or defense of improper copyright notice is affirmatively pleaded. Forster Music Publisher, Inc. v Fred Fisher Music Co. (1944, DC NY) 6 FRD 314, 63 USPQ 60, 63 USPQ 112.

Averment, in answer to bill for infringement of copyright, that plaintiff was greatly benefited, and not damaged, is immaterial and must be stricken out. Harms v Cohen (1922, DC Pa) 279 F 276.

Answer alleging that defendant obtained copyrighted matter from third persons required trial as to defendant and other persons named, irrespective of conspiracy or collusion. Pathe Exchange, Inc. v International Alliance, T.S.E., etc. (1932, DC NY) 3 F Supp 63.

Defendant urges that Congress exceeded its power in Copyright Act in designating employer for hire as "author"; this is without foundation, but, not being in answer, it is not open to defendant since no opportunity is given plaintiff to meet it or court to notify attorney general that constitutionality of act is brought in question. Vitaphone Corp. v Hutchinson Amusement Co. (1939, DC Mass) 28 F Supp 526, 42 USPQ 431.

112. —Counterclaim

In action wherein defendant is charged with copyright infringement and unfair competition on account of defendant's licensing television performance of copyrighted motion pictures allegedly owned by plaintiff, defendant interposes affirmative defense of estoppel alleging that additional defendants, now in control of plaintiff, had at one time acted as counsel for defendant in acquisition of television rights at issue; counterclaim against plaintiff and additional defendants is related to estoppel defense, since it charges that additional defendants conspired to deprive defendant of its rights in order to cement their own position in control of plaintiff; action is alleged to be one of series of harassing maneuvers designed to interfere with defendant's proper exploitation of rights acquired on advice of additional defendants; pleadings disclose sufficient logical relationship so that, in interest of avoiding circuity and multiplicity of action, counterclaim should be considered compulsory. United Artists Corp. v Masterpiece Productions, Inc. (1955, CA2 NY) 221 F2d 213, 105 USPQ 52.

113. —General denial

Defendant cannot enlarge scope and meaning of averment of bill for infringement by expand-

ing his denial beyond allegations of bill. Osgood v A. S. Aloe Instrument Co. (1895, CC Mo) 69 F 291.

Defendant may answer by pleading general denial to all averments of bill for infringement of copyright, and thereunder, upon trial, "give special matter in evidence." Johnston v Klopsch (1898, CC NY) 88 F 692.

Waiver of answer under oath will not permit filing of answer which is mere general denial not responding to interrogatories in bill for infringement of copyright which requested usual discovery. John Church Co. v Zimmerman (1904, CC Wis) 131 F 652.

Complaint's factual allegations giving court jurisdiction of subject matter are not defeated by defendants' denials. Southern Music Pub. Co. v Walt Disney Productions (1947, DC NY) 73 F Supp 580, 74 USPQ 145.

D. Discovery

114. Generally

Particulars were refused as to material claimed to have been used by defendants and manner in which used; if defendants used script, they knew what use they made of it since they had copy; particulars were granted as to whom plaintiff submitted script; defendants are corporations and should be apprized of identity of persons to whom it is claimed communication was made; particulars were granted as to approximate date when it is claimed each defendant made infringing use; particulars granted as to what orchestra it was claimed defendants retained in connection with broadcasts referred to in amended complaint, although orchestra was named in original complaint and defendants objected to it as immaterial and redundant; particulars from plaintiff were refused as to dates and other data of defendants' alleged submission of plaintiff's script to others, as well as to time of broadcast and radio stations broadcasting. Buckley v Music Corp. of America (1942, DC Del) 2 FRD 328, 54 USPQ 70.

To enable defendants in copyright infringement suit properly to prepare answers, they are entitled to particulars as to specific literary material, incidents, episodes, dialogue, similarities, and publicity values used in defendants' radio broadcast which plaintiff claims were taken from six copyrighted books; action under copyright laws is similar in many respects to action under patent laws and like rules of practice are applicable; particulars should be allowed with same liberality as in patent cases. Cole v Allen (1942, DC NY) 3 FRD 236, 58 USPQ 56.

Assignor's status is material inquiry on examination before trial and any facts bearing on subject are relevant to subject matter involved in action; on examination, before trial, witness, officer of plaintiff's assignor, is not required to produce mat or plate supplied to specific newspaper for printing copyrighted comic. Detective Comics, Inc. v Fawcett Publications, Inc. (1944, DC NY) 4 FRD 237, 64 USPQ 116.

Ordinarily, plaintiff is not permitted to obtain discovery on question of damages in copyright infringement suit until after question of his right to damages and accounting is determined; thus, discovery is refused in nonjury case where extensive inquiry is contemplated, parties are competitors, discovery might unnecessarily disclose defendant's business affairs to plaintiff, and no prejudice will result to plaintiff. Orgel v Clark Boardman Co. (1956, DC NY) 20 FRD 31, 111 USPQ 435.

Defendant may demur to parts of bill for infringement which seek discovery, and which may subject him to anything in nature of penalty or forfeiture. Chapman v Ferry (1882, CC Or) 12 F 693.

Copies of plaintiff's copyrighted map and alleged infringement filed pursuant to motion for bill of particulars become part of complaint. Christianson v West Pub. Co. (1944, DC Cal) 53 F Supp 454, 60 USPQ 279, aff'd (CA9 Cal) 149 F2d 202, 65 USPQ 263.

Defendant is not required, on examination before trial, to answer question as to names and locations of theaters in which allegedly infringing motion picture has been shown and number of screenings given picture in each theater, although after refusal to furnish information, plaintiff attempted to make separate infringements elements of cause of action, since question goes to amount of damages; if accounting is ordered, plaintiff may renew motion. Jerome v Twentieth Century-Fox Film Corp. (1944, DC NY) 58 F Supp 13, 63 USPQ 206.

In taking depositions in copyright infringement suits, plaintiffs' attorneys presumptuously and arbitrarily directed witnesses to refuse to answer questions; although they would have warranted disciplinary action against attorneys or summary ruling touching further prosecution of cases by plaintiffs, defendants did not seasonably seek such remedies; court will not, after trial, allow incidents to intercept ruling on merits. Remick Music Corp. v Interstate Hotel Co. (1944, DC Neb) 58 F Supp 523, 63 USPQ 327, aff'd (CA8 Neb) 157 F2d 744, 71 USPQ 138, cert den 329 US 809, 91 L Ed 691, 67 S Ct 622, reh den 330 US 854, 91 L Ed 1296, 67 S Ct 769.

Plaintiff is required to furnish bill of particulars containing copy of material alleged to infringe his uncopyrighted work; he must specify when, where, and of whom he demanded that infringing material be retracted or corrected and whether demands were written or oral. Fiske v Hitchcock (DC NY) 76 USPQ 299.

Court compels answers to deposition questions involving broadcasting of songs by radio station without performing rights license, even though questions relate to songs and broadcast dates not specifically alleged in complaint, and even though attorney asking questions is not admitted to practice before court, but was accompanied by attorney of record. Broadcast Music, Inc. v J. B. Broadcasting of Baltimore, Ltd. (1974, DC Md) 184 USPQ 478.

115. Interrogations and requests for admission

In copyright infringement suit wherein plaintiff has burden of proving execution of assignment of copyright registration, plaintiff should be allowed to prove case in its own way and obtain this evidence by way of interrogatories; all objections which defendants make, on motion for order that evidence shall not be taken on interrogatories, with respect to competency and materiality of interrogatories will be before court at trial and if objections are then sustained, there will be no injury or prejudice to defendants; court will permit oral examination of witness in lieu of written interrogatories on condition that party objecting to written interrogatories will pay opponent's attorney his reasonable expenses to attend at oral examination. Houghton Mifflin Co. v Stackpole Sons, Inc. (1940, DC NY) 1 FRD 506, 47 USPQ 228.

Where defendant in copyright infringement suit propounds written interrogatories to witnesses in foreign country, under Rule 31(a) of Federal Rules of Civil Procedure, plaintiff may within ten days after receipt of direct interrogatories serve cross-interrogatories on defendant; although courts have varied from regular practice, court refuses leave to plaintiff to serve cross-interrogatories after receipt of answers to direct interrogatories, since this may lead to upset of accepted practice in copyright cases as well as in other matters; defendant's interrogatories are usual ones in copyright case; answers to direct and cross-interrogatories are to be filed simultaneously with court; in view of alleged difficulty of which plaintiff complains, court will allow him to propound additional cross-interrogatories within five days after filing of such answers; court refuses to permit oral examination of witnesses at defendant's expense. Baron v Leo Feist, Inc. (1946, DC NY) 7 FRD 71, 72 USPQ 107.

In copyright infringement action, plaintiff has right, before trial establishing liability, to inquire by interrogatories as to information relevant solely to issue of damages. Greenbie v Noble (1955, DC NY) 18 FRD 414, 107 USPQ 356.

Interrogatories in copyright infringement suit calling for disclosure of all facts relative to operation of defendant's place of entertainment concerning use of copyrighted musical compositions were refused as being attempt to pry into defendant's affairs; where answer in copyright infringement suit denied that compositions were original, interrogatories asking defendant to state names of composers, authors, and publishers and titles of original composition from which copyrighted compositions are copied were refused. Buck v Virgo (1938, DC NY) 22 F Supp 156, 37 USPQ 325.

Interrogatories in copyright infringement suit calling for defendant's witnesses and defendant's evidence are objectionable. Michelson v Crowell Pub. Co. (1938, DC Mass) 25 F Supp 653, 39 USPQ 336.

In suit for copyright infringement interrogatory was refused insofar as inquiring into contents of communication addressed to plaintiff's agent; in suit for copyright infringement interrogatory whether S. received or read plaintiff's story for defendant was allowed, since plaintiff was entitled to show by interrogatory that defendant's agent read story. O'Rourke v RKO Radio Pictures, Inc. (1939, DC Mass) 27 F Supp 996, 41 USPQ 725.

It was ruled by agreement that defendant might submit interrogatories as to license but they were never issued by defendant; this is to be construed against him especially when connected later with proof by plaintiff as to licenses. Famous Music Corp. v Melz (1939, DC La) 28 F Supp 767, 42 USPQ 573.

In copyright infringement suit, interrogatory for deposition inquiring whether story related by means of specific motion picture is similar to another story is improper; in copyright infringement suit, interrogatory for deposition inquiring whether witness had seen screening or exhibition of specific motion picture is proper but witness may not be asked if motion picture was in its entirety based on specific scenario or script. Upham v Warner Bros. Pictures, Inc. (DC NY) 49 USPQ 504.

In copyright infringement action, plaintiffs must answer request for admission that defendants' work was not copied from plaintiff's copyrighted work, but need not answer request calling upon them to admit that defendants' work does not infringe, since this request is improper as calling for mixture of opinion and conclusion of law. Breffort v I Had A Ball Co. (1967, DC NY) 271 F Supp 623, 155 USPQ 391.

Defendant need not answer interrogatory asking that defendant state substance of report analyzing involved musical compositions, since there is no showing that analysis of compositions cannot be obtained by plaintiff's own research; defendant must answer interrogatory as to its belief as to whether composition was original and copyrightable and its factual basis for negative belief and interrogatory as to its knowledge and belief as to whether plaintiff's copyrighted musical composition was copied or patterned after prior source, and, if so, produce copy of such source. Acuff-Rose Publications, Inc. v Silver Star Publishing Co. (1967, DC Tenn) 155 USPQ 455.

116. Production of documents

Provision of interlocutory decree for examination of defendants and for production by them of their account books and papers is proper in suit in equity for infringement. Callaghan v Myers (1888) 128 US 617, 32 L Ed 547, 9 S Ct 177.

In action for infringement of copyright court can issue subpena duces tecum for purpose of bringing in books of defendant. American Lithographic Co. v Werckmeister (1911) 221 US 603, 55 L Ed 873, 31 S Ct 676.

In an action for infringement of copyright, defendant cannot be compelled to produce articles which may be used as evidence against himself. Johnson v Donaldson (1880, CC NY) 3 F 22.

In copyright infringement suit, defendant is not required to serve on plaintiff specific documents referred to in defendant's deposition interrogatories to specific witnesses, since defendant has offered to make documents available to plaintiff at office of defendant's counsel at any time within reasonable business hours and will provide accommodations where he may make such excerpts as he may desire. Upham v Warner Bros. Pictures, Inc. (DC NY) 49 USPQ 504.

Subpena duces tecum is issued against witness, plaintiff's licensee, to furnish names, addresses, and dates of newspapers in which were published plaintiff's cartoon strip and continuity with respect to which plaintiff may charge defendant infringed or was chargeable with unfair competition, as alleged in complaint; plaintiff should state what particular continuities it claims defendant infringed or as to which it unfairly competed. Detective Comics, Inc. v Fawcett Publications, Inc. (DC NY) 61 USPQ 435.

Subpenas duces tecum to examine plaintiff's officers and employees are quashed in copyright infringement suit as far as they seek to elicit evidence to aid court in determining legislative intent and whether compulsory license provision of Copyright Act was intended to apply to plaintiff's electrical transcription; they are not quashed so far as examination seeks to establish characteristics of plaintiff's device. Longines-Wittnauer Watch Co. v T. B. Harms Co. (DC NY) 76 USPQ 97.

Defendants are ordered to permit inspection of papers used in creation or preparation of script of allegedly infringing dramatico-musical composition, but need not produce papers pertaining to screen play, planning, execution, and recordation since such inspection is too broad. Breffort v I Had A Ball Co. (1965, DC NY) 240 F Supp 1018, 144 USPQ 708.

In suit for copyright infringement for copying substantial portions of catalogs of automotive parts, plaintiff's objection to production of catalogs is without merit, and defendant's request for production of all contracts and communications between plaintiff and certain other companies is denied as overly broad. Everco Industries, Inc. v O.E.M. Products Co. (1973, DC Ill) 362 F Supp 204.

E. Summary Judgment

117. Generally

Although defendant's motion for judgment on pleadings is denied since motion concedes access and copying, this does not mean that suit must go to trial; on motion for summary judgment, supported by defendant's author's deposition or perhaps even affidavit, it might be established that there was neither access nor copying. MacDonald v Du Maurier (1944, CA2 NY) 144 F2d 696, 62 USPQ 394, later app (DC NY) 75 F Supp 653 and later app (DC NY) 75 F Supp 655.

When copyrighted work and alleged infringement are before court, capable of examination and comparison, noninfringement can be determined on motion to dismiss. Christianson v West Pub. Co. (1945, CA9 Cal) 149 F2d 202, 65 USPQ 263.

District courts treat motions for summary judgment in plagiarism suits with caution. Millstein v Leland Hayward, Inc. (1950, DC NY) 10 FRD 198, 85 USPQ 448.

When court has opportunity of comparing two works in question, it has all data necessary to decide question of infringement, which it may do on motion where works are set forth in complaint. Park v Warner Bros. (1934, DC NY) 8 F Supp 37, 23 USPQ 202.

Where two copyrighted works in extenso are before court by stipulation, on motion by defendant for summary decree of dismissal, works themselves supersede and control any allegations of conclusions of fact about them or descriptions of them in complaint, for courts deal with actualities of situations before them, not with interested comments thereon. Shipman v R. K. O.

Radio Pictures, Inc. (1937, DC NY) 20 F Supp 249, 35 USPQ 242, affd (CA2 NY) 100 F2d 533, 40 USPQ 211.

Determination of notice to dismiss on ground that plaintiff has failed to state claim on which relief can be granted depends on whether allegations of plaintiff's pleadings, taken as true, establish threatened infringement by defendant of his copyright. Long v Jordan (1939, DC Cal) 29 F Supp 287, 43 USPQ 176.

On granting plaintiff's motion for summary judgment in copyright infringement suit, action is referred to master to fix damages and profits. Houghton Mifflin Co. v Stackpole Sons, Inc. (1940, DC NY) 31 F Supp 517, 44 USPQ 668, mod on other grounds (CA2 NY) 113 F2d 627, 46 USPQ 296.

On motions for summary judgment in copyright infringement case court examines depositions of principals on their examination before trial, extensive pleadings including plaintiff's detailed bill of particulars, two plays with several versions of defendants' play, the book, and articles by defendant author from which he claims his idea was developed, and complete briefs of parties. Rose v Connelly (1941, DC NY) 38 F Supp 54, 49 USPQ 170.

On defendants' motion for summary judgment in copyright infringement suit, access to and use of work claimed to be plagiarized is admitted; issue is whether comparison of two works establishes as matter of law that defendants have not made unfair use of sufficient amount of plaintiff's copyrightable matter to justify holding of infringement; motion is denied since enough similarity between both works in theme, characters, locale, and incidents is found to preclude holding that there is no infringement as matter of law. Solomon v R. K. O. Radio Pictures, Inc. (1941, DC NY) 40 F Supp 625, 49 USPQ 647.

Copyright infringement suit is not dismissed on ground that plaintiff's attorneys have no authority to represent specific plaintiff (enemy alien) where authority was not questioned until trial and there is no evidence overcoming presumption that attorney who appears for litigant has authority to do so. Select Theatres Corp. v Ronzoni Macaroni Co. (DC NY) 59 USPQ 288.

Motion to dismiss is addressed solely to pleading which in instant case is complaint as supplemented by bill of particulars; for purposes of motion, allegations of complaint and bill of particulars must be deemed admitted. Jerry Vogel Music Co. v Edward B. Marks Music Corp. (1944, DC NY) 56 F Supp 779, 63 USPQ 1.

Copyright infringement complaint is dismissed on motion for failure to state claim upon which relief can be granted, if copyrighted publication discloses invalidity on examination. Kanover v Marks (DC NY) 91 USPQ 370.

Copyright infringement suit is decided on motion to dismiss for failure to state claim upon which relief can be granted, since court has before it copies of plaintiff's copyrighted print and of defendants' publications; these are all data necessary to decide infringement; comparison of material may be made; issue of infringement should be speedily determined whenever possible. Lewis v Kroger Co. (1952, DC W Va) 109 F Supp 484, 95 USPQ 359.

Summary judgment is awarded defendant in action for infringement of common-law copyright if similarity between plaintiff's play and defendant's motion picture is in public domain or is inconsequential; however, since it is assumed for purposes of motion that defendant copied, motion is denied if jury could reasonably find that there was unlawful appropriation. Malkin v Dubinsky (1956, DC NY) 146 F Supp 111, 112 USPQ 263.

Action for copyright infringement may be disposed of on motion for summary judgment. Tralins v Kaiser Aluminum & Chemical Corp. (1958, DC Md) 160 F Supp 511, 117 USPQ 79.

Partial summary judgments determining liability are entered in copyright infringement actions against sellers of records of pirated songs since documents before court show plaintiff's title to copyrighted songs and sellers' liability for unauthorized use through sale of records published, without plaintiff's consent, by third party; also, sellers have same attorneys as manufacturer and cannot contend that they lacked knowledge of copying. Harms, Inc. v F. W. Woolworth Co. (1958, DC Cal) 163 F Supp 484, 118 USPQ 436.

Whether defendant's motion picture infringes plaintiff's copyrighted short story is matter for trial, not summary judgment; summary judgment for defendant is not entered in copyright infringement action even if complaint does not sufficiently allege facts incident to plaintiff's equitable ownership of copyright; plaintiff should be granted opportunity to come forward with proof in support of this contention. Brennan v Paramount Pictures Corp. (1962, DC NY) 209 F Supp 150, 135 USPQ 356.

Where copyrighted luggage label and allegedly infringing label are before court for side-by-side comparison, court may properly determine whether substantial similarity exists and grant summary judgment on issue of infringement. International Luggage Registry v Avery Products Corp. (1974, DC Cal) 184 USPQ 66.

Summary judgment of noninfringement is granted on record showing that first possible infringement occurred after plaintiff assigned copyright to third party, and publication by third party without notice forfeited copyright so that no infringement could occur after reassignment to plaintiff. Walker v University Books, Inc. (1977, DC Cal) 193 USPQ 596.

118. Questions of fact, generally

In copyright infringement action, if claimed custom requires interpretation of contract conveying rights in copyright to defendant which would exclude rights claimed by defendant and, if in absence of such custom such rights were included in transfer, issue as to existence of custom is material issue and defendant's motion for summary judgment should be denied. Murphy v Warner Bros. Pictures, Inc. (1940, CA9 Cal) 112 F2d 746, 46 USPQ 2.

Summary judgment dismissing copyright infringement suit is granted where defendants' affidavits prove license and plaintiff merely denies license, presenting no facts in support thereof, thus raising no issue; there is no genuine issue concerning material fact. Piantadosi v Loew's Inc. (1943, CA9 Cal) 137 F2d 534, 59 USPQ 174.

Summary judgment of noninfringement of copyright is proper where no genuine issue of material fact is raised. Miner v Employers Mut. Liability Ins. Co. (1956) 97 App DC 152, 229 F2d 35, 108 USPQ 100.

Issues of fact in instant copyright infringement action are not to be resolved by merely briefly describing method of compilation of copyrighted maps; examination of source material is needed to see if end product met standards of copyrightability; summary judgment dismissing complaint is refused. Trowler v Phillips (1958, CA9 Cal) 260 F2d 924, 119 USPQ 164.

In an action in which it was held that plastic scale model airplanes are a proper subject matter for copyright protection, the existence of material factual issues involving possible plagiarism, sufficiency of copyright notice, and the extent of subject matter protected was held to preclude a summary judgment for the plaintiff. Monogram Models, Inc. v Industro Motive Corp. (1971, CA6 Mich) 448 F2d 284, later app (CA6 Mich) 492 F2d 1281, cert den 419 US 843, 42 L Ed 2d 71, 95 S Ct 76.

Summary judgment that defendant's commercial did not infringe plaintiff's copyrighted TV show is reversed because disputed issues of fact exist, and important issues were not argued by the parties or decided by the court below. Goodson-Todman Enterprises, Ltd. v Kellogg Co. (1975, CA9 Cal) 513 F2d 913, 185 USPQ 193.

Summary judgment dismissing infringement and related actions is vacated because contracts between parties leave questions of fact for trial as to time limits of contracts and estoppel to deny termination, and case is remanded for trial on merits. Zolar Publishing Co. v Doubleday & Co. (1975, CA2 NY) 529 F2d 663, 188 USPQ 609.

On plaintiff's motion for summary judgment in copyright infringement suit, consideration of affidavits and exhibits reveals sharp issue of fact as to whether plaintiff's musical composition is in public domain. Edward B. Marks Music Corp. v Stasny Music Corp. (1941, DC NY) 1 FRD 720, 49 USPQ 553.

Plaintiff's motion for summary judgment in copyright infringement action is denied where answer pleads affirmative defense that plaintiff induced defendant to copy plaintiff's copyrighted literary composition. Curtis Pub. Co. v Union Leader Corp. (1952, DC NH) 12 FRD 341, 93 USPQ 360.

Defendant's assertion that sketch from which its alleged infringement was made was purchased in good faith is insufficient to raise issue for trial on plaintiff's motion for summary judgment. Home Art, Inc. v Glensder Textile Corp. (1948, DC NY) 81 F Supp 551, 79 USPQ 12.

Summary judgment is refused in copyright infringement suit since defendants' denial of essential allegations of complaint puts in issue validity of copyright; that is sufficient to raise questions of fact not determinable on motion for summary judgment; it is not controlling that defendants' affidavits do not controvert plaintiffs' assertions of validity; issue of validity will be disposed of at trial and not on affidavits; also, defendants deny infringement, and question of damages must be determined. McCulloch v Zapun Ceramics, Inc. (DC NY) 97 USPQ 12.

In order to maintain action for copyright infringement, plaintiff must show that there is genuine issue with respect to claim of similarity; there being no genuine issue as to similarity, summary judgment dismissing complaint is entered. Buckler v Paramount Pictures, Inc. (1955, DC NY) 133 F Supp 223, 106 USPQ 256.

Ordinarily, copyright infringement suits should be tried, but summary judgment may be granted where it is apparent upon face of pleadings and other matters of record that there is no genuine and material issue of fact; summary judgment is granted in copyright infringement action since no amount of expert or lay testimony could change obvious contents of plaintiff's play, defendant's motion picture, and source works, and expert testimony could not affect spontaneous and immediate impression of plaintiff's and defendant's literary works upon mind of ordinary observer. Costello v Loew's, Inc. (1958, DC Dist Col) 159 F Supp 782, 116 USPQ 372.

Summary judgment dismissing copyright infringement action is entered in view of fact that court of appeals, which had respective fabrics before it, reversed order granting temporary injunction inasmuch as court of appeals held that there was no infringement; whatever evidence plaintiff might offer, it could not outweigh evidence of fabrics themselves; no amount of expert testimony could overcome crucial difference between fabrics. Millworth Converting Corp. v Slifka (1960, DC NY) 188 F Supp 629, 128 USPQ 143.

Summary judgment for plaintiff is appropriate for action for public performance for profit of copyrighted songs in place of entertainment, where defendants did not respond to requests for admissions and otherwise failed to present any issues of fact for trial. Shapiro, Bernstein & Co. v "Log Cabin Club Asso." (1973, DC W Va) 365 F Supp 325, 180 USPQ 316.

Defendant's motion for summary judgment in copyright infringement case should be granted only in rarest instances, and is denied where issues of fact remain for trial of infringement of story by television production. Reyher v Children's Television Workshop (1974, DC NY) 377 F Supp 411, 181 USPQ 729.

Evidence showing access, extensive similarity, and duplication of errors in defendant's catalog of equipment similar to plaintiff's shows probability of copying, but ordinary observers might disagree about "substantial and material similarity" so that questions of fact remain for jury; summary judgment denied. Rexnord, Inc. v Modern Handling Systems, Inc. (1974, DC Del) 379 F Supp 1190, 183 USPQ 413.

Since questions of fact exist as to similarity between novels and motion pictures based on novels, summary judgment for infringement by televising motion pictures is denied. Filmvideo Releasing Corp. v Hastings (1976, DC NY) 426 F Supp 690, 193 USPQ 305.

Summary judgment is denied for infringement of preschool reading skills kit by kit having similar content, format, and sequence, because of possible question of fact that public domain kits may also exist having similar content, format and sequence, although preliminary injunction is granted because of likelihood of success of plaintiff. Grolier, Inc. v Educational Reading Aids Corp. (1976, DC NY) 193 USPQ 632.

Questions of fact remain as to intended scope of previous release signed in settlement of previous infringement action so that case is remanded to trial court for determination of whether release applies to defendant. Mount v Book-of-the Month Club, Inc. (1977, CA2) 194 USPQ 245.

119. —Copying as disputed matter

In copyright infringement suit, defendant in response to demand filed bill of particulars giving "cutting continuity" as synopsis of its motion-picture play and then plaintiff in response to demand filed bill of particulars showing alleged infringement, based on "cutting continuity"; defendant then moved to dismiss and after comparing continuity with plaintiff's copyrighted and uncopyrighted version of play court dismissed bill; this procedure was not permissible as plaintiff was not bound to accept continuity and is deprived of day in court; by basing its particulars on continuity it did not accept it but was entitled to try out issue whether it faithfully represented film; judge need not see film if continuity is accurate representation. Dellar v Samuel Goldwyn, Inc. (1939, CA2 NY) 104 F2d 661, 42 USPQ 164.

Cutting continuity of motion picture was submitted and bill dismissed for lack of infringement, but plaintiff argues that it is not fair representation of film, and decree is reversed and remanded; if court on new hearing determines that continuity is fair representation it should dismiss bill; view of picture may be best means of reaching satisfactory conclusion. Collins v Metro-Goldwyn Pictures Corp. (1939, CA2 NY) 106 F2d 83, 42 USPQ 553.

In order to succeed on motion for summary judgment in action for copyright infringement, plaintiff must conclusively demonstrate that there are no genuine issues of fact with regard to any essential element comprising claim of copyright infringement; if examination of works indicates that similarities are so overwhelming and pervasive that trial judge would be justified in directing verdict for plaintiff, judgment can be granted on motion despite defendant's contentions that there was no copying. Hammond & Co. v International College Globe, Inc. (1956, DC NY) 146 F Supp 514, 112 USPQ 291.

Summary judgment is appropriate for fair-use defense, because no issues of fact remain for trial, and where facts show copying of copyrighted letters was small and formed insignificant part of work involving matters of historical interest, summary judgment dismissing action is granted. Meeropol v Nizer (1976, DC NY) 417 F Supp 1201, 191 USPQ 346, application den (US) 50 L Ed 2d 729, 97 S Ct 687.

F. Trial

1. In General

120. Generally

In suit for infringement of copyright and its renewal, amended bill omitted renewal but defendant counterclaimed for declaration of invalidity of renewal and plaintiff conceded invalidity at trial; there was no error in awarding judgment on counterclaim. Yardley v Houghton Mifflin Co. (1939, CA2 NY) 108 F2d 28, 44 USPQ 1, cert den 309 US 686, 84 L Ed 1029, 60 S Ct 891.

Courts do not examine copyrighted work for intrinsic worth or merit. Jackson v Quickslip Co. (1940, CA2 NY) 110 F2d 731, 45 USPQ 6.

Findings of judge on motion to dismiss as to validity and infringements of copyright should not be disturbed by coordinate judge, and his decision is law of case unless at trial facts shown are different from facts alleged in complaint and admitted by implication on motion. Basevi v Edward O'Toole Co. (1939, DC NY) 26 F Supp 41, 40 USPQ 333.

Copyright infringement suit is heard ex parte when defendant is absent at calling of case for trial. Buck v Coe (1940, DC Pa) 32 F Supp 829, 45 USPQ 230.

It is proper to compare literary attainments and reputation of plaintiffs and defendants and to ask whether defendants are type who would be likely to plagiarize. Shurr v Warner Bros. Pictures, Inc. (DC NY) 59 USPQ 49, affd (CA2 NY) 144 USPQ 200, 62 USPQ 60.

Court must determine whether fact of infringement is proved; opinion of experts, although helpful, may not be substituted for court's judgment. Allegrini v De Angelis (1944, DC Pa) 59 F Supp 248, 64 USPQ 165, affd (CA3 Pa) 149 F2d 815, 65 USPQ 589.

Since court finds no copyright infringement, it is unnecessary to probe question of copyright's validity. Dunham v General Mills, Inc. (1953, DC Mass) 116 F Supp 152, 99 USPQ 372.

In action for misappropriation of literary property and infringement of common-law copyright, questions of originality, similarity, and copying are questions of law, in first instance, and may be determined by court upon demurrer. Glane v General Mills, Inc. (1956, Cal App) 298 P2d 626, 110 USPQ 391, hear gr by sup ct, app dismd.

121. Jury trial, generally

In suit at law for infringement, it is question for jury to decide whether or not defendant has copied. Blunt v Patten (1828, CC NY) F Cas No 1579.

Although copyright infringement suit, where infringed and infringing works are books or other long literary compositions, should preferably be tried before court without jury, issue of infringement in instant case (short song) is comparatively simple and should not take long to try; infringement issue is to be tried to jury.

Pallant v Sinatra (1945, DC NY) 7 FRD 293, 65 USPQ 158.

Right to jury trial would not be lost even if plaintiffs waived all damages other than statutory minimum, and plaintiffs' waiver, if they get any verdict, does not deprive defendant of right to have jury pass on question, for example, of whether defendant ever performed copyrighted music. Chappell & Co. v Cavalier Cafe, Inc. (1952, DC Mass) 13 FRD 321, 95 USPQ 243.

Causes for infringement of statutory and common-law copyrights are triable by court without jury since they are causes of action in equity. Pallant v Sinatra (1945, DC NY) 59 F Supp 684, 64 USPQ 326.

Similarity, access, and actionable copying are issues of fact for jury in copyright infringement action. Costello v Loew's, Inc. (1958, DC Dist Col) 159 F Supp 782, 116 USPQ 372.

On issue of unlawful appropriation of copyrighted musical comparison where test is response of ordinary lay hearer, jury is particularly well fitted to make finding; it is only where it is abundantly clear that there is complete dissimilarity in melody and accompaniment of two pieces that directed verdict on issue would be warranted; verdict is directed for defendant where there was no competent evidence to support plaintiff's claims, either as to copying or unlawful appropriation. O'Brien v Thall (DC Conn) 127 USPQ 325, affd (CA2 Conn) 283 F2d 741, 127 USPQ 296.

California Code of Civil procedure, providing for attachment to complaint of compositions of both parties in action for infringement of rights in literary production, provides method for considering alleged infringed and infringing productions upon demurrer; this in no way deprives plaintiff of right to jury trial; if, from comparison of productions, question of fact is shown to exist, cause should be submitted to jury. Kurlan v Columbia Broadcasting System, Inc. (1953) 40 Cal 2d 799, 256 P2d 962, 97 USPQ 556.

In action for plagiarism and for breach of implied contract to pay for use of original radio program, questions of whether plaintiff had original expression of ideas reduced to concrete form and whether defendant copied ideas and their expression are questions for jury. Kurlan v Columbia Broadcasting System, Inc. (1951, Cal App) 233 P2d 936, 90 USPQ 267, superseded 40 Cal 2d 799, 256 P2d 962, 97 USPQ 556.

122. —Right to jury trial as affected by relief sought

Although copyright infringement suit as originally brought contained prayer for injunctive relief, plaintiff is entitled to jury trial since he has waived claim for injunction and only other issues, copyright infringement and damages, are properly determinable by a jury; formal waiver of claim for injunctive relief is to be filed by plaintiff. Frazier v New England Newspaper Pub. Co. (1941, DC Mass) 1 FRD 734, 49 USPQ 497.

Jury trial was refused in copyright infringement suit seeking damages, profits, and injunctive relief and alleging inadequate remedy at law, since complaint was essentially equitable in nature and demand for damages was merely incidental to main relief. Young v Loew's, Inc. (1942, DC NY) 2 FRD 350, 53 USPQ 169.

Where plaintiff seeks injunction and accounting, alleging that without injunction infringement will continue and that remedy at law is inadequate, he has no right to jury trial. Arnstein v Twentieth Century Fox Film Corp. (1943, DC NY) 3 FRD 58, 56 USPQ 511.

First count for damages for breach of motion-picture contract is cognizable at law and to be tried to jury; second count is claim of co-author which belongs in equity; third count is for piracy of literary property which may be prosecuted both at law and equity; there is no such interdependence between first count and other counts as requires that all should be tried in equity but on motion second and third counts are transferred to nonjury calendar to be tried first. Bercovici v Chaplin (1944, DC NY) 3 FRD 409, 60 USPQ 409, mod on other grounds (DC NY) 7 FRD 61, 72 USPQ 340.

Interpleader is almost entirely equitable, although not wholly unknown at common law; specific performance is solely equitable; action striking records (copyright renewal and assignments) in copyright office is solely equitable; accounting is usually equitable; these remedies sought do not leave any matter triable by jury; remedy of declaring title to song and rights thereunder is equitable; demand for jury trial is stricken on motion. Edward B. Marks Music Corp. v Wonnell (1944, DC NY) 4 FRD 146, 63 USPQ 4.

Count pleads more than quantum meruit since it alleges collaboration to produce motion picture, extent of profits earned by defendant collaborator, and that compensation implied by law by reason of collaboration is 50% of net profits; plaintiff brought self into equity and is not entitled to jury trial. Bercovici v Chaplin (1946, DC NY) 7 FRD 61, 72 USPQ 340.

Where plaintiff asks for injunction, accounting, and damages, court cannot say that damages sought are merely incidental, and defendant is entitled to jury trial of issues of infringement and damages. Berlin v Club 100, Inc. (1951, DC Mass) 12 FRD 129, 91 USPQ 237.

Judge may determine issues of fact in disposing of equitable claim in copyright infringement action, so that no issues of fact are left to be tried by jury when legal claim (damages) is reached, but this does not justify striking of defendant's jury claim at outset of case, for judge can follow usual course of having legal claim tried first. Chappell & Co. v Cavalier Cafe, Inc. (1952, DC Mass) 13 FRD 321, 95 USPQ 243.

Defendant was entitled to jury trial of alleged infringement where no right of injunction appeared in bill. Metro-Goldwyn-Mayer Distributing Corp. v Fisher (1935, DC Md) 10 F Supp 745, 25 USPQ 341.

Parties by appearing before court and submitting evidence on all questions involved waived jury trial; if plaintiff is entitled to legal relief only, court will allow damages only but, if he is entitled to injunction, court is empowered to grant that relief also. Towle v Ross (1940, DC Or) 32 F Supp 125, 45 USPQ 143.

Where original complaint sought damages and accounting of profits, but amended complaint, with which was filed demand for jury trial, sought damages only, plaintiff is entitled to jury trial. Tynan v R. K. O. Radio Pictures, Inc. (1947, DC NY) 77 F Supp 238, 76 USPQ 387.

Jury trial of action for copyright infringement and unfair competition is refused since prayer for damages is incidental to equitable relief requested. Boucher v Du Boyes, Inc. (1955, DC NY) 137 F Supp 639, 109 USPQ 10.

Alleged copyright infringer is entitled to jury trial on issue whether just damages are payable where complaint seeks in one count both an injunction and just damages in lieu of actual damages and profits. Chappell & Co. v Palermo Cafe, Inc. (1956, DC Mass) 146 F Supp 867, 112 USPQ 378, affd in part and app dismd in part on other grounds (CA1 Mass) 249 F2d 77, 115 USPQ 205.

Defendant's request for jury trial is denied in action for infringement of performing rights, because action seeks only injunction and statutory minimum damages which are automatically set by court on finding of infringement, and there is no request for compensatory or punitive damages to raise legal issue for trial by jury. Cayman Music, Ltd. v Reichenberger (1975, DC Wis) 403 F Supp 794, 189 USPQ 301.

123. Stay of proceedings

Stay of action for copyright infringement and defamation of character in other districts is affirmed where prospective paperback publisher joined in first suit on same issues and has privity with hardbound publisher of same book because of indemnification agreement, so that plaintiffs have all rights preserved in first case making stay

of second case proper. Meeropol v Nizer (1974, CA2 NY) 505 F2d 232, 183 USPQ 513.

Trial of copyright infringement actions against sellers of records of pirated songs is not deferred until decision of actions against manufacturers. Harms, Inc. v F. W. Woolworth Co. (1958, DC Cal) 163 F Supp 484, 118 USPQ 436.

2. Evidentiary Matters

124. Generally

Court's problem primarily is to compare magazines to see whether defendants' copies plaintiff's. Official Aviation Guide Co. v American Aviation Associates (1945, CA7 Ill) 150 F2d 173, 65 USPQ 553, cert den 326 US 776, 90 L Ed 469, 66 S Ct 267, reh den 326 US 811, 90 L Ed 495, 66 S Ct 335.

It is not necessary for plaintiff to prove his title to copyright when he avers such fact in bill and defendant expressly admits it in answer. Historical Pub. Co. v Jones Bros. Pub. Co. (1916, CA3 Pa) 231 F 638.

In a suit for infringement of copyright and literary property by moving picture, where district court judge compared "cutting continuity" with plaintiff's version of play, it is not necessary that he see film if cutting continuity is reasonably fair synopsis of film in words. Dellar v Samuel Goldwyn, Inc. (1939, CA2 NY) 104 F2d 661, 42 USPQ 164.

As fair use is determined by considering all evidence, so, likewise, is question of infringement one of fact solved by study of evidence. Mathews Conveyer Co. v Palmer-Bee Co. (1943, CA6 Mich) 135 F2d 73, 57 USPQ 219.

Book must be produced in court before any witnesses will be permitted to testify concerning identical parts in such book. Boucicault v Fox (1862, CC NY) F Cas No 1691.

Where it was alleged that copyrighted article has been infringed, copyrighted article and alleged infringing article, or so much thereof as may be necessary for intelligent comparisons, must be included in proofs. Encyclopedia Britannica Co. v American Newspaper Asso. (1904, CC NJ) 130 F 460, affd (CA3 NJ) 134 F 831.

In suit for infringement of copyright, court may take into consideration evidence of facts arising subsequent to filing of bill, but before final decree. Record & Guide Co. v Bromley (1909, CC Pa) 175 F 156.

Complainant must make proof of copyright, even in absence of denial. Huebsch v Arthur H. Crist Co. (1914, DC NY) 209 F 885.

Question of infringement is one of fact on which previous decisions are not controlling precedents. Park v Warner Bros. (1934, DC NY) 8 F Supp 37, 23 USPQ 202.

Uncopyrighted variations cannot be utilized in suit in which jurisdiction is predicated on copyright laws. Davies v Columbia Pictures Corp. (1937, DC NY) 20 F Supp 809, 35 USPQ 187.

True facts as to asserted compliance with requirements as to copyright notice are integral part of plaintiffs' affirmative case. Winkler v New York Evening Journal, Inc. (1940, DC NY) 32 F Supp 810, 45 USPQ 562.

Before deciding copyright infringement case court views defendant's motion picture in presence of counsel for both parties, hears evidence, observes witnesses on stand, reads depositions and plaintiff's copyrighted play, and hears arguments of counsel. Gropper v Warner Bros. Pictures, Inc. (1941, DC NY) 38 F Supp 329, 49 USPQ 17.

When court has opportunity of comparing two works in copyright case, it has before it all necessary data to decide infringement. Christianson v West Pub. Co. (1944, DC Cal) 53 F Supp 454, 60 USPQ 279, affd (CA9 Cal) 149 F2d 202, 65 USPQ 263.

Inasmuch as there is question as to whether two defendants handled allegedly infringing figurines for sale and since third defendant disputes accuracy of number of figurines it is alleged to have marketed, defendants are required to produce, at taking of depositions, all records relating to purchase, sale, and handling of allegedly infringing figurines. McCulloch v Zapun Ceramics, Inc. (DC NY) 97 USPQ 12.

In order to prevail in copyright infringement action, plaintiff must prove access, substantial similarity, and copying of copyrighted work. Dugan v American Broadcasting Corp. (1963, DC Cal) 216 F Supp 763, 137 USPQ 238.

Proof necessary to recover for use of literary composition upon theory of contract implied in law is same as that required by tort action for plagiarism; there can be no recovery where defendant has not used protectible portion of composition, since implied contract cannot arise, as defendants have used no property belonging to plaintiff. Weitzenkorn v Lesser (1953) 40 Cal 2d 778, 256 P2d 947, 97 USPQ 545.

125. Admissibility and competency

It might be better practice to receive evidence as to plaintiff's damage even if it falls short of establishing measure of liability, for when recovery for copyright infringement may be awarded without any proof of injury, it may aid exercise of discretion to hear any evidence on subject that has probative value; however, defendant cannot complain of its exclusion in response to its objections. F. W. Woolworth Co. v Contemporary Arts, Inc. (1952) 344 US 228, 97 L Ed 276,

73 S Ct 222, 95 USPQ 396, motion den 350 US 810, 100 L Ed 727, 76 S Ct 37.

In suit for infringement testimony of witnesses who have compared paragraphs from complainant's book, and others from defendant's book should not be rejected as incompetent evidence insofar as their testimony refers to specific instances of copying, and points out close comparisons; offer to give evidence as to rate of speed of legal editors in writing headnotes for cases was properly rejected. West Pub. Co. v Lawyers' Coop. Pub. Co. (1897, CA2 NY) 79 F 756.

Evidence which relates to history of copyrighted picture may be admitted. Hegeman v Springer (1901, CA2 NY) 110 F 374, affd 189 US 505, 47 L Ed 921, 23 S Ct 849.

If defendant, in pleading to whole of bill for infringement, alleges that complainant's composition has been publicly exhibited without proper copyright notice, complainant's evidence of exclusiveness of exhibition is admissible and competent without amendment of bill. Werckmeister v American Lithographic Co. (1904, CA2 NY) 134 F 321.

Under broad allegations describing object of copyright explanatory evidence was admissible. Korzybski v Underwood & Underwood, Inc. (1929, CA2 NY) 36 F2d 727, 3 USPQ 242.

Defendants' silence, when requested to admit that telephone numbers in both plaintiff's and defendants' directories were in error, is tantamount to admission and is admissible to prove that books contain identical errors; plaintiff need not prove that telephone numbers were in error. Adventures in Good Eating, Inc. v Best Places to Eat, Inc. (1942, CA7 Ill) 131 F2d 809, 56 USPQ 242.

Testimony is admissible to interpret "printed copy" in contracts assigning interest in copyrights by author of song and supports finding that "printed copy" does not refer to "folios." Gumm v Jerry Vogel Music Co. (1946, CA2 NY) 158 F2d 516, 71 USPQ 285.

Testimony as to reissue and remake value of one of plaintiff's silent motion pictures is excluded as having little relevance in determining value of plaintiff's talking picture infringed by defendants; copyright owner may testify as to value of property misappropriated by defendants; owner of personal property may always testify to its value; he may testify to value of intangibles, advertising scheme, and good will of business; literary property is not distinguished from other personal property, is subject to same rules, and is likewise protected. Universal Pictures Co. v Harold Lloyd Corp. (1947, CA9 Cal) 162 F2d 354, 73 USPQ 317.

Statement of officer of corporation was incompetent evidence against corporation touching question of complainant's damages from infringement. Chils v Gronlund (1890, CC NY) 41 F 145.

Remedies provided for infringement of copyright are penal rather than remedial, and therefore evidence given by defendant in another suit is inadmissible and cannot be used against him for enforcement of penalty. Daly v Brady (1895, CC NY) 69 F 285, later app (CA2 NY) 83 F 1007, affd 175 US 148, 44 L Ed 109, 20 S Ct 62.

Signed memorandum of Librarian of Congress, that two copies of copyrighted work were received, is competent evidence to prove deposit of copies with Librarian of Congress although memorandum was not under seal. Suderman v Saake (1909, CC Pa) 166 F 815.

Rules of evidence in copyright cases are same as in other cases, and receipt showing settlement between plaintiff and infringer from whom defendant obtained his picture is not admissible for purpose of defeating action, but it may be admitted as bearing upon equities between parties. Altman v New Haven Union Co. (1918, DC Conn) 254 F 113.

In copyright infringement suit, court overrules plaintiff's objections to introduction in evidence of copyright certificate of third party's composition not reproduced for sale, of copyright certificate of orchestral arrangement thereof, and of copyright certificate of composition as published work, although no copy of words or music is submitted but only piano portion of chorus arrangement. Remick Music Corp. v Interstate Hotel Co. (1944, DC Neb) 58 F Supp 523, 63 USPQ 327, affd (CA8 Neb) 157 F2d 744, 71 USPQ 138, cert den 329 US 809, 91 L Ed 691, 67 S Ct 622, reh den 330 US 854, 91 L Ed 1296, 67 S Ct 769.

When noninfringement is plain, court is not justified in hearing so-called expert opinion testimony of literary agents, newspaper men, and instructors in dramatics called by plaintiff. Burns v Twentieth Century-Fox Film Corp. (1948, DC Mass) 75 F Supp 986, 76 USPQ 515.

Dissection of plaintiff's copyrighted work and defendant's work by use of parallel column analysis and expert testimony is proper when used in determination of issue of copying, but not when it is offered with respect to issue of unlawful appropriation or substantiality or materiality. Morse v Fields (1954, DC NY) 127 F Supp 63, 104 USPQ 54.

It is difficult for court to see materiality, on question of infringement of copyrighted design, of evidence that one customer, who found both plaintiff's and defendants' fabrics equally suitable, refused to reorder from plaintiff until its price was reduced to that charged by defendants.

Millworth Converting Corp. v Slifka (1960, DC NY) 188 F Supp 629, 128 USPQ 143.

In suit by licensor of motion-picture rights to drama against his licensee, parol evidence of licensor's title to drama was competent. Hart v Fox (1917, Sup) 166 NYS 793.

Evidence of repeated public production of the play is proper for purpose of showing that defendant may have obtained his play through memory. Keene v Clarke, 28 NY Super Ct 38.

126. Judicial notice

In copyright infringement suit court takes judicial notice that, at time plaintiff's play and defendant's motion picture were written, main theme thereof was uppermost in public mind. Gropper v Warner Bros. Pictures, Inc. (1941, DC NY) 38 F Supp 329, 49 USPQ 17.

Court takes judicial notice that copyrighted song is well-known and popular. Robbins Music Corp. v Weinstock (1952, DC NY) 107 F Supp 102, 94 USPQ 107.

Judge may draw upon his own knowledge of literary matters in determining whether pattern is of type which, having been used in other words, can be given protection of copyright law, or whether copying was permissible or illicit; expert testimony, even of highest type, need not be substituted for judge's own conclusion arrived at from his own study. Bradbury v Columbia Broadcasting System, Inc. (1959, DC Cal) 174 F Supp 733, 123 USPQ 10, revd on other grounds (CA9 Cal) 287 F2d 478, 128 USPQ 376, cert dismd 368 US 801, 7 L Ed 2d 15, 82 S Ct 19.

127. Presumptions and burden of proof

Question of burden of proof as to apportionment of profits did not arise since defendants voluntarily assumed and sustained burden. Sheldon v Metro-Goldwyn Pictures Corp. (1940) 309 US 390, 84 L Ed 825, 60 S Ct 681, 44 USPQ 607.

Burden is on plaintiff to prove valid copyright. Public Ledger Co. v Post Printing & Publishing Co. (1923, CA8 Mo) 294 F 430.

Plaintiff has burden of proving infringement by fair preponderance of evidence, and it is not necessary for defendant to prove intellectual alibi. Oxford Book Co. v College Entrance Book Co. (1938, CA2 NY) 98 F2d 688, 39 USPQ 7.

Burden of showing access is on plaintiff. Sarkadi v Wiman (1943, CA2 NY) 135 F2d 1002, 57 USPQ 361.

Plaintiff established prima facie case by producing copyright certificate, and, while ultimate burden was on it to establish right to declaratory judgment of sole ownership of copyrighted publication, defendant had burden of establishing affirmative defense of coauthorship. Jerry Vogel

Music Co. v Forster Music Publishers, Inc. (1945, CA2 NY) 147 F2d 614, 64 USPQ 417, cert den 325 US 880, 89 L Ed 1996, 65 S Ct 1573.

Plaintiff in copyright infringement suit has burden of proving, as to any comic strip it puts in suit, that it was validly copyrighted. National Comics Publications, Inc. v Fawcett Publications, Inc. (1952, CA2) 198 F2d 927, 94 USPQ 289.

In order to establish infringement of copyrighted musical composition, plaintiff has burden to prove that challenged composition is similar in substantial respects to copyrighted composition, and that similarity is due to copying; substantial similarity which is product of independent work is not actionable as infringement. Schultz v Holmes (1959, CA9 Cal) 264 F2d 942, 121 USPQ 117.

Evidence of access and substantial similarity create inference of copying copyrighted work and establish prima facie case of copying; when plaintiff has made a strong prima facie case of copying by proving access and similarity, burden of going forward shifts to defendant, and he must offer evidence to negative probability of copying. Blumcraft of Pittsburg v Newman Bros., Inc. (1967, CA6 Ohio) 373 F2d 905, 153 USPQ 91.

In an action for copyright infringement plaintiff does not have the burden of proving that all publications were with copyright notice; the burden rests on the defendants to establish invalidation of the copyright. Tennessee Fabricating Co. v Moultrie Mfg. Co. (1970, CA5 Ga) 421 F2d 279, 164 USPQ 481 cert den 398 US 928, 26 L Ed 2d 91, 90 S Ct 1819.

In suit for infringement burden is upon complainant to prove by competent evidence his title to copyright, as well as to prove infringement. Chase v Sanborn (1874, CC NH) F Cas No 2628.

In action for infringement complainant's copyright is prima facie evidence that he is author of work, and burden of proof is upon defendant to show contrary. Reed v Carusi (1845, CC Md) F Cas No 11642.

Authors take their rights under and subject to copyright laws, and when attacked, burden is upon them to show literal compliance with each and every statutory requirement in the nature of conditions precedent. Osgood v A. S. Aloe Instrument Co. (1897, CC Mo) 83 F 470.

Plaintiff who introduced certificates of registration of copies of allegedly copyrighted publications and copy of defendant's alleged infringing publication had the burden to prove publication of notice of copyright. Harms v Pure Milk Assn. (DC Ill) 37 USPQ 575.

In order for plaintiff to prevail in suit for copyright infringement he must prove ownership to painting and nonpublication prior to copyright; and upon failure to sustain this burden of proof, case is dismissed. Vaughan v Real Detective Publishing Co. (DC NY) 42 USPQ 500.

In any country in which musical composition may be copyrighted and proprietor of copyright is entitled to protection of that country's law, it cannot, in absence of proof, be presumed that particular composition is within public domain, and, therefore, proponent of proposition has burden of proving that specific composition is in fact in public domain in foreign country. Paine v Electrical Research Products, Inc. (1939, DC NY) 30 F Supp 260, 43 USPQ 240.

Burden of proof is on plaintiff to show that defendant copied its catalogue, but plaintiff having made out prima facie case, burden is thrown on defendant of going forward with evidence to explain similarities; it is unnecessary to show intent to infringe but such intention may be shown to aggravate infringement. R. R. Donnelley & Sons Co. v Haber (1942, DC NY) 43 F Supp 456, 52 USPQ 445.

To recover, plaintiff has burden of proving (1) that he is proprietor of valid copyright by proving (a) work was original, (b) he took necessary steps to comply with registration statute, (c) work had not been published before securing copyright, and (d) he has title to copyright, and (2) that defendants have infringed. Freudenthal v Hebrew Pub. Co. (1942, DC NY) 44 F Supp 754, 53 USPQ 466.

Defendant's mere denial of plaintiff's allegation that work always carried proper copyright notice does not impose undue burden on plaintiff; defense need not be asserted affirmatively; on mere denial, plaintiff is required in first instance to substantiate allegation; on affirmative defense, defendant's prima facie case is complete in introduction into evidence of copies carrying improper notices; burden then shifts to plaintiff to explain how improper notices came about; from practical standpoint, plaintiff's burden is same irrespective of manner in which defense is pleaded. Forster Music Publisher, Inc. v Fred Fisher Music Co. (DC NY) 63 USPQ 112.

Court will not engage in speculation or conjecture to find that defendant had access to plaintiff's work; plaintiff has burden of proving access. Alexander v Irving Trust Co. (1955, DC NY) 132 F Supp 364, 106 USPQ 74, affd (CA2 NY) 228 F2d 221, 108 USPQ 24, cert den 350 US 996, 100 L Ed 860, 76 S Ct 545.

Once copying is demonstrated and there is minimal similarity between works, question of improper appropriation presents, in first instance, issue of fact. Malkin v Dubinsky (1956, DC NY) 146 F Supp 111, 112 USPQ 263.

Although burden of proof remains on plaintiff throughout the case, if plaintiff shows that infringing work contains substantial copyrightable matter which was appropriated from plaintiff's book, plaintiff need not prove that such matter was not derived by author from sources available in public domain; plaintiff has burden of proving that defendant's novel contains substantial quantity of copyrightable matter which was appropriated from plaintiff's book; however, by establishing prima facie case of infringement, plaintiff shifts to defendant burden of going forward with evidence. Greenbie v Noble (1957, DC NY) 151 F Supp 45, 113 USPQ 115.

Copyright owner is presumed to suffer irreparable damage when his right to exclusive use of copyrighted material is invaded. Walco Products, Inc. v Kittay & Blitz, Inc. (1972, DC NY) 354 F Supp 121.

Plaintiff fails to meet burden of proving copying by defendant of molds for making ceramic objects, because evidence as to business practices and types of plaster used is conflicting and most likely conclusion is that accused's molds were actually made by plaintiff. S-K Potteries & Mold Co. v Sipes (1976, DC Ind) 192 USPQ 537.

Burden of proving access is on plaintiff, as it is on plaintiff to prove every fact necessary to constitute plagiarism charged. Cantor v Mankiewicz (1960, Sup) 203 NYS2d 626, 125 USPQ 598.

In action for infringement of play, defendant had burden of proving that he came into possession of play in lawful manner. Palmer v De Witt, 40 How Pr 293, 32 NY Super Ct 530, affd 47 NY 532.

128. Sufficiency, generally

In suit for infringement, plaintiff's parol evidence concerning his title was sufficient prima facie evidence of title. Callaghan v Myers (1888) 128 US 617, 32 L Ed 547, 9 S Ct 177.

Evidence, in action for infringement of copyright of two paintings, was insufficient to show original authorship and nonpublication before copyright was secured by plaintiff under his assignment. Bosselman v Richardson (1909, CA2 NY) 174 F 622.

In an action for infringement, where plaintiff was unable to produce original painting or copies deposited in copyright office so as to prove his identity with copyright, production of print of copyrighted picture upon which appeared title and notice of copyright was sufficient to establish his identity; it is not enough to show that work was without statutory notice when it came into defendant's possession; it must appear that it left

plaintiff copyright holder's possession in that condition. Gerlach-Barklow Co. v Morris & Bendien, Inc. (1927, CA2 NY) 23 F2d 159.

Where plaintiff produced testimony of originality and utility and evidence warranted inference of direct copying by defendant, and defendant presented no real challenge, being content to rest without offer of any testimony, judgment against defendant was affirmed. Colonial Book Co. v Amsco School Publications, Inc. (1944, CA2 NY) 142 F2d 362, 61 USPQ 391.

In action for infringement of copyrighted statue of dog, plaintiff does not fail to establish basis for claim of infringement by failing to show which of its commercial models is copy of model upon which copyright certificate issued; statement of plaintiff's counsel in offering models as exhibits, which was corroborated later by testimony, that models embody copyrighted statue is enough to establish plaintiff's prima facie case. F. W. Woolworth Co. v Contemporary Arts, Inc. (1951, CA1 Mass) 193 F2d 162, 92 USPQ 4, affd 344 US 228, 97 L Ed 276, 73 S Ct 222, 95 USPQ 396, motion den 350 US 810, 100 L Ed 727, 76 S Ct 37.

Defendant's burden of proof to overcome presumption of copying arising from "access" and substantial similarity does not require "strong, convincing and persuasive evidence", and instruction to jury to consider "any evidence" explaining or accounting for similarity is not clearly erroneous; and judgment of noninfringement is affirmed. Granite Music Corp. v United Artists Corp. (1976, CA9 Cal) 532 F2d 718, 189 USPQ 406.

Evidence was sufficient to warrant conclusion that plaintiff had a good copyright in his book. Emerson v Davies (1845, CC Mass) F Cas No 4436.

General testimony showing compliance with copyright statutes regarding inscription of notice upon complainant's book was sufficient to establish prima facie case; production of lithograph from complainant's photograph which bore no notice of copyright was insufficient evidence to overthrow complainant's prima facie case of compliance with copyright statutes. Falk v Gast Lith. & Eng. Co. (1889, CC NY) 40 F 168.

Evidence was sufficient to support finding that defendant's dictionary infringed complainant's. Chils v Gronlund (1890, CC NY) 41 F 145.

Evidence showed infringement of plaintiff's book in defendant's advertising calendars only to extent of actual copying. Warren v White & Wyckoff Mfg. Co. (1930, DC NY) 39 F2d 922.

Evidence proved copyrighted musical compositions were infringed where plaintiff's witnesses testified that copyrighted music was played and defendant's witnesses could not remember what music was played. Leo Feist, Inc. v Demarie (1935, DC La) 16 F Supp 827, 32 USPQ 122.

Where music alleged to be infringed was in public domain, and there was no noticeable similarity between such music and that alleged to infringe, evidence was insufficient to sustain claim of infringement. Hirsch v Paramount Pictures, Inc. (1937, DC Cal) 17 F Supp 816, 32 USPQ 233.

Testimony of inspector for plaintiffs from dated memorandum that music was played in restaurant on date specified should be accepted as against specific denial of orchestra leader based entirely on memory of two years afterward. Buck v Lisa (1939, DC NY) 28 F Supp 379, 42 USPQ 116.

Fact that defendant published song with music pirated from another song does not prove that it pirated words from plaintiff's song. Newcomb v Young (1942, DC NY) 43 F Supp 744, 52 USPQ 373.

Fact that evidence of infringement comes from hired "music detectives" or "spotters" who went to defendants' places of public entertainment in order to assemble evidence as foundation for infringement goes only to question of their credibility. Remick Music Corp. v Interstate Hotel Co. (1944, DC Neb) 58 F Supp 523, 63 USPQ 327, affd (CA8 Neb) 157 F2d 744, 71 USPQ 138, cert den 329 US 809, 91 L Ed 691, 67 S Ct 622, reh den 330 US 854, 91 L Ed 1296, 67 S Ct 769.

In civil action for copyright infringement, plaintiffs are not required to establish case beyond reasonable doubt, but merely by preponderance of evidence. Harms, Inc. v Sansom House Enterprises, Inc. (1958, DC Pa) 162 F Supp 129, 117 USPQ 272, affd (CA3 Pa) 267 F2d 494.

Revolutionary number of changes in defendant's design, all in the direction of plaintiff's copyright, at the least, adds substantial weight to prima facie case of copying based upon evidence of access and substantial similarity. Such reinforced prima facie case does not alter plaintiff's eventual and basic burden of proof, but it calls from defendant an explanation at least equivalent to the prima facie case, to say nothing of the reinforcement. Blumcraft of Pittsburgh v Newman Bros., Inc. (1968, DC Ohio) 159 USPQ 166.

Record held sufficient to establish infringement of plaintiff's statutory and common law copyrights of children's songs by defendants, who were manufacturers, rather than mere pressers, of offending records. Rosette v Rainbo Record Mfg. Corp. (1973, DC NY) 354 F Supp 1183, affd (CA2 NY) 546 F2d 461.

Jury determined similarity after play was read to it and after it viewed motion picture, and on no other evidence; sufficiency of evidence to sustain finding of similarity can be determined by appellate court only by reading play and seeing picture. Golding v R. K. O. Pictures, Inc. (1949, Cal) 208 P2d 1, 82 USPQ 136, subsequent op on reh 35 Cal 2d 690, 221 P2d 95, 86 USPQ 537.

129. —Sufficiency as to access

Charge of copyright infringement does not fail merely because infringer was not caught in act since access may be inferred or found circumstantially. Cholvin v B. & F. Music Co. (1958, CA7 Ill) 253 F2d 102, 116 USPQ 491.

In the copyright field, access means not merely opportunity to have read or known contents of work, but means actual reading or knowledge thereof; evidence of access by defendant to plaintiff's copyrighted works, considered with noteworthy similarities in defendant's production, is strong and persuasive evidence of copying which requires defendant to counter with strong convincing and persuasive evidence to contrary; mere denial of copying is insufficient. Bradbury v Columbia Broadcasting System, Inc. (1961, CA9 Cal) 287 F2d 478, 128 USPQ 376, cert dismd 368 US 801, 7 L Ed 2d 15, 82 S Ct 19.

Without direct proof of access or of reasonable possibility of access, access and copying may be implied only if similarities of plays are so striking and of such nature as to preclude possibility of coincidence, accident, or independent creation. Scott v Wkjg, Inc. (1967, CA7 Ind) 376 F2d 467, 153 USPQ 493, cert den 389 US 832, 19 L Ed 2d 91, 88 S Ct 101.

If there is actual infringement, priority is sufficient to show access. Echevarria v Warner Bros. Pictures, Inc. (1935, DC Cal) 12 F Supp 632, 28 USPQ 213.

Access has been established because plaintiff's magazine was on all newsstands for about year before defendant's magazine was published. Detective Comics, Inc. v Bruns Publications, Inc. (1939, DC NY) 28 F Supp 399, 41 USPQ 182, mod on other grounds (CA2 NY) 111 F2d 432, 45 USPQ 291.

Evidence of submission of scenario to scenario company is insufficient where form received from company, and now bearing title of scenario, shows erasure where title is typewritten and all other correspondence with company is with reference to another scenario. Sheets v Twentieth Century Fox Film Corp. (1940, DC Dist Col) 33 F Supp 389, 46 USPQ 120.

Plaintiff's only proof of access is his claim of having left copies of his song in 1919 with defendants and that they were not returned, but no proof was offered that he had demanded return; complaint does not allege such access and it first appeared in answer to interrogatories; in view of slight resemblance between plaintiff's song and defendants', copyrighted in 1926, proof of access is too meager for copyright infringement suit to be predicated thereon. Davilla v Harms, Inc. (1940, DC NY) 36 F Supp 843, 48 USPQ 103.

Failure to prove direct access does not foreclose recovery since access may be inferred from similarity of two compositions; but mere similarity is not sufficient since independent reproduction of copyrighted musical work is not infringement, and nothing short of plagiarism will serve. Allen v Walt Disney Productions, Ltd. (1941, DC NY) 41 F Supp 134, 50 USPQ 365.

Finding of access cannot be based on tenuous disclosure of similarity. McMahon v Harms, Inc. (1942, DC NY) 42 F Supp 779, 52 USPQ 321.

Plaintiffs submitted play to defendant motion-picture company and synopsis has been in defendant's archives since 1936 together with synopsis of each of thousands of other manuscripts submitted; that motion-picture producer made contract with defendant to use defendant's studio does not show access by producer in 1940. Shurr v Warner Bros. Pictures, Inc., (DC NY) 59 USPQ 49, affd (CA2 NY) 144 F2d 200, 62 USPQ 60.

Improbability of access to copyrighted unpublished composition is inferable from standing instructions of register of copyrights forbidding access to unpublished filings. Remick Music Corp. v Interstate Hotel Co. (1944, DC Neb) 58 F Supp 523, 63 USPQ 327, affd (CA8 Neb) 157 F2d 744, 71 USPQ 138, cert den 329 US 809, 91 L Ed 691, 67 S Ct 622, reh den 330 US 854, 91 L Ed 1296, 67 S Ct 769.

Access means that person charged with pirating another's work saw first person's work; it must be shown that person having access communicated information to those who created story; person's denial of communication is corroborated by his disapproval of story and by his separation from company during period when final form of story took shape. Schwarz v Universal Pictures Co. (1945, DC Cal) 85 F Supp 270, 83 USPQ 153.

Identity in measurement and conformation of sculptures to minutest detail could not be result of coincidence, hence it precludes contention that defendant did original and independent work. Contemporary Arts, Inc. v F. W. Woolworth Co. (1950, DC Mass) 93 F Supp 739, 86 USPQ 476, affd (CA1 Mass) 193 F2d 162, 92 USPQ 4, affd 344 US 228, 97 L Ed 276, 73 S Ct 222, 95 USPQ 396, motion den 350 US 810, 100 L Ed 727, 76 S Ct 37.

Mere possibility of access to synopsis of plaintiff's play in defendant's files or to play itself is not enough to overcome testimony of writer, producer, and director of defendant's motion picture that they did not see plaintiff's work and did not copy from it. Pinci v Twentieth Century-Fox Film Corp. (1951, DC NY) 95 F Supp 884, 88 USPQ 475.

Proof that plaintiff submitted play to defendant's New York office in 1931 would not warrant inference that authors of defendant's screen play had synopsis of plaintiff's play or copy of play before them when they wrote screen play in 1945. Meyer v Universal Pictures Co. (DC NY) 89 USPQ 496.

Copying may be inferred from evidence of access, although evidence of access will not prove copying if there are no similarities. Jones v Supreme Music Corp. (1951, DC NY) 101 F Supp 989, 92 USPQ 347.

Copyrighted song, which had acquired folk song notoriety, was contained in four published song books enjoying wide publicity and distribution; it is probable that defendant either consciously or unconsciously had access to song; infringement is found since examination of two songs shows that defendant's was taken directly from plaintiff's despite defendant's contrary testimony. Edward B. Marks Music Corp. v Borst Music Pub. Co. (1953, DC NJ) 110 F Supp 913, 97 USPQ 394.

Mere fact of access is not fatal to defense in copyright case. Greenbie v Noble (1957, DC NY) 151 F Supp 45, 113 USPQ 115.

Since plaintiff failed to establish access to her copyrighted play by defendants, she must, to succeed in copyright infringement action, show such striking and extensive similarities between two plays that conclusion is compelled that defendants' play could not have been written except by copying and plagiarism of her work. Morris v Wilson (1960, DC NY) 189 F Supp 565, 128 USPQ 419, affd (CA2 NY) 295 F2d 36, 131 USPQ 130, cert den 368 US 1004, 7 L Ed 2d 543, 82 S Ct 639.

Access alone without copying is insufficient to find copyright infringement. Burnett v Lambino (1962, DC NY) 204 F Supp 327, 133 USPQ 325.

Proof that plaintiff's work was published year prior to alleged copying prima facie shows access, not merely inference of access. Blazon, Inc. v De Luxe Game Corp. (1965, DC NY) 268 F Supp 416, 156 USPQ 195.

In infringement action, evidence of reasonable opportunity to view or read plaintiff's work is all that is needed to show access by defendant; even if access cannot be so established, nevertheless it may be inferred where accused work is strikingly similar to copyrighted work. Stratchborneo v Arc Music Corp. (1973, DC NY) 357 F Supp 1393.

Evidence of access to copyrighted compilation of executive desk calendar, letters to trade saying that infringing calendar is similar to copyrighted calendar, and nearly identical arrangement of infringing calendar supports finding of infringement. Baldwin Cooke Co. v Keith Clark, Inc. (1974, DC Ill) 383 F Supp 650, 183 USPQ 209, affd without opinion (CA7 Ill) 505 F2d 1250, 183 USPQ 769, and supp op (DC Ill) 420 F Supp 404.

Decorative tray bearing New York City scenes similar in many respects to copyrighted tray infringes copyright in spite of incredible testimony of independent creation by direct competitor who admitted checking on copyright proprietor's wares occasionally, and access and copying can be inferred from circumstantial evidence of direct competition and close similarity in works. Arrow Novelty Co. v Enco Nat. Corp. (1974, DC NY) 393 F Supp 157, 187 USPQ 413, affd without op (CA2 NY) 515 F2d 504.

Proof of opportunity of access together with proof of substantial similarities is sufficient to support implied finding of access and copying. Kovacs v Mutual Broadcasting System, Inc. (1950) 99 Cal App 2d 56, 221 P2d 108, 86 USPQ 547.

It is not important whether persons who prepared defendant's infringing radio program had access to plaintiff's material, since other responsible employees in charge of program production admitted access. Stanley v Columbia Broadcasting System, Inc. (1948, Cal App) 192 P2d 495, 77 USPQ 404, superseded (Cal) 208 P2d 9, 82 USPQ 123, subsequent op on reh 35 Cal 2d 653, 221 P2d 73, 86 USPQ 520, 23 ALR2d 216.

Proof of substantial similarity between plaintiff's and defendant's literary properties gives rise to inference of defendant's access to plaintiff's material and copying by defendant. Glane v General Mills, Inc. (1956, Cal App) 298 P2d 626, 110 USPQ 391, hear gr by sup ct, app dismd.

In common-law copyright, to constitute tortious appropriation of musical property, proof should establish priority of plaintiff's composition and that defendant with animus furandi obtained access to and copied it; access is indispensable ingredient in proof of piracy. Smith v Berlin (1955) 207 Misc 862, 141 NYS2d 110, 105 USPQ 296.

Access may be proven by direct proof, circumstantial evidence, or upon such frequent and striking resemblances between the two works as to compel inference of access; mere suspicion is not proof of access; question is not whether it is possible that defendant had access, but whether court is convinced from all the proof that he did; it is important that defendant testified that he did not know of plaintiff or of subject of plaintiff's biography. Cantor v Mankiewicz (1960, Sup) 203 NYS2d 626, 125 USPQ 598.

130. —Sufficiency as to copying

In copyright infringement suit, plaintiff must prove copying by defendant; plaintiff may create inference of copying by establishing access to copyrighted work by defendant and similarity or identity between works; defendant may rebut inference by affirmative proof of his prior composition; stronger prima facie case established by plaintiff, correspondingly more persuasive must be rebuttal evidence; however, it is incorrect rule of law to hold that defendant never can rebut inference by mere preponderance of evidence, but must establish defense by clear and convincing evidence or beyond reasonable doubt. Overman v Loesser (1953, CA9 Cal) 205 F2d 521, 98 USPQ 177, cert den 346 US 910, 98 L Ed 407, 74 S Ct 241.

Presumption of copying from "access" to copyrighted song and similarity of alleged infringement is overcome by preponderance of evidence showing use of common musical phrase in other songs, differences in alleged infringement, and lack of copying by infringer. Granite Music Corp. v United Artists Corp. (1976, CA9 Cal) 532 F2d 718, 189 USPQ 406.

In suit for infringement of cuts contained in copyrighted catalogue, complainant's evidence was sufficient to show copying by defendant. Da Prato Statuary Co. v Giuliani Statuary Co. (1911, CA8 Minn) 189 F 90.

Evidence showed that defendant constructed cemetery monument, with several changes, from copyrighted design of plaintiff and was guilty of infringement. Jones Bros. Co. v Underkoffler (1936, DC Pa) 16 F Supp 729, 31 USPQ 197.

In action for infringement of common-law copyright, plaintiff must establish copying by preponderance of evidence; copying is normally shown by establishing access and similarity. Herwitz v National Broadcasting Co. (1962, DC NY) 210 F Supp 231, 135 USPQ 96.

In action for infringement of copyrighted popular song, substantial similarity between songs, so as to justify inference of copying, will not be found if only small, common phrase appears in both songs, unless reappearing phrase is especially unique or qualitatively important; copying may be inferred where accused work is strikingly similar to copyrighted work; expert testimony may and should be used to aid court in analyzing works involved in order to draw such inference. Stratchborneo v Arc Music Corp. (1973, DC NY) 357 F Supp 1393.

Decorative tray bearing New York City scenes similar in many respects to copyrighted tray infringes copyright in spite of incredible testimony of independent creation by direct competitor who admitted checking on copyright proprietor's wares occasionally, and access and copying can be inferred from circumstantial evidence of direct competition and close similarity in works. Arrow Novelty Co. v Enco Nat. Corp. (1974, DC NY) 393 F Supp 157, 187 USPQ 413, affd without op (CA2 NY) 515 F2d 504.

Copying may be shown by (a) direct evidence of copying, which includes direct evidence that defendants had seen or heard plaintiff's work or direct evidence of access by defendants to plaintiff's work, or (b) similarities appearing from words themselves so strong as to compel inference; mere similarities carry no right of action for infringement. Heywood v Jericho Co. (1948) 193 Misc 905, 85 NYS2d 464, 79 USPQ 450.

3. Judgments

131. Generally

Where court finds copyright infringed, counsel for plaintiff must forthwith prepare and submit through clerk's office findings of fact following complaint with such additions as counsel may be advised, as pictures in papers on motion for preliminary injunction and comparison of texts as in plaintiff's trial brief and conclusions of law; defendants to be notified and to submit criticism; only findings and conclusions signed by judge will be part of record; Supreme Court in Interstate Circuit, Inc. v United States (1938) 304 US 55, 82 L Ed 1146, 58 S Ct 768, ended practice of opinion standing as findings and conclusions. Detective Comics, Inc. v Bruns Publications, Inc. (1939, DC NY) 28 F Supp 399, 41 USPQ 182, mod on other grounds (CA2 NY) 111 F2d 432, 45 USPQ 291.

Counsel for defendants must prepare and submit findings of ultimate facts and simple conclusions of law, not details of facts; plaintiff may, within five days, submit and serve his criticisms; only findings and conclusions signed by court will be filed as part of record; counterfinding by plaintiff will not avail him anything; he must take objections to findings by way of appropriate assignments of error on appeal. Arnstein v American Soc. of Composers, etc. (1939, DC NY) 29 F Supp 388, 42 USPQ 581.

Partial final judgment under Rule 54(b) of Federal Rules of Civil Procedure determining liability for copyright infringement is refused since it would establish nothing with finality and would require defendants to appeal to protect their rights; infringement cannot be dissociated

from relief by way of injunction and damages provided by Copyright Act; to establish liability under Rule 54(b) of Federal Rules of Civil Procedure would force defendants to litigate merits of case piecemeal. Harms, Inc. v Tops Music Enterprises, Inc. (1958, DC Cal) 160 F Supp 77, 117 USPQ 72.

Where consent decree was entered which settled all liabilities of the defendant for infringement, such decree could not be used by another person to avoid payment for infringing books which he had purchased from such defendant. Edward Thompson Co. v Pakulski (1915) 220 Mass 96, 107 NE 412.

132. Declaratory judgment

Complaint seeking declaratory judgment as to title to copyrights did not allege infringement and consequent damages, but this did not waive right to demand damages, in addition to declaratory and injunctive relief, upon declaration that plaintiff has title to copyrights; also, complaint asked for such further relief as may be necessary or proper. Edward B. Marks Music Corp. v Charles K. Harris Music Publishing Co. (1958, CA2 NY) 255 F2d 518, 117 USPQ 308, cert den 358 US 831, 3 L Ed 2d 69, 79 S Ct 51.

Declaratory judgment action relative to copyright infringement is dismissed where evidence shows defendant does not threaten plaintiff with copyright infringement, has retracted and apologized, and has brought action on other grounds in state court. Mailer v Zolotow (1974, DC NY) 380 F Supp 894, 184 USPQ 20.

Under federal Declaratory Judgment Act [28 USCS §§ 2201, 2202], one need not wait until he has actually been charged with infringement before beginning action. Broadcast Music, Inc. v Taylor (1945) 10 Misc 2d 9, 55 NYS2d 94, 65 USPQ 503.

G. Appeal

133. Generally

Admission of copyrighted photograph in evidence, though it is irrelevant testimony, is not error, where it does not operate to prejudice defendant. Springer Lithographing Co. v Falk (1894, CA2 NY) 59 F 707.

Where invalidity of copyright was not raised in lower court, and ownership was admitted by stipulation, it was too late to raise questions on appeal. Johns & Johns Printing Co. v Paull-Pioneer Music Corp. (1939, CA8 Mo) 102 F2d 282, 41 USPQ 3.

On appeal from interlocutory decree taken after thirty days, Court of Appeals held that plaintiff was not author of copyrighted song; Supreme Court on certiorari held that appeal was too late and reversed with directions to dismiss appeal; accounting was concluded and final decree entered by plaintiff; on appeal therefrom, Court of Appeals adhered to its previous opinion. Victor Talking Mach. Co. v George (1939, CA3 NJ) 105 F2d 697, 42 USPQ 346, cert den 308 US 611, 84 L Ed 511, 60 S Ct 176, reh den 308 US 638, 84 L Ed 530, 60 S Ct 294 and reh den 309 US 693, 84 L Ed 1034, 60 S Ct 466.

Final determinations of separate controversies involved in single suit are separately appealable, such as where claims for infringement of separate patents were asserted in single suit. Collins v Metro-Goldwyn Pictures Corp. (1939, CA2 NY) 106 F2d 83, 42 USPQ 553.

Court of Appeals is asked to disregard finding of noninfringement of copyright because, from what District Judge said at trial, he seems to have supposed that anticipation invalidates copyright; court is not sure that he meant this but, if he did, cannot assume that he did not intend to make finding on which court relies; if plaintiff had wished to rid himself of that handicap, he should have done so before he appealed; while it stands, it is fatal to his success. Darrell v Joe Morris Music Co. (1940, CA2 NY) 113 F2d 80, 46 USPQ 167.

On prior appeal from dismissal of bill for failure to state facts sufficient to constitute cause of action, court of appeals reversed and remanded for further proceedings; case was tried before district court which found no infringement of plaintiff's common-law copyright; issue of infringement was not before court of appeals on first appeal and was not then decided; issue was before district court at trial of case and court of appeals affirmed since issue was properly decided. Dezendorf v Twentieth Century Fox Film Corp. (1941, CA9 Cal) 118 F2d 561, 49 USPQ 133.

Where plaintiff failed to prove access either directly or indirectly, court of appeals will not disturb judgment based on failure to prove copyright infringement. Sarkadi v Wiman (1943, CA2 NY) 135 F2d 1002, 57 USPQ 361.

Appellant's brief did not discuss ownership of 1914 renewal copyright, so appellate court did not discuss it; discussion is refused on motion to clarify opinion, but it does not follow that district court's ruling thereon was left undisturbed and must be incorporated in judgment on mandate; appellate court reversed and remanded "for entry of a judgment consistent with this opinion"; this permits district judge to enter any judgment which he thinks consistent with opinion; he may consider whether principles enunciated with respect to 1912 renewal copyright are applicable to 1914 version. Shapiro, Bernstein &

Co. v Jerry Vogel Music Co. (1946, CA2 NY) 161 F2d 406, 73 USPQ 5, cert den 331 US 820, 91 L Ed 1837, 67 S Ct 1310.

In copyright infringement and unfair competition action against motion-picture producer, its president, and motion-picture distributor, complaint alleges that producer produced and distributor distributed motion picture which infringes plaintiffs' uncopyrighted story and copyrighted book; since complaint sets forth combined action by defendants to bring picture to public, plaintiffs have only single claim, not to be broken into separate parts for purpose of immediate appeal as to one such part only; hence, where president was personally served and distributor does not challenge that it was doing business in district, order quashing service on producer is not immediately appealable; appeal is dismissed. Gauvreau v United States Pictures, Inc. (1959, CA2 NY) 267 F2d 861, 121 USPQ 541.

Test of copyright infringement is of necessity vague; that this is true is more reason why court of appeals cannot say that trial court erred, as matter of law, finding no infringement. Caddy-Imler Creations, Inc. v Caddy (1962, CA9 Cal) 299 F2d 79, 132 USPQ 384.

It is of little moment in copyright infringement action whether court should first determine originality of copyrighted work or its appropriation by defendant since, for purposes of appellate review, it is desirable that both questions be considered. Tralins v Kaiser Aluminum & Chemical Corp. (1958, DC Md) 160 F Supp 511, 117 USPQ 79.

134. Appeal of fact determinations

Findings of trial judge may have somewhat less significance than that of jury or that of some administrative agencies, and trial judge's finding may be clearly erroneous, although apparently supported by oral testimony, where testimony is in conflict with contemporaneous documents of such character that it would be unreasonable to believe witnesses. United States v United States Gypsum Co. (1948) 333 US 364, 92 L Ed 746, 68 S Ct 525, 76 USPQ 430, reh den 333 US 869, 92 L Ed 1147, 68 S Ct 788.

Judgment that licensee's publication of copyrighted pictures was within license should be affirmed if evidence supports finding. Swift v Collegian Press, Inc. (1942, CA2 NY) 131 F2d 900, 55 USPQ 472.

Appellate court must consider that trial judge was in more advantageous position to determine credibility of witnesses and that he had better position to weigh effect of evidence that defendant's agent saw plaintiff's play. Twentieth Century-Fox Film Corp. v Stonesifer (1944, CA9 Cal) 140 F2d 579, 60 USPQ 392.

Although interlocutory judgment for plaintiff was granted before copyright was held unoriginal and anticipated in suit against another defendant, appellate court could not retry case on different basis than it was tried in trial court. Colonial Book Co. v Amsco School Publications, Inc. (1944, CA2 NY) 142 F2d 362, 61 USPQ 391.

Rule that fact finding may be set aside only when clearly erroneous is as applicable to action for copyright infringement as to any other action. Sawyer v Crowell Publishing Co. (1944, CA2 NY) 142 F2d 497, 61 USPQ 389, cert den 323 US 735, 89 L Ed 589, 65 S Ct 74.

Nothing short of conviction that finding that composer created song at specific time was clearly erroneous will suffice for reversal of finding. Baron v Leo Feist, Inc. (1949, CA2 NY) 173 F2d 288, 80 USPQ 535.

District judge is not obliged to accept as true oral testimony of witness as to performance of copyrighted music which is uncontradicted, unimpeached by anything in record, and not inherently improbable; findings rejecting testimony are not clearly erroneous; judge's estimate of orally-testifying witness may stem from judge's application of absurd rule-of-thumb, but appellate court cannot correct error unless judge reveals of record that he used irrational test of credibility. Broadcast Music, Inc. v Havana Madrid Restaurant Corp. (1949, CA2 NY) 175 F2d 77, 81 USPQ 506.

Plaintiff having given evidence of access and similarity which court credited over contrary evidence, presumption of copying could reasonably be inferred; despite fact that burden of proving plagiarism remains at all times on plaintiff, defendant then had duty to go forward by offering evidence of prior composition, which, if believed, would make finding of copying untenable; trial court weighed such evidence and concluded that defendant's work was composed prior to plaintiff's; since finding involved credibility of witnesses, and since it is supported by substantial evidence, it is conclusive on appeal. Overman v Loesser (1953, CA9 Cal) 205 F2d 521, 98 USPQ 177, cert den 346 US 910, 98 L Ed 407, 74 S Ct 241.

Since issues of copying and improper appropriation of copyright song are issues of fact, and

since findings thereon are not clearly erroneous, findings cannot be disturbed by court of appeals. Cholvin v B. & F. Music Co. (1958, CA7 Ill) 253 F2d 102, 116 USPQ 491.

When district court's determination of infringement hinges upon such purely factual question as to whether defendant had access to plaintiff's copyrighted materials and whether physical acts of copying or selling actually occurred, scope of review on appeal is limited to determining if district court's conclusions are clearly erroneous, but appellate court's power of review need not be so constrained where facts are undisputed and issue of infringement depends merely upon legal conclusion to be drawn from a consideration of parties' relationship. Shapiro, Bernstein & Co. v H. L. Green Co. (1963, CA2 NY) 316 F2d 304, 137 USPQ 275.

Lack of specific finding of substantial similarities supporting infringement decision would ordinarily require remand, but since no question of credibility is involved, and Court of Appeals can compare wall charts for exercise machines at issue, court reviews matter and finds sufficient dissimilarity to vacate infringement judgment. Universal Athletic Sales Co. v Salkeld (1975, CA3 Pa) 511 F2d 904, 185 USPQ 76, cert den 423 US 863, 46 L Ed 2d 92, 96 S Ct 122.

Trial court's finding of similarities between copyrighted book and magazine article is reversed by appellate court because determination rests solely on comparison of works rather than on credibility of witnesses or other evidence. Reyher v Children's Television Workshop (1976, CA2 NY) 533 F2d 87, 190 USPQ 387, cert den 429 US 980, 50 L Ed 2d 588, 97 S Ct 492.

On appeal from judgment entered on jury's verdict for plaintiffs in plagiarism case, mere existence of two dramatic works in record does not, per se, constitute sufficient evidence of similarity; it is necessary for appellate court to read or view works to see if they present any substantial similarity insofar as plaintiff's property in his work is concerned; this is not to say that court substitutes itself for jury to decide what it thinks of issue of similarity, but it is merely question of determining if there is any substantial evidence of similarity to support jury's finding. Golding v R. K. O. Pictures, Inc. (1949, Cal) 208 P2d 1, 82 USPQ 136, subsequent op on reh 35 Cal 2d 690, 221 P2d 95, 86 USPQ 537.

§ 502. Remedies for infringement: Injunctions

(a) Any court having jurisdiction of a civil action arising under this title [17 USCS §§ 101 et seq.] may, subject to the provisions of section 1498 of

315

title 28 [28 USCS § 1498], grant temporary and final injunctions on such terms as it may deem reasonable to prevent or restrain infringement of a copyright.

(b) Any such injunction may be served anywhere in the United States on the person enjoined; it shall be operative throughout the United States and shall be enforceable, by proceedings in contempt or otherwise, by any United States court having jurisdiction of that person. The clerk of the court granting the injunction shall, when requested by any other court in which enforcement of the injunction is sought, transmit promptly to the other court a certified copy of all the papers in the case on file in such clerk's office.
(Added Oct. 19, 1976, P. L. 94-553, Title I, § 101, 90 Stat. 2584.)

HISTORY; ANCILLARY LAWS AND DIRECTIVES

Effective date of section:
Section 102 of Act Oct. 19, 1976, P. L. 94-553, 90 Stat. 2598 provided that this section "becomes effective on January 1, 1978".

CROSS REFERENCES

Infringement actions against United States, 28 USCS § 1498.
This section referred to in 17 USCS §§ 111, 115, 116, 411, 510.

RESEARCH GUIDE

Am Jur:
18 Am Jur 2d, Copyright and Literary Property §§ 134, 144, 147.

Forms:
6 Federal Procedural Forms L Ed, Copyrights §§ 17:51, 17:52, 17:69, 17:70.

INTERPRETIVE NOTES AND DECISIONS

I. IN GENERAL (notes 1–2)
II. RIGHTS PROTECTABLE BY IN-JUNCTION (notes 3–9)
III. EQUITIES RELEVANT TO INJUNC-TIONS (notes 10–14)
IV. TEMPORARY OR PRELIMINARY INJUNCTIONS (notes 15–22)
V. PRACTICE AND PROCEDURE (notes 23–32)

5. Derivative works (as specified in 17 USCS § 106(2))
6. Distribution of copies (as specified in 17 USCS § 106(3))
7. Performance or display, generally (as specified in 17 USCS § 106(4,5))
8. —Musical works
9. Importation (as specified in 17 USCS § 602)

I. IN GENERAL

1. Generally
2. Jurisdictional matters

II. RIGHTS PROTECTABLE BY INJUNCTION

3. Generally
4. Copying (as specified in 17 USCS § 106(1))

III. EQUITIES RELEVANT TO INJUNCTIONS

10. Generally
11. Persons enjoinable
12. Persons entitled to injunction
13. Threat of future infringement
14. Unclean hands; violation of law

I. IN GENERAL

1. Generally

Forfeitures and penalties may not be recovered in suit for injunction for infringement of copyright. Stevens v Gladding (1855) 58 US 447, 15 L Ed 155.

Author is enjoined from asserting claim that insurance forms, copyright on which has been forfeited, are copyrighted; however, since, in general, insurance forms are copyrightable, injunction extends no further than to forms on which copyright has been forfeited. Continental Casualty Co. v Beardsley (1958, CA2 NY) 253 F2d 702, 117 USPQ 1, cert den 358 US 816, 3 L Ed 2d 58, 79 S Ct 25.

Fact that qui tam action for penalty allowed by law was pending did not affect right to injunction against infringement of copyright. Schumacher v Schwencke (1885, CC NY) 25 F 466.

Suit cannot be maintained to secure injunction to prevent printing of opinions of judges, since they are not subjects of copyright. Banks & Bros. v West Pub. Co. (1886, CC Minn) 27 F 50.

Injunction will not issue to protect system of stenography which is described in copyrighted book, since copyright does not cover system. Griggs v Perrin (1892, CC NY) 49 F 15.

Where infringement has been established appropriate relief is by injunction and accounting for profits. Fishel v Lueckel (1892, CC NY) 53 F 499.

Complainant cannot maintain suit for injunc-

tion when statutory provisions for form of copyright notice have not been complied with. Louis De Jonge & Co. v Breuker & Kessler Co. (1910, CC Pa) 182 F 150, affd (CA3 Pa) 191 F 35, affd 235 US 33, 59 L Ed 113, 35 S Ct 6.

Violation of copyright is tort and is analogous to trespass on real estate, for injunctive purposes. Metro-Goldwyn-Mayer Distributing Corp. v Fisher (1935, DC Md) 10 F Supp 745, 25 USPQ 341.

Owner of copyright of picture who omitted his name from all copies thereof was not entitled to restrain infringer. Goes Lithographing Co. v Apt Lithographic Co. (1936, DC NY) 14 F Supp 620, 30 USPQ 119.

In connection with advertising of its products, plaintiff produces puzzle contests; copyrighted entry blank for contests states that entries will be disqualified for outside, professional, or compensated help; defendant, expert in puzzle contests, distributes to those paying him fee his solution to puzzle together with material copied from copyrighted blank; defendant is preliminarily enjoined from continuing such unethical and unlawful conduct; selling answers to puzzle contest is unlawful interference with plaintiff's business and copyright and induces spurious and fraudulent performances by prospective contestants. Proctor & Gamble Co. v Moskowitz (DC NY) 127 USPQ 523.

2. Jurisdictional matters

Predecessor section does not create any new cause of action, but relates only to jurisdiction and procedure to protect rights secured by the copyright laws. Goldwin Pictures Corp. v Howells Sales Co. (1922, CA2 NY) 282 F 9.

Claim that several infringements of copyrights are joined in bill for injunctive relief, in order to prevent multiplicity of suits, and inclusion in bill of prayer for discovery, under facts of case, did not justify retention of bill to assess damages after denial of injunctive relief. Hutchinson Amusement Co. v Vitaphone Corp. (1937, CA1 Mass) 93 F2d 176, 36 USPQ 1.

Where copyright has terminated by abandonment at time suit is brought, and only relief sought is injunction, bill must be dismissed. Atlantic Monthly Co. v Post Pub. Co. (1928, DC Mass) 27 F2d 556.

II. RIGHTS PROTECTABLE BY INJUNCTION

3. Generally

Injunction may be granted to prevent infringement of motion-picture film where notice of copyright was placed on one end. Edison v

Lubin (1903, CA3 Pa) 122 F 240, app dismd 195 US 624, 49 L Ed 349, 25 S Ct 790.

Federal court has no authority to enjoin publication of uncopyrighted work. Bentley v Tibbals (1915, CA2 NY) 223 F 247.

Common-law copyright of author in his manuscripts is entitled to protection by injunction. Bartlett v Crittenden (1849, CC Ohio) F Cas No 1076.

Injunction will be granted to protect only such publications as are already in existence. Centennial Catalogue Co. v Porter (1876, CC Pa) F Cas No 2546.

Injunction denied where facts showed no infringement and defendant agreed to discontinue his acts of unfair competition; where defendant's opera does not infringe upon copyright, no injunction can be had against him unless he advertises so as to mislead public that his opera is that of complainants. The Iolanthe Case (1883, CC Md) 15 F 439.

Motion for injunction was denied where defendant did not appropriate any copyrighted articles, and his actions did not evince unfair competition. Black v Ehrich (1891, CC NY) 44 F 793.

While anyone may reprint dictionary after copyright expires, anyone so doing will be restrained from advertising such reprint in manner to lead public to believe that it is new edition of plaintiff's dictionary which is copyrighted. Merriam v Texas Siftings Pub. Co. (1892, CC NY) 49 F 944.

Protection by injunction is not afforded under the copyright laws to title, separate from book. Corbett v Purdy (1897, CC NY) 80 F 901.

Owner of motion-picture rights in play popular under particular name was allowed injunction against use of colorable imitation of name for competing play. National Picture Theatres, Inc. v Foundation Film Corp. (1920, CA2 NY) 266 F 208.

Owner of copyright on label for shoe boxes may enjoin defendant from using such labels on his boxes, pending trial of issues. Hoague-Sprague Corp. v Frank C. Meyer Co. (1928, DC NY) 27 F2d 176.

To allow others to benefit financially by artist's work and skill would be unfair trade practice and equity will enjoin such effort. Waring v Dunlea (1939, DC NC) 26 F Supp 338, 41 USPQ 201.

Author's failure to seek to enjoin filming of motion picture does not bar him from maintaining plagiarism action after production of picture since producer had informed him that author's script was not being used in picture and that producer could not pay author for writing of script unless picture were produced. Szekely v Eagle Lion Films, Inc. (1956, DC NY) 140 F Supp 843, 109 USPQ 348, affd (CA2 NY) 242 F2d 266, 113 USPQ 98, cert den 354 US 922, 1 L Ed 2d 1437, 77 S Ct 1382.

Where book title has secondary meaning, owner can enjoin another threatening to use or using it as title for motion picture. Johnston v Twentieth Century-Fox Film Corp. (1947) 82 Cal App 2d 796, 187 P2d 474, 76 USPQ 131.

Where complainant is assignee of copyrighted play under contract with defendant which requires him to produce play specified number of times within year, he may enjoin defendant from assigning right to another, so long as there is still time in which to produce it required number of times. Widmer v Greene (NY) 56 How Pr 91.

Title of uncopyrighted play will be protected, and its use on another play will be restrained when such use will confuse, although another play may have been copyrighted by that title. Dickey v Mutual Film Corp. (1916, Sup) 160 NYS 609, mod on other grounds 186 App Div 701, 174 NYS 784.

Injunction may issue to prevent use of title of copyrighted play by another. Shook v Wood (Pa) 10 Phila 373.

4. Copying (as specified in 17 USCS § 106(1))

Injunction should be granted to restrain printing of copyrighted map by one who purchased copperplate engraving of map at sheriff's sale. Stephens v Cady (1853) 55 US 528, 14 L Ed 528.

Though plaintiff may not, in law, have any ground for complaint because state officers have manuscript in their possession, he may nevertheless invoke aid of court of equity to restrain defendants from printing or publishing such manuscript, if printing or publication thereof would infringe his rights under copyright laws. Howell v Miller (1898, CA6 Mich) 91 F 129.

Where there is proof that considerable number of errors common to both defendant's and complainant's book of citations, occurred first in complainant's book, prima facie case of copying is made, and unless defendant satisfactorily explains such errors, his publication will be enjoined. Frank Shepard Co. v Zachary P. Taylor Pub. Co. (1912, CA2 NY) 193 F 991.

One who so embodies copyrighted with uncopyrighted matter that one reading his work cannot distinguish between two may not have injunction to restrain others from republishing his works. Bentley v Tibbals (1915, CA2 NY) 223 F 247.

Failure of copyright proprietor to deposit two copies of second volume will be important only on issue of damages, if then; defendants' edition being in one volume must be enjoined in any event. Houghton Mifflin Co. v Stackpole Sons, Inc. (1940, CA2 NY) 113 F2d 627, 46 USPQ 296.

Retracing, reproducing, and multiplying material portions of copyrighted map constituted infringement warranting issuance of injunction. Sanborn Map & Pub. Co. v Dakin Pub. Co. (1889, CC Cal) 39 F 266.

Although work is uncopyrighted defendant will be enjoined from publishing lectures of complainant when defendant's publication does not present them fully or correctly. Drummond v Altemus (1894, CC Pa) 60 F 338.

Where post cards are not copyrighted, another person cannot be restrained from copying them. Bamforth v Douglass Post Card & Mach. Co. (1908, CC Pa) 158 F 355.

Evidence and instances of copying was too insignificant in amount to demand injunction against defendant's books; right given to author to multiply copies of his work, and to prevent appropriation of his work by other persons, includes right to injunction where such is appropriate and accessory remedy. West Publishing Co. v Edward Thompson Co. (1909, CC NY) 169 F 833, mod on other grounds (CA2 NY) 176 F 833.

Injunction prohibiting further infringement and order for inspection of customer records results from copyright infringement by copying and using portions of mail order tool catalog. Bliss & Laughlin Industries, Inc. v Starvaggi (1975, DC NY) 188 USPQ 89.

Preliminary injunction is made permanent as to entire infringing book, because in addition to 11 percent admitted plagiarism, organizational pattern of entire book shows substantial additional copying and relatively little independent research. Meredith Corp. v Harper & Row, Publishers, Inc. (1975, DC NY) 192 USPQ 92.

Defendant will not be enjoined from manufacturing and selling for his own benefit, volumes of reports of state supreme court, containing matter prepared by state, when such matter was not protected by copyright, although defendant unlawfully used manuscripts intrusted to him by the state. State v State Journal Co. (1905) 75 Neb 275, 106 NW 434, motion den 77 Neb 752, 110 NW 763, application den 77 Neb 771, 111 NW 118.

5. Derivative works (as specified in 17 USCS § 106(2))

Where motion-picture company filmed novel after negotiating only with author when it had notice publisher had exclusive license in motion-picture rights of novel, publisher was entitled to injunction restraining picture irrespective of large investment of picture company therein. L. C. Page & Co. v Fox Film Corp. (1936, CA2 NY) 83 F2d 196, 29 USPQ 386.

TV dramatization of copyrighted script was limited by copyright license from proprietors of script, so that deleterious editing of dramatization for insertion of commercials and broadcast on TV comes outside scope of license and infringes copyright of authors to justify injunction of further broadcasts. Gilliam v American Broadcasting Co. (1976, CA2) 192 USPQ 1.

Contract provided for author to write motion-picture script, title to be vested in author until payment of specified sum; he had common-law literary property in script until payment of such sum; author not having received sum and not having consented to utilization of script for production of motion picture, use of his literary ideas in picture constituted deprivation of literary property for which he is entitled to issuance of injunction and award of damages. Szekely v Eagle Lion Films, Inc. (1956, DC NY) 140 F Supp 843, 109 USPQ 348, affd (CA2 NY) 242 F2d 266, 113 USPQ 98, cert den 354 US 922, 1 L Ed 2d 1437, 77 S Ct 1382.

Since copyrights in rock opera "Jesus Christ Superstar" are valid and although based on material in public domain, work includes original music and lyrics and is not pirated from previous book "The Passover Plot", defendants will be permanently enjoined from threatened making of movie production of "Jesus Christ Superstar". Leeds Music, Ltd. v Robin (DC Ohio) 358 F Supp 650, 36 Ohio Misc 1, 65 Ohio Ops 2d 20, 179 USPQ 413.

Evidence of title of a play was sufficient to enable plaintiff to maintain a suit to enjoin defendant from exhibiting and distributing a motion picture based on plaintiff's play. O'Neill v General Film Co. (1916) 171 App Div 854, 157 NYS 1028.

6. Distribution of copies (as specified in 17 USCS § 106(3))

Defendant cannot be restrained from selling copyrighted books below certain price when he purchased full title to books, although they contained notice that sale at different price would be treated as infringement. Bobbs-Merrill Co. v Straus (1908) 210 US 339, 52 L Ed 1086, 28 S Ct 722.

Although plaintiffs placed legend ("this periodical may not be sold except by authorized dealers and . . . shall not be sold or distributed with any part of its cover or markings removed . . .") on copyrighted comics, this does not, ipso facto, entitle them to injunction against resale of coverless comics; they have burden of showing that all facts (including presence of legend) rightly call for injunctive relief; enforcement of legend is denied where totality of facts does not provide proper foundation for issuance of injunction; moreover, under Copyright Act, legend is unenforcible since there is no privity of contract between parties. Independent News Co. v Williams (1961, CA3 Pa) 293 F2d 510, 129 USPQ 377.

Book dealer may be enjoined from selling copyrighted book, in action brought by author, when author sold only through agents and then only on subscription. Henry Bill Pub. Co. v Smythe (1886, CC Ohio) 27 F 914.

Owner of copyright may not restrain, by virtue of copyright laws, sale of copy of copyrighted book, title to which he has transferred, but which is being sold in violation of agreement; where owner of copyright has transferred title to copy of copyrighted work, to another, he cannot restrain, as infringement of his copyright, work from being sold in violation of agreement; his only remedy is for breach of contract. Harrison v Maynard, M. & Co. (1894, CA2 NY) 61 F 689.

Where copyrighted manuscripts are printed without authority, such publication may be enjoined. Bartlett v Crittenden (1849, CC Ohio) F Cas No 1076.

It is no defense in suit to restrain publication of a book that book had already been printed. Bunkley v De Witt (1855, CC NY) F Cas No 2134.

Where copyrighted books were sold by agent to book dealer contrary to instructions of copyright owner and contrary to known method by which plaintiff sold his books, such dealer will be enjoined from selling copies in his possession. Henry Bill Pub. Co. v Smythe (1886, CC Ohio) 27 F 914.

Where encyclopedia is reprinted, with exception of certain copyrighted articles, which were substituted by others, defendants cannot be enjoined from publishing such work when they do not make misleading statements as to publication of work. Black v Ehrich (1891, CC NY) 44 F 793.

Since defendant deliberately copied plaintiffs' copyrighted design and since copyright notice was adequate, plaintiffs are entitled to permanent injunction regardless of alleged lack of knowledge of copyright by defendant at time of initial infringement; after actual notice and after service of complaint, defendant must discontinue selling infringing copy regardless of its claim of innocence at inception. Peter Pan Fabrics, Inc. v Dixon Textile Corp. (1960, DC NY) 188 F Supp 235, 127 USPQ 329.

7. Performance or display, generally (as specified in 17 USCS § 106(4, 5))

Although uncopyrighted play is performed publicly, defendant will be restrained from producing such play when he obtained knowledge of play through unpublished manuscript and not through such public presentation. Keene v Wheatley (1861, CC Pa) F Cas No 7644.

Where unprinted drama is produced, person in audience may be restrained from reproducing drama from memory, although drama was not copyrighted. Crowe v Aiken (1870, CC Ill) F Cas No 3441; Tompkins v Halleck (1882) 133 Mass 32.

Owner of uncopyrighted opera may restrain another from producing opera without his permission. Goldmark v Kreling (1885, CC Cal) 25 F 349.

Performance of operetta "Nanon" similar to play of same title to which exclusive American rights had been purchased by plaintiffs before its publication in Europe was enjoined. Goldmark v Kreling (1888, CC Cal) 35 F 661.

Actor is not entitled to injunction against motion-picture producer licensing copyrighted motion-picture films, in which actor starred under expired contracts, for exhibition on television in connection with sponsored advertising. Autry v Republic Productions, Inc. (1952, DC Cal) 104 F Supp 918, 93 USPQ 284, mod on other grounds (CA9 Cal) 213 F2d 667, 101 USPQ 478, cert den 348 US 858, 99 L Ed 676, 75 S Ct 83.

Contract between author and motion-picture producer provided that title to author's motion-picture script should be vested in author until payment of specified sum; sum was not paid, but picture using script was produced and distributed; although author is awarded damages for plagiarism against distributor equal to specified sum, distributor also is enjoined from further distribution of picture. Szekely v Eagle Lion Films, Inc. (1956, DC NY) 140 F Supp 843, 109 USPQ 348, affd (CA2 NY) 242 F2d 266, 113 USPQ 98, cert den 354 US 922, 1 L Ed 2d 1437, 77 S Ct 1382.

In action to enjoin exhibition or distribution of motion picture, evidence was sufficient to warrant that defendants had used plaintiff's dramatization in making such motion picture. O'Neill v General Film Co. (1916) 171 App Div 854, 157 NYS 1028.

8. —Musical works

Legend on records prohibiting use except on phonographs at home is valid in Pennsylvania but invalid under copyright law and New York federal court will not enjoin radio broadcasting of records reception of which will be had in

Pennsylvania since to do so broadcaster would have to be enjoined from broadcasting throughout United States and Canada. RCA Mfg. Co. v Whiteman (1940, CA2 NY) 114 F2d 86, 46 USPQ 324, cert den 311 US 712, 85 L Ed 463, 61 S Ct 393 and cert den 311 US 712, 85 L Ed 463, 61 S Ct 394.

Use on another program without permission of electrical transcription bearing notice that use was limited to radio station for definite program was enjoined. Waring v Dunlea (1939, DC NC) 26 F Supp 338, 41 USPQ 201.

Plaintiff is entitled to injunction, damages, costs, and reasonable attorney's fee for infringement of copyrighted music by playing at place of entertainment. Shapiro, Bernstein & Co. v Mitchell (DC Miss) 41 USPQ 646.

Hotel and club having infringed copyrighted musical compositions by their performance in club, which is facility of hotel, hotel and club are not only enjoined from publicly performing compositions in club, but are enjoined from such performance in any place owned, controlled, or conducted by them and are enjoined from aiding or abetting such performance in any such place or otherwise. Porter v Marriott Motor Hotels, Inc. (DC Tex) 137 USPQ 473.

Injunction should restrain further performance of defendants' musical play, at least as long as it remains substantially in its present form, which infringes plaintiffs' copyrighted musical play; injunction should not extend to independent rendition of music or lyrics of defendants' play or preclude their being performed or used other than integral part of defendants' play. Breffort v I Had A Ball Co. (1967, DC NY) 271 F Supp 623, 155 USPQ 391.

Plaintiff played music composed by another for recording and records as sold were marked "Not licensed for Radio Broadcast"; title to physical substance and right to use of literary or artistic property printed upon or embodied in it are distinct and independent of each other; use on radio by one who purchased record and got license from owner of copyright on music was enjoined. Waring v WDAS Broadcasting Station, Inc. (1937) 327 Pa 433, 194 A 631, 35 USPQ 272.

9. Importation (as specified in 17 USCS § 602)

Fact that defendant's unlawful importation of foreign-printed books did not effect injury to defendant, was not defense to plaintiff's suit to enjoin infringement of copyright. Bentley v Tibbals (1915, CA2 NY) 223 F 247.

Plastic version of Uncle Sam mechanical bank copying public domain bank but changing proportions slightly for plastic fabrication is "merely trivial variation" and does not evidence artistic skill contributing to work so that motion for preliminary injunction is granted to compel copyright proprietor to cancel recordation of copyright with United States Customs Service, thereby allowing entry of competing product into country. L. Batlin & Son, Inc. v Snyder (1975, DC NY) 394 F Supp 1389, 187 USPQ 91, affd (CA2 NY) 536 F2d 486, cert den 429 US 857, 50 L Ed 2d 135, 97 S Ct 156.

III. EQUITIES RELEVANT TO INJUNCTIONS

10. Generally

Where infringement is slight and result of imposition of injunction would be inequitable, copyright owner will be remitted to his remedy at law. Dun v Lumbermen's Credit Asso. (1908) 209 US 20, 52 L Ed 663, 28 S Ct 335.

One who innocently reproduces work from which copyright notice has been removed may be enjoined. Falk v Gast Lithograph & Engraving Co. (1893, CA2 NY) 54 F 890.

Injunction is denied where proportion of work taken is insignificant compared to injury resulting from stopping use of large volume of independently acquired information. Mathews Conveyer Co. v Palmer-Bee Co. (1943, CA6 Mich) 135 F2d 73, 57 USPQ 219.

Where infringement is patent, and injunction will not result in any serious injury, such order is not usually refused as to so much of work as is plain infringement of prior publication. Banks v McDivitt (1875, CC NY) F Cas No 961.

Where there is doubt upon question of defendant's infringement, injunction will be denied. Blunt v Patten (1828, CC NY) F Cas No 1580.

Injunction will issue, though only part of subsequent work infringes original. Emerson v Davies (1845, CC Mass) F Cas No 4436.

To obtain injunction for infringement of copyright it is not necessary that whole or even large part of copyrighted work be infringed. Greene v Bishop (1858, CC Mass) F Cas No 5763.

Injunction will not be granted in copyright cases where infringement is slight, if there is no proof of bad motive, or where title to copyright is in doubt, or where there has been long acquiescence in infringement, or laches or negligence in seeking redress, especially if it appear that delay has misled defendant. Lawrence v Dana (1869, CC Mass) F Cas No 8136.

Injunction will be refused if there is reasonable doubt as to plaintiff's right, or validity of his copyright. Miller v McElroy (1839, CC Pa) F Cas No 9581.

If it does not satisfactorily appear that what defendant has done is, or what he intends to do will be, infringement of copyright, injunction will be denied. Smith v Johnson (1859, CC NY) F Cas No 13066.

Intent of infringer may have material bearing upon complainants' right to injunction. Webb v Powers (1847, CC Mass) F Cas No 17323.

Where defendant eliminated from his publication copied list and revised book so that no plagiarism was shown, and delivered up to court copied sheets and master cards for destruction, there was no reason for injunction; plaintiff was not entitled to injunctive relief where proportion of infringing items in defendant's rating list to items of original work by defendant was very small. Cravens v Retail Credit Men's Asso. (1924, DC Tenn) 26 F2d 833.

Destruction of infringing plates of copyrighted photograph did not bar injunctive relief. Cory v Physical Culture Hotel, Inc. (1936, DC NY) 14 F Supp 977, 30 USPQ 353, affd (CA2 NY) 88 F2d 411, 33 USPQ 58.

If injunction should not be granted it matters not that reason for refusing issuance is based partly on facts occurring after suit began. Basevi v Edward O'Toole Co. (1939, DC NY) 26 F Supp 41, 40 USPQ 333.

Injunction was refused after only one infringing sale. Larsen v Goldblatt Bros., Inc. (DC Ill) 53 USPQ 287.

Where defendants were on notice, which they ignored, that unauthorized use of any portions of illustrations in plaintiff's catalog would subject them to prosecution and where, despite willful infringement, plaintiff suffered no immediate financial loss, defendants were subject to (1) injunction restraining infringement, (2) deliver up for destruction all infringing catalogs together with all plates, molds, matrices, or other means for making infringing catalogs, and (3) pay to plaintiff, as damages, one dollar for each catalog distributed. Amplex Mfg. Co. v A. B. C. Plastic Fabricators, Inc. (1960, DC Pa) 184 F Supp 285, 125 USPQ 648.

Where injunctive relief is sought against copyright infringement, copier from copier is in no better position than one who copies directly from author; if, however, action were one for damages, result might be different. Perkins Marine Lamp & Hardware Corp. v Long Island Marine Supply Corp. (1960, DC NY) 185 F Supp 353, 126 USPQ 169.

In action for injunctive relief based on copyright infringement, lack of intent is not defense although it may bar award of damages. Massapequa Publishing Co. v Observer, Inc. (DC NY) 126 USPQ 229.

11. Persons enjoinable

Proprietor of copyright may be granted injunctive relief against defendant for infringement,

though such relief will interfere with performance of duties imposed upon defendant by state. Howell v Miller (1898, CA6 Mich) 91 F 129.

Bill for injunction will be dismissed when defendant is officer of corporation which is alleged to have infringed complainant's work and such corporation is not made party defendant. Stuart v Smith (1895, CC NY) 68 F 189.

Individual defendants who organized corporation and controlled and directed its activities while infringing acts were committed can be held liable to injunction and damages and may be joined as defendants with corporation. National Geographic Soc. v Classified Geographic, Inc. (1939, DC Mass) 27 F Supp 655, 41 USPQ 719.

Where defendants, employees of United States, reproduced copyrighted map for use of United States but reproductions were never used, no injunction is necessary except against reproduction of map by defendants personally or through their cooperation; use by United States of maps which are owned by them must be protected. Towle v Ross (1940, DC Or) 32 F Supp 125, 45 USPQ 143.

Performer who makes phonograph record and causes to be affixed thereto notice of restriction that it is not licensed for commercial radio broadcast may restrain its use by radio station but this restraint cannot be extended to advertiser who has and exerts no control over conduct of broadcasts during or between which advertising announcements, with no relation to broadcast entertainment, are read. National Asso. of Performing Artists v Wm. Penn Broadcasting Co. (1941, DC Pa) 38 F Supp 531, 49 USPQ 563.

Where copyright is renewed by heirs of one coauthor, license by surviving coauthor gives licensee sufficient equitable interest in composition to bar injunction against it. Edward B. Marks Music Corp. v Jerry Vogel Music Co. (1942, DC NY) 47 F Supp 490, 55 USPQ 288, 55 USPQ 489, affd (CA2 NY) 140 F2d 266, 60 USPQ 257, and mod (CA2 NY) 140 F2d 268, 60 USPQ 256.

Had local retail store infringing copyright continued as independent concern, its mere assurance of good intention might be acceptable in lieu of injunction against infringement which ceased upon notice, but store has become branch of national organization and thus injunction is required. Malsed v Marshall Field & Co. (1951, DC Wash) 96 F Supp 372, 88 USPQ 552.

12. Persons entitled to injunction

Officers of state cannot interpose their official character, or orders of state, in suit for injunction to enjoin infringement.

Injunction is denied to corporation in copyright infringement action where it is instrument of individual, created principally for purpose of suppressing biography of individual. Rosemont Enterprises, Inc. v Random House, Inc. (1966, CA2 NY) 366 F2d 303, 150 USPQ 715, 23 ALR3d 122, cert den 385 US 1009, 17 L Ed 2d 546, 87 S Ct 714.

Where by contract, state gives person right to publish and copyright volumes containing opinions of courts of state, such person may enjoin others from printing such books. Little v Gould (1851, CC NY) F Cas No 8394.

Injunction will not be denied to holder of legal title of copyright because he is merely trustee for benefit of third party who is "author" or "proprietor." Hanson v Jaccard Jewelry Co. (1887, CC Mo) 32 F 202.

Nondomiciled resident Canadian cannot maintain suit for injunction. G. Ricordi & Co. v Columbia Graphophone Co. (1919, DC NY) 256 F 699.

Preliminary injunction for copyright infringement of lace is denied where defendant alleges that plaintiff is nonexclusive licensee and does not have standing to sue unless joined by owner of copyright. Klauber Bros., Inc. v Westchester Lace Work, Inc. (1974, DC NY) 181 USPQ 523.

Where plaintiff had purchased right to produce German play in this country but did not copyright it, he cannot restrain another from producing play in this country when author had published book of play, although such publication was in violation of his contract. Daly v Walrath (1899) 40 App Div 220, 57 NYS 1125.

One co-owner of copyright cannot bring suit to restrain production of play by third person, unless he can prove that such person was not licensed by his co-owner. Herbert v Fields (1915, Sup) 152 NYS 487.

13. Threat of future infringement

Where bill avers that plaintiffs had title to copyright at date of filing, and answer admits averment, and defendant was threatening to infringe copyright, plaintiff is entitled to injunction, although actual infringement has not taken place. Historical Pub. Co. v Jones Bros. Pub. Co. (1916, CA3 Pa) 231 F 638.

In suit for copyright infringement, which apparently was friendly suit instigated and financed by plaintiff and in which defendant said he would not be damaged by injunction, and where infringement had not occurred but it was stated that he threatened to infringe, and where decision against plaintiff in court in another jurisdiction was not brought to attention of court, suit was dismissed for want of equity. Seltzer v Corem (1939, CA7 Ind) 107 F2d 75, 43 USPQ 245.

District court was not required to grant permanent injunction after finding sale infringed, upon further finding that there was no likelihood that appellee would again infringe. Shapiro, Bernstein & Co. v 4636 S. Vermont Ave., Inc. (1966, CA9 Cal) 367 F2d 236, 151 USPQ 231.

Injunction will not issue upon mere threat or intent to print infringing book. Centennial Catalogue Co. v Porter (1876, CC Pa) F Cas No 2546.

Although there has been no infringement or threat of infringement since complainant acquired copyright, any infringement furnished ground for injunction, and fact that infringement has ceased may take away occasion but not right to injunction. Gilmore v Anderson (1889, CC NY) 38 F 846.

Although there does not appear to be any immediate danger of further infringement, injunction may issue as recognition of plaintiff's technical right. M. Witmark & Sons v Calloway (1927, DC Tenn) 22 F2d 412.

Injunction would not issue to restrain copyright infringement where there was little likelihood of repetition, but jurisdiction of court was not divested. Vitaphone Corp. v Hutchinson Amusement Co. (1937, DC Mass) 19 F Supp 359, 33 USPQ 422.

Bill prays for injunction restraining copyright infringement; there is no evidence of threatened continuation of infringement but threat may be inferred from evidence and injunction is granted. Eliot v Geare-Marston, Inc. (1939, DC Pa) 30 F Supp 301, 43 USPQ 249.

Injunction is unnecessary and is denied since copyright infringer has no intention to violate copyright in future. Phillips v Constitution Publishing Co. (DC Ga) 72 USPQ 69.

Copyright proprietor was not enjoined from advising competitor's customers that competitor was infringing copyrights, and he was not liable for damages, where proprietor's conduct occurred prior to institution of suit (which found no infringement of any valid copyright) and before any adjudication of his rights and was based upon belief that he had valid copyright which was being infringed; to enjoin proprietor for past activities would be expression of belief by court that he would probably continue them after adjudication; evidence did not justify such belief; also, competitor was unable to show any actual compensable damage. Davis-Robertson Agency v Duke (1953, DC Va) 119 F Supp 931, 100 USPQ 211.

Despite fact that former licensee has returned unused mats of copyrighted advertisements and several years have elapsed without repetition of infringement, injunction is granted since former licensee continues to assert that he had right to do that which court has said to be infringement. Local Trademarks, Inc. v Grantham (1957, DC Neb) 166 F Supp 494, 117 USPQ 335.

14. Unclean hands; violation of law

Where assignee of copyright fails to put proper notice of copyright upon his publication he cannot maintain suit for injunction, whether against his assignor or any other. Thompson v Hubbard (1889) 131 US 123, 33 L Ed 76, 9 S Ct 710.

Although complainant violated copyright law in importing English editions, such misconduct is unconnected with suit to enjoin infringing publication, and defense of unclean hands because of such importation cannot be applied in suit for injunction. Bentley v Tibbals (1915, CA2 NY) 223 F 247.

There is nothing in fact that injunction is asked to protect copyright which will take case out of general principle of equity that plaintiff must come into court with clean hands; where complainant has wrongfully conducted himself in respect to matter in litigation, he cannot obtain injunction. T. B. Harms & Francis, Day & Hunter v Stern (1916, CA2 NY) 231 F 645.

Fact that defendant violated copyright laws in publishing score card with copyright notice when there was no copyright registration does not entitle rival score card vendor and ball club to relief by injunction; if true it would mean only that defendant is subject to proceedings for violation of copyright statutes. Penn Sportservice, Inc. v Goldstein (1940, DC Pa) 35 F Supp 706, 47 USPQ 210.

Injunction and damages are refused in copyright infringement suit where copyright monopoly has been illegally extended. M. Witmark & Sons v Jensen (1948, DC Minn) 80 F Supp 843, 79 USPQ 6, app dismd (CA8 Minn) 177 F2d 515.

IV. TEMPORARY OR PRELIMINARY INJUNCTIONS

15. Generally

Court is not bound, on trial of copyright infringement action, to find absence of infringement by reason of prior denial of preliminary injunction by another judge; issue on motion for preliminary injunction was not whether there was infringement as matter of law, but whether on evidence before court judge was so convinced that plaintiff would prevail that he should exercise discretion and grant preliminary injunction; decision denying injunction meant only that within judge's appropriate discretion he was not

so convinced. American Visuals Corp. v Holland (1958, CA2 NY) 261 F2d 652, 119 USPQ 482.

Preliminary injunction will not be granted when it is doubtful whether or not there has been infringement. Blunt v Patten (1828, CC NY) F Cas No 1580; Colliery Engineer Co. v United Correspondence Schools Co. (1899, CC NY) 94 F 152; Benton v Van Dyke (1909, CC NY) 170 F 203; Bobbs-Merrill Co. v Equitable Motion Pictures Corp. (1916, DC NY) 232 F 791.

Where court is in doubt whether book of engravings, issued for trade purposes, is intrinsically valuable as work of art, preliminary injunction will not be granted. Lamb v Grand Rapids School Furniture Co. (1889, CC Mich) 39 F 474.

To be entitled to preliminary injunction, a complainant must show affirmatively, beyond any doubt, that he has complied with copyright laws. American Trotting Register Asso. v Gocher (1895, CC Ohio) 70 F 237.

Where from affidavits of parties it is impossible to decide to what extent, if at all, defendant has trespassed upon complainant's copyright rights, motion for preliminary injunction will be denied. Littleton v Fischer (1905, CC NY) 137 F 684.

Complainant's objection to an oral license, under which defendant has proceeded, may not be interposed for first time upon motion for preliminary injunction, as ground for such order. G. Ricordi & Co. v Hammerstein (1907, CC NY) 150 F 450.

On motion for preliminary injunction against copyright infringement, district court regards decision by its court of appeals, in action against another defendant, as dispositive of issue of validity of copyright for purposes of motion. Rushton Co. v F. W. Woolworth Co. (1955, DC NY) 135 F Supp 317, 108 USPQ 80.

Author's failure to apply for preliminary injunction does not bar him from maintaining plagiarism action. Szekely v Eagle Lion Films, Inc. (1956, DC NY) 140 F Supp 843, 109 USPQ 348, affd (CA2 NY) 242 F2d 266, 113 USPQ 98, cert den 354 US 922, 1 L Ed 2d 1437, 77 S Ct 1382.

Preliminary injunction may be granted against innocent copyright infringer. Peter Pan Fabrics, Inc. v Acadia Co. (1959, DC NY) 173 F Supp 292, 121 USPQ 81, affd (CA2 NY) 274 F2d 487, 124 USPQ 154.

For purposes of motion for preliminary injunction, court may resolve issues by reliance on sworn admissions of defendants, undisputed portions of plaintiff's affidavits, and most particularly, visual inspection of infringing articles as compared with plaintiff's goods, where there are no disputed facts requiring hearing to take testimony. Walco Products, Inc. v Kittay & Blitz, Inc. (1972, DC NY) 354 F Supp 121.

Plastic version of Uncle Sam mechanical bank copying public domain bank but changing proportions slightly for plastic fabrication is "merely trivial variation" and does not evidence artistic skill contributing to work so that motion for preliminary injunction is granted to compel copyright proprietor to cancel recordation of copyright with United States custom service, thereby allowing entry of competing product into country. L. Batlin & Son, Inc. v Snyder (1975, DC NY) 394 F Supp 1389, 187 USPQ 91, affd (CA2 NY) 536 F2d 486, cert den 429 US 857, 50 L Ed 2d 135, 97 S Ct 156.

Preliminary injunction is not barred by laches because delay after preliminary negotiations involved waiting for actual infringement to occur and time lost after death of company president. Selchow & Righter Co. v Book-of-the-Month Club, Inc. (1976, DC NY) 192 USPQ 530.

16. Irreparable harm

Preliminary injunctions are granted more readily in dramatic than in other cases because delay involved in waiting for final decree would generally amount to denial of justice. Chappell & Co. v Fields (1914, CA2 NY) 210 F 864.

Once a prima facie case of infringement is made out, a preliminary injunction should issue, even in absence of showing of irreparable injury, where dramatico-musical works are concerned, since irreparable injury may be presumed. Robert Stigwood Group Ltd. v Sperber (1972, CA2 NY) 457 F2d 50, 173 USPQ 258.

Where preliminary injunction will not cause serious injury, it will ordinarily be granted against so much of defendant's work as plainly infringes upon plaintiff's work. Banks v McDivitt (1875, CC NY) F Cas No 961.

Preliminary injunction will not be granted where it appears that author had permitted foreign publisher to use work, and injury to defendant caused by injunction would be greater than any injury plaintiff might suffer by its refusal. Scribner v Stoddart (1879, CC Pa) F Cas No 12561.

Preliminary injunction will be refused where fact of infringement is not clear, and issuance of such order would work irreparable damage to defendant. Colliery Engineer Co. v United Correspondence Schools Co. (1899, CC NY) 94 F 152; Benton v Van Dyke (1909, CC NY) 170 F 203.

Where two songs, though different in character and theme, have same words, "I hear you calling me," and where these words are impressive part of song, and music accompanying these words is similar in both songs, temporary injunction will be granted when it appears that defendant may not be financially able to pay damages. Boosey v Empire Music Co. (1915, DC NY) 224 F 646.

Where foreword states defendant's book is condensed edition with all important parts presented; although sold at much less price, it will damage plaintiff, and preliminary injunction should issue as there is real competition, possibly more competition than expensive book edition. Houghton Mifflin Co. v Noram Pub. Co. (1939, DC NY) 28 F Supp 676, 42 USPQ 370.

Granting of preliminary injunction is exercise of far-reaching power to be indulged in only in case clearly demanding it; moving papers should establish that denial will cause irreparable injury, during pendency of action. H. M. Chandler Co. v Penn Paper Products, Inc. (1950, DC NY) 88 F Supp 753, 84 USPQ 128.

In action for copyright infringement by owner of copyrighted play who licensed defendant to make moving picture based upon play, defendant is preliminarily enjoined from releasing picture before release date fixed by license; if injunction were not granted, computation of plaintiff's damages would be difficult, although damages may be substantial; there is no easy way of measuring comparison of return to stage production of play under a condition without film competition and that with film competition. Inge v Twentieth Century-Fox Film Corp. (1956, DC NY) 143 F Supp 294, 111 USPQ 153.

Detailed showing of irreparable harm need not be made out by copyright proprietor as prerequisite to preliminary injunction since infringement is plain; if there be any inconvenience or loss to defendants arising from issuance of injunction, that fact does not appeal to court's conscience where infringement is blatant. Geo-Physical Maps, Inc. v Toycraft Corp. (1958, DC NY) 162 F Supp 141, 117 USPQ 316.

Since plaintiff's copyrighted dinnerware pattern was sold with notice of copyright thereon, any sale by defendant of dinnerware bearing substantially same design would violate copyright and should be restrained by court; infringement is preliminarily enjoined since its continuance will cause plaintiff immediate and irreparable harm. Syracuse China Corp. v Stanley Roberts, Inc. (1960, DC NY) 180 F Supp 527, 125 USPQ 62.

Copyrighted design printed on batik is original reproduction of original work of art; defendants infringe by selling "Chinese" copies thereof in competition with plaintiff and at substantially lower prices; infringement has caused considerable loss of sales to plaintiff and, since merchandise is highly seasonable in character, plaintiff will be irreparably injured; plaintiff's motion for preliminary injunction is granted. H. M. Kolbe Co. v Armgus Textile Co. (1960, DC NY) 184 F Supp 423, 126 USPQ 11, affd (CA2 NY) 279 F2d 555, 126 USPQ 1.

Preliminary injunction is proper remedy for copyright proprietor; thus, where proprietor is "converter" which buys uncolored cloth upon which it prints copyrighted design which it sells to dressmakers, proprietor is entitled to preliminary injunction against dress manufacturer which obtains from an unnamed source fabrics bearing infringing design, which fabrics defendant makes into dresses which it sells; denial of injunction would irreparably harm proprietor. Peter Pan Fabrics, Inc. v Candy Frocks, Inc. (1960, DC NY) 187 F Supp 334, 126 USPQ 171.

Plaintiff's original copyrighted textile designs were obtained at considerable expense; plaintiff's business is that of style leader for customers willing to pay for distinctive patterns; defendant's offering of infringing patterns in garments at lower prices than similar garments made by plaintiff's customers from plaintiff's copyrighted reproductions robs plaintiff's goods of their distinctive appeal; life of new design is short, and unless preliminary injunction is issued, plaintiff will suffer substantial and irreparable injury from defendant's competition during significant part of period during which designs will have value. Defendant is preliminarily enjoined. Loomskill, Inc. v Puritan Dress Co. (DC NY) 134 USPQ 20.

Preliminary injunction against infringement of copyrighted dolls representing members of currently popular musical group is granted inasmuch as promotional nature of dolls has life span which may be extraordinarily short with concentration of business within brief period, and opportunity to realize upon heavy investment is restricted to immediate present. Remco Industries, Inc. v Goldberger Doll Mfg. Co. (DC NY) 141 USPQ 898.

Plaintiffs' motion for temporary injunction is denied for lack of irreparable injury since, once license was granted to defendant, anyone could manufacture and sell records under compulsory license provision. American Metropolitan Enterprises of New York, Inc. v Warner Bros. Records, Inc., (1967, DC NY) 154 USPQ 311.

After prima facie showing of copyright validity and infringement, plaintiff need not make detailed showing of danger of irreparable harm to warrant preliminary injunction, but injunction may be denied if damages appear to be trivial or if there is not sufficient likelihood of immediate irreparable injury. Blazon, Inc. v Deluxe Game Corp. (1965, DC NY) 268 F Supp 416, 156 USPQ 195.

Detailed showing of irreparable harm is not necessary to obtain preliminary injunction in copyright infringement suit once prima facie case is made out; however, irreparable harm is not shown where there is no reason why money damages will not serve as an adequate remedy, and plaintiff's delays in bringing suit and moving for injunction suggest that plaintiff does not feel the urgency his request demands. Short selling life of copyrighted design compounds court's difficulty in understanding delays. American Fabrics Co. v Lace Art, Inc. (1968, DC NY) 291 F Supp 589, 160 USPQ 366.

Plaintiff need not show danger of irreparable injury as basis for preliminary injunction against copyright infringement; further, injunction is not barred merely because defendants have ceased infringement, pursuant to advice of counsel; this cessation is some indication that the hurt to them from being restrained is likely to be bearable. National Chemsearch Corp. v Easton Chemical Co. (1969, DC NY) 160 USPQ 537.

Owners of copyrighted tape recordings are entitled to preliminary injunction against defendants' use in their stores of coin-operated electronic systems whereby customers purchase blank tapes and obtain recordings of plaintiffs' tapes furnished by defendants, since prima facie case of irreparable harm to warrant preliminary injunctive relief is established by showing that defendants' customers obtained copies of plaintiffs' $6.00 tapes at a cost of less than $2.00; defendants' activities are not outside scope of sound recording reproduction right either because individual rather than mass-duplication was involved, or because reproductions were made by self-service of customers rather than defendants' active reproduction—electronic tape reproducing system not being comparable to photocopy machine in public library. Elektra Records Co. v Gem Electronic Distributors, Inc. (1973, DC NY) 360 F Supp 821.

Since immediate compromise of "Mickey Mouse March" will result from use of work on sound track of movie during sex scene, use is preliminarily enjoined and parties are ordered not to commercialize decision under penalty of contempt. Walt Disney Productions v Mature Pictures Corp. (1975, DC NY) 389 F Supp 1397, 186 USPQ 48.

Showing of irreparable harm from competition by inferior fabric products, combined with startling similarity of infringing works with copyrighted works, supports right to preliminary injunction which is not defeated by delay of several months by plaintiff or questions of adequacy of copyright notice of portion of works infringed in single fabric. American Greetings

Corp. v Kleinfab Corp. (1975, DC NY) 400 F Supp 228, 188 USPQ 297.

Some evidence of irreparable harm or balance of hardships must be presented to justify preliminary injunction for copyright infringement, and although test for preliminary injunction of copyright infringement is less severe than test for preliminary injunction for trademark infringement, lack of any showing of irreparable harm precludes preliminary injunction for book about playing SCRABBLE, especially considering that money damages appear to be adequate. Selchow & Righter Co. v Book-of-the-Month Club, Inc. (1976, DC NY) 192 USPQ 530.

Proof of access and similarity in content, format, and sequence between preschool reading skills kits establishes plaintiff's likelihood of success on merits and justifies preliminary injunction in spite of possible question of fact that copyrighted kit may be based on public domain kit having similar format. Grolier, Inc. v Educational Reading Aids, Inc. (1976, DC NY) 193 USPQ 632.

Preliminary injunction is granted upon showing of likelihood of success on merits and irreparable injury from infringement because of copying of substantial portions of air travel guide, including copying of error. Reuben H. Donnelley Corp. v Guides to Multinational Business, Inc. (1976, DC Ill) 193 USPQ 791.

Copyright owner's marketing of garments on basis of limited and exclusive additions shows irreparable harm from infringing copies of garments by defendant to support preliminary injunction and order of recall. Nik-Nik Industries, Inc. v Walt Disney Productions, Inc. (1976, DC NY) 194 USPQ 108.

17. Likelihood of success on merits

On motion for preliminary injunction in copyright infringement action, in addition to validity of copyrights, plaintiff must make out prima facie case of infringement and must present facts which indicate sufficient likelihood of immediate irreparable injury; also, plaintiff must demonstrate likelihood of ultimately prevailing upon final decision after trial. Platt & Munk Co. v Republic Graphics, Inc. (1962, DC NY) 218 F Supp 262, 137 USPQ 412.

Record establishes substantial likelihood of defendants' infringement of plaintiff's copyrighted Christmas tree ornament kit, photographs, catalogue, and book, warranting preliminary injunction, where lay observer would find substantial similarity in design of defendants' ornament kit and plaintiff's copyrighted work of art, and where defendants had access to plaintiff's work. Walco Products, Inc. v Kittay & Blitz, Inc. (1972, DC NY) 354 F Supp 121.

In determining right to preliminary injunction, principal question is ordinarily whether plaintiff has shown valid copyright and infringement, thus indicating probability of success; purposes of preliminary injunction is to preserve state of noninfringement and uninterrupted recognition of copyright, to prevent release of infringing articles into market which should be destroyed and impounded during action to eliminate undesirable and unsatisfactory resort to vindictive damages, and to preserve the plaintiff's market, which is the correct measure of its remedial as well as its substantive right. Uneeda Doll Co. v Regent Baby Products Corp. (1972, DC NY) 355 F Supp 438.

Preliminary injunction cannot be issued merely on prima facie case of plaintiffs' statutory copyright and defendants' quotation of portions of copyrighted letters, and court in copyright case must consider likelihood of success, irreparable harm, clean hands and other equitable factors; plaintiffs are denied injunctive relief against continued sales of book quoting portions of letters of Ethel and Julius Rosenberg for not meeting burden of establishing likelihood of success at trial where quoted letters are small part of book and are likely to be fair use, some of letters may be public domain, plaintiffs may be guilty of laches, defendants may have had permission to copy, and harm to defendants outweighs potential rights of plaintiffs. Meeropol v Nizer (1973, DC NY) 361 F Supp 1063.

Preliminary injunction is awarded to proprietor of fabric design for infringing design strikingly similar in configuration and practically identical in coloring where copyrighted design was sufficiently original to support copyright and copyright proprietor is likely to succeed at trial. Primcot Fabrics, Dept. of Prismatic Fabrics, Inc. v Kleinfab Corp. (1974, DC NY) 368 F Supp 482, 181 USPQ 443.

Wallpaper design meeting test of substantial similarity to copyrighted design in eyes of ordinary lay observer is preliminarily enjoined where plaintiff is likely to succeed on merits, even though licensee of design under contract obligation to use copyright notice may have sold copies without notice. Judscott Handprints, Ltd. v Washington Wall Paper Co. (1974, DC NY) 377 F Supp 1372, 182 USPQ 601.

Since defendants' T-shirt pendants are substantially similar to copyrighted pendant and differ only in minor details, plaintiff has shown probability of success and is entitled to preliminary injunction against infringement. Cynthia Designs, Inc. v Robert Zentall, Inc. (1976, DC NY) 416 F Supp 510, 191 USPQ 35.

Plaintiff fails to establish likelihood of success to support preliminary injunction under claim that defendant uses data from plaintiff's horse racing publication to select and display some relevant information in different manner in defendant's publication. Triangle Publications, Inc. v Sports Eye, Inc. (1976, DC Pa) 193 USPQ 50.

18. Prima facie case

Where plaintiff has made prima facie case in regard to existence of copyright and infringement, temporary injunction will, as general rule, be issued. American Code Co. v Bensinger (1922, CA2 NY) 282 F 829.

In copyright cases, if plaintiff makes prima facie showing of his right, preliminary injunction should issue where two editions of book of great popular interest are being actively promoted in competition. Houghton Mifflin Co. v Stackpole Sons, Inc. (1939, CA2 NY) 104 F2d 306, 42 USPQ 96, cert den 308 US 597, 84 L Ed 499, 60 S Ct 131.

When prima facie case for copyright infringement has been made, plaintiffs are entitled to preliminary injunction without detailed showing of danger of irreparable harm; injunction is granted where defendants do not controvert allegation that market for copyrighted item is seasonal and likely to be exhausted in few months. Rushton v Vitale (CA2) 103 USPQ 158.

Having made prima facie showing of validity of copyright and of infringement by defendants, plaintiff is entitled to injunction pending suit. H. M. Koibe Co. v Armgus Textile Co. (1960, CA2 NY) 279 F2d 555, 126 USPQ 1.

Usual rationale for granting preliminary injunction upon showing of prima facie copyright infringement does not apply where copyright covers musical compositions, mechanically reproduced, since copyright holder does not have any right of exclusivity once he permits use; no irreparable injury may be presumed in such situation. American Metropolitan Enterprises, Inc. v Warner Bros. Records, Inc. (1968, CA2 NY) 389 F2d 903, 157 USPQ 69.

To warrant preliminary injunction complainant must make clear and convincing showing of infringement, and not merely scattered and incidental resemblance between two works. Simonton v Gordon (1924, DC NY) 297 F 625.

Plaintiffs sell for 10 cents within ball park copyrighted score card containing news items, baseball statistics and rules, editorials, and line-ups, and numbers of players; defendant's score card sold at 5 cents outside of park contains line-ups and numbers of players; defendant contends that it does not infringe copyrighted card and is not unfairly competing since names and numbers of players are public information; preliminary injunction is denied as court is not satisfied that infringement of copyright or unfair

competition has been shown so clearly and certainly as to warrant preliminary injunction. Penn Sportservice, Inc. v Goldstein (1940, DC Pa) 33 F Supp 944, 45 USPQ 706.

As general rule in copyright infringement cases, preliminary injunction is granted where plaintiff makes out prima facie case as to existence of copyright and its infringement. Robbins Music Corp. v Weinstock (1952, DC NY) 107 F Supp 102, 94 USPQ 107.

Defendant's denial of access to and copying of plaintiff's copyrighted costume jewelry is not convincing; this, together with substantial identity of defendant's product to plaintiff's article, establishes prima facie case of infringement; market for article being seasonal, preliminary injunction is warranted. Trifari, Krussman & Fishel, Inc. v Charel Co. (1955, DC NY) 134 F Supp 551, 107 USPQ 48.

In order to grant preliminary injunction against copyright infringement, there must be clear and convincing impression of plagiarism. American Visuals Corp. v Holland (1957, DC NY) 162 F Supp 14, 117 USPQ 180, affd (CA2 NY) 261 F2d 652.

Preliminary injunction should issue in copyright infringement cases when plaintiff makes prima facie showing that copyright is valid and that defendant has infringed; detailed proof that plaintiff will suffer substantial and irreparable injury, unless afforded preliminary relief, is not required. Peter Pan Fabrics, Inc. v Acadia Co. (1959, DC NY) 173 F Supp 292, 121 USPQ 81, affd (CA2 NY) 274 F2d 487, 124 USPQ 154.

Plaintiff is entitled to preliminary injunction without detailed showing of danger of irreparable harm since it has made prima facie case of copyright validity and infringement; showing is adequate where infringing designs sell at lower prices and business expected by plaintiff has failed to materialize except for small sales at reduced prices; not only loss of sales and profits is involved, but also quick obsolescence of plaintiff's inventory robbed of its distinctive appeal by sales of infringing fabrics at lower prices, and attendant loss of good will. Scarves by Vera, Inc. v United Merchants & Mfrs., Inc. (1959, DC NY) 173 F Supp 625, 121 USPQ 578.

Preliminary injunction should issue in copyright infringement cases when plaintiff makes prima facie showing that copyright is valid and that defendant has infringed. Cortley Fabrics Co. v Slifka (1959, DC NY) 175 F Supp 66, 122 USPQ 321.

Having made out prima facie showing of ownership and validity of copyright and of its infringement, copyright proprietor is entitled to preliminary injunction restraining infringement; proprietor is in midst of season for specific goods; to await trial would be to lose value of copyrighted design since, at conclusion of season, question of exclusivity of design would be virtually academic; infringer's activities have caused and are continuing to cause proprietor irreparable harm. Fabrex Corp. v Scarves by Vera, Inc. (DC NY) 129 USPQ 392.

Preliminary injunction should issue in copyright infringement case when plaintiff makes prima facie showing that copyright is valid and that defendant has infringed; detailed proof of likelihood of immediate irreparable harm is not required to justify granting of preliminary injunction in copyright infringement case; injunction is granted where plaintiff makes out prima facie case that it will suffer immediate substantial and irreparable injury unless afforded preliminary relief. Prestige Floral, Societe Anonyme v California Artificial Flower Co. (1962, DC NY) 201 F Supp 287, 132 USPQ 350.

If plaintiff has valid copyrights which have not been lost by failure to affix proper copyright notice, it is entitled to preliminary injunction on finding that defendant has infringed without a detailed showing of irreparable injury. Royalty Designs, Inc. v Thrifticheck Service Corp. (1962, DC NY) 204 F Supp 702, 133 USPQ 148.

For the purposes of obtaining a preliminary injunction for infringement of a copyright the plaintiff must present a prima facie case and show a probability of success on the merits. Robert Stigwood Group Ltd. v Sperber (1971, DC NY) 332 F Supp 1206, 171 USPQ 684.

Upon establishing prima facie case of infringement, plaintiff is entitled to preliminary injunction where there is any substantial risk of further infringement, notwithstanding defendant's voluntary undertaking to temporarily halt its activities, and notwithstanding absence of detailed showing of danger of irreparable harm. Walco Products, Inc. v Kittay & Blitz, Inc. (1972, DC NY) 354 F Supp 121.

Preliminary injunction cannot be issued merely on prima facie case of plaintiffs' statutory copyright and defendants' quotation of portions of copyrighted letters, and court in copyright case must consider likelihood of success, irreparable harm, clean hands and other equitable factors. Meeropol v Nizer (1973, DC NY) 361 F Supp 1063.

No detailed showing of irreparable harm is necessary to support preliminary injunction for copyright infringement of turtle doll where prima facie infringement is shown, and delay in registering copyright may affect damages before registration, but does not affect right to injunction. Samet & Wells, Inc. v Shalom Toy Co. (1975, DC NY) 185 USPQ 36.

Exact copying and sale of supplement pages for "Outline of Internal Medicine" is preliminarily enjoined on showing of prima facie case of copyright validity and infringement, and proof of irreparable harm is not required, because it is clear from facts presented on motion. Neal v Glickman (1975, DC Tex) 391 F Supp 1088, 185 USPQ 549.

Advertisements copying from illustrations in plaintiff's copyrighted book make out a prima facie case of copyright infringement which is coupled with likelihood of irreparable harm to justify preliminary injunction. Sensory Research Corp. v Pasht, Inc. (1976, DC NY) 192 USPQ 168.

19. Specific circumstances and issues, generally

Preliminary injunction was properly denied where defendants purchased from trustee without notice of trust agreement. Brady v Reliance Motion Picture Corp. (1916, CA2 NY) 229 F 137.

Motion for preliminary injunction to prevent publication of copyrighted work by author thereof, in newspaper, will be denied when complainant is holder of copyright through contract requiring him to use his best efforts to secure sale of book, and his compliance with such contract is doubtful. Worthington v Batty (1889, CC NY) 40 F 479.

Preliminary injunction may be granted to restrain infringement of form chart, containing data of race horses, although it may be used by persons for gambling purposes, when complainant's affidavit states that it is read by others than those engaged in gambling upon races. Egbert v Greensberg (1900, CC Cal) 100 F 447.

Where there is no doubt of infringement and no defense rendering it inequitable to grant relief prayed for, preliminary injunction will be granted. Encyclopedia Britannica Co. v American Newspaper Asso. (1904, CC NJ) 130 F 460, affd (CA3 NJ) 134 F 831.

Evidence of abandonment of words of a song, although there is no proof that abandonment was authorized by composer, may be taken into consideration by court on motion for preliminary injunction. Savage v Hoffmann (1908, CC NY) 159 F 584.

Where two plays, one copyrighted and other not, are adapted from same novel, copyright of which had expired, and both use title of novel, preliminary injunction will not be granted to restrain use of title on uncopyrighted play. Glaser v St. Elmo Co. (1909, CC NY) 175 F 276.

Court should be particularly hesitant about granting preliminary injunction after months of delay, where it appears that defendants did not know of existence of plaintiff's manuscript until suit was brought. Eichel v Marcin (1913, DC NY) 241 F 404.

Until master's report, defendants are not enjoined from using material set up in type since plaintiffs have exaggerated number of recent infringements and old infringements of racing charts rapidly lose potency. Triangel Publications, Inc. v New England Newspaper Pub. Co. (1942, DC Mass) 46 F Supp 198, 54 USPQ 171.

Injunction pendente lite against publication of manuscript is denied where facts are in dispute, prospective publisher has agreed not to publish without plaintiff's consent, and it is unlikely that any other publisher would undertake publication before dispute as to ownership is terminated. Leland v Morin (1952, DC NY) 104 F Supp 401, 93 USPQ 258.

Where there is no reasonable ground for believing that there will be repetition of copyright infringement, court will not grant preliminary injunction, especially where injunction would inflict damages upon defendants out of proportion to benefit inuring to plaintiff. Rushton Co. v F. W. Woolworth Co. (1955, DC NY) 135 F Supp 317, 108 USPQ 80.

In usual case of copyright infringement when infringer had notice of valid copyright, plaintiff is entitled to preliminary injunction without detailed showing of danger of irreparable harm; even if defendants had no knowledge of copyright prior to suit, they have notice of copyright by virtue of suit and would be preliminarily enjoined if they proposed to go on with manufacture and distribution of infringements; however, court exercises discretion to refuse injunction where defendants do not intend to infringe during pendency of action. Trifari, Krussman & Fishel, Inc. v B. Steinberg-Kaslo Co. (1956, DC NY) 144 F Supp 577, 110 USPQ 487.

On motion for preliminary injunction in action for copyright infringement and unfair competition, defendants' change from accused labels and panel to ones which cannot be confused with plaintiff's, and defendants' assurance that old labels and panel will not be used, make consideration of these items unnecessary. Autoyre Co. v Yagoda (1957, DC NY) 148 F Supp 447, 112 USPQ 380.

Plaintiff is entitled to temporary injunction to protect its copyrighted merchandise display card, since infringing card was adopted solely as instrument of duress in price; injunction also covers leaflets which reproduce infringing card modified only in unimportant respects. Comptone Co. v Raytex Corp. (1957, DC NY) 158 F Supp 241, 116 USPQ 120, affd in part and app dismd in part (CA2 NY) 251 F2d 487, 116 USPQ 105.

Plaintiff was aware of defendants' activities for about year before it brought action for copyright and patent infringement; this inaction disentitles it to preliminary injunction. Klauber Brothers, Inc. v Lady Marlene Brassiere Corp. (1968, DC NY) 285 F Supp 806, 157 USPQ 338.

Defendants' allegation that they have discontinued production of fabric bearing design infringing plaintiffs' copyright is no ground for denying preliminary injunction, since court's power to hear case and grant injunction survives discontinuance of wrongful conduct and defendants have heavy burden to demonstrate that they have no reasonable expectation of committing wrong anew. United Merchants & Mfrs., Inc. v Sutton (1967, DC NY) 282 F Supp 588, 157 USPQ 487.

Preliminary injunction granted against publication of child psychology textbook clearly plagiarizing successful copyrighted textbook. Meredith Corp. v Harper & Row, Publishers, Inc. (1974, DC NY) 378 F Supp 686, 182 USPQ 609, affd (CA2 NY) 500 F2d 1221, 182 USPQ 577.

Preliminary injunction is justified to prevent further infringement of copyright in script by broadcasting edited version of dramatization as derived from script, because editing is outside of scope of license given for broadcasting of dramatization. Gilliam v American Broadcasting Co. (1976, CA2) 192 USPQ 1.

Troughs, waves, and lines formed in molded shoe bottom cannot be identified and do not exist independently of utilitarian function of shoe bottom as copyrightable work of art so that copyright on shoe bottom applies to molded bicycle design not appearing on alleged infringement so that preliminary injunction is denied. SCOA Industries, Inc. v Famolare, Inc. (1976, DC NY) 192 USPQ 216.

Balance of hardship must be shown by some evidence to support preliminary injunction which is denied relative to book about playing SCRABBLE. Selchow & Righter Co. v Book-of-the-Month Club, Inc. (1976, DC NY) 192 USPQ 530.

Strong showing of copying from similarity of fabric design for garments, coupled with copyright owner's marketing on basis of limited and exclusive designs, shows likelihood of success, irreparable injury and justifies preliminary injunction and order of recall of infringing garments. Nik-Nik Industries, Inc. v Walt Disney Productions, Inc. (1976, DC NY) 194 USPQ 108.

Temporary injunction will not be granted where two motion pictures are different with exception of title, and one is seven reel film, whole being shown at one time and other series of two reel films to be shown on different days. Gillette v Stoll Film Co. (1922) 120 Misc 850, 200 NYS 787.

In determining plaintiff's motion for temporary injunction against defendants' use of "Invasion" in "March of Time, Invasion" as motion-picture title, paramount issue is whether use of title creates confusion with plaintiff's copyrighted motion picture "Invasion" to plaintiff's detriment; injunction is refused where plaintiff's film is six reel feature film and defendants' is two reel newsreel short; films are not shown in same type of theaters; fact issues can be determined on speedy trial; temporary injunction would greatly damage defendants but refusal will not greatly damage plaintiff; it is no defense that defendants would not have used title if they had known of plaintiff's use but it is considered since defendant's title cannot be changed, distribution having taken place. Adventure Films, Inc. v Twentieth Century-Fox Film Corp. (Misc) 59 USPQ 76.

20. —Copying or extent of copying issue

In application for preliminary injunction, plaintiff's affidavits should satisfactorily show that defendant has actually copied into his book copyrighted matter taken from plaintiff's work. American Code Co. v Bensinger (1922, CA2 NY) 282 F 829.

Plaintiff is entitled to preliminary injunction against copyright infringement since defendant's affidavits do not challenge validity of copyrights, since there is little doubt of deliberate copying, and since defendant's affidavits do not deny copying. Joshua Meier Co. v Albany Novelty Mfg. Co. (1956, CA2 NY) 236 F2d 144, 111 USPQ 197.

Preliminary injunction will not be granted when there is nothing to show which parts of Bible were claimed to have been copyrighted. Flint v Jones (1875, CC Pa) F Cas No 4872.

Although plaintiff shows copyright of book, and copy of book having same title, and that defendant is publishing book containing extracts from it, preliminary injunction will not be granted when plaintiff has not shown that such copy as shown, is copy of copyrighted book. Humphreys' Homeopathic Medicine Co. v Armstrong (1887, CC NY) 30 F 66.

Complainant was granted injunction pendente lite where three pages of its books were being used as copy from which to print defendant's book, and defendant made no satisfactory explanation therefor. Chicago Directory Co. v United States Directory Co. (1902, CC NY) 122 F 189.

Defendants' unsatisfactory explanation of reproduction of errors occurring in plaintiffs' book and failure to present copy of its book to court

entitled plaintiffs to preliminary injunction. Trow Directory Printing & Bookbinding Co. v United States Directory Co. (1903, CC NY) 122 F 191.

Evidence of copying either language or dramatic situations of play was insufficient to form basis for preliminary injunction; where two plays use same device that is common property, and in analyzing details of such device points of essential difference outnumber points of similarity, preliminary injunction will not be granted. Hubges v Belasco (1904, CC NY) 130 F 388.

Where same errors, admissions, and similarity of language occur in alleged infringing work as in original work, complainant is entitled to preliminary injunction. George T. Bisel Co. v Welsh (1904, CC Pa) 131 F 564.

Where character and extent of dedication to public through uncopyrighted publication of musical composition cannot be determined upon affidavit and inspection of respective scores, and it does not appear that defendant is unable to respond in damages, preliminary injunction should not be granted. Littleton v Fischer (1905, CC NY) 137 F 684.

Where court is unable to determine extent of matter copied, it will not grant preliminary injunction to restrain publication of certain parts of work. White v Bender (1911, CC NY) 185 F 921.

Evidence showing that same errors appeared in infringing work as in original work is sufficient for extending of preliminary injunction until final hearing. George T. Bisel Co. v Bender (1911, CC NY) 190 F 205.

Manufacturer of shoe boxes, employing special decorative design on which he has obtained copyright, was entitled to preliminary injunction against defendant using same design on similar boxes. Hoague-Sprague Corp. v Frank C. Meyer Co. (1928, DC NY) 27 F2d 176.

Preliminary injunction issued at suit of telephone company on ground that defendant had infringed copyright of plaintiff's telephone directory. Cincinnati & Suburban Bell Tel. Co. v Brown (1930, DC Ohio) 44 F2d 631.

Where there is evidence of extensive copying of plaintiff's copyrighted directories by defendant, there is sufficient proof of infringement to warrant granting of injunction pendente lite. Chain Store Business Guide, Inc. v Wexler (1948, DC NY) 79 F Supp 726, 77 USPQ 656.

Temporary injunction is refused in action for infringement of copyrighted catalogue where, although defendant's catalogue contains 2,000 items, only 25 illustrations are alleged to be similar in appearance to those in copyrighted catalogue; also, there is no showing of duplication of errors. Miller Harness Co. v Arcaro &

Dan's Saddlery, Inc. (1956, DC NY) 142 F Supp 634, 110 USPQ 190.

Preliminary injunction lies in copyright infringement action only if defendants' acts constitute copying within meaning of copyright laws. Peter Pan Fabrics, Inc. v Acadia Co. (1959, DC NY) 173 F Supp 292, 121 USPQ 81 affd (CA2 NY) 274 F2d 487, 124 USPQ 154.

Preliminary injunction against copyright infringement is not warranted merely because combination of similar colors used in designs which are similar in style results in fabrics which have roughly same aesthetic effect since there is no correlation between designs although fabrics are similar in general appeal; there is important difference between slavish copy which alters few details and independent work executed in similar colors and in similar style; fact that style of plaintiff's fabric is derived from works of art in public domain entitles it to less broad protection than if style were wholly original with it. Manes Fabrics Co. v Acadia Co. (DC NY) 139 USPQ 339.

Preliminary injunction granted against publication of child psychology textbook clearly plagiarizing successful copyrighted textbook; copying is not excused under fair use doctrine because of amount copied, extensive paraphrasing, and commercial effect of plagiarization. Meredith Corp. v Harper & Row, Publishers, Inc. (1974, DC NY) 378 F Supp 686, 182 USPQ 609, affd (CA2 NY) 500 F2d 1221, 182 USPQ 577.

Preliminary injunction against sale of fabric design is denied where both parties' designs are based on public domain "Tree of Life" design, designs are dissimilar, and accused infringer offered evidence of independent creation of design from several public domain versions. Deering Milliken, Inc. v Quaker Fabric Corp. (1975, DC NY) 187 USPQ 288.

Preliminary injunction is denied for defendant's use of raw data from plaintiff's horse racing publication to select information presented in different way in defendant's publication, because plaintiff's copyright protects form of expression and not underlying data or ideas. Triangle Publications, Inc. v Sports Eye, Inc. (1976, DC Pa) 193 USPQ 50.

21. —Ownership of copyright issue

Where there was dispute between plaintiff and defendant as to ownership of copyrighted play, injunction pendente lite against defendant restraining performance of copyrighted play or similar play was continued. Eisfeldt v Campbell (1909, CC NY) 171 F 594.

Where plaintiff's title to right in copyrighted work is denied in answer, and plaintiff does not introduce new evidence to prove title, preliminary injunction will not be granted. Ginn v Apollo Pub. Co. (1913, DC Pa) 209 F 713.

Where defendant claims to have given performance under implied license from plaintiff and plaintiff claims that such authority had been revoked prior to alleged infringement, preliminary injunction will not be granted. Jerome H. Remick & Co. v General Electric Co. (1924, DC NY) 4 F2d 160.

Preliminary injunction for copyright infringement of lace is denied where defendant raises substantial questions of fact relative to standing of plaintiff to sue and to adequacy of copyright notice. Klauber Bros., Inc. v Westchester Lace Work, Inc. (1974, DC NY) 181 USPQ 523.

Preliminary injunction for infringement of copyrighted teddy bears is denied where plaintiffs lack evidence of authorship of distinctions from prior teddy bears and distinctions are so trivial as to be nearly nonexistent. Kuddle Toy, Inc. v Pussycat-Toy Co. (1974, DC NY) 183 USPQ 642.

Plaintiff's proof of exclusive right to dramatize "Sherlock Holmes" was insufficient to warrant issuance of preliminary injunction against defendant's use of such character in motion-picture play. Gillette v Stoll Film Co. (1922) 120 Misc 850, 200 NYS 787.

22. —Validity of copyright issue

Denial of temporary injunction against copyright infringement is proper where affidavits raise question as to validity of plaintiff's copyright and do not show that money damages will not be adequate remedy or that plaintiff will suffer irreparable injury if temporary injunction is denied. American Visuals Corp. v Holland (1955, CA2 NY) 219 F2d 223, 104 USPQ 222.

Where validity of plaintiff's copyright is doubtful, and it appears that defendant will be able to pay damages, preliminary injunction will not be granted. Miller v McElroy (1839, CC Pa) F Cas No 9581.

If there be doubt as to validity of plaintiff's copyright, preliminary injunction will be refused. Scribner v Stoddart (1879, CC Pa) F Cas No 12561.

If, on motion for preliminary injunction, it is impossible to determine that one work is infringement of original, or that copyright of original is valid, injunction will not issue; where two plays are adapted from same novel and defendants' play resembles book in some particulars which were not found in plaintiff's play, and validity of plaintiff's copyright was questioned, preliminary injunction cannot be granted. Nixon v Doran (1909, CC NY) 168 F 575.

Preliminary injunction was denied where it was not clearly established that pirated "gags" were original with complainant, or that any serious damage would result to him; where defendant avers under oath that expressions in a copyrighted monologue were not new with complainant, but common property, preliminary injunction should not issue. Hoffman v Le Traunik (1913, DC NY) 209 F 375.

Since affidavits raise question as to validity of plaintiff's copyright, it is improper to grant plaintiff's motion for temporary injunction based on strength of allegation of copyright infringement. Kramer Jewelry Creations, Inc. v Capri Jewelry, Inc. (1956, DC NY) 143 F Supp 120, 111 USPQ 151.

In ruling on motion for preliminary injunction against copyright infringement, court considers whether affidavits raise question as to copyright's validity, whether plaintiff made prima facie showing of copyright's validity, and whether there is likelihood of plaintiff's ultimate success. Ross Products, Inc. v New York Merchandise Co. (1964, DC NY) 233 F Supp 260, 141 USPQ 652.

Copyright office issuance of certificate of registration for alleged infringing design after comparison with plaintiff's copyrighted design is not binding on courts, and after independent judicial comparison finding differences in designs, preliminary injunction is denied. Soptra Fabrics Corp. v Stafford Knitting Mills, Inc. (1973, DC NY) 365 F Supp 1199, 180 USPQ 362, revd on other grounds (CA2 NY) 490 F2d 1092, 180 USPQ 545, 26 ALR Fed 402.

Preliminary injunction for copyright infringement of map copied by defendant is denied where evidence shows plaintiff prepared map by copying from available government maps and did not use sufficient originality to support copyright. Alaska Map Service, Inc. v Roberts (1973, DC Alaska) 368 F Supp 578, 181 USPQ 296.

Preliminary injunction is awarded to proprietor of fabric design for infringing design strikingly similar in configuration and practically identical in coloring where copyrighted design was sufficiently original to support copyright and copyright proprietor is likely to succeed at trial. Primcot Fabrics, Dept. of Prismatic Fabrics, Inc. v Kleinfab Corp. (1974, DC NY) 368 F Supp 482, 181 USPQ 443.

V. PRACTICE AND PROCEDURE

23. Generally

On motion for preliminary injunction for infringement court may refer question of infringement and its extent to master for examination and report, which court will hear when further proceedings in cause are had. Story v Derby (1846, CC Ohio) F Cas No 13496.

24. Bond requirements

Where defendant has expended $15,000 on alleged infringing work and has on hand books valued at $50,000, bond given by complainant in sum of $250 upon issuance of preliminary injunction is insufficient. American Code Co. v Bensinger (1922, CA2 NY) 282 F 829.

Where terms of contract have not been determined and there is doubt as to whether there has been infringement, preliminary injunction will not be granted, but defendant will be required to give bond pending final hearing. Hubbard v Thompson (1882, CC Mo) 14 F 689.

Although moving papers make out very strong prima facie case, when preliminary injunction would be in effect, judgment in advance of trial, which would work irreparable injury on defendant, it will not be granted, provided defendant furnishes sufficient bond. Trow Directory, Printing & Bookbinding Co. v Boyd (1899, CC NY) 97 F 586.

Where it is doubtful whether subject matter is proper subject for copyright, injunction will not be granted provided defendant furnishes bond to indemnify complainants against damage. Louis De Jonge & Co. v Breuker & Kessler Co. (1906, CC Pa) 147 F 763.

Where defendant's directory is shown to contain same errors as plaintiff's, but defendant, by affidavit alleges that such names were copied from voters lists in which errors occurred, and shows manner in which directory was compiled, no preliminary injunction will be granted provided defendant files sufficient bond. Gopsill v C. E. Howe Co. (1907, CC Pa) 149 F 905.

Where alleged infringing work is song of such character that usually has temporary vogue, and financial showing of defendant is not satisfactory, temporary injunction will be granted but will be suspended when defendant files sufficient bond and files statement of sales. Boosey v Empire Music Co. (1915, DC NY) 224 F 646.

25. Pleading requirements

In suit to enjoin infringement of copyright defense of unclean hands need not be pleaded, but when evidence discloses such fact court will apply maxim of its own motion. Bentley v Tibbals (1915, CA2 NY) 223 F 247.

Owner of equitable title to copyright is not mere licensee and may sue in equity to restrain infringement, especially where owner of legal title is infringer, but he must connect himself with legal title by proper averment; ordinarily equitable owner must join owner of legal title as party plaintiff. Ted Browne Music Co. v Fowler (1923, CA2 NY) 290 F 751.

Allegation in bill of complaint that each copy contained statutory copyright notice justifies finding that plaintiff has sought to comply with Copyright Act, and when not controverted by defendant there is prima facie case for injunction. Gerlach-Barklow Co. v Morris & Bendien, Inc. (1927, CA2 NY) 23 F2d 159.

Where a bill for injunction did not allege facts justifying relief, it was error for the district court to retain jurisdiction for the purpose of awarding damages. Hutchinson Amusement Co. v Vitaphone Corp. (1937, CA1 Mass) 93 F2d 176, 36 USPQ 1.

Owner of copyrighted "bank night" scheme for cash prizes to be given by places of amusement was not entitled to restrain theater owner from using such scheme in absence of allegations showing infringement of copyright. Affiliated Enterprises, Inc. v Gantz (1936, CA10 Okla) 86 F2d 597, 31 USPQ 397.

Bill for injunction, not intended to be used as evidence, need not be verified. Black v Henry G. Allen Co. (1890, CC NY) 42 F 618.

Allegation in the bill, that complainant is "author, inventor, designer and proprietor of a certain photograph and negative thereof" and giving title under which it was copyrighted is sufficient in suit for injunction without giving detailed description of steps taken in producing photograph. Falk v Schumacher (1891, CC NY) 48 F 222.

It sometimes happens that redress by injunction must be speedily obtained in order to prevent irreparable injury, and that plaintiff may not have copy of manuscript at hand to file with petition, in which case he can describe substance of subject matter, but satisfactory reasons must be given for its absence. Tully v Triangle Film Corp. (1916, DC NY) 229 F 297.

Bill of complaint in suit for protection of copyright must allege facts which show performance of conditions precedent to copyright. Pathe Exchange, Inc. v International Alliance, T.S.E., etc. (1932, DC NY) 3 F Supp 63.

Federal equity rules, insofar as applicable, apply to equity copyright action. Gross v Twentieth Century Fox Film Corp. (DC NY) 38 USPQ 399.

26. Evidentiary matters, generally

Where defendant desires some parts of his work to be exempted from injunction, opportunity may be given him to clearly prove noninfringement in respect to such parts. W. H. Anderson Co. v Baldwin Law Pub. Co. (1928, CA6 Ohio) 27 F2d 82.

Fact that court of appeals held prima facie proof of identity of person who signed assignment of copyright and his authority to act for copyright proprietor sufficient for temporary injunction is not conclusive on motion for summary judgment of permanent injunction; prima facie case will serve if justice demands but plaintiff was party to assignment and presumably has access to evidence; defendants are not required to accept very general conclusions of plaintiff's affidavits but evidence should be produced in regular way and witnesses should be submitted to cross-examination. Houghton Mifflin Co. v Stackpole Sons, Inc. (1940, CA2 NY) 113 F2d 627, 46 USPQ 296.

Whenever bill for injunction is to be used as evidence, either upon motion for preliminary injunction or in any other way, it must be verified; but there is no imperative rule requiring verification of bill, at time it is signed. Black v Henry G. Allen Co. (1890, CC NY) 42 F 618.

27. —Weight and sufficiency of evidence

Although fictitious items which appeared in complainant's book of credit ratings also appeared in defendant's book, when it is shown by evidence manner in which defendant obtained original information at great expense and proportion of such names is insignificant, no injunction will be granted. Dun v Lumbermen's Credit Asso. (1908) 209 US 20, 52 L Ed 663, 28 S Ct 335.

Evidence of piracy as shown by reproduction of common errors and exhibits was sufficient to deny defendant's motion for dismissal from interlocutory order of injunction. Chicago Dollar Directory Co. v Chicago Directory Co. (1895, CA7 Ill) 66 F 977.

Evidence is not sufficient to support bill for injunction, unless it shows that defendant was doing or threatening something subject to be enjoined or that there was present continuous wrongful infringement. McCaleb v Fox Film Corp. (1924, CA5 La) 299 F 48.

Upon application for injunction to restrain infringement, it is not necessary to show that violation of copyright is so extensive that piratical work is substitute for original work. Reed v Holliday (1884, CC Pa) 19 F 325.

In suit for injunction it is not necessary that complainant prove that notice of copyright appeared upon each one of his copies, but general testimony is sufficient to establish prima facie case. Falk v Gast Lith. & Eng. Co. (1889, CC NY) 40 F 168.

If plaintiff shows infringement of his copyright, injunction will be granted without proof of damages. Fishel v Lueckel (1892, CC NY) 53 F

499; Macmillan Co. v King (1914, DC Mass) 223 F 862.

To entitle complainant to injunction, he must show affirmatively beyond any doubt, that he has complied with copyright law. American Trotting Register Asso. v Gocher (1895, CC Ohio) 70 F 237.

Where legislature has determined that public interests require new compilation of laws of state, and work is completed, court should not interfere by injunction, unless right to relief asked is clearly manifest from evidence. Howell v Miller (1898, CA6 Mich) 91 F 129.

While court of equity will not and should not permit enforcement of oral license to use copyrighted musical production, without satisfactory and convincing proof, where complainant by his own affidavits shows that he never objected to defendant's application for license, motion for injunction will be denied. G. Ricordi & Co. v Hammerstein (1907, CC NY) 150 F 450.

Proof of actual damage is not necessary for issuance of injunction if infringement appears and damage may probably follow from its continuance. Macmillan Co. v King (1914, DC Mass) 223 F 862; Henry Holt & Co. v Liggett & Myers Tobacco Co. (1938, DC Pa) 23 F Supp 302, 37 USPQ 449.

28. Order or decree, generally

Decree awarding preliminary injunction and accounting which is still pending, is not final decree and conclusive of infringement of copyright, and cannot be admitted as evidence in later case involving same persons and same facts. Hills & Co. v Hoover (1906, CC Pa) 142 F 904.

Copying of 18 cuts from complainant's catalogue into defendant's was sufficient to justify granting of injunction limited to 18 cuts copied. Da Prato Statuary Co. v Giuliani Statuary Co. (1911, CA8 Minn) 189 F 90.

29. —Conditions or scope

Where, by misconduct of defendant's employees, part of complainant's copyrighted work has been appropriated by defendant and so mingled with original matter in publication, that no one except defendant's employees can segregate pirated from original matter, and they do not make segregation, whole work should be enjoined. West Pub. Co. v Lawyers' Co-op. Pub. Co. (1897, CA2 NY) 79 F 756.

Injunction should not extend to those distinct parts of book which are not affected by complainant's copyrights. Historical Pub. Co. v Jones Bros. Pub. Co. (1916, CA3 Pa) 231 F 638; Story v Holcombe (1847, CC Ohio) F Cas No 13497; Webb v Powers (1897, CC Mass) F Cas

No 17323; List Pub. Co. v Keller (1887, CC NY) 30 F 772; Farmer v Elstner (1888, CC Mich) 33 F 494; Social Register Ass'n v Murphy (1904, CC RI) 128 F 116; Sampson & Murdock Co. v Seaver-Radford Co. (1905, CA1 Mass) 140 F 539.

If infringing parts of book cannot be separated from original parts, publication of whole may be enjoined. Investment Service Co. v Fitch Pub. Co. (1923, CA7 Ill) 291 F 1010; Lawrence v Dana (1869, CC Mass) F Cas No 8136; Farmer v Elstner (1888, CC Mich) 33 F 494; Williams v Smythe (1901, CC Pa) 110 F 961; Social Register Ass'n v Murphy (1904, CC RI) 128 F 116; Dam v Kirke La Shelle Co. (1908, CC NY) 166 F 589, affd (CA2 NY) 175 F 902 (ovrld on other grounds Sheldon v Metro-Goldwyn Pictures (CA2 NY) 106 F2d 45, affd 309 US 390, 84 L Ed 825, 60 S Ct 681); Park & Pollard Co. v Kellerstrass (1910, CC Mo) 181 F 431.

Where injunction is awarded in favor of plaintiff, defendant will be permitted to show that certain parts of his published works do not constitute infringement in order that they may be exempted from restraining order. W. H. Anderson Co. v Baldwin Law Pub. Co. (1928, CA6 Ohio) 27 F2d 82.

Defendant was permitted to publish catalogues with infringing cuts eliminated. Kaeser & Blair, Inc. v Merchants' Asso. (1933, CA6 Ohio) 64 F2d 575.

If copyrighted work is infringed, but only part of new work actually infringes upon copyright of original, injunction may issue only against that part. Story v Holcombe (1847, CC Ohio) F Cas No 13497; List Pub. Co. v Keller (1887, CC NY) 30 F 772.

Where there is lack of positive evidence that infringement will cause irreparable injury, court may grant conditional injunction. Ladd v Oxnard (1896, CC Mass) 75 F 703.

Where objectionable parts of play are seemingly inseparable from theme of play, play as whole must be enjoined, but if it can be revamped to eliminate objectionable imitations the injunction will simply cover objectionable portions. Dam v Kirke La Shelle Co. (1908, CC NY) 166 F 589, affd (CA2 NY) 175 F 902 (ovrld on other grounds Sheldon v Metro-Goldwyn Pictures (CA2 NY) 106 F2d 45, affd 309 US 390, 84 L Ed 825, 60 S Ct 681).

Preliminary injunction will be granted where pirated matter is so interwoven in same book that defendant cannot use what is his own without using that which is not; and court will not assume task of separating what is proper from improper, but after defendant has made separation he may have modification of decree. Park &

Pollard Co. v Kellerstrass (1910, CC Mo) 181 F 431.

Although only 18 cuts were copied from complainant's catalogue of 2,813 cuts, and printed in defendant's catalogue of 393 cuts, it is sufficient to justify granting of injunction, as to 18 cuts. Da Prato Statuary Co. v Giuliani Statuary Co. (1911, CA8 Minn) 189 F 90.

Where motion picture is found to infringe upon copyright, its exhibition will be restrained only until the events, incidents, and situations that infringe are eliminated. International Film Service Co. v Affiliated Distributors, Inc. (1922, DC NY) 283 F 229.

Defendant infringed copyrighted telephone directories published periodically by publishing directories copied from telephone directories; defendant is permanently enjoined from infringing plaintiff's copyrights in any and all directories published by plaintiff in course of its business, for which it holds or may hereafter hold copyright, whether said directories have been heretofore published or shall, in future, be published, and whether copyright thereto has been heretofore granted, or shall, in future, be granted, and from otherwise interfering with plaintiff's business by printing, publishing, and selling any directories containing names of plaintiff's subscribers, or containing telephone numbers or addresses of subscribers, information for which has been obtained from any directory of plaintiff to which plaintiff has acquired, or in future may acquire, copyright. Southern Bell Tel. & Tel. Co. v Donnelly (1940, DC Fla) 35 F Supp 425, 48 USPQ 11.

Neither past infringement of copyright on motion-picture films, nor mere prayer for injunction and for discovery as to past infringements, is in itself sufficient to justify present issuance of injunction against defendant from infringement of any other films, whether now or hereafter to be copyrighted by plaintiff and subsequently furnished to defendant under contractual arrangements for exhibition. Universal Pictures Corp. v Marsh (1940, DC W Va) 36 F Supp 241, 48 USPQ 319.

Although defendants do not infringe copyright or unfairly compete by using plaintiff's indices and charts solely to secure clues, they are enjoined from so doing since they have infringed by copying portions of charts and exception to injunction would make it in practice unenforceable in view of defendants' prior record of infringement. Triangle Publications, Inc. v New England Newspaper Pub. Co. (1942, DC Mass) 46 F Supp 198, 54 USPQ 171.

30. —Dissolution or modification

Denials and allegations affecting complainant's copyright title made merely on information and belief was insufficient to entitle defendant to dissolution of injunction; where preliminary injunction has been issued in suit for infringement of copyright, court, in absence of any pretense of fraud or mistake, will not, upon motion to dissolve order, consider any questions arising upon complainant's right to bring suit. Farmer v Calvert Lithographing, etc., Co. (1872, CC Mich) F Cas No 4651.

Defendant was not entitled to damages suffered by reason of injunction which prevented him from selling his song, where such order was later discharged on ground that copyright on original song was invalid. Broder v Zeno Mauvais Music Co. (1898, CC Cal) 88 F 74.

Where court cannot separate parts of directory that are free from charge of piracy and those that are not, whole book will be enjoined, but if defendant can sever parts and eliminate pirated matter he may be entitled to modification of restraining order. Williams v Smythe (1901, CC Pa) 110 F 961.

Motion for new trial on ground of newly-discovered evidence and surprise in entry of judgment is denied on merits when filed six months after perpetual injunction against copyright infringement and reference to master for accounting; although same court in subsequent suit against third party on same copyright found unclean hands and that plaintiff did not originate copyrighted drawings, defendant has not sustained burden of diligence; evidence is not newly discovered since facts were pleaded in other suit of which defendant was aware seven months before trial in instant case but were not raised, other defenses being relied on at trial. Colonial Book Co. v Amsco School Publications, Inc. (1942, DC NY) 48 F Supp 794, 56 USPQ 265, affd (CA2 NY) 142 F2d 362, 61 USPQ 391.

31. Contempt

Defendants had not become liable for contempt by using names found in city directory to aid in forming their architects' directory. Colliery Engineer Co. v Ewald (1903, CC NY) 126 F 843.

Circumstances surrounding sales of books against which injunctive order was in effect did not warrant adjudication that defendant was guilty of contempt. Encyclopaedia Britannica Co. v American Newspaper Asso. (1904, CC NJ) 130 F 493.

In copyright infringement action, court issued restraining order which in substance forbade plaintiff from utilizing existence of litigation to impair defendant's business; plaintiff is held in contempt where it (1) stated to trade that defendant's trophies infringed plaintiff's copyrights, threatened to sue defendant's customers, and informed such customers of pendency of litigation, and (2) apprised specific prospective customer of existence of litigation and possible liability of customer, with result that customer refused to do business with defendant. Dodge, Inc. v General Classics, Inc. (DC Ill) 125 USPQ 431.

Defendant is held in contempt of court and subject to damages provable by plaintiff for making only minor effort to retrieve offending catalog pages as ordered and stop sales of infringements, but court does not apply penalty fine provisions in original injunction, because these were to secure performance, rather than to punish, and can no longer have desired effect. Andre Matenciot, Inc. v David & Dash, Inc. (1976, DC NY) 189 USPQ 360.

Contempt citation is granted against modified drapery fabric pattern similar in overall design to copyrighted fabric to extent that average lay observer would find substantial similarity in design and take one design to be same as other. Comptoir de L'Industrie Textile de France v Tilbury Fabrics, Inc. (1975, DC NY) 189 USPQ 442.

32. Appeal

Appeal from order denying motion to dissolve preliminary injunction will be dismissed, when evidence of repetition of errors was produced at trial. Chicago Dollar Directory Co. v Chicago Directory Co. (1895, CA7 Ill) 66 F 977.

Order for preliminary injunction will not be set aside on appeal unless it appear that there has been abuse of discretion, or that court below was mistaken in its view of situation. Werner Co. v Encyclopaedia Britannica Co. (1905, CA3 NJ) 134 F 831.

Plaintiff may appeal if injunction be refused or dissolved by interlocutory order or decree. His-

torical Pub. Co. v Jones Bros. Pub. Co. (1916, CA3 Pa) 231 F 638.

General rule, applicable to interlocutory decree in action for copyright infringement, is that propriety of granting of other relief than injunction forms no part of subject matter of appeal and is not before court of appeals, not being final decision; in equitable action for infringement of copyrighted moving picture, where trial judge, recognizing nonexistence of actual or threatened continued infringement, correctly denied injunction, but inadvertently included injunction in interlocutory decree, appeal from that part of decree was properly taken. Sheldon v Moredall Realty Corp. (1938, CA2 NY) 95 F2d 48, 37 USPQ 286.

On appeal from grant of summary judgment for plaintiff, only question is whether there is any issue, relevant to merits of case, which deserved trial, where court of appeals on previous appeal had passed on rights of parties in affirming issuance of temporary injunction. Houghton Mifflin Co. v Stackpole Sons, Inc. (1940, CA2 NY) 113 F2d 627, 46 USPQ 296.

In reviewing order granting preliminary injunction against infringement of copyrighted fabric design, court of appeals is bound by Rule 52 of Federal Rules of Civil Procedure; however, court of appeals is in as good position as trial judge to determine issue of infringement where record contains almost no evidence on issue other than the fabrics themselves. Millworth Converting Corp. v Slifka (1960, CA2 NY) 276 F2d 443, 125 USPQ 506.

Reference to master to ascertain damages for copyright infringement and report back renders judgment interlocutory; hence, only propriety of temporary injunction can be considered on appeal. Reeve Music Co. v Crest Records, Inc. (1960, CA2 NY) 285 F2d 546, 128 USPQ 24.

§ 503. Remedies for infringement: Impounding and disposition of infringing articles

(a) At any time while an action under this title [17 USCS §§ 101 et seq.] is pending, the court may order the impounding, on such terms as it may deem reasonable, of all copies or phonorecords claimed to have been made or used in violation of the copyright owner's exclusive rights, and of all plates, molds, matrices, masters, tapes, film negatives, or other articles by means of which such copies or phonorecords may be reproduced.

(b) As part of a final judgment or decree, the court may order the destruction or other reasonable disposition of all copies or phonorecords found to have been made or used in violation of the copyright owner's exclusive rights, and of all plates, molds, matrices, masters, tapes, film

negatives, or other articles by means of which such copies or phonorecords may be reproduced.
(Added Oct. 19, 1976, P. L. 94-553, Title I, § 101, 90 Stat. 2585.)

HISTORY; ANCILLARY LAWS AND DIRECTIVES

Effective date of section:
Section 102 of Act Oct. 19, 1976, P. L. 94-553, 90 Stat. 2598 provided that this section "becomes effective on January 1, 1978".
"Copies" defined, 17 USCS § 101.
"Copyright owner" defined, 17 USCS § 101.
"Phonorecords" defined, 17 USCS § 101.
Infringement of copyright, 17 USCS § 501.
Forfeiture and destruction as consequence of criminal infringement, 17 USCS § 506(b).
This section referred to in 17 USCS §§ 111, 115, 116, 411, 510.

RESEARCH GUIDE

Am Jur:
18 Am Jur 2d, Copyright and Literary Property § 146.

Forms:
6 Federal Procedural Forms L Ed, Copyrights § 17:61.

Annotations:
Construction and application of §§ 1(c) and 1(d) of Copyright Act (17 USCS §§ 101(c), 101(d)), providing for impounding of articles alleged to infringe copyright and for destruction of infringing copies or devices. 22 ALR Fed 487.

INTERPRETIVE NOTES AND DECISIONS

1. Generally
2. Impoundment during trial [17 USCS § 503(a)]
3. Destruction or disposition as part of final judgment or decree [17 USCS § 503(b)]

1(d) of Copyright Act (17 USCS §§ 101(c), 101(d)), providing for impounding of articles alleged to infringe copyright and for destruction of infringing copies or devices. 22 ALR Fed 487.

1. Generally
Infringing copies of city directory in hands of users, not infringers, are immune from seizure. Jewelers' Circular Pub. Co. v Keystone Pub. Co. (1921, DC NY) 274 F 932, affd (CA2 NY) 281 F 83, 26 ALR 571, cert den 259 US 581, 66 L Ed 1074, 42 S Ct 464.

Although, in appropriate circumstances, court may order that infringer surrender for destruction all means of copying copyrighted material, such order is purposeless where infringer has long since surrendered such material. Local Trademarks, Inc. v Grantham (1957, DC Neb) 166 F Supp 494, 117 USPQ 335.

Annotations:
Construction and application of §§ 1(c) and

2. Impoundment during trial [17 USCS § 503(a)]
Loss of probable profits may be measure of damages upon vacation of writ for impounding. Universal Film Mfg. Co. v Copperman (1914, CA2 NY) 218 F 577, cert den 235 US 704, 59 L Ed 433, 35 S Ct 209.

Attachment is not proper remedy in suit involving infringement of copyright. Dixon v Corinne Runkel Stock Co. (1914, DC NC) 214 F 418.

On dismissing infringement suit and releasing defendant's plates, he is not entitled to damages from plaintiff for physical injury to plates after seizure by marshal; there is no showing how injury occurred or why plaintiff should be charged. Rudolf Lesch Fine Arts, Inc. v Metal (1943, DC NY) 51 F Supp 69, 58 USPQ 668.

Provisions of predecessor act relating to destruction of infringing copies and plates do not apply where violation of copyrights consists of use of mechanical reproduction of musical works; however, matrices and other matter upon which copyrighted musical compositions may be recorded, or from which parts serving to reproduce mechanically said compositions may be made, are impounded until decreed royalties and triple damages be paid and until statutory notice of intention to use work be given. Miller v Goody (1954, DC NY) 125 F Supp 348, 103 USPQ 292.

Annotations:

Construction and application of §§ 1(c) and 1(d) of Copyright Act (17 USCS §§ 101(c), 101(d)), providing for impounding of articles alleged to infringe copyright and for destruction of infringing copies or devices. 22 ALR Fed 487.

3. Destruction or disposition as part of final judgment or decree [17 USCS § 503(b)]

When action was brought for recovery of infringing matter, and goods were seized and turned over to plaintiff, action cannot be brought later for penalties, since all relief under statute must be had in single action. Hills & Co. v Hoover (1911) 220 US 329, 55 L Ed 485, 31 S Ct 402.

Action for assumpsit for purpose of recovering statutory penalty for copies of infringing article in possession of defendant, must be brought after there is forfeiture, and there can be no forfeiture until there is finding by court. Falk v Curtis Pub. Co. (1901, CA3 Pa) 107 F 126; Child v New York Times Co. (1901, CC NY) 110 F 527.

District court erred in ordering return of impounded tape recording equipment and machinery, blank tapes, cartridges, cassettes and packaging materials used by defendant in mechanically reproducing for sale plaintiffs' copyrighted musical works, on grounds that these items, unlike recordings themselves, did not embody a mechanical and/or electronic impression of plaintiffs' works; Congress intended to impound and destroy "the whole of the paraphernalia" used for making infringing copies, including those items which may be used for other purposes. Duchess Music Corp. v Stern (1972, CA9 Ariz) 458 F2d 1305, 22 ALR Fed 475, cert den 409 US 847, 34 L Ed 2d 88, 93 S Ct 52.

Where defendant willfully violates injunction against sale of infringing dress-making charts, she must surrender all published charts, together with plates on which they are printed. Drury v Ewing (1862, CC Ohio) F Cas No 4095.

Copyright infringer is commanded to deliver up on oath to marshal of court all copies of infringing books, as well as all plates, molds, matrices, and other means for making copies of books in his possession, and marshal is directed to destroy them within five days after their delivery to him and to make return of his act to court. Southern Bell Tel. & Tel. Co. v Donnelly (1940, DC Fla) 35 F Supp 425, 48 USPQ 11.

Injunction issues with order that infringing defendants deliver up for destruction all infringing copies, as well as all plates, molds, and other means for making such copies. Sammons v Larkin (1940, DC Mass) 38 F Supp 649, 49 USPQ 350, mod on other grounds (CA1 Mass) 126 F2d 341, 53 USPQ 71.

Infringing prints and plates are subject to destruction. Rudolf Lesch Fine Arts, Inc. v Metal (1943, DC NY) 51 F Supp 69, 58 USPQ 668.

Plaintiff is entitled to delivery and destruction of all infringing products and materials in defendant's hands which may have been used in infringement of plaintiff's copyrights. Curt Teich & Co. v Beals Lithograph & Printing Co. (DC Iowa) 61 USPQ 434.

Summary judgment for defendants is granted as to plaintiff's prayer that infringing copies, be delivered for destruction, since defendants' affidavits state, without contradiction by plaintiff, that copies, were destroyed prior to start of suit. Local Trademarks, Inc. v Rogers (1947, DC Ala) 73 F Supp 907, 75 USPQ 336.

Where defendant's catalogue contains cuts copied from plaintiff's copyrighted catalogue, defendant is required to block out copied cuts, together with script referring thereto, from all catalogues in its possession or under its control and must surrender all plates, molds, and other matter used for producing infringements. Perkins Marine Lamp & Hardware Co. v Goodwin Stanley Co. (1949, DC NY) 86 F Supp 630, 83 USPQ 32.

Predecessor of this section contemplates destruction of infringement copies, but fact of infringement first must be judicially established. Lampert v Hollis Music, Inc. (1952, DC NY) 105 F Supp 3, 94 USPQ 226.

Injunction required copyright infringer to deliver for destruction all infringing copies and plates, including all books on consignment but still owned by infringer. Ziegelheim v Flohr (1954, DC NY) 119 F Supp 324, 100 USPQ 189.

Default judgment cannot order destruction of matrices used to produce phonograph records infringing musical copyright where complaint makes no assertion, and seeks no relief, upon basis of violation of this section; hence, defendant is not in default as to such contention. Miller v Goody (1954, DC NY) 125 F Supp 348, 103 USPQ 292.

Copyright infringers are required to deliver up for destruction all infringing copies, articles, records, and devices in their possession or under their control as well as all plates, molds, matrices, or other means of making such infringements. Dorchester Music Corp. v National Broadcasting Co. (1959, DC Cal) 171 F Supp 580, 120 USPQ 429.

Twelve technical manuals copying substantial portions of 6 copyrighted technical manuals for computers and components warrants destruction of all infringing copies under control of infringer. Telex Corp. v International Business Machines Corp. (DC Okla) 367 F Supp 258, 179 USPQ 777, affd in part and revd in part on other grounds (CA10 Okla) 510 F2d 894, cert dismd 423 US 802, 46 L Ed 2d 244, 96 S Ct 8.

Infringing brochures copying material from competitor's brochures on automotive lamps and lighting equipment is ordered removed or blocked out in lieu of destruction because it makes up small portion of defendant's catalog. Foreign Car Parts, Inc. v Auto World, Inc. (1973, DC Pa) 366 F Supp 977, 181 USPQ 162.

United States has right to sue for destruction of equipment used in tape piracy of copyrighted musical works as parens patriae, as enforcer of its copyright laws, and as protector of copyrights under international treaties. United States v Brown (1975, DC Miss) 400 F Supp 656, 189 USPQ 612.

Annotations:

Construction and application of §§ 1(c) and 1(d) of Copyright Act (17 USCS §§ 101(c), 101(d)), providing for impounding of articles alleged to infringe copyright and for destruction of infringing copies or devices. 22 ALR Fed 487.

§ 504. Remedies for infringement: Damages and profits

(a) In general. Except as otherwise provided by this title [17 USCS §§ 101 et seq.], an infringer of copyright is liable for either—

(1) the copyright owner's actual damages and any additional profits of the infringer, as provided by subsection (b); or

(2) statutory damages, as provided by subsection (c).

(b) Actual damages and profits. The copyright owner is entitled to recover the actual damages suffered by him or her as a result of the infringement, and any profits of the infringer that are attributable to the infringement and are not taken into account in computing the actual damages. In establishing the infringer's profits, the copyright owner is required to present proof only of the infringer's gross revenue, and the infringer is required to prove his or her deductible expenses and the elements of profit attributable to factors other than the copyrighted work.

(c) Statutory damages. (1) Except as provided by clause (2) of this subsection, the copyright owner may elect, at any time before final judgment is rendered, to recover, instead of actual damages and profits, an award of statutory damages for all infringements involved in the action, with respect to any one work, for which any one infringer is liable individually, or for which any two or more infringers are liable jointly and severally, in a sum of not less than $250 or more than $10,000 as the court considers just. For the purposes of this subsection, all the parts of a compilation or derivative work constitute one work.

(2) In a case where the copyright owner sustains the burden of proving, and the court finds, that infringement was committed willfully, the court in its discretion may increase the award of statutory damages to a sum

of not more than $50,000. In a case where the infringer sustains the burden of proving, and the court finds, that such infringer was not aware and had no reason to believe that his or her acts constituted an infringement of copyright, the court in its discretion may reduce the award of statutory damages to a sum of not less than $100. The court shall remit statutory damages in any case where an infringer believed and had reasonable grounds for believing that his or her use of the copyrighted work was a fair use under section 107 [17 USCS § 107], if the infringer was: (i) an employee or agent of a nonprofit educational institution, library, or archives acting within the scope of his or her employment who, or such institution, library, or archives itself, which infringed by reproducing the work in copies or phonorecords; or (ii) a public broadcasting entity which or a person who, as a regular part of the nonprofit activities of a public broadcasting entity (as defined in subsection (g) of section 118 [17 USCS § 118(g)]) infringed by performing a published nondramatic literary work or by reproducing a transmission program embodying a performance of such a work.
(Added Oct. 19, 1976, P. L. 94-553, Title I, § 101, 90 Stat. 2585.)

HISTORY; ANCILLARY LAWS AND DIRECTIVES

Effective date of section:
Section 102 of Act Oct. 19, 1976, P. L. 94-553, 90 Stat. 2598 provided that this section "becomes effective on January 1, 1978".

CROSS REFERENCES

"Copyright owner" defined, 17 USCS § 101.
Fair use, 17 USCS § 107.
Infringement of copyright, 17 USCS § 501.
Injunction as remedy for infringement, 17 USCS § 502.
Impounding and disposition of infringing articles, 17 USCS § 503.
This section referred to in 17 USCS §§ 111, 115, 116, 405, 411, 412, 510.

RESEARCH GUIDE

Forms:
6 Federal Procedural Forms L Ed, Copyrights § 17:118.

Annotations:
Measurement of damages for copyright infringement under 17 USCS § 101. 97 L Ed 283.
Apportionment and computation of profits for which copyright infringer is liable. 2 ALR3d 1211.

Law Review Articles:
Originality and Monetary Remedies Under The Copyright Act. 23 Buffalo L Rev 97.

INTERPRETIVE NOTES AND DECISIONS

I. IN GENERAL [17 USCS § 504(a)]

1. Generally
2. Interest on damage awards

II. ACTUAL DAMAGES AND PROFITS [17 USCS § 504(b)]

A. Actual Damages

3. Generally
4. Lost profits to complainant as measure of actual damage
5. Specific amounts awarded

B. Profits to Infringer

6. Generally
7. Apportionment of profits
8. Deductions from profits
9. Specific amounts awarded

III. STATUTORY DAMAGES [17 USCS § 504(c)]

10. Generally
11. Innocent or unintentional infringement
12. Maximum and minimum limits
13. Number of infringement
14. Parts of compilations and derivative works
15. Specific amounts awarded
16. Willful infringement

IV. PRACTICE AND PROCEDURE

17. Generally
18. Accounting for damages and profits
19. Evidentiary matters
20. Jury determinations
21. Orders or decrees
22. Appeals

I. IN GENERAL [17 USCS § 504(a)]

1. Generally

Defendant is liable only for copies in his possession and not for every copy that he has published or procured to be published. Bolles v Outing Co. (1899) 175 US 262, 44 L Ed 156, 20 S Ct 94.

Copyright statute differs from patent and trade-mark statutes, and injunction is not condition precedent for accounting and award of damages for copyright infringement. Sheldon v Moredall Realty Corp. (1938, CA2 NY) 95 F2d 48, 37 USPQ 286.

Damages and profits from copyright infringement are distinct items of recovery and are awarded on different legal principles. Sammons v Colonial Press, Inc. (1942, CA1 Mass) 126 F2d 341, 53 USPQ 71.

Since statute provides method of finding dam-

ages when actual damages cannot be proven, patent rule that measure of damages in such cases is established or reasonable royalty has no application to copyright cases. Widenski v Shapiro, Bernstein & Co. (1945, CA1 RI) 147 F2d 909, 64 USPQ 448.

Damages can be recovered for injury to personal property (copyrighted motion picture) although market value cannot be shown. Universal Pictures Co. v Harold Lloyd Corp. (1947, CA9 Cal) 162 F2d 354, 73 USPQ 317.

Action for damages by reason of copyright infringement sounds in tort. Turton v United States (1954, CA6 Ky) 212 F2d 354, 101 USPQ 164.

Measure of recovery is cumulative, encompassing both net profits of infringer and damages of copyright holder; although in some cases it may be assumed that copyright holder would have made identical number of sales had not infringer made such sales, such assumption is not permissible as basis for award of damages in case where parties sold fabrics of different quality at different prices in different markets. Peter Pan Fabrics, Inc. v Jobela Fabrics, Inc. (1964, CA2 NY) 329 F2d 194, 140 USPQ 631.

The Copyright Act allows only a single recovery for a single sale, and where multiple defendants are all connected with the same infringement, their liability is joint and several and recovery from one reduces the liability of the others, regardless of whether or not it is so agreed at the time of payment and whether or not the settling defendant is actually liable to a copyright holder. Screen Gems-Columbia Music, Inc. v Metlis & Lebow Corp. (1972, CA2 NY) 453 F2d 552, 172 USPQ 261.

Where infringement is slight and merely technical, court may only require defendant to pay small royalty to plaintiff. Myers v Callaghan (1883, CC Ill) 20 F 441.

Where value of complainant's rights in its copyright have been so injured by defendant's piracy that injunctive relief will be of no avail, the plaintiff may have decree for accounting and costs. Hartford Printing Co. v Hartford Directory & Pub. Co. (1906, CC Conn) 146 F 332.

Position of defendants as employees of United States cannot protect them from award of damages for copyright infringement; acts done were for benefit of government but that does not immunize its agents as well as government. Towle v Ross (1940, DC Or) 32 F Supp 125, 45 USPQ 143.

All defendants participating in production of infringing play are jointly liable for all of plaintiff's damages resulting from infringement; defendants, who published infringing play, are jointly liable for plaintiff's damages resulting from publication and are jointly and severally liable for profits received from its publication and for royalties received from producers of infringing play. Harris v Miller (DC NY) 50 USPQ 625.

Damages for copyright infringement are not merely incidental to equitable relief, since right to damages is provided as distinct and separate remedy from injunctive relief; damages are not limited to such damages as court might award as incident to injunctive relief, but include also statutory damages, which are peculiar to copyright cases; court is empowered to award such damages only because of statute, and not by virtue of general equity powers. Chappell & Co. v Cavalier Cafe, Inc. (1952, DC Mass) 13 FRD 321, 95 USPQ 243.

Statutory damages under Copyright Act cannot be recovered in common-law action depending on diversity of citizenship and requisite jurisdictional amount; having no evidence of specific damages resulting from conduct of defendant complained of, plaintiff cannot state common-law claim against defendant within jurisdiction of federal court. Smith v George E. Muehlehach Brewing Co. (1956, DC Mo) 140 F Supp 729, 110 USPQ 177.

Ordinarily, law allows victim of infringement upon his literary rights to recover profits made by infringer or damages suffered by himself; profits customarily are determined upon accounting; that defendant may not have made profits is not conclusive on issue of damages, since right to damages is alternative to right to recover infringer's profits. Szekely v Eagle Lion Films, Inc. (1956, DC NY) 140 F Supp 843, 109 USPQ 348, affd (CA2 NY) 242 F2d 266, 113 USPQ 98, cert den 354 US 922, 1 L Ed 2d 1437, 77 S Ct 1382.

In terms of remedy, actions for copyright infringement and suits for statutory royalties are quite different; under former, accounting of profits based upon sales is available to aid determination of appropriate damages, while, under compulsory license, royalty fixed by statute limits pecuniary remedy of copyright proprietor, irrespective of profits which may be involved. ABC Music Corp. v Janov (1960, DC Cal) 186 F Supp 443, 126 USPQ 429.

Individual defendants, who caused corporate defendant to publish articles infringing plaintiff's copyright, are jointly and severally liable together with corporate defendant for damages sustained by plaintiff; all who participate in infringement are jointly and severally liable. Massapequa Publishing Co. v Observer, Inc. (1961, DC NY) 191 F Supp 261, 128 USPQ 418.

Successful plaintiff in copyright infringement action can recover his damages or defendant's profits. Orgel v Clark Boardman Co. Ltd. (DC NY) 128 USPQ 531, mod on other grounds (CA2 NY) 301 F2d 119, 133 USPQ 94, 2 ALR3d 1203, cert den 371 US 817, 9 L Ed 2d 58, 83 S Ct 31.

It is within discretion of court and available proof to determine damages that should be awarded for copyright infringement; object is to take profit out of copyright infringement when profits can be ascertained or, in lieu thereof, permit award of statutory damages based on number of infringing articles involved. Neal v Thomas Organ Co. (1965, DC Cal) 241 F Supp 1020, 145 USPQ 315.

Liability for damages must rest upon substantial evidence of similarity between plaintiffs' literary property and defendants' moving picture; owner of property is competent to testify as to its worth; rule permits owner of play to testify as to its value as basis for ascertainment of damages incurred by its infringement. Golding v R. K. O. Pictures, Inc. (1949, Cal) 208 P2d 1, 82 USPQ 136, subsequent op on reh 35 Cal 2d 690, 221 P2d 95, 86 USPQ 537.

Recovery in California state court upon contract implied in law not to use literary composition without paying for same must be limited solely to reasonable value of composition, or portion of it, which was used; there can be no recovery of damages for failure to give screen credit to plaintiff. Weitzenkorn v Lesser (1953) 40 Cal 2d 778, 256 P2d 947, 97 USPQ 545.

Unauthorized use of the literary production of another furnishes no ground for recovery of damages, except through federal copyright laws. State v State Journal Co. (1905) 75 Neb 275, 106 NW 434, motion den 77 Neb 752, 110 NW 763, application den 77 Neb 771, 111 NW 118.

Although defendants are enjoined from using book title, plaintiff is not entitled to receive profits from book merely because title, which had acquired no secondary significance, had been improperly appropriated by defendants. Biltmore Pub. Co. v Grayson Pub. Corp. (1947) 272 App Div 504, 71 NYS2d 337, 74 USPQ 241.

Annotations:

Measurement of damages for copyright infringement under 17 USCS § 101. 97 L Ed 283.

2. Interest on damage awards

Interest on recoveries in copyright infringement suit is computed from date of master's report. Harris v Miller (DC NY) 57 USPQ 190.

Interest is allowed at 6% on unpaid royalties admitted to be due on account of sale of copyrighted music. Pallma v Fox (DC NY) 87 USPQ 395.

Author is entitled to interest on damages, awarded for plagiarism of his motion-picture script, from date of first exhibition of motion picture to date of judgment. Szekely v Eagle Lion Films, Inc. (1956, DC NY) 140 F Supp 843, 109 USPQ 348, affd (CA2 NY) 242 F2d 266, 113 USPQ 98, cert den 354 US 922, 1 L Ed 2d 1437, 77 S Ct 1382.

II. ACTUAL DAMAGES AND PROFITS [17 USCS § 504(b)]

A. Actual Damages

3. Generally

Where infringement works some considerable injury, court may estimate damages within statutory limits, without being bound by usual legal proofs; it was intention of Congress (1) to preserve right of plaintiff to pursue damages and profits by historic methods of equity if he chooses so to do; and (2) to give new right of application to court for such damages as shall 'appear to be just,' in lieu of actual damages; words present no difficulty in interpretation; 'actual' means 'real' as opposed to 'nominal'; it means 'existent,' without precluding thought of change; 'in lieu' means in place of thing modified by quoted phrase. S. E. Hendricks Co. v Thomas Pub. Co. (1917, CA2 NY) 242 F 37.

Damages alone are awarded where copyright infringer's profits are less than damages sustained by plaintiff. Universal Pictures Co. v Harold Lloyd Corp. (1947, CA9 Cal) 162 F2d 354, 73 USPQ 317.

Discretion to award damages for copyright infringement is that of trial court, not of court of appeals; in lieu of actual damages, damages may be such as to court shall appear to be just, but must be within limits of predecessor section; discretion respecting allowance of attorney fees to prevailing party is also that of trial court. Wihtol v Crow (1962, CA8 Iowa) 309 F2d 777, 135 USPQ 385.

Right given to author to multiply copies of his work, and to prevent appropriation of his work by other persons, includes right to recover damages for infringement where such can be proven. West Publishing Co. v Edward Thompson Co. (1909, CC NY) 169 F 833, mod on other grounds (CA2 NY) 176 F 833.

Recovery of damages on account of copyright infringement by manufacturer of infringing figurines does not bar recovery of damages from one who purchases figurines from manufacturer and resells them; damages assessed against manufacturer were assessed as result of manufacturer's infringement and not infringement of purchaser

from manufacturer. McCulloch v Zapun Ceramics, Inc. (DC NY) 97 USPQ 12.

Although acts of copyright infringement, for which plaintiff is awarded damages, also constitute acts of unfair competition, plaintiff is not entitled to recover damages for acts of unfair competition. Dorchester Music Corp. v National Broadcasting Co. (1959, DC Cal) 171 F Supp 580, 120 USPQ 429.

Copyright proprietor is entitled to award of amount of damages or infringer's profits, whichever is higher. Runge v Lee (1969, DC Cal) 161 USPQ 770.

Annotations:

Measurement of damages for copyright infringement under 17 USCS § 101. 97 L Ed 283.

4. Lost profits to complainant as measure of actual damage

Lost profits to complainant may be assessed as damages even though infringer derived no profit from sale of infringing copies. Gross v Van Dyk Gravure Co. (1916, CA2 NY) 230 F 412.

Measure of damages is profits which plaintiffs would have made on sales of their copyrighted book had not infringing book competed; infringer's profits may bear no relation to, and are wholly unreliable as indication of, plaintiff's damages, that is profits which he would have made but for infringement. Sammons v Colonial Press, Inc. (1942, CA1 Mass) 126 F2d 341, 53 USPQ 71.

Damages for infringement of architectural plans for factory are fair market value of plans, and case is remanded for proof of fair value of plans; and previous determination that infringer did not benefit from use of plans is binding on parties. Nucor Corp. v Tennessee Forging Steel Service, Inc. (1975, CA8 Ark) 513 F2d 151, 185 USPQ 332.

Diminution of plaintiff's sales up to time of suit may be considered in measuring damages in absence of proof of amount of sales by infringer. Chils v Gronlund (1890, CC NY) 41 F 145.

For infringement of name alone of copyrighted work, preventing author from exhibiting work as motion-picture scenario, sale value of such scenario is measure of damages. Paramore v Mack Sennett, Inc. (1925, DC Cal) 9 F2d 66.

Copyright proprietor was not awarded statutory damages of one dollar for each copy of infringing book, but was awarded lesser sum based upon his lost sales and defendant's profits; lost sales were computed by comparing actual sales with average sales in previous two years; more than cost of printing and binding should have been included in cost of publication of defendant's books. Ziegelheim v Flohr (1954, DC NY) 119 F Supp 324, 100 USPQ 189.

Where defendant plagiarizes plaintiff's literary property by distribution of motion picture incorporating plaintiff's motion-picture script, plaintiff is entitled to damages based upon special value of script to him; such value is value of security interest which he had in manuscript inasmuch as contract between plaintiff and motion-picture producer provided that plaintiff would retain title to script as security for payment of specific sum; defendant is liable for such sum; plaintiff may not base damages upon what third party might have paid for script, since producer was only market available to him, nor may plaintiff recover punitive damages since plaintiff recognized that his best chance of securing payment of amount due from producer was to allow production and distribution of picture. Szekely v Eagle Lion Films, Inc. (1956, DC NY) 140 F Supp 843, 109 USPQ 348, affd (CA2 NY) 242 F2d 266, 113 USPQ 98, cert den 354 US 922, 1 L Ed 2d 1437, 77 S Ct 1382.

In determining damages for copyright infringement, court considers facts that defendant inflicted deliberate injury upon plaintiff's business and that plaintiff's fabric had demonstrated high degree of commercial success when defendant copied and sold exact reproductions of copyrighted design to cheaper market, thereby aborting any further exploitation of design by plaintiff in higher priced, specialized market in which plaintiff customarily did business. Plaintiff is awarded damages for loss of potential market. Fruit of The Loom, Inc. v Andris Fabrics, Inc. (1963, DC NY) 227 F Supp 977, 141 USPQ 484.

When the damages from infringement take the form of claiming the entire profit on the defendant's sale, on the lost-sale-to-plaintiff theory, the amount so claimed is inclusive of both damages and profits. Fedtro, Inc. v Kravex Mfg. Corp. (1970, DC NY) 313 F Supp 990, 164 USPQ 510.

In action on implied contract to pay for reasonable value of use of literary material wherein defendant contends that use was trivial, unsubstantial, and insignificant, jury might take into account nature of matter involved and likelihood that, by adoption of fundamental ideas in plaintiff's scripts, particular material was deprived of its substance and rendered of no further value on market. Yadkoe v Fields (1944) 66 Cal App 2d 150, 151 P2d 906, 63 USPQ 103.

5. Specific amounts awarded

Where 5000 copies of infringing map were sold, but it did not appear that plaintiff's business was materially injured, allowance of $2000 damages was adequate. General Drafting Co. v Andrews (1930, CA2 NY) 37 F2d 54.

Even if plaintiff's biography was not success and has long been out of print and even if there is no evidence that defendants gained anything from using infringing material in their novel and that plaintiff suffered actual damage, court is justified in awarding plaintiff damages and attorney's fees. Toksvig v Bruce Pub. Co. (1950, CA7 Wis) 181 F2d 664, 85 USPQ 339.

Deliberate infringer (distributor of motion picture) should not be able to say that screen play common-law copyright was worthless because infringer did not make expenses on infringement, in face of its payment to producer of amount in excess of amount as security for which author retained rights in screen play; infringer cannot cast on holder of rights burden of unscrambling elements of value in picture, when it deliberately infringed with notice of rights in it held as security; author may recover security value placed upon play. Szekely v Eagle Lion Films, Inc. (1957, CA2 NY) 242 F2d 266, 113 USPQ 98, cert den 354 US 922, 1 L Ed 2d 1437, 77 S Ct 1382.

In action for damages for infringement of copyright, where plaintiff did not distribute, or attempt to distribute or sell single copy after publication of infringing work in newspaper, court is unable to determine what damage resulted to plaintiff from such publication. D'Ole v Kansas City Star Co. (1899, CC Mo) 94 F 840.

Where plaintiff had suffered no actual damage by reason of the infringing acts court allowed nominal damages of six cents. F. A. Mills, Inc. v Standard Music Roll Co. (1915, DC NJ) 223 F 849, affd (CA3 NJ) 241 F 360.

Five hundred dollars based on value of play and publicity author would have received had his name been upon advertisements of the play were allowed as damages for infringement. Stodart v Mutual Film Corp. (1917, DC NY) 249 F 507.

Where contract gave defendant, proprietor of grocery store, exclusive right to use plaintiff's copyrighted advertisements in defendant's community, and defendant continued to use advertisements after termination of contract, plaintiff is not entitled to receive $1 for each copy of newspaper containing infringement, or nominal damages of $250, but only amount of sale price of subscription during period of infringement. Advertisers Exchange, Inc. v Hinkley (1951, DC Mo) 101 F Supp 801, 92 USPQ 313, affd (CA8 Mo) 199 F2d 313, 95 USPQ 124, cert den 344 US 921, 97 L Ed 710, 73 S Ct 388.

It makes little difference, in assessing damages from defendant's showing of plaintiff's copyrighted motion picture, whether or not each showing was separate infringement; total value of picture did not exceed $3,000; hence, sum of the parts (separate showings) cannot exceed the whole; damages cannot exceed $3,000. Pickford Corp. v De Luxe Laboratories, Inc. (1958, DC Cal) 169 F Supp 118, 120 USPQ 521.

Infringement of architectural plans by unauthorized taking and copying of plans and starting to build house according to plans justifies damages of $9,000 reasonable architectural fee plus additional $5,000 for unauthorized taking and copying, plus full attorney fees and costs of plaintiff. Herman Frankel Organization, Inc. v Wolfe (1974, DC Mich) 184 USPQ 819.

Uncorroborated and speculative evidence of estimates of lost profits of copyright proprietor is insufficient for damage computation; proof of infringer's sales invoices is insufficient to determine infringer's profits because noninfringing sales are mixed in with infringing sales, so court applies "in lieu" damages and on finding that infringement was wilful, awards $2500 each for infringement of 9 castings for lamp bases, and $250 each for infringing copyrighted photographs of lamp base castings plus $2500 attorney fees to plaintiff. L & L White Metal Casting Corp. v Joseph (1975, DC NY) 387 F Supp 1349, 185 USPQ 269.

Plaintiff submitted his uncopyrighted but fully developed radio program to defendant, with recording of actual studio broadcast; defendant subsequently produced and broadcast program found by jury to be based on plaintiff's uncopyrighted program; verdict for $35,000 was sustained. Stanley v Columbia Broadcasting System, Inc. (1948, Cal App) 192 P2d 495, 77 USPQ 404, superseded (Cal) 208 P2d 9, 82 USPQ 123, subsequent op on reh 35 Cal 2d 653, 221 P2d 73, 86 USPQ 520, 23 ALR2d 216.

In suit for plagiarism, plaintiff's testimony that value of his format for radio program was $100,-000 and that it had no value after defendants' use thereof, was sufficient to support award of $25,000 damages. Kovacs v Mutual Broadcasting System, Inc. (1950) 99 Cal App 2d 56, 221 P2d 108, 86 USPQ 547.

B. Profits to Infringer

6. Generally

In passing Copyright Act apparent intention of Congress was to assimilate remedy with respect to recovery of profits to that already recognized in patent cases; fact that defendants are guilty of deliberate plagiarism is no ground for saying that in awarding profits to copyright proprietor as means of compensation, court may make award of profits not shown to be due to infringement. Sheldon v Metro-Goldwyn Pictures Corp. (1940) 309 US 390, 84 L Ed 825, 60 S Ct 681, 44 USPQ 607.

By coming forward with undisputed admission

of its profit from copyright infringement, defendant cannot tie hands of court and limit recovery to that amount. F. W. Woolworth Co. v Contemporary Arts, Inc. (1952) 344 US 228, 97 L Ed 276, 73 S Ct 222, 95 USPQ 396, motion den 350 US 810, 100 L Ed 727, 76 S Ct 37.

If proprietor whose copyright has been infringed waives his action for damages, he may have accounting of profits. Stevens v Gladding (1856, CC RI) F Cas No 13399.

Evidence showing sales and exchanges of infringing books, but failing to show the sum defendant received from such sales and exchanges, was insufficient to prove any profits. Gilmore v Anderson (1890, CC NY) 42 F 267.

Amounts received from advertisers should be included in accounting for profits on infringing directory. Hartford Printing Co. v Hartford Directory & Printing Co. (1906, CC Conn) 148 F 470.

Rule that defendant is to account for every copy of his book sold as if it had been copy of complainant's book, and to pay complainant profit which latter would have received from sale of so many additional copies was inapplicable, and damages were assessed on basis of defendant's profits from sale of his infringing book. Scribner v Clark (1888, CC Ill) 50 F 473, affd 144 US 488, 36 L Ed 514, 12 S Ct 734.

Where defendant is found guilty of infringement, complainant is entitled to take account of profits gained from sale of infringing book, and to full costs and reasonable attorney's fees. Huebsch v Arthur H. Crist Co. (1914, DC NY) 209 F 885.

Composer of infringing music is chargeable with profits in amount of royalties received from infringing song. Wilkie v Santly Bros., Inc. (1940, DC NY) 36 F Supp 574, 47 USPQ 380, affd (CA2 NY) 139 F2d 264, cert den 322 US 740, 88 L Ed 1574, 64 S Ct 1058.

Nominal recovery of statutory minimum of $250 will not compensate plaintiff, in view of defendants' probable profits from infringement, so accounting is ordered. Khan v Leo Feist, Inc. (1947, DC NY) 70 F Supp 450, 73 USPQ 104, affd (CA2 NY) 165 F2d 188, 76 USPQ 27.

It is cardinal principle in patent and copyright actions that plaintiff may recover only for actual profits from sales that he is able by proof to establish; similarly, infringer is accountable only for those profits which may be justly apportioned to sale of infringing products; in accounting for profits, court is not interested in what parties would have priced infringements at had they been able to foresee infringement suit; defendant is limited to actual sales price as of time of sales contract just as plaintiff is restricted in recovery to actual profits. Alfred Bell & Co. v Catalda

Fine Arts, Inc. (1949, DC NY) 86 F Supp 399, 82 USPQ 273, mod on other grounds (CA2 NY) 191 F2d 99, 90 USPQ 153.

Defendant having failed to disclose amount of sales resulting from publication of infringing contract advertisement, plaintiff is awarded as damages sum based on sales made and commissions paid by defendant to plaintiff in prior contest conducted under valid contract whereby defendant used plaintiff's copyrighted advertisement. Gordon v Weir (1953, DC Mich) 111 F Supp 117, 97 USPQ 387, affd (CA6 Mich) 216 F2d 508, 104 USPQ 40.

When damages take form of claiming infringer's entire profits on sales, on the lost sale to plaintiff theory, amount so claimed is inclusive of both damages and profits. Fedtro, Inc. v Kravex Mfg. Corp. (1970, DC NY) 313 F Supp 990, 164 USPQ 510.

Right to account of profits is incident to right to injunction in copyright cases. Stevens v Gladding (1855) 58 US 447, 15 L Ed 155; Belford v Scribner (1892) 144 US 488, 36 L Ed 514, 12 S Ct 734; Stevens v Cady (1854, CC RI) F Cas No 13395; Fishel v Lueckel (1892, CC NY) 53 F 499; Falk v Gast Lithograph & Engraving Co. (1893, CA2 NY) 54 F 890; McCaleb v Fox Film Corp. (1924, CA5 La) 299 F 48.

Annotations:

Measurement of damages for copyright infringement under 17 USCS § 101. 97 L Ed 283.

Apportionment and computation of profits for which copyright infringer is liable. 2 ALR3d 1211.

7. Apportionment of profits

Where lawful cannot be separated from unlawful parts of book, owner of copyright is entitled to recover entire profits. Callaghan v Myers (1888) 128 US 617, 32 L Ed 547, 9 S Ct 177; Belford v Scribner (1892) 144 US 488, 36 L Ed 514, 12 S Ct 734.

Where it is impossible to separate defendant's profits on published matter to which copyright does not extend from profits on matter covered by copyright, defendant, being responsible for blending of lawful with unlawful, has to abide consequences and is liable for entire profits. Sheldon v Metro-Goldwyn Pictures Corp. (1940) 309 US 390, 84 L Ed 825, 60 S Ct 681, 44 USPQ 607.

Where defendant contended that since phonograph disc was double record, only one side of which infringed, profits should be divided but offered no proof as to cost of making up each composition or as to sales advantages of one over the other, it was sufficient for plaintiff to establish number of sales of its composition, and,

in absence of proof of every element of cost, defendant's claim could not be sustained. Davilla v Brunswick-Balke Collender Co. (1938, CA2 NY) 94 F2d 567, 36 USPQ 398, cert den 304 US 572, 82 L Ed 1536, 58 S Ct 1040.

In patent and copyright cases, co-infringers, unless partners, are severally accountable only for profits each has received. Sammons v Colonial Press, Inc. (1942, CA1 Mass) 126 F2d 341, 53 USPQ 71.

Indirect overhead, which was neither increased nor decreased by infringement, is apportioned according to number of songs published, and not according to number of copies sold although infringing song was best seller. Wilkie v Santly Bros., Inc. (1943, CA2 NY) 139 F2d 264, 60 USPQ 46, cert den 322 US 740, 88 L Ed 1574, 64 S Ct 1058.

One infringer is not liable for profits which other infringers derive from same infringement; appellant cannot complain of fact that apportionment of profits between infringing and noninfringing parts of book, though liberal to him, is not mathematically exact. Washingtonian Pub. Co. v Pearson (1944) 78 App DC 287, 140 F2d 465, 60 USPQ 224.

Where portion of profits of infringing work (motion picture) is attributable to appropriated work (play), to avoid unjustly giving originator all profits where infringer's labor and artistry have also to extent contributed to ultimate result, there may be reasonable approximation and apportionment of profits; plaintiff is awarded one fifth of profits from infringing motion pictures and attorney fees. Twentieth Century-Fox Film Corp. v Stonesifer (1944, CA9 Cal) 140 F2d 579, 60 USPQ 392.

In ascertaining profits derived by exhibitor from infringing motion picture, profits derived from picture and other portions of show were apportioned. Sheldon v Moredall Realty Corp. (1939, DC NY) 29 F Supp 729, 43 USPQ 81.

Producers of infringing play were severally liable for profits they received from production of play. Harris v Miller (DC NY) 50 USPQ 306, mod on other grounds 50 USPQ 625.

Profits from play infringing biography are apportioned 50% for acting of star of play, 35% for script, 10% for direction of specific infringer, and 5% for "other factors"; plaintiff is allowed profits attributable to script and direction; apportionment between infringing and noninfringing material in script is not possible or practicable. Harris v Miller (DC NY) 57 USPQ 103.

Equity is concerned with making fair apportionment between profits from infringement and profits not from infringement; principle of apportioning profits has been used in patent law to prevent doing of manifest injustice, namely, to award all profits from sale of machine to owner of patent that was infringed by only part of machine; result sought is rational separation of net profits so that neither may have what rightfully belongs to other; doctrine has been extended to accounting for profits in copyright cases. Alfred Bell & Co. v Catalda Fine Arts, Inc. (1949, DC NY) 86 F Supp 399, 82 USPQ 273, mod on other grounds (CA2 NY) 191 F2d 99, 90 USPQ 153.

Although only 35% of copyright infringer's book contains plagiarized material, he is liable for his entire profits from book since there is no evidence as to how much of profits resulted from plagiarism; for aught that appears legitimate 65% of book may have been without influence in the sales. Orgel v Clark Boardman Co. (DC NY) 128 USPQ 531, mod on other grounds (CA2 NY) 301 F2d 119, 133 USPQ 94, 2 ALR3d 1203, cert den 371 US 817, 9 L Ed 2d 58, 83 S Ct 31.

While copyright protection does not extend to specific phonograph records, which comprise part of copyrighted instruction course, records have no purpose when separated from instruction manual; profit cannot be apportioned between records and instructional manual since profit was not derived from sale of records alone. Neal v Thomas Organ Co. (1965, DC Cal) 241 F Supp 1020, 145 USPQ 315.

Publisher's profit from sale of infringing book is not apportioned, although plagiarized material constituted only comparatively small part of plaintiff's work, since profit was due to book as whole, not to any particular part thereof. Smith v Little, Brown & Co. (1967, DC NY) 273 F Supp 870, affd (CA2 NY) 396 F2d 150, 154 USPQ 473.

Where defendants' infringing display cards bear noninfringing articles, plaintiff is not entitled to profits from sale of articles, but is entitled to the whole profit from sale of cards, even though such profit is not entirely due to infringing material, inasmuch as defendants made no adequate apportionment of profits. Fedtro, Inc. v Kravex Mfg. Corp. (1970, DC NY) 313 F Supp 990, 164 USPQ 510.

Annotations:

Apportionment and computation of profits for which copyright infringer is liable. 2 ALR3d 1211.

8. Deductions from profits

Profits made on infringement are arrived at by deducting actual and legitimate manufacturing cost from selling price. Callaghan v Myers (1888) 128 US 617, 32 L Ed 547, 9 S Ct 177.

Gross profits are not what copyright owner is entitled to recover from infringer, but only such profits as remain after defendant reduces them by proof of allowable elements of costs. F. W. Woolworth Co. v Contemporary Arts, Inc. (1952) 344 US 228, 97 L Ed 276, 73 S Ct 222, 95 USPQ 396, motion den 350 US 810, 100 L Ed 727, 76 S Ct 37.

In accounting for infringement by motion picture, overhead which does not assist in production of infringement should not be credited to infringer but that which does should be and where picture was one of over forty made by defendants, using same staff and organization, they were as much condition on production of infringing picture as scenery or play. Sheldon v Metro-Goldwyn Pictures (1939, CA2 NY) 106 F2d 45, 42 USPQ 540, affd 309 US 390, 84 L Ed 825, 60 S Ct 681, 44 USPQ 607.

Defendant has burden of proving every element of cost, blanket undifferentiated item of overhead is insufficient; only if evidence shows that amount owing from infringing publisher to infringing printer is uncollectible will printer be entitled to deduction therefor in computing its net profits; deduction is properly made of proper proportion of general overhead expenses which assisted in production of copyright infringement, at least where infringement was not conscious and deliberate. Sammons v Colonial Press, Inc. (1942, CA1 Mass) 126 F2d 341, 53 USPQ 71.

Fact that publisher of many songs operated at over-all loss gives it no immunity from accounting for profits from infringement of common-law copyright of plaintiff's song merely because they were less than enough to make entire business profitable; if publisher lost less because of infringement, to that extent infringement gave it profit for which it must account. Wilkie v Santly Bros., Inc. (1943, CA2 NY) 139 F2d 264, 60 USPQ 46, cert den 322 US 740, 88 L Ed 1574, 64 S Ct 1058.

Publisher is entitled to treat royalties paid to author of infringing book as an element of its cost in computing profits which plaintiff is entitled to recover from publisher. Plaintiff may sue author for such royalties. Smith v Little, Brown & Co. (1968, CA2 NY) 396 F2d 150, 158 USPQ 177.

In determining profits of play, each season is to be taken as unit, and losses sustained in one season cannot be deducted from earnings of next season. Dam v Kirk La Shelle Co. (1911, CC NY) 189 F 842.

In copyright cases where purpose is to find amount of profits or damages, plaintiff may show only receipts from infringing sales and put upon defendant burden of proving cost of production.

Ginn & Co. v Apollo Pub. Co. (1915, DC Pa) 228 F 214.

Although defendants must bare any inaccuracies arising out of accounting because they are wrongdoers, it is not equitable to deprive them arbitrarily of money rightly theirs. Pallma v Fox (DC NY) 74 USPQ 130.

Plaintiff can recover profits only on infringements actually sold by defendant; likewise, defendant is limited to deductions for cost of infringements sold; defendant may not deduct, from profits of infringements sold, cost of infringements not sold; sales discounts, freight and cartage outward, salesmen's salaries and commissions, commissions to dealers, shipping, and packing are sales overhead expense properly deductible from gross profits. Alfred Bell & Co. v Catalda Fine Arts, Inc. (1949, DC NY) 86 F Supp 399, 82 USPQ 273, mod on other ground (CA2 NY) 191 F2d 99, 90 USPQ 153.

Direct cost of production of infringements and percentage of indirect cost of doing business are deductible from infringer's gross receipts from infringing sales. Neal v Thomas Organ Co. (1965, DC Cal) 241 F Supp 1020, 145 USPQ 315.

Annotations:

Apportionment and computation of profits for which copyright infringer is liable. 2 ALR3d 1211.

9. Specific amounts awarded

Award of $1 per copy as damages for copies of song found in possession of infringer was improper, and award was reduced to maximum profit which owner of copyright would have made on retail sale of such copies. Turner & Dahnken v Crowley (1918, CA9 Cal) 252 F 749.

Plaintiff is awarded defendant's profits of $629 from four infringements, without deduction of losses of $23 from three additional infringements. Curt Teich & Co. v Beals Lithograph & Printing Co. (DC Iowa) 61 USPQ 434.

Infringer sold infringing books for $10,600, but has submitted no evidence as to cost of publication, so plaintiff recovers $10,600 as infringer's profits, and in addition recovers $250 damages for infringement. Whitman Publishing Co. v Writesel (DC Ohio) 83 USPQ 535.

Defendant who admitted infringement by selling shirts having copyrighted fabric design, who promptly stopped infringement, and whose failure to respond to a warning letter was due to attorney oversight, is assessed $300 damages equal to net profits rather than larger "in lieu" damages. Printempo Fabrics, Inc. v G & G Shops, Inc. (1975, DC NY) 186 USPQ 327.

Annotations:

Apportionment and computation of profits for which copyright infringer is liable. 2 ALR3d 1211.

III. STATUTORY DAMAGES [17 USCS § 504(c)]

10. Generally

Provision of predecessor statute that infringer shall be liable to pay "in lieu of actual damages and profits, such damages as to the court shall appear just" is not applicable where profits have been proved and only question is as to their apportionment. Sheldon v Metro-Goldwyn Pictures Corp. (1940) 309 US 390, 84 L Ed 825, 60 S Ct 681, 44 USPQ 607.

Recovery of penalty for copies infringing painting, may be had for all such copies made by defendant whether in his possession or not. American Lithographic Co. v Werckmeister (1911) 221 US 603, 55 L Ed 873, 31 S Ct 676.

Rule of liability which merely takes away profits from copyright infringement would offer little discouragement to infringers; statutory rule does not merely compel restitution of profit and reparation for injury, but also is designed to discourage wrongful conduct; court's discretion is wide enough to permit resort to statutory damages for such purpose; even for uninjurious and unprofitable invasions of copyright, court may impose liability within statutory limits. F. W. Woolworth Co. v Contemporary Arts, Inc. (1952) 344 US 228, 97 L Ed 276, 73 S Ct 222, 95 USPQ 396, motion den 350 US 810, 100 L Ed 727, 76 S Ct 37.

Sums specified in predecessor section are not fixed sums to be allowed as damages under any circumstances of infringement after notice, but it is duty of court to award damages as justified by nature and circumstances of case as developed on trial; and where no proof of actual damage is offered award should have relation to such inferences as are reasonably deductible from whole case of infringement without reference to any idea of punishment. Turner & Dahnken v Crowley (1918, CA9 Cal) 252 F 749.

Where damages are indirect and not capable of ascertainment, compensation which the copyright proprietor shall receive is committed to discretion of trial judge. Campbell v Wireback (1920, CA4 Md) 269 F 372, 17 ALR 743.

In suit for statutory penalty for violation of copyright, strict construction and proof are required. Caliga v Inter Ocena Newspaper Co. (1907, CA7 Ill) 157 F 186, affd 215 US 182, 54 L Ed 150, 30 S Ct 38.

Whether profits shall be awarded or statutory damages allowed in copyright infringement suit is not matter of choice with plaintiff and where there was ample evidence to make award of damages on basis of actual profits, master and court below were in error in granting statutory damages. Davilla v Brunswick-Balke Collender Co. (1938, CA2 NY) 94 F2d 567, 36 USPQ 398, cert den 304 US 572, 82 L Ed 1536, 58 S Ct 1040.

Although infringer had actual notice of copyright before infringement, limitation applies since there was no law suit of which he had notice and he was not then "a defendant"; if limitation were inapplicable, plaintiff would be left to such damages as to court shall appear just, arrived at in exercise of judicial discretion up to dollar per copy. Advertisers Exchange, Inc. v Hinkley (1952, CA8 Mo) 199 F2d 313, 95 USPQ 124, cert den 344 US 921, 97 L Ed 710, 73 S Ct 388.

Since there was no showing on amount of damages arising from copyright infringement, plaintiff was entitled to be compensated in manner provided in predecessor of this section; it was inappropriate for court of appeals to assess these damages; this highly discretionary function was best performed by trier of facts, especially since defendant distributed its infringing catalogues with notice of plaintiff's copyright, and therefore trial court was not confined by statutory limitations in its assessment of damages. Markham v A. E. Borden Co. (1953, CA1 Mass) 206 F2d 199, 98 USPQ 346.

Court has discretion to grant lesser statutory amount rather than copyright infringer's actual profits. American Visuals Corp. v Holland (1958, CA2 NY) 261 F2d 652, 119 USPQ 482.

Since predecessor of this section is clear that lack of proof of damages and profits does not preclude recovery of larger amount where warranted, it is error for court not to consider as within its discretion propriety of statutory award for damages suffered even though incapable of exact proof in addition to actual profits shown to have been made by infringer; proof of one element of award does not curtail exercise of discretion under "in lieu" clause. Peter Pan Fabrics, Inc. v Jobela Fabrics, Inc. (1964, CA2 NY) 329 F2d 194, 140 USPQ 631.

In case where court found copyright infringement, but damages and profits were not shown, it was required to apply mandatory statutory damage provisions of predecessor section. Shapiro, Bernstein & Co. v 4636 S. Vermont Ave., Inc. (1966, CA9 Cal) 367 F2d 236, 151 USPQ 231.

Predecessor of this section is inapplicable, in discretion of court, to case disclosing infringement covering musical composition where there is no proof of actual damage. Atlantic Monthly Co. v Post Pub. Co. (1928, DC Mass) 27 F2d 556.

Damage because of defendant's infringement of copyrighted mezzotint engraving cannot be more than nominal since plate for engraving has been destroyed for many years and most, if not all, of proofs taken from it have been sold by plaintiff. Alfred Bell & Co. v Catalda Fine Arts, Inc. (1947, DC NY) 74 F Supp 973, 75 USPQ 66, later app (DC NY) 86 F Supp 399, mod on other grounds (CA2 NY) 191 F2d 99, 90 USPQ 153.

Since there is no showing of actual damages suffered by plaintiff, it is entitled to be compensated for copyright infringement under predecessor of this section, which authorizes court to allow such damages as shall appear to be just; in its discretion, court may allow amounts stated in statute. M. J. Golden & Co. v Pittsburgh Brewing Co. (1956, DC Pa) 137 F Supp 455, 108 USPQ 250.

It was not intent of Congress to award statutory damages of $1.00 per copy for books which are fraudulent in that they are used for sole and express purpose of falsely inducing public to believe that cash discounts on merchandise are obtained through use of books, whereas same discounts are given to all members of public in ordinary course of business; however, court allows specific sum as statutory damages because of difficulty of proving actual damage. Advisers, Inc. v Wiesen-Hart, Inc. (1958, DC Ohio) 161 F Supp 831, 117 USPQ 330.

Since no evidence is presented as to infringer's profits, all copies of infringing publication have been recalled, and defendant is no longer actively in business, there is no need for further relief in addition to award of statutory damages; evidence as to cost of preparing copyrighted directory and as to losses of sales due to infringement is vague and conjectural; court cannot with any reasonable accuracy find actual damages suffered by plaintiff; in lieu thereof, statutory damages of $1.00 for each infringing copy are awarded. Greenfield v Tanzer (1960, DC Mass) 186 F Supp 795, 125 USPQ 392.

Predecessor of this section provides in essence that court may award to copyright proprietor either actual damages he suffered due to infringement, plus infringer's profits, or damages in amount to be computed in accordance with arbitrary standard set forth in statute; where there is no evidence as to damage suffered by proprietor or profits realized by infringer, court is justified in awarding statutory damages. Doran v Sunset House Distributing Corp. (1961, DC Cal) 197 F Supp 940, 131 USPQ 94, affd (CA9 Cal) 304 F2d 251, 134 USPQ 4, and (disapproved on other grounds L. Batlin & Son, Inc. v Snyder (CA2 NY) 536 F2d 486, cert den 429 US 857, 50 L Ed 2d 135, 97 S Ct 156).

Court exercises its discretion to award statutory damages to plaintiff since plaintiff was unable to prove actual damages and testimony as to amount of profits from copyright infringement is in conflict; such damages may be awarded when there is uncertainty as to amount of damages or profits. Holdredge v Knight Publishing Corp. (1963, DC Cal) 214 F Supp 921, 136 USPQ 615.

Damages for infringement of plaintiff's copyrights on video-taped television rerun programs were, in District Court's discretion, granted an amount which appeared just, rather than on basis of evidence of plaintiff's actual damages or defendant's profits resulting from infringements. Smothers v Columbia Broadcasting System, Inc. (1973, DC Cal) 359 F Supp 723.

Uncorroborated and speculative evidence of estimates of lost profits of copyright proprietor is insufficient for damage computation; proof of infringer's sales invoices is insufficient to determine infringer's profits because noninfringing sales are mixed in with infringing sales, so court applies "in lieu" damages and on finding that infringement was wilful, awards $2500 each for infringement of 9 castings for lamp bases, and $250 each for infringing copyrighted photographs of lamp base castings plus $2500 attorney fees to plaintiff. L & L White Metal Casting Corp. v Joseph (1975, DC NY) 387 F Supp 1349, 185 USPQ 269.

Copying of portions of copyrighted technical brochures is copyright infringement and is not excused by salesmen's unauthorized grant of permission, but lack of wilfulness of infringement results in award of statutory minimum damages of $250 per infringement. USAchem, Inc. v Sands (1975, DC NM) 185 USPQ 387.

Annotations:

Measurement of damages for copyright infringement under 17 USCS § 101. 97 L Ed 283.

11. Innocent or unintentional infringement

Although defendant was entirely innocent in publication of copyrighted article and had taken it from copyrighted magazine with permission of magazine, when there is technical violation of copyright, some damages should be awarded. Insurance Press v Ford Motor Co. (1918, CA2 NY) 255 F 896.

Where prints of copyright owner lacked notice by accident or mistake and defendant stopped infringing on actual notice, he is innocent infringer and not responsible for damages for prior infringement. Smith v Wilkinson (1938, CA1 NH) 97 F2d 506, 38 USPQ 1.

Innocent copier of screen play, whether copyrighted or not, is liable for damages; while Copyright Act makes significant distinctions in

certain instances based on innocent or willful infringement, it does not do so in general provision for award of profits and actual damages, or statutory sums allowable in court's discretion in lieu of actual damages. De Acosta v Brown (1944, CA2 NY) 146 F2d 408, 63 USPQ 311, cert den 325 US 862, 89 L Ed 1983, 65 S Ct 1197 and cert den 325 US 862, 89 L Ed 1983, 65 S Ct 1198.

Provision restricting recovery to $5,000 where motion-picture producer is unaware of infringement, applies to statutory damages, not where court is awarding actual damages. Universal Pictures Co. v Harold Lloyd Corp. (1947, CA9 Cal) 162 F2d 354, 73 USPQ 317.

In suit against innocent infringer who has been misled by omission of copyright notice, complainant is not entitled to recover damages but may recover all profits gained from infringement. Strauss v Penn Printing & Pub. Co. (1915, DC Pa) 220 F 977.

Plaintiff has right to damages and accounting for profits under copyright law, regardless of innocence of defendant. Haas v Leo Feist (1916, DC NY) 234 F 105.

In awarding damages in lieu of actual damages for infringement of map copyright, by newspaper publisher acting in good faith, court may treat publication in several editions of newspaper as single infringement. Sauer v Detroit Times Co. (1917, DC Mich) 247 F 687.

Although defendant was innocent infringer of copyright, and no damage is shown to have resulted to plaintiff, defendant must be assessed minimum damages. Altman v New Haven Union Co. (1918, DC Conn) 254 F 113.

Where 50,000 infringing pamphlets were printed and 10,000 of them distributed, and defendant did not know that it was copyrighted work he had copied, award of $3000 damages was just. Norris v No-Leak-O Piston Rings Co. (1921, DC Md) 271 F 536, affd (CA4 Md) 277 F 951.

Where defendants continued after notice from plaintiff's attorney but by advice of their own attorney that their activities would not constitute infringement, they should not be severely penalized, especially where venture has not been successful and injunction and destruction of books will entail further loss. National Geographic Soc. v Classified Geographic, Inc. (1939, DC Mass) 27 F Supp 655, 41 USPQ 719.

Where infringement was printed in defendant's magazine through misapprehension of rights and apology and retraction were offered, $1000 damages were assessed. Zenn v National Golf Review (1939, DC NY) 27 F Supp 732, 41 USPQ 535.

Lack of intention to infringe where there was due notice of copyright did not release from liability. Advertisers Exch., Inc. v Laufe (1939, DC Pa) 29 F Supp 1, 38 USPQ 93.

Owner of theatre exhibiting motion picture which infringes copyright is innocent infringer and may deduct from gross receipts what it paid in federal income taxes on profits from exhibition, investment, interest, and depreciation. Sheldon v Moredall Realty Corp. (1939, DC NY) 29 F Supp 729, 43 USPQ 81.

One who markets infringing figurines made by another infringes copyright irrespective of innocence of infringement and is liable for damages therefor. McCulloch v Zapun Ceramics, Inc. (DC NY) 97 USPQ 12.

Lack of knowledge of copyright infringement does not relieve defendants of liability; however, their infringement consisted of use of infringing advertisement under copyright issued to plagiarist which appeared valid on its face; there must be some point at which innocent infringer should be protected from liability other than accounting of profits which he would not have made but for use of copyrighted matter; also, he should not be liable for damages realized by coinfringer; therefore, there being no proof that defendants profited from infringement, and it not being shown that plaintiff sustained actual damages except for commission which he, rather than plagiarist, would have received, no damages are assessed against defendants except on defendant who used infringing material second time after notice of infringement. Gordon v Weir (1953, DC Mich) 111 F Supp 117, 97 USPQ 387, affd (CA6 Mich) 216 F2d 508.

Defense of innocence of ignorance of copyright applies only insofar as it may be relevant to question of damages assessed against infringer. Peter Pan Fabrics, Inc. v Dixon Textile Corp. (1960, DC NY) 188 F Supp 235, 127 USPQ 329.

Question as to defendant's actual knowledge of plaintiffs' copyright does not bear on issue of liability but goes only to issue of amount of damages. Peter Pan Fabrics, Inc. v Puritan Dress Co. (1962, DC NY) 207 F Supp 563, 133 USPQ 678.

12. Maximum and minimum limits

Court's conception of what is just in particular case, considering nature of copyright, circumstances of infringement, and like, is made measure of damages to be paid, but with express qualification that in every case assessment must be within prescribed limitations; that is to say, neither more than maximum nor less than minimum; within these limitations court's discretion and sense of justice are controlling, but it has no discretion when proceeding under predecessor provision to go outside of them. L. A. Westermann Co. v Dispatch Printing Co. (1919) 249 US 100, 63 L Ed 499, 39 S Ct 194.

Where there is no proof of actual damages court is bound by minimum amount of $250; maximum and minimum provisions are applicable alike to all types of infringement except those for which statute makes other specific provisions. Jewell-La Salle Realty Co. v Buck (1931) 283 US 202, 75 L Ed 978, 51 S Ct 407.

Where there is no proof of damages it is within discretion of court to award damages of one dollar for each infringing copy, and such award cannot be disturbed on appeal so long as award is not less than $250 or more than $5,000. Douglas v Cunningham (1935) 294 US 207, 79 L Ed 862, 55 S Ct 365, 24 USPQ 153.

Effect of limitations on amount of damages, is that it gives more substantial relief in event only small number of copies is found and is less oppressive on defendant where maximum number of copies is found. Boston Traveler Co. v Purdy (1905, CA1 Mass) 137 F 717.

Where defendant had obtained article from copyrighted magazine with permission of magazine, and without knowledge that it was otherwise copyrighted, and printed it in booklet which he distributed free to owners of automobiles, plaintiff was awarded minimum amount of $250. Insurance Press v Ford Motor Co. (1918, CA2 NY) 255 F 896.

For infringement of copyright of musical composition minimum amount assessable is $250 instead of the amount stated in predecessor of this section. Irving Berlin, Inc. v Daigle (1929, CA5 La) 31 F2d 832.

Damages for infringement of copyright of musical composition for public performance is minimum of $250 for each performance for profit, and not $10 penalty. Lutz v Buck (1930, CA5 Tex) 40 F2d 501, 5 USPQ 452, cert den 282 US 880, 75 L Ed 776, 51 S Ct 83.

In absence of proof of both actual damages and profits, trial court is required to award minimum statutory sum of $250. Johns & Johns Printing Co. v Paull-Pioneer Music Corp. (1939, CA8 Mo) 102 F2d 282, 41 USPQ 3; Burndy Engineering Co. v Sheldon Serv. Corp. (1942, CA2 NY) 127 F2d 661, 53 USPQ 409.

Judgment of $250 for each infringement is proper since this is minimum amount permitted by Copyright Act where actual damages are not established. Interstate Hotel Co. v Remick Music Corp. (1946, CA8 Neb) 157 F2d 744, 71 USPQ 138, cert den 329 US 809, 91 L Ed 691, 67 S Ct 622, reh den 330 US 854, 91 L Ed 1296, 67 S Ct 769.

Since, within minimum and maximum limits set by predecessor of this section, district court's discretion is controlling in its award of statutory damages, only question before court of appeals is whether district court awarded less than statutory minimum for each infringement. Markham v A. E. Borden Co. (1955, CA1 Mass) 221 F2d 586, 105 USPQ 199.

Damage award of $5000 for selling infringing copies of poem is affirmed as within limits prescribed by predecessor statute, where actual damages to copyright proprietor are unascertainable. Bell v Pro Arts, Inc. (1975, CA6 Ohio) 511 F2d 451, 185 USPQ 6, cert den 423 US 829, 46 L Ed 2d 46, 96 S Ct 47.

Statutory "in lieu" damages, although ambiguous hodgepodge of improvisation, requires court to follow statutory minimum of $250 for each infringement that was separate, and court erred in awarding lesser amount reflecting "such damages as to the court shall appear just"; and provisions in statute for damages for infringements for performances of dramatical-musical compositions and musical compositions are guidelines that do not apply until statutory minimum of $250 has been awarded; and District Court is directed to enter judgment for minimum statutory amount of $250 for each copyright infringed for each performance given of infringing rock opera or such greater sum "as to the court shall appear just". Robert Stigwood Group, Ltd. v O'Reilly (1976, CA2 Conn) 530 F2d 1096, 189 USPQ 453, cert den 429 US 848, 50 L Ed 2d 121, 97 S Ct 135.

Predecessor section in providing for minimum damages of $250 and maximum of $5000 does not bind court to decree at least statutory minimum of damages where court is of opinion that there are no damages, or that they are less than $250. Woodman v Lydiard-Peterson Co. (1912, CC Minn) 192 F 67, affd (CA8 Minn) 204 F 921, reh den (CA8 Minn) 205 F 900.

Damages for infringement of copyright of musical composition are governed by predecessor of this section, providing that damages shall not exceed $5000 or be less than $250; provision of said predecessor section fixing damages at $10 for every infringing performance, applies only within limits of $5000 and $250. Waterson, Berlin & Snyder Co. v Tollefson (1918, DC Cal) 253 F 859.

Minimum damages allowable are $250, irrespective of extent of use of copyrighted article, and smallness of damage does not require reduction of attorney fees to be allowed. M. Witmark & Sons v Calloway (1927, DC Tenn) 22 F2d 412.

Magazine was not included within exceptions stated to higher range of allowable damages.

Cory v Physical Culture Hotel, Inc. (1936, DC NY) 14 F Supp 977, 30 USPQ 353, affd (CA2 NY) 88 F2d 411, 33 USPQ 58.

Court was required to assess damages of not less than $250 against defendant infringing copyright scheme, though contrary to justice in case. Doll v Libin (1936, DC Mont) 17 F Supp 546, 33 USPQ 17.

Plaintiff is entitled to some damages for copyright infringement on mere showing of infringing acts; there must have been some actual damage but this damage is without proof raised to statutory amount ($250) if amount of damage cannot be ascertained. Towle v Ross (1940, DC Or) 32 F Supp 125, 45 USPQ 143.

Publisher is liable only under "in lieu" clause of predecessor section on account of printing of allegedly infringing book, since copyright owner suffered no damage from printing and only printer made profits therefrom; "in lieu" damages are no more than $250, since no effective damage took place until publication and sale. Greenbie v Noble (1957, DC NY) 151 F Supp 45, 113 USPQ 115.

Since actual damages from copyright infringement are not shown, statutory minimum for each infringement may be applied. Harms, Inc. v Sansom House Enterprises, Inc. (1958, DC Pa) 162 F Supp 129, 117 USPQ 272, affd (CA3 Pa) 267 F2d 494.

F. W. Woolworth Co. v Contemporary Arts, Inc., 344 US 228, 97 L Ed 276, 73 SCR 222, 95 USPQ 362, gives to copyright owner, under statutory mandate, measure of damages greater than mere licensing fee to which proprietor of copyrighted music would have been entitled had license been sought; courts have discretion to determine damages, within maximum and minimum statutory limits, as their sense of justice may determine. Harms, Inc. v F. W. Woolworth Co. (1958, DC Cal) 163 F Supp 484, 118 USPQ 436.

Where plaintiff proves copyright infringement, but has not submitted proof of actual damages, award of $250 as minimum damages in each cause of action is mandatory. Bourne, Inc. v Romero (1959, DC La) 23 FRD 292, 122 USPQ 129 (disapproved on other grounds Securities & Exchange Com. v Research Automation Corp. (CA2) 521 F2d 585).

Where plaintiffs in copyright infringement action prove infringement, but do not submit proof of actual damages, award of $250 as minimum damages in each cause of action is mandatory under predecessor section. Edwin H. Morris & Co. v Burton (1961, DC La) 201 F Supp 36, 132 USPQ 680.

Copyright proprietor is not entitled to minimum sum of $250 for each infringed song, regardless of actual damages suffered by proprietor and regardless of profits made by infringing vendor; it is matter of judicial discretion as to whether it is more just that recovery be based upon proven profits of defendant and damages to plaintiff or be within statutory limits; plaintiff's motion for summary judgment is denied; parties should be put to their proof as to plaintiff's damages and defendant's profits before court is in position to exercise discretion which might result in imposition of statutory minimum of damages. Shapiro, Bernstein & Co. v Bleeker (1963, DC Cal) 224 F Supp 595, 140 USPQ 111.

Statutory minimum of $250 and maximum of $5000 apply to each separate infringement; they apply to all types of infringement except those for which statute makes other specific provision; within limitation of this minimum and maximum, trial court has complete discretion to award any damages which it thinks are just and, in fixing such damages, may use statutory formula as guide; each copying by defendant, for use in either or both of its catalogs, of separately prepared illustration in plaintiff's catalog must be regarded as separate infringement for purpose of computing damages under "in lieu" provision. Hedeman Products Corp. v Tap-Rite Products Corp. (1964, DC NJ) 228 F Supp 630, 141 USPQ 381.

Considering deliberate infringement of zodiac pins and sudden drop in sales of copyrighted pins after infringement began, and considering difficulty in measuring profits, court awards maximum "in lieu" damages of $5,000 per infringement for 8 infringements plus $1617 as defendants' profits, plus $1 per infringing copy sold after notice. Jerry De Nicola, Inc. v Genesco, Pakula & Co. (1975, DC NY) 188 USPQ 306.

Maximum and minimum limits of damages set by predecessor of this section do not apply to infringements after notice. Loew's Inc. v Superior Court of Los Angeles County (1941) 18 Cal 2d 419, 115 P2d 983, 50 USPQ 641.

13. Number of infringement

Each infringement of single copyright on entire periodical justifies separate minimal damage award; newspaper publication separately and independently of six pictorial illustrations, designed for advertising purposes and separately copyrighted by proprietor, five of which were published once and other one twice, constituted seven separate and distinct infringements. L. A. Westermann Co. v Dispatch Printing Co. (1919) 249 US 100, 63 L Ed 499, 39 S Ct 194.

Where there is no showing of actual loss court must allow minimum amount and may in his discretion, if there are sufficient number of infringing copies or performances, employ schedule as provided for in predecessor of this section as basis for assessing additional damages. Jewell-La Salle Realty Co. v Buck (1931) 283 US 202, 75 L Ed 978, 51 S Ct 407.

Where damages awarded were within limit for one infringement and there was no denial of at least one infringement, it was not necessary to decide whether there was more than one infringement. Cory v Physical Culture Hotel, Inc. (1937, CA2 NY) 88 F2d 411, 33 USPQ 58.

In case wherein infringer caused 29 publications of copyrighted advertisements in newspaper printing 3261 copies of each publication, and in which plaintiff does not prove actual damages or profits, "in lieu" provision of predecessor section does not require that plaintiff be awarded one dollar for each infringing copy of newspaper or 29 times 3261 dollars. Advertisers Exchange, Inc. v Hinkley (1952, CA8 Mo) 199 F2d 313, 95 USPQ 124, cert den 344 US 921, 97 L Ed 710, 73 S Ct 388.

In copyright infringement action wherein court finds 13 copyrights to be valid and infringed, it is error for court to award $250 as total amount of damages since plaintiff is entitled to statutory award of not less than $250 nor more than $5,000 for each of the 13 separate and distinct infringed copyrights; court's discretion in assessing damages is limited by statutory minimum of $250 and maximum of $5,000; while court of appeals ordinarily would remand with direction that district court fix damages within statutory limits, it is not necessary in instant case since plaintiff states that it is unable to prove damages in more than statutory minimum amount on each infringement; plaintiff, therefore, is entitled only to $250 for each of 13 copyrights infringed. Universal Statuary Corp. v Gaines (1962, CA5 Tex) 310 F2d 647, 135 USPQ 483.

District Court is directed to award minimum damages of $48,000 for infringement of four copyrights at $250 per infringement times 48 infringing performances for one rock opera, and $13,500 on same formula for infringement of other rock opera; three overlapping copyrights on dramatical-musical portion of rock opera are regarded as single copyright for infringement purposes, and minimum damages of $250 per copyright infringement are awarded for infringement of three musical compositions plus dramatical-musical work for each performance of infringing rock opera, since there is no reason to merge successive performances into single infringement. Robert Stigwood Group, Ltd. v O'Reilly (1976, CA2 Conn) 530 F2d 1096, 189

USPQ 453, cert den 429 US 848, 50 L Ed 2d 121, 97 S Ct 135.

Discretion of special master in fixing amount of recovery in lieu of damages did not extend to number of infringing articles. Fleischer Studios, Inc. v Ralph A. Freundlich, Inc. (1936, DC NY) 14 F Supp 401, 30 USPQ 125.

Publication of infringing copies of copyrighted photograph in advertisements in successive issues of magazine constituted separate infringements. Cory v Physical Culture Hotel, Inc. (1936, DC NY) 14 F Supp 977, 30 USPQ 353, affd (CA2 NY) 88 F2d 411, 33 USPQ 58.

Where plaintiff had copyright of book of 52 illustrations and defendant used four illustrations in four advertisements on four different dates, this constituted four infringements, and statutory damages of four times $250 are awarded. Lindsay & Brewster, Inc. v Verstein (1937, DC Me) 21 F Supp 264, 35 USPQ 494.

Award of $4000 as statutory damages for copyright infringement is proper where there were 14 cases of infringement contained in six separate printings of defendant's trade catalogue and gross sale price of items sold by defendant, which covers items mentioned in infringing pages of catalogue, is over $52,000, and taking into consideration general nature of defendant's business and fact that no notice was given defendant of infringement until suit was brought. Burndy Engineering Co. v Penn-Union Electric Corp. (1940, DC Pa) 32 F Supp 671, 45 USPQ 80, adhered to (DC Pa) 36 F Supp 35 and affd (CA3 Pa) 122 F2d 932, 51 USPQ 548.

Five publications in infringing advertisement in newspaper constituted five separate acts of infringement; court awards $250 damages for each infringement. Zuckerman v Dickson (1940, DC Pa) 35 F Supp 903, 47 USPQ 514.

Defendants infringed three copyrights on catalogue by four separate printings; this constituted 12 infringements for which award of $250 statutory damages each was proper as was allowance of one dollar for each of 500 copies of one infringing page printed separately. Burndy Engineering Co. v Sheldon Service Corp. (1941, DC NY) 39 F Supp 274, 50 USPQ 24, affd (CA2 NY) 127 F2d 661, 53 USPQ 409.

There being no proof as to plaintiff's actual damage or defendants' profits, court allows statutory damages of ten dollars for each infringing radio performance; composition was performed three times with chain hook-ups of 67, 66, and 85 stations; damages of $2180 are awarded on theory that there were 218 performances, not three; $250 attorneys' fee is allowed. Law v National Broadcasting Co. (1943, DC NY) 51 F Supp 798, 58 USPQ 669.

Court awarded one dollar for each infringing copy where large number of items was copied from plaintiff's catalogue, but awarded statutory minimum of $250 for infringement which only copied two items from plaintiff's catalogue; $250 also was awarded as to infringement where it was likely that substantial numbers of infringing copies were distributed during period wherein recovery was barred by statute of limitations. Harry Alter Co. v A. E. Borden Co. (1954, DC Mass) 121 F Supp 941, 102 USPQ 2.

Simultaneous network telecast of infringing play over 162 stations constitutes only one infringement by network, sponsor, advertising agency, producer, person in charge of production, and script writers. Davis v E. I. Du Pont De Nemours & Co. (1966, DC NY) 249 F Supp 329, 148 USPQ 328.

Separate radio broadcasts at monthly intervals of copyrighted musical compositions each constitute separate infringement since broadcasts are not merely continuation or repetition of first; if infringements had been confined to period of few days rather than several years, damages would have been limited by $5,000 maximum for single infringement instead of sum represented by multiple of minimums. Baccaro v Pisa (1966, DC NY) 252 F Supp 900, 149 USPQ 296.

Fourteen separate infringements in 12 technical manuals copying substantial portions of 6 copyrighted technical manuals at $250 for each infringement plus $1 for each additional infringing copy results in judgment of $13,776. Telex Corp. v International Business Machines Corp. (DC Okla) 367 F Supp 258, 179 USPQ 777, affd in part and revd in part on other grounds (CA10 Okla) 510 F2d 894, cert dismd 423 US 802, 46 L Ed 2d 244, 96 S Ct 8.

Wilful and deliberate infringement with full notice of copyright in musical compositions eliminates maximum damage provision of $5,000, and in absence of proof of profits of infringer, court awards $250 per infringement for unauthorized arrangements, copies, and several thousand performances in promoting Arizona State Fair. Mills Music, Inc. v Arizona (1975, DC Ariz) 187 USPQ 22.

14. Parts of compilations and derivative works

Where law provides penalty for each copy of infringed copyright, and two infringements are printed on every sheet, it is proper for penalty to be $800 when 400 of such sheets were printed. Journal Pub. Co. v Drake (1912, CA9 Or) 199 F 572.

Under prior act which provided penalty for every "sheet" found in possession of defendant, although more than one copyrighted picture was printed on a sheet, such sheet constituted but one article on which penalty could be had. Falk v Heffron (1893, CC NY) 56 F 299.

Defendant who used five newspaper advertisements from plaintiff's copyrighted book, after expiration of contract with plaintiff, was guilty of but one infringement, not five. Doll v Libin (1936, DC Mont) 17 F Supp 546, 33 USPQ 17.

15. Specific amounts awarded

Where infringer proved gross profit of $899.16 and trial court excluded or struck most of copyright owner's proof of actual damages on ground that authority to allow statutory damages rendered such proof unnecessary, statute empowered trial court in its sound exercise of judicial discretion on all facts to allow statutory damages in amount of $5,000. F. W. Woolworth Co. v Contemporary Arts, Inc. (1952) 344 US 228, 97 L Ed 276, 73 S Ct 222, 95 USPQ 396, motion den 350 US 810, 100 L Ed 727, 76 S Ct 37.

Where 2800 copies of an infringing work had been sold, $2500 damages were not erroneous. S. E. Hendricks Co. v Thomas Pub. Co. (1917, CA2 NY) 242 F 37.

Minimum of $250, recovered, and which equaled award of one dollar for all catalogues distributed, was proper where plaintiff had not been damaged. Russell & Stoll Co. v Oceanic Electrical Supply Co. (1936, CA2 NY) 80 F2d 864, 28 USPQ 203.

Thirty-five hundred dollars damages are allowed; defendants sold 3500 books at fifty cents while plaintiff sold 180,000 copies at $1.50 each. Adventures in Good Eating, Inc. v Best Places to Eat, Inc. (1942, CA7 Ill) 131 F2d 809, 56 USPQ 242.

It is not abuse of discretion to award damages of $1000 and attorney's fees of $500 where infringing author received $3000 in connection with sale of book and infringing publisher sold 14,262 copies at net profit of five to ten cents per book. Toksvig v Bruce Pub. Co. (1950, CA7 Wis) 181 F2d 664, 85 USPQ 339.

Award of $5000 damages under predecessor section is justified, despite fact that infringing publication was not profitable, in view of abrupt drop in sales of copyrighted chart and authors' fee paid by infringer. Nikanov v Simon & Schuster, Inc. (1957, CA2 NY) 246 F2d 501, 114 USPQ 89.

Damage award of $25,000 in lieu of actual damages and profits is proper and within court's discretion where infringer failed to answer interrogatories as to number and dollar amounts of sales of infringing model airplane kits. Monogram Models, Inc. v Industro Motive Corp. (1974, CA6 Mich) 492 F2d 1281, 181 USPQ 425, cert den 419 US 843, 42 L Ed 2d 71, 95 S Ct 76.

For admitted copying of part of plaintiff's book for use in advertising calendar not sold for profit, and which caused no actual damage to plaintiff, $1000 as damages and same amount as attorney's fees were awarded. Warren v White & Wyckoff Mfg. Co. (1930, DC NY) 39 F2d 922.

Twenty-five hundred dollars were awarded for infringement of advertising card, where claims of parties varied greatly. Sebring Pottery Co. v Steubenville Pottery Co. (1934, DC Ohio) 9 F Supp 384.

Plaintiff was entitled to $250, defendant having submitted its catalogue to plaintiff before issue. North & Judd Mfg. Co. v Krischer's Mfg. Co. (1935, DC Conn) 11 F Supp 739, 27 USPQ 224.

Five thousand dollars were awarded for infringement of copyright photograph, where infringing copies were used in advertisements in seven issues of magazine. Cory v Physical Culture Hotel, Inc. (1936, DC NY) 14 F Supp 977, 30 USPQ 353, affd (CA2 NY) 88 F2d 411, 33 USPQ 58.

Court in following cases awarded minimum damages of $250 for each song or musical selection sung or played. Society of European State Authors & Composers, Inc. v New York Hotel Statler Co. (1937, DC NY) 19 F Supp 1, 34 USPQ 6; Buck v Russo (1938, DC Mass) 25 F Supp 317, 39 USPQ 377; Buck v Ridgway Const. Co. (1938, DC Mass) 25 F Supp 690, 39 USPQ 376; Buck v Newsreel, Inc. (1938, DC Mass) 25 F Supp 787, 40 USPQ 20; Buck v Spanish Gables, Inc. (1938, DC Mass) 26 F Supp 36, 40 USPQ 19; Buck v Dacier (1938, DC Mass) 26 F Supp 37, 40 USPQ 14; Buck v Savoia Restaurant, Inc. (1938, DC NY) 27 F Supp 289, 41 USPQ 138; Buck v Lisa (1939, DC NY) 28 F Supp 379, 42 USPQ 116; Buck v Crescent Gardens Operating Co. (1939, DC Mass) 28 F Supp 576, 42 USPQ 435; Shapiro, Bernstein & Co. v Veltin (1942, DC La) 47 F Supp 648, 55 USPQ 335; Remick Music Corp. v Interstate Hotel Co. (1944, DC Neb) 58 F Supp 523, 63 USPQ 327, affd (CA8 Neb) 157 F2d 744, 71 USPQ 138, cert den 329 US 809, 91 L Ed 691, 67 S Ct 622, reh den 330 US 854, 91 L Ed 1296, 67 S Ct 769; Buck v LaFontaine (DC Mass) 39 USPQ 377; Buck v Deane (DC Mass) 39 USPQ 381; Buck v Royal Palms (DC Mass) 39 USPQ 382; Buck v Columbus Restaurant, Inc. (DC Mass) 39 USPQ 382; Buck v Yin Ho Co. (DC Mass) 39 USPQ 383; Buck v Melanson (DC Mass) 39 USPQ 384; Buck v Parker (DC Mass) 40 USPQ 13; Buck v Valenti (DC Mass) 40 USPQ 16; Buck v Ricci (DC Mass) 40 USPQ 17; Buck v Sunbeam (DC Mass) 40 USPQ 18; Buck v Repertory Theatre, Inc. (DC Mass) 40 USPQ 23; Buck v Holyoke Theatre, Inc. (DC

Mass) 40 USPQ 24; Buck v Wrentham Show Boat, Inc. (DC Mass) 40 USPQ 25; Buck v Levin (DC Mass) 40 USPQ 27.

Where M procured N to reproduce copyrighted matter for M to distribute, on finding of infringement, damages of $2000 were allowed, to be paid by M. Freedman v Milnag Leasing Corp. (1937, DC NY) 20 F Supp 802, 35 USPQ 184.

Infringing printer which made no profits from infringement is liable for $250 as statutory damages and costs; infringing author is liable for $7600 profits and costs. Sammons v Larkin (1940, DC Mass) 38 F Supp 649, 49 USPQ 350, mod on other grounds (CA1 Mass) 126 F2d 341, 53 USPQ 71.

Motion picture having infringed play by copying substantial and material part, and having made $19,800 profit, court assesses $3960 as damages. Stonesifer v Twentieth Century-Fox Film Corp. (1942, DC Cal) 48 F Supp 196, 56 USPQ 94, affd (CA9 Cal) 140 F2d 579, 60 USPQ 392.

Although infringer could have obtained license for $90 per year or $10 per month, plaintiff's actual damages are not confined to loss of license fee; in lieu of actual damages and profits, $250 damages and $100 attorney's fee are awarded for one infringing performance of copyrighted song. Shapiro, Bernstein & Co. v Widenski (1944, DC RI) 54 F Supp 780, 61 USPQ 91, affd (CA1 RI) 147 F2d 909, 64 USPQ 448.

In cases wherein plaintiff offered no proof of damages or profits, master awarded statutory damages of $22,720 against one defendant and $18,000 against another defendant, but court reduces amounts to $5000 and $2000. Foreign & Domestic Music Corp. v Michael M. Wyngate, Inc. (DC NY) 74 USPQ 296.

Predecessor section gives court broad discretion in granting statutory damages in lieu of actual damages; award of statutory damages is called for in case where plaintiff is unable to show actual damages and defendant fails to prove its costs; minimum statutory allowance of $250 justly compensates plaintiff and discourages further infringement by defendant where product involved is inexpensive. Morser v Bengor Products Co. (1968, DC NY) 283 F Supp 926, 159 USPQ 267.

Court awards full statutory damages of $5,000 for infringement of poem copied onto posters where defendants repeatedly failed to provide information on poster sales and were unable to produce records of posters sold, although circumstances do not justify punitive damages. Bell v Pro Arts, Inc. (DC Ohio) 366 F Supp 474, 180 USPQ 517, affd (CA6 Ohio) 511 F2d 451, cert den 423 US 829, 46 L Ed 2d 46, 96 S Ct 47.

Publication of telephone directory infringing copyrighted telephone directory is subject to $500 damages. Southwestern Bell Tel. Co. v Nationwide Independent Directory Service, Inc. (1974, DC Ark) 371 F Supp 900, 182 USPQ 193.

Considering deliberate infringement of zodiac pins and sudden drop in sales of copyrighted pins after infringement began, and considering difficulty in measuring profits, court awards maximum "in lieu" damages of $5,000 per infringement for 8 infringements plus $1617 as defendants' profits, plus $1 per infringing copy sold after notice. Jerry De Nicola, Inc. v Genesco, Pakula & Co. (1975, DC NY) 188 USPQ 306.

16. Willful infringement

Defendant who, with wanton or malicious disregard of rights of the plaintiff, publishes previously unpublished ode in violation of common-law rights to such ode may be charged with exemplary damages. Press Pub. Co. v Monroe (1896, CA2 NY) 73 F 196, error dismd 164 US 105, 41 L Ed 367, 17 S Ct 40.

In fixing punitive damages, court may take into consideration intent and acts of defendant in failing to make payment and its willful disregard of provisions of Copyright Act. Leo Feist, Inc. v American Music Roll Co. (1918, DC Pa) 253 F 860.

Where defendants are conscious and deliberate infringers, credits for income tax payments are refused. Harris v Miller (DC NY) 57 USPQ 103.

Inasmuch as defendant continued to account for royalties on basis of records sold, rather than on basis of records manufactured, despite plaintiff's repeated protests, damages awarded are assessed at three times amount found to be due as a royalty; in awarding such damages, court considers intent and acts of defendant in failing to make payment and its wilful disregard of Copyright Act; such damages are in addition to royalty to which plaintiffs are entitled. Famous Music Corp. v Seeco Records, Inc. (1961, DC NY) 201 F Supp 560, 132 USPQ 342.

Belated notices of intent to use and specious tenders of payment are transparent attempt to build defense in infringement action; they will not limit amount of recovery of compensatory or punitive damages and will not bar award of attorney's fees. Pickwick Music Corp. v Record Productions, Inc. (1968, DC NY) 292 F Supp 39, 159 USPQ 228.

Uncorroborated and speculative evidence of estimates of lost profits of copyright proprietor is insufficient for damage computation; proof of infringer's sales invoices is insufficient to determine infringer's profits because noninfringing sales are mixed in with infringing sales, so court applies "in lieu" damages and on finding that infringement was wilful, awards $2500 each for infringement of 9 castings for lamp bases, and $250 each for infringing copyrighted photographs of lamp base castings plus $2500 attorney fees to plaintiff. L & L White Metal Casting Corp. v Joseph (1975, DC NY) 387 F Supp 1349, 185 USPQ 269.

Wilful and deliberate infringement with full notice of copyright in musical compositions eliminates maximum damage provision of $5,000, and in absence of proof of profits of infringer, court awards $250 per infringement for unauthorized arrangements, copies, and several thousand performances in promoting Arizona State Fair. Mills Music, Inc. v Arizona (1975, DC Ariz) 187 USPQ 22.

In addition to award of $1617 as defendants' profits, court awards maximum in lieu damages for deliberate infringement of zodiac pins. Jerry De Nicola, Inc. v Genesco, Pakula & Co. (1975, DC NY) 188 USPQ 306.

IV. PRACTICE AND PROCEDURE

17. Generally

Issuance of writ of execution is proper process with respect to portion of decree awarding money damages and costs for copyright infringement. Raymor Ballroom Co. v Buck (1940, CA1 Mass) 110 F2d 207, 45 USPQ 2.

In copyright suit, interrogatories pertaining solely to question of damages may be issued only when liability of defendants shall have been established. Michelson v Crowell Pub. Co. (1938, DC Mass) 25 F Supp 968, 39 USPQ 520.

Annotations:

Measurement of damages for copyright infringement under 17 USCS § 101. 97 L Ed 283.

18. Accounting for damages and profits

Where bill for infringement of copyright prays for general relief, but not expressly for accounting, equity may decree accounting. Stevens v Gladding (1855) 58 US 447, 15 L Ed 155.

If bill for infringement contains no prayer for account, or prayer for general relief, an accounting will not be decreed. Stevens v Cady (1854, CC RI) F Cas No 13395.

Where accounting of profits is claimed, such can be decreed under general prayer for relief. Gilmore v Anderson (1889, CC NY) 38 F 846.

Defendant filed affidavit stating amount of total sales infringing copyright and opposes reference to master for accounting; plaintiff is not bound by defendant's affidavit and questions correctness of amount; on motion, master is appointed for accounting. Burndy Engineering

Co. v Sheldon Service Corp. (DC NY) 44 USPQ 103.

In copyright infringement case, plaintiff's filing of 60 exceptions, contained in 22 typewritten pages, to master's report on accounting is unreasonable where exceptions only raise two questions necessary to be passed on. Burndy Engineering Co. v Penn-Union Electric Corp. (1940, DC Pa) 32 F Supp 671, 45 USPQ 80, adhered to (DC Pa) 36 F Supp 35 and affd (CA3 Pa) 122 F2d 932, 51 USPQ 548.

19. Evidentiary matters

In action of infringement for penalty of one dollar for every copy found in defendant's possession, exclusion of testimony regarding plaintiff's damage from sale of defendant's copies was proper. Springer Lithographing Co. v Falk (1894, CA2 NY) 59 F 707.

Architect's testimony that his plans, which defendant used in violation of common-law copyright, are worth stated sum is admissible in evidence; such sum is limit of claim since there is no other evidence as to damages. Ashworth v Glover (1967) 20 Utah 2d 85, 433 P2d 315, 156 USPQ 219.

20. Jury determinations

Jury was authorized to allow plaintiff damages for infringement on basis of fifty cents for every sheet found in possession of defendant. Dwight v Appleton (1843, CC NY) F Cas No 4215.

Issue of damages for infringement has been made jury issue in number of copyright cases. Pallant v Sinatra (1945, DC NY) 7 FRD 293, 65 USPQ 158.

Jury trial is refused where plaintiff demands accounting of profits. Tynan v R. K. O. Radio Pictures, Inc. (1947, DC NY) 77 F Supp 238, 76 USPQ 387.

In copyright infringement action seeking injunction, damages, and accounting, plaintiff is entitled to jury trial as to damages whether or not damages are sought in same count as injunction and accounting. Russell v Laurel Music Corp. (1952, DC NY) 104 F Supp 815, 94 USPQ 63.

21. Orders or decrees

Decree which established validity of copyright and determined that scene in play was dramatic composition entitled to protection under the copyright laws is conclusive as between parties in action at law for damages for violation of copyright. Brady v Daly (1899) 175 US 148, 44 L Ed 109, 20 S Ct 62.

In action for infringement of copyrighted trade catalogue, only damages recoverable under final decree were such as interlocutory decree adjudged. Russell & Stoll Co. v Oceanic Electrical Supply Co. (1936, CA2 NY) 80 F2d 864, 28 USPQ 203.

22. Appeals

Appellate court cannot review action of trial judge in assessing amount in lieu of actual damages, where amount awarded is within the limits imposed by Copyright Act. Douglas v Cunningham (1935) 294 US 207, 79 L Ed 862, 55 S Ct 365, 24 USPQ 153.

Supreme Court does not disturb deductions allowed by court of appeals in computing net profits in copyright infringement case where questions of fact, which have been determined by court below on evidence, are involved. Sheldon v Metro-Goldwyn Pictures Corp. (1940) 309 US 390, 84 L Ed 825, 60 S Ct 681, 44 USPQ 607.

Where no proof of actual damages was offered or received on trial and court made no finding on subject, discretion of trial court in assessing statutory damages instead of actual damages for copyright infringement is not reviewable on appeal. Johns & Johns Printing Co. v Paull-Pioneer Music Corp. (1939, CA8 Mo) 102 F2d 282, 41 USPQ 3.

No evidence of actual damages having been given, if infringer made no profits for which it is accountable, assessment of statutory damages of $250 cannot be reviewed on appeal; but, if after further hearing on remand court finds infringer liable for profits, amount of profits will be measure of recovery and it will no longer be permissible to decree statutory damages. Sammons v Colonial Press, Inc. (1942, CA1 Mass) 126 F2d 341, 53 USPQ 71.

§ 505. Remedies for infringement: Costs and attorney's fees

In any civil action under this title [17 USCS §§ 101 et seq.], the court in its discretion may allow the recovery of full costs by or against any party other than the United States or an officer thereof. Except as otherwise provided by this title [17 USCS §§ 101 et seq.], the court may also award a reasonable attorney's fee to the prevailing party as part of the costs. (Added Oct. 19, 1976, P. L. 94-553, Title I, § 101, 90 Stat. 2586.)

HISTORY; ANCILLARY LAWS AND DIRECTIVES

Effective date of section:
Section 102 of Act Oct. 19, 1976, P. L. 94-553, 90 Stat. 2598 provided that this section "becomes effective on January 1, 1978".

CROSS REFERENCES

This section referred to in 17 USCS §§ 111, 115, 116, 411, 412, 510.

RESEARCH GUIDE

Am Jur:
18 Am Jur 2d, Copyright and Literary Property § 152.

Annotations:
Prevailing party's right to recover counsel fees in federal courts. 8 L Ed 2d 894.

INTERPRETIVE NOTES AND DECISIONS

I. IN GENERAL

1. Generally
2. Discretion of court
3. Good faith in litigation
4. Innocent or unintentional infringement
5. Order and decree
6. Willful infringement

II. PARTICULAR FEES AND COSTS

7. Attorney's fees, generally
8. —Initial amount determination
9. —Appeal of fee award
10. Costs, generally
11. —Apportionment of costs
12. —Specific amounts awarded

I. IN GENERAL

1. Generally

Liability for costs and attorney fees is statutory and copyright law exempts officers of United States from this liability; allowance of costs and attorney fees is discretionary with court and allowance would be made if defendants were acting as individuals, but is not made against employees of Bonneville administration even if they are not technically officers of United States. Towle v Ross (1940, DC Or) 32 F Supp 125, 45 USPQ 143.

Copyright infringers are jointly and severally liable for damages resulting from infringement, but accountability for profits, which originates in equity, is peculiarly personal, presupposition being that infringer obtained something which it is unreasonable for him to keep; infringers are not jointly accountable, but individually accountable, for profits which each received, not being held for profits received by co-infringer; but responsibility for costs and attorneys' fees under statute is joint and several. Alfred Bell & Co. v Catalda Fine Arts, Inc. (1949, DC NY) 86 F Supp 399, 82 USPQ 273, mod on other grounds (CA2 NY) 191 F2d 99, 90 USPQ 153.

On question of costs and attorney's fee in copyright action wherein plaintiff was successful only in part, court considers primarily who was infringer. Shapiro Bernstein & Co. v Jerry Vogel Music Co. (1953, DC NY) 115 F Supp 754, 98 USPQ 438, 99 USPQ 381, revd on other grounds (CA2 NY) 221 F2d 569, 105 USPQ 178, adhered to (CA2 NY) 223 F2d 252, 105 USPQ 460.

In suit for copyright infringement, court may award reasonable attorney fee to such party as part of costs. Alexander v Irving Trust Co. (1955, DC NY) 132 F Supp 364, 106 USPQ 74, affd (CA2 NY) 228 F2d 221, 108 USPQ 24, cert den 350 US 996, 100 L Ed 860, 76 S Ct 545.

Counsel fees may be awarded where party seeks declaratory judgment with respect to ownership of renewed copyright; purpose of award of counsel fees in copyright cases is as much to penalize losing party as to compensate prevailing party; losing party is not penalized for seeking determination of effect in his situation of doctrine applied in cited case, but his refusal to accept decision of Supreme Court in another cited case was frivolous; as to latter point, prevailing party is awarded counsel fees; also, prevailing party is entitled to counsel fees and expenses involved in preparing to meet losing party's claim which was not pressed at trial. Rose v Bourne, Inc. (1959, DC NY) 176 F Supp 605, 123 USPQ 29, affd (CA2 NY) 279 F2d 79, 125 USPQ 509, cert den 364 US 880, 5 L Ed 2d 103, 81 S Ct 170.

2. Discretion of court

Award of attorney fees to defendant is not justified where court of appeals finds that plaintiff's copyright was infringed, since such fees may be allowed, in discretion of court, only to prevailing party; fact that plaintiff had mentioned criminal prosecution in letter to defendant, and fact that plaintiff was accused of perjury in regard to an immaterial matter, do not justify judgment against plaintiff or allowance of attorney fees to defendant. Wihtol v Crow (1962, CA8 Iowa) 309 F2d 777, 135 USPQ 385.

Court exercises discretion to refuse counsel fees to successful plaintiff in copyright infringement suit. Edward B. Marks Music Corp. v Borst Music Pub. Co. (1953, DC NJ) 110 F Supp 913, 97 USPQ 394.

Penalty element is important factor in award of counsel fees in copyright cases; court can see little reason why unsuccessful party in bona fide dispute over copyright matter should pay opponent's lawyers' fees any more than he should in the general run of litigation; court is not inclined to charge copyright litigant with opponent's lawyers' fees except to penalize conduct which seems to merit a penalty. Rose v Bourne, Inc. (DC NY) 127 USPQ 187, affd (CA2 NY) 279 F2d 79, 125 USPQ 509.

Under predecessor statute, it is discretionary with court as to whether to allow reasonable attorney's fee as part of costs; such fee is awarded only where dictated by equity and good conscience; fee is allowed where defendants deliberately copied copyrighted figure and then, in effort to capitalize on good will enjoyed by plaintiffs' advertisements, included picture of plaintiffs' product, also imitated plaintiffs' advertisements, included picture of plaintiffs' product with their product, and used plaintiffs' registered trademark and trade name; defendants' product was inferior to plaintiffs' and sold for less, with overall result that defendants not only captured part of plaintiffs' market but also injured reputation of plaintiffs' product. Doran v Sunset House Distributing Corp. (1961, DC Cal) 197 F Supp 940, 131 USPQ 94, affd (CA9 Cal) 304 F2d 251, 134 USPQ 4, and (disapproved on other grounds L. Batlin & Son, Inc. v Snyder (CA2 NY) 536 F2d 486, cert den 429 US 857, 50 L Ed 2d 135, 97 S Ct 156).

Award of attorney fees in copyright cases to prevailing party is not matter of right, but is within sound discretion of court; elements to consider are no different than in other cases, such as, amount involved, time necessarily spent, and skill, professional standing and reputation of attorneys; however, court need not make award to prevailing party on basis of its attorneys usual charges, but may award lesser sum, especially since plaintiff prevailed on only one aspect of litigation. Key West Hand Print Fabrics, Inc. v Serbin, Inc. (1966, DC Fla) 269 F Supp 605, 155 USPQ 130, affd (CA5 Fla) 381 F2d 735, 155 USPQ 113.

3. Good faith in litigation

Attorney fees are refused to prevailing party on appeal in copyright infringement case where case was hard fought, principal question presented was complex question of law, and appeal was not pursued in bad faith. Official Aviation Guide Co. v American Aviation Associates (1947, CA7 Ill) 162 F2d 541, 74 USPQ 45; Overman v Loesser (1953, CA9 Cal) 205 F2d 521, 98 USPQ 521, cert den 346 US 910, 98 L Ed 407, 74 S Ct 241.

Allowance of attorney fee is usually appropriate where copyright proprietor recovers for infringement, but fee is denied where prevailing proprietor attempted to inflate and exaggerate claims under "in lieu" provision of predecessor section; "in lieu" provision is not to accomplish imposition of a penalty, but is equitable substitute for cases which present difficulty or impossibility of proof as to damages and profits. Advertisers Exchange, Inc. v Hinkley (1952, CA8 Mo) 199 F2d 313, 95 USPQ 124, cert den 344 US 921, 97 L Ed 710, 73 S Ct 388.

Although in copyright cases court of appeals has discretionary power to allow attorney fees for services in prosecuting appeal, unsuccessful plaintiff should not thus be penalized where litigation was not vexatious but involved novel question of statutory interpretation. Edward B. Marks Music Corp. v Continental Record Co. (1955, CA2 NY) 222 F2d 488, 105 USPQ 171, 105 USPQ 350, cert den 350 US 861, 100 L Ed 764, 76 S Ct 101.

Losing plaintiff in copyright infringement action is not assessed attorney fees where close question as to infringement was involved. Eisenschiml v Fawcett Publications, Inc. (1957, CA7 Ill) 246 F2d 598, 114 USPQ 199, cert den 355 US 907, 2 L Ed 2d 262, 78 S Ct 334.

In copyright infringement action wherein attorney fees were allowed by district court, court of appeals makes additional allowance to plaintiffs, for services of counsel on appeal, in view of deliberate nature of infringement and lack of substance to defendants' contention on appeal. Boucher v Du Boyes, Inc. (1958, CA2 NY) 253 F2d 948, 117 USPQ 156, cert den 357 US 936, 2 L Ed 2d 1550, 78 S Ct 1384.

Discretionary award of moderate counsel fees is proper where assignor's copyright infringement action against assignee is dismissed on ground that assigned rights had not reverted to assignor; although assignor's claim was not synthetic or capricious, it was unreasonable since it represented attempt to employ highly technical argument as means of extracting unfair penalty assessment from assignee. Mailer v RKO Teleradio Pictures, Inc. (1964, CA2 NY) 332 F2d 747, 141 USPQ 462.

Where plaintiff, by combination of circumstances, was led to belief that his work had been appropriated and brought suit in good faith, though there was no infringement, costs will not be awarded against him. Vernon v Sam S. & Lee Shubert (1915, DC NY) 220 F 694.

Defendant's motion to dismiss action for copyright infringement filed in good faith, having been sustained on question of law not heretofore passed on in reported decisions, attorney fees are refused defendant. Corcoran v Montgomery Ward & Co. (1940, DC Cal) 32 F Supp 421, 45 USPQ 115, affd (CA9 Cal) 121 F2d 575, 50 USPQ 277; Corcoran v Montgomery Ward & Co. (1940, DC Cal) 32 F Supp 422, 45 USPQ 114.

Prevailing defendant is refused costs since it misled plaintiff as to its interest in his plan and thus brought about litigation. Ketcham v New York World's Fair 1939, Inc. (1940, DC NY) 34 F Supp 657, 46 USPQ 307, affd (CA2 NY) 119 F2d 422, 49 USPQ 756.

Defendant, not guilty of infringement but only of fair use, was refused counsel fee where suit was well brought. American Institute of Architects v Fenichel (1941, DC NY) 41 F Supp 146, 51 USPQ 29.

Infringers must pay substantial allowance for attorney fees since they deliberately brought about court test of validity of plaintiff's copyrights, contending that they were invalid, knowing that, if unsuccessful, they would incur liability for attorney fees. Alfred Bell & Co. v Catalda Fine Arts, Inc. (1949, DC NY) 86 F Supp 399, 82 USPQ 273, mod on other grounds (CA2 NY) 191 F2d 99, 90 USPQ 153.

Defendant was not entitled to award of attorney fees upon dismissal of plaintiff's infringement suit based on ground that plaintiff's statuette was not subject for copyright, if suit was in good faith due to perfect copy of statuette by defendant. Stein v Expert Lamp Co. (1952, DC Ill) 107 F Supp 60, 94 USPQ 137.

Court exercises discretion to refuse counsel fee to prevailing defendant in copyright infringement suit where plaintiff's claim was not capricious or unreasonable and court found noninfringement only after thorough and difficult consideration of evidence and inferences drawn therefrom. Morse v Fields (1954, DC NY) 127 F Supp 63, 104 USPQ 54.

Although court has discretionary power to award attorney fees to prevailing party in copyright infringement action, it refuses award where case was treated as test case, there being no authorities squarely in point to guide litigants. Loew's, Inc. v Columbia Broadcasting System, Inc. (1955, DC Cal) 131 F Supp 165, 105 USPQ 302, affd (CA9 Cal) 239 F2d 532, 112 USPQ 11, affd 356 US 43, 2 L Ed 2d 583, 78 S Ct 667, 116 USPQ 479, reh den 356 US 934, 2 L Ed 2d 764, 78 S Ct 770.

Although court finds no copyright infringement by defendant author, it exercises discretion to refuse attorney fees, since plaintiff was sincerely convinced that there was infringement, especially since jury, in prior action against author's publisher, had found infringement. Warshawsky v Carter (1955, DC Dist Col) 132 F Supp 758, 107 USPQ 80.

Counsel fees are awarded to prevailing defendants as matter of discretion in copyright infringement action wherein multiplicity of procedural activities, including plaintiff's motion for appointment of receiver of one defendant, intervened between start of action and its coming to trial. Lampert v Hollis Music, Inc. (1956, DC NY) 138 F Supp 505, 109 USPQ 242.

Prevailing defendants are not awarded counsel fees since plaintiff commenced copyright infringement action in good faith. Greenbie v Noble (1957, DC NY) 151 F Supp 45, 113 USPQ 115.

Losing defendants should not be unduly burdened where elaborate briefs were in part necessitated by fact that case is one of first impression. Harms, Inc. v Sansom House Enterprises, Inc. (1958, DC Pa) 162 F Supp 129, 117 USPQ 272, affd (CA3 Pa) 267 F2d 494.

While, in the event of voluntary dismissal with prejudice which ended copyright infringement action, defendant would presumably be entitled to counsel fees, this is not situation in instant action wherein, prior to voluntary dismissal of complaint without prejudice, plaintiffs' offer to discontinue action with prejudice was rejected by defendant, which desired to obtain adjudication of declaratory judgment counterclaim; although defendant prevailed on counterclaim, plaintiffs should not be charged with defendant's expenses in obtaining resolution of difficult and open legal question; however, as to issues raised by reply to counterclaim and which plaintiffs insisted remain in case but as to which plaintiffs offered no evidence, defendant is entitled to reasonable counsel fees; same is true as to legal issue which plaintiffs raised and which unnecessarily added to defendant's attorneys' labors. Rose v Bourne, Inc. (DC NY) 127 USPQ 187, affd (CA2 NY) 279 F2d 79, 125 USPQ 509.

As a matter of discretion, counsel fees are not allowed to prevailing defendants in action for copyright infringement and unfair competition since plaintiff did not harass defendants and action was brought in good faith. C. S. Hammond & Co. v International College Globe, Inc. (1962, DC NY) 210 F Supp 206, 135 USPQ 56.

Attorney fees are refused to successful defendant in copyright infringement action where determinative legal issue was novel and presented substantial questions, plaintiff's claim of infringement was not clearly unreasonable or in bad faith, and plaintiff's conduct of litigation was not vexatious or unduly burdensome. Bartsch v Metro-Goldwyn-Mayer, Inc. (1967, DC NY) 155 USPQ 577.

Belated notices of intent to use and specious tenders of payment are transparent attempt to build defense in infringement action; they will not limit amount of recovery of compensatory or punitive damages and will not bar award of attorney fees. Pickwick Music Corp. v Record Productions, Inc. (1968, DC NY) 292 F Supp 39, 159 USPQ 228.

Counsel fees are awarded only where defendant resisted a valid claim with a defense that is so lacking in merit as to present no arguable question of law or fact, or where defense was designed to annoy or harass plaintiff. Counsel fees are refused, although infringement was fairly clear, since defendants' decision to resist claim for sizeable damages in a case involving an inexpensive product cannot be deemed a mere ploy to annoy or harass plaintiff. Morser v Bengor Products Co. (1968, DC NY) 283 F Supp 926, 159 USPQ 267.

Full costs and attorney fees are awarded to copyright proprietor where suit was necessary primarily because of infringer's failure to supply information on sales of posters copying poem. Bell v Pro Arts, Inc. (DC Ohio) 366 F Supp 474, 180 USPQ 517, affd (CA6 Ohio) 511 F2d 451, cert den 423 US 829, 46 L Ed 2d 46, 96 S Ct 47.

Attorney fees are awarded against party copying and using copyrighted mail order tool catalog, especially considering warnings and opportunities to desist before litigation. Bliss & Laughlin Industries, Inc. v Starvaggi (1975, DC NY) 188 USPQ 89.

Considering that suit bordered on unreasonable but did not appear frivolous or brought in bad faith, and considering economic circumstances of plaintiff, court awards attorney disbursements, as distinct from fees, to be taxed as costs in favor of defendants. Gardner v Nizer (1975, DC NY) 396 F Supp 63, 190 USPQ 318.

4. Innocent or unintentional infringement

Assessment of attorney fees against several

defendants did not apply to one of defendants who had infringed innocently. Gross v Van Dyk Gravure Co. (1916, CA2 NY) 230 F 412.

Complainant was entitled to attorney fee although infringement was shown to have been innocently done. Strauss v Penn Printing & Pub. Co. (1915, DC Pa) 220 F 977.

No attorney fee is awarded since infringer sincerely ordered orchestra leader not to play nonlicensed American Society of Composers, Authors, and Publishers music and it is likely that the society, of which plaintiffs are members maintains attorneys on yearly salary basis. Shapiro, Bernstein & Co. v Veltin (1942, DC La) 47 F Supp 648, 55 USPQ 335.

Attorney fee was refused prevailing defendant which had innocently copied material published with defective copyright notice. Metro Associated Services, Inc. v Webster City Graphic, Inc. (1953, DC Iowa) 117 F Supp 224, 100 USPQ 88.

Attorney fees were not awarded against copyright infringer, where it was common practice for publishers of prayer books to copy freely from each other, much of plaintiff's book was in public domain, and defendant honestly, but mistakenly, believed that plaintiff was illegally attempting to copyright and monopolize printing of ancient prayers. Ziegelheim v Flohr (1954, DC NY) 119 F Supp 324, 100 USPQ 189.

Fixation of damage for copyright infringement is left to court's discretion; in action wherein defendants printed infringing articles in their newspaper, but testified that they knew nothing of copying, had no intent to infringe, and had no knowledge of copyright law, court awards statutory minimum damages of $250 plus costs as well as $250 for attorney's fees. Massapequa Publishing Co. v Observer, Inc. (1961, DC NY) 191 F Supp 261, 128 USPQ 418.

5. Order and decree

Decree dismissing complaint for infringement of copyright should carry costs including reasonable counsel fee, to be fixed before costs are taxed. Shipman v R. K. O. Radio Pictures, Inc. (1937, DC NY) 20 F Supp 249, 35 USPQ 242, affd (CA2 NY) 100 F2d 533, 40 USPQ 211; Caruthers v R. K. O. Radio Pictures, Inc. (1937, DC NY) 20 F Supp 906, 35 USPQ 115, 35 USPQ 542.

Final decree will be submitted through clerk's office on usual notice, but only after costs, damages, and attorney fees are fixed so they may be included in decree. Detective Comics, Inc. v Bruns Publications, Inc. (1939, DC NY) 28 F Supp 399, 41 USPQ 182, mod on other grounds (CA2 NY) 111 F2d 432, 45 USPQ 291.

6. Willful infringement

Although defendant prevailed it was not granted costs or counsel fee because it admitted it knowingly copied plaintiff's pictures. Basevi v Edward O'Toole Co. (1939, DC NY) 26 F Supp 41, 40 USPQ 333.

Court refuses allowance to successful defendants since they knowingly copied plaintiff's pictures and made use of them to their own profit; plaintiff's action was brought in good faith but complaint was dismissed for defective copyright notice. Krafft v Cohen (1941, DC Pa) 38 F Supp 1022, 49 USPQ 648.

Printer of copyright infringements, as well as its co-infringers, is liable for attorney fees, since it knew copyrights and pursued its course with knowledge that, if defense of copyright invalidity were overruled, it would be liable for attorney fees. Alfred Bell & Co. v Catalda Fine Arts, Inc. (1949, DC NY) 86 F Supp 399, 82 USPQ 273, mod on other grounds (CA2 NY) 191 F2d 99, 90 USPQ 153.

Plaintiff's voluntary dismissal of copyright infringement action, after defendant had taken depositions and moved for more definite statement, makes defendant prevailing party, but defendant is refused award of reasonable attorney fees, since exhibits show that defendant appropriated plaintiff's copyrighted material, but plaintiff will be required to pay such fees if it later reinstitutes copyright action. Uniflow Mfg. Co. v Superflow Mfg. Corp. (1950, DC Ohio) 10 FRD 589, 87 USPQ 89.

Where techniques of copying and vending articles infringing copyright are tinged with bad faith, plaintiffs are entitled to reasonable attorney fees; such fees cannot be allowed for any services of attorneys except those reasonably necessary to redress infringement and procure injunction against further infringement. Stein v Rosenthal (1952, DC Cal) 103 F Supp 227, 92 USPQ 402, affd (CA9 Cal) 205 F2d 633, 98 USPQ 180.

In determining amount of proper attorney fee for plaintiff, which prevailed on its main contention in copyright infringement suit, court takes into consideration fact that considerable amount of attorney's time was devoted to factual issue on which plaintiff was unsuccessful. Shapiro Bernstein & Co. v Jerry Vogel Music Co. (1953, DC NY) 115 F Supp 754, 98 USPQ 438, 99 USPQ 381, revd on other grounds (CA2 NY) 221 F2d 569, 105 USPQ 178, adhered to (CA2 NY) 223 F2d 252.

Plaintiff is entitled to recover reasonable attorneys' fees since defendant's copyright infringement was wilful and deliberate. Gelles-Widmer Co. v Milton Bradley Co. (DC Ill) 132 USPQ 30, affd (CA7 Ill) 313 F2d 143, 136 USPQ 240, cert den 373 US 913, 10 L Ed 2d 414, 83 S Ct 1303.

Court retains discretion as to whether to award reasonable attorney's fee as part of costs; such fee is awarded where losing defendant deliberately reproduced almost all of plaintiff's copyrighted catalog, with full knowledge of copyright notice imprinted thereon. B & B Auto Supply, Inc. v Plesser (1962, DC NY) 205 F Supp 36, 133 USPQ 247.

Court retains discretion as to whether to award reasonable attorney's fee as part of costs; fee is awarded upon clear showing of infringement and deliberate copying. Nom Music, Inc. v Kaslin (1964, DC NY) 227 F Supp 922, 141 USPQ 22, affd (CA2 NY) 343 F2d 198.

Purpose of award of attorney fees to plaintiffs is to deter infringement while award to defendants represents penalty imposed upon plaintiffs for institution of a baseless, frivolous, or unreasonable suit, or one instituted in bad faith; plaintiffs are entitled to award where defendants deliberately infringed with knowledge of plaintiffs' copyrighted play, after it had been entrusted to them for purpose of developing English adaption. Breffort v I Had A Ball Co. (1967, DC NY) 271 F Supp 623, 155 USPQ 391.

Infringement by copying substantial portions of 6 technical manuals into 12 technical manuals for competing equipment justifies award of reasonable costs and attorney fees. Telex Corp. v International Business Machines Corp. (DC Okla) 367 F Supp 258, 179 USPQ 777, affd in part and revd in part on other grounds (CA10 Okla) 510 F2d 894, cert dismd 423 US 802, 46 L Ed 2d 244, 96 S Ct 8.

II. PARTICULAR FEES AND COSTS

7. Attorney's fees, generally

Court is well within its discretion in not awarding attorney fees to alleged infringer despite holding that copyright is not infringed and was forfeited for publication without statutory notice. Continental Casualty Co. v Beardsley (1958, CA2 NY) 253 F2d 702, 117 USPQ 1, cert den 358 US 816, 3 L Ed 2d 58, 79 S Ct 25.

Request denied to increase trial court's attorney fee award for work done on appeal in copyright case. Sunset House Distributing Corp. v Doran (1962, CA9 Cal) 304 F2d 251, 134 USPQ 4.

Where defendant prevailed in copyright infringement suit tried before master, all costs, including counsel fees of defendants, were taxed to plaintiff, and bond given by plaintiff on temporary injunction was held until all costs and fees were paid. Seltzer v Sunbrock (1938, DC Cal) 22 F Supp 621, 37 USPQ 491.

Where publication of infringing article did not damage plaintiff or profit defendant, attorney fee was not awarded. Vinick v Charm Publications, Inc. (DC NY) 46 USPQ 510.

Where infringement was not willful or deliberate and no damage resulted, attorney fee was not allowed. Washingtonian Publishing co. v Pearson (DC DC) 56 USPQ 23, aff'd 78 App DC 287, 140 F2d 465, 60 USPQ 224.

Although complaint is dismissed since plaintiff's bookkeeping forms are uncopyrightable, defendant is refused attorneys' fee, which is within court's discretion, since plaintiff's system and forms were valuable, cost defendant nothing, and were appropriated by defendant. Aldrich v Remington Rand, Inc. (1942, DC Tex) 52 F Supp 732, 59 USPQ 210.

Even though copyright infringer is liable for profits of only $4199, it is not improper to make it liable, with co-infringers, jointly and severally for attorneys' fees of $7750, especially since judgment gives it right to recover from other infringers; in determining liability for attorneys' fees, court is not influenced by amount of profits each infringer gained from infringement, but by part each played in causing legal test of validity of copyrights. Alfred Bell & Co. v Catalda Fine Arts, Inc. (1949, DC NY) 86 F Supp 399, 82 USPQ 273, mod on other grounds (CA2 NY) 191 F2d 99, 90 USPQ 153.

In action for declaratory judgment as to title of renewal copyright and for injunction restraining infringement, wherein defendant asks for like relief, prevailing defendant is awarded reasonable counsel fees in view of clear and settled nature of the authorities governing issues. Tobias v Joy Music, Inc. (1962, DC NY) 204 F Supp 556, 133 USPQ 181.

Defendants, prevailing in copyright infringement suit by showing that plaintiff's marking of point count values on playing cards was not copyrightable expression, are not entitled to attorney fees as part of costs in absence of compelling reasons for levying penalty against plaintiff. Freedman v Grolier Enterprises, Inc. (1973, DC NY) 179 USPQ 476.

Attorney fees are denied to successful plaintiff for copyright infringement forming small portion of case also involving trademark infringement, with court exercising reasonable discretion. SmokEnders, Inc. v Smoke No More, Inc. (1975, DC Fla) 184 USPQ 646.

Award of attorney fees is discretionary with court and requires close scrutiny of circumstances surrounding settlement of case before trial, and court awards attorney fees to prevailing party even though case was settled before trial. Balcaen v Herschberger (1976, DC Wis) 193 USPQ 562.

8. —Initial amount determination

Attorney fee of $1500 was allowed against infringing publisher which made over $7000 profits; no fee was allowed against infringing printer liable only for $250 statutory damages. Sammons v Colonial Press, Inc. (CCA 1), 126 F2d 341, 53 USPQ 71.

Counsel fee of $2000 was not excessive in case awarding $3500 statutory damages where defendant's series of infringements (two catalogues, one of which went to three printings) rendered issues multifarious both as to law and facts. Burndy Engineering Co. v Sheldon Serv. Corp. (1942, CA2 NY) 127 F2d 661, 53 USPQ 409.

Prevailing party in copyright infringement case is awarded $500 attorney fee for services on appeal. F. W. Woolworth Co. v Contemporary Arts, Inc. (1951, CA1 Mass) 193 F2d 162, 92 USPQ 4, affd 344 US 228, 97 L Ed 276, 73 S Ct 222, 95 USPQ 396, motion den 350 US 810, 100 L Ed 727, 76 S Ct 37.

Award of $20,644.81 as reasonable attorney's fee is proper and within court's discretion where infringer failed to answer interrogatories relative to infringement of copyright on model airplane kits, but additional award of $13,689.91 for attorney fees for appeal is denied where issues on appeal are not complex and generous award was made in District Court. Monogram Models, Inc. v Industro Motive Corp. (1974, CA6 Mich) 492 F2d 1281, 181 USPQ 425, cert den 419 US 843, 42 L Ed 2d 71, 95 S Ct 76.

Attorney fees are not to be reduced because damages are small, though amount of such fees is to be based on magnitude of the interest involved, amount recovered in damages, and volume of work required and accomplished; in this case where there was single use of copyrighted music roll fee of $250 was reasonable. M. Witmark & Sons v Calloway (1927, DC Tenn) 22 F2d 412.

Where plaintiff was unsuccessful in proving infringement, defendants were allowed $3500 attorney fees. Lowenfels v Nathan (1932, DC NY) 2 F Supp 73, 16 USPQ 421.

Eighteen hundred dollars was reasonable attorney fee where advertising card for dishes was infringed resulting in award therefor of $2500. Sebring Pottery Co. v Steubenville Pottery Co. (1934, DC Ohio) 9 F Supp 384.

Where court awarded $5000 damages for seven infringements when it could have awarded $35,000, it could fix $2500 as reasonable allowance for counsel fees. Cory v Physical Culture Hotel, Inc. (1936, DC NY) 14 F Supp 986, 30 USPQ 360, affd (CA2 NY) 88 F2d 411, 33 USPQ 58.

Where orchestra in restaurant played copyrighted music with no proof of special damages, $50 attorney fee was allowed. Buck v Lisa (1939, DC NY) 28 F Supp 379, 42 USPQ 116.

One hundred dollars attorney fee was allowed where $150 damages were awarded for nonwillful infringement. Druley v Thompson (DC Pa) 44 USPQ 284.

Copyright suit was dismissed in part without leave to amend and in part plaintiff was ordered to file better statement with respect to publication with notice of copyright and with respect to deposit in copyright office; without filing better statement plaintiff moved to dismiss without prejudice and with costs taxed against plaintiff; motion was granted and it appearing that defendants had been wrongfully subjected to expense of legal services, award of $400 attorney fees is made to each of two defendants in addition to all other costs. Corcoran v Montgomery Ward & Co. (1940, DC Cal) 32 F Supp 421, 45 USPQ 115, affd (CA9 Cal) 121 F2d 575, 50 USPQ 277; Corcoran v Montgomery Ward & Co. (1940, DC Cal) 32 F Supp 422, 45 USPQ 115.

On fixing attorney fee, court confirming master's report cannot close eyes to finding of invalidity of copyright in action by same plaintiff against another defendant decided after same court had held copyright valid and infringed. Colonial Book Co. v Amsco School Publications, Inc. (DC NY) 57 USPQ 36, affd (CA2 NY) 142 F2d 362, 61 USPQ 391.

Regard being had to nature of 11 infringement cases, their presentation together, work of counsel, and other factors, court allows $150 fee in each single count case and $300 in each multiple count case irrespective of number of counts; fees allowed are inadequate for services rendered, but indulgence is allowed defendants since they had ostensible grant of right to perform compositions under state law which court holds invalid. Remick Music Corp. v Interstate Hotel Co. (1944, DC Neb) 58 F Supp 523, 63 USPQ 327, affd (CA8 Neb) 157 F2d 744, 71 USPQ 138, cert den 329 US 809, 91 L Ed 691, 67 S Ct 622, reh den 330 US 854, 91 L Ed 1296, 67 S Ct 769.

In determining attorney fee awarded plaintiff in copyright infringement suit, master is entitled to consider generally fee sought by defendant's counsel. Alfred Bell & Co. v Catalda Fine Arts, Inc. (1949, DC NY) 86 F Supp 399, 82 USPQ 273, mod on other grounds (CA2 NY) 191 F2d 99, 90 USPQ 153.

In determining reasonable fee, court considers, among other elements, amount of work necessary, amount of work done, skill employed, monetary amount involved, and result achieved.

Cloth v Hyman (1956, DC NY) 146 F Supp 185, 112 USPQ 254.

Allowance of attorney fees to prevailing plaintiff in copyright infringement action would be unreasonably burdensome, especially since damages have been awarded and since there is no evidence by which court could determine amount of fees. Local Trademarks, Inc. v Grantham (1957, DC Neb) 166 F Supp 494, 117 USPQ 335.

In light of facts that copyright infringement complaint was prepared by plaintiffs' staff attorneys, that judgment was obtained by default, that only minimum damages were suffered, and that action is a consolidated one, single award of $100 attorneys fees is sufficient. Robbins Music Corp. v Southington Inn, Inc. (1967, DC Conn) 156 USPQ 489.

A $10,000 fee was reasonable where the standard fee for a case of the kind involved had to be materially increased to compensate for the needless difficulties introduced by the misconduct of the defendants during the litigation. Fedtro, Inc. v Kravex Mfg. Corp. (1970, DC NY) 313 F Supp 990, 164 USPQ 510.

Attorney fees of $2,000 awarded for publishing telephone directory infringing copyrighted directory. Southwestern Bell Tel. Co. v Nationwide Independent Directory Service, Inc. (1974, DC Ark) 371 F Supp 900, 182 USPQ 193.

Attorney fees of $750 are awarded for infringing performance for profit of four songs. Quackenbush Music, Ltd. v Wood (1974, DC Tenn) 381 F Supp 904, 184 USPQ 210.

Unauthorized taking and copying of architectural plans and starting construction of building according to plans justifies award of all plaintiff's court costs plus all plaintiff's attorney fees on hourly basis of about $7,000 in addition to damages. Herman Frankel Organization, Inc. v Wolfe (1974, DC Mich) 184 USPQ 819.

Defendant whose attorney neglected to reply to warning letter, but who otherwise admitted infringement in selling shirts of copyrighted fabric is assessed $500 attorney fees rather than requested $2,000, because matter might have been settled by plaintiff's attorney calling to check on matter before filing lawsuit. Printempo Fabrics, Inc. v G & G Shops, Inc. (1975, DC NY) 186 USPQ 327.

Court considers deliberateness of infringement of zodiac pins, success and expertise of plaintiff's attorneys in recovering over $57,000 damages, plus attorney time spent on trials in awarding reasonable attorney fees of $25,000. Jerry De Nicola, Inc. v Genesco, Pakula & Co. (1975, DC NY) 188 USPQ 306.

Court considers defendant's unreasonable refusals of settlement offers and inadequate offer of judgment relative to total infringing sales of over $3,000 and awards attorney fees to plaintiff of $4,500. Goldman-Morgen, Inc. v Dan Brechner & Co. (1976, DC NY) 190 USPQ 478.

9. —Appeal of fee award

Order making award to attorney of defendants was appealable though in discretion of trial court; appeal from order finally fixing award to attorney for defendant properly included order dismissing bill of plaintiff and order of reference, though such orders were not appealable. Cohan v Richmond (1936, CA2 NY) 86 F2d 680, 32 USPQ 298.

On reversal of district court's judgment for defendant in copyright infringement suit, case is remanded to district court for appropriate action as to injunction, damages, and accounting and court of appeals states that any issues concerning attorney's fee in either court may be settled by district court in its final judgment. College Entrance Book Co. v Amsco Book Co. (1941, CA2 NY) 119 F2d 874, 49 USPQ 517.

Under predecessor statute, question of awarding attorney's fee to prevailing copyright infringement suit defendant was for discretion of trial court; appellate court affirms refusal of fee since no abuse of discretion appears. Advertisers Exchange, Inc. v Anderson (1944, CA8 Iowa) 144 F2d 907, 63 USPQ 39.

10. Costs, generally

In suit for infringement involving two distinct musical compositions, where complainant prevails as to one and fails as to other, court does not abuse its discretion in making a division of costs. M. Witmark & Sons v Standard Music Roll Co. (1915, CA3 NJ) 221 F 376.

Reference made necessary by defendants could not be charged to plaintiff. Cohan v Richmond (1936, CA2 NY) 86 F2d 680, 32 USPQ 298.

In copyright infringement suit, resident plaintiff complied with local rule by posting $25 cash bond and neither marshal nor clerk applied to court for further cost deposits; court has no right to require plaintiff to post $500 cost bond and to dismiss cause with prejudice with award of $150 attorney fee to defendant on plaintiff's failure to post such bond. Williams v Hodge (1941, CA6 Tenn) 119 F2d 394, 49 USPQ 687.

Plaintiff was not required to bear half of master's compensation where it did not unnecessarily prolong suit. Burndy Engineering Co. v Sheldon Serv. Corp. (1942, CA2 NY) 127 F2d 661, 53 USPQ 409.

Full costs are mandatory in favor of successful or prevailing party in copyright infringement suit; court has no discretion as to ordinary costs, and fact that defendants' counterclaim for copyright infringement was dismissed does not change situation. Official Aviation Guide Co. v American Aviation Associates (1947, CA7 Ill) 162 F2d 541, 74 USPQ 45.

It is error for judgment dismissing copyright infringement action to provide that each party bear its own costs. Amsterdam v Triangle Publications, Inc. (1951, CA3 Pa) 189 F2d 104, 89 USPQ 468.

Since one defendant prevailed in copyright infringement action, it is entitled to full costs. H. M. Kolbe Co. v Armgus Textile Co. (1963, CA2 NY) 315 F2d 70, 137 USPQ 9, 99 ALR2d 390.

Judgment taxing costs against defendants convicted of tape piracy is remanded to separate costs involved in convictions under other counts of mail fraud. United States v Taxe (1976, CA9 Cal) 540 F2d 961, 192 USPQ 204.

Right to elect to try issue of infringement before jury was granted upon payment of ordinary taxable costs of suit already accrued. Emerson v Davies (1845, CC Mass) F Cas No 4436.

In copyright suit plaintiff if unsuccessful is chargeable with costs and, within discretion of court, may be required to pay attorney fee of defendant; therefore, on motion, plaintiff is required to post bond to cover costs and fee. Williams v Hodge (DC Tenn) 44 USPQ 25.

Award of full costs to "prevailing party" is mandatory, and settlement of case before trial does not deprive successful party of costs award.

Balcaen v Herschberger (1976, DC Wis) 193 USPQ 562.

11. —Apportionment of costs

Defendants (authors, printers, and publishers) are jointly and severally liable for costs although no defendant is liable for damages and one defendant is not liable for profits. Washingtonian Publishing Co. v Pearson, (DC DC) 56 USPQ 23, affd 78 App DC 287, 140 F2d 465, 60 USPQ 224.

Costs, including attorney fee, are not apportioned among defendants where they are jointly and severally liable. Harris v Miller (DC NY) 57 USPQ 190.

12. —Specific amounts awarded

Fee of $800 was allowed master for services on accounting. Jones Brothers Co. v Underkoffler (DC Pa) 35 USPQ 448.

Fee of $1000 was allowed for special master fixing recovery. Sheldon v Moredall Realty Corp. (1939, DC NY) 29 F Supp 729, 43 USPQ 81.

Court in copyright infringement case referred to master for accounting considers master's petition for allowance of $1825, considers time spent by master, as well as nature and extent of his report, and finds that $1000 is fair and reasonable fee, which is allowed together with disbursements. Wilkie v Santly Bros., Inc. (1940, DC NY) 36 F Supp 574, 47 USPQ 380, affd (CA2 NY) 139 F2d 264, 60 USPQ 46, cert den 322 US 740, 88 L Ed 1574, 64 S Ct 1058.

§ 506. Criminal offenses

(a) Criminal infringement. Any person who infringes a copyright willfully and for purposes of commercial advantage or private financial gain shall be fined not more than $10,000 or imprisoned for not more than one year, or both: *Provided, however,* That any person who infringes willfully and for purposes of commercial advantage or private financial gain the copyright in a sound recording afforded by subsections (1), (2), or (3) of section 106 [17 USCS § 106(1), (2), or (3)] or the copyright in a motion picture afforded by subsections (1), (3), or (4) of section 106 [17 USCS § 106(1), (3) or (4)] shall be fined not more than $25,000 or imprisoned for not more than one year, or both, for the first such offense and shall be fined not more than $50,000 or imprisoned for not more than two years, or both, for any subsequent offense.

(b) Forfeiture and destruction. When any person is convicted of any violation of subsection (a), the court in its judgment of conviction shall, in addition to the penalty therein prescribed, order the forfeiture and destruction or other disposition of all infringing copies or phonorecords and all implements, devices, or equipment used in the manufacture of such infringing copies or phonorecords.

(c) Fraudulent copyright notice. Any person who, with fraudulent intent, places on any article a notice of copyright or words of the same purport that such person knows to be false, or who, with fraudulent intent, publicly distributes or imports for public distribution any article bearing such notice or words that such person knows to be false, shall be fined not more than $2,500.

(d) Fraudulent removal of copyright notice. Any person who, with fraudulent intent, removes or alters any notice of copyright appearing on a copy of a copyrighted work shall be fined not more than $2,500.

(e) False representation. Any person who knowingly makes a false representation of a material fact in the application for copyright registration provided for by section 409 [17 USCS § 409], or in any written statement filed in connection with the application, shall be fined not more than $2,500.
(Added Oct. 19, 1976, P. L. 94-553, Title I, § 101, 90 Stat. 2586.)

HISTORY; ANCILLARY LAWS AND DIRECTIVES

Effective date of section:
Section 102 of Act Oct. 19, 1976, P. L. 94-553, 90 Stat. 2598 provided that this section "becomes effective on January 1, 1978".

CROSS REFERENCES

Notice of copyright, 17 USCS §§ 401–406.
Application for copyright registration, 17 USCS § 409.
Impounding and disposition of infringing articles, 17 USCS § 503.
This section referred to in 17 USCS §§ 111, 115, 116, 411, 509.

RESEARCH GUIDE

Am Jur:
18 Am Jur 2d, Copyright and Literary Property §§ 154, 155.

INTERPRETIVE NOTES AND DECISIONS

1. Criminal infringement, generally [17 USCS § 506(a)]
2. —Importation
3. —Motion pictures
4. —Sound recordings
5. Forfeiture and destination [17 USCS § 506(b)]
6. Fraudulent copyright notice [17 USCS § 506(c)]
7. Fraudulent removal of copyright notice [17 USCS § 506(d)]
8. False representation [17 USCS § 506(e)]

1. Criminal infringement, generally [17 USCS § 506(a)]

Indictment for infringing copyright need not allege "copying" or expressly negative possibility that defendant's broadcast was original composition. Marx v United States (1938, CA9 Cal) 96 F2d 204, 37 USPQ 380.

Willful copying of copyrighted figurines constituting criminal violation is shown by defendant taking figurines to third party with instructions to make figurines resembling copyrighted figurines as closely as possible without "copyright trouble"; figurines so made are in most respects copies of copyrighted figurines and were deliberately made and deliberately sold by defendant for profit. United States v Backer (1943, CA2 NY) 134 F2d 533, 57 USPQ 133.

Sentence more severe than that given coconspirator and amounting to 2 year probation and $5000 fine for record piracy is well within statutory limits and is affirmed. United States v Malicoate (1976, CA10 Okla) 531 F2d 439, 189 USPQ 691.

Predecessor statute satisfies constitutional standards of certainty and is not overly broad in providing criminal penalties for vending of copyrighted motion pictures. United States v Wise (1977, CA9) 194 USPQ 59.

Predecessor section applies only to such articles as may be copyrighted. Rosenbach v Dreyfuss (1880, DC NY) 2 F 217.

United States district court has jurisdiction of suits to recover penalties under copyright laws. Taft v Stephens Lithographing & Engraving Co. (1889, CC Mo) 37 F 726.

No offense is committed if article is one that could not be copyrighted. Taft v Stephens Lithographing & Engraving Co. (1889, CC Mo) 38 F 28.

If upon different days, under different circumstances, defendant printed separate copies, each transaction thus separate would constitute separate offense, yet when printing of many copies is single continuous act, only one offense is committed. Taft v Stephens Lithographing & Engraving Co. (1889, CC Mo) 39 F 781.

Indictment charging defendant with "inciting, counseling, and procuring an infringement" was not ambiguous or uncertain. United States v Schmidt (1936, DC Pa) 15 F Supp 804.

Liability for willful copyright infringement is not affected or discharged by bankruptcy. Gordon v Weir (1953, DC Mich) 111 F Supp 117, 97 USPQ 387, affd (CA6 Mich) 216 F2d 508.

2. —Importation

Unlawful importation and vending of foreign-printed book is offense against United States of which it alone may complain. Bentley v Tibbals (1915, CA2 NY) 223 F 247.

3. —Motion pictures

Conviction for sale of copyrighted motion pictures is affirmed upon showing that motion pictures could not have been purchased, infringement was willful following consent decree signed by defendant, and government need not show that actual profit was made. United States v Wise (1977, CA9) 194 USPQ 59.

Before convicting for wilful infringement court must analyze arrangements involved in previous transfers of 16mm motion picture films to determine whether they come within first sale doctrine or whether their possession is so unauthorized as to be wilful infringement; search warrant is invalidated and seized 16mm motion picture films are returned to collector for lack of probable cause of wilful infringement because evidence was insubstantial that films were collected for profit or were not acquired under first sale doctrine, and possible violations of contract provisions in acquiring title to films is distinguished from wilful infringement. United States v Bily (1975, DC Pa) 406 F Supp 726, 188 USPQ 344.

Motion picture dealer's sale and lease of copyrighted movies infringes copyrights of proprietors and is not excused as transfer of copy lawfully obtained, because evidence falls far short of showing that copies purchased from individuals in other states were lawfully obtained, and plaintiffs' evidence shows elaborate system to protect copyright in movie distribution activities. Avco Embassy Pictures Corp. v Korshnak (1974, DC Pa) 189 USPQ 303.

4. —Sound recordings

Conviction of conspiracy and record piracy is affirmed even though information erroneously cited wrong statutory subsection, because record shows that defendant was not misled or prejudiced by error. United States v Malicoate (1976, CA10 Okla) 531 F2d 439, 189 USPQ 691.

Tape piracy conviction is not erroneous because information cited wrong section of statute under circumstances that did not mislead defendant, and conviction is affirmed as based on adequate evidence. United States v Blanton (1975, CA10 Okla) 531 F2d 442, 191 USPQ 21, cert den 425 US 935, 48 L Ed 2d 176, 96 S Ct 1666, reh den 426 US 912, 48 L Ed 2d 838, 96 S Ct 2238.

Information charging crime of record piracy is adequate in alleging copyrighted sound recording was manufactured, used or sold without authorization, willfully and for profit whether defendants infringed directly or willfully aided and abetted infringement. United States v Bodin (1974, DC Okla) 375 F Supp 1265, 183 USPQ 345.

Infringement for criminal purposes exists for tapes made by rerecording copyrighted tapes and copying more than trivial part of copyrighted tapes even though slight changes were made by speeding up, slowing down, deleting certain frequencies, and adding echoes or synthesizer sounds, especially where changes were insubstantial to human ear and were intended to be so. United States v Taxe (1974, DC Cal) 380 F Supp 1010, 184 USPQ 5, affd in part and vacated in part on other grounds (CA9 Cal) 540 F2d 961.

Sound Recording Act of 1971 added additional remedy for wilful infringement for profit by applying criminal sanctions and did not change law as to what constitutes infringement, and in view of court rulings that tape pirates are not entitled to compulsory license provisions and infringe copyright, then criminal sanctions are applicable to recordings fixed before Feb 1972 if infringement is wilful and for profit. Heilman v Levi (1975, DC Wis) 391 F Supp 1106, 185 USPQ 682.

5. Forfeiture and destination [17 USCS § 506(b)]

United States Government, in its capacity as parens patriae by reason of its interest in enforcing copyright laws, could, under predecessor statute, bring action seeking destruction of allegedly infringing magnetic tape recordings. United States v Brown (1975, DC Miss) 400 F Supp 656.

6. Fraudulent copyright notice [17 USCS § 506(c)]

Parts of English edition of dictionary being different from the American edition copyrighted in this country, notice of copyright on English edition would be violation. G. & C. Merriam Co. v United Dictionary Co. (1906, CA7 Ill) 146 F 354, affd 208 US 260, 52 L Ed 478, 28 S Ct 290.

Distinct penalty was not provided for each article marked, but for each separate offense of marking. London v Everett H. Dunbar Corp. (1910, CA1 Mass) 179 F 506.

One inserting false notice of copyright may be punished, whether or not notice appears in position provided in Copyright Act; complaint must aver that article falsely impressed has not been copyrighted. Rigney v Raphael Tuck & Sons Co. (1896, CC NY) 77 F 173.

To publish prints which were taken from cut that was falsely impressed constituted violation. Rigney v Dutton (1896, CC NY) 77 F 176.

False notice which omits date of copyright will not sustain action for penalty. Hoertel v Raphael Tuck Sons & Co. (1899, CC NY) 94 F 844.

7. Fraudulent removal of copyright notice [17 USCS § 506(d)]

Plaintiff does not show property interest independent of predecessor section by its argument that, when defendant purchases towels embodying plaintiff's copyrighted designs, removes copyright notice, and uses towels in manufacture of handbags which are sold to public, defendant is placing designs in public domain, exposing them to use by public, and thereby destroying copyright; argument falls short because defendant by its actions cannot place copyrighted designs in public domain; in order for designs to be placed in public domain, it must be shown that copyrighted works left plaintiff's possession without required notice, and this burden is on defendant. Scarves by Vera, Inc. v American Handbags, Inc. (1960, DC NY) 188 F Supp 255, 127 USPQ 47.

8. False representation [17 USCS § 506(e)]

Failure to reveal on copyright form previous publication of ring similar to ring of application to register copyright, together with false and misleading warning to infringers, is such inequitable conduct as to constitute misuse of copyright. Vogue Ring Creations, Inc. v Hardman (1976, DC RI) 190 USPQ 329. 410 F Supp 609, 190 USPQ 329.

§ 507.   Limitations on actions

(a) Criminal proceedings. No criminal proceeding shall be maintained under the provisions of this title [17 USCS §§ 101 et seq.] unless it is commenced within three years after the cause of action arose.

(b) Civil actions. No civil action shall be maintained under the provisions of this title [17 USCS §§ 101 et seq.] unless it is commenced within three years after the claim accrued.

(Added Oct. 19, 1976, P. L. 94-553, Title I, § 101, 90 Stat. 2586.)

HISTORY; ANCILLARY LAWS AND DIRECTIVES

Effective date of section:

Section 102 of Act Oct. 19, 1976, P. L. 94-553, 90 Stat. 2598 provided that this section "becomes effective on January 1, 1978".

CROSS REFERENCES

Infringement of copyright, 17 USCS § 501.
Criminal infringement, 17 USCS § 506.

RESEARCH GUIDE

Am Jur:

18 Am Jur 2d, Copyright and Literary Property §§ 130, 157.

Forms:

6 Federal Procedural Forms L Ed, Copyrights § 17:100.

Annotations:

Construction and application of provision of Federal Copyright Act (17 USCS § 115(b)) requiring that civil action arising out of copyright infringement be commenced within 3 years after claim accrued. 13 ALR Fed 922.

INTERPRETIVE NOTES AND DECISIONS

1. Generally
2. Accrual of cause of action
3. Laches or delay, generally
4. —Specific time periods
5. Tolling of limitations statute

1. Generally

Prior to 1958, copyright law contained no limitation of time within which civil action could be maintained under it, but predecessor section was amended in 1957 (effective in 1958) so that it provides that action shall not be maintained "unless same is commenced within three years after the claim accrued"; effect of amendment evidently has been to establish bar within three-year period whether claim accrued before or after effective date of amendment; before amendment, maximum term in which author of copyrighted song could sue for infringement was governed by law of state where action was brought; amendment imposes three-year limitation in all civil actions brought under Copyright Act. Vance v American Soc. of Composers, etc. (1959, CA8 Mo) 271 F2d 204, 123 USPQ 296, cert den 361 US 933, 4 L Ed 2d 355, 80 S Ct 373.

Where plaintiff brought replevin action to recover copies in defendant's possession he could not, after case was barred by statute, amend his pleadings by adding cause of action for statutory penalty. Hills & Co. v Hoover (1914, CA3 Pa)

211 F 241, cert den 238 US 634, 59 L Ed 1499, 35 S Ct 938.

Suit in December 1936 for copyright infringement by publication in August 1934 was barred by statute of limitations. Norm Co. v John A. Brown Co. (1939, DC Okla) 26 F Supp 707, 40 USPQ 419.

Exhibition of motion picture allegedly infringing common-law or statutory copyright is more analogous to republication or new publication and each exhibition gives rise to separate cause of action to which, respectively, statute of limitations applies. Stein v RKO Radio Pictures, Inc. (DC NY) 53 USPQ 294.

Estoppel exists if copyright owner, with knowledge of alleged infringement, permitted defendants to spend large sums on manufacture of alleged infringing book without making infringement claim. Christie v Raddock (1959, DC NY) 169 F Supp 48, 120 USPQ 76.

Copyright infringement action being barred by statute of limitations, plaintiff is not entitled to damages; however, inasmuch as defendant obtained invalid renewal certificate of copyright validly renewed by plaintiff, plaintiff is entitled to injunction against infringement of copyright, to receive from defendant any copies of composition which are in his possession by reason of possessing invalid renewal copyright, to receive from defendant all materials in his possession which could be used for printing or stamping copies of composition, and to assignment by defendant of invalid renewal copyright. Austin v

Steiner (1962, DC Ill) 207 F Supp 776, 134 USPQ 561.

Annotations:

Construction and application of provision of Federal Copyright Act (17 USCS § 115(b)) requiring that civil action arising out of copyright infringement be commenced within 3 years after claim accrued. 13 ALR Fed 922.

2. Accrual of cause of action

Three-year statutory bar applies to all printing and publishing activity of defendant more than 3 years before suit is started, so that only remainder sale of allegedly infringing work is within 3-year limitation and possible infringes. Mount v Book-of-the-Month Club, Inc. (1977, CA2) 194 USPQ 245.

Statute of limitations does not bar complaint alleging that after March 1944 and up to present time defendant has infringed and is infringing plaintiff's copyright; this is not affirmative statement that plaintiff knew in March 1944 that the defendant was infringing; although "after March 1944" could refer to any date between March 1944 and February 1956, which would fall within period subject to statute, words also can refer to any date between February 1956 and date of filing of complaint, which is period not barred thereunder. Rodriguez Serra v Matias Photo Shop (1957, DC Puerto Rico) 21 FRD 188, 116 USPQ 258.

Three-year limitation runs from date of last infringing act, not from date of initial infringement. Baxter v Curtis Industries, Inc. (1962, DC Ohio) 201 F Supp 100, 133 USPQ 78.

Date of accrual of action for infringement by manufacture of records of unpublished musical compositions which had been previously recorded by plaintiff is date when plaintiff filed notice of use of composition on records; plaintiff may not recover for infringements occurring prior to filing of notice or for infringements occurring more than 3 years before commencement of action. Rosette v Rainbo Record Mfg. Corp. (1973, DC NY) 354 F Supp 1183, affd (CA2 NY) 546 F2d 461.

3. Laches or delay, generally

Laches, as ground for refusing preliminary injunction, was inapplicable where neither complainant nor its predecessors had any knowledge or notice of alleged prior infringement of complainant's copyrights. Werner Co. v Encyclopaedia Britannica Co. (1905, CA3 NJ) 134 F 831.

Laches of complainant may be taken into consideration in action for injunction and accounting of profits. West Pub. Co. v Edward Thompson Co. (1910, CA2 NY) 176 F 833.

Copyright owner may not deliberately delay prosecution and thereby speculate without risk with another's money to determine success of exploitation. Universal Pictures Co. v Harold Lloyd Corp. (1947, CA9 Cal) 162 F2d 354, 73 USPQ 317.

Action for infringement of distribution rights in copyrighted motion picture is barred by plaintiff's long delay in suing during period when defendant or its predecessors had valid license, but defendant's expenditures in exploiting picture, if not made under valid license, should not be used as basis for defense of laches or estoppel. Machaty v Astra Pictures, Inc. (1952, CA2 NY) 197 F2d 138, 93 USPQ 51, cert den 334 US 827, 97 L Ed 644, 73 S Ct 29.

Copyright infringement action against distributor of motion picture is not barred by estoppel where distributor had notice of plaintiff's claim before distribution, which continued after further warning and for some years after suit was brought. Szekely v Eagle Lion Films, Inc. (1957, CA2 NY) 242 F2d 266, 113 USPQ 98, cert den 354 US 922, 1 L Ed 2d 1437, 77 S Ct 1382.

Where there has been long acquiescence in infringement, or culpable laches and negligence in seeking redress, especially if it appears that delay has misled respondent, equity will not afford complainant relief. Lawrence v Dana (1869, CC Mass) F Cas No 8136.

Complainant's laches in prosecuting defendant's infringements did not bar issuance of temporary injunction in absence of any showing that defendant had been prejudiced by delay. Hein v Harris (1910, CC NY) 175 F 875, affd (CA2 NY) 183 F 107.

Promptly after hearing of presentation of defendants' January, 1952, television show, plaintiff claimed copyright infringement; on learning in June, 1953, that defendants were preparing similar show, plaintiffs promptly brought suit charging both shows with infringement; plaintiffs are not guilty of laches; fact that plaintiffs did not commence action in January, 1952, was not waiver; dispute over infringement was never settled. Loew's, Inc. v Columbia Broadcasting System, Inc. (1955, DC Cal) 131 F Supp 165, 105 USPQ 302, affd (CA9 Cal) 239 F2d 532, 112 USPQ 11, affd 356 US 43, 2 L Ed 2d 583, 78 S Ct 667, 116 USPQ 479, reh den 356 US 934, 2 L Ed 2d 764, 78 S Ct 770.

When copyright holder has acquiesced in, or failed to object to, acts constituting alleged infringement so as to induce infringer to incur financial obligations, such delay in bringing suit gives rise to equitable defense of laches; also, in determining whether suit should be dismissed, court is guided by applicable statute of limitations; action commenced approximately six years after plaintiff acquired knowledge of alleged infringement is not dismissed, especially since plaintiff did not acquiesce in publication of alleged infringement, but notified defendant of copyright claim and objected to publication. Greenbie v Noble (1957, DC NY) 151 F Supp 45, 113 USPQ 115.

Laches, resulting from long delay in enforcing one's rights, followed by change of position of party relying on other party's inaction, might result in denial of equitable relief such as injunction and recovery of profits, but it would not stand in way of granting damages for unauthorized copying of copyrighted work or of injunction against future violations; to contrary, estoppel destroys very rights which it is sought to assert. Hayden v Chalfant Press, Inc. (1959, DC Cal) 177 F Supp 303, 123 USPQ 475, affd (CA9 Cal) 281 F2d 543, 126 USPQ 483.

4. —Specific time periods

Laches will not be imputed from complainant's delay of one year before prosecuting defendant's infringement, where circumstances refute rather than suggest acquiescence in infringement. Wooster v Crane & Co. (1906, CA8 Kan) 147 F 515.

Where plaintiff knew of defendant's catalogue short time following its first printing and made no protest or complaint until filing suit over three years later, during which time defendant incurred great expense in printing and distribution of catalogues, plaintiff was estopped from asserting claim of infringement. Edwin L. Wiegand Co. v Harold E. Trent Co. (1941, CA3 Pa) 122 F2d 920, 50 USPQ 243, cert den 316 US 667, 86 L Ed 1743, 62 S Ct 1033.

Additional relief in the form of damages for infringement is not refused for laches in action seeking declaratory judgment as to copyright title, although there was delay of 11 years between institution of action and trial, inasmuch as defendant consented to or joined in applications for delays and no specific prejudice is shown; it is unfair to tax plaintiff, rightful owner, rather than defendant, infringer, with penalties for delay in which they both participated; although not brought until six years after notice of defendant's threatened infringement, plaintiff's action based on numerous copyrighted songs by same author is not barred by laches since three years after notice plaintiff sued defendant as to one of these songs and defendant advanced same defense as to title as was raised in instant action; such prior suit was discontinued after defendant withdrew claim to song, which would indicate that defendant then believed that it had no title under conveyance relied upon in instant action. Edward B. Marks Music Corp. v Charles K. Harris

Music Publishing Co. (1958, CA2 NY) 255 F2d 518, 117 USPQ 308, cert den 358 US 831, 3 L Ed 2d 69, 79 S Ct 51.

Few weeks' delay on the part of the plaintiff after knowledge of infringement, before taking action, may debar him from any accounting for profits. Haas v Leo Feist (1916, DC NY) 234 F 105.

Owner of copyrighted map who delayed seven years before bringing infringement suit was not entitled to injunction or accounting, but it was entitled to enjoin defendant from using its maps in other than its business, and to compensatory damages, and costs. Blackburn v Southern California Gas Co. (1936, DC Cal) 14 F Supp 553, 29 USPQ 437.

While plaintiff denies having heard defendant's song, copyrighted in 1926, played in any manner before 1937, it is highly improbable, in view of plaintiff's residing in large city and engaging in music publishing business, that he did not between 1926 and 1937 have some knowledge of song; this constitutes laches barring suit alleging infringement of plaintiff's copyright by defendants' song. Davilla v Harms, Inc. (1940, DC NY) 36 F Supp 843, 48 USPQ 103.

Copyright proprietor is not guilty of laches in bringing infringement suit since defendants were notified of infringement within two months of proprietor learning of publication of infringing play and its performance. Harris v Miller (DC NY) 50 USPQ 306, mod on other grounds 50 USPQ 625.

Copyright infringement suit brought in 1937 is barred by laches where plaintiff heard of defendant's composition in 1922 and brought prior suit against defendant in 1932, suit being dismissed in 1932 for lack of jurisdiction over defendant; defendant's song has become very popular, and while there is no evidence as to how much money defendant spent in exploiting song it is assumed that change in position resulted from plaintiff's failure to prosecute. McMahon v Harms, Inc. (1942, DC NY) 42 F Supp 779, 52 USPQ 321.

Delay in applying for copyright of 22 years after composition of song, and of 11 years after defendant first published song, constitutes laches barring infringement suit; composer's laches are chargeable to assignee. Egner v E. C. Schirmer Music Co. (1942, DC Mass) 48 F Supp 187, 56 USPQ 214, affd (CA1 Mass) 139 F2d 398, 60 USPQ 74, cert den 322 US 730, 88 L Ed 1565, 64 S Ct 947.

Where plaintiff did not learn of probable infringement until January, came to United States from Trinidad in March and wrote defendant in same month, and plaintiff's United States copyright was secured in June and suit was filed 42 days later, suit is not barred by laches. Khan v Leo Feist, Inc. (1947, DC NY) 70 F Supp 450, 73 USPQ 104, affd (CA2 NY) 165 F2d 188, 76 USPQ 27.

Delay of 27 months before filing suit for copyright infringement was not unreasonable although delay prejudiced defendant in that key witness died one month before trial. Amsterdam v Triangle Publications, Inc. (1950, DC Pa) 93 F Supp 79, 87 USPQ 90, mod on the ground (CA3 Pa) 189 F2d 104, 89 USPQ 468.

Ordinarily, failure to take action against stranger does not give rise to estoppel, but copyright proprietor's knowing failure for over 19 years to institute proceedings against automobile club constitutes estoppel not only against club but also against defendants who were authorized by club to reproduce club's maps which proprietor now claims were, in turn, copied from his; defendants can assert estoppel whether or not they are assignees of club's copyright. Hayden v Chalfant Press, Inc. (1959, DC Cal) 177 F Supp 303, 123 USPQ 475, affd (CA9 Cal) 281 F2d 543, 126 USPQ 483.

Plaintiffs in copyright infringement action are barred by limitations and laches from obtaining part of relief sought since they took no action for several years despite knowledge of defendants' extensive use of copyright work. Klasmer v Baltimore Football, Inc. (1961, DC Md) 200 F Supp 255, 132 USPQ 36.

Delay of several months in bringing copyright infringement action after discovery of allegedly infringing fabric bearing copyrighted design was not laches since plaintiffs were required to spend some time investigating the origin of fabric. United Merchants & Mfrs., Inc. v K. Gimbel Accessories, Inc. (1968, DC NY) 294 F Supp 151, 161 USPQ 147.

Inaction of renewal copyright proprietor during many showings of motion picture throughout 19 year period is not abandonment of copyright or estoppel to assert infringement where there is no evidence proprietor knew of infringement and proprietor took no action indicating intent to surrender rights. Rohauer v Killiam Shows, Inc. (1974, DC NY) 379 F Supp 723, 183 USPQ 592, revd on other grounds (CA2 NY) 551 F2d 484.

5. Tolling of limitations statute

Intent of predecessor statute was that equitable considerations would apply to suspend the running of the statute, and these equitable considerations must be derived from general principles applicable to every federal form, not those peculiar to a local jurisdiction; inability of plaintiff in an infringement action to procure a copy of the book in question is insufficient to show the successful concealment under general equitable doctrines necessary to toll the statute of limitations. Prather v Neva Paperbacks, Inc. (1971, CA5 Fla) 446 F2d 338, 170 USPQ 378, 13 ALR Fed 916.

Defendant's mere holding of invalid renewal certificate of copyright validly renewed by plaintiff does not toll statute of limitations applicable to infringement actions. Austin v Steiner (1962, DC Ill) 207 F Supp 776, 134 USPQ 561.

§ 508. Notification of filing and determination of actions

(a) Within one month after the filing of any action under this title [17 USCS §§ 101 et seq.], the clerks of the courts of the United States shall send written notification to the Register of Copyrights setting forth, as far as is shown by the papers filed in the court, the names and addresses of the parties and the title, author, and registration number of each work involved in the action. If any other copyrighted work is later included in the action by amendment, answer, or other pleading, the clerk shall also send a notification concerning it to the Register within one month after the pleading is filed.

(b) Within one month after any final order or judgment is issued in the case, the clerk of the court shall notify the Register of it, sending with the notification a copy of the order or judgment together with the written opinion, if any, of the court.

(c) Upon receiving the notifications specified in this section, the Register shall make them a part of the public records of the Copyright Office. (Added Oct. 19, 1976, P. L. 94-553, Title I, § 101, 90 Stat. 2586.)

HISTORY; ANCILLARY LAWS AND DIRECTIVES

Effective date of section:
Section 102 of Act Oct. 19, 1976, P. L. 94-553, 90 Stat. 2598 provided that this section "becomes effective on January 1, 1978".

CROSS REFERENCES

Copyright Office records, 17 USCS § 705.
Notification of filing of patent infringement action, 35 USCS § 290.

INTERPRETIVE NOTES AND DECISIONS

Right of holder of trade-mark, patent, or copyright to warn others of infringement suits does not depend upon validity of mark, patent, or copyright so long as holder believes his claims are valid. Lucien Lelong, Inc. v Dana Perfumes, Inc. (1955, DC Ill) 138 F Supp 575, 108 USPQ 101.

§ 509. Seizure and forfeiture

(a) All copies or phonorecords manufactured, reproduced, distributed, sold, or otherwise used, intended for use, or possessed with intent to use in violation of section 506(a) [17 USCS § 506(a)], and all plates, molds, matrices, masters, tapes, film negatives, or other articles by means of which such copies or phonorecords may be reproduced, and all electronic, mechanical, or other devices for manufacturing, reproducing, or assembling such copies or phonorecords may be seized and forfeited to the United States.

(b) The applicable procedures relating to (i) the seizure, summary and judicial forfeiture, and condemnation of vessels, vehicles, merchandise, and baggage for violations of the customs laws contained in title 19 [19 USCS §§ 1 et seq.], (ii) the disposition of such vessels, vehicles, merchandise, and baggage or the proceeds from the sale thereof, (iii) the remission or mitigation of such forfeiture, (iv) the compromise of claims, and (v) the award of compensation to informers in respect of such forfeitures, shall apply to seizures and forfeitures incurred, or alleged to have been incurred, under the provisions of this section, insofar as applicable and not inconsistent with the provisions of this section; except that such duties as are imposed upon any officer or employee of the Treasury Department or any other person with respect to the seizure and forfeiture of vessels, vehicles, merchandise; and baggage under the provisions of the customs laws contained in title 19 [19 USCS §§ 1 et seq.] shall be performed with respect to seizure and forfeiture of all articles described in subsection (a) by such officers, agents, or other persons as may be authorized or designated for that purpose by the Attorney General.

(Added Oct. 19, 1976, P. L. 94-553, Title I, § 101, 90 Stat. 2587.)

HISTORY; ANCILLARY LAWS AND DIRECTIVES

Effective date of section:
Section 102 of Act Oct. 19, 1976, P. L. 94-553, 90 Stat. 2598 provided that this section "becomes effective on January 1, 1978".

Impounding and disposition of infringing articles, 17 USCS § 503.
Forfeiture and destruction as consequence of criminal infringement, 17 USCS
§ 506(b).
Customs laws, 19 USCS §§ 1 et seq.
This section referred to in 17 USCS §§ 111, 115, 116, 411.

RESEARCH GUIDE

Forms:
6 Federal Procedural Forms L Ed, Copyrights §§ 17:62–17:68.

§ 510. Remedies for alteration of programing by cable systems

(a) In any action filed pursuant to section 111(c)(3) [17 USCS § 111(c)(3)],
the following remedies shall be available:

(1) Where an action is brought by a party identified in subsections (b) or
(c) of section 501 [17 USCS § 501], the remedies provided by sections
502 through 505 [17 USCS §§ 502–505], and the remedy provided by
subsection (b) of this section; and

(2) When an action is brought by a party identified in subsection (d) of
section 501 [17 USCS § 501], the remedies provided by sections 502 and
505 [17 USCS §§ 502–505], together with any actual damages suffered
by such party as a result of the infringement, and the remedy provided
by subsection (b) of this section.

(b) In any action filed pursuant to section 111(c)(3) [17 USCS § 111(c)(3)],
the court may decree that, for a period not to exceed thirty days, the cable
system shall be deprived of the benefit of a compulsory license for one or
more distant signals carried by such cable system.
(Added Oct. 19, 1976, P. L. 94-553, Title I, § 101, 90 Stat. 2587.)

HISTORY; ANCILLARY LAWS AND DIRECTIVES

Effective date of section:
Section 102 of Act Oct. 19, 1976, P. L. 94-553, 90 Stat. 2598 provided
that this section "becomes effective on January 1, 1978"

CROSS REFERENCES:

Secondary transmissions by cable systems, 17 USCS § 111(c).
"Distant signal equivalent" defined, 17 USCS § 111(f).
Infringement of copyright, 17 USCS § 501.
Remedies for infringement, 17 USCS § 502–505.
This section referred to in 17 USCS §§ 111, 411.

CHAPTER 6. MANUFACTURING REQUIREMENTS AND IMPORTATION

§ 601. Manufacture, importation, and public distribution of certain copies

(a) Prior to July 1, 1982, and except as provided by subsection (b), the importation into or public distribution in the United States of copies of a work consisting preponderantly of nondramatic literary material that is in the English language and is protected under this title [17 USCS §§ 101 et seq.] is prohibited unless the portions consisting of such material have been manufactured in the United States or Canada.

(b) The provisions of subsection (a) do not apply—

(1) where, on the date when importation is sought or public distribution in the United States is made, the author of any substantial part of such material is neither a national nor a domiciliary of the United States or, if such author is a national of the United States, he or she has been domiciled outside the United States for a continuous period of at least one year immediately preceding that date; in the case of a work made for hire, the exemption provided by this clause does not apply unless a substantial part of the work was prepared for an employer or other person who is not a national or domiciliary of the United States or a domestic corporation or enterprise;

(2) where the United States Customs Service is presented with an import statement issued under the seal of the Copyright Office, in which case a total of no more than two thousand copies of any one such work shall be allowed entry; the import statement shall be issued upon request to the copyright owner or to a person designated by such owner at the time of registration for the work under section 408 [17 USCS § 408] or at any time thereafter;

(3) where importation is sought under the authority or for the use, other than in schools, of the Government of the United States or of any State or political subdivision of a State;

(4) where importation, for use and not for sale, is sought—

(A) by any person with respect to no more than one copy of any work at any one time;

377

(B) by any person arriving from outside the United States, with respect to copies forming part of such person's personal baggage; or

(C) by an organization operated for scholarly, educational, or religious purposes and not for private gain, with respect to copies intended to form a part of its library;

(5) where the copies are reproduced in raised characters for the use of the blind; or

(6) where, in addition to copies imported under clauses (3) and (4) of this subsection, no more than two thousand copies of any one such work, which have not been manufactured in the United States or Canada, are publicly distributed in the United States; or

(7) where, on the date when importation is sought or public distribution in the United States is made—

(A) the author of any substantial part of such material is an individual and receives compensation for the transfer or license of the right to distribute the work in the United States; and

(B) the first publication of the work has previously taken place outside the United States under a transfer or license granted by such author to a transferee or licensee who was not a national or domiciliary of the United States or a domestic corporation or enterprise; and

(C) there has been no publication of an authorized edition of the work of which the copies were manufactured in the United States; and

(D) the copies were reproduced under a transfer or license granted by such author or by the transferee or licensee of the right of first publication as mentioned in subclause (B), and the transferee or the licensee of the right of reproduction was not a national or domiciliary of the United States or a domestic corporation or enterprise.

(c) The requirement of this section that copies be manufactured in the United States or Canada is satisfied if—

(1) in the case where the copies are printed directly from type that has been set, or directly from plates made from such type, the setting of the type and the making of the plates have been performed in the United States or Canada; or

(2) in the case where the making of plates by a lithographic or photoengraving process is a final or intermediate step preceding the printing of the copies, the making of the plates has been performed in the United States or Canada; and

(3) in any case, the printing or other final process of producing multiple copies and any binding of the copies have been performed in the United States or Canada.

(d) Importation or public distribution of copies in violation of this section does not invalidate protection for a work under this title [17 USCS §§ 601 et seq.]. However, in any civil action or criminal proceeding for infringement of the exclusive rights to reproduce and distribute copies of the work, the infringer has a complete defense with respect to all of the nondramatic literary material comprised in the work and any other parts of the work in which the exclusive rights to reproduce and distribute copies are owned by the same person who owns such exclusive rights in the nondramatic literary material, if the infringer proves—

(1) that copies of the work have been imported into or publicly distributed in the United States in violation of this section by or with the authority of the owner of such exclusive rights; and

(2) that the infringing copies were manufactured in the United States or Canada in accordance with the provisions of subsection (c); and

(3) that the infringement was commenced before the effective date of registration for an authorized edition of the work, the copies of which have been manufactured in the United States or Canada in accordance with the provisions of subsection (c).

(e) In any action for infringement of the exclusive rights to reproduce and distribute copies of a work containing material required by this section to be manufactured in the United States or Canada, the copyright owner shall set forth in the complaint the names of the persons or organizations who performed the processes specified by subsection (c) with respect to that material, and the places where those processes were performed.
(Added Oct. 19, 1976, P. L. 94-553, Title I, § 101, 90 Stat. 2588.)

HISTORY; ANCILLARY LAWS AND DIRECTIVES

Effective date of section:
Section 102 of Act Oct. 19, 1976, P. L. 94-553, 90 Stat. 2598 provided that this section "becomes effective on January 1, 1978".

CODE OF FEDERAL REGULATIONS

19 CFR Part 133

CROSS REFERENCES

"Publication" defined, 17 USCS § 101.
"United States" defined, 17 USCS § 101.
Identification of manufacturer in application for copyright registration, 17 USCS § 409.
Customs laws, 19 USCS §§ 1 et seq.
This section referred to in 17 USCS §§ 409, 602, 708.

RESEARCH GUIDE

Am Jur:
18 Am Jur 2d, Copyright and Literary Property §§ 27, 64, 74–76, 114.

Law Review Articles:
Copyright Symposium, 22 New York Law School Law Review 193.

INTERPRETIVE NOTES AND DECISIONS

Fact that foreign edition of domestic book was printed in foreign country from plates made in this country did not authorize infringer to import such foreign edition and, by making copies, infringe copyrighted domestic book. G. & C. Merriam Co. v United Dictionary Co. (1906, CA7 Ill) 146 F 354, affd 208 US 260, 52 L Ed 478, 28 S Ct 290.

Sale of copies of copyrighted work printed from type not set in United States does not debar copyright holder from relief against infringement. Bentley v Tibbals (1915, CA2 NY) 223 F 247.

Importation of editions of Meccano copyrighted manuals printed in England and accompanying Meccano outfits sold in United States was not a violation of predecessor section. Meccano, Ltd. v Wagner (1916, DC Ohio) 234 F 912, mod (CA6 Ohio) 246 F 603.

Infringing phonograph records which have gone through eight of nine processes involved in their making, and have then been shipped to Canada for ninth process, are "manufactured" within United States and subject to payment of royalty. G. Ricordi & Co. v Columbia Graphophone Co. (1920, DC NY) 270 F 822.

Silk screen process for making copyrighted fabric design, even when positive is made with photographic process, is not within meaning of terms "photo engraving" or "lithography" as used in predecessor statute, which was not intended to cover all printing processes, and court preliminary enjoins continued infringement of fabric designs. Huk-A-Poo Sportswear, Inc. v Franshaw, Inc. (1976, DC NY) 411 F Supp 15, 189 USPQ 747.

Provisions of predecessor act which require books to be printed from type set within limits of United States are not complied with by printing from type set within Philippine Islands, when Congress has not extended copyright laws to Philippines. 25 OAG 25; 25 OAG 179.

Books copyrighted under laws of United States and printed from type set and plates made in this country, printed sheets of which were sent to Belgium and there bound, cannot be legally returned to or imported into United States. 28 OAG 90.

Application for registration of copyright should be denied where copy, printed and bound in accordance with manufacturing provisions of predecessor section, is only fragment of work. 28 OAG 176.

Copyrighted books which have been printed from type set within United States, and printing and binding both performed within limits thereof, may be rebound abroad and imported without violation of predecessor section. 28 OAG 209.

§ 602. Infringing importation of copies or phonorecords

(a) Importation into the United States, without the authority of the owner of copyright under this title [17 USCS §§ 101 et seq.], of copies or phonorecords of a work that have been acquired outside the United States is an infringement of the exclusive right to distribute copies or phonorecords under section 106 [17 USCS § 106], actionable under section 501 [17 USCS § 501]. This subsection does not apply to—

(1) importation of copies or phonorecords under the authority or for the use of the Government of the United States or of any State or political subdivision of a State, but not including copies or phonorecords for use in schools, or copies of any audiovisual work imported for purposes other than archival use;

(2) importation, for the private use of the importer and not for distribution, by any person with respect to no more than one copy or phonorecord of any one work at any one time, or by any person arriving from outside the United States with respect to copies or phonorecords forming part of such person's personal baggage; or

(3) importation by or for an organization operated for scholarly, educational, or religious purposes and not for private gain, with respect to no

more than one copy of an audiovisual work solely for its archival purposes, and no more than five copies or phonorecords of any other work for its library lending or archival purposes, unless the importation of such copies or phonorecords is part of an activity consisting of systematic reproduction or distribution, engaged in by such organization in violation of the provisions of section 108(g)(2) [17 USCS § 108(g)(2)].

(b) In a case where the making of the copies or phonorecords would have constituted an infringement of copyright if this title [17 USCS §§ 101 et seq.] had been applicable, their importation is prohibited. In a case where the copies or phonorecords were lawfully made, the United States Customs Service has no authority to prevent their importation unless the provisions of section 601 [17 USCS § 601] are applicable. In either case, the Secretary of the Treasury is authorized to prescribe, by regulation, a procedure under which any person claiming an interest in the copyright in a particular work may, upon payment of a specified fee, be entitled to notification by the Customs Service of the importation of articles that appear to be copies or phonorecords of the work.

(Added Oct. 19, 1976, P. L. 94-553, Title I, § 101, 90 Stat. 2589.)

HISTORY; ANCILLARY LAWS AND DIRECTIVES

Effective date of section:
Section 102 of Act Oct. 19, 1976, P. L. 94-553, 90 Stat. 2598 provided that this section "becomes effective on January 1, 1978".

CODE OF FEDERAL REGULATIONS

19 CFR Part 133

CROSS REFERENCES

Exclusive rights in copyrighted works, 17 USCS § 106.
Exemption for reproduction by library or archives, 17 USCS § 108(g)(2).
Infringement of copyright, 17 USCS § 501.
Manufacturing requirement, 17 USCS § 601.
Customs laws, 19 USCS §§ 1 et seq.
This section referred to in 17 USCS §§ 501, 603.

INTERPRETIVE NOTES AND DECISIONS

Defendants who imported foreign publication contrary to copyright law, and reprinted it, had no valid rights to so reprint to injury of American owner of copyright of same work. Harper & Bros. v M. A. Donohue & Co. (1905, CC Ill) 144 F 491, affd (CA7 Ill) 146 F 1023.

Uncopyrighted lithographs may be imported although copies of copyrighted paintings. 20 OAG 753.

Article which is prohibited importation cannot gain admission through being attached to article which is not prohibited; importation of reprints of musical compositions copyrighted in United States is prohibited. 22 OAG 29.

Importation of a book printed in original French from type not set within United States, where copyright therefor for United States was secured by Paris publisher, is prohibited. 23 OAG 353.

Tariff act which provides when and under what circumstances certain articles are exempt from duty on importation, does not repeal, modify, or abrogate any part of Copyright Act. 23 OAG 445.

§ 603. Importation prohibitions: Enforcement and disposition of excluded articles

(a) The Secretary of the Treasury and the United States Postal Service shall separately or jointly make regulations for the enforcement of the provisions of this title [17 USCS §§ 101 et seq.] prohibiting importation.

(b) These regulations may require, as a condition for the exclusion of articles under section 602 [17 USCS § 602]—

(1) that the person seeking exclusion obtain a court order enjoining importation of the articles; or

(2) that the person seeking exclusion furnish proof, of a specified nature and in accordance with prescribed procedures, that the copyright in which such person claims an interest is valid and that the importation would violate the prohibition in section 602 [17 USCS § 602]; the person seeking exclusion may also be required to post a surety bond for any injury that may result if the detention or exclusion of the articles proves to be unjustified.

(c) Articles imported in violation of the importation prohibitions of this title [17 USCS §§ 101 et seq.] are subject to seizure and forfeiture in the same manner as property imported in violation of the customs revenue laws. Forfeited articles shall be destroyed as directed by the Secretary of the Treasury or the court, as the case may be; however, the articles may be returned to the country of export whenever it is shown to the satisfaction of the Secretary of the Treasury that the importer had no reasonable grounds for believing that his or her acts constituted a violation of law. (Added Oct. 19, 1976, P. L. 94-553, Title I, § 101, 90 Stat. 2590.)

HISTORY; ANCILLARY LAWS AND DIRECTIVES

References in text:
"Customs revenue laws", referred to in subsec. (c), appear generally as 19 USCS §§ 1 et seq.

Effective date of section:
Section 102 of Act Oct. 19, 1976, P. L. 94-553, 90 Stat. 2598 provided that this section "becomes effective on January 1, 1978".

CODE OF FEDERAL REGULATIONS
19 CFR Part 133

CROSS REFERENCES
Infringing importation of copies or phonorecords, 17 USCS § 602.
Customs laws, 19 USCS §§ 1 et seq.

RESEARCH GUIDE
Am Jur:
18 Am Jur 2d, Copyright and Literary Property § 75.

INTERPRETIVE NOTES AND DECISIONS

Importation of a foreign book printed from type set in England is unlawful, and books so imported are subject to forfeiture. Bentley v Tibbals (1915, CA2 NY) 223 F 247.

Rules of Secretary of Treasury and Postmaster General may provide for destruction of book imported into this country in violation of copyright laws. 22 OAG 29.

Secretary of Treasury and Postmaster General may provide for destruction of prohibited articles, without judicial proceeding when value of property involved is trifling. 22 OAG 70.

CHAPTER 7. COPYRIGHT OFFICE

---

§ 701. The Copyright Office: General responsibilities and organization

(a) All administrative functions and duties under this title [17 USCS §§ 101 et seq.], except as otherwise specified, are the responsibility of the Register of Copyrights as director of the Copyright Office of the Library of Congress. The Register of Copyrights, together with the subordinate officers and employees of the Copyright Office, shall be appointed by the Librarian of Congress, and shall act under the Librarian's general direction and supervision.

(b) The Register of Copyrights shall adopt a seal to be used on and after January 1, 1978, to authenticate all certified documents issued by the Copyright Office.

(c) The Register of Copyrights shall make an annual report to the Librarian of Congress of the work and accomplishments of the Copyright Office during the previous fiscal year. The annual report of the Register of Copyrights shall be published separately and as a part of the annual report of the Librarian of Congress.

(d) Except as provided by section 706(b) [17 USCS § 706(b)] and the regulations issued thereunder, all actions taken by the Register of Copyrights under this title [17 USCS §§ 101 et seq.] are subject to the provisions of the Administrative Procedure Act of June 11, 1946, as amended (c. 324, 60 Stat. 237, Title 5, United States Code, Chapter 5, Subchapter II and Chapter 7).

(Added Oct. 19, 1976, P. L. 94-553, Title I, § 101, 90 Stat. 2591.)

HISTORY; ANCILLARY LAWS AND DIRECTIVES

References in text:
"Administrative Procedure Act of June 11, 1946, as amended", referred to in subsec. (d), was repealed and similar provisions were reenacted as 5 USCS §§ 551 et seq., 701 et seq.

Effective date of section:
Section 102 of Act Oct. 19, 1976, P. L. 94-553, 90 Stat. 2598 provided that this section "becomes effective on January 1, 1978".

Other provisions:
National Commission on New Technological Uses of Copyrighted Works. Act Dec. 31, 1974, P. L. 93-573, Title II, §§ 201–208, 88 Stat. 1873, as amended by Act June 21, 1976, P. L. 94-314, 90 Stat. 692, provided:

"ESTABLISHMENT AND PURPOSE OF COMMISSION

"Sec. 201. (a) There is hereby created in the Library of Congress a National Commission on New Technological Uses of Copyrighted Works (hereafter called the Commission).

"(b) The purpose of the Commission is to study and compile data on:

"(1) the reproduction and use of copyrighted works of authorship—

"(A) in conjunction with automatic systems capable of storing, processing, retrieving, and transferring information, and

"(B) by various forms of machine reproduction, not including reproduction by or at the request of instructors for use in face-to-face teaching activities; and

"(2) the creation of new works by the application or intervention of such automatic systems or machine reproduction.

"(c) The Commission shall make recommendations as to such changes in copyright law or procedures that may be necessary to assure for such purposes access to copyrighted works, and to provide recognition of the rights of copyright owners.

"MEMBERSHIP OF THE COMMISSION

"Sec. 202. (a) The Commission shall be composed of thirteen voting members, appointed as follows:

"(1) Four members, to be appointed by the President, selected from authors and other copyright owners;

"(2) Four members, to be appointed by the President, selected from users of copyright works:

"(3) Four nongovernmental members to be appointed by the President, selected from the public generally, with at least one member selected from among experts in consumer protection affairs;

"(4) The Librarian of Congress.

"(b) The President shall appoint a Chairman, and a Vice Chairman who shall act as Chairman in the absence or disability of the Chairman or in the event of a vacancy in that office, from among the four members selected from the public generally, as provided by clause (3) of subsection (a). The Register of Copyrights shall serve ex officio as a nonvoting member of the Commission.

"(c) Seven voting members of the Commission shall constitute a quorum.

"(d) Any vacancy in the Commission shall not affect its powers and shall be filled in the same manner as the original appointment was made.

"COMPENSATION OF MEMBERS OF COMMISSION

"Sec. 203. (a) Members of the Commission, other than officers or employees of the Federal Government, shall receive compensation at the rate of $100 per day while engaged in the actual performance of Commission duties, plus reimbursement for travel, subsistence, and other necessary expenses in connection with such duties.

"(b) Any members of the Commission who are officers or employees of the Federal Government shall serve on the Commission without compensation, but such members shall be reimbursed for travel, subsistence, and other necessary expenses in connection with the performance of their duties.

"STAFF

"Sec. 204. (a) To assist in its studies, the Commission may appoint a staff which shall be an administrative part of the Library of Congress. The staff shall be headed by an Executive Director, who shall be responsible to the Commission for the Administration of the duties entrusted to the staff.

"(b) The Commission may procure temporary and intermittent services to the same extent as is authorized by section 3109 of title 5 [5 USCS § 3109], United States Code but at rates not to exceed $100 per day.

"EXPENSES OF THE COMMISSION

"Sec. 205. There are hereby authorized to be appropriated such sums as may be necessary to carry out the provisions of this title until and including the day on which the Commission terminates.

"REPORTS

"Sec. 206. (a) Within one year after the first meeting of the Commission it shall submit to the President and the Congress a preliminary report on its activities.

"(b) Within three years after the enactment of this Act [enacted Dec. 31, 1974] the Commission shall submit to the President and the Congress a final report on its study and investigation which shall include its recommendations and such proposals for legislation and administrative action as may be necessary to carry out its recommendations.

"(c) In addition to the preliminary report and final report required by this section, the Commission may publish such interim reports as it may determine, including but not limited to consultant's reports, transcripts of testimony, seminar reports, and other Commission findings.

"POWERS OF THE COMMISSION

"Sec. 207. (a) The Commission or, with the authorization of the Commission, any three or more of its members, may, for the purpose of carrying out the provisions of this title [this note], hold hearings, administer oaths, and require, by subpoena or otherwise, the attendance and testimony of witnesses and the production of documentary material.

"(b) With the consent of the Commission, any of its members may hold any meetings, seminars, or conferences considered appropriate to provide a forum for discussion of the problems with which it is dealing.

"TERMINATION

"Sec. 208. On the sixtieth day after the date of the submission of its final report, the Commission shall terminate and all offices and employment under it shall expire."

CROSS REFERENCES

Administrative Procedure Act, 5 USCS §§ 551, 701.
Copyright Office regulations, 17 USCS § 702.
Copies of Copyright Office records, 17 USCS § 706.

RESEARCH GUIDE

Am Jur:
18 Am Jur 2d, Copyright and Literary Property § 54.

Law Review Articles:
Copyright Symposium, 22 New York Law School Law Review 193.

INTERPRETIVE NOTES AND DECISIONS

In appointing Register of Copyrights, Librarian of Congress is bound by Library's personnel regulations and may not disregard findings of administrative hearing office, supported by record, that applicant for position had been discriminated against on basis of race and sex in Librarian's appointment of another; court will set aside appointment of such other person and order Librarian's compliance with regulations, but court does not have power to appoint new Register of Copyrights. Ringer v Mumford (1973, DC Dist Col) 355 F Supp 749.

Copyright office, while within the Library of Congress, is separate and distinct office; register of copyrights must perform those duties charged upon him by law, is liable under his bond for their faithful performance, and cannot escape this responsibility by any delegation of authority; it is not intended, however, that he must perform all details personally. 39 OAG 429.

Provision that Register of Copyrights shall perform his duties under direction and supervision of Librarian of Congress does not warrant demand by counsel that librarian personally examine upon its merits claim for copyright registration denied by Register. 40 OAG 27, 48 USPQ 439.

§ 702. Copyright Office regulations

The Register of Copyrights is authorized to establish regulations not inconsistent with law for the administration of the functions and duties made the responsibility of the Register under this title [17 USCS §§ 101 et seq.]. All regulations established by the Register under this title [17 USCS §§ 101 et seq.] are subject to the approval of the Librarian of Congress.
(Added Oct. 19, 1976, P. L. 94-553, Title I, § 101, 90 Stat. 2591.)

HISTORY; ANCILLARY LAWS AND DIRECTIVES

Effective date of section:
Section 102 of Act Oct. 19, 1976, P. L. 94-553, 90 Stat. 2598 provided
that this section "becomes effective on January 1, 1978".

CODE OF FEDERAL REGULATIONS

37 CFR Part 201–202 (Copyright Office Regulations)

CROSS REFERENCES

General responsibilities and organization of Copyright Office, 17 USCS
§ 701.
USCS Administrative Rules, Copyrights, 37 CFR Parts 201 and 202.

RESEARCH GUIDE

Am Jur:
18 Am Jur 2d, Copyright and Literary Property § 65.

INTERPRETIVE NOTES AND DECISIONS

Acceptance of application which did not contain statement of citizenship or nationality operated as a waiver of administrative regulation and copyright obtained thereon was valid. Campbell v Wireback (1920, CA4 Md) 269 F 372, 17 ALR 743.

§ 703. Effective date of actions in Copyright Office

In any case in which time limits are prescribed under this title [17 USCS §§ 101 et seq.] for the performance of an action in the Copyright Office, and in which the last day of the prescribed period falls on a Saturday, Sunday, holiday, or other nonbusiness day within the District of Columbia or the Federal Government, the action may be taken on the next succeeding business day, and is effective as of the date when the period expired. (Added Oct. 19, 1976, P. L. 94-553, Title I, § 101, 90 Stat. 2591.)

HISTORY; ANCILLARY LAWS AND DIRECTIVES

Effective date of section:
Section 102 of Act Oct. 19, 1976, P. L. 94-553, 90 Stat. 2598 provided
that this section "becomes effective on January 1, 1978".

CROSS REFERENCES

General responsibilities and organization of Copyright Office, 17 USCS
§ 701.

§ 704. Retention and disposition of articles deposited in Copyright Office

(a) Upon their deposit in the Copyright Office under sections 407 and 408 [17 USCS §§ 407 and 408], all copies, phonorecords, and identifying material, including those deposited in connection with claims that have been refused registration, are the property of the United States Government.

(b) In the case of published works, all copies, phonorecords, and identifying material deposited are available to the Library of Congress for its collections, or for exchange or transfer to any other library. In the case of unpublished works, the Library is entitled, under regulations that the Register of Copyrights shall prescribe, to select any deposits for its collections or for transfer to the National Archives of the United States or to a Federal records center, as defined in section 2901 of title 44 [44 USCS § 2901].

(c) The Register of Copyrights is authorized, for specific or general categories of works, to make a facsimile reproduction of all or any part of the material deposited under section 408 [17 USCS § 408], and to make such reproduction a part of the Copyright Office records of the registration, before transferring such material to the Library of Congress as provided by subsection (b), or before destroying or otherwise disposing of such material as provided by subsection (d).

(d) Deposits not selected by the Library under subsection (b), or identifying portions or reproductions of them, shall be retained under the control of the Copyright Office, including retention in Government storage facilities, for the longest period considered practicable and desirable by the Register of Copyrights and the Librarian of Congress. After that period it is within the joint discretion of the Register and the Librarian to order their destruction or other disposition; but, in the case of unpublished works, no deposit shall be knowingly or intentionally destroyed or otherwise disposed of during its term of copyright unless a facsimile reproduction of the entire deposit has been made a part of the Copyright Office records as provided by subsection (c).

(e) The depositor of copies, phonorecords, or identifying material under section 408 [17 USCS § 408], or the copyright owner of record, may request retention, under the control of the Copyright Office, of one or more of such articles for the full term of copyright in the work. The Register of Copyrights shall prescribe, by regulation, the conditions under which such requests are to be made and granted, and shall fix the fee to be charged under section 708(a)(11) [17 USCS § 708(a)(11)] if the request is granted. (Added Oct. 19, 1976, P. L. 94-553, Title I, § 101, 90 Stat. 2591.)

HISTORY; ANCILLARY LAWS AND DIRECTIVES

Effective date of section:
Section 102 of Act Oct. 19, 1976, P. L. 94-553, 90 Stat. 2598 provided that this section "becomes effective on January 1, 1978".

CROSS REFERENCES

Deposit of copies or phonorecords for Library of Congress, 17 USCS § 407.
Administrative classification and optional deposit as element of copyright registration, 17 USCS § 408(c).

General responsibilities and organization of Copyright Office, 17 USCS § 701.
Copyright Office fees, 17 USCS § 708.
Federal records center, 44 USCS § 2901.

RESEARCH GUIDE

Am Jur:
18 Am Jur 2d, Copyright and Literary Property § 63.

§ 705. Copyright Office records: Preparation, maintenance, public inspection, and searching

(a) The Register of Copyrights shall provide and keep in the Copyright Office records of all deposits, registrations, recordations, and other actions taken under this title [17 USCS §§ 101 et seq.], and shall prepare indexes of all such records.

(b) Such records and indexes, as well as the articles deposited in connection with completed copyright registrations and retained under the control of the Copyright Office, shall be open to public inspection.

(c) Upon request and payment of the fee specified by section 708 [17 USCS § 708], the Copyright Office shall make a search of its public records, indexes, and deposits, and shall furnish a report of the information they disclose with respect to any particular deposits, registrations, or recorded documents.
(Added Oct. 19, 1976, P. L. 94-553, Title I, § 101, 90 Stat. 2592.)

HISTORY; ANCILLARY LAWS AND DIRECTIVES

Effective date of section:
Section 102 of Act Oct. 19, 1976, P. L. 94-553, 90 Stat. 2598 provided that this section "becomes effective on January 1, 1978".

CROSS REFERENCES

General responsibilities and organization of Copyright Office, 17 USCS § 701.
Retention and disposition of articles deposited in Copyright Office, 17 USCS § 704.
Copyright Office fees, 17 USCS § 708.
This section referred to in 17 USCS § 708.

RESEARCH GUIDE

Am Jur:
18 Am Jur 2d, Copyright and Literary Property §§ 54, 63.

§ 706. Copies of Copyright Office records

(a) Copies may be made of any public records or indexes of the Copyright Office; additional certificates of copyright registration and copies of any public records or indexes may be furnished upon request and payment of the fees specified by section 708 [17 USCS § 708].

(b) Copies or reproductions of deposited articles retained under the control of the Copyright Office shall be authorized or furnished only under the conditions specified by the Copyright Office regulations.
(Added Oct. 19, 1976, P. L. 94-553, Title I, § 101, 90 Stat. 2592.)

HISTORY; ANCILLARY LAWS AND DIRECTIVES

Effective date of section:
Section 102 of Act Oct. 19, 1976, P. L. 94-553, 90 Stat. 2598 provided that this section "becomes effective on January 1, 1978".

CROSS REFERENCES

General responsibilities and organization of Copyright Office, 17 USCS § 701.
Copyright Office regulations, 17 USCS § 702.
Retention and disposition of articles deposited in Copyright Office, 17 USCS § 704.
Copyright Office records, 17 USCS § 705.
Copyright Office fees, 17 USCS § 708.
This section referred to in 17 USCS §§ 701, 708.

§ 707. Copyright Office forms and publications

(a) **Catalog of copyright entries.** The Register of Copyrights shall compile and publish at periodic intervals catalogs of all copyright registrations. These catalogs shall be divided into parts in accordance with the various classes of works, and the Register has discretion to determine, on the basis of practicability and usefulness, the form and frequency of publication of each particular part.

(b) **Other publications.** The Register shall furnish, free of charge upon request, application forms for copyright registration and general informational material in connection with the functions of the Copyright Office. The Register also has the authority to publish compilations of information, bibliographies, and other material he or she considers to be of value to the public.

(c) **Distribution of publications.** All publications of the Copyright Office shall be furnished to depository libraries as specified under section 1905 of

title 44 [44 USCS § 1905], and, aside from those furnished free of charge, shall be offered for sale to the public at prices based on the cost of reproduction and distribution.
(Added Oct. 19, 1976, P. L. 94-553, Title I, § 101, 90 Stat. 2592.)

HISTORY; ANCILLARY LAWS AND DIRECTIVES

Effective date of section:
Section 102 of Act Oct. 19, 1976, P. L. 94-553, 90 Stat. 2598 provided that this section "becomes effective on January 1, 1978".

CROSS REFERENCES

General responsibilities and organization of Copyright Office, 17 USCS § 701.
Copyright registration in general, 17 USCS § 408.
Depository libraries, 44 USCS § 1905.

§ 708. Copyright Office fees

(a) The following fees shall be paid to the Register of Copyrights:

(1) for the registration of a copyright claim or a supplementary registration under section 408 [17 USCS § 408], including the issuance of a certificate of registration, $10;

(2) for the registration of a claim to renewal of a subsisting copyright in its first term under section 304(a) [17 USCS § 304(a)], including the issuance of a certificate of registration, $6;

(3) for the issuance of a receipt for a deposit under section 407 [17 USCS § 407], $2;

(4) for the recordation, as provided by section 205 [17 USCS § 205], of a transfer of copyright ownership or other document of six pages or less, covering no more than one title, $10; for each page over six and each title over one, 50 cents additional;

(5) for the filing, under section 115(b) [17 USCS § 115(b)], of a notice of intention to make phonorecords, $6;

(6) for the recordation, under section 302(c) [17 USCS § 302(c)], of a statement revealing the identity of an author of an anonymous or pseudonymous work, or for the recordation, under section 302(d) [17 USCS § 302(d)], of a statement relating to the death of an author, $10 for a document of six pages or less, covering no more than one title; for each page over six and for each title over one, $1 additional;

(7) for the issuance, under section 601 [17 USCS § 601], of an import statement, $3;

(8) for the issuance, under section 706 [17 USCS § 706], of an additional certificate of registration, $4;

(9) for the issuance of any other certification, $4; the Register of Copyrights has discretion, on the basis of their cost, to fix the fees for

preparing copies of Copyright Office records, whether they are to be certified or not;

(10) for the making and reporting of a search as provided by section 705 [17 USCS § 705], and for any related services, $10 for each hour or fraction of an hour consumed;

(11) for any other special services requiring a substantial amount of time or expense, such fees as the Register of Copyrights may fix on the basis of the cost of providing the service.

(b) The fees prescribed by or under this section are applicable to the United States Government and any of its agencies, employees, or officers, but the Register of Copyrights has discretion to waive the requirement of this subsection in occasional or isolated cases involving relatively small amounts.

(c) All fees received under this section shall be deposited by the Register of Copyrights in the Treasury of the United States and shall be credited to the appropriation for necessary expenses of the Copyright Office. The Register may, in accordance with regulations that he or she shall prescribe, refund any sum paid by mistake or in excess of the fee required by this section; however, before making a refund in any case involving a refusal to register a claim under section 410(b) [17 USCS § 410(b)], the Register may deduct all or any part of the prescribed registration fee to cover the reasonable administrative costs of processing the claim.

(Added Oct. 19, 1976, P. L. 94-553, Title I, § 101, 90 Stat. 2593; Aug. 5, 1977, P. L. 95-94, § 406(b), 91 Stat. 682.)

HISTORY; ANCILLARY LAWS AND DIRECTIVES

Effective date of section:
Section 102 of Act Oct. 19, 1976, P. L. 94-553, 90 Stat. 2598 provided that this section "becomes effective on January 1, 1978".

Amendments:
1977. Act Aug. 5, 1977, effective 1/1/78, substituted, in subsec. (c), "All fees received under this section shall be deposited by the Register of Copyrights in the Treasury of the United States and shall be credited to the appropriation for necessary expenses of the Copyright Office." for "The Register of Copyrights shall deposit all fees in the Treasury of the United States in such manner as the Secretary of the Treasury directs.".

CROSS REFERENCES

"Anonymous work" defined, 17 USCS § 101.
"Pseudonymous work" defined, 17 USCS § 101.
Filing of notice of intention to obtain compulsory license, 17 USCS § 115(b).
Recordation of transfers and other documents, 17 USCS § 205.
Recordation of statement revealing identity of author of anonymous or pseudonymous work, 17 USCS § 302(c).
Recordation of statement relating to death of author, 17 USCS § 302(d).

Registration of claim to renewal of subsisting copyright in its first term, 17 USCS § 304(a).
Deposit of copies or phonorecords for Library of Congress, 17 USCS § 407.
Copyright registration in general, 17 USCS § 408.
Refusal to register claim, 17 USCS § 410(b).
Import statement, 17 USCS § 601.
General responsibilities and organization of Copyright Office, 17 USCS § 701.
Copyright Office regulations, 17 USCS § 702.
Additional certificate of copyright registration, 17 USCS § 706.
Searching of Copyright Office records, 17 USCS § 705(c).
This section referred to in 17 USCS §§ 205, 407, 408, 704–706.

§ 709. Delay in delivery caused by disruption of postal or other services

In any case in which the Register of Copyrights determines, on the basis of such evidence as the Register may by regulation require, that a deposit, application, fee, or any other material to be delivered to the Copyright Office by a particular date, would have been received in the Copyright Office in due time except for a general disruption or suspension of postal or other transportation or communications services, the actual receipt of such material in the Copyright Office within one month after the date on which the Register determines that the disruption or suspension of such services has terminated, shall be considered timely.
(Added Oct. 19, 1976, P. L. 94-553, Title I, § 101, 90 Stat. 2594.)

HISTORY; ANCILLARY LAWS AND DIRECTIVES

Effective date of section:
Section 102 of Act Oct. 19, 1976, P. L. 94-553, 90 Stat. 2598 provided that this section "becomes effective on January 1, 1978".

CROSS REFERENCES

General responsibilities and organization of Copyright Office, 17 USCS § 701.
Copyright Office regulations, 17 USCS § 702.

§ 710. Reproduction for use of the blind and physically handicapped: Voluntary licensing forms and procedures

The Register of Copyrights shall, after consultation with the Chief of the Division for the Blind and Physically Handicapped and other appropriate officials of the Library of Congress, establish by regulation standardized forms and procedures by which, at the time applications covering certain specified categories of nondramatic literary works are submitted for registration under section 408 of this title [17 USCS § 408], the copyright owner may voluntarily grant to the Library of Congress a license to reproduce the copyrighted work by means of Braille or similar tactile symbols, or by fixation of a reading of the work in a phonorecord, or both, and to distribute the resulting copies or phonorecords solely for the use of the blind and physically handicapped and under limited conditions to be specified in the standardized forms.

(Added Oct. 19, 1976, P. L. 94-553, Title I, § 101, 90 Stat. 2594.)

HISTORY; ANCILLARY LAWS AND DIRECTIVES

Effective date of section:

Section 102 of Act Oct. 19, 1976, P. L. 94-553, 90 Stat. 2598 provided that this section "becomes effective on January 1, 1978".

CROSS REFERENCES

Copyright registration in general, 17 USCS § 408.
General responsibilities and organization of Copyright Office, 17 USCS § 701.

CHAPTER 8.   COPYRIGHT ROYALTY TRIBUNAL

---

§ 801.   Copyright Royalty Tribunal: Establishment and purpose

(a) There is hereby created an independent Copyright Royalty Tribunal in the legislative branch.

(b) Subject to the provisions of this chapter [17 USCS §§ 801 et seq.], the purposes of the Tribunal shall be—

(1) to make determinations concerning the adjustment of reasonable copyright royalty rates as provided in sections 115 and 116 [17 USCS §§ 115 and 116], and to make determinations as to reasonable terms and rates of royalty payments as provided in section 118 [17 USCS § 118]. The rates applicable under sections 115 and 116 [17 USCS §§ 115 and 116] shall be calculated to achieve the following objectives:

(A) To maximize the availability of creative works to the public;

(B) To afford the copyright owner a fair return for his creative work and the copyright user a fair income under existing economic conditions;

(C) To reflect the relative roles of the copyright owner and the copyright user in the product made available to the public with respect to relative creative contribution, technological contribution, capital investment, cost, risk, and contribution to the opening of new markets for creative expression and media for their communication;

(D) To minimize any disruptive impact on the structure of the industries involved and on generally prevailing industry practices.

(2) to make determinations concerning the adjustment of the copyright royalty rates in section 111 [17 USCS § 111] solely in accordance with the following provisions:

(A) The rates established by section 111(d)(2)(B) [17 USCS § 111(d)(2)(B)] may be adjusted to reflect (i) national monetary inflation or deflation or (ii) changes in the average rates charged cable

396

subscribers for the basic service of providing secondary transmissions to maintain the real constant dollar level of the royalty fee per subscriber which existed as of the date of enactment of this Act [enacted Oct. 19, 1976]: *Provided,* That if the average rates charged cable system subscribers for the basic service of providing secondary transmissions are changed so that the average rates exceed national monetary inflation, no change in the rates established by section 111(d)(2)(B) [17 USCS § 111(d)(2)(B)] shall be permitted: *And provided further,* That no increase in the royalty fee shall be permitted based on any reduction in the average number of distant signal equivalents per subscriber. The Commission may consider all factors relating to the maintenance of such level of payments including, as an extenuating factor, whether the cable industry has been restrained by subscriber rate regulating authorities from increasing the rates for the basic service of providing secondary transmissions.

(B) In the event that the rules and regulations of the Federal Communications Commission are amended at any time after April 15, 1976, to permit the carriage by cable systems of additional television broadcast signals beyond the local service area of the primary transmitters of such signals, the royalty rates established by section 111(d)(2)(B) [17 USCS § 111(d)(2)(B)] may be adjusted to insure that the rates for the additional distant signal equivalents resulting from such carriage are reasonable in the light of the changes effected by the amendment to such rules and regulations. In determining the reasonableness of rates proposed following an amendment of Federal Communications Commission rules and regulations, the Copyright Royalty Tribunal shall consider, among other factors, the economic impact on copyright owners and users: *Provided,* That no adjustment in royalty rates shall be made under this subclause with respect to any distant signal equivalent or fraction thereof represented by (i) carriage of any signal permitted under the rules and regulations of the Federal Communications Commission in effect on April 15, 1976, or the carriage of a signal of the same type (that is, independent, network, or noncommercial educational) substituted for such permitted signal, or (ii) a television broadcast signal first carried after April 15, 1976, pursuant to an individual waiver of the rules and regulations of the Federal Communications Commission, as such rules and regulations were in effect on April 15, 1976.

(C) In the event of any change in the rules and regulations of the Federal Communications Commission with respect to syndicated and sports program exclusivity after April 15, 1976, the rates established by section 111(d)(2)(B) [17 USCS § 111(d)(2)(B)] may be adjusted to assure that such rates are reasonable in light of the changes to such rules and regulations, but any such adjustment shall apply only to the affected television broadcast signals carried on those systems affected by the change.

(D) The gross receipts limitations established by section 111(d)(2)(C) and (D) [17 USCS § 111(d)(2)(C) and (D)] shall be adjusted to reflect national monetary inflation or deflation or changes in the average rates charged cable system subscribers for the basic service of providing secondary transmissions to maintain the real constant dollar value of the exemption provided by such section; and the royalty rate specified therein shall not be subject to adjustment; and

(3) to distribute royalty fees deposited with the Register of Copyrights under sections 111 and 116 [17 USCS § 111 and 116], and to determine, in cases where controversy exists, the distribution of such fees.

(c) As soon as possible after the date of enactment of this Act [enacted Oct. 19, 1976], and no later than six months following such date, the President shall publish a notice announcing the initial appointments provided in section 802 [17 USCS § 802], and shall designate an order of seniority among the initially-appointed commissioners for purposes of section 802(b) [17 USCS § 802(b)].

(Added Oct. 19, 1976, P. L. 94-553, Title I, § 101, 90 Stat. 2594.)

HISTORY; ANCILLARY LAWS AND DIRECTIVES

Effective date of section:

Act Oct. 19, 1976, P. L. 94-553, Title I, § 102, 90 Stat. 2598, provided in part that this section takes "effect upon the enactment of this Act [enacted Oct. 19, 1976]."

CROSS REFERENCES

Compulsory license for secondary transmissions by cable systems, 17 USCS § 111(d).

Royalty payable under compulsory license for making and distributing phonorecords, 17 USCS § 115(c).

Distribution of royalties from public performances by means of coin-operated phonorecord players, 17 USCS § 116(c).

Membership of Copyright Royalty Tribunal, 17 USCS § 802.

This section referred to in 17 USCS §§ 802, 804, 810.

RESEARCH GUIDE

Law Review Articles:

Copyright Symposium, 22 New York Law School Law Review 193.

§ 802. Membership of the Tribunal

(a) The Tribunal shall be composed of five commissioners appointed by the President with the advice and consent of the Senate for a term of seven years each; of the first five members appointed, three shall be designated to serve for seven years from the date of the notice specified in section 801(c) [17 USCS § 801(c)], and two shall be designated to serve for five years from such date, respectively. Commissioners shall be compensated at the highest rate now or hereafter [enacted Oct. 19, 1976] prescribe [prescribed] for grade 18 of the General Schedule pay rates (5 USC 5332) [5 USCS § 5332].

(b) Upon convening the commissioners shall elect a chairman from among the commissioners appointed for a full seven-year term. Such chairman shall serve for a term of one year. Thereafter, the most senior commissioner who has not previously served as chairman shall serve as chairman for a period of one year, except that, if all commissioners have served a full term as chairman, the most senior commissioner who has served the least number of terms as chairman shall be designated as chairman.

(c) Any vacancy in the Tribunal shall not affect its powers and shall be filled, for the unexpired term of the appointment, in the same manner as the original appointment was made.
(Added Oct. 19, 1976, P. L. 94-553, Title I, § 101, 90 Stat. 2596.)

HISTORY; ANCILLARY LAWS AND DIRECTIVES

Effective date of section:
Act Oct. 19, 1976, P. L. 94-553, Title I, § 102, 90 Stat. 2598, provided in part that this section takes "effect upon enactment of this Act [enacted Oct. 19, 1976]."

CROSS REFERENCES

General Schedule pay rates, 5 USCS § 5332.
Establishment and purpose of Copyright Royalty Tribunal, 17 USCS § 801.
Notice of appointment to Copyright Royalty Tribunal, 17 USCS § 801(c).
This section referred to in 17 USCS §§ 118, 801.

§ 803. Procedures of the Tribunal

(a) The Tribunal shall adopt regulations, not inconsistent with law, governing its procedure and methods of operation. Except as otherwise provided in this chapter, the Tribunal shall be subject to the provisions of the Administrative Procedure Act of June 11, 1946, as amended (c. 324, 60 Stat. 237, Title 5, United States Code, Chapter 5, Subchapter II and Chapter 7).

(b) Every final determination of the Tribunal shall be published in the Federal Register. It shall state in detail the criteria that the Tribunal determined to be applicable to the particular proceeding, the various facts that it found relevant to its determination in that proceeding, and the specific reasons for its determination.
(Added Oct. 19, 1976, P. L. 94-553, Title I, § 101, 90 Stat. 2596.)

HISTORY; ANCILLARY LAWS AND DIRECTIVES

References in text:
"Administrative Procedure Act of June 11, 1946, as amended", referred to in subsec. (a), was repealed and similar provisions were reenacted as 5 USCS §§ 551 et seq., 701 et seq.

Effective date of section:

Act Oct. 19, 1976, P. L. 94-553, Title I, § 102, 90 Stat. 2598, provided in part that this section takes "effect upon enactment of this Act [enacted Oct. 19, 1976]."

CROSS REFERENCES

Administrative Procedure Act, 5 USCS §§ 551, 701.
Establishment and purpose of Copyright Royalty Tribunal, 17 USCS § 801.
This section referred to in 17 USCS §§ 808, 809.

§ 804. Institution and conclusion of proceedings

(a) With respect to proceedings under section 801(b)(1) [17 USCS § 801(b)(1)] concerning the adjustment of royalty rates as provided in sections 115 and 116 [17 USCS §§ 115 and 116], and with respect to proceedings under section 801(b)(2)(A) and (D) [17 USCS § 801(b)(2)(A) and (D)]—

(1) on January 1, 1980, the Chairman of the Tribunal shall cause to be published in the Federal Register notice of commencement of proceedings under this chapter [17 USCS §§ 801 et seq.]; and

(2) during the calendar years specified in the following schedule, any owner or user of a copyrighted work whose royalty rates are specified by this title [17 USCS §§ 101 et seq.], or by a rate established by the Tribunal, may file a petition with the Tribunal declaring that the petitioner requests an adjustment of the rate. The Tribunal shall make a determination as to whether the applicant has a significant interest in the royalty rate in which an adjustment is requested. If the Tribunal determines that the petitioner has a significant interest, the Chairman shall cause notice of this determination, with the reasons therefor, to be published in the Federal Register, together with notice of commencement of proceedings under this chapter [17 USCS §§ 801 et seq.].

(A) In proceedings under section 801(b)(2)(A) and (D) [17 USCS § 801(b)(2)(A) and (D)], such petition may be filed during 1985 and in each subsequent fifth calendar year.

(B) In proceedings under section 801(b)(1) [17 USCS § 801(b)(1)] concerning the adjustment of royalty rates as provided in section 115 [17 USCS § 115], such petition may be filed in 1987 and in each subsequent tenth calendar year.

(C) In proceedings under section 801(b)(1) [17 USCS § 801(b)(1)] concerning the adjustment of royalty rates under section 116 [17 USCS § 116], such petition may be filed in 1990 and in each subsequent tenth calendar year.

(b) With respect to proceedings under subclause (B) or (C) of section 801(b)(2) [17 USCS § 801(b)(2)(B) or (C)], following an event described in either of those subsections, any owner or user of a copyrighted work whose royalty rates are specified by section 111 [17 USCS § 111], or by a rate established by the Tribunal, may, within twelve months, file a petition with the Tribunal declaring that the petitioner requests an adjustment of the rate. In this event the Tribunal shall proceed as in subsection (a)(2), above. Any change in royalty rates made by the Tribunal pursuant to this subsection may be reconsidered in 1980, 1985, and each fifth calendar year thereafter, in accordance with the provisions in section 801(b)(2)(B) or (C) [17 USCS § 801(b)(2)(B) or (C)], as the case may be.

(c) With respect to proceedings under section 801(b)(1) [17 USCS § 801(b)(1)], concerning the determination of reasonable terms and rates of royalty payments as provided in section 118 [17 USCS § 118], the Tribunal shall proceed when and as provided by that section.

(d) With respect to proceedings under section 801(b)(3) [17 USCS § 801(b)(3)], concerning the distribution of royalty fees in certain circumstances under sections 111 or 116 [17 USCS §§ 111 or 116], the Chairman of the Tribunal shall, upon determination by the Tribunal that a controversy exists concerning such distribution, cause to be published in the Federal Register notice of commencement of proceedings under this chapter [17 USCS §§ 801 et seq.].

(e) All proceedings under this chapter [17 USCS §§ 801 et seq.] shall be initiated without delay following publication of the notice specified in this section, and the Tribunal shall render its final decision in any such proceeding within one year from the date of such publication.
(Added Oct. 19, 1976, P. L. 94-553, Title I, § 101, 90 Stat. 2597.)

HISTORY; ANCILLARY LAWS AND DIRECTIVES

Effective date of section:
Act Oct. 19, 1976, P. L. 94-553, Title I, § 102, 90 Stat. 2598, provided in part that this section takes "effect upon enactment of this Act [enacted Oct. 19, 1976]."

CROSS REFERENCES

Compulsory license for secondary transmissions by cable systems, 17 USCS § 111(d).
Royalty payable under compulsory licensing for making and distributing phonorecords, 17 USCS § 115(c).
Distribution of royalties from public performances by means of coin-operated phonorecord players, 17 USCS § 116(c).
Royalty payments for use of certain works in connection with noncommercial broadcasting, 17 USCS § 118(b).
Purpose of Copyright Royalty Tribunal, 17 USCS § 801(b).

§ 805. Staff of the Tribunal

(a) The Tribunal is authorized to appoint and fix the compensation of such employees as may be necessary to carry out the provisions of this chapter [17 USCS §§ 801 et seq.], and to prescribe their functions and duties.

(b) The Tribunal may procure temporary and intermittent services to the same extent as is authorized by section 3109 of title 5 [5 USCS § 3109]. (Added Oct. 19, 1976, P. L. 94-553, Title I, § 101, 90 Stat. 2598.)

HISTORY; ANCILLARY LAWS AND DIRECTIVES

Effective date of section:

Act Oct. 19, 1976, P. L. 94-553, Title I, § 102, 90 Stat. 2598, provided in part that this section takes "effect upon enactment of this Act [enacted Oct. 19, 1976]."

CROSS REFERENCES

Authorization of Copyright Royalty Tribunal to procure temporary and intermittent services, 5 USCS § 3109.

§ 806. Administrative support of the Tribunal

(a) The Library of Congress shall provide the Tribunal with necessary administrative services, including those related to budgeting, accounting, financial reporting, travel, personnel, and procurement. The Tribunal shall pay the Library for such services, either in advance or by reimbursement from the funds of the Tribunal, at amounts to be agreed upon between the Librarian and the Tribunal.

(b) The Library of Congress is authorized to disburse funds for the Tribunal, under regulations prescribed jointly by the Librarian of Congress and the Tribunal and approved by the Comptroller General. Such regulations shall establish requirements and procedures under which every voucher certified for payment by the Library of Congress under this chapter [17 USCS §§ 801 et seq.] shall be supported with a certification by a duly authorized officer or employee of the Tribunal, and shall prescribe the responsibilities and accountability of said officers and employees of the Tribunal with respect to such certifications. (Added Oct. 19, 1976, P. L. 94-553, Title I, § 101, 90 Stat. 2598.)

HISTORY; ANCILLARY LAWS AND DIRECTIVES

Effective date of section:

Act Oct. 19, 1976, P. L. 94-553, Title I, § 102, 90 Stat. 2598, provided in part that this section takes "effect upon enactment of this Act [enacted Oct. 19, 1976]."

CROSS REFERENCES

Establishment and purpose of Copyright Royalty Tribunal, 17 USCS § 801.
Staff of Copyright Royalty Tribunal, 17 USCS § 805.

§ 807. Deduction of costs of proceedings

Before any funds are distributed pursuant to a final decision in a proceeding involving distribution of royalty fees, the Tribunal shall assess the reasonable costs of such proceeding.
(Added Oct. 19, 1976, P. L. 94-553, Title I, § 101, 90 Stat. 2598.)

HISTORY; ANCILLARY LAWS AND DIRECTIVES

Effective date of section:
Act Oct. 19, 1976, P. L. 94-553, Title I, § 102, 90 Stat. 2598, provided in part that this section takes "effect upon enactment of this Act [enacted Oct. 19, 1976]."

CROSS REFERENCES

Effective date of final determinations of Copyright Royalty Tribunal, 17 USCS § 809.

§ 808. Reports

In addition to its publication of the reports of all final determinations as provided in section 803(b) [17 USCS § 803(b)], the Tribunal shall make an annual report to the President and the Congress concerning the Tribunal's work during the preceding fiscal year, including a detailed fiscal statement of account.
(Added Oct. 19, 1976, P. L. 94-553, Title I, § 101, 90 Stat. 2598.)

HISTORY; ANCILLARY LAWS AND DIRECTIVES

Effective date of section:
Act Oct. 19, 1976, P. L. 94-553, Title I, § 102, 90 Stat. 2598, provided in part that this section takes "effect upon enactment of this Act [enacted Oct. 19, 1976]."

CROSS REFERENCES

Publication in Federal Register of every final determination of Copyright Royalty Tribunal, 17 USCS § 803(b).

§ 809. Effective date of final determinations

Any final determination by the Tribunal under this chapter [17 USCS §§ 801 et seq.] shall become effective thirty days following its publication in the Federal Register as provided in section 803(b) [17 USCS § 803(b)], unless prior to that time an appeal has been filed pursuant to section 810 [17 USCS § 810], to vacate, modify, or correct such determination, and notice of such appeal has been served on all parties who appeared before the Tribunal in the proceeding in question. Where the proceeding involves the distribution of royalty fees under sections 111 or 116 [17 USCS §§ 111 or 116], the Tribunal shall, upon the expiration of such thirty-day period,

distribute any royalty fees not subject to an appeal filed pursuant to section 810 [17 USCS § 810].
(Added Oct. 19, 1976, P. L. 94-553, Title I, § 101, 90 Stat. 2598.)

HISTORY; ANCILLARY LAWS AND DIRECTIVES

Effective date of section:
Act Oct. 19, 1976, P. L. 94-553, Title I, § 102, 90 Stat. 2598, provided in part that this section takes "effect upon enactment of this Act [enacted Oct. 19, 1976]."

CROSS REFERENCES

Compulsory license for secondary transmissions by cable systems, 17 USCS § 111(d).
Distribution of royalties from public performances by means of coin-operated phonorecord players, 17 USCS § 116(c).
Publication in Federal Register of every final determination of Copyright Royalty Tribunal, 17 USCS § 803(b).
Judicial review of decisions of Copyright Royalty Tribunal, 17 USCS § 810.

§ 810. Judicial review

Any final decision of the Tribunal in a proceeding under section 801(b) [17 USCS § 801(b)] may be appealed to the United States Court of Appeals, within thirty days after its publication in the Federal Register by an aggrieved party. The judicial review of the decision shall be had, in accordance with chapter 7 of title 5 [USCS §§ 701 et seq.], on the basis of the record before the Tribunal. No court shall have jurisdiction to review a final decision of the Tribunal except as provided in this section.
(Added Oct. 19, 1976, P. L. 94-553, Title I, § 101, 90 Stat. 2598.)

HISTORY; ANCILLARY LAWS AND DIRECTIVES

Effective date of section:
Act Oct. 19, 1976, P. L. 94-553, Title I, § 102, 90 Stat. 2598, provided in part that this section takes "effect upon enactment of this Act [enacted Oct. 19, 1976]."

CROSS REFERENCES

Judicial review provision of Administrative Procedure Act, 5 USCS §§ 701 et seq.
Purpose of Copyright Royalty Tribunal, 17 USCS § 801(b).
Publication in Federal Register of every final determination of Copyright Royalty Tribunal, 17 USCS § 803(b).
This section referred to in 17 USCS §§ 116, 809.

RESEARCH GUIDE

Am Jur:
18 Am Jur 2d, Copyright and Literary Property § 153.

Forms:
2 Federal Procedural Forms L Ed Appeal, Certiorari, and Review § 3:15.

INDEX

INDEX

TITLE 17—COPYRIGHTS

CHILDREN
Definition, 17 § 101
Duration of copyrights, 17 § 304

CHOREOGRAPHIC WORKS
Pantomimes and Choreographic Works (this index)

COIN-OPERATED PHONORECORD PLAYERS
Defined, copyright law, 17 § 116
Exclusive rights in public performances by means of, 17 § 116

COLLECTIVE WORKS
Contributions to collective works, copyright of, 17 §§ 201, 404
Definitions, 17 § 101
Notice of copyright, contributions to collective works, 17 § 404
Registration of copyright, deposit for, 17 § 408

COMPENSATION
Wages and Compensation (this index)

COMPILATIONS
Definition, 17 § 101
Subject matter of copyright, 17 § 103

COMPULSORY LICENSES
Coin-operated phonorecord players, 17 § 116
Phonorecords, making and distributing, 17 § 115

COMPUTERS
Information systems, use of copyright material in conjunction with computers and, 17 § 117

CONFLICTING TRANSFER AND LICENSES
Priorities between, 17 § 205

CONSTRUCTIVE NOTICE
Recordation as constructive notice, 17 § 205

CONVENTIONS
Universal Copyright Convention, see separate volume **USCS Administrative Rules,** Universal Copyright Convention

COPIES
Reproductions or Copies (this index)

COPYRIGHT OFFICE
Generally, 17 §§ 701 to 710
Administrative rules of procedure before Copyright Office, see separate volume **USCS Administrative Rules** Copyrights
Blind and physically handicapped, reproductions for use of, 17 § 710
Date of actions, effective, 17 § 703
Delivery, delay caused by disruption of postal service, 17 § 709

COPYRIGHT OFFICE—Cont'd
Fees, 17 § 708
Forms and publications, 17 §§ 707, 710
Records, 17 §§ 705, 706
Registration of Copyrights (this index)
Regulations, 17 § 702; also see separate volume **USCS Administrative Rules,** Copyrights
Responsibilities and organization, 17 § 701
Retention and disposition of articles deposited in, 17 § 704
Voluntary licensing forms and procedures, 17 § 710

COPYRIGHT OWNER
Definition, 17 § 101

COPYRIGHT ROYALTY TRIBUNAL
Royalty Tribunal (this index)

CORRECTIONS
Registration, correction of copyright, 17 § 408

COSTS AND EXPENSES
Attorney's fees, awarding of costs, 17 §§ 412, 505
Copyright office fees, 17 § 708
Royalty Fees (this index)
Royalty Tribunal, deduction of cost of proceedings, 17 § 807

COURT OF APPEALS
Royalty Tribunal, appeal to Court of Appeals, 17 § 810

CREATED
Definition, 17 § 101

CRIMES AND OFFENSES
Fines and Penalties (this index)

DAMAGES
Cable systems, remedy for alteration of programing by, 17 § 510
Infringement actions, damages and profits in, 17 § 504

DATE OR TIME
Time or Date (this index)

DEAF PERSONS
Handicapped Persons (this index)

DEATH OF AUTHOR
Fee for recording statement, 17 § 708
Presumptions, 17 § 302
Records, 17 § 302
Renewal terms, transfers and licenses, termination of, 17 § 304
Transfers and licenses, termination of, 17 § 203

DEDUCTIONS
Royalty Tribunal, deduction of costs of proceedings, 17 § 807

DEFINITIONS
Anonymous work, 17 § 101
Audiovisual works, 17 § 101
Best edition, 17 § 101
Cable system, 17 § 111
Children, 17 § 101
Coin-operated phonorecord player, 17 § 116
Collective work, 17 § 101
Compilation, 17 § 101
Copies, 17 § 101
Copyright owner, 17 § 101
Created, 17 § 101
Derivative work, 17 § 101
Device, 17 § 101
Display, 17 § 101
Distance signal equivalent, 17 § 111
Fixed, 17 § 101
Including, 17 § 101
Independent station, 17 § 111
Joint work, 17 § 101
Literary works, 17 § 101
Local service area of primary transmitter, 17 § 111
Machine, 17 § 101
Motion pictures, 17 § 101
Network station, 17 § 111
Noncommercial educational station, 17 § 111
Operator, 17 § 116
Perform, 17 § 101
Performing rights society, 17 § 116
Phonorecords, 17 § 101
Pictorial, graphic and sculptural works, 17 § 101
Primary transmission, 17 § 111
Process, 17 § 101
Pseudonymous work, 17 § 101
Publication, 17 § 101
Public broadcasting, 17 § 118
Publicly, 17 § 101
Secondary transmission, 17 § 111
Sound recordings, 17 § 101
State, 17 § 101
Such as, 17 § 101
Transfer of copyright ownership, 17 § 101
Transmission program, 17 § 101
Transmit, 17 § 101
United States, 17 § 101
Useful article, 17 § 101
Widow or widower, 17 § 101
Work made for hire, 17 § 101
Work of the United States government, 17 § 101

DELIVERY
Delay in delivery of application or deposit caused by disruption of postal service, 17 § 709

DEPOSITS
Library of Congress, deposit of copies or phonorecords for, 17 § 407
Copyright Office, retention and disposition of articles deposited in, 17 § 704
Register of Copyrights, deposit of fees collected by, 17 § 708
Registration of copyright, deposit required, 17 § 408

DERIVATIVE WORKS
Definitions, 17 § 101
Exclusive rights in copyrighted works, 17 § 106
Subject matter of copyright, 17 § 103

DESTRUCTION
Articles made or used in violation of copyright, 17 § 503
Import prohibitions, 17 § 603
Criminal infringement, destruction of infringing copies and phonorecords 17 § 506

DETERMINATIONS
Royalty Tribunal, effective date of final determinations of, 17 § 809

DEVICE
Definition, 17 § 101

DISPLAYS
Definition, 17 § 101
Infringement, exemption from copyright, 17 § 110

DISPOSITION
Copyright office, articles deposited in, 17 § 704
Criminal infringing copies and phonorecords, 17 § 506
Import prohibitions, disposition of excluded articles, 17 § 603
Infringing articles, disposition of, 17 § 503

DISTANCE SIGNAL EQUIVALENT
Definition, 17 § 111

DISTRIBUTION
Copies, manufacture, importation, and distribution of, 17 § 601
Exclusive rights in nondramatic musical works, phonorecords, 17 § 115

DRAMATIC WORKS
Exclusive rights in, 17 § 106
Subject matter of copyright, 17 § 102

DURATION
Time or Date (this index)

EDUCATION
Damages for infringement, 17 § 504
Fair use limitation on exclusive rights, 17 § 107

References are to title and sections

MEMBERSHIP

Royalty Tribunal, membership of, 17 § 802

MOTION PICTURES AND AUDIOVISUAL WORKS

Definition, 17 § 101

Ephemeral recordings, 17 § 112

Exclusive rights in copyrighted works, 17 § 106

Libraries and archives, prohibition against reproduction, 17 § 108

Sound recordings, scope of exclusive rights in, 17 § 114

Subject matter of copyright, 17 § 102

Television and Radio (this index)

MUSICAL WORKS

Exclusive rights in copyrighted works, 17 § 106

Libraries and archives, prohibition against reproduction, 17 § 108

Noncommercial broadcasting, use of nondramatic musical works, 17 § 118

Nondramatic musical works, exclusive rights in, 17 §§ 106, 115, 116

Performance and display of musical works as exempt from copyright infringement, 17 § 110

Sound Recordings (this index)

Subject matter of copyright, 17 102

NAMES

Notice of copyright, error in name on, 17 § 406

NATIONAL ORIGIN

Author, subject matter of copyright, 17 § 104

NETWORK STATION

Definition, 17 § 111

NEW REPORTS

Photographs, use of, 17 § 113

NEWS REPORTING

Fair use as limitation on exclusive rights, 17 § 107

NONCOMMERCIAL EDUCATIONAL STATION

Definition, 17 § 111

NONDRAMATIC MUSICAL WORKS

Exclusive rights in, 17 §§ 106, 115, 116

NONPROFIT

Charities (this index)

Education (this index)

Ephemeral recordings by nonprofit organizations, 17 § 112

Performance or display of nondramatic literary or musical works as exempt from copyright infringement, 17 § 110

Exclusive rights, use of certain works in connection with noncommercial broadcasting, 17 § 118

NOTICE OR KNOWLEDGE

Generally, 17 §§ 401 to 406

Collective works, contributions to, 17 § 404

Dates, errors in, 17 § 406

Fraudulent copyright notice, criminal penalty for, 17 § 506

Infringement actions, notification of determination of, 17 § 508

Names, errors in, 17 § 406

Omission of notice, 17 § 405

Position of notice, 17 §§ 401, 402

Sound recordings, phonorecords of, 17 § 402

United States government works, publications incorporating, 17 § 403

Visually perceptible copies, 17 § 401

Recordation as constructive notice, 17 § 205

Register of copyrights, notification of filing of action, 17 § 508

Renewal term, termination of transfers and licenses covering extended, 17 § 304

Royalty Tribunal, publication of notice of commencement of proceedings, 17 § 804

Termination of transfers or licenses, 17 §§ 203, 304

OFFENSES

Fines and Penalties (this index)

OPERATOR

Defined, 17 § 116

ORIGINAL WORKS

Subject matter of, 17 § 102

OWNERSHIP AND TRANSFER

Generally, 17 §§ 201 to 205; see also **Sales or Transfers** (this index)

PANTOMIMES AND CHOREOGRAPHIC WORKS

Exclusive rights in copyrighted works, 17 § 106

Subject matter of copyright, 17 § 102

PENALTIES

Fines and Penalties (this index)

PERFORMING RIGHTS SOCIETY

Defined, 17 § 116

PERFORM OR PERFORMANCES

Definition, 17 § 101

Infringement, exemptions from copyright, 17 § 110

PERMITS

Licenses and Permits (this index)

PETITIONS

Royalty Tribunal, petition for adjustment of rate, 17 § 804

References are to title and sections

PHONOGRAPHS
Coin-operated phonographs, public performances by, 17 § 116

PHONORECORDS
Defined, 17 § 101
Sound Recordings (this index)

PHOTOGRAPHS
Pictorial, Graphic and Sculptural Works (this index)

PHYSICALLY HANDICAPPED
Handicapped Persons (this index)

PICTORIAL, GRAPHIC AND SCULPTURAL WORKS
Definition, 17 § 101
Exclusive rights, scope of, 17 § 113
Fair use limitations on exclusive rights, 17 § 107
Libraries and archives, prohibition against reproduction, 17 § 108
Noncommercial broadcasting, use of, 17 § 118
Subject matter of copyright, 17 § 102

POSITION OF COPYRIGHT NOTICE
Generally, 17 §§ 401, 402

POSTAL SERVICE
United States Postal Service (this index)

PREEMPTION
Duration of copyright, preemption with respect to other laws, 17 § 301

PRESUMPTIONS
Author's death, presumption as to, 17 § 302

PRIMA FACIE EVIDENCE
Certificate of registration, 17 § 410

PRIMARY TRANSMISSION
Definition, 17 § 111

PRIORITIES
Conflicting transfers, priority between, 17 § 205

PROCEDURES
Copyright Office (this index)
Seizure and forfeiture of infringing articles, procedure for, 17 § 509
Royalty Tribunal, 17 § 803

PROCEEDINGS
Copyright Office (this index)
Royalty Tribunal, 17 §§ 804, 807

PROCESS
Definition, 17 § 101

PROFITS
Infringement, remedy for, 17 § 504

PROGRAMING
Cable systems, remedies for alteration of programing by, 17 § 510

PSEUDONYMOUS WORKS
Definition, 17 § 101
Duration of copyright, 17 § 302
Fee for recording statement revealing identity of author, 17 § 708

PUBLICATIONS
Catalog of copyright entries, 17 § 707
Copyright Office, 17 § 707
Definition, 17 § 101
Royalty Tribunal, publication of final determinations of, 17 § 803

PUBLIC BROADCASTING
Defined, copyright law, 17 § 118
Exclusive rights, scope of, 17 § 118
Infringement, damages for, 17 § 504
Public broadcasting entity, defined, 17 § 118

PUBLIC DISTRIBUTION
Copies, 17 § 601

PUBLICLY
Definition, 17 § 101

PUBLISHED WORKS
Author, subject matter of copyright, national origin of, 17 § 104
Duration of copyrights on works published after January 1, 1978, 17 § 303

RADIO
Television and Radio (this index)

RECORDINGS
Sound Recordings (this index)

RECORD PLAYERS
Coin-operated phonographs, public performances by, 17 § 116

RECORDS AND RECORDATION
Coin-operated phonographs, 17 § 116
Copyright Office records and copies of records, 17 §§ 705, 706
Fees, copyright office, 17 § 708
Death of author, records relating to, 17 § 302
Transfers and other documents, recordation of, 17 § 205

REGISTER OF COPYRIGHTS
See more specific lines throughout this index

REGISTRATION OF COPYRIGHTS
Generally, 17 §§ 408 to 412
Application for copyright registration, 17 § 409
Claim, registration of, 17 § 410
False representation on application for copyright registration, criminal penalty for, 17 § 506
Fee of Copyright Office, 17 § 708
Infringement, registration as prerequisite to remedies for, 17 §§ 411, 412
Issuance of certificate, 17 § 410

REGULATIONS
Rules and Regulations (this index)

RELIGION
Ephemeral recordings, 17 § 112
Performance or display of nondramatic literary or musical works as exempt from copyright infringement, 17 § 110

REMEDIES
Infringement (this index)

RENEWALS
Registration of copyright, 17 §§ 304, 408

REPORTS
Copyright Office, 17 § 701
Register of Copyrights, annual report of, 17 § 701
Royalty Tribunal, 17 § 808

REPRODUCTIONS OR COPIES
Blind and physically handicapped, reproduction by Register of Copyrights for use of, 17 § 710
Definition of copies, 17 § 101
Exclusive rights in copyrighted works, 17 § 106
Importation, generally, 17 §§ 601 to 603
Impounding and disposition of infringing articles, 17 § 503
Infringing importations of, 17 § 602
Libraries and archives, reproduction as limitation on exclusive rights, 17 § 108
Library of Congress, deposit of copies for, 17 § 407
Limitation on exclusive rights, effect of transfer, 17 § 109
Manufacture and distribution, 17 § 601
Notice of copyright, visually perceptible copies, 17 § 401
Records in Copyright Office, 17 § 706
Retention and disposition of articles deposited in Copyright Office, 17 § 704
Sound Recordings (this index)

RETENTION
Copyright Office, articles in, 17 § 704

REVERSION
Termination of grants, 17 § 203

REVIEW
Royalty Tribunal, judicial review of decisions, 17 § 810

ROYALTY FEES
Cable systems, 17 § 111
Coin-operated phonographs, public performances by means of, 17 § 116
Noncommercial broadcasting, 17 § 118
Phonorecords, compulsory license for making and distributing, 17 § 115
Royalty Tribunal, adjustment of royalty fees by, 17 § 801

ROYALTY TRIBUNAL
Generally, 17 §§ 801 to 810
Administrative support, 17 § 806
Deduction of costs of proceedings, 17 § 807
Establishment and purpose, 17 § 801
Final determination, effective date of, 17 § 809
Institution and conclusion of proceedings, 17 § 804
Judicial review, 17 § 810
Membership, 17 § 802
Procedures, 17 § 803
Proceedings instituted by, 17 § 804
Reports, 17 § 808
Staff, 17 § 805

RULES AND REGULATIONS
Copyright Office, 17 § 702; see also separate volume **USCS Administrative Rules,** Copyrights
Royalty Tribunal, 17 § 803

SALES OR TRANSFERS
Generally, 17 §§ 201 to 205
Exclusive rights, transfer of copies or phonorecords as limitation on, 17 § 109
Execution of transfer of copyright ownership, 17 § 204
Involuntary transfer, 17 § 201
Licenses, termination of, 17 § 203
Material object, ownership of copyright distinguished from ownership of, 17 § 202
Recordation of transfers and other documents, 17 § 205
Renewals, termination of transfers and licenses covering extended renewal term, 17 § 304
Termination of transfers, 17 § 203
Transfer of copyright ownership, deined, 17 § 101

SCULPTURAL WORKS
Pictorial, Graphic and Sculptural Works (this index)

SEARCHES
Record searches, Copyright Office, 17 § 705
Fee for, 17 § 708

SECONDARY TRANSMISSIONS
Definition, 17 § 111

References are to title and sections

SECONDARY TRANSMISSIONS—Cont'd
Exemption from copyright infringement, 17 § 111
Infringement of copyright, 17 § 501

SECRETARY OF TREASURY
Importation prohibitions, enforcement of, 17 § 603

SEIZURES AND FORFEITURES
Copies or phonorecords, infringing, 17 § 509
Criminal infringement, 17 § 506
Import prohibitions, seizure and forfeiture of articles violating, 17 § 603
Remedies for infringement, impoundment and disposition, 17 § 503

SEVERABILITY OF STATUTORY PROVISIONS
Generally, 17 § 101 note

SOUND RECORDINGS
Coin-operated phonorecord players, exclusive rights in performances using, 17 § 116
Copyright Office, retention and disposition of articles deposited in, 17 § 704
Definition, 17 § 101
Ephemeral recordings as limitation on exclusive rights, 17 § 112
Exclusive rights in, 17 §§ 106, 114, 115
Fair use limitations on exclusive rights, 17 § 107
Importation, generally, 17 §§ 601 to 603
Impounding and disposition of infringing articles, 17 § 503
Infringing importation of, 17 § 602
Library of Congress, deposit of phonorecords, 17 § 407
License for making and distributing phonorecords, 17 § 115
Limitations on exclusive rights, effect of transfer, 17 § 108
Notice of copyright, phonorecords of sound recordings, 17 § 402
Phonographs, public performance by coin-operated, 17 § 116
Pre-emption with respect to other laws, 17 § 301
Registration of copyright, deposit for, 17 § 408
Seizure and forfeiture of infringing phono records, 17 § 509
Subject matter of copyright, 17 § 102
Television and Radio (this index)

STAFF
Royalty Tribunal, 17 § 805

STATE
Definition, 17 § 101

STATUTE OF LIMITATIONS
Civil and criminal actions, 17 § 507

SUBJECT MATTER AND SCOPE OF COPYRIGHT
Generally, 17 §§ 101 et seq.
Compilation and derivative works, subject matter of copyright, 17 § 103
Compulsory license for making and distributing phonorecords, scope of exclusive rights in nondramatic musical works, 17 § 115
Computers and similar information systems, scope of exclusive rights, 17 § 117
Definitions, 17 § 101
Ephemeral recordings as limitation on exclusive rights, 17 § 112
Exclusive rights. See lines throughout this topic
Fair use, limitation on exclusive rights, 17 § 107
Libraries and archives, reproduction as limitation on exclusive rights, 17 § 108
Limitations on exclusive rights, 17 §§ 107-112
National origin, subject matter of copyright, 17 § 104
Noncommercial broadcasting, scope of exclusive rights where works are used in connection with, 17 § 118
Performances and displays exempt from exclusive rights, 17 § 110
Pictorial, graphic and sculptural works, scope of exclusive rights in, 17 § 113
Public performances by means of coin-operated phonorecord players, scope of exclusive rights in nondramatic musical works, 17 § 116
Reproduction by libraries and archives, 17 § 108
Scope of exclusive rights, 17 §§ 113-118
Secondary transmission as limitation on exclusive rights, 17 § 111
Sound recordings, scope of exclusive rights in, 17 § 114
Transfer of particular copy or phonorecord, effect on exclusive rights, 17 § 109
United States government works, subject matter of copyright, 17 § 101

SUBSISTING COPYRIGHTS
Duration of, 17 § 304

SUCH AS
Definition, 17 § 101

TELEVISION AND RADIO
Cable Systems (this index)
Definitions, 17 § 111
Fair use in news reporting, 17 § 107
Infringement, exemptions and actions, 17 §§ 110, 501
Noncommercial broadcasting, use of certain works in, 17 § 118
Public Broadcasting (this index)
Scope of exclusive rights in sound recordings, 17 § 114

TERMINATION
Author, transfers and licenses granted by, 17 § 203
Date of copyright, 17 § 305
Transfer and licenses covering extended renewal term, 17 § 304

TERM OF OFFICE
Royalty Tribunal, members of, 17 § 802

TIME OR DATE
Copyright Office, effective date of actions in, 17 § 703
Duration of copyrights, generally, 17 §§ 301-305
Errors, notice of, 17 § 406
Notice of copyright, error in name or date, 17 § 406
Postal service, delay in delivery caused by disruption of, 17 § 709
Preemption with respect to other laws, 17 § 301
Royalty Tribunal, effective date of final terminations, 17 § 809
Subsisting copyrights, 17 § 304
Terminal date, 17 § 305
Term of office of members of Royalty Tribunal, 17 § 802
Work created before or after January 1, 1978, 17 §§ 302, 303

TRANSFER OF COPYRIGHT OWNERSHIP
Definition, 17 § 101
Sales or Transfers (this index)

TRANSMISSION PROGRAM
Definition, 17 § 101

TRANSMIT
Definition, 17 § 101

TREASURY, SECRETARY OF
Importation prohibitions, enforcement of, 17 § 603

TREATIES
Universal Copyright Convention, see separate volume **USCS Administrative Rules,** Universal Copyright Convention

UNITED STATES WORKS
Definition, 17 § 101
Notice of copyright for publication incorporating government works, 17 § 403
Postal service, enforcement of importation prohibitions, 17 § 603
Subject matter of copyright, 17 § 105

UNITED STATES POSTAL SERVICE
Copyright office, delays in deliveries caused by disruption of services, 17 § 709
Importation prohibitions, enforcement of, 17 § 603

USEFUL ARTICLE
Definition, 17 § 101

VACANCIES
Royalty Tribunal, vacancy in, 17 § 802

VIDEOTAPES
Cable system, use of videotapes by, 17 § 111

WAGES OR COMPENSATION
Royalty Tribunal, members of, 17 § 802
Staff of Royalty Tribunal, 17 § 805

WIDOW OR WIDOWER
Definition, 17 § 101
Duration of copyrights, 17 § 304

WORK OF UNITED STATES GOVERNMENT
United States Works (this index)

WORK MADE FOR HIRE
Definition, 17 § 101
Duration of copyright on, 17 § 302
Ownership of, 17 § 201

WRITERS
Deaths of Authors (this index)
National origin of, 17 § 104

WRITING
Transfer of ownership, writing required for, 17 § 204